Environmental
Science

YOUR WORLD, YOUR TURN

SAVVAS
LEARNING COMPANY

ISBN-13: 978-1-4183-3635-6

ISBN-10:   1-4183-3635-1

6 22

About the Author

Jay Withgott is author of two college textbooks on environmental science: *Environment: The Science Behind the Stories* and *Essential Environment.*

A science writer with extensive experience in research and teaching, he holds degrees from Yale University, the University of Arkansas, and the University of Arizona. As a researcher, Jay has published scientific papers on topics in ecology, evolution, animal behavior, and conservation biology in journals including *Proceedings of the National Academy of Sciences, Proceedings of the Royal Society of London B, Evolution*, and *Animal Behavior.* As an instructor, he has taught university-level laboratory courses in ecology, ornithology, vertebrate diversity, anatomy, and general biology. As a science writer, Jay has authored articles for a variety of journals and magazines including *Science, New Scientist, BioScience, Smithsonian, Current Biology, Conservation in Practice*, and *Natural History.* He strives to combine his scientific knowledge with his past experience as a reporter and editor for daily newspapers to make science accessible and engaging for students and for general audiences.

Jay lives with his wife, biologist Susan Masta, in Portland, Oregon.

Contributors

Marylin Lisowski, Ph.D.
Professor
Eastern Illinois University (adjunct)
Pittsburgh Regional Center for Science Teaching
Pittsburgh, PA

Judith Scotchmoor
University of California Museum of Paleontology
Berkeley, CA

Anastasia Thanukos, Ph.D.
University of California Museum of Paleontology
Berkeley, CA

Reviewers

ENVIRONMENTAL SCIENCE TEACHER PANEL

Anthony Derriso
Teacher
Mountain Brook High School
Birmingham, AL

Mark Francis
Teacher of Environmental
 Science
Lawrence North High School
Indianapolis, IN

Grace D. Hanners, M.S.
Science Teacher
Huntingtown High School
Huntingtown, MD

Daniel Hyke, M.A.
Science Department Chair,
 Environmental Science
 Instructor
Alhambra High School
Alhambra, CA

Margaret Scot Smith
Upper School Principal, Science
 Faculty
Canterbury School of Florida
St. Petersburg, FL

Gary Swick
Environmental Science Teacher
Dundee-Crown High School
Carpentersville, IL

Mark Van Hecke
Economics and Geography
 Instructor
Anchor Bay High School
Fair Haven, MI

Marilyn Zaragoza, Ed.D.
Science Teacher/Coach
Everglades High School
Pembroke Pines, FL

HIGH SCHOOL REVIEWERS

Ophelia M. Barizo, M.S.
Chair, Science Department/
 Science Teacher
Highland View Academy
Hagerstown, MD

Joseph A. Condello, M.A.
Science Teacher
Goshen High School
Goshen, NY

Geoffrey Gailey, M.A.T.
Biology, Environmental Science
 Teacher
Boston Public Schools
Knowles Science Teaching
 Foundation
Boston, MA

Rebecca Grella, M.A.
Teacher of Science
Brentwood High School
Brentwood, NY

Courtney Mayer
Teacher
Winston Churchill High School
San Antonio, TX

Hugh Graham McBride
AP Environmental Science
 Instructor,
 AP Biology Instructor
Woodberry Forest School
Woodberry Forest, VA

Michelle L. Odierna, M.A.T.
Biology Teacher
Hopkinton High School
Hopkinton, MA

Jennifer K. Perrella, MSCAR
Department Chairperson
César Chavez Public Charter
 School for Public Policy
Washington, D.C.

Tracy Shisler, M.Ed.
Science Teacher, Department
 Chair
Cape Hatteras Secondary School
 of Coastal Studies
Buxton, NC

Evan P. Silberstein, M.S.
Chemistry Teacher
The Frisch School
Paramus, NJ

Judith Treharne, M.S.
Science Teacher (retired)
Ocean Township High School
Oakhurst, NJ

Carol Widegren, M.A.
Teacher
Chicago Public Schools
Chicago, IL

Derrick Willard, M.Ed.
AP Environmental Science
 Teacher
Providence Day School
Charlotte, NC

Table of Contents

 GO ONLINE to access your digital course.

GO ONLINE to access your digital course.

UNIT 3 Humans and the Environment.....225

🖥 **GO ONLINE** to access your digital course.

x

GO ONLINE to access your digital course.

In-text Labs and Activities

Quick Lab

Map it

Real Data

Go Outside

Online Labs and Activities

 **GO ONLINE** to access your digital course.

Phenomena-Driven Instruction

ANCHORING PHENOMENON

Launch every unit with an engaging Anchoring Phenomenon that introduces and unifies the upcoming environmental science concepts. Students ask questions and gather evidence about the phenomenon on their sense-making journey. At the end of the unit, students solidify their mastery of the concepts behind the Anchoring Phenomenon.

ANCHORING PHENOMENON

What are the effects of dead zones on both people and the environment?

NAME_____ DATE_____ CLASS_____

ANCHORING PHENOMENON PROJECT
Costs of Excess Nutrients Reaching Aquatic Ecosystems

When excess nutrients reach aquatic ecosystems, such as rivers, lakes, and oceans, it can set off a chain of events that impact the abiotic and biotic factors in the ecosystem, as well as people who depend on the ecosystem for income, food, or recreation. For example, large amounts of excess nutrients reach the Gulf of Mexico in spring each year. Algae take up the excess nutrients and reproduce in great numbers, resulting in an algal bloom. When the algae die, bacteria decompose their remains, using much or all of the oxygen in the water. An area of hypoxic, or low-oxygen, water called a dead zone is created. Fish, shellfish, and other aquatic organisms cannot survive in the hypoxic water and die in large numbers. Think about how these events affect people who rely on this ecosystem for income, whether it is from fishing or tourism; food; or recreation. These impacts are part of the external costs associated with excess nutrients in aquatic ecosystems.

In this _____ conduct research to learn more about the costs of excess _____ people who depend on these ecosystems. Then

Students build understanding with an **Anchoring Phenomenon Project** that accompanies every unit.

REVISIT
ANCHORING PHENOMENON

These questions will help you apply what you have learned in this Unit to the Anchoring Phenomenon.

1. **SEP Asking Questions** Research more information about harmful algal blooms (HABs). Suppose you plan to attend a public meeting about how your local or state government is working to reduce the environmental and economic impacts of HABs. Write a list of questions you would ask officials at the meeting.

2. **SEP Developing and Using Models** Make models of the carbon cycle, the phosphorus cycle, and the nitrogen cycle to show both the short-term and long-term effects of excess nitrogen and phosphorus in runoff. How does making the model help you visualize the impacts of excess nutrients on ecosystems?

GO ONLINE

For activities that will give you an opportunity to demonstrate what you have learned.

CLAIM-EVIDENCE-REASONING Revisit your Anchoring Phenomenon CER with the information you have learned in this unit.

ANCHORING PHENOMENON PROJECT Design a solution to reduce external costs associated with excess nutrients in oceans and waterways.

Revisit the Anchoring Phenomenon as more knowledge is uncovered.

NAME_____ DATE_____ CLASS_____

CLAIM-EVIDENCE-REASONING
What is Causing the Fish to Die?

Think about the Anchoring Phenomenon question. What is the science behind the phenomenon? To help you build an understanding of the phenomenon, you will construct and revise a scientific argument.

Build Your Argument Through Claim, Evidence, and Reasoning

1. **SEP Ask Questions** Write a question about the phenomenon or event that you would like to discuss with your classmates. (Your teacher may also provide you with one.)

2. **SEP Construct Written Arguments** Use the Claim-Evidence-Reasoning framework to build a scientific argument about the phenomenon. After stating your claim, support it with evidence and scientific reasoning.

Make a Claim Your claim should be a response _____ only what you

Students track their knowledge in a **Claims-Evidence-Reasoning or Modeling Worksheet** as they learn more about the phenomenon.

INVESTIGATIVE PHENOMENON

Introduce every chapter with an Investigative Phenomenon Central Case Study. This engaging real-world case encourages students to draw connections between environmental science and their life. Interacting with the central case provides opportunities for students to gather the knowledge necessary to make sense of the Anchoring Phenomenon.

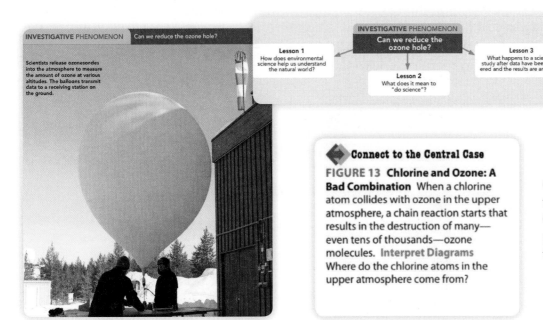

INVESTIGATIVE PHENOMENON   Can we reduce the ozone hole?

Scientists release ozonesondes into the atmosphere to measure the amount of ozone at various altitudes. The balloons transmit data to a receiving station on the ground.

INVESTIGATIVE PHENOMENON
Can we reduce the ozone hole?

Lesson 1
How does environmental science help us understand the natural world?

Lesson 2
What does it mean to "do science"?

Lesson 3
What happens to a scientific study after data have been gathered and the results are analyzed?

Connect to the Central Case

FIGURE 13 **Chlorine and Ozone: A Bad Combination** When a chlorine atom collides with ozone in the upper atmosphere, a chain reaction starts that results in the destruction of many—even tens of thousands—ozone molecules. **Interpret Diagrams** Where do the chlorine atoms in the upper atmosphere come from?

Chapter content ties back to the **Central Case**, providing a storyline for students to follow.

Defend Your Case

The Central Case in this chapter explored how science led to the discovery of how certain chemicals were affecting the ozone layer. Use examples from the Central Case and throughout the chapter to provide evidence on how science often relies not only on individuals, but the entire scientific community and beyond to achieve its goals.

Students **Defend Their Case** at the end of the chapter – giving them the opportunity to gather evidence, analyze data, and use scientific reasoning to support their claim.

REVISIT

3. **INVESTIGATIVE** PHENOMENON

Why is the process of science better represented by the diagram shown in **Figure 10** than by a diagram like the one seen here?

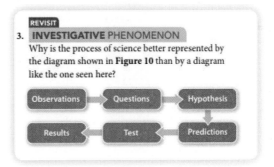

Observations → Questions → Hypothesis

Results ← Test ← Predictions

Assessment questions repeatedly encourage students to revisit the phenomenon.

EVERYDAY PHENOMENON

Every lesson begins with an Everyday Phenomenon, setting the stage for inquiry. Teacher materials provide optional activities to extend students' thinking.

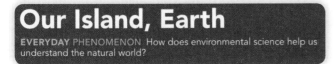

Our Island, Earth

EVERYDAY PHENOMENON How does environmental science help us understand the natural world?

EVERYDAY PHENOMENON

FOCUS Have students write for two minutes about the term *environmental science*. Then, have them review what they have written. Call on volunteers to share what they wrote with the class. Use students' responses to launch a class discussion on how environmental science can promote understanding of the natural world.

Student-Centered Experiences

Environmental Science combines high-interest, real-world content with cutting-edge digital support and a variety of hands-on inquiry investigations to help ensure student success in environmental science. Acclaimed author and active researcher Jay Withgott shows students why learning environmental science is vital.

The Central Case

The **Central Case** highlights real issues in today's world – issues students will be excited to investigate.

Lesson 1	Lesson 2	Lesson 3	Lesson 4
Matter and the Environment	Systems in Environmental Science	Earth's Spheres	Biogeochemical Cycles

The Gulf of Mexico's Dead Zone

LOUISIANA'S FISHING PROFESSIONALS haul in more seafood than those of any other U.S. state except Alaska. Each year they send more than 400 million kilograms (almost 1 billion pounds) of fish, shrimp, and other shellfish to our dinner tables. They are doing this despite the impact that the "dead zone" has on the Gulf of Mexico each year.

The Gulf's "dead zone" is a region of water so depleted of oxygen that marine organisms are killed or driven away. The low concentrations of dissolved oxygen in the bottom waters of the dead zone indicate hypoxia, or low oxygen levels. Aquatic animals obtain oxygen from water that passes over their gills, and, like us, these animals die without oxygen. Well-oxygenated water contains 10 parts per million (ppm) of oxygen. When concentrations drop below 2 ppm, animals that can leave an affected area do so. Below 1.5 ppm, most marine organisms die. In the Gulf's hypoxic zone, oxygen concentrations frequently drop below 2 ppm.

The dead zone appears each spring and grows until fall, when storms stir in some oxygen. It starts off the coast of Louisiana, near the mouths of the Mississippi and Atchafalaya rivers. In 2017, the dead zone reached a record 22,729 square kilometers (8776 square miles)—an area larger than the state of New Jersey.

Why are these waters depleted of oxygen? According to scientists, farming practices and other human causes are to blame. The Gulf, they say, is essentially being fertilized by nitrogen and phosphorus flowing down the Mississippi River. These excess nutrients come from fertilizers used on farms far up the Mississippi and Atchafalaya rivers, as well as from other human sources, including industrial waste, fossil fuel emissions, and sewage treatment plants. The nutrients allow an

GO ONLINE
• Take It Local   • 3-D Geo Tour

overgrowth of plankton whose wastes and remains nourish bacteria that deplete oxygen from the waters at the bottom of the Gulf.

The U.S. government has acted, proposing that farmers in states upriver from the Gulf—such as Ohio, Iowa, and Illinois—cut down on fertilizer use. Farmers' advocates protest that farmers are being singled out while other sources are ignored. The debate continues.

Scientists have also documented dead zones in 200 other bodies of water worldwide, including the Chesapeake Bay. Scientists have been tracking the size of the dead zone in the Chesapeake Bay since the 1980s. In 2019, the dead zone lasted for 136 days with oxygen levels too low for many fish and crabs to survive. Clearly, scientists need to investigate these dead zones in order to protect our food supply and economy. Doing so will require that they continue to research complex environmental systems and their interactions.

Earth's Environmental Systems **63**

GO ONLINE
• Take It Local   • 3-D Geo Tour

Learn About Local Issues

Take It Local activities on Realize encourage students to find a similar situation in their local environment. This extension personalizes the case for students and leads to deeper understanding.

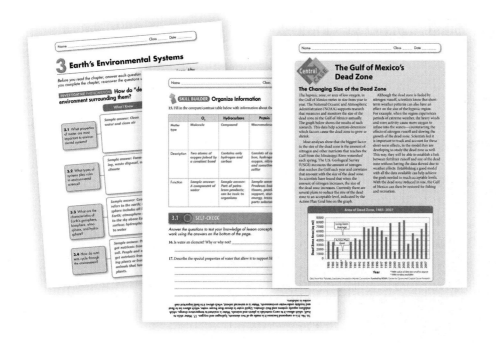

More Practice!

Students can study and reinforce their knowledge with lesson-level vocabulary and activities such as Skill Builder, Think Visually, Central Case activities, and 21st Century Skills in the Study Workbook.

Hands-On Inquiry

Editable hands-on inquiry activities, such as In Your Neighborhood labs, Modeling labs, and Claim-Evidence-Reasoning documents support student understanding of the anchoring and investigative phenomenon under study. The Teachers Guide to Fieldwork provides suggestions for outdoor lab studies.

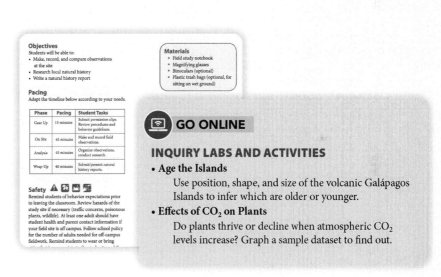

GO ONLINE

INQUIRY LABS AND ACTIVITIES

- **Age the Islands**
  Use position, shape, and size of the volcanic Galápagos Islands to infer which are older or younger.
- **Effects of CO₂ on Plants**
  Do plants thrive or decline when atmospheric CO_2 levels increase? Graph a sample dataset to find out.

Analyze Data

A student took water samples from a small pond every three hours and measured their pH. The results are plotted on the graph. Use the graph to answer the questions.

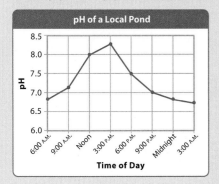

Reinforce Math Skills

- Real data in activities and graphs make the math problems more relevant.

- The Skills Handbook at the back of this book is an easy-to-use refresher for "must-know" math concepts and applications.

- Graphing tutorials on Realize encourage real-world practice.

- Additional math support in the Study Workbook provides more clarity.

Assessment and e-Learning

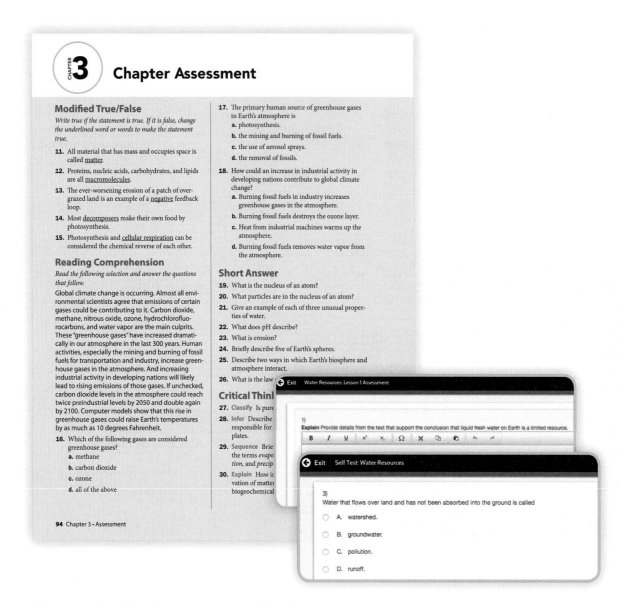

Customizable Assessment Tools

- Lesson and chapter assessments in the Student Edition require students to think critically, apply chapter concepts, and connect to the phenomena.

- Differentiate with two levels of unit and chapter assessments. Customize assessments with editable documents.

- Students self-assess with chapter self-tests on SavvasRealize.com. These pre-tests give students and teachers an opportunity to gauge their knowledge before an exam.

- ExamView® Assessment Suite lets teachers create and print custom tests in minutes to meet specific needs.

An Interactive Digital Experience

SavvasRealize.com is your online digital platform for Environmental Science. With Savvas Realize™, you can go digital with the online Student Edition, online Teacher Edition, and editable Teacher Resources.

Access a wealth of interactive content, editable lesson plans, and assessment tools in one location. The Realize Reader app allows for **offline access**– giving students and teachers even more flexibility to learn anywhere they want.

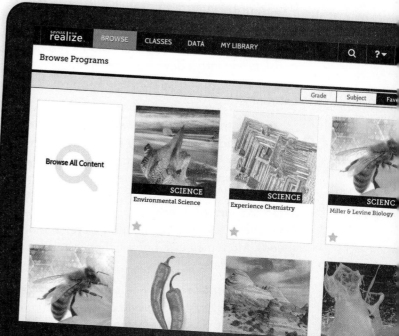

Data-Driven Decisions

- Access data on standards mastery by student, small group, or whole class.
- Monitor student progress with online quizzes and chapter tests.
- Get real-time data on student activity and usage.

Google Partnership

Realize is a partner with Google Classroom™. Sharing content, assessments, and rosters is now easier than ever when working with both Realize and Google G Suite™ for Education.

Google and the Google logo are registered trademarks of Google, LLC.

OpenEd Resources

Search and assign OpenEd resources, making it quick and easy to add thousands of reliable, vetted resources.

Dear Student:

You are coming of age at a unique and momentous time in history. Within your lifetime, our global society must chart a promising course for a sustainable future—or risk falling into a downward spiral of decay. The stakes could not be higher, and the path we take will depend largely on how we choose to interact with our environment.

Today we live long lives enriched with astonishing technologies, in societies more free, just, and equal than ever before. We enjoy wealth on a scale our ancestors could hardly have dreamed of. Yet we have purchased these wonderful things at a price. By tapping into Earth's resources and ecological services, we are depleting our planet's bank account and running up its credit card. Never before has Earth been asked to support so many people making so many demands upon it. We are altering our planet's land, air, water, nutrient cycles, biodiversity, and climate at dizzying speeds. More than ever before, the future of our society rests with how we treat the world around us.

Environmental science helps show us how Earth's systems function and how we influence these systems, giving us a big-picture understanding of the world and our place within it. Studying environmental science helps us comprehend the problems we create, and it illuminates ways to fix those problems. Clearly, environmental science is not just some subject you learn about in school. It's something that relates to everything around you for your whole life!

I have written this book because today's students will shape tomorrow's world. At this unique moment in history, students of your generation are key to achieving a sustainable future for our civilization. Given the vital importance of environmental science today, I want to do my best to engage, educate, and inspire you. In this book I will show you how science can help us toward a sustainable society. Along the way I aim to maintain balance and to encourage you to think critically as we flesh out the social debate over environmental issues.

I also try to focus on providing hope and solutions. For although the many challenges that face us can seem overwhelming, I want you to feel encouraged and motivated. Each dilemma is also an opportunity; for every problem that human carelessness has managed to create, human ingenuity can devise an answer. Now is the time for innovation and creativity and the fresh perspectives that a new generation can offer. Your own ideas and energy will make a difference. You are the solution!

Sincerely,

Jay Withgott

It's Your World

THERE IS A PHRASE, commonly seen on bumper stickers, T-shirts, and reusable bags, that serves as a kind of mantra for individuals and organizations striving to improve the environment: *Think globally, but act locally.* Thinking globally can be overwhelming. The size of our population is climbing along with global temperatures. Our appetite for technology is increasing, yet the resources needed to support technology are dwindling. But our situation is far from hopeless. Every day, all over the world, people are acting locally and making a difference. Will you be next?

To assist student groups and their teachers, the National Science Teachers Association has formed a partnership with the Toyota Motor Corporation to offer grants for innovative projects to schools or school districts. Since 1991, more than 1000 Toyota TAPESTRY grants have been awarded to fund innovative science classroom projects. Awards totaling more than $6.8 billion have supported community gardens, classroom recycling, habitat restoration, and even racing pigeons! A few of the environmental action projects funded by Toyota TAPESTRY are described in the following pages.

Through these projects, you will be able to explore what students like you have done for their communities' environments. Perhaps their efforts can serve as inspiration for you and your classmates. Whether you begin now or in the future, every action you take can make a difference. It just may be *your turn* to help the environment.

Share your knowledge.

Use less and recycle more.

Be curious about your world.

Lend a hand.

Stewards-in-Training

How can policymakers make decisions that affect the environment if they do not understand how the environment functions? Rebecca Grella, a science teacher at Brentwood High School on Long Island, New York, thinks that there is nothing more important than having the future generation of policymakers get involved in environmental projects. Ms. Grella applied for a Toyota TAPESTRY grant that would do just that—get students outside exploring their surroundings and learning to be stewards of their environment.

The area around Brentwood High School is known as the Bishop Tract Preserve. It is one of the last remaining open spaces in the area. In partnership with Brookhaven National Laboratory and Suffolk County, students use GIS (geographic information system) technology to sample and monitor a 15.4 hectare (38 acre) plot within the preserve with an aim to preserving and protecting it for years to come. In particular, the students were interested in the spread of invasive species, a persistent problem on Long Island. The data gathered by students were used to inform their community members, nature groups, and local government about the status and health of the preserve. Perhaps more importantly, however, the project gave students productive and meaningful after-school experiences.

Centaurea nigrescens, also known as Tyrol knapweed, is an invasive species that Ms. Grella's students tracked.

Students present data on the invasion of *Centaurea nigrescens* in the Bishop Tract Preserve.

Milkweed beetles atop milkweed

Students analyze some of their GIS data.

Ms. Grella's students engaged in a challenging and rigorous academic program grounded in relevant real-world experiences. Further, they came to realize that their voices and actions matter—to their community, to the larger academic world, and to professional scientists. Participating students not only achieved academically, they were recognized by the community for their active roles in environmental preservation and local policymaking. Additionally, students presented their data to professional scientists at a meeting of the Brookhaven National Laboratory Open Space Stewardship Program.

Students collect data in an area dense with *Centaurea nigrescens*

A student presents his data at the Open Space Stewardship Conference hosted by Brookhaven National Laboratory.

Students analyze some of their GIS data.

Taking notes in the field

One of many artificial reefs built by students

Several students snorkel on an artificial reef they created in Pamlico Sound.

Students record data relayed to them by the snorkelers.

Students come out of Pamlico Sound after working on an oyster reef.

A Pearl of a Project

Hatteras Island, North Carolina, is one of the barrier islands off the mid-Atlantic coast. Pamlico Sound, a large lagoon separated from the Atlantic Ocean by the barrier islands, supports an active commercial fishing industry. The sound's most important commercial resource is oysters. Young oysters, called *spat*, need something to attach to so they can continue their life cycle. Severe storms, such as nor'easters and hurricanes, have caused a decline in suitable attachment sites. This loss, coupled with uncontrolled harvesting and disease outbreaks, has caused serious declines in the area's oyster population.

Students at Cape Hatteras Secondary School in Buxton, North Carolina, are hoping they can reverse this trend. They have partnered with the University of North Carolina's Coastal Studies Institute and North Carolina State University in an effort to supply protected attachment sites for spat and restock the sound with disease-resistant oysters. It is a big project—but the students are already seeing encouraging results.

Since Hatteras Island has cultural and economic ties to the fishing industry, teacher Tracy Shisler made sure her students understood how modern society affects the ecology of Pamlico Sound and surrounding estuaries. Once these fundamentals were established, the students developed a hatchery program. Local oyster larvae are raised in the classroom and released near offshore artificial reefs that students have built. Local oysters seem to have resistance to the diseases that are prevalent among nonnative oyster populations in the sound. The artificial reefs serve as attachment sites for the released spat. By restocking the reef with local oysters, Ms. Shisler's class hopes to reduce population decline due to disease.

Students take a population sample of oysters on a new reef.

Two students collect aquatic organisms in nets.

Oyster reefs provide habitat for many fish species, and students quickly realized that not only could they help replenish oyster populations, but they also could help in some small way to increase fish populations. Since it began in 2007, the hatchery project has expanded to include several fish species important to the sound, such as black sea bass, flounder, red drum, and pompano. The newest addition to their endeavor is the construction of an oyster research sanctuary reef behind the school in the sound. After just three months, 43 percent of the sanctuary reef was covered in new spat.

These exciting results are why many of the students work on weekends, holidays, and over summer vacation to help tend the hatchery, build oyster reefs, and collect data. Students share their progress and results with the community and local government, generating interest in oyster reef restoration.

Each year as a new sixth grade class enters the secondary school, more parents volunteer and want to be involved. Ms. Shisler is convinced that the project has been so successful because it connects students to their community, and the community is cheering them on.

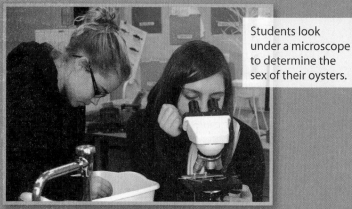
Students look under a microscope to determine the sex of their oysters.

John McCord of the Coastal Studies Institute demonstrates how to open oyster shells and take tissue samples.

Ms. Shisler and a student prepare oysters for spawning.

Collecting organisms on a cloudy day

Make an impact.

Explore nature.

Volunteer.

Restore balance.

It's *Your Turn*

Whether you're participating in a large project, like the ones described here, or simply remembering to turn off lights, recycling, and reusing—everything you do matters.

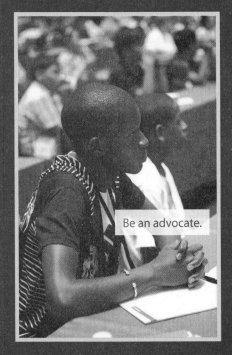
Be an advocate.

Leave the environment better than you found it.

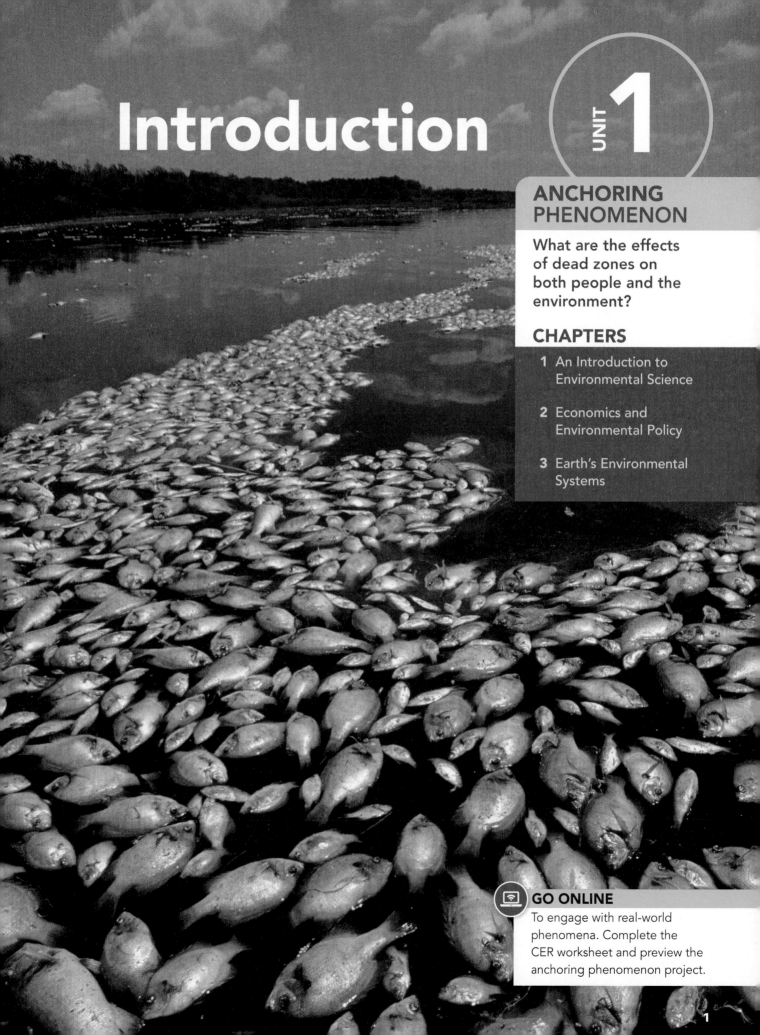

Introduction

ANCHORING PHENOMENON

What are the effects of dead zones on both people and the environment?

CHAPTERS

1 An Introduction to Environmental Science

2 Economics and Environmental Policy

3 Earth's Environmental Systems

GO ONLINE

To engage with real-world phenomena. Complete the CER worksheet and preview the anchoring phenomenon project.

CHAPTER **1**

An Introduction to Environmental Science

INVESTIGATIVE PHENOMENON | Can we reduce the ozone hole?

Scientists release ozonesondes into the atmosphere to measure the amount of ozone at various altitudes. The balloons transmit data to a receiving station on the ground.

Lesson 1
Our Island, Earth

Lesson 2
The Nature of Science

Lesson 3
The Community of Science

Fixing a Hole in the Sky

WHAT HAPPENS to the chemicals that humans release into the atmosphere? Sometimes, they seem to do nothing. Other times, however, the effects are devastating ... and life-threatening.

In the atmosphere, reactions constantly take place between oxygen atoms (O), oxygen gas (O_2), and ozone (O_3). Ultraviolet light from the sun breaks oxygen gas into two oxygen atoms: $O_2 \rightarrow 2O$. These oxygen atoms collide and react with oxygen gas, forming ozone: $O + O_2 \rightarrow O_3$. And oxygen atoms collide with ozone, releasing two oxygen molecules: $O + O_3 \rightarrow 2O_2$.

Despite the constant reactions between O, O_2, and O_3, a certain amount of ozone remains concentrated within a layer of the atmosphere known as the stratosphere. This concentrated area of ozone, called the "ozone layer," blocks harmful ultraviolet (UV) rays from reaching Earth's surface. UV rays can cause skin cancer, cell mutations, and other harmful effects in organisms including humans.

In the 1960s and '70s, Dutch scientist Paul Crutzen began to investigate and form hypotheses about the regulation of atmospheric ozone levels. He suspected that gases from fertilizer and jet exhaust had the potential to significantly deplete the ozone layer and warned that human activities could damage the atmosphere.

Meanwhile, English scientist James Lovelock invented an instrument that could detect atmospheric chemicals including CFCs, or chlorofluorocarbons. CFCs are synthetic compounds of carbon, fluorine, and chlorine atoms that were once found in many manufactured products—from shaving cream cans to asthma inhalers, refrigerators to air conditioners. The amount of CFCs Lovelock found in the atmosphere made it clear that CFCs did not break down well. They remained intact in our atmosphere.

Two scientists in California, Mario Molina and Sherwood Rowland, heard about Lovelock's findings and began to investigate what effect CFCs might have on the atmosphere. They looked at

 GO ONLINE
• Take It Local   • 3-D Geo Tour

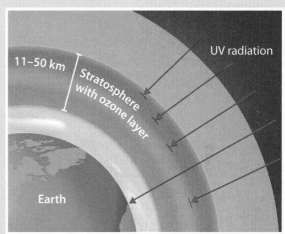

how CFCs move through the atmosphere and react with other chemicals. They also tried to calculate exactly how many CFCs were being released. What they found out was frightening: CFCs had the potential to destroy Earth's protective ozone layer.

When Molina and Rowland published their results in 1974, Paul Crutzen recognized the significance of these findings and began to model the process of ozone depletion in more detail. In 1985, Molina, Rowland, and Crutzen's concerns were shown to be justified: Scientists discovered that the ozone layer over Antarctica had become dangerously thin, so thin that it was called an "ozone hole." For their research, Molina, Rowland, and Crutzen shared the 1995 Nobel Prize in Chemistry.

With the discovery of the ozone hole, most nations agreed to phase out the use of CFCs and other ozone-destroying chemicals. Nonetheless, CFCs can remain in the atmosphere for up to a century. The ozone hole continues to appear over Antarctica every year from August to October. Scientists estimate it will take until 2050 for the ozone layer to recover significantly. Without the efforts of the entire scientific community, however, the problem could have been much worse.

Our Island, Earth

EVERYDAY PHENOMENON How does environmental science help us understand the natural world?

Knowledge and Skills

- Explain the focus of environmental science.
- Describe the recent trends in human population and resource consumption.

Reading Strategy and Vocabulary

✅ **Reading Strategy** Create a KWL chart for each of the vocabulary terms in this lesson. Before you read, fill in what you know and what you want to learn. After reading, fill in what you learned.

Vocabulary environment, environmental science, environmentalism, natural resource, renewable natural resource, nonrenewable natural resource, sustainable, fossil fuel, ecological footprint

VIEWED FROM SPACE, our home planet resembles a small blue marble suspended against a vast inky-black backdrop. Earth may seem vast here on its surface, but an astronaut's perspective reveals that Earth and its natural systems are limited. It has become clear that as our population and technological powers increase, so does our ability to change our planet and possibly damage the very systems that keep us alive.

Our Environment

From space, Earth looks simple—blue oceans, green and brown land masses, white clouds—but this is not a complete picture of the environment. The **environment** includes all the living and nonliving things with which organisms interact. It includes the continents, oceans, clouds, and icecaps visible in the photo of Earth from space, but it also includes the animals, plants, forests, and farms that you cannot see from such a great distance. The environment includes remote areas rarely visited by people, but it also includes all of the buildings, urban centers, and houses that people have built, as well as the complex webs of social relationships that shape our daily lives.

Humans and the Environment Unfortunately, *environment* is often used to mean the nonhuman or "natural" world. But humans are part of nature. Like all other species on Earth, we interact with our environment and rely on a healthy, functioning planet for everything we need—including air, water, food, and shelter. Without a healthy environment, we cannot survive. Studying environmental science reminds us that we are part of the natural world and how we interact with it matters a great deal.

Understanding Human Influences Many people today enjoy longer life spans, better health, and greater material wealth than ever before. We can fly around the world with ease and cure previously incurable diseases with a pill. However, these improvements have often harmed the natural systems that sustain us, destroying habitats and polluting the water and atmosphere. The discovery that synthetic chemicals were harming Earth's ozone layer served as a wake-up call, illustrating how human influences can ultimately threaten long-term health and survival.

Environmental science is the study of how the natural world works, how our environment affects us, and how we affect our environment. Understanding interactions between humans and the environment is the first step toward solving environmental problems. The size and scope of these problems can seem overwhelming. However, with these problems also come countless opportunities for devising creative solutions. In the case of ozone depletion, a very real and effective solution has been found to a seemingly impossible problem. Scientists now predict that within fifty years, ozone depletion will be reversed and the ozone hole will be gone.

Environmental scientists study issues that are important to our world and its future. Right now, global conditions are changing quickly, but so is our knowledge and understanding of the natural world. With such large challenges and opportunities, this particular moment in history is a very exciting time to be studying environmental science.

 Reading Checkpoint *Why do people need the natural world?*

FIGURE 1 Humans in the Environment For better or worse, people—just like every other species—affect the environment. Unlike other species, however, our actions have the ability to do great harm, or great good, on a global scale.

FIGURE 2 Environmentalism or Environmental Science? Can you tell which is which? **(a)** Environmentalists protest commercial whaling in London, UK, in 2019. **(b)** Environmental scientists from the New England Aquarium, in Boston, Massachusetts, collect data on right whales that will help them understand how the whales live in the wild.

Environmental Science vs. Environmentalism Many environmental scientists are motivated by a desire to develop solutions to environmental problems. Studying our interactions with our environment is a complex endeavor that requires expertise from many disciplines, including ecology, earth science, chemistry, biology, economics, political science, and others. Environmental science is thus an *interdisciplinary* field, one that borrows techniques from numerous disciplines and brings research results from these disciplines together.

Although many environmental scientists are interested in solving problems, it would be incorrect to confuse environmental science with environmentalism, or environmental activism. They are *not* the same, as shown in **Figure 2**. Environmental science is the pursuit of knowledge about the workings of the environment and our interactions with it. **Environmentalism** is a social movement dedicated to protecting the natural world—and, by extension, people—from undesirable changes brought about by human actions. Although environmental scientists may study many of the same issues environmentalists care about, they try to maintain an objective approach in their work, avoiding bias whenever possible. *Bias* is a preference or viewpoint that is personal, not scientific. Attempting to remain free from bias, open to whatever conclusions the data demand, is a hallmark of the effective scientist.

Population Up, Resources Down

Inhabitants of an island must cope with limited materials, whether food, water, or other supplies. On our island Earth, human beings, like all living things, ultimately face environmental constraints. Specifically, there are limits to many of our **natural resources,** materials, and energy sources found in nature, that humans need to survive.

Renewable natural resources
• Sunlight
• Wind energy
• Wave energy
• Geothermal energy

• Fresh water
• Forest products
• Agricultural crops
• Soil

Nonrenewable natural resources
• Crude oil
• Natural gas
• Coal
• Copper, aluminum, and other metals

FIGURE 3 Natural Resources
Natural resources lie along a continuum from always available and completely renewable to nonrenewable. Completely renewable resources, such as sunlight and wind energy, will always be there for us. Nonrenewable resources, such as oil and coal, exist in limited amounts that could one day be gone. Resources such as timber, soil, and fresh water can be renewed naturally if we are careful not to use them faster than nature can replace them.

Renewable or Nonrenewable? Nature "makes" natural resources in different ways and at varied speeds. Some natural resources, such as fruits and grains, are naturally replenished, or renewed, over short periods. These resources are **renewable natural resources.** In contrast, resources such as coal and oil are **nonrenewable natural resources** because they are naturally formed much more slowly than we use them. Once nonrenewable resources are completely depleted, or used up, they are gone forever.

▶ *A Renewability Continuum* As shown in **Figure 3,** the renewability of natural resources can be visualized as a continuum. Some renewable resources, such as sunlight, wind, and wave energy, are essentially available at all times. Nonrenewable resources, such as coal and oil, are at the other end of the continuum—for example, it takes millions of years of intense heat and pressure to form oil, but only a few hours to burn through a tank of gasoline.

▶ *Sustainability* In between these two extremes are natural resources such as fresh water, timber, and soil. These resources can renew themselves, but it takes some time—not millions of years like nonrenewable resources, but still months, years, or decades. These types of renewable resources may become nonrenewable if they are not used at a sustainable rate. Resource use is considered **sustainable** if it can continue at the same rate into the foreseeable future.

If nonrenewable resources and the "in between" resources like timber and water are used unsustainably, then we can run out of them. For example, lakes and reservoirs can dry up if the freshwater supplies are drained faster than rainfall and snowmelt can refill them. In recent years, consumption of natural resources has increased to unsustainable levels, driven by the growth of the largest human population in history.

 How do we use resources sustainably?

World Population Growth

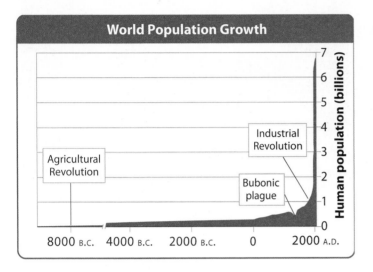

FIGURE 4 Human Population Growth For almost all of human history, our population was low and relatively stable. It increased significantly due to two events: the Agricultural Revolution and the Industrial Revolution. The only significant drop in population occurred when 25 million people died of bubonic plague in the 1300s.

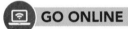

GO ONLINE

• **Graph It** An Introduction to Graphing

FIGURE 5 Less Time, More Power Technologies developed during the Industrial Revolution have made many tasks easier, but many of them require the use of nonrenewable resources. For example, **(a)** horses used to power plows, like this one from 1903, but **(b)** today gasoline powers plows.

Human Population Growth For nearly all of human history, only a few million people lived on Earth at any one time. Although past populations cannot be calculated precisely, **Figure 4** gives you some idea of just how recently and suddenly our population has grown to about 7.8 *billion* people. We add about 78 million people to the planet each year—that's more than 200,000 people each day. Today, the rate of population growth is slowing, but our absolute numbers continue to increase and shape our interactions with one another and with our environment.

▶ *The Agricultural Revolution* The remarkable increases in population size can be attributed to two events in recent human history. The first was the transition from a hunter-gatherer lifestyle to an agricultural way of life. This change began around 10,000 years ago and is known as the *Agricultural Revolution*. As people began to grow crops, raise domestic animals, and live in villages, they found it easier to meet their nutritional needs. As a result, they began to live longer and to produce more children who survived to adulthood.

▶ *The Industrial Revolution* About 320 years ago in the early 1700s, the second event, known as the Industrial Revolution began. The *Industrial Revolution* describes the shift from rural life, with animal-powered agriculture, and handmade manufacturing, to an urban society powered by nonrenewable energy sources. These nonrenewable energy resources, such as oil, coal, and natural gas, are known as **fossil fuels.** The Industrial Revolution introduced many improvements. Medical technology advanced, sanitation improved, and agricultural production increased with the use of fossil-fuel-powered equipment and chemical fertilizers. Humans lived longer, had healthier lives, and over time, enjoyed new technologies like telephones, automobiles, and computers.

The Problem With Population Growth

At the outset of the Industrial Revolution in England, population growth was regarded as a good thing. For parents, high birthrates meant more children to support them in old age. For society, it meant a greater pool of labor for factory work. British economist Thomas Malthus had a different opinion, however. Malthus claimed that unless population growth was controlled, the number of people would outgrow the available food supply until starvation, war, or disease arose and reduced the population. Malthus expressed his ideas in *An Essay on the Principle of Population*, published in 1798.

More recently, biologists Paul and Anne Ehrlich of Stanford University have warned that population growth will have disastrous effects on human welfare. In his book *The Population Bomb*, published in 1968, Paul Ehrlich predicted that the rapidly increasing human population would unleash famine and conflict that would consume civilization by the end of the twentieth century. Luckily for us, Ehrlich's forecasts have not materialized on the scale he predicted. Some, such as economist Julian Simon, think this dire prediction unlikely and maintain that technology can stretch our resources. However, concerned scientists warn that a global population crisis is still possible.

Ecological Footprints

Population growth unquestionably leads to many environmental problems. However, it is not just the number of people on Earth, but how much we consume, that is to blame. Resource consumption can be quantified using the concept of the "ecological footprint," developed in the 1990s by environmental scientists Mathis Wackernagel and William Rees. An **ecological footprint** expresses the environmental effects of an individual or population in terms of the total amount of land and water required: (1) to provide the raw materials the individual or population consumes and (2) to dispose of or recycle the waste the individual or population produces. The ecological footprint concept is most commonly applied to humans, but every organism and natural or synthetic object has a footprint.

FIGURE 6 Too Many People, Too Little Space For residents of Mumbai, India, there simply aren't enough resources to go around. Many people live in extreme poverty within slums. This slum, Dharavi, is the largest in Mumbai. It is estimated to have a population of around 1 million people—the densest population of any city on Earth.

WHAT DO YOU THINK?

What do you think accounts for the variation in sizes of ecological footprints among societies? Do you think that nations with larger footprints should have to reduce their effects on the environment, to leave more resources available for nations with smaller footprints?

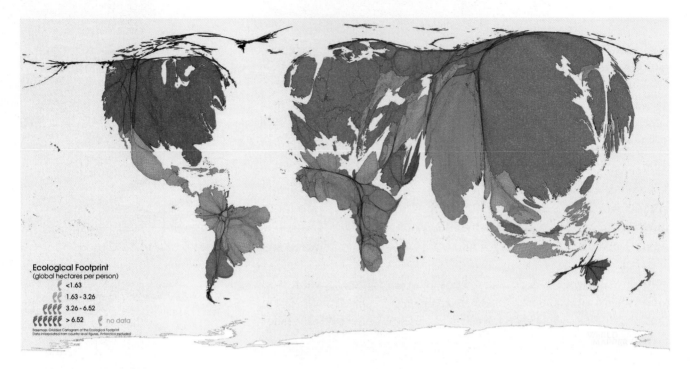

Ecological Footprint
(global hectares per person)
<1.63
1.63 - 3.26
3.26 - 6.52
> 6.52   no data

Basemap: Gridded Cartogram of the Ecological Footprint
Data interpolated from country-level figures, Antarctica excluded

FIGURE 7 Relative Footprints In this map, nations in green have a sustainable ecological footprint. Nations in orange, red, and dark red have exceeded a sustainable footprint. These nations are increased in size on the map to show their disproportionate use of resources. Nations in dark red have the least sustainable ecological footprint.

There is no universal way to calculate an ecological footprint. When looking at the footprint for a potato, for example, one group of researchers may include only the resources needed to grow the potato, while another group of researchers might include the resources needed to cook the potato as well. When comparing footprints, however, it does not matter what approach is used to calculate footprint values as long as it is used consistently. In this way, ecological footprints can be enormously useful as a tool to compare resource use across individuals or populations.

For example, by one set of calculations, the average American has an ecological footprint about 3.5 times that of the global average. Residents of other nations, such as Canada, Chile, and Australia, however, are consuming resources at a rate less than the global average. **Figure 7** shows one research group's summary of how footprints compare across the globe.

Map it

Comparing Ecological Footprints

The map in **Figure 7** uses data from the Global Footprint Network and the Socioeconomic Data and Applications Center to compare resource consumption in the world's nations. Each nation's shape has been stretched in proportion to its relative ecological footprint size. Color also serves to indicate how a nation compares to the world average.

1. **Interpret Maps** Describe how color is used in the map. What does green indicate? What do orange, red, and dark red indicate?

2. **Interpret Maps** Use the Internet or an atlas to identify five of the nations shown in the darkest shades of red.

3. **Infer** Use the Internet or other reference material to look up the ten nations with the largest gross national product (GNP), a measure of a nation's wealth. How does the wealth of a nation relate to its relative ecological footprint?

The Tragedy of the Commons What will happen if we use resources globally at an unsustainable rate? Increased resource use can cause what Garrett Hardin of the University of California at Santa Barbara called a *tragedy of the commons.* According to Hardin, unless resources are regulated, we will eventually be left with nothing.

▶ *The Original "Commons"* Hardin bases his argument on a scenario described in an 1833 English pamphlet describing public pastures, or "commons," that were open to unregulated community grazing. Hardin argues that the commons model, in which a resource is left unregulated, motivates individuals to increase their resource consumption. If the common is open to public use, why would anyone turn it down? But as more and more people acted in their own self-interest, in this case by adding animals to graze upon the pasture, a problem arose: The animals ate the grass faster than it could regrow. Eventually, no grass was left and all of the animals suffered. Hardin argues that when resources are unregulated, everyone takes what he or she can until the resource is depleted. No *one* takes responsibility, so *every*one eventually loses. As shown in **Figure 8,** tragedies of the commons still occur today.

▶ *Learning From the Past* How can the tragedy of the commons be avoided? The most obvious solution, perhaps, is for people sharing a common resource to voluntarily organize, cooperate, and enforce responsible use. Some have argued that this type of management is often impractical, and that private ownership of natural resources is the better option. With resource privatization, a regulating body, such as a government, gives each person a share of the resource that he or she controls instead of leaving resources open to everyone. While this strategy has potential with discrete resources such as minerals, fish, or farmland, privatization does not work as well with continuous, global resources such as the oceans or the ozone layer.

It is important for individuals and governments to consider every kind of solution for the diverse problems facing us today. One way or another, environmental scientists warn, we must address the rate at which resources are consumed—and soon.

FIGURE 8 A Modern-Day Tragedy of the Commons Many parts of southern Africa are experiencing a tragedy of the commons today. Vast forested regions have been cleared to enable farming and ranching. Improper techniques coupled with overuse, however, are causing the land to dry up, making it unsuitable for the very crops and animals it was intended for.

LESSON 1 Assessment

1. **Apply Concepts** Ecology is the study of how organisms interact with their environments. How is environmental science different from ecology? In what way is ecology part of environmental science? Explain.

2. **Form an Opinion** Do you think it is possible to have the benefits of the Agricultural and Industrial revolutions without the environmental costs? Explain why or why not.

3. **THINK IT** *THROUGH* Suppose you make your living fishing for lobster. You and everyone else are free to set out as many traps as you like. As more and more traps are set up, however, fewer and fewer lobsters are caught. Soon, lobster catches are too small to support your families. A meeting is coming up where you and your fellow lobster fishers will present possible solutions to this problem. What will you propose to combat this tragedy of the commons and restore the fishery?

The Nature of Science

EVERYDAY PHENOMENON What does it mean to "do science"?

Knowledge and Skills

- Explain what science is.
- Describe the process of science.

Reading Strategy and Vocabulary

☑ **Reading Strategy** Before you read, write *process of science* on a piece of paper and draw a circle around it. As you read, make a cluster diagram using this circled phrase as your main idea.

Vocabulary hypothesis, prediction, independent variable, dependent variable, controlled study, data

THE END OF THE WORLD AS WE KNOW IT? It seems like predictions of environmental catastrophe come out every day. Constantly, scientists are on television, the radio, in the newspapers, or on the Internet explaining their latest data—of a warming Earth, rising seas, and declining resources. On the other hand, there are reports that these environmental concerns are exaggerated and the science is flawed. How do we sort fact from fiction? Studying environmental science will outfit you with the tools that can help you to evaluate information on environmental change and to think critically and creatively about possible actions to take in response.

What Science Is and Is Not

What is science? Modern scientists describe it as a systematic process for learning about the world and testing our understanding of it. The term *science* also refers to the accumulated body of knowledge that arises as a result of this process. Therefore, science is both a process of learning about the natural world and a summary of what we have already learned. Many scientists are motivated by the potential for developing useful applications of scientific knowledge and a desire to understand how the world works. Science is essential if we hope to develop solutions to the problems—environmental and otherwise—that we face.

Science and the Natural World Whether storm chasers waiting for tornadoes, or bird watchers waiting for a rare species, scientists work exclusively within the natural world. This includes every part of our physical environment, from the smallest atom to the largest galaxy. The natural world also includes the forces and energies that operate on and within our environment, such as gravity and solar radiation.

FIGURE 9 **Gathering Evidence**
A scientist takes and records readings as Mount Etna, a volcano in Sicily, Italy, erupts nearby.

Science assumes that the natural world functions in accordance with rules that do not change unpredictably from time to time or from place to place. The boiling point of pure water at sea level, for example, is 100°C. As long as you're at sea level, water will boil at 100°C today, tomorrow, and 1000 years from now, because boiling point is determined by rules of molecular attraction and bonding that do not change. The goal of science is to discover how the rules of the natural world operate and what effect they have. Science does *not* deal with the supernatural, which includes anything not governed by the rules of the natural world.

Science and Evidence Scientists examine the workings of the natural world by collecting evidence. They rely on their senses and test results for evidence. Then they use their reasoning abilities to figure out what that evidence suggests about the underlying processes at work. Ideas that cannot be tested against evidence gathered and analyzed in this way cannot be evaluated by science. For example, science cannot determine which flower is prettier, a rose or a tulip, even though roses and tulips are part of the natural world. The answer to this question is an opinion rooted in personal preference and not in scientific evidence. However, science can examine what percent of people prefer roses to tulips and under what conditions they might change their minds. Science can also help us learn about the chemical processes these flowers use to perform photosynthesis.

Science, Skepticism, and Change Nothing in science can be absolutely proven no matter how much evidence is collected. Instead, ideas can only be repeatedly supported by rigorous scientific testing. Effective scientists, therefore, are always skeptical, meaning that they do not simply accept what they hear from others. Instead, scientists actively seek evidence that provides answers to scientific questions, and are open to results that change, or even refute, a previously accepted idea. Scientists are critical thinkers, and will either accept or reject ideas based on the strength of evidence that supports them. Note that scientists "accept"—rather than "believe in"—scientific ideas, because believing in something often means accepting something without supporting evidence.

 What does it mean if a scientific idea is "accepted"?

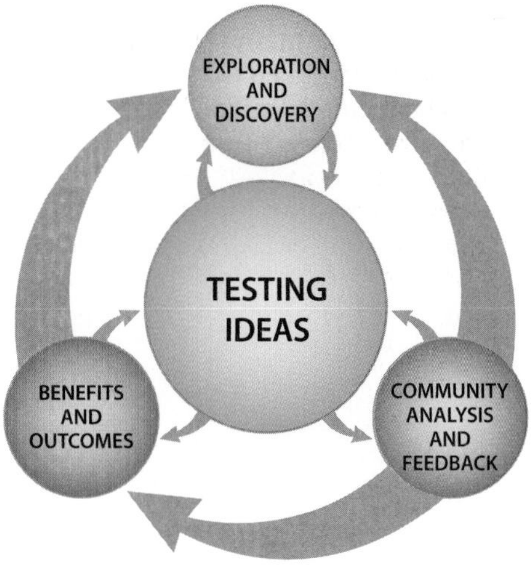

The Process of Science

In their quest for understanding, scientists engage in many different activities: They ask questions, make observations, seek evidence, share ideas, and analyze data. These activities are all part of the dynamic process of science. There is nothing mysterious about the process of science; it uses the same reasoning abilities and logical steps that any of us might naturally follow, using common sense, to resolve a question. As practiced by individual researchers or research teams, the process of science typically consists of the components shown in **Figure 10.** Notice that the parts of the process do not proceed in a linear fashion. Real science usually involves many activities that loop back on themselves, building up knowledge as they proceed. In fact, science is at its heart a creative endeavor. Scientists take many different paths through the process depending on the questions they are investigating and the resources available to them.

Exploration and Discovery Scientific investigations begin in many different ways, but the early stages of an investigation often involve the observation of some phenomenon that the scientist wishes to explain. Observations also function throughout the process as scientists gather evidence about their ideas. Observations can be made simply with the eye, or they can require sensitive instruments. Observations can happen unexpectedly, or they can be carefully planned after reading about other ideas and studies. Alternatively, by exploring the scientific literature, a scientist can stumble upon an interesting idea or phenomenon to test. Inspiration for scientific investigations can come from almost anywhere.

As scientists begin an investigation, they usually ask many questions. Curiosity is a fundamental human characteristic. As soon as we can speak, we begin asking questions. As scientists explore these questions, they may discuss them with their colleagues and read about similar questions in the scientific literature. Sharing ideas, like questioning, often plays an important role in the beginning of an investigation. James Lovelock, an independent scientist, presented his CFC research at a scientific meeting in 1972. Sherwood Rowland was at the same meeting, and when he heard Lovelock's presentation, he may have asked: "What are the effects of CFCs in our atmosphere?"

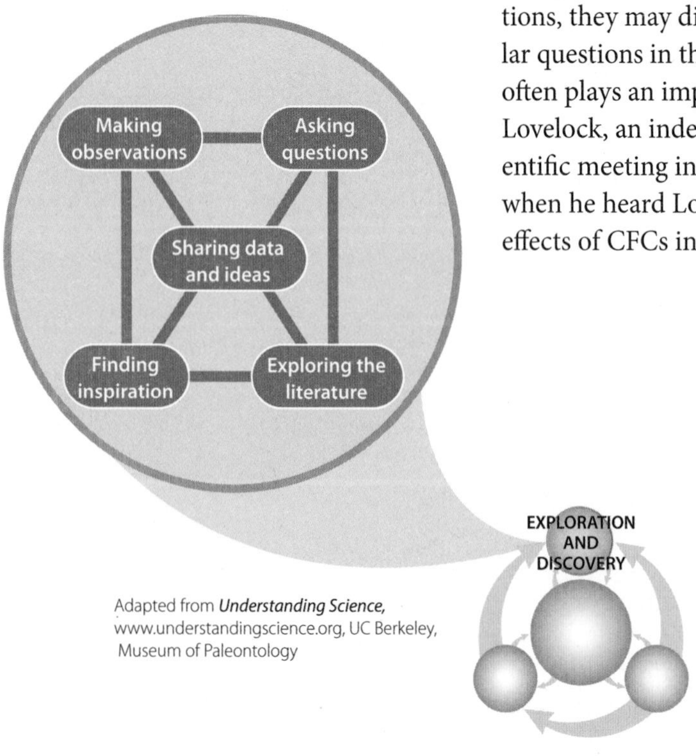

Adapted from *Understanding Science,*
www.understandingscience.org,
UC Berkeley, Museum of Paleontology

FIGURE 10 The Process of Science
Science involves many different people doing many different activities at different points in time. Testing ideas is at the heart of science, but it relies on constant interactions among scientists, society, and the larger scientific community. These interactions make science an ongoing, unpredictable, and dynamic process.

Adapted from *Understanding Science,*
www.understandingscience.org, UC Berkeley,
Museum of Paleontology

FIGURE 11 Exploration and Discovery Observing, questioning, sharing ideas, and exploring the literature are all ways in which scientists can be inspired to investigate a phenomenon or problem.

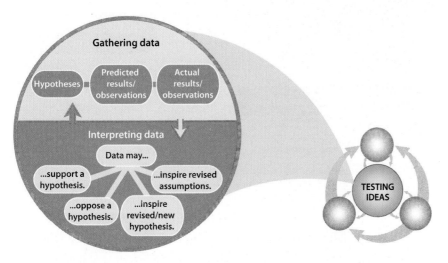

Adapted from *Understanding Science*, www.understandingscience.org, UC Berkeley, Museum of Paleontology

FIGURE 12 Testing Ideas Gathering and interpreting data are at the center of scientific investigations. Generally, data either support or contradict a hypothesis, but occasionally data suggest that a test is not working as expected or inspire a new potential explanation.

◆ **Connect to the Central Case**

FIGURE 13 Chlorine and Ozone: A Bad Combination When a chlorine atom collides with ozone in the upper atmosphere, a chain reaction starts that results in the destruction of many—even tens of thousands—ozone molecules. **Interpret Diagrams** Where do the chlorine atoms in the upper atmosphere come from?

Testing Scientific Ideas

As **Figure 12** shows, scientists attempt to answer their questions by devising explanations that they can test. A **hypothesis** is a testable idea that attempts to explain a phenomenon or answer a scientific question. Scientists often explore many hypotheses at the same time. Rowland, together with Mario Molina, developed the hypothesis that CFCs break down in the upper atmosphere and react with ozone, destroying it in the process.

Molina and Rowland came to this hypothesis after a review of the scientific literature on CFCs revealed no known process that affects CFCs in the lower atmosphere. Because nothing destroyed them, CFCs would eventually diffuse to the upper atmosphere. Both Molina and Rowland had backgrounds in chemistry and knew that solar radiation is far more intense in the upper atmosphere than in the lower atmosphere. Intense solar radiation, they reasoned, would break apart CFC molecules. What else was in the upper atmosphere for CFCs to react with? Ozone.

Molina and Rowland hypothesized that chlorine released from CFCs would react with the oxygen in ozone, as shown in **Figure 13.** These reactions are similar to the destructive reactions between nitrogen compounds and ozone that Paul Crutzen had studied more than five years before. Molina and Rowland calculated that one chlorine atom could destroy about 100,000 ozone molecules.

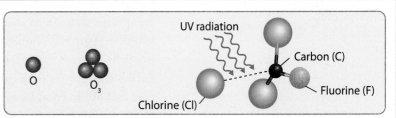

The ozone layer is full of ozone (O_3) and loose oxygen molecules (O). UV radiation breaks down CFC molecules, releasing chlorine atoms (Cl).

A single chlorine atom reacts with O_3...   producing chlorine monoxide (ClO) and molecular oxygen (O_2).

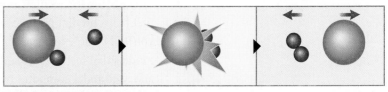

The ClO molecule then reacts with a loose oxygen atom...   producing Cl and O_2.

This leaves the chlorine atom (Cl) free to start the process all over again and destroy another ozone molecule.

Adapted from *Understanding Science*, www.understandingscience.org, UC Berkeley, Museum of Paleontology

FIGURE 14 Molina-Rowland Hypothesis and Predictions Molina and Rowland's hypothesis that CFCs break down only in the upper atmosphere where they react with, and destroy, the ozone layer generated two key predictions: (1) Chlorine monoxide (ClO), a byproduct of CFC-ozone reactions, will be present in the upper atmosphere; and (2) more CFCs will be present at lower altitudes than higher altitudes.

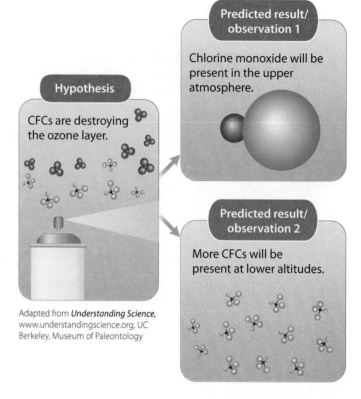

Adapted from *Understanding Science,* www.understandingscience.org, UC Berkeley, Museum of Paleontology

▶ *Predictions* Scientists use hypotheses to generate **predictions,** which are specific statements about what we would expect to observe if the hypotheses are true. Sometimes figuring out what predictions a hypothesis generates is straightforward, but sometimes it is more difficult. The Earth's atmosphere is an immensely complex system. In fact, it is so complex that Molina and Rowland's fellow scientists, including Paul Crutzen, had to use mathematical models to generate predictions about what should be happening in the atmosphere if Rowland and Molina's ideas were correct.

▶ *Modeling* Scientists often use models to generate predictions when they cannot observe a phenomenon directly. Geologists, for example, cannot easily perform experiments to test the effects of tectonic plate motion! Instead, they build computer or mathematical models that represent the system they are studying. Later in this book, you will use a mathematical equation to calculate population sizes—a simple mathematical model that helps predict population size under a given set of conditions. While you will be able to solve the population equation easily, the mathematical models that tested Rowland and Molina's ideas were far more complicated and required a computer to solve.

The atmospheric models generated two predictions based on the Molina-Rowland hypothesis: (1) chlorine monoxide (ClO) should be present in the upper atmosphere, and (2) more CFCs will be present at lower altitudes. These predictions are shown in **Figure 14.**

 ✓ Reading Checkpoint *What did Molina and Rowland hypothesize about the ozone layer?*

FIGURE 15 **Caught on Camera**
Remote, motion-activated cameras
help scientists gather data on hard-to-
find rainforest animals.

Gathering Data Scientists test predictions by gathering evidence. If
the evidence matches their predictions, the hypothesis is supported, and
if the evidence doesn't match the predictions, the hypothesis is con-
tradicted. There are many different ways to test predictions, including
experiments and observational studies. Depending on the scientific question being investigated, one type of test might be more useful than others.

▶ *Experiments* An *experiment* is an activity designed to test the validity of a prediction or a hypothesis. It involves manipulating *variables,*
or conditions that can change. Consider the hypothesis that fertilizers
stimulate algal growth. This hypothesis generates the prediction that adding agricultural fertilizers to a pond will cause the quantity of algae in the
pond to increase. A scientist could test this prediction by selecting two
similar ponds and adding fertilizer to one while leaving the other in its
natural state. In this example, fertilizer input is an **independent variable,**
a variable the scientist manipulates, whereas the quantity of algae that
results is the **dependent variable,** one that depends on the conditions set
up in the experiment.

Of course, some hypotheses cannot easily be tested with experiments.
In these cases, the appropriate experiment might take too long or might
be too expensive, dangerous, or ethically questionable. For example, a
doctor studying the effects of solar radiation on humans would not know-
ingly place human subjects in potentially harmful conditions. And in
other cases, experiments are simply impossible. Earth only has one atmosphere and CFCs were already present in it when Molina and Rowland
began investigating a possible link to ozone destruction. A simple experiment could not answer their question. Experiments are just one way that
scientists carry out their research.

 Reading
Checkpoint   *What is the difference between an independent and
dependent variable?*

FIGURE 16 Up in the Air James Anderson and his team collected data using weather balloons and a NASA ER-2 stratospheric research aircraft like this one.

▶ *Observational Studies* Observational studies provide another key source of scientific evidence. In an observational study, scientists look for evidence in the natural world that would help confirm or contradict the predictions generated by their hypotheses. Observational studies often rely on *correlation*, a meaningful and predictable relationship among variables. In the mid-1970s, scientists searched for evidence about whether or not CFCs were destroying the ozone layer using observational studies. They used planes and high-altitude balloons to collect data about CFC and chlorine monoxide concentrations at different altitudes. They were looking for the predicted correlations between altitude and the levels of these chemicals. If Molina and Rowland were right, the evidence should show high CFC levels at low altitudes and chlorine monoxide at high altitudes.

▶ *Controlled Variables and Repetition* Scientists studying cause-and-effect relationships are careful to manage the variables in their tests; that is, they try to keep all variables constant except the one whose effect they are testing in a study. *Controlled variables* are variables kept constant in a study. **Controlled studies,** in which all variables are controlled except one, allow scientists to be more confident that any differences observed were caused by the factor they are investigating.

Controlled variables are important in both experimental and observational tests. For example, in the pond experiment described earlier, the scientist would try to pick two ponds that are as similar as possible—same geographic region, same temperature, and so on—in order to be confident that any difference in algal growth was caused by the fertilizer and not one of the other variables. In the tests of the Molina-Rowland hypothesis, the scientists tried to make their observations of CFC levels at different altitudes in exactly the same way—same instruments, same technique, and so on—to be confident that the different levels detected were related to altitude and were not a result of the measurement technique.

Whenever possible, it is best to repeat the same test many times. For example, our wetlands scientist could perform the same experiment on, say, ten pairs of ponds, adding fertilizer to one of each pair. Repetition is also important in observational tests. To test the Molina-Rowland hypothesis, James Anderson and the other scientists studying chlorine monoxide levels in the atmosphere repeated the same measurements on three different days in order to be more confident in their results.

 Reading Checkpoint *What does it mean for variables to show correlation?*

FIGURE 17 Underwater Science A diver surveys a coral reef in West Papua, Indonesia.

Adapted from *Understanding Science*, www.understandingscience.org, UC Berkeley, Museum of Paleontology

FIGURE 18 What Can Data Do for You? Most data gathered and analyzed in the course of a scientific investigation will either lend support to a hypothesis or will help to refute it. Data cannot prove or disprove any hypothesis.

▶ *Interpreting Data* Scientists collect and record **data,** or information, from their studies. They particularly value *quantitative* data (information expressed using numbers) because numbers provide precision and are easy to compare. The scientists testing the first CFC model prediction quantified the concentration of chlorine monoxide in the upper atmosphere. For the second prediction, that CFCs should remain intact in the lower atmosphere but break apart in the upper atmosphere, scientists quantified the concentration of CFCs at different altitudes.

Generally, data in the form of results and observations either lend support to or help to refute a hypothesis, as shown in **Figure 18.** If many tests refute a hypothesis, the scientist will ultimately have to reject that hypothesis. It is important to remember, though, that science is always tentative: We can never completely *prove* or *disprove* an idea. Science is always willing to revise its ideas if warranted by new evidence.

In 1975, two research groups measured CFC concentrations at various altitudes. Their data matched the predictions of the mathematical models, and therefore supported the hypothesis that CFCs destroy the ozone layer. And in 1976, James Anderson's team detected chlorine monoxide concentrations in the upper atmosphere consistent with the predictions of atmospheric models, providing further support.

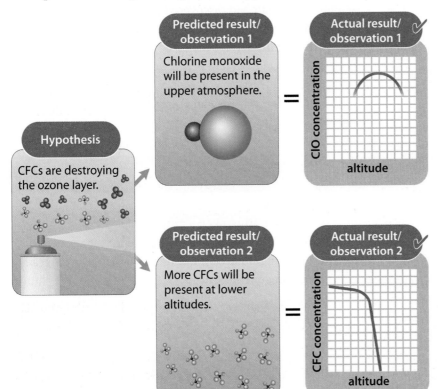

Adapted from *Understanding Science*, www.understandingscience.org, UC Berkeley, Museum of Paleontology

Go Outside

Measure for Measure

❶ Use string, scissors, and a marker to capture the diameter of three trees in your neighborhood.

❷ Use both a yard stick and a meter stick to record the diameter of each tree. Place the data in a comparison table, using both inches and centimeters. Be as precise as you can in taking the measurements.

❸ Calculate the average diameter of the three trees, in inches and centimeters.

❹ Convert your average into yards and meters.

Analyze and Conclude

1. **Compare and Contrast** Which type of measure was easiest to work with and why?

2. **Communicate** What everyday objects use metric units?

◆ Connect to the Central Case

FIGURE 19 Gathering Support Both of the predictions generated by the Molina-Rowland CFC hypothesis were supported by data gathered by researchers in the mid-1970s. **Interpret Graphs** Describe how CFC concentration changes with altitude according to the graph.

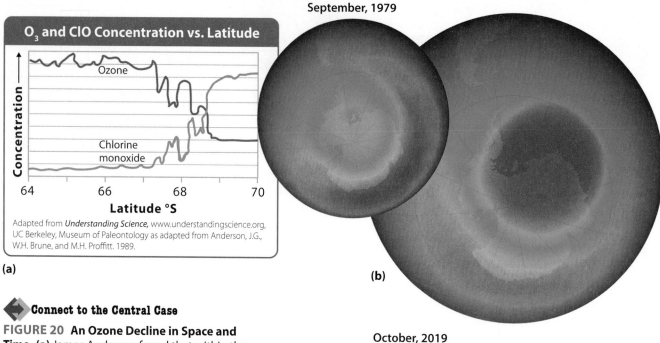

September, 1979

O_3 and ClO Concentration vs. Latitude

Ozone

Chlorine monoxide

Concentration

Latitude °S

64   66   68   70

Adapted from *Understanding Science,* www.understandingscience.org, UC Berkeley, Museum of Paleontology as adapted from Anderson, J.G., W.H. Brune, and M.H. Proffitt. 1989.

(a)

(b)

October, 2019

◆ **Connect to the Central Case**

FIGURE 20 An Ozone Decline in Space and Time (a) James Anderson found that within the "ozone hole," ozone levels are low and ClO levels are high—just as predicted by the Molina-Rowland hypothesis. **(b)** NASA satellite data confirm Joseph Farman's ozone findings—increasingly low levels of ozone (blue) over Antarctica beginning around 1979. **Interpret Graphs** According to the graph, at what latitudes are ozone concentrations the lowest?

Then, in 1982, a scientist named Joseph Farman detected a 40 percent drop in ozone concentration over the Antarctic. He had been collecting ozone readings since 1957 and had never encountered such a dramatic shift. The following year, he detected another steep decline. Reanalyzing data he had collected since 1977, Farman realized that ozone concentration had been steadily declining. Together with NASA scientists, Farman had discovered the "ozone hole," a region of depleted ozone the size of the United States in the atmosphere above Antarctica. The extent of ozone damage was greater than scientists had predicted. Further study showed that clouds of ice particles over Antarctica sped up ozone destruction. The evidence all pointed to one fact—CFCs were indeed destroying the ozone layer.

LESSON ② Assessment

1. **Compare and Contrast** What makes science different from other subjects you study in school, such as writing, history, or language?

2. **Explain** Some people think that *science* can be defined as "a collection of facts." Explain why that is an inaccurate definition, and, in your own words, write your own definition of science.

REVISIT

3. **INVESTIGATIVE** PHENOMENON
Why is the process of science better represented by the diagram shown in **Figure 10** than by a diagram like the one seen here?

Observations → Questions → Hypothesis

Results ← Test ← Predictions

LESSON 3

The Community of Science

EVERYDAY PHENOMENON What happens to a scientific study after data have been gathered and the results are analyzed?

Knowledge and Skills

- Describe the major roles of the scientific community in the process of science.
- Explain the study of environmental ethics.

Reading Strategy and Vocabulary

✅ **Reading Strategy** As you read, make a T-chart that identifies and explains the main concepts of this lesson.

Vocabulary peer review, theory, ethics, environmental ethics

SCIENTIFIC WORK takes place within the context of a community of peers. Molina and Rowland built upon the observations of James Lovelock and others. Other scientists, including James Anderson, tested the predictions of Molina and Rowland. With each discovery, the scientists talked with peers and published their work, making their data accessible to the entire scientific community.

Community Analysis and Feedback

When a researcher's work on a particular test or idea is done, he or she writes up the findings. Frequently, scientists will present their work at professional conferences, where they interact with colleagues and receive informal comments on their research. Such feedback from colleagues can help improve the quality of a scientist's work before it is submitted to a journal for publication.

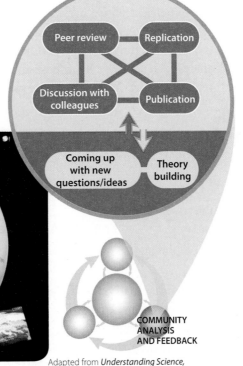

Peer review — Replication

Discussion with colleagues — Publication

Coming up with new questions/ideas — Theory building

COMMUNITY ANALYSIS AND FEEDBACK

Adapted from *Understanding Science*, www.understandingscience.org, UC Berkeley, Museum of Paleontology

FIGURE 21 Community Analysis and Feedback Science does not end in the lab or field. Interactions within the scientific community help ensure accuracy and build consensus.

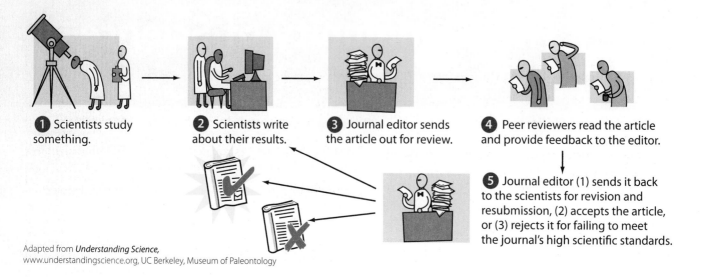

1. Scientists study something.
2. Scientists write about their results.
3. Journal editor sends the article out for review.
4. Peer reviewers read the article and provide feedback to the editor.
5. Journal editor (1) sends it back to the scientists for revision and resubmission, (2) accepts the article, or (3) rejects it for failing to meet the journal's high scientific standards.

Adapted from *Understanding Science,*
www.understandingscience.org, UC Berkeley, Museum of Paleontology

FIGURE 22 Peer Review Results published in peer-reviewed journals are the most respected in science because they have passed through a rigorous evaluation process involving feedback from multiple sources.

Peer Review Once a manuscript is submitted for publication, several other scientists specializing in the topic of the paper examine it. This procedure, known as **peer review,** is a more formal way for the researcher to get comments and criticism from the scientific community. If the reviewers feel the article should be published, the journal may publish it as is or ask the scientists to address comments and turn in a final paper. If, however, the peer reviewers are not satisfied with the work, the journal will not publish the article. Peer review is a valuable guard against faulty science contaminating the literature on which all scientists rely. The peer review process is summarized in **Figure 22.**

Replication Sound science is based on replication rather than a one-time occurrence. Even when a hypothesis appears to explain observed phenomena, scientists are always willing to consider other scientific explanations. After test results are published, other scientists may attempt to reproduce the results by performing their own experiments and data analysis. Generally, a hypothesis must be repeatedly tested and results replicated in various ways before scientists are willing to accept it.

Quick Lab

Can You Repeat That?

1. Together with a partner, arrange ten objects, such as pencils or blocks, into an unusual shape or structure.
2. Write directions that another team can use to replicate your shape or structure without seeing it.
3. Exchange directions with another team. Replicate that team's shape or structure by following their directions. You may not ask questions of the team or look at their original design.
4. Compare each replicated shape or structure to the original.

Analyze and Conclude

1. **Evaluate and Revise** Identify the places where you could have written clearer instructions. Revise your instructions and swap them with another team. Did the instructions work better the second time?
2. **Infer** Why is it important that procedures be included in published scientific papers?

Self-Correction in Science

As the scientific community accumulates data in any given area of research, interpretations may change. Most of the time, the changes are minor, small adjustments rather than complete revisions. However, science may go through revolutions in which one strongly held scientific view is abandoned for another.

For example, before the sixteenth century, scientists thought that Earth was at the center of the universe. Their data on the movements of planets fit that concept quite well, yet the idea was eventually shown to be false by Nicolaus Copernicus. Such revolutions in scientific thought demonstrate the strength and vitality of science, showing it to be a process that refines and improves itself through time. Science is self-correcting, and understanding how science works is vital to assessing how scientific ideas and interpretations change through time as new information accrues.

Scientific Theory-Building

Hypotheses are explanations for a fairly narrow set of phenomena, while **theories** are broader explanations that apply to a wider range of situations and observations. For example, Molina, Rowland, and others formed specific hypotheses about the ozone-depleting chain of chemical reactions in the upper atmosphere. These specific hypotheses were based on broader chemical and physical theories that deal with how *all* atoms and molecules interact with one another. It is not always clear when an explanation should be called a hypothesis and when it should be called a theory. Some scientists view Molina and Rowland's set of ideas about ozone depletion as a *theory*, and others view it as a *hypothesis*. Regardless of what we choose to call it, their explanation has been supported by many different lines of evidence and is broadly accepted by the scientific community.

Note that scientific use of the word *theory* differs from popular usage of the word. In everyday language when we say something is "just a theory," we are suggesting it is an idea without much substance. Scientists, however, mean just the opposite when they use the term. To be accepted as a *scientific theory,* an idea must effectively explain a phenomenon, make accurate predictions in a wide range of situations, and have undergone extensive, rigorous testing. Scientists are extremely confident in accepted theories. Darwin's theory of evolution by natural selection, for example, has been supported and elaborated upon by many thousands of studies over 150 years of intensive research. Other prominent scientific theories include atomic theory, cell theory, the big bang theory, plate tectonics, and the theory of general relativity.

 Reading Checkpoint *Why isn't anything in science "just" a theory?*

FIGURE 23 The Evolution of a Theory Paleontologist Neil Shubin sketches a 375-million-year-old fossil of *Tiktaalik roseae*. It is a fish, but has many characteristics of a land animal. Near Dr. Shubin is a fossil of an ancient whale. Notice its legs, evidence that whales evolved from terrestrial ancestors. Scientists have been adding to and refining Darwin's theory of natural selection for more than 150 years, making it among the strongest theories in science.

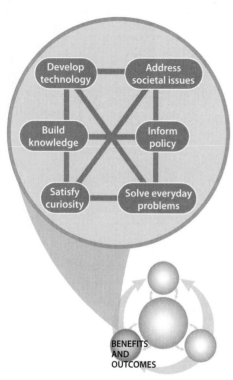

Adapted from *Understanding Science,*
www.understandingscience.org,
UC Berkeley, Museum of Paleontology

FIGURE 24 Benefits and Outcomes
Science does not occur in isolation.
Society, especially its ethical standards
and worldview, influences science, just
as science influences society. Science
and society work together to build
knowledge, satisfy curiosity, address
issues, inform policy, solve problems,
and develop technology. One scientific
benefit and outcome is this green
roof atop the California Academy of
Sciences building in San Francisco.
Green roofs like this one reduce energy
demands and provide wildlife habitat.

Benefits and Outcomes

Environmental scientists ask questions, test hypotheses, conduct experiments, gather and analyze data, and draw conclusions about environmental processes. Beyond the simple satisfaction of generating results, their work has helped contribute to our overall knowledge of the environment and has led to the development of new technologies. But the work does not end with the science. To address environmental problems, we need more than an understanding of the science—we also need to understand how people value their environment. To value something is to think it is important. Economics, covered in the next chapter, deals with how things are valued in terms of money. Ethics deals with how things are morally valued. Scientific knowledge can affect our social, ethical, and economic decision making.

Ethics Ethics is a branch of philosophy that involves the study of behavior: good and bad, right and wrong. The term *ethics* can also refer to the set of moral principles or values held by a person or a society. Ethical standards are grounded in values—for instance, promoting human welfare, maximizing individual freedom, or minimizing pain and suffering. We all use our own set of ethical standards as tools for making decisions, consciously or unconsciously, in our everyday lives. Governments and decision makers also employ ethics when deciding on public policy.

Culture and Worldview People of different cultures may differ in their ethical standards. *Culture* is the ensemble of knowledge, beliefs, values, and learned ways of life shared by a group of people. Culture, together with personal experience, influences each person's perception of the world and his or her place within it, something described as the person's *worldview*. Worldview and culture can influence what a scientist chooses to study or where to look for inspiration. Worldview reflects a person's or group's beliefs about the meaning, operation, and essence of the world.

You may be wondering why we are discussing beliefs in a book about science—especially because we have said that scientists do not *believe* in a scientific idea, they accept or reject it based on evidence. Although scientists strive to be objective, worldview influences how society interprets and acts on the results science produces. People with different worldviews can study the same situation and review identical data yet draw dramatically different conclusions.

For example, scientific investigations led to the conclusion that CFCs were destroying the ozone layer. A discovery such as this is neither good nor bad, it is just fact. What is done with the information, however, is influenced by worldview, and may be seen differently by different people. On May 11, 1977, the United States government announced that it was phasing out CFCs. In 1987, nations began to sign on to the Montreal Protocol, an agreement to control the production and use of ozone-depleting substances. Within a few years, nations that had adopted the treaty agreed to a complete ban of CFCs and other chemicals. Environmentalists viewed these developments as a triumph, but many people who worked in industries that relied on CFCs were angered.

Ethics and the Environment Did we, as humans, have a responsibility to ban CFCs and protect the ozone layer? The application of ethical standards to relationships between humans and their environment is known as **environmental ethics.** This relatively new branch of ethics arose once people became aware of environmental changes brought about by industrialization. Human interactions with the environment frequently give rise to ethical questions that can be difficult to resolve. For example, does the present generation have an obligation to conserve resources for future generations? What if protecting those resources means people today will suffer because they have fewer resources available to them? Answers to questions like these depend partly on what ethical standards a person chooses to use. Three important ethical standards in environmental ethics are *anthropocentrism, biocentrism,* and *ecocentrism.*

◆ **Connect to the Central Case**

FIGURE 25 Phasing Out Mario Molina gave a speech celebrating the Protocol's success at the twentieth anniversary celebration seminar on the Montreal Protocol, September 16, 2007, in Montreal, Canada. **Infer** Why might the Montreal Protocol not have been as successful if very few nations had signed on?

▶ **Anthropocentrism** *Anthropocentrism* describes a human-centered view of our relationship with the environment. An anthropocentrist places the highest value on humans and human welfare. In evaluating a decision, someone with this worldview would likely consider the impacts on human health and economies more important than the impacts on other aspects of the environment.

▶ **Biocentrism** In contrast to anthropocentrism, *biocentrism* gives value to all living things. In this perspective, nonhuman life has ethical standing, so a biocentrist evaluates actions in terms of their overall effect on living things, both human and nonhuman. Some biocentrists advocate equal consideration of all living things, whereas others advocate that some types of organisms should receive more consideration than others.

▶ **Ecocentrism** *Ecocentrism* judges actions in terms of their benefit or harm to the integrity of whole ecological systems, which consist of both living and nonliving elements and the relationships among them. An ecocentrist would value the well-being of species, communities, or ecosystems over the welfare of a given individual. Implicit in this view is that the preservation of larger systems generally protects their components.

Environmental Justice In recent years, people of all persuasions have increasingly realized the connection between environmental quality and human quality of life. Unfortunately, disadvantaged people tend to be exposed to a greater share of pollution, hazards, and environmental degradation than are affluent people. In addition, just as wealthy people often impose their pollution on poorer people, wealthy nations often do the same to poorer nations. The *environmental justice movement* promotes the fair and equitable treatment of all people with respect to environmental policy and practice, regardless of their income, race, or ethnicity. As we explore environmental issues from a scientific standpoint, we will also encounter the social aspects of these issues, and the concept of environmental justice will arise again and again.

 What does it mean to have an ecocentric worldview?

FIND OUT MORE

Where are the factories, waste dumps, and polluting facilities located in your city or town? Prepare a short oral presentation of your findings.

Ecocentric

Biocentric

Anthropocentric

FIGURE 26 Ethical Views Individuals vary in how much value they give living things and the environment. People with an anthropocentric worldview tend to measure the costs and benefits of actions primarily according to their effect on humans. Biocentric individuals consider the costs and benefits to all living things. Ecocentrists tend to think that whole ecological systems, involving living and nonliving parts, should be protected over individuals.

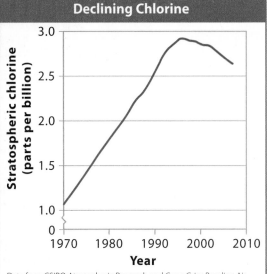

Declining Chlorine

Data from CSIRO Atmospheric Research and Cape Grim Baseline Air Pollution Station, Australian Antarctic Division and Australian Bureau of Meteorology as appears in *Understanding Science,* www.understandingscience.org, UC Berkeley, Museum of Paleontology

Toward the Future Finding effective ways of living peacefully, healthfully, and sustainably on our diverse and complex planet will require a thorough scientific understanding of both natural and social systems. Environmental science helps us understand our intricate relationship with the environment and informs our attempts to solve and prevent environmental problems. The work involving CFCs, for example, is a success story for environmental science. Since the ban of CFCs, chlorine levels in the atmosphere have fallen dramatically, as shown in **Figure 27.** Scientists predict that the ozone hole should be fully repaired sometime this century.

It is important to keep in mind that identifying a problem is the first step in devising a solution to it. Many of the trends detailed in this book may cause us worry, but others give us reason to hope. One often-heard criticism of environmental science courses and textbooks is that too often they emphasize the negative. In this book, we attempt to balance the discussion of environmental problems with a corresponding focus on solutions. Solving environmental problems can move us toward health, longevity, peace, and prosperity. Science in general, and environmental science in particular, can aid us in our efforts to develop balanced and workable solutions to the many environmental dilemmas we face today and to create a better world for ourselves and our children.

Connect to the Central Case

FIGURE 27 A Positive Decline Since the late 1990s, scientists have measured a steady decline in the chlorine concentration in the stratosphere. The trend suggests that efforts to prevent ozone-destroying chemicals from entering the atmosphere have been successful. The Live Earth concerts of 2007 proved to be another successful environmental effort. They raised money for international environmental programs and global awareness of environmental issues such as climate change. **Interpret Graphs** In what year was chlorine concentration highest?

LESSON ③ Assessment

1. **Apply Concepts** Your doctor recommends that someone in your family start taking a new drug to lower cholesterol. Where would you recommend looking for information: articles published in peer-reviewed journals or materials published by the drug company? Explain.

2. **Explain** Explain how although science itself is objective, it can be affected by subjective influences such as worldview and culture.

3. **THINK IT** *THROUGH* Suppose you are the head of a major funding agency that gives money to researchers investigating environmental science issues. Describe how you would decide what types of projects to fund.

An Introduction to Environmental Science **27**

THE LESSON OF
EASTER ISLAND

When European explorers first reached Easter Island in the 1700s, there were an estimated 2000 or fewer people living there. There were not many trees on the island, and the native people, called the *Rapa Nui,* could only grow enough food to support their small population. But the island also had more than 800 moai statues, the largest of which stands 10 meters (33 feet) high and weighs 75 metric tons (82 tons)—bigger than a two-story house!

The large number of moai and other archaeological evidence suggest that the island may have once supported as many as 10,000 people. What happened to the large population that built the moai, and how had so many people survived on such a barren island?

KEY

🗿 Stone statues

0 — 4 mi

0 — 4 km

map area

SOUTH PACIFIC OCEAN

Easter Island (CHILE)

SOUTH AMERICA

PROOF IN THE POLLEN

By studying ancient coastal settlements, archaeologists determined that the island natives likely arrived from Polynesia between A.D. 700 and 1100. Not much was known however, about what the island was like before that time. In the 1980s, geographer John Flenley drilled long cylinders, or cores, of mud out of the bottom of lakes on Easter Island. The mud contained fossilized pollen grains. How deep the pollen was buried showed when different plant species lived on the island. By analyzing the pollen, Flenley found that before people arrived, the island was covered with a variety of large palm trees and many other plants.

A LOST JUNGLE

Pollen cores taken by Flenley and other researchers showed that shortly after the Polynesians arrived on the island, all of the tall trees had disappeared. By A.D. 1400, most species of plants had vanished from the island as well. Some researchers hypothesize that the people on the island cut down the trees, using them to build canoes and houses, and, most likely, to transport the moai. In addition to overharvesting, changes in climate may have contributed to the deforestation of Easter Island.

THE DECLINE

Without trees, the island's soil washed away, disrupting fresh water sources and making it hard to grow food. Famine and war reduced the native island population from nearly 10,000 to 2000 or 3000 by the time Europeans arrived. The civilization that built the moai declined because the resources it needed to survive disappeared, in part because the people of the island had overused them.

CAREER **Environmental Policy Analyst**

Environmental policy analysts study economic, scientific, and other available data to provide information on various environmental issues. Go Online and research careers in environmental policy. Write a brief summary of your findings.

INVESTIGATIVE PHENOMENON

Can we reduce the ozone hole?

Lesson 1
How does environmental science help us understand the natural world?

Lesson 2
What does it mean to "do science"?

Lesson 3
What happens to a scientific study after data have been gathered and the results are analyzed?

LESSON 1 Our Island, Earth

- Environmental scientists study how the natural world works, and how humans and the environment affect each other. Environmentalism, on the other hand, is a social movement dedicated to protecting the natural world from negative human influences.
- In the last several hundred years, both human population and natural resource consumption have risen dramatically.
- A natural resource is any material or energy source provided by nature that humans need to survive.

environment (4)
environmental science (5)
environmentalism (6)
natural resource (6)
renewable natural resources (7)
nonrenewable natural resources (7)
sustainable (7)
fossil fuel (8)
ecological footprint (9)

LESSON 2 The Nature of Science

- Science is both an organized and methodical way of studying the natural world and the body of knowledge gained from such studies.
- The process of science involves making observations, asking questions, developing hypotheses, making and testing predictions, and analyzing and interpreting results—often many times and in many changing orders.
- Experiments and observational studies involve variables. Independent variables are manipulated by a scientist. Dependent variables depend on the conditions of the experiment or study. Controlled variables are kept constant. Controlled studies and experiments involve only one manipulated variable—all other variables are held constant.

hypothesis (15)	dependent variable (17)
prediction (16)	controlled study (18)
independent variable (17)	data (19)

LESSON 3 The Community of Science

- The scientific community, through peer review and replication, helps to verify the accuracy of results and contributes to the establishment of scientific theories.
- Environmental ethics explores how environmental science interacts with, and is guided by, a society's morals and principles.
- There are three important ethical standards involved in environmental ethics: anthropocentrism, biocentrism, and ecocentrism. Anthropocentrism is a human-centered view of the world in which humans and human welfare are given the highest value. Biocentrism gives value to all living things equally. Ecocentrism assigns less value to individual organisms than to whole populations, species, communities, and ecosystems.

peer review (22)
theory (23)
ethics (24)
environmental ethics (25)

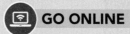 **GO ONLINE**

INQUIRY LABS AND ACTIVITIES

- **Modeling Finite Resources**
  How does the "tragedy of the commons" really work? See it in action by simulating fishing in a shared lake.
- **Green vs. Conventional Cleaners**
  Can homemade, environmentally friendly cleaners work as well as toxic ones? Design an experiment to find out.
- **Local Research Studies**
  What current environmental studies are happening near you? Find out how, where, and why one local study is being conducted.

Chapter Assessment

Defend Your Case

The Central Case in this chapter explored how science led to the discovery of how certain chemicals were affecting the ozone layer. Use examples from the Central Case and throughout the chapter to provide evidence on how science often relies not only on individuals, but the entire scientific community and beyond to achieve its goals.

Review Concepts and Terms

1. The environment contains
   a. living things only.
   b. nonliving things only.
   c. both living and nonliving things.
   d. only artificial things.

2. Which of the following is NOT an example of a natural resource?
   a. coal   c. timber
   b. sunlight   d. plastic

3. Which of the following is ALWAYS a nonrenewable natural resource?
   a. wind   c. oil
   b. fresh water   d. soil

4. "A testable idea that attempts to explain a phenomenon or answer a scientific question" is the definition of a (an)
   a. prediction.
   b. hypothesis.
   c. theory.
   d. experiment.

5. Which of the following phrases is missing below?

   Predicted results/ observations ≠ **Actual results/ observations** → **?**

   a. supports hypothesis
   b. proves hypothesis
   c. refutes hypothesis
   d. disproves hypothesis

6. Experiments or observational studies in which only one variable is manipulated are described as
   a. controlled.   c. dependent.
   b. observed.   d. independent.

7. The branch of philosophy that deals with good, bad, right, and wrong is called
   a. logic.   c. science.
   b. ethics.   d. culture.

8. Which of the following is the primary difference between a theory and a hypothesis?
   a. A theory deals only with the natural world, a hypothesis does not.
   b. A theory is tested, a hypothesis is not.
   c. A theory is not tested, a hypothesis is.
   d. A theory is broader than a hypothesis, dealing with a wider range of situations and observations.

9. The variable a scientist manipulates in an experiment is called the
   a. controlled variable.
   b. observation variable.
   c. dependent variable.
   d. independent variable.

Modified True/False

Write true if the statement is true. If it is false, change the underlined word or words to make the statement true.

10. <u>Environmentalism</u> is the study of how the natural world works, how our environment affects us, and how we affect our environment.

11. At the start of the <u>Industrial Revolution,</u> about 10,000 years ago, humans began planting crops and domesticating animals.

12. <u>Independent variables</u> depend on experimental conditions.

13. The process by which the scientific community examines a paper before its publication is called <u>peer review.</u>

14. <u>Anthropocentrism</u> describes a worldview in which all components of an ecosystem have value.

Chapter Assessment

Reading Comprehension

Read the following selection and answer the questions that follow.

There is historical evidence that civilizations can crumble when pressures from population and consumption overwhelm resource availability. Indeed, many great civilizations have fallen after depleting resources from their environments, and each has left devastated landscapes in its wake. Plato wrote of the deforestation and environmental degradation accompanying ancient Greek cities, for example. Archaeologists, historians, and paleoecologists study past societies and landscapes and have accumulated evidence of environmental collapse, from the Greek and Roman empires to the Maya, the Anasazi, and other civilizations of the New World. Scientist and author Jared Diamond in his 2005 book, *Collapse,* formulated sets of reasons why civilizations succeed and persist, or fail and collapse. Success and persistence, it turns out, depend largely on how societies interact with their environments.

15. From the passage, it is possible to infer that the Anasazi were an ancient civilization that
    a. collapsed after the Greek Empire.
    b. lived in the New World.
    c. were part of the Roman Empire.
    d. persisted and live in the New World today.

16. Which of the following would be the BEST title for this passage?
    a. "The Mayan Civilization"
    b. "Paleoecology Today"
    c. "The Danger of Depleting Resources"
    d. "Plato's Warning"

17. Which of the following is a synonym (word with a similar definition) for the word *degradation,* used in line 8 of the passage?
    a. health
    b. ruin
    c. gradation
    d. evaluation

Short Answer

18. What is "the tragedy of the commons"?

19. Who was Thomas Malthus, and what did he suggest about human population growth?

20. What does it mean to use a resource sustainably?

21. Why do scientists use models?

22. Sometimes variables are described as "manipulated" and "responding." Which do you think is the alternative name for the independent variable? Explain.

23. What is the environmental justice movement?

Critical Thinking

24. **Compare and Contrast** Briefly explain the Agricultural and Industrial revolutions and how they affected the human population.

25. **Classify** Classify each of the following natural resources as renewable, nonrenewable, or "in between": (a) wave energy, (b) oil, (c) soil, (d) sunlight, (e) fresh water, and (f) timber. Explain what it means to be an "in between" resource.

26. **Compare and Contrast** What are the similarities and differences between experiments and observational studies?

27. **Apply Concepts** Why do scientists try to control most variables in an experiment or observational study?

28. **Evaluate** A scientist repeats an experiment ten times. Nine out of ten times, the results support her predictions. She thinks she knows what caused the one trial to produce the unexpected result. Should she report all of the results in her paper, or just the nine that supported her hypothesis? Explain your reasoning.

29. **Explain** What does it mean that science is "self-correcting"?

30. **Relate Cause and Effect** What is a worldview, and what impact does it have on science?

Analyze Data

Environmental scientists study phenomena that range in size from individual molecules to the entire planet, and that occur over periods lasting seconds to billions of years. To meaningfully represent these varied data, scientists have devised a variety of techniques, such as exponential notation and logarithmic scales. The graphs below show the same data, a hypothetical population's growth over 900 generations, in two different ways. Use the graphs to answer the questions.

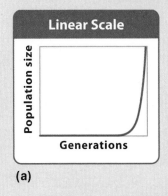

(a)

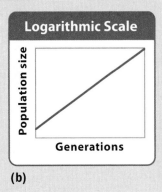

(b)

31. Interpret Graphs What impression does Graph A give about population change over the 900 generations shown? What impression does Graph B give?

32. Apply Concepts Describe a situation in which you would use Graph A. Describe a situation in which you would use Graph B.

Write About It

33. Creative Writing There are many misconceptions about what science is. To help address them, create a full-page ad called "This Is Science." Use images, words, or a combination of images and words to accurately describe what science is and is not.

34. **REVISIT** **INVESTIGATIVE** PHENOMENON
Science almost always starts with observations and asking questions. In this way, nearly every person participates in the process of science every day. Think of three observations you have made or questions you have asked recently. Write them down and then briefly describe a way you might investigate each further. Remember, to be science, these observations and questions need to be about the natural world.

Ecological Footprints

Read the information below. Copy the table into your notebook and record your calculations. Then, answer the questions that follow.

Mathis Wackernagel and his colleagues at the Global Footprint Network reported in 2006 that the average person has an ecological footprint of about 2.23 hectares (5.4 acres). That means that each person on Earth, on average, requires 2.23 hectares of functioning ecosystem to recycle wastes and produce the energy and resources required to live. The ecological footprints of several nations are shown in the table.

1. Which nation included in the table has an ecological footprint closest to the world's average? Which nation has the smallest footprint? Which nation has the largest footprint?

2. Why do you think that there is such a large difference in footprint size between the nation with greatest footprint and the nation with the smallest footprint?

Nation	Ecological Footprint (hectares per person)	Proportion Relative to World Average Footprint
Bangladesh	0.5	
Colombia	1.3	
Mexico	2.6	
Sweden	6.1	
Thailand	1.4	
United States	9.6	

Data from *Living planet report 2006.* WWF International, Zoological Society of London, and Global Footprint Network.

3. In 2005, Wackernagel estimated that there are about 1.8 hectares (4.4 acres) available to each person in the world, but the average footprint is 2.23 hectares. By these calculations, by about what percentage are we "overshooting" the resources available to us?

MATH SUPPORT For help with ratio and proportion calculations, see the Math Handbook.

Economics and Environmental Policy

How do economic factors influence environmental policy?

Sometimes the amount of sewage and other toxins from the Tijuana River leads to beach closures in San Diego, CA.

Lesson 1
Economics

Lesson 2
United States
Environmental Policy

Lesson 3
International Environmental
Policy and Approaches

Cleaning the Tides of San Diego and Tijuana

THE TIJUANA RIVER winds northwestward through the arid landscape of northern Mexico, crossing the U.S. border just south of San Diego. On the Mexican side of the border, the river and its creeks are lined with farms, apartments, shanties, and factories, as well as aging and leaky sewage treatment plants and toxic dump sites. Rains wash pollutants from all these sources into the creeks that enter the river.

Although pollution has flowed into the Tijuana River for at least 70 years, the problem has grown worse in recent decades because the region's population almost tripled between 1972 and 2000. The opening of U.S.-owned factories on the Mexican side of the border has contributed to the river's pollution with waste disposal and by attracting more workers to the already crowded region.

Eventually this water, polluted with disease-causing raw sewage and debris, makes its way north across the U.S. border, where it is expelled into the Pacific Ocean along San Diego's coast. The pollution is at its worst after heavy rains when the system of pipes that are supposed to divert the polluted water to wastewater treatments plants overflow. San Diego officials regularly close beaches and issue hundreds of health advisories due to the harmful pollutants.

This pollution problem is a difficult one to solve because it involves two nations with their own laws. The polluted water that flows into the Pacific Ocean violates the Clean Water Act. But the Clean Water Act is a United States law and cannot be enforced in Mexico.

When beaches are closed, the San Diego area loses money from tourists and other beachgoers. And someone has to pay for the cleanup. But what about the citizens of the Tijuana area whose everyday lives are affected by this pollution? Since U.S.-owned factories have contributed

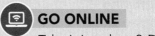

GO ONLINE
• Take It Local   • 3-D Geo Tour

to the pollution problem, is the United States responsible for helping to solve it? Or is it Mexico's responsibility to keep pollution from entering the United States? Clearly, this problem requires cooperation between the two nations.

Both countries have contributed funds to help solve the environmental and public health issue. The United States and Mexico agreed to the construction of the South Bay International Wastewater Treatment Plant just over the U.S. border, which would be completed in two phases. Mexico, in turn, agreed to improve its ability to sanitize wastewater.

However, the pumps diverting the water to treatment plants can't keep up with the wastewater. Recently, the United States has evaluated approaches to handle the secondary treatment phase, including building wastewater treatment plants on the U.S. side of the border. Mexico and the United States continue to work together to find solutions for this pollution problem.

Economics

EVERYDAY PHENOMENON How is sustainability affected by economics?

Knowledge and Skills

- Describe two basic concepts of economics.
- Explain the relationship between economics and the environment.
- Describe ways that economies are working toward sustainability.

Reading Strategy and Vocabulary

✅ **Reading Strategy** Before you start reading, skim the lesson. Look at the headings and the highlighted vocabulary. Skim any charts, tables, and maps. Read the captions for photographs and diagrams. Write down (1) what you think this lesson will be about and (2) what you want to learn from this lesson.

Vocabulary economics, supply, demand, cost-benefit analysis, ecological economics, environmental economics, non-market value, market failure, ecolabeling

BECAUSE PEOPLE RELY on the resources around them to make products or provide services to earn a living, the environment and economics are closely associated with each other. The word *economic* and the word *ecology* come from the same Greek root, *oikos*, meaning "household." In its broadest sense, the human "household" is Earth.

What Is Economics?

When you hear the word *economics*, the first word that may come to your mind is *money*. But economics also has a lot to do with human behavior and how people interact with nature. **Economics** is the study of how resources are converted into goods and services and how these goods and services are distributed and used. *Goods* are the manufactured materials and products that individual consumers and businesses buy. *Services* are the work that someone or a company does for others as a form of business, such as home repairs.

There are three types of economies. In a *centrally planned economy,* the government decides what is made, how it is made, and who gets what. Socialist and communist governments generally operate this type of economy. In a *free market economy,* individuals decide what is made, how it is made, and how much is made. In a *mixed economy,* both the government and individuals play roles in making these decisions. Almost all modern economies are mixed economies. The degree of government involvement versus individual choice differs from nation to nation. The U.S. economy, for example, leans toward the free market.

Economics is closely tied to decisions that people make every day about their needs and wants. Economists, people who study economics, spend a lot of time examining the factors that influence the decisions of buyers and sellers.

Supply and Demand The amount of a product offered for sale at a given price is supply. The amount of a product people will buy at a given price if free to do so is **demand.** Sellers aim to sell the most product at the highest price consumers will pay before they turn to other options. When demand is low, the seller may drop the price and slow production. When demand is high, the seller may raise the price and increase production. Under those conditions, the market is expected to reach equilibrium—the point when the amount of product produced is equal to the demand for the product **(Figure 1).**

Cost-Benefit Analysis Decision makers commonly use a method called cost-benefit analysis in which they compare what they will sacrifice and gain by a specific action. For example, when a company considers developing a new product, or a city considers improving a transportation system, all of the costs and benefits are considered. If the costs outweigh the benefits, then often the idea will be revised or abandoned. If the benefits outweigh the costs, the action is often pursued. Cost-benefit analyses can be quite complicated and controversial because, as you will learn, not all costs and benefits can be easily identified or defined.

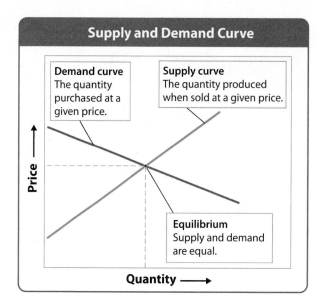

FIGURE 1 **Supply and Demand** In a basic supply-and-demand graph, the demand curve indicates the quantity of a good or service that consumers desire at each price. The supply curve indicates the quantity produced at each price. The market tends to move toward equilibrium, the point at which supply equals demand.

Economics and the Environment

Economies depend on materials from the environment to produce products, and on Earth's systems, such as the water cycle, to handle production wastes. But there are consequences to relying on natural resources and ecological systems in an ever-growing world economy.

 **Quick Lab**

Cost-Benefit Analysis

Maria finishes a jar of peanut butter while making a sandwich. She starts to rinse out the jar so that she can throw it in the recycling bin. But the remaining peanut butter is quite stuck to the inside of the jar. As more and more water flows down the drain, she thinks, "I know that recycling is important, but so is water conservation. At what point should I just throw this jar in the trash?"

Analyze and Conclude

1. **Explain** How is Maria's decision similar to the cost-benefit analysis that a company might perform?

2. **Summarize** In a table, list the costs and benefits of Maria's two choices: continuing to prepare the jar for the recycling bin or throwing it out.

3. **Pose Questions** Maria decides to research her question. List three questions that Maria should try to answer as she does her research.

Some resources are naturally recycled.

The resources for economies come from ecosystems.

(a)

Economies convert resources to goods and pay wages to households. Households buy products and supply labor to make the products.

Ecosystems take the waste from economies.

(c)

(b)

FIGURE 2 **Economic Activity**
Traditionally, economics focused on processes of production and consumption between households and businesses. Traditional economists only considered the interactions that occur in **(b).** More recently, economists have started to view economies as existing within the natural environment, and consider the interactions that occur among **(a), (b),** and **(c).**

Support From the Environment Natural resources are the various substances and forces people need to survive, such as the sun's energy, fresh water, trees, rocks, and fossil fuels. We can think of natural resources as "goods" produced by nature. Without these resources there would be no economics. Ecological systems provide "ecosystem services" as they purify air and water, cycle nutrients, and serve as containers and recycling centers for the wastes produced by economic activities.

Impact on the Environment When economic activity depletes natural resources or produces too much pollution, ecological systems can be harmed. In return, this will harm economies. For example, what happens to a vacation destination when the local sewage treatment facility can no longer keep up with the waste being generated? Wastes pollute the water, swimming areas are closed, tourists stop coming, and local businesses suffer.

Interactions between economies and the environment, shown in **Figure 2,** may seem obvious. But, they are not always considered during the cost-benefit analyses discussed earlier. Traditionally, many environmental factors such as beautiful views, fresh air, and clean water don't have a monetary value assigned to them. Some long-held assumptions of economics have led to negative outcomes for the environment.

 Reading Checkpoint   *Briefly describe how economies receive support from the environment and affect the environment.*

▶ **Internal Costs and Benefits** Economists tend to assume that costs and benefits only affect buyers and sellers directly involved in transactions. These factors are known as *internal* costs and benefits. However, beach closures due to Tijuana River pollution lead to economic losses for restaurants and hotels that did not contribute to the pollution. The costs of this pollution are not figured into cost-benefit analyses of new factories opening in Tijuana because their owners will not be paying these costs. Such factors, which involve parties other than a buyer or seller, are known as *external* costs and benefits.

▶ **Short-Term Effects** Often in planning, short-term costs and benefits are given more weight than long-term costs and benefits. Because many environmental problems unfold slowly, less attention is given to the effects of resource depletion and pollution on future generations.

▶ **Endless Resources** Economists often do not consider that resources can run out. People may assume that any resource can be substituted with something else. It is true that some resources can be substituted. For example, machines now do work previously done by animals. But some resources, such as fossil fuels, cannot be replaced. Some renewable resources, such as fresh water, can be overused until supply does not meet demand.

▶ **Growth** Another assumption of economists is that continued growth is required to keep employment high and maintain social order. The rate of economic growth in recent decades has never been seen before. More and more goods are produced and sold. Some argue that because Earth's resources are limited, nonstop economic growth is not sustainable. Others argue that technology will continue to overcome obstacles to economic growth and that growth is sustainable.

◆ **Connect to the Central Case**
FIGURE 3 External Costs Ethically, water pollution poses problems because in most cases pollution from upstream users affects downstream users, who are not responsible for the pollution. **Apply Concepts** Describe how the opening of more factories in Tijuana became a cost for beachfront businesses in southern California.

Economics and Sustainability

Can economic growth continue indefinitely with ever-advancing technology, or do we need a more balanced system? An emerging field of economics, **ecological economics,** applies the principles of Earth's systems to economics. These systems, which include complex relationships among living and non-living things, generally have a near-perfect balance of inputs and outputs. Ecological economists argue that history suggests civilizations do not overcome their resource limitations. Many ecological economists advocate economies that do not grow or shrink, but rather are stable and sustainable—like Earth's systems.

Another field, called **environmental economics,** agrees that economies are unsustainable if resource use is not made more efficient. However, these economists argue that economies can become sustainable if environmental challenges are addressed. Some of these challenges include assigning market values to ecosystem services and addressing market failure.

FIGURE 4 Non-market Value
Keeping in mind non-market values such as those shown here may help people make better environmental and economic decisions.

(a) Aesthetic value

(b) Cultural value

(c) Scientific value

Types of Non-Market Values	
Non-market value	**Is the worth we attach to things…**
Use value	that we use directly, such as a river for boating.
Option value	that we do not use now but might use later, such as timber in an uncut forest.
Aesthetic value	that we appreciate for their beauty or emotional appeal.
Cultural value	that sustain or help define our culture.
Scientific value	that may be the subject of scientific research.
Educational value	that may teach us about ourselves and the world.
Existence value	simply because they exist, even though we may never experience them directly, such as animals in far-off places.

Assign Market Values Ecosystem services provided by Earth's systems are said to have **non-market values**—values not usually included in the price of goods or services. Because many ecosystem services do not have a value associated with them, people tend to exploit them. **Figure 4** gives some examples of non-market values.

Environmental and ecological economists have developed ways to assign values to services provided by Earth's systems. In one method—surveys—they may ask people to estimate how much they would pay for specific non-market goods, such as clean beaches or preservation of a beautiful view.

Another method is to compare transactions for similar goods or services that only differ because one is associated with a non-market good and the other is not. For example, a comparison could be made of the sale prices of similar homes some of which overlook a woodlot and some of which do not. This comparison could estimate the value of the woodlot.

Address Market Failure When markets do not reflect the full costs and benefits of actions, they are said to fail. **Market failure** occurs when markets do not consider the environment's positive effects on economies, such as ecosystem services, or when they do not reflect the negative effects of economic activity on the environment or on people, such as external costs.

For example, smokestacks emit chemicals that may harm trees and pollute water sources hundreds of miles away. Traditionally, the company emitting the chemicals has not been held responsible for these lost resources, cleanup costs, or effects on human health. Instead, another group (usually taxpayers) pays for some of the costs related to the company's activities.

To counteract such external costs, governments sometimes introduce policies that give companies economic incentives to conserve resources and reduce pollution, or that penalize them with taxes or fines for not doing so. These types of policies will be examined more closely in the next two lessons.

 Reading Checkpoint *How could addressing market failure help make an economy more environmentally sustainable?*

WHAT DO YOU THINK?

Do you think we should attempt to quantify and assign market values to ecosystem services and other entities that have only non-market values? Why or why not?

Examples of Ecolabels	
Ecolabel	**Meaning**
FAIR TRADE CERTIFIED	The Fair Trade Certified™ standards aim to ensure that farmers in developing nations receive fair prices and encourage sustainable farming methods. TransFair USA, a nonprofit organization, is the certifier of fair trade goods in the United States.
USDA ORGANIC	This seal indicates that a food is produced, processed, and certified to consistent national standards that were developed and are monitored by the U.S. Department of Agriculture's National Organic Program.
energy ENERGY STAR	The ENERGY STAR label identifies products that are approved as energy efficient by the Environmental Protection Agency. Purchasing products with this label should lead to lower energy bills, help to conserve energy, and lower greenhouse gas emissions.

FIGURE 5 Ecolabeling Ecolabeling allows businesses to promote products that have low environmental impact. These pineapples, grown in Costa Rica, carry a Fair Trade Certified label.

Changing Consumer Values Changing consumer values have become a driving force in encouraging corporations and businesses to pursue sustainability goals. Markets are already adapting to the call for sustainable goods and services. For example, manufacturers of certain products explain on their labels how the products were grown, harvested, or manufactured. This method, called **ecolabeling,** tells consumers which brands are made with processes that do not harm the environment. By choosing ecolabeled products, consumers give businesses a powerful incentive to switch to more sustainable processes. **Figure 5** shows examples of ecolabels you might see on products sold in the United States.

Corporate Responses As more consumers and investors demand sustainable products and services, more industries, businesses, and corporations are finding that they can make money and improve their public image by supplying the market with these products. Many corporations are finding ways to increase energy efficiency, reduce use of toxic substances, increase the use of recycled materials, and reduce greenhouse gas emissions.

LESSON ① Assessment

1. **Summarize** What is the expected outcome of the relationship between supply and demand? What is the goal of a cost-benefit analysis?

2. **Relate Cause and Effect** Describe four assumptions traditionally made in economics that can have a negative effect on the environment.

3. **Infer** What are two benefits that a company can achieve by operating its business in an environmentally sustainable way?

REVISIT

4. **INVESTIGATIVE** PHENOMENON
Suppose you were developing a survey to determine the non-market value for an ecosystem service in your community. Describe the ecosystem service and list three questions you would put on the survey that would help you determine the value of the service to members of your community.

United States Environmental Policy

EVERYDAY PHENOMENON How do environmental policies protect the environment?

Knowledge and Skills

- Explain the purpose of environmental policy.
- Describe the history of U.S. environmental policy.
- Describe the direction of current U.S. environmental policy.

Reading Strategy and Vocabulary

✔ **Reading Strategy** Before you read, create an outline using the blue and green headings in this lesson. As you read, fill in key phrases or sentences about each heading. If you have a question or an insight, record it on your outline.

Vocabulary policy, environmental policy, Environmental Impact Statement (EIS)

ONCE UPON A TIME the natural resources of the United States seemed absolutely endless. Settlers who forged into the vast western reaches of the continent probably could never imagine that such careful management of these resources is required today.

Two centuries later, the United States is a much different place. Industrialization made everyday lives easier in countless ways. But it also led to the rapid use of natural resources, pollution, ecosystem degradation, and other problems that affect human health and economic well-being. A challenge of the twenty-first century is maintaining the benefits of industrialization, while both repairing and preventing further damage to the environment.

What Is Environmental Policy?

When a society concludes that a problem needs a solution, it may persuade its leaders to resolve the problem through policy. **Policy** consists of a formal set of general plans and principles for addressing problems and guiding decision making. In particular, **environmental policy** consists of general plans and principles that address the interactions between humans and the environment. Modern-day environmental policy aims to protect environmental quality, protect natural resources, and ensure that resources are shared fairly.

In making environmental policy, government interacts with citizens, organizations, and businesses. Producing effective environmental policy requires input from science, ethics, and economics. Science provides information and analysis needed to identify, understand, and devise potential solutions for problems. Ethics and economics offer criteria to assess problems and to help clarify how society could address them.

The United States provides a good focus for understanding environmental policy in democracies worldwide. It has pioneered innovative environmental policies that have served as models—of both success and failure—for many other nations. Each of the three branches of government—legislative, executive, and judicial—are involved in environmental policy.

Legislative Branch A policy enters the realm of the federal government when legislation—a proposed law—is introduced by either the House of Representatives or the Senate. If both houses of Congress pass the bill, its next stop is the executive branch.

Executive Branch Legislation is enacted (approved) or vetoed (rejected) by the President. Enacted legislation becomes law and is assigned to an executive agency that puts it into action and enforces it. Dozens of executive agencies influence environmental policy, but a few examples are the Environmental Protection Agency, the U.S. Forest Service, and the Natural Resources Conservation Service.

Judicial Branch The judicial branch, which consists of the Supreme Court and lower courts, interprets laws. This is necessary because society changes over time and Congress writes broad laws to ensure they apply across the nation. Environmental advocates and organizations use lawsuits as tools to ensure corporations and government agencies comply with laws. Courts also hear complaints from businesses and individuals challenging environmental laws that they feel infringe on their rights.

State and Local Policy Important environmental policy is also created at the state and local levels. The structure of the federal government is mirrored at the state level with legislatures, governors, agencies, and judiciaries. However, state laws cannot violate the U.S. Constitution. If state and federal laws conflict, federal laws take precedence.

The strength of environmental policy differs somewhat from area to area. Environmental protection is often considered a great priority in cities, such as Pittsburgh, that have dealt with the impact of human health issues and messy cleanups **(Figure 6)**. California, New York, and Massachusetts are examples of states with strong environmental laws and well-funded environmental agencies. Among states that have not experienced environmental catastrophes, laws may favor development of local economies over environmental protection.

FIGURE 6 One City's Transformation Pittsburgh was once known as the Smoky City because of the air pollution from its steel mills. Its waterways and land were heavily polluted with industrial wastes. Although many problems still persist, the fall of the steel industry and strong local environmental policy have transformed Pittsburgh into a much cleaner and more environmentally friendly city.

(a) Etching of Pittsburgh, 1833

(b) David L. Lawrence Convention Center, a green building in downtown Pittsburgh

History of U.S. Environmental Policy

The laws that make up historical U.S. environmental policy can be divided into three periods. The first period ranged from the 1780s to late-1800s, the second period from the late-1800s to mid-1900s, and the third from the mid-1900s to the late-1900s. As you read, note how U.S. environmental policy through these three periods was related to the perceptions and goals of the nation.

The First Period (1780s to late-1800s) The laws enacted during this period dealt primarily with the management of public lands—federally owned lands—and accompanied the westward expansion of the nation. U.S. environmental policy of this era reflected the perception that the amount of land and natural resources in the West was endless. **Figure 7** describes some of the important laws of this period.

Western expansion provided settlers with opportunities to be successful, while relieving crowded conditions in eastern cities. However, this expansion was at the cost of millions of Native Americans who were displaced from lands they had long inhabited.

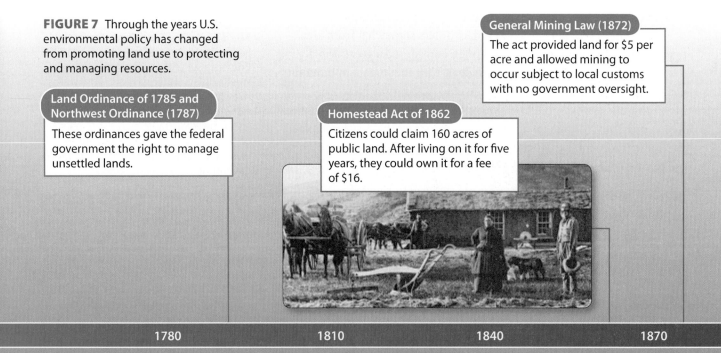

FIGURE 7 Through the years U.S. environmental policy has changed from promoting land use to protecting and managing resources.

Land Ordinance of 1785 and Northwest Ordinance (1787)
These ordinances gave the federal government the right to manage unsettled lands.

Homestead Act of 1862
Citizens could claim 160 acres of public land. After living on it for five years, they could own it for a fee of $16.

General Mining Law (1872)
The act provided land for $5 per acre and allowed mining to occur subject to local customs with no government oversight.

1780   1810   1840   1870

National Park Service (1916)
Congress created the National Park Service to manage the growing number of national parks and monuments.

The Second Period (late-1800s to mid-1900s) Due to the policies of the first period, the West did become more populated, but at the expense of many natural resources that were overused or exploited. Public perception and government policy toward natural resources began to shift. Laws of this period, ranging from the Forest Reserve Act of 1891 to soil conservation laws of the 1930s to the Wilderness Act of 1964, aimed to reduce some of the environmental problems associated with westward expansion. They reflected a new understanding that the West's resources could be used up and required legal protection. The policies of this time eventually led to the national forest system, national wildlife refuge system, and national park system that still serve as global models.

The Third Period (mid- to late-1900s) Further social changes in the mid- to late-twentieth century gave rise to the third major period of U.S. environmental policy. America was now an even more densely populated country driven by technology, heavy industry, and intensive resource consumption. Many Americans found themselves better off economically, but living amid dirtier air, dirtier water, and more waste and toxic chemicals. During the 1960s and 1970s several events triggered increased awareness of environmental problems and brought about a shift in public priorities and public policy. Two of these events were the publication of *Silent Spring* by Rachel Carson, and fires on the oil-polluted Cuyahoga River (**Figure 8**).

FIGURE 8 Cuyahoga River Fires
During the 1950s and 1960s, the oil- and waste-polluted Cuyahoga River in Ohio caught fire more than half a dozen times and sometimes burned for days. Events such as this moved the public to prompt the government to do more to protect the environment.

 Reading Checkpoint *During which period did policy form that would lead to the national forest system and national parks?*

Silent Spring (1962)
In this book, Rachel Carson, a writer and scientist, awakened the public to the negative ecological and health effects of industrial chemicals and pesticides such as DDT.

National Environmental Policy Act (1969)
This act declared that the federal government, in cooperation with state and local governments and the public, would act "to create and maintain conditions under which man and nature can exist in productive harmony."

Earth Day (1970)
The first Earth Day, founded by Senator Nelson of Wisconsin, consisted of about 20 million Americans demonstrating their desires for a healthier environment.

1900	1930	1960	1990

Emergency Conservation Work Act (1933)
President Franklin Roosevelt signed this act during the Great Depression. The act gave unemployed men jobs planting trees, fighting soil erosion, and improving wildlife habitats throughout the country.

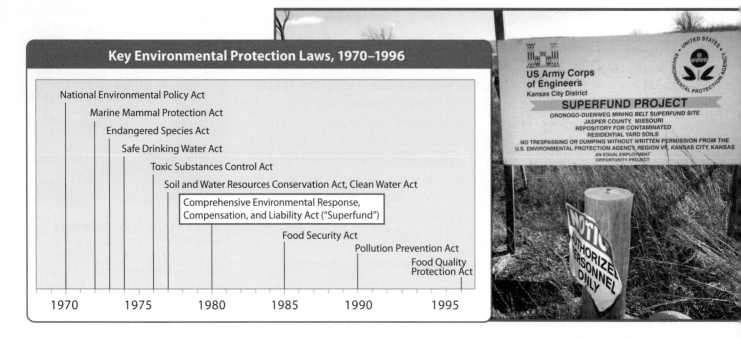

Key Environmental Protection Laws, 1970–1996

National Environmental Policy Act
Marine Mammal Protection Act
Endangered Species Act
Safe Drinking Water Act
Toxic Substances Control Act
Soil and Water Resources Conservation Act, Clean Water Act
Comprehensive Environmental Response, Compensation, and Liability Act ("Superfund")
Food Security Act
Pollution Prevention Act
Food Quality Protection Act

1970   1975   1980   1985   1990   1995

US Army Corps of Engineers
Kansas City District
SUPERFUND PROJECT
ORONOGO-DUENWEG MINING BELT SUPERFUND SITE
JASPER COUNTY, MISSOURI
REPOSITORY FOR CONTAMINATED
RESIDENTIAL YARD SOILS
NO TRESPASSING OR DUMPING WITHOUT WRITTEN PERMISSION FROM THE
U.S. ENVIRONMENTAL PROTECTION AGENCY, REGION VII, KANSAS CITY, KANSAS
AN EQUAL EMPLOYMENT
OPPORTUNITY PROJECT

FIGURE 9 Key Environmental Protection Laws Many environmental laws of the late twentieth century focus on cleaning up the environment. For example, the Superfund program identifies sites polluted with hazardous chemicals, such as this mining site in Missouri, and takes action to clean them up.

Modern U.S. Environmental Policy

Today, largely because of environmental policies enacted during the late twentieth century, pesticides are more regulated, and many areas of the nation have cleaner air and water. Examples of key environmental protection laws are provided in **Figure 9.** The public outcry for environmental protection that spurred such advances remains strong today. Such support is evident each year in April, when millions of people worldwide celebrate Earth Day. Since the first Earth Day on April 22, 1970, participation in this event has grown and spread to nearly every country in the world. Besides Earth Day, two other federal actions marked the modern era of environmental policy, the National Environmental Policy Act (NEPA) and the formation of the Environmental Protection Agency (EPA).

National Environmental Policy Act On January 1, 1970, President Nixon signed the National Environmental Policy Act into law. NEPA created an agency called the Council on Environmental Quality and required that an Environmental Impact Statement be prepared for any major federal action that might significantly affect the environment. An **Environmental Impact Statement (EIS)** requires government agencies and any businesses that contract with them to evaluate the impact of a project, such as a new dam, highway, or building, on the environment before proceeding with the design. EISs involve citizens in the policy process because the statements must be made available to the public for comment.

Environmental Protection Agency Six months later, Nixon issued an executive order calling for a new approach to environmental policy based on the understanding that environmental problems are interrelated. Now tasks such as regulation of water quality, air pollution, and solid waste that had been divided up among many agencies could be overseen by a single major entity—the EPA.

The EPA is responsible for conducting and evaluating research, monitoring environmental quality, and setting and enforcing standards for pollution levels. It also educates the public and assists states in meeting federal standards.

Other Important Laws Ongoing public demand for a cleaner environment resulted in a number of laws that remain key to U.S. environmental policy. For pollution problems like those of the Tijuana River, a crucial law has been the Clean Water Act of 1977. Prior to passage of such federal laws, pollution problems were handled by local and state governments or were addressed through lawsuits. The flaming waters of the Cuyahoga, for example, showed many people that local and state governments weren't doing enough and that federal legislation was needed.

Due to restrictions on pollutants by the Federal Water Pollution Control Acts of 1948 and 1972, and later the Clean Water Act, waterways began to recover. These laws regulate the discharge of wastes, especially from industry, into rivers and streams. The Clean Water Act also aimed to protect wildlife and establish a system for granting companies permits to discharge pollutants on a limited basis.

Post-1980 The 1960s and 1970s were a time of major advances in environmental reform. At that time, evidence of environmental problems became clear. Also, the political climate was ideal due to a supportive public and leaders who were willing to act.

Starting in the 1980s there was a backlash against these environmental policies. Many felt that some laws imposed too great an economic burden on businesses and individuals. During the next couple of decades, many efforts were made to weaken federal environmental laws.

Since then, environmental policy has been strengthened or weakened, depending upon the priorities of the current administration. However, awareness and concern over climate change issues and environmental protections has climbed steadily for the American public over the last decade. Citizens and many companies have become more focused on conserving energy, supporting renewable energy technologies, and reducing carbon emissions, reflecting the environmental efforts found in developed nations worldwide.

FIND OUT MORE

Choose a local department or agency that handles the management of natural resources in your area. Find out about the projects the office is currently working on and those planned for the future.

LESSON 2 Assessment

1. **Synthesize** Draw a cluster diagram that shows how science, economics, ethics, and politics are related to environmental policy.

2. **Compare and Contrast** Compare and contrast the first period of U.S. environmental policy with the third period.

3. **Explain** Why do you think that 1970 could be considered the first year of modern environmental policy in the United States?

4. **THINK IT** *THROUGH* You are probably familiar with titles that historians have given to specific periods in history such as Pax Romana, the Renaissance, and the Victorian Era. What title would you give to each of the three periods of U.S. environmental policy discussed in this lesson? Explain your choices.

International Environmental Policy and Approaches

EVERYDAY PHENOMENON How can governments work with each other and their citizens to form sound environmental policy?

Knowledge and Skills

- Identify major international institutions involved in environmental policy.
- Discuss different approaches to environmental policy.
- List the steps involved in the environmental policy process.

Reading Strategy and Vocabulary

✓ **Reading Strategy** As you read the section under each blue heading, stop and write a brief summary of what you just read.

Vocabulary command-and-control approach, subsidy, green tax, cap-and-trade, lobbying

WE ALL INHABIT the same small planet. Ocean and wind currents have no regard for each nation's individual environmental policies. The currents move around the globe carrying pollution from one region of the world to another. The planet also has a limited amount of nonrenewable and renewable resources that must be shared for there to be peace. Solving many environmental problems requires creativity and cooperation among nations.

International Environmental Policy

Environmental problems are not restricted to the national borders drawn on maps. Because the laws of one nation have no authority in other nations, international laws are needed to solve issues that involve more than one nation. Following are some examples of environmental issues that involve more than one nation, which are sometimes called *transboundary problems.*

- Many rivers flow through more than one nation. Like the Tijuana River, they may carry water pollution across borders.
- Air pollutants that are emitted in one nation may travel on wind currents far across the globe.
- Migrating animals travel across international borders both on land and in the oceans. Over-hunting and over-fishing in one area of the world can affect food availability or the success of a fishing industry in another part of the world.
- Multinational companies operate outside of national laws and may not conserve resources or conduct business in sustainable ways.

International laws may arise from multinational conventions or treaties, such as those mentioned in **Figure 10.** Many international organizations have emerged to help promote problem solving and cooperation among nations. Most of these organizations do not have power to enforce laws, but they can influence the behavior of nations by providing funding, applying peer pressure, or directing media attention toward a problem.

SOME MAJOR INTERNATIONAL TREATIES

The Antarctic Treaty System 1959 The treaty and related protocols that followed require that Antarctica be used for peaceful purposes and scientific research only.

Convention on International Trade in Endangered Species of Wild Fauna and Flora (CITES) 1975 CITES ensures that the trade of an animal or plant across national borders will not threaten the survival of the species.

Kyoto Protocol 1997 Nations that signed the treaty (the United States did not) promised to reduce emissions of six greenhouse gases to levels below those of 1990. Nations that were not considered industrialized were not held to the same standard as industrialized nations.

Montreal Protocol on Substances That Deplete the Ozone Layer 1987 The purpose of the treaty is to end ozone layer damage by restricting the production of chemicals that deplete it. By the twentieth anniversary of the treaty, all 197 UN member nations had signed it and evidence suggested that the thinning of the ozone layer had slowed.

Paris Climate Agreement 2015 Ratified by 189 nations, the Paris Climate Agreement seeks commitment from nations worldwide to reduce greenhouse gas emissions and holds them accountable through self-reporting of strategies and progress. The Trump administration formally announced that the U.S. would withdraw from the agreement in 2019. If the U.S decides to rejoin the Paris Climate Agreement in the future, it would be legally binding after 30 days.

The United Nations (U.N.) In 1945, representatives of 50 nations founded the U.N. Today, 197 nations are members. Headquartered in New York City, this organization's purpose is to promote peace and to help solve economic, social, cultural, and humanitarian problems. The U.N. has helped shape international environmental policy. The United Nations Environment Programme, based in Nairobi, Kenya, is an example of a program that promotes sustainable development with research and programs that provide information to international policymakers.

The European Union (EU) The EU, which currently consists of 27 member nations, was formed after World War II with the goal of promoting Europe's economic and social progress. The EU can sign treaties and enact regulations that have the same authority as national laws in each member nation. The main objective of the EU's European Environment Agency is to produce thorough, current environmental data and analyses that can be used to guide policymakers.

FIGURE 10 Treaties When nations sign international treaties, they agree to abide by and enforce the treaties' terms. The figure describes just a few of the many treaties related to international environmental policy.

The World Trade Organization (WTO)

The WTO, which was established in 1995, promotes free trade and enforces fair trade practices among its member nations. The WTO has authority to impose financial penalties on nations that do not comply with its directives. Critics have charged that the WTO often adds to environmental problems. For example, in 1995, the EPA issued regulations requiring cleaner-burning gasoline in U.S. cities. Brazil and Venezuela complained that the new rules discriminated against their petroleum products. The WTO agreed and the EPA had to change its regulations.

FIGURE 11 Non-Governmental Organizations Conservation International teamed up with a Swiss fragrance company and community members to discourage illegal logging in the Caura River basin of Venezuela.

World Bank Established in 1944, the World Bank is owned by 189 member nations and provides interest-free credits, low-interest loans, or grants to poor nations for projects that will improve their citizens' living standards. The institution shapes environmental policy by funding projects such as dams and irrigation systems. The World Bank's mission may be admirable, but critics say that in its efforts to help growing human populations in poor nations, it sometimes funds projects that are not environmentally sustainable.

Non-Governmental Organizations (NGOs) Many environmental organizations that are not affiliated with governments exert influence over international environmental policy. Groups such as Greenpeace, Population Connection, and Conservation International (shown in **Figure 11**) attempt to shape policy through research, lobbying, education, and protest. NGOs contribute considerable funding, expertise, and research toward solving environmental problems.

 Reading Checkpoint *Make a table with a list of the international agencies that affect environmental policy and a brief description of their roles.*

Approaches to Environmental Policy

Over the years, a great deal of environmental policy throughout the world has used a **command-and-control approach.** With this approach, a government body sets rules and threatens punishment for violations. In the United States, most federal policy consists of legislation from Congress and regulations from administrative agencies. This simple and direct approach to policymaking has given the nation cleaner air, cleaner water, safer workplaces, and healthier neighborhoods. A cost-benefit analysis performed by the White House Office of Management and Budget in 2003 revealed that the benefits of this approach outweighed the costs by even more than people estimated.

Although the command-and-control approach has had many successes, there have also been failures. Sometimes government actions are well meaning, but not well informed, which leads to unexpected circumstances. Policy can also fail if a government does not live up to its promises or if citizens view laws and regulations as restrictions on their freedom.

The most common critique of the command-and-control approach is the argument that companies competing in a free market will produce better solutions at lower cost than the government can produce. To answer this critique, policymakers now often try to combine the approaches of government and of private industries. One example of this alternative approach is ecolabeling, which you read about in the last lesson. Other examples often involve economic incentives for companies such as tax breaks and subsidies.

Real Data

Analyzing Graphs

Water is a very limited resource on the border between the United States and Mexico. The pressure of population growth, along with farming and industry, has negatively affected both water quality and water quantity.

The U.S.–Mexico Border Water Infrastructure Program (BWIP) is a cooperative effort between the two nations to deliver safe drinking water and adequate sanitation for people living in the area.

The graphs below show first-time households connected through pipes to safe drinking water sources and adequate waste removal systems.

1. **Analyze Data** At first glance, the graphs look similar. They both show annual progress and cumulative progress over time. What is very different about the two graphs?

2. **Infer** What factors do you think affect how many homes are newly hooked up to water supplies and wastewater treatment services per year?

3. **Evaluate** Which of these services likely has more impact on the health of the Tijuana River and the San Diego beaches that are affected by pollution from the river? Explain.

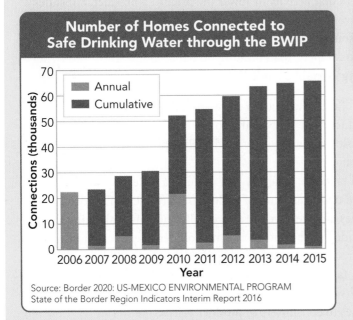

Number of Homes Connected to Safe Drinking Water through the BWIP

Source: Border 2020: US-MEXICO ENVIRONMENTAL PROGRAM
State of the Border Region Indicators Interim Report 2016

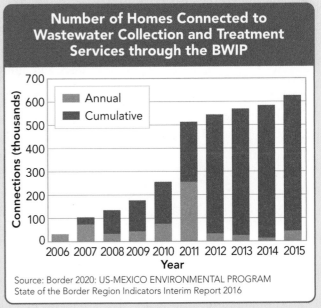

Number of Homes Connected to Wastewater Collection and Treatment Services through the BWIP

Source: Border 2020: US-MEXICO ENVIRONMENTAL PROGRAM
State of the Border Region Indicators Interim Report 2016

FIGURE 12 Financial Incentives
Companies that build green buildings or that make green changes to existing buildings may receive incentives such as tax breaks. The solar panels and pond seen here are two features of this energy efficient office building in Vermont.

Tax Breaks and Subsidies Governments may give tax breaks to businesses or individuals who participate in environmentally friendly actions, such as producing electricity from coal with new technologies that reduce emissions. Lowering their taxes encourages them to continue with the activity.

Governments also may provide subsidies to some industries. A subsidy is a giveaway of cash or public resources that is intended to encourage a particular activity or lower the price of a product. Subsidies are often controversial. In the United States, some subsidy money goes to renewable resources. However, enormous subsidies are provided for nonrenewable fossil fuels, road building in national forests for removing trees, and mining on public lands.

Green Taxes Taxes imposed on companies that participate in activities or produce products that are harmful to the environment are known as green taxes. These taxes are widely used in Europe, but are not as popular in the United States.

Under green taxation, a factory that pollutes a waterway would pay extra taxes based on the amount of pollution it produces. The idea is to give companies an incentive to reduce pollution, while allowing the company to decide how best to do it. One polluter may decide to invest in technologies to reduce its pollution and avoid taxes. Another may choose to pay the green tax. The government could then apply the tax money to the cleanup. A disadvantage of green taxes is that businesses may pass their tax expenses to consumers in product prices.

Cap-and-Trade In a cap-and-trade system, a government determines the overall amount of pollution it will accept for a specific pollutant and issues permits that allow polluters to emit a certain fraction of that amount. These permits then can be bought, sold, and traded among companies, utilities, or industries.

For example, suppose a factory owner has permits to release 10 units of a pollutant. The factory becomes more efficient and releases only five units. Now the owner can sell his extra five permits to another factory that releases more pollution than is allowed. Ideally, this system allows the owner to make money, meets the needs of the other factory, and does not increase pollution levels. In some cases, environmental agencies may buy surplus permits and "retire" them, which reduces pollution.

The cap-and-trade system does not always have positive results in every situation. Although the system can reduce pollution overall, it does allow concentrated areas of pollution to occur around companies that buy extra permits. Critics also say that giving companies permission to pollute will not solve environmental problems in the long run.

Local Incentives Many policy tools of local governments involve financial incentives. Local governments may charge residents for waste disposal based on how much waste they generate. Rebates may be given to residents who buy water-efficient toilets and other appliances, because these products will save the town or city money over time.

At all levels of government from local to international, market-based incentives can reduce environmental impact, reduce industry costs, and ease concerns about government regulation. Market-based approaches can be more complicated than command-and-control approaches, but they can lessen environmental impact at a lower overall cost.

 Reading Checkpoint *In a cap-and-trade system, what does the term* cap *refer to and what does the term* trade *refer to?*

FIGURE 13 Reducing Acid Rain With Cap-and-Trade The 1990 amendments to the Clean Air Act called for reduced emissions of sulfur dioxide, a contributor to acid rain. A cap-and-trade system was put into place. The cap-and-trade, along with other factors, led to a 35 percent drop in sulfur dioxide emissions, which protects other trees from the acid rain damage suffered by those in this photograph.

The Environmental Policy Process

In constitutional democracies like the United States, it is true that each and every person has a political voice and can make a difference. However, this is not always as easy as it sounds! Individuals who push for a policy must be ambitious, resourceful, and persistent, and must understand how the system works. **Figure 14** on the next page illustrates the steps of environmental policy process.

❶ Identify the Problem The first step is to clearly identify an environmental problem. Identifying a problem requires curiosity, observation, recordkeeping, and an awareness of the relationship between people and their environment. For example, assessing the contamination of San Diego- and Tijuana-area beaches required an understanding of the ecological and health effects of untreated wastewater.

FIGURE 14 Policy Process Steps Understanding the steps of the policy process is an essential element of solving environmental problems.

❶ Identify the problem.

❷ Identify specific causes of the problem.

❸ Envision a solution and set goals.

❹ Get organized.

❺ Gain access to influential people.

❻ Manage drafting of bill and development of policy.

❷ *Identify Causes* Discovering specific causes of the problem is the next step in the policy process. Identifying causes often requires scientific research. A person seeking causes for pollution in the Tijuana River might notice that pollution became worse once U.S.-based companies began opening factories in Mexico. Much of a scientist's work at this step would also involve risk assessment—evaluating the extent of a problem and judging the risk to public health and the environment.

❸ *Envision a Solution* Science plays a vital role in proposing solutions to environmental problems. The solutions often involve social or political actions. In San Diego, activists wanted Tijuana to be encouraged to enforce its own pollution laws more effectively. This began to happen once San Diego city employees helped train their Mexican counterparts on keeping hazardous waste out of the sewage treatment system.

❹ *Get Organized* Once a problem has been identified, researched, and a solution is proposed, it is time to organize. When it comes to getting the attention of elected officials, organizations are generally more effective than individuals. One reason is that organizations are more effective at raising funds that can be contributed to political campaigns. But even small groups and individuals who are motivated, informed, and organized can find ways to get their ideas heard.

❺ *Gain Access* Now that the group is organized, the next step in the policy process is gaining access to officials who have the ability to sponsor new bills. This is often done through lobbying and campaign contributions. **Lobbying** involves efforts to influence an elected official into supporting a specific interest. Anyone can lobby, but it is more difficult for the average citizen rather than the thousands of lobbyists employed by businesses and organizations. Supporting a candidate's reelection efforts is another way to make one's voice heard.

6 *Help a Solution Become Policy* Once access to elected officials has been gained, the next step is to prepare a bill that describes the desired policy. Anyone can draft a bill, but a member of the legislature has to introduce it and follow it until it is passed. If it gets through these steps, the bill may become law, but there are still obstacles to its long-term survival. The law may undergo changes once it is passed to the administrative agency that will implement and regulate it.

Getting Involved The policy process is long and often difficult. But it has yielded effective results across the nation. However, what can you do if you aren't even old enough to vote? What influence can young people have on environmental policy?

Many national environmental policies began as movements in towns and small cities inspired by one person or a small group of people. Many Web sites such as those for the EPA and the United Nations recommend ways that young people can make an impact on environmental policy from the smallest to the grandest scales. These tasks could include pinpointing a specific way a school could improve energy efficiency, joining a local environmental group, or even taking part in a city-wide rally for climate action like the people in **Figure 15.**

FIGURE 15 Many people join together to march over environmental concerns in San Francisco.

LESSON ③ Assessment

1. **Explain** In your own words, explain why international environmental laws are needed.

2. **Compare and Contrast** Compare and contrast green taxes and subsidies.

3. **Summarize** Describe the environmental policy process, from identification of a problem through enactment of a federal law.

4. **THINK IT** *THROUGH* You are the new head of the EPA. New legislation from Congress says water pollution caused by oil spillage from commercial and recreational boats needs to be reduced by 25 percent within ten years. What policy approaches would you pursue to carry out these instructions? Explain your choices.

Economics and Environmental Policy **55**

FIGHTING FOR
CLEAN WATER

By the end of the 1980s, Tijuana, Mexico, was growing faster than it could treat its sewage. Wastewater from the city was flowing down the Tijuana River, polluting the land and ocean around San Diego, California. In 1990, the United States and Mexico agreed to construct the South Bay International Wastewater Treatment Plant in the U.S. portion of the Tijuana River Valley. Because of limited funding, the EPA decided to open the plant in two phases. The first phase would remove solid waste and particles.

Other pollutants, such as toxic metals and bacteria, would still be released into the ocean until a secondary treatment facility was completed.

Until the second phase could be built, the EPA planned to treat the sewage with an "activated sludge" process, which uses giant vats of bacteria to detoxify wastewater. Several parties filed a lawsuit against the EPA, asking the agency to instead use ponds filled with algae as a temporary secondary treatment because they are better at filtering heavy metals. One person involved in the lawsuit was local activist Lori Saldaña.

San Diego

Tijuana

Tijuana River Estuary

FURTHER DELAYS

The suit was eventually settled out of court. The EPA agreed to use secondary treatment ponds until the second phase of the plant was completed. However, the EPA never started construction of the ponds and the secondary treatment facility was delayed through the 1990s. Meanwhile, sewage continued to flow into the ocean.

OCEAN POLLUTION

In 1999, Saldaña and oceanographer Tim Baumgartner tested the quality of the treated sewage near its release site. Although computer simulations predicted that this released wastewater would be diluted enough to meet federal and state pollution standards, Saldaña and Baumgartner's work suggested otherwise. They posted their results on the Internet and urged policymakers to speed construction of the secondary treatment plant.

RECOGNITION

Saldaña's efforts did not go unnoticed. President Clinton appointed her to the Border Environment Cooperation Commission's Advisory Council in 1999 to work on water quality improvement projects in San Diego and Tijuana. In 2004, Saldaña was elected to the California State Assembly. Partly because of Saldaña's continuing efforts, construction to upgrade the original plant to meet Clean Water Act standards was complete in 2011.

21st Century Skills **Media Literacy** Use online and print news sources to research an environmental issue or movement in your region. Identify the various groups involved. Who wants the change? Who doesn't? Has either side used scientific evidence to support its claims?

Study Guide

INVESTIGATIVE PHENOMENON

How do economic factors influence environmental policy?

Lesson 1
How is sustainability affected by economics?

Lesson 2
How do environmental policies protect the environment?

Lesson 3
How can governments work with each other and their citizens to form sound environmental policy?

LESSON 1 Economics

- Supply and demand and cost-benefit analyses are two economics concepts that greatly contribute to decision making and are especially related to economics and the environment.
- All economies depend on the environment for resources and for management of wastes, but these connections are often overlooked.
- A new trend in economics is the recognition that suppliers of goods and services need to consider how to conserve resources and reduce harm to the environment.

economics (36)
supply (37)
demand (37)
cost-benefit analysis (37)
ecological economics (39)
environmental economics (39)
non-market value (40)
market failure (40)
ecolabeling (41)

LESSON 2 United States Environmental Policy

- Environmental policy makes use of science, ethics, economics, and an understanding of the political process to solve environmental problems.
- Many times throughout its history, the United States government has reinvented its approach to the relationship between its goals and the environment.
- Modern U.S. environmental policy reveals lessons learned from past misuses of resources and strives for a sustainable future.

policy (42)
environmental policy (42)
Environmental Impact Statement (EIS) (46)

LESSON 3 International Environmental Policy and Approaches

- International organizations, laws, and treaties help governments of the world come to agreement on environmental issues.
- Approaches to environmental policy may include direct laws from a government body or policies with economic incentives.
- Steps of the environmental policy process include identifying a problem, finding the cause, proposing solutions, getting organized, gaining access to policymakers, and guiding the solution to law.

command-and-control approach (50)
subsidy (52)
green tax (52)
cap-and-trade (53)
lobbying (54)

 GO ONLINE

INQUIRY LABS AND ACTIVITIES

- **Working Trees**

   Choose where to plant neighborhood trees. Then, calculate the dollar value of the services and benefits your trees provide.

- **Pending Legislation**

   Download a summary for one pending environmental bill in your state. Analyze the costs and benefits. Then make recommendations.

- **Choose an Approach**

   A sustainable practice is proposed. Which approach do you think policymakers should take—tax breaks, subsidies, incentives, or penalties?

Chapter Assessment

Defend Your Case

The Central Case looked at a water pollution problem that affects both Mexico and the United States. Use evidence from the Central Case and throughout the chapter to suggest a solution to this problem that will help both nations. How you would use the environmental policy process to see this solution implemented?

Review Concepts and Terms

1. If a nonrenewable resource such as oil suddenly became scarce while demand remained constant
   a. the equilibrium price would increase.
   b. the equilibrium price would decrease.
   c. demand would increase.
   d. demand would decrease.

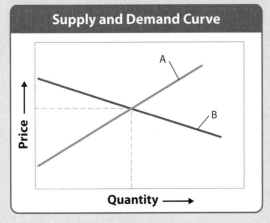

Supply and Demand Curve

2. Which is an example of an external cost?
   a. raw materials
   b. electricity payments
   c. wages
   d. depleted natural resources

3. The executive branch of the United States government includes
   a. the House of Representatives.
   b. agencies that monitor the enforcement of laws.
   c. the Senate.
   d. the Supreme Court.

4. The first laws in U.S. environmental policy
   a. banned use of certain chemicals.
   b. dealt primarily with the management of private land.
   c. promoted settlement of the West.
   d. promoted preservation of endangered species.

5. Which federal government creation led to the use of Environmental Impact Statements?
   a. Clean Water Act
   b. National Environmental Policy Act
   c. Environmental Protection Agency
   d. Superfund

6. If one nation's laws make it impossible for another nation to sell its goods there, which organization is most likely to get involved?
   a. the World Bank
   b. the United Nations
   c. the World Trade Organization
   d. the Environmental Protection Agency

7. Which agreement led to the reduced release of chemicals that harm the ozone layer?
   a. Kyoto Protocol
   b. Antarctic Treaty
   c. United Nations Environment Programme
   d. Montreal Protocol

8. When a government gives cash to an industry to support an activity of the industry, this is known as
   a. a tax break.
   b. a subsidy.
   c. a green tax.
   d. command-and-control.

9. During which part of the environmental policy process is lobbying used?
   a. pinpointing a problem
   b. proposing a solution
   c. getting organized
   d. gaining access

Chapter Assessment

Modified True/False

Write true if the statement is true. If it is false, change the underlined word or words to make the statement true.

10. In a <u>centrally planned economy</u>, both the government and individuals play a role in the direction the economy takes.

11. <u>The Land Ordinance of 1785</u> gave the government the right to manage unsettled lands.

12. Companies that pay green taxes produce <u>less</u> pollution than companies that do not pay them.

13. The most common critique of the <u>cap-and-trade system</u> is that companies competing in a free market will produce better solutions at lower cost than the government can.

Reading Comprehension

Read the following selection and answer the questions that follow.

The Fifth Amendment to the U.S. Constitution ensures that private property shall not "be taken for public use without just compensation." Courts have interpreted the *takings clause* to ban regulatory taking. Regulatory taking occurs when the government, by means of law or regulation, deprives a property owner of economic uses of the property.

This led to a landmark case, *Lucas v. South Carolina Coastal Council.* In 1986, Lucas purchased beachfront property in South Carolina. In 1988, before Lucas started to build homes, the state passed a law banning construction on eroding beaches, including Lucas's property. Lucas claimed that this was regulatory taking and asked a state court to overrule the law. The case eventually reached the U.S. Supreme Court , which ruled that the state law deprived Lucas of economic use of his land. Today, homes stand on the land, but they face damage due to the eroding beach. This case reveals the sensitive balance between private rights and public good.

14. The law that South Carolina passed in 1988 was meant to

   a. take private land from beachfront owners.

   b. prevent construction on eroding beaches.

   c. fix beach erosion.

   d. support the Fifth Amendment.

15. What was Lucas's argument against the new South Carolina law?

   a. The state cannot ban construction in a particular area.

   b. The state's assessment of the erosion problem was not accurate.

   c. The state was preventing him from making economic use of his property.

   d. The new law was not in the interest of the public good.

Short Answer

16. What is the purpose of an EIS?

17. What is the difference between an *internal* cost or benefit and an *external* cost or benefit?

18. Name four ways that the environment contributes to economies.

19. List four types of economic assumptions that can negatively affect the environment.

20. Briefly describe the mission of the EPA.

21. What are three actions an individual citizen can take to influence an environmental policy?

Critical Thinking

22. **Apply Concepts** How could addressing market failure lead to a more sustainable future?

23. **Compare and Contrast** Compare and contrast the views of typical economists and ecological economists.

24. **Summarize** Describe the roles of the legislative, executive, and judicial branches of government in the environmental policy process.

25. **Explain** Why are environmental regulations sometimes considered to be unfair barriers to trade?

26. **Evaluate** Describe an advantage and a disadvantage of the command-and-control approach.

27. **Explain** Describe in your own words the meaning of the term *transboundary problem*. Use an example to support your explanation.

Analyze Data

The data table lists beach closures in the San Diego area during the first month of 2020, including the source of the water contamination and the dates of the closure.

San Diego Beach Closures				
Beach	Cause	Source	Start	End
Imperial Beach	Sewage/ grease	Tijuana River associated	1/1/20	1/7/20
Border Field	Sewage/ grease	Tijuana River associated	1/1/20	1/1/20
Imperial Beach	Sewage/ grease	Tijuana River associated	1/10/20	1/11/20
Imperial Beach	Sewage/ grease	Tijuana River associated	1/17/20	1/23/20

Data from California State Water Control Boards

28. **Interpret Data** How many of the closures were due to Tijuana River overflow?

29. **Calculate** What is the average number of days that San Diego County beaches were closed due to pollution from the Tijuana River in January 2020?

Write About It

30. **Summary** Interview your grandparents or other older adults about how environmental conditions have changed during their lifetimes. Summarize their answers to your questions.

31. **Description** Think of an environmental problem in your area that you would like to see solved. Using the environmental policy process, describe how you think you could guide your ideas through the process to address the problem.

32. **REVISIT INVESTIGATIVE** PHENOMENON Consider how the focus of U.S. environmental policy has changed over the years. What issues might environmental policy need to address 50 years from now? Do you think there will be more or less environmental policy?

Ecological Footprints

Read the information below. Copy the table into your notebook and record your calculations. Then, answer the questions.

According to the U.S. Geological Survey, the nation withdrew about 281 billion gallons of fresh water per day in 2015. Seventy percent of these withdrawals were from surface water, and 29 percent were from groundwater. Thermoelectric power plants (generating electricity) accounted for 41 percent; irrigation for 37 percent; public water supplies for 12 percent; and industrial, livestock, and mining for 7 percent. (Percentages add up to 97 percent because of rounding.) The population of the United States was about 325 million in 2015. Use these statistics and recent statistics for your hometown to fill in the number of gallons used for each category.

MATH SUPPORT For help with multiplying with percentages, see the Math handbook.

1. How many gallons of the nation's daily water came from surface water?

2. What policies would you recommend to reduce water use? Provide one example of a command-and-control approach and one example of a market-based policy tool.

	Population	Electricity	Irrigation	Public Water Supply	Industrial/ Livestock/ Mining
You	1				
Your class					
Your hometown					
United States					

Data from U.S. Geological Survey, *Estimated use of water in the United States, 2015.*

Earth's Environmental Systems

CHAPTER

INVESTIGATIVE PHENOMENON   How do "dead zones" affect the environment surrounding them?

Sediments from the
Mississippi River and
other sources reach the
Gulf of Mexico.

Lesson 1
Matter and the
Environment

Lesson 2
Systems in
Environmental Science

Lesson 3
Earth's Spheres

Lesson 4
Biogeochemical
Cycles

The Gulf of Mexico's Dead Zone

LOUISIANA'S FISHING PROFESSIONALS

haul in more seafood than those of any other U.S. state except Alaska. Each year they send more than 400 million kilograms (almost 1 billion pounds) of fish, shrimp, and other shellfish to our dinner tables. They are doing this despite the impact that the "dead zone" has on the Gulf of Mexico each year.

The Gulf's "dead zone" is a region of water so depleted of oxygen that marine organisms are killed or driven away. The low concentrations of dissolved oxygen in the bottom waters of the dead zone indicate *hypoxia*, or low oxygen levels. Aquatic animals obtain oxygen from water that passes over their gills, and, like us, these animals die without oxygen. Well-oxygenated water contains 10 parts per million (ppm) of oxygen. When concentrations drop below 2 ppm, animals that can leave an affected area do so. Below 1.5 ppm, most marine organisms die. In the Gulf's hypoxic zone, oxygen concentrations frequently drop below 2 ppm.

The dead zone appears each spring and grows until fall, when storms stir in some oxygen. It starts off the coast of Louisiana, near the mouths of the Mississippi and Atchafalaya rivers. In 2017, the dead zone reached a record 22,729 square kilometers (8776 square miles)—an area larger than the state of New Jersey.

Why are these waters depleted of oxygen? According to scientists, farming practices and other human causes are to blame. The Gulf, they say, is essentially being fertilized by nitrogen and phosphorus flowing down the Mississippi River. These excess nutrients come from fertilizers used on farms far up the Mississippi and Atchafalaya rivers, as well as from other human sources, including industrial waste, fossil fuel emissions, and sewage treatment plants. The nutrients allow an

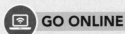

GO ONLINE
• Take It Local   • 3-D Geo Tour

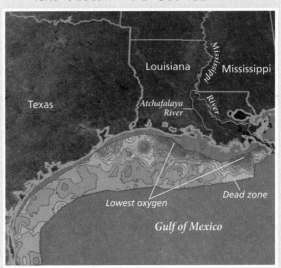

overgrowth of plankton whose wastes and remains nourish bacteria that deplete oxygen from the waters at the bottom of the Gulf.

The U.S. government has acted, proposing that farmers in states upriver from the Gulf—such as Ohio, Iowa, and Illinois—cut down on fertilizer use. Farmers' advocates protest that farmers are being singled out while other sources are ignored. The debate continues.

Scientists have also documented dead zones in 200 other bodies of water worldwide, including the Chesapeake Bay. Scientists have been tracking the size of the dead zone in the Chesapeake Bay since the 1980s. In 2019, the dead zone lasted for 136 days with oxygen levels too low for many fish and crabs to survive. Clearly, scientists need to investigate these dead zones in order to protect our food supply and economy. Doing so will require that they continue to research complex environmental systems and their interactions.

Matter and the Environment

EVERYDAY PHENOMENON What properties of matter are most important to environmental systems?

Knowledge and Skills

- Differentiate among an atom, an element, a molecule, and a compound.
- Discuss how various macromolecules are essential to life.
- Identify some unusual properties of water.

Reading Strategy and Vocabulary

✓ **Reading Strategy** Before you read, create an outline using the dark blue, green, and light blue headings in this lesson. As you read, fill in key phrases or sentences about each heading.

Vocabulary matter, atom, element, nucleus, molecule, compound, hydrocarbon, solution, macromolecule, protein, nucleic acid, carbohydrate, lipid, pH

EXAMINE ANY ENVIRONMENTAL ISSUE, and you will likely find chemistry at its core. Chemistry is crucial to understanding how pollutants cause acid rain; how gases such as carbon dioxide and methane contribute to global climate change; how pesticides and other manufactured chemicals affect our health and the health of wildlife and the environment; and how matter is cycled through the environment. Chemistry is central, too, in understanding water pollution and wastewater treatment, hazardous waste and its cleanup and disposal, the atmospheric "ozone hole," and most energy issues.

Chemistry is also central to many solutions to environmental problems. For example, some organisms can help clean up certain kinds of pollution. Bacteria and fungi that consume the harmful substances in gasoline can be used to clean up soil beneath leaky gasoline tanks that threaten drinking water supplies. Other microorganisms can be used to break down pesticide residue in soil. Plants as different as wheat, tobacco, water hyacinth, and cattails have helped clean up toxic waste sites, often by absorbing toxic metals into their roots. These are all instances of *bioremediation*, the reduction of chemical pollution using organisms that consume or neutralize the polluting substances. Using bioremediation requires both knowledge of the chemical makeup of the pollution and of the biological and chemical makeup of the organisms used. There is no escape from chemistry.

Building Blocks of Chemistry

To appreciate the chemistry involved in environmental science, we must begin with a basic fact. All material in the universe that has mass and occupies space is called **matter.**

Atoms and Elements **Atoms** are the basic units of matter. An **element** is a chemical substance with a given set of properties that cannot be broken down into substances with other properties.

Every atom has a **nucleus,** or central core, containing particles called protons and neutrons. *Protons* are positively charged; *neutrons* have no electric charge. The atoms of each element have a defined number of protons, called the *atomic number*. Carbon, for example, has six protons in its nucleus; so its atomic number is 6. An atom's nucleus is surrounded by negatively charged particles known as *electrons*, which usually balance the positive charge of the protons (**Figure 1**).

Chemists currently recognize 94 elements occurring naturally, as well as about 24 others that scientists have made. Each element is assigned a chemical symbol. The *periodic table of the elements* in Appendix D summarizes information on the elements. Carbon, nitrogen, hydrogen, and oxygen are elements especially abundant in living things.

Bonding When atoms combine, it is called *bonding*. Atoms bond because of an attraction that involves sharing or transfer of their electrons. Because the strength of this attraction varies among elements, atoms bond in different ways, according to whether and how they share or transfer electrons. When atoms share electrons, they generate a *covalent bond* and form a molecule. For example, two atoms of hydrogen (H) bond to form hydrogen gas, H_2, by sharing electrons equally. Atoms in a covalent bond can also share electrons unequally, with one atom exerting a greater pull. Such is the case with water, in which oxygen attracts electrons more strongly than hydrogen, forming what are termed polar covalent bonds (**Figure 2a**). These polar bonds are responsible for some of the unusual properties of water that you'll learn about later. If the strength of attraction is unequal enough, an electron may be transferred from one atom to another. Such a transfer creates oppositely charged atoms, or *ions*, that form *ionic bonds*. Table salt (NaCl) contains ionic bonds (**Figure 2b**).

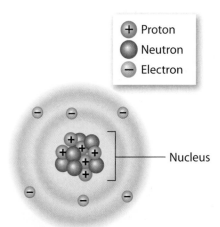

FIGURE 1 **Atom** In an atom, protons and neutrons are held in the nucleus, and electrons move around the nucleus. Each chemical element has a different total of protons, neutrons, and electrons. The carbon atom above has six of each. Electrons actually move around the nucleus in more complex ways than is implied in the diagrams on this page.

(a) Covalent Bonding
Water molecule (H_2O)

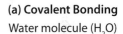
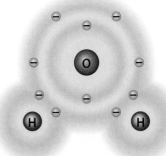

FIGURE 2 **Bonding** In a water molecule **(a),** each hydrogen atom shares two electrons with the oxygen atom, forming a covalent bond. In table salt **(b),** the sodium atom loses an electron to the chlorine atom, forming an ionic bond.

(b) Ionic Bonding
Salt (NaCl)

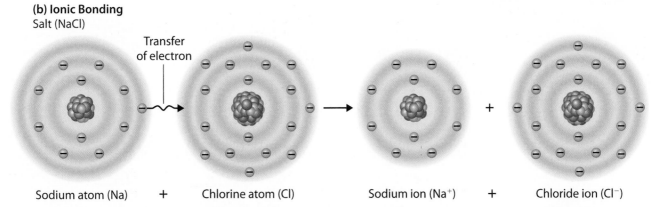

Transfer of electron

Sodium atom (Na)   +   Chlorine atom (Cl)   Sodium ion (Na⁺)   +   Chloride ion (Cl⁻)

Molecules and Compounds Atoms joined by covalent bonds are called molecules. A **molecule** is a combination of two or more atoms of the same type or of different types joined by covalent bonds. Common molecules include those of oxygen (O_2) and nitrogen (N_2). A substance composed of atoms of two or more different elements is called a **compound.** Water is a compound made up of two hydrogen atoms bonded to one oxygen atom, so it is represented by the chemical formula H_2O. Another compound is carbon dioxide, consisting of one carbon atom bonded to two oxygen atoms; its chemical formula is CO_2.

▶ *Organic and Inorganic Compounds* Living things are made of organic compounds, and they produce organic compounds. Organic compounds consist of carbon atoms (and usually hydrogen atoms) joined by covalent bonds. Other elements may also be present. Carbon's unusual ability to build elaborate molecules has resulted in millions of different organic compounds. Because of the diversity of organic compounds and their importance in living organisms, chemists differentiate organic compounds from *inorganic compounds,* which lack carbon-to-carbon bonds.

▶ *Hydrocarbons* Crude oil and petroleum products are made up primarily of hydrocarbons. **Hydrocarbons** are organic compounds containing only hydrogen and carbon. Some hydrocarbons, and products of their burning, are hazardous, so hydrocarbons are common topics in environmental science. For example, *polycyclic aromatic hydrocarbons,* or PAHs, can evaporate from spilled or incompletely burned oil and gasoline and can mix with water. They can be toxic to aquatic animals such as fish. PAH particles can also result from burning and may be present in wood smoke, charred parts of meat, and cigarette smoke (**Figure 3a**). Some PAH particles have been shown to cause cancer in people. Other hydrocarbons, such as those emitted in automobile exhaust, can cause smog when exposed to sunlight (**Figure 3b**).

 Reading Checkpoint   *How do organic and inorganic compounds differ?*

(a) Cigarette smoke

FIGURE 3 Hydrocarbons
(a) Cigarette smoke contains harmful polycyclic aromatic hydrocarbons.
(b) Other hydrocarbons include those from auto emissions that cause smog.

(b) Traffic and smog in Beijing

Solutions Elements, molecules, and compounds can also come together in mixtures without bonding chemically. A mixture in which all the ingredients are evenly distributed is called a **solution.** Solutions can be liquids, gases, or solids. Air, for example, is a solution formed mostly of nitrogen, oxygen, water, carbon dioxide, methane (CH_4), and ozone (O_3). Ocean water, carbonated water, plant sap, and metal alloys such as brass are also solutions.

Macromolecules

Organic compounds sometimes combine to form long chains of repeated molecules. Some of these chains, called *polymers*, play key roles as building blocks of life. Three types of polymers are essential to life: proteins, nucleic acids, and carbohydrates. Lipids are not polymers but are also essential to life. Proteins, nucleic acids, carbohydrates, and lipids are called **macromolecules** because of their large size.

Proteins **Proteins** are polymers that serve many functions in organisms. They are organic compounds made up of carbon, hydrogen, oxygen, nitrogen, and sometimes sulfur. Some help produce tissues and provide support. For example, the production of bones, skin, hair, muscles, and some other body tissues relies on proteins **(Figure 4).** Other proteins store energy, transport substances, or work within the immune system. Still others act as *hormones*, molecules that serve as chemical messengers within an organism. Proteins can also serve as *enzymes*, molecules that promote certain chemical reactions.

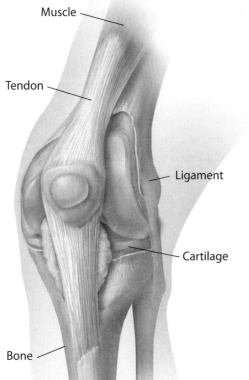

Muscle

Tendon

Ligament

Cartilage

Bone

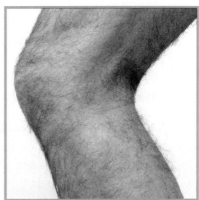

FIGURE 4 Proteins Proteins are needed for the development of the bones, muscles, tendons, ligaments, and cartilage (left), as well as the skin and hair (above), that make up a knee.

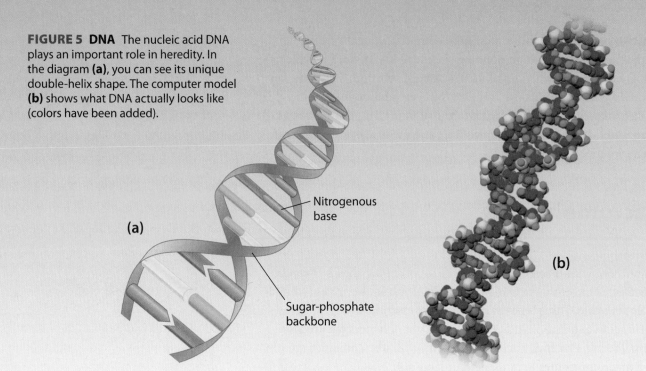

FIGURE 5 DNA The nucleic acid DNA plays an important role in heredity. In the diagram **(a)**, you can see its unique double-helix shape. The computer model **(b)** shows what DNA actually looks like (colors have been added).

(a)

Nitrogenous base

Sugar-phosphate backbone

(b)

Nucleic Acids Nucleic acids are macromolecules that direct protein production. *Deoxyribonucleic acid (DNA)* carries hereditary information and is responsible for passing traits from parents to offspring. *Ribonucleic acid (RNA)* are copies of DNA segments that are involved in making proteins. Nucleic acids are composed of long chains of nucleotides, each of which contains a sugar molecule, a phosphate group, and a nitrogenous base. DNA's double strands can be pictured as ladder rungs twisted into a spiral, giving the molecule a shape called a double helix **(Figure 5)**. RNA is generally single-stranded and contains a different sugar than DNA does.

Very generally, heredity works this way: The parts of DNA that "order" the production of certain proteins are called *genes*. Information that has been inherited is encoded in DNA and rewritten to a molecule of RNA. RNA then directs the order in which amino acids assemble to build proteins. Genetic information in DNA is passed from one generation to another during cell division and egg or sperm formation. In most organisms, the set of all of an individual's genes is divided into *chromosomes*.

Carbohydrates Carbohydrates are polymers that consist of atoms of carbon, hydrogen, and oxygen. A simple carbohydrate, or sugar, has three to seven carbon atoms and a formula that is some multiple of CH_2O. Glucose, for example, is $C_6H_{12}O_6$. Glucose is one of the most common and important sugars because it provides the energy that fuels plant and animal cells. Glucose also serves as a building block for complex carbohydrates, such as starch. Plants use starch to store energy, and animals acquire starch when they eat plants.

In addition, the structures that support the bodies of most plants and animals contain complex carbohydrates. Insects and crustaceans form hard outer coverings from the carbohydrate chitin. Cellulose is a complex carbohydrate found in the cell walls of plants.

 Reading Checkpoint   *Name two nucleic acids.*

Lipids		
Lipid type	**Characteristics**	**Examples**
Fats and oils	Store energy, which is released when they burn; hydrocarbons with chemical structures similar to gasoline	Animal fats, vegetable oils, petroleum
Phospholipids	Primary component of cell membranes; similar to fats	Primary component of lecithin
Waxes	Make up biological structures such as honeycombs in beehives; eaten by some organisms	Beeswax
Steroids and steroid hormones	Cell membrane component (steroids); produce bodily changes, such as sexual development (steroid hormones)	Cholesterol (steroid); androgen, estrogen, testosterone (steroid hormones)

FIGURE 6 **Lipids** Lipids include fats, oils, phospholipids, waxes, steroids, and steroid hormones.

Lipids Lipids are a chemically diverse group of macromolecules that are classified together because they do not dissolve in water. Lipids are made up of carbon, hydrogen, oxygen, and sometimes phosphorus. Fats, oils, phospholipids, waxes, and steroids are common lipids. You can learn more about lipids, including their roles in living things, in **Figure 6.**

Water

Water covers more than 70 percent of Earth's surface. Water's abundance is a primary reason there is life on Earth. Scientific evidence demonstrates that life originated in water and stayed there for 3 billion years before moving onto land. Every organism, even if it lives only on land, relies on water for its survival.

Properties of Water Water is our most familiar compound. The water molecule's amazing capacity to support life results from its unique chemical properties. A water molecule's single oxygen atom attracts electrons more strongly than its two hydrogen atoms, resulting in a polar molecule with a partial negative charge at the oxygen end and a partial positive charge at the hydrogen end. Because of this configuration, water molecules adhere to one another in a special type of attraction called a *hydrogen bond*, in which the oxygen atom of one water molecule is weakly attracted to one or two hydrogen atoms of another **(Figure 7).** These loose connections among molecules give water several properties important in supporting life and stabilizing Earth's climate.

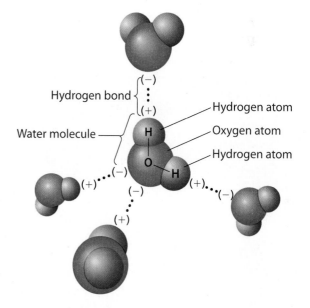

FIGURE 7 **Water Molecule** Water molecules have a negative charge at the oxygen end and a positive charge at the hydrogen end, which causes them to adhere to one another in hydrogen bonds. These bonds give water several properties essential to life.

FIGURE 8 Cohesion of Water
Because cohesion between water molecules is so strong, insects such as this raft spider can actually walk across it.

▶ *Cohesion* Water sticks to itself. (Think of how water droplets on a surface join when you touch them to one another.) This property, called *cohesion*, allows the transport of materials, such as nutrients and waste, in plants and animals. Cohesion between water molecules is so strong that certain animals, such as the raft spider in **Figure 8,** can actually walk on water!

▶ *Resistance to Temperature Change* Heating weakens the hydrogen bonds in water, but it does not initially increase the molecular motion, which is what causes temperature to rise. As a result, water can absorb a large amount of energy with only small changes in its temperature. This resistance to temperature change helps stabilize aquatic environmental systems and the climates in which they exist. It also explains why people like to live and vacation on the coast. Because it takes bodies of water longer to heat up and cool down, coastal areas are cooler in hot weather and warmer in cold weather.

▶ *Ice Density* Water molecules in ice are farther apart than in liquid water (**Figure 9),** so ice is less dense than liquid water— the reverse pattern of most other compounds, which become denser as they freeze. This is why ice floats on liquid water. Floating ice insulates bodies of water, preventing them from freezing solid in winter, allowing animals and plants to survive in the water at the bottom.

▶ *Universal Solvent* Water molecules bond well with other polar molecules, because the positive end of one molecule bonds easily to the negative end of another. As a result, water can hold in solution, or dissolve, many other molecules, including chemicals vital for life. Because of this property, water is often called "the universal solvent."

FIGURE 9 Density of Ice Icebergs float on top of bodies of water because ice is less dense than liquid water.

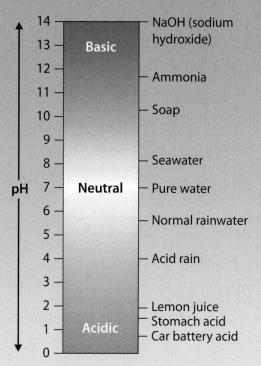

FIGURE 10 pH The pH scale describes how acidic or basic a substance is. Lemon juice is rather acidic and soap is rather basic.

Acids, Bases, and pH In any water solution, a small number of water molecules separate into *ions*, or charged atoms. Each separation results in a hydrogen ion (H^+) and a hydroxide ion (OH^-). Pure water contains equal numbers of these ions, so we say that it has a neutral pH. Most water solutions, however, contain different concentrations of the two ions. Solutions in which the H^+ concentration is greater than the OH^- concentration are *acidic,* whereas solutions in which the OH^- concentration exceeds the H^+ concentration are *basic,* or *alkaline.*

The acidity or alkalinity of a solution is described by **pH.** The pH scale runs from 0 to 14. A pH of 7 is perfectly neutral—pure water has a pH of 7. Solutions with a pH less than 7 are acidic, and those with a pH greater than 7 are basic. Each point on the scale represents a tenfold difference in hydrogen ion concentration. Thus, a substance with a pH of 6 is 10 times as acidic as a substance with a pH of 7, and a substance with a pH of 8 is one-tenth as acidic as one with a pH of 7. **Figure 10** shows the a pH of several common substances.

LESSON ① Assessment

1. **Classify** Is table salt (NaCl) a compound? How can you tell?

2. **Review** List the four types of macromolecules. What is one role played in the body by each?

3. **Apply Concepts** How would each of the four properties of water referred to in this lesson help a fish living in a pond?

4. **THINK IT** *THROUGH* What would you say to a classmate who said that he wanted to fulfill his science requirement by taking environmental science so he could avoid chemistry?

Systems in Environmental Science

EVERYDAY PHENOMENON What types of systems play roles in environmental science?

Knowledge and Skills

- Describe two major ways that Earth's systems interact.
- Define Earth's geosphere, lithosphere, biosphere, atmosphere, and hydrosphere.

Reading Strategy and Vocabulary

✓ **Reading Strategy** As you read the section on feedback loops, draw a cycle diagram showing the negative feedback loop involved in a thermostat's regulation of the heat in a house.

Vocabulary feedback loop, erosion, geosphere, lithosphere, biosphere, atmosphere, hydrosphere

A *SYSTEM* **IS A NETWORK** of relationships among parts, elements, or components that interact with and influence one another through the exchange of energy, matter, or information. Systems receive *inputs* of energy, matter, or information; process these inputs; and produce *outputs* of energy, matter, or information.

Earth's environment consists of complex, interlinked systems. Earth's systems include the complex webs of relationships among species and the interactions of living organisms with the nonliving objects around them. Earth's systems also include cycles that shape landscapes and guide the flow of chemical elements and compounds that support life and regulate climate.

Interacting Systems

Systems seldom have well-defined boundaries, so deciding where one system ends and another begins can be difficult. Consider a laptop computer system. What are its boundaries? Is the system made up of just what arrives in the shipping box and sits on your desk? Or does it also include the network you connect it to? What about the energy grid you plug it into, with its distant power plants and transmission lines—is that part of the system, too? Does the system include the Internet?

Whenever we try to define a system, we run into connections to other systems. Systems may exchange energy, matter, and information with other systems, and they may contain or be contained within other systems. So the boundaries we draw for a system usually depend on our focus at the moment. In our discussions of Earth's systems then, you may infer connections to other systems that are not being discussed at the moment. Don't worry—we'll get to them.

Earth's Systems Inputs into Earth's systems include energy, information, and matter. Energy inputs to Earth's environmental systems include solar energy as well as energy released by geothermal activity, the life processes of organisms, and human activities such as fossil fuel combustion. Information inputs can come in the form of sensory cues or genes. Inputs of matter occur when chemicals or physical materials move among systems, such as when seeds are dispersed long distances or when plants convert carbon in the air to living tissue via photosynthesis.

For example, as a system, the Gulf of Mexico receives inputs of fresh water, sediments, nutrients, and pollutants from the Mississippi and other rivers. Fishers harvest some of the Gulf system's output: matter and energy in the form of fish and shellfish, such as shrimp and scallops (**Figure 11**). This output then becomes input to the global economic system and to the digestive systems of the many people who consume the fish and shellfish.

FIGURE 11 Earth's Systems The scallops caught here are an output of the Gulf of Mexico system. The scallops will become inputs for several human systems.

Feedback Loops Sometimes an event is both a cause, or input, and an effect, or output, in the same system, a cyclical process called a **feedback loop.** A feedback loop can be either negative or positive.

▶ *Negative Feedback Loops* In a *negative feedback loop* (**Figure 12**), the output of a system moving in one direction acts as input that causes the system to move in the other direction. Input and output respond to each other's effects, canceling them out and stabilizing the system.

A thermostat, for example, stabilizes a room's temperature by turning the furnace on when the room gets cold and shutting it off when the room gets hot. One environmental example of negative feedback is a system in which predator and prey populations—wolves and moose, for example—rise and fall in response to each other. Most systems in nature involve negative feedback loops. Negative feedback loops enhance stability, and in the long run, only stable systems persist.

✓ **Reading Checkpoint** *What would you call a process in which an event is both an input and output of the same system?*

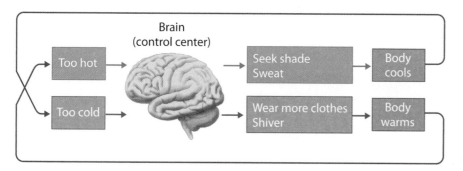

FIGURE 12 Negative Feedback Loop Negative feedback loops stabilize systems and are common in nature. The human body's responses to heat and cold involve a negative feedback loop.

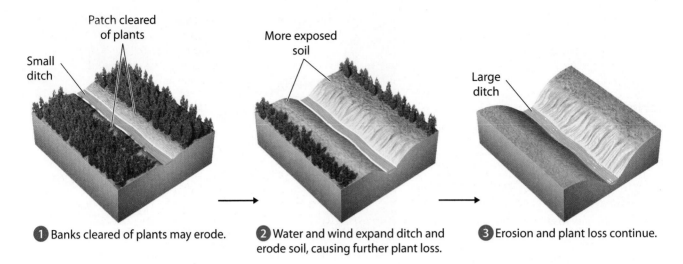

① Banks cleared of plants may erode.

② Water and wind expand ditch and erode soil, causing further plant loss.

③ Erosion and plant loss continue.

FIGURE 13 Positive Feedback Loop
Positive feedback loops destabilize systems and push them toward extremes. For example, the clearing of plants from land can lead to uncontrolled soil erosion. Water flowing through an eroded ditch may expand it and lead to further erosion. Positive feedback loops are rare in natural systems, but common in systems altered by humans, such as on land that has been grazed too much by livestock.

▶ *Positive Feedback Loops* *Positive feedback loops* have the opposite effect of negative feedback loops. Rather than stabilizing a system, they drive it toward an extreme. **Erosion,** the removal of soil by water, wind, ice, or gravity, can lead to a positive feedback loop. Once plants have been cleared from an area and soil is exposed, erosion may increase if the effects of water or wind surpass the rate of plant regrowth **(Figure 13)**. (You will learn more about erosion in a later chapter.) Because positive feedback destabilizes a system and drives it toward an extreme, it can alter a system drastically. This may be the reason that positive feedback loops are relatively rare in natural environmental systems. They are, however, common in environmental systems changed by people.

Earth's "Spheres"

Despite the challenges discussed earlier, categorizing Earth's environmental systems can help make Earth's complexity and environmental issues easier to understand. So scientists often divide Earth into spheres, some of which are described more by their makeup than by their location **(Figure 14)**. Earth's **geosphere** is made of all the rock at and below Earth's surface. The **lithosphere** is the hard rock on and just below Earth's surface—the outermost layer of the geosphere. The **biosphere** consists of all the planet's living or once-living things and the nonliving parts of the environment with which they interact. The **atmosphere** consists of the layers of gases surrounding our planet. The **hydrosphere** encompasses all water—salt, fresh, liquid, ice, and vapor—on Earth's surface, underground, and in the atmosphere. You will learn more about Earth's spheres in the next lesson.

 Reading Checkpoint *What are the components of the biosphere?*

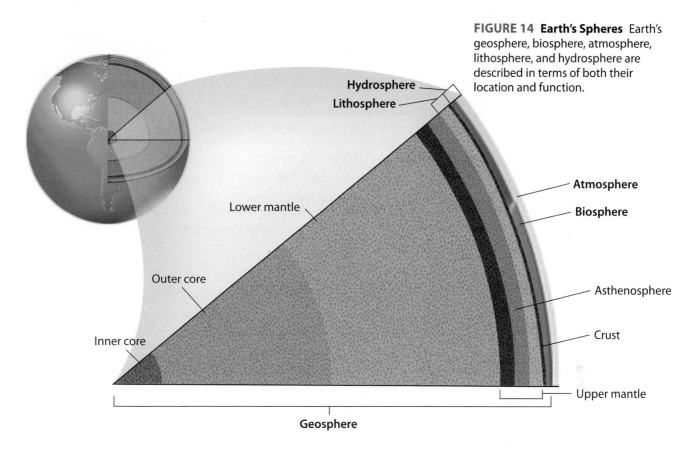

FIGURE 14 **Earth's Spheres** Earth's geosphere, biosphere, atmosphere, lithosphere, and hydrosphere are described in terms of both their location and function.

Hydrosphere
Lithosphere
Atmosphere
Biosphere
Asthenosphere
Crust
Upper mantle
Lower mantle
Outer core
Inner core
Geosphere

Although these spheres are useful models, keep in mind that they both overlap and interact. For example: Picture a robin plucking an earthworm from the ground after a rainstorm and then flying to a tree. You are witnessing the robin (an organism) eating the earthworm (another organism) that has been tunneling through the soil (the lithosphere)—all made possible because rain (from the hydrosphere) has dampened the ground. The robin might then fly through the air (the atmosphere) and land in a tree (another organism), in the process respiring (combining oxygen from the atmosphere with glucose from the organism, and adding water to the hydrosphere and carbon dioxide and heat to the atmosphere). Finally, the bird might release waste, adding nutrients to the soil (the lithosphere). And it all takes place in the biosphere. The study of the complex interactions in such apparently simple events is typical of environmental science.

LESSON 2 Assessment

1. **Compare and Contrast** What are the two types of feedback loops? How are they similar? How are they different?

2. **Classify** Suppose your lab partner were to empty a beaker of mud onto your lab table and ask you which of Earth's spheres it was part of. How would you answer? Explain.

3. **THINK IT** *THROUGH* As snow melts on a city street, it exposes some darker-colored pavement. Dark-colored surfaces absorb more sunlight and heat than light-colored surfaces. Would you expect a feedback process to result from this situation? If so, which type? Explain your answer.

Earth's Spheres

EVERYDAY PHENOMENON What are the characteristics of Earth's geosphere, biosphere, atmosphere, and hydrosphere?

Knowledge and Skills

- Describe the parts of Earth's geosphere.
- Describe Earth's biosphere and atmosphere.
- Discuss the water cycle.

Reading Strategy and Vocabulary

✔ **Reading Strategy** As you read, draw a concept map that relates Earth's geosphere, lithosphere, mantle, and core.

Vocabulary crust, mantle, core, tectonic plate, landform, deposition, evaporation, transpiration, precipitation, condensation, aquifer, groundwater

YOU MAY BE THINKING of Earth's geosphere, biosphere, atmosphere, and hydrosphere as a set of concentric spheres or Russian dolls, fitting neatly together but separate. As you will learn in the next two lessons, however, Earth's spheres interact with each other. You could think of each sphere as a different highway in the same area. Cars on the highways can travel independently of one another. But at interchanges, there is an intricate dance between cars traveling on a highway and those entering or exiting it.

The Geosphere

Earth's geosphere consists of the rock and minerals (including soil) on Earth's surface and below it. It includes the crust, the mantle, and the core. Tectonic plates that carry the continents move with the mantle, whose movement is fueled by heat from Earth's core.

Earth's Crust and Mantle Earth's **crust** is a thin layer of relatively cool rock that forms Earth's outer skin both on dry land and in the ocean. Below the crust is the **mantle**, a layer of very hot but mostly solid rock. The crust and the uppermost part of the mantle make up the lithosphere. The lithosphere is carried on a softer, hot layer of rock called the *asthenosphere*. The lower part of the lithosphere and the asthenosphere are included in the upper mantle. Below the upper mantle is the solid rock of the lower mantle.

The Core Beneath the lower mantle is Earth's **core**. Earth's outer core is made of molten metals such as iron and nickel that are almost as hot as the surface of the sun. Earth's inner core is a dense ball of solid metal. The heat from the outer core pushes the asthenosphere's soft rock upward (as it warms). The rock then sinks downward as it cools, like a gigantic conveyor belt. This process is called *convection*.

Plate Tectonics As the asthenosphere moves, it drags along large plates of lithosphere called **tectonic plates.** Earth's surface consists of about 15 major tectonic plates, most of which include some combination of ocean floor and continent (**Figure 15a**). Imagine peeling an orange and putting the pieces of peel back onto the fruit; the ragged pieces of peel are like the plates of Earth's crust. These plates move about 2 to 15 centimeters (1 to 6 inches) per year. This movement has influenced Earth's climate and life's evolution as the continents have combined, separated, and recombined. By studying ancient rock formations throughout the world, geologists have determined that, at least twice, all the world's continents were combined as a supercontinent. Scientists call the most recent super-continent *Pangaea* (**Figure 15b**).

These collisions and separations of plates result in **landforms**— features such as mountains (above and beneath the ocean's surface), islands, and continents. Landforms created by tectonic processes influence climate by altering patterns of rainfall, wind, ocean currents, heating, and cooling. These climate characteristics, in turn, affect the rates of soil formation, erosion, and **deposition** (the depositing of eroded soil at a new location). And climate, soil formation, erosion, and deposition affect the ability of a given plant or animal to inhabit a region. Thus, plate tectonics affects the types of animals that can live in an area.

Map it

Pangaea

Trace Pangaea and the boundaries drawn on it in **Figure 15b.** Then refer to **Figure 15a** as you respond to the items below.

1. **Compare and Contrast** Compare the shapes drawn on Pangaea to the shapes of today's continents. Aside from Antarctica, can you match each of those shapes, to one of today's continents?

2. **Interpret Maps** On your tracing, label the shapes that correspond to modern North America, South America, Eurasia, Africa, India, and Australia.

(b) Pangaea, 225 million years ago

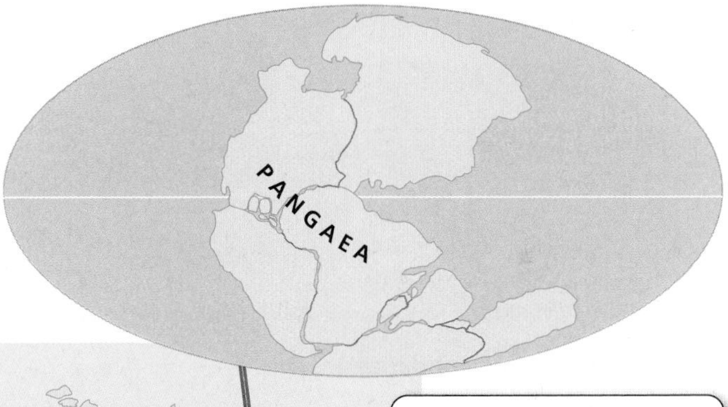

FIGURE 15 Tectonic Plates Earth's crust consists of about 15 major plates **(a)** that move very slowly by the process of plate tectonics. Today's continents were joined in the supercontinent Pangaea **(b)** about 225 million years ago.

(a) Tectonic plates

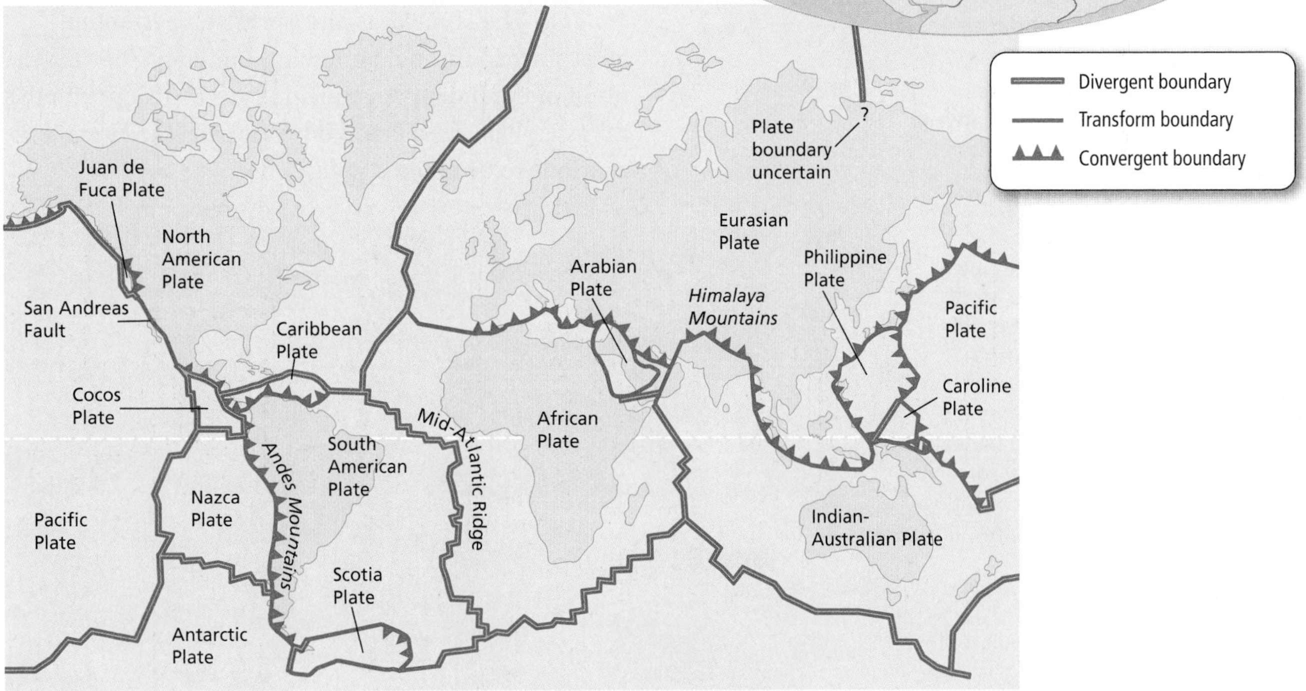

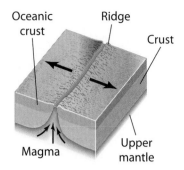

Oceanic crust · Ridge · Crust · Magma · Upper mantle

(a) Divergent plate boundary

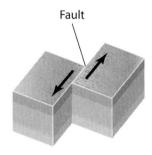

Fault

(b) Transform plate boundary

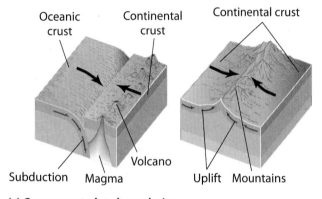

Oceanic crust · Continental crust · Continental crust · Subduction · Magma · Volcano · Uplift · Mountains

(c) Convergent plate boundaries

FIGURE 16 Plate Boundaries
Different types of boundaries between tectonic plates result in different geologic processes (above). At a divergent plate boundary **(a)**, magma surges up through the crust, and the two plates move gradually away like conveyor belts. At a transform plate boundary **(b)**, two plates slide alongside each other, producing friction that leads to earthquakes. At a convergent plate boundary **(c)**, one plate may be subducted beneath another, leading to volcanoes, or both plates may be uplifted, resulting in mountain ranges, such as the Himalayas (right).

Types of Plate Boundaries Plates interact in different ways based on the type of boundary between them. The type of plate boundary also determines the type of landform that results from a collision. Plate boundaries are either divergent, transform, or convergent.

▶ *Divergent Plate Boundaries* At *divergent plate boundaries, magma,* or molten rock, surges upward to the surface and pushes plates apart, creating new crust as it cools **(Figure 16a)**. A prime example is the Mid-Atlantic Ridge, part of a 74,000-kilometer (46,000-mile) system that cuts across the ocean floor. Plates expanding outward from divergent plate boundaries at mid-ocean ridges bump against other plates, forming transform or convergent plate boundaries.

▶ *Transform Plate Boundaries* When two plates meet, they may slip and grind alongside one another, forming a *transform plate boundary* **(Figure 16b)**. The friction between plates at transform plate boundaries often spawns earthquakes. The Pacific Plate and the North American Plate, for example, rub against each other along California's San Andreas Fault, the origin of many of North America's most severe earthquakes.

▶ *Convergent Plate Boundaries* When plates collide at *convergent plate boundaries,* one of two events happens **(Figure 16c)**. One plate of crust may slide beneath another in a process called *subduction.* The subducted crust is heated as it dives into the mantle, and it may send up magma that erupts through the surface in volcanoes. Mount Saint Helens in Washington, which erupted violently in 1980 and became active again in 2004, is fueled by magma from this process of subduction.

Alternately, the two plates may collide, slowly lifting material from both plates in a process called *mountain-building.* The Himalayas, the world's highest mountains, formed through mountain-building. They are the result of the Indian-Australian Plate's collision with the Eurasian Plate 40–50 million years ago. The Himalayas continue to be uplifted today.

The Biosphere and Atmosphere

Like all of Earth's systems, Earth's biosphere and atmosphere interact. The gases used and expelled by organisms in the biosphere affect the composition of gases in the atmosphere. In turn, the gases in the atmosphere protect and support the organisms in the biosphere.

The Biosphere The part of Earth in which living things interact with nonliving things is Earth's biosphere, which you could call "the living Earth." You may think that all of Earth has living things, but remember that Earth is not an empty shell. It is filled with hot rock and metal—and scientists know of no organisms living in Earth's mantle or core.

The Atmosphere When you look at a photo of Earth from space, the atmosphere looks like a very thin blue line **(Figure 17).** But that thin blue line is an ocean of gases that support and protect the entire biosphere. The atmosphere contains the gases, such as oxygen, that organisms use for their life processes. It also contains *ozone*, a gas made up of oxygen molecules that each have three oxygen atoms. A layer of ozone protects the biosphere from the sun's radiation—it is a sort of global sunscreen.

The atmosphere also includes gases that keep Earth warm enough to support life, protecting the biosphere from the bitter cold of space. These gases, which include carbon dioxide and methane, are called greenhouse gases because the way they keep Earth warm is analogous to the way the sun's energy, enhanced by the windows of a greenhouse, keeps plants warm. The process is called the greenhouse effect. As you may already know, human activities can affect it. You will read more about the greenhouse effect in a later chapter.

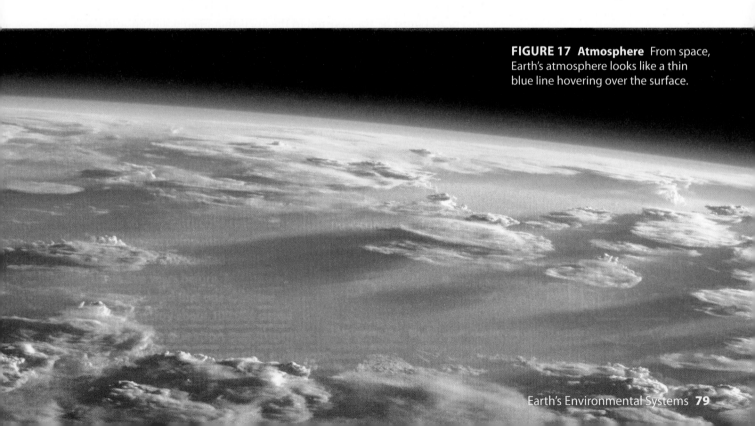

FIGURE 17 Atmosphere From space, Earth's atmosphere looks like a thin blue line hovering over the surface.

FIGURE 18 Distribution of Earth's Water Most of Earth's water is salt water, which cannot be used for drinking or for watering crops. Only 2.5 percent of Earth's water is fresh water, and 79 percent of that is frozen. A tiny percentage of Earth's water is vapor.

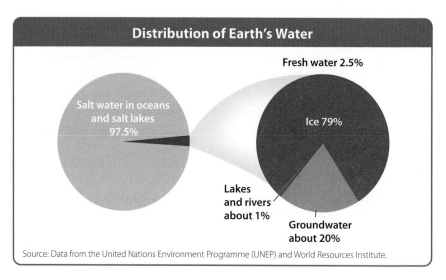

Distribution of Earth's Water

Salt water in oceans and salt lakes 97.5%

Fresh water 2.5%

Ice 79%

Lakes and rivers about 1%

Groundwater about 20%

Source: Data from the United Nations Environment Programme (UNEP) and World Resources Institute.

The Hydrosphere

Water is essential to life, but we frequently take it for granted. As a means of transport and as a solvent, water plays key roles in nearly every environmental system, including all the other cycles of matter and the life processes of every organism in the biosphere.

Earth's Water Most of Earth's water is salt water (**Figure 18**). The salt water in oceans and salt lakes makes up about 97.5 percent of Earth's water. So only 2.5 percent of Earth's water is fresh water. And more than three quarters of that fresh water is ice. (The ice-covered parts of Earth are sometimes called the *cryosphere.*) Only about 0.5 percent of Earth's water is unfrozen fresh water that might be used for drinking or watering crops. Most of that water is underground, in groundwater, and must be brought to the surface via pumps and/or wells. The rest is in lakes and rivers and must be transported to the areas that need it. Given water's importance and its limited accessibility, it is easy to see how shortages and conflicts over its use occur.

Quick Lab

Distribution of Earth's Water

1. Fill a 1-liter plastic bottle with water. This amount represents all of Earth's water.
2. Pour 97.5 percent, or 975 milliliters, of the water into a large bowl. This amount represents Earth's salt water.
3. Label cups *Ice, Groundwater,* and *Lakes and Rivers.*
4. Using **Figure 18,** calculate how much of the remaining 25 milliliters should be poured into each cup.
5. Use a graduated cylinder to measure and pour the correct amount of water into each cup.

Analyze and Conclude

1. **Infer** Which cup(s) represent water that humans can easily use for drinking or watering crops?
2. **Calculate** Calculate the percentage of Earth's water that those cups represent, combined.
3. **Draw Conclusions** Some regions have water shortages even though they are located on ocean coasts. How could that be the case?

FIGURE 19 The Water Cycle The water cycle summarizes the many routes that water molecules take through Earth's spheres. In this diagram, labels in boxes refer to sources of water, and italic labels refer to processes of the water cycle.

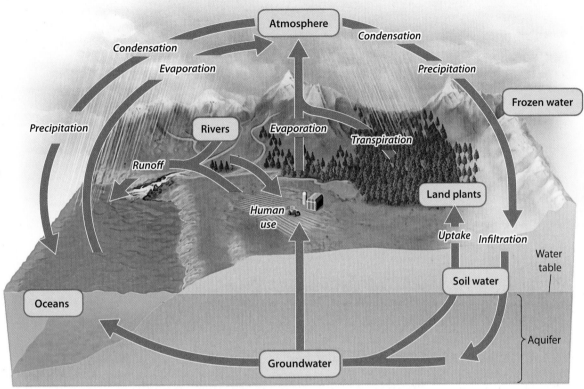

Adapted from Schlesinger, W.H. 1997. *Biogeochemistry: An analysis of global change, 2nd ed.* London: Academic Press

The Water Cycle The *water cycle,* or *hydrologic cycle* (**Figure 19**), summarizes the roles that water—liquid, gaseous, and solid—plays in our environment. Evaporation, transpiration, precipitation, and condensation are the major processes of the water cycle.

▶ *Evaporation and Transpiration* Water moves from bodies of water and moist soil into the atmosphere by **evaporation,** the conversion of a substance from a liquid to a gas. Warm temperatures and strong winds speed evaporation. Exposed soil loses moisture very quickly—a logged area or an area converted to farms or buildings will lose moisture faster than a similar-sized area covered with natural vegetation. Water also enters the atmosphere by **transpiration,** the release of water vapor by plants through their leaves. Evaporation and transpiration distill water naturally, creating pure water by filtering out minerals and pollutants. Small amounts of water also enter the atmosphere as byproducts of cellular respiration and combustion.

▶ *Precipitation and Condensation* Water returns from the atmosphere to Earth's surface as **precipitation** such as rain or snow. Precipitation occurs when water vapor undergoes **condensation,** a change in state from a gas to a liquid. Precipitation may be taken up by plants and used by animals, but much of it flows as *runoff* into bodies of surface water such as rivers, lakes, and oceans.

FIND OUT MORE

your world • your turn

Are there any conflicts over water use in your area? What pollution threats does the water supply in your town face? Given your knowledge of the water cycle, what solution would you propose for one of the water problems in your area?

FIGURE 20 Human Impacts on the Water Cycle People draw groundwater out of aquifers to water crops, such as those planted on these circular fields near Dimmitt, Texas. Crops are planted on circular fields so that they can be efficiently watered by a sprayer pipe that extends across the radius of the circle.

▶ *Groundwater* Some precipitation and surface water soaks down through soil and rock to recharge underground reservoirs, or storage areas, known as **aquifers.** Aquifers are layers of rock and soil that hold **groundwater,** fresh water found underground. The upper limit of groundwater held in an aquifer is called the *water table.* Groundwater can take hundreds or even thousands of years to recharge fully after being depleted, if it *ever* recharges, so it is an extremely precious resource.

▶ *Human Impacts* Human activity can affect every aspect of the water cycle. By clearing plants from Earth's surface, we increase runoff and erosion, increase evaporation, and reduce transpiration. By spreading water on farm fields, we can deplete surface water and groundwater and increase evaporation (**Figure 20**). And by releasing certain pollutants into the atmosphere, we cause precipitation to become more acidic. Perhaps most threatening to our future, we are depleting groundwater with unrestrained use by irrigation and industry. The depletion is so severe in some areas, such as South Asia, the Middle East, and the American West, that water shortages have given rise to political, or even armed, conflicts.

LESSON ③ Assessment

1. **Apply Concepts** What parts of the geosphere are involved in plate tectonics? What are their functions in that process?

2. **Use Analogies** Use an anology to describe one way that gases in Earth's atmosphere protect the biosphere.

3. **Relate Cause and Effect** Describe the two processes by which most water moves into the atmosphere.
   REVISIT

4. **INVESTIGATIVE** PHENOMENON How are the processes of the water cycle essential to an unpolluted biosphere?

4 Biogeochemical Cycles

EVERYDAY PHENOMENON How do nutrients cycle through the environment?

Knowledge and Skills

- Explain how the law of conservation of matter applies to the behavior of nutrients in the environment.
- Describe the carbon cycle.
- Describe the events of the phosphorus cycle.
- Explain the importance of bacteria to the nitrogen cycle.

Reading Strategy and Vocabulary

✔ **Reading Strategy** Before you read, preview **Figure 21.** Make a list of questions you have about the carbon cycle. As you read, try to answer those questions.

Vocabulary law of conservation of matter, nutrient, biogeochemical cycle, primary producer, photosynthesis, consumer, decomposer, cellular respiration, eutrophication, nitrogen fixation

CONSIDER THIS: A carbon atom in your fingernail today might have helped make up the muscle of a cow a year ago, may have belonged to a blade of grass a month before that, and may have been part of a dinosaur's tooth 100 million years ago. Matter is never used up, and it never goes away. It just keeps cycling around and around.

Nutrient Cycling

Why does matter, such as water, cycle through the environment, never getting used up? Here's the answer: Matter may be transformed from one type to another, but it cannot be created or destroyed. This principle is called the **law of conservation of matter.** It explains why the amount of matter in the environment stays the same as it flows through matter cycles, such as the water cycle.

Nutrients are matter that organisms require for their life processes. Organisms need several dozen nutrients. The nutrients required in relatively large amounts are called *macronutrients* and include nitrogen, carbon, and phosphorus. The nutrients needed in small amounts are called *micronutrients*. Nutrients circulate endlessly throughout the environment in complex cycles called **biogeochemical cycles,** or nutrient cycles. Carbon, oxygen, phosphorus, and nitrogen are nutrients that cycle through all of Earth's spheres and organisms. The water cycle plays parts in all the biogeochemical cycles.

The Carbon Cycle

From fossil fuels to DNA, from plastics to medicines, carbon (C) atoms are everywhere. The *carbon cycle* describes the routes that carbon atoms take through the environment.

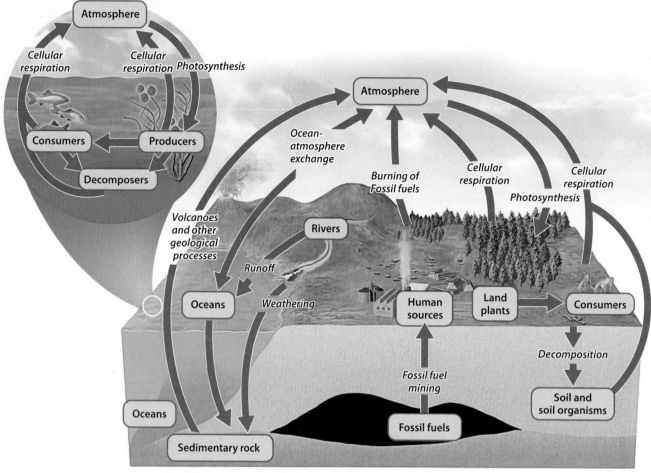

Adapted from Schlesinger, W.H. 1997. *Biogeochemistry: An analysis of global change, 2nd ed.* London: Academic Press

FIGURE 21 Carbon Cycle The carbon cycle describes the routes that carbon atoms take as they move through the environment. In this diagram, labels in boxes refer to reservoirs, or pools, of carbon, and italic labels refer to processes of the carbon cycle.

Producers Primary producers are organisms, including plants and algae, that produce their own food. Producers use the sun's energy or chemical energy along with carbon dioxide to produce carbohydrates. The carbohydrates are used as food by the producers.

Most producers make their own food by using the sun's energy in photosynthesis. In **photosynthesis,** producers pull carbon dioxide out of their environment and combine it with water in the presence of sunlight. The chemical bonds in carbon dioxide (CO_2) and water (H_2O) are then broken, producing oxygen (O_2) and carbohydrates (such as glucose, $C_6H_{12}O_6$). (The numbers in front of the chemical formulas below are numbers of molecules.)

$$6CO_2 + 6H_2O + \text{the sun's energy} \rightarrow C_6H_{12}O_6 \text{ (sugar)} + 6O_2$$

Consumers and Decomposers The carbon in a producer may be passed on to another organism, either a consumer that eats it or a decomposer that breaks down its wastes or remains. **Consumers** are organisms, mainly animals, that must eat other organisms to obtain nutrients. **Decomposers** are organisms such as bacteria and fungi that break down wastes and dead organisms.

Cellular Respiration Cellular respiration does *not* refer to *breathing*. Cellular respiration is the process by which organisms use oxygen to release the chemical energy of sugars and release CO_2 and water. In general terms, it is the chemical reverse of photosynthesis.

$$C_6H_{12}O_6 \text{ (sugar)} + 6O_2 \rightarrow 6CO_2 + 6H_2O + \text{energy}$$

Most organisms undergo cellular respiration constantly, releasing carbon back into the atmosphere and oceans. Organisms do not release all the carbon they take in, however. They use some of it for their life processes. In fact, the abundance of plants and the fact that they use so much carbon for photosynthesis and other processes makes them a major carbon *sink*. (A sink is a reservoir of a substance that accepts more of that substance than it releases.)

Carbon in Sediments When organisms die in water, their remains may settle in sediments. As new layers of sediment accumulate, pressure on earlier layers increases. These conditions can convert soft tissues into fossil fuels, and shells and skeletons into sedimentary rock such as limestone. Limestone and other sedimentary rock make up the largest reservoir of carbon. Sedimentary rock releases some of its carbon through erosion and volcanic eruptions. Fossil fuel deposits contain a great deal of carbon, which is released when we extract the fossil fuels.

Carbon in Oceans The world's oceans are the second-largest carbon reservoir **(Figure 22)**. They absorb carbon compounds from the atmosphere, from runoff, from undersea volcanoes, and from the wastes and remains of organisms. The rates at which seawater absorbs and releases carbon depend on many factors, including the water temperature and the numbers of marine organisms living in it.

Human Impacts Humans shift carbon to the atmosphere in many ways. By extracting fossil fuels, we remove carbon from storage in the lithosphere. By then burning those fossil fuels, we move carbon dioxide into the atmosphere. The cutting of forests and burning of forests to plant farm fields also increase carbon in the atmosphere, both by releasing it from storage in plants and by reducing the plants available to use it. Producers cannot absorb enough carbon to keep up with human activities.

The Missing Carbon Sink Our understanding of the carbon cycle is not complete. Scientists have long been baffled by a missing carbon sink. Of the carbon dioxide humans release, scientists have measured how much is returned to the atmosphere and oceans, and more than 1–2 billion metric tons (1.1–2.2 billion tons) are unaccounted for. Many researchers think it must be taken up by the northern forests. But they'd like to know for sure.

FIGURE 22 Carbon in the Oceans
It's hard to believe that this beautiful blue-green wave is full of carbon. Oceans are Earth's second-largest carbon reservoir.

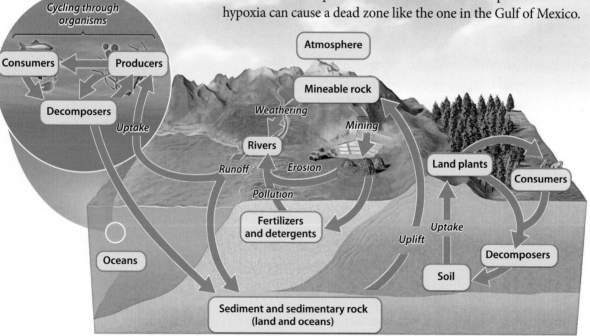

The Phosphorus Cycle

The *phosphorus cycle* (**Figure 23**) involves mainly the lithosphere and the oceans. Phosphorus is a key component of cell membranes and of several molecules essential to life, including DNA and RNA. Although phosphorus is essential to life, the amount of phosphorus in organisms is dwarfed by the vast amounts in rocks, soil, sediments, and the oceans. Phosphorus is released naturally only when rocks are worn down by water or wind. Because most phosphorus is bound up in rock, the phosphorus available to organisms at any time tends to be very low. This scarcity, along with the need that organisms have for phosphorus, explains why plant and algae growth often jumps dramatically when phosphorus is added to their environments.

Organisms in the Phosphorus Cycle Plants can take up phosphorus through their roots only when it is dissolved in water. Consumers acquire phosphorus from the water they drink and the organisms they eat. The waste of consumers contains phosphorus that decomposers return to the soil.

Human Impacts People influence the phosphorus cycle in several ways. We mine phosphorus to use as fertilizer. People also release phosphorus-rich wastewater from their houses and businesses. (Phosphorus compounds are added to many detergents to improve their cleaning power.) Wastewater containing fertilizers and detergents that runs off or leaches into waterways adds phosphorus to them. The addition of phosphorus to bodies of water can lead to an overgrowth of producers (usually algae) in a process called **eutrophication.** In extreme cases, eutrophication can lead to *hypoxia,* or extremely low levels of oxygen in a body of water, as decomposers break down all the dead producers. Widespread hypoxia can cause a dead zone like the one in the Gulf of Mexico.

FIGURE 23 Phosphorus Cycle The phosphorus cycle describes the routes that phosphorus atoms take through the environment. In this diagram, labels in boxes refer to reservoirs of phosphorus, and italic labels refer to processes of the phosphorus cycle.

Adapted from Schlesinger, W.H. 1997. *Biogeochemistry: An analysis of global change, 2nd ed.* London: Academic Press

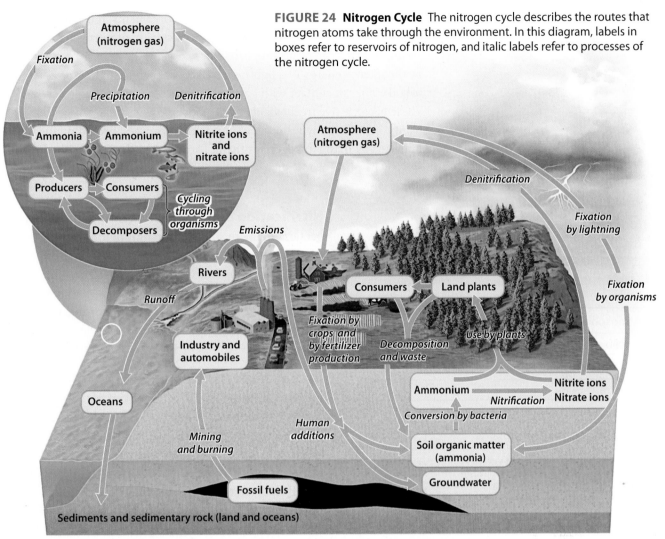

FIGURE 24 Nitrogen Cycle The nitrogen cycle describes the routes that nitrogen atoms take through the environment. In this diagram, labels in boxes refer to reservoirs of nitrogen, and italic labels refer to processes of the nitrogen cycle.

Adapted from Schlesinger, W.H. 1997. *Biogeochemistry: An analysis of global change, 2nd ed.* London: Academic Press

The Nitrogen Cycle

Nitrogen makes up 78 percent of our atmosphere by mass, and is the sixth most abundant element. It is an essential ingredient in the proteins, DNA, and RNA that build our bodies. Like phosphorus, nitrogen is an essential nutrient for plant growth. Thus the *nitrogen cycle* (**Figure 24**) is of vital importance to us and to all other organisms. Despite its abundance, nitrogen gas cannot cycle out of the atmosphere and into organisms. For this reason, nitrogen is relatively scarce in the lithosphere, hydrosphere, and in organisms. However, once nitrogen undergoes the right kind of chemical change—assisted by lightning, specialized bacteria, or human technology—it becomes usable to the organisms that need it. Those nitrogen compounds can act as potent fertilizers in the biosphere.

 Why is nitrogen scarce in the biosphere?

Nitrogen Fixation To become usable to organisms, nitrogen gas (N_2) must be "fixed." **Nitrogen fixation** is the conversion of nitrogen gas into ammonia. This can be accomplished in two naturally occurring ways: by the intense energy of a lightning strike, or when air in the top layer of soil comes in contact with particular types of *nitrogen-fixing bacteria*. These bacteria live freely in soil or in association with many types of plants, including soybeans, clover, and other legumes, providing them nutrients by fixing nitrogen for them. Farmers have long nourished their soils by planting crops, such as legumes, whose roots host nitrogen-fixing bacteria.

Nitrification and Denitrification Other types of bacteria living in soil use ammonium ions from nitrogen fixation or from the waste of decomposers to perform *nitrification*. In this process, the ammonium ions are first converted into nitrite ions (NO_2^-), then into nitrate ions (NO_3^-). Plants can take up nitrate ions. The nitrogen cycle is complete when *denitrifying bacteria* convert nitrates in soil or water back to nitrogen gas.

Human Impacts The slow rate of natural nitrogen fixation limits the flow of nitrogen out of the atmosphere and into the biosphere. But humans can also fix nitrogen. The process was developed shortly before World War I, when German scientist Fritz Haber found a way to synthesize ammonia, a nitrogen compound. Carl Bosch, another German scientist, later built on Haber's work to produce ammonia on a large scale. The Haber-Bosch process enabled people to overcome the limits on plant productivity imposed by the natural scarcity of nitrogen. Today, humans fix at least as much nitrogen artificially as is fixed naturally.

Sources of Nitrogen into Gulf of Mexico	
Source	Percent
Atmospheric deposition	26%
Fertilizers	41%
Fixation and other legume sources	9%
Manure	10%
Urban areas	7%
Wastewater treatment plants	7%

Data from USGS SPARROW model estimates of sources of total nitrogen and total phosphorus transported from Mississippi River Basin to Gulf of Mexico (Robertson and Saad 2013).

 Connect to the Central Case

FIGURE 25 Nitrogen in the Gulf of Mexico The table shows the sources of nitrogen added to the Gulf of Mexico from the Mississippi River basin (photo). **Interpret Data** What has been the largest source of added nitrogen in the Gulf of Mexico?

 Reading Checkpoint *What are two ways in which nitrogen fixation can occur naturally?*

By fixing atmospheric nitrogen, we increase its flow out of the atmosphere and into other reservoirs. We also affect other parts of the nitrogen cycle. When we burn forests and fields, we force nitrogen out of soils and vegetation and into the atmosphere. When we burn fossil fuels, we increase the rate at which nitric oxide (NO) enters the atmosphere and reacts to form nitrogen dioxide (NO_2). This compound can lead to acid precipitation. These and other human activities unbalance the nitrogen cycle.

Conflicting Interests Nitrogen's natural scarcity and its importance to organisms mean that when it is introduced by people, problems similar to those of introduced phosphorus, such as eutrophication, can occur. The impacts of excess nitrogen from agriculture and other human activities along the Mississippi River (**Figure 25**) are painfully evident to fishers and scientists with an interest in the Gulf of Mexico. Yet, farmers upstream also need to continue making a living, so there is a conflict.

The federal government has tried to help resolve that conflict. In 1998, the U.S. Congress passed the Harmful Algal Bloom and Hypoxia Research and Control Act. This law called for an "integrated assessment" of hypoxia in the northern Gulf to address the extent, nature, and causes of the dead zone, as well as its ecological and economic impacts. The assessment report published two years later outlined potential solutions and their estimated social and economic costs. The report proposed that the federal government work with Gulf Coast and Midwestern communities to carry out several proposals, which you can see in **Figure 26.** In 2017, Congress reauthorized the Act, extending it to fiscal year 2023.

Proposals for Reducing Gulf of Mexico Dead Zone

- Reduce nitrogen fertilizer use on Midwestern farms.
- Change the timing of fertilizer use to minimize runoff during the rainy season.
- Plant alternative crops.
- Manage nitrogen-rich livestock manure more effectively.
- Restore nitrogen-absorbing wetlands in the Mississippi River basin.
- Construct artificial wetlands to filter farm runoff.
- Improve sewage treatment.
- Restore frequently flooded lands to reduce runoff.
- Restore wetlands near the Mississippi River's mouth to improve nitrogen-absorbing ability.

 Connect to the Central Case

FIGURE 26 Potential Solutions to the Dead Zone A 2000 assessment of hypoxia in the Gulf of Mexico led to these proposals. Congress continues to work on refining laws concerning the addition of nutrients to the Mississippi River basin in efforts to reduce the dead zone. **Infer** According to these proposals, what group will bear much of the responsibility for reducing the dead zone?

LESSON ④ Assessment

1. **Review** Describe the law of conservation of matter.
2. **Infer** Why is it said that photosynthesis and cellular respiration are reverse chemical processes?
3. **Sequence** Describe the roles of organisms in the phosphorus cycle.
4. **Classify** A classmate describes a bacterium to you as living on the roots of clover and providing nutrients to the plant. Would you classify this bacterium as nitrogen-fixing, nitrifying, or denitrifying? Explain.
5. **THINK IT** *THROUGH* You've been noticing that a local pond has developed a green scum that is getting thicker and thicker. When you look into the water, you see fewer fish and other animals than you used to, and you see fewer birds around the pond. Based on what you learned in this chapter, what is this process called? What are two possible causes?

Nutrients

Carbon, nitrogen, and phosphorus are the most abundant nutrients in the biosphere, but there are many secondary nutrients that are also vital for life. Plants, for example, require 13 nutrients to grow; humans and animals require several more. Some of these are *macronutrients,* which are nutrients required in large quantities. Others are *micronutrients,* which are required only in small quantities. Potassium, calcium, and iron are three important nutrients that are required by almost every organism on Earth for survival.

POTASSIUM

Potassium comes from weathered mineral salts in the Earth's crust. Plants need large amounts of potassium for the transport of water and nutrients through their stems—some plant species need even more potassium than nitrogen. Old, highly weathered acidic soils, however, such as those in rain forests and savannas near the equator, tend to be low in potassium, making potassium fertilizer necessary for agriculture in these regions. For animals, potassium is a micronutrient, that is needed to keep animal muscles and brains functioning.

Tropical soils are often leached of potassium.

CALCIUM

Calcium is best known as the mineral that strengthens bones in humans and other vertebrates, but plants need calcium, too. In fact, calcium can be just as important as nitrogen and phosphorus for plants. This is particularly true for plants growing in acidic soils where levels of calcium tend to be low. For these plants, calcium is often in short supply, which can limit growth. Calcium is also important for ocean creatures such as corals, snails, and tiny microscopic organisms that build shells or plates out of calcium carbonate ($CaCO_3$).

Calcium carbonate is the major component of clam shells and corals.

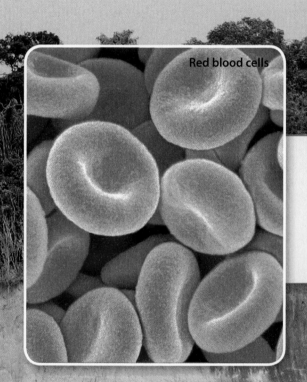

Red blood cells

IRON

Iron is a micronutrient, necessary only in small quantities, but nearly every organism on Earth depends on it for survival. In animals, iron is needed for transporting oxygen in the blood. In plants and bacteria, iron is necessary for photosynthesis.

CAREER **Nutritionist** Nutritionists advise people on what to eat based on specific dietary or medical needs. Nutritionists work in hospitals and private settings. Go Online and research careers in nutrition. Write a brief summary of your findings.

Study Guide

INVESTIGATIVE PHENOMENON

How do "dead zones" affect the environment surrounding them?

Lesson 1
What properties of matter are most important to environmental systems?

Lesson 2
What types of systems play roles in environmental science?

Lesson 3
What are the characteristics of Earth's geosphere, biosphere, atmosphere, and hydrosphere?

Lesson 4
How do nutrients cycle through the environment?

LESSON 1 Matter and the Environment

- Atoms and elements are the basic building blocks of chemistry.
- Proteins, nucleic acids, carbohydrates, and lipids are the building blocks of life.
- Water is a unique compound with several unusual properties that make it essential to life.

matter (64)	solution (67)
atom (64)	macromolecule (67)
element (64)	protein (67)
nucleus (65)	nucleic acid (68)
molecule (66)	carbohydrate (68)
compound (66)	lipid (69)
hydrocarbon (66)	pH (71)

LESSON 2 Systems in Environmental Science

- An output of one of Earth's systems is often also an input to that or another system.
- Earth's geosphere, lithosphere, biosphere, atmosphere, and hydrosphere are defined according to their functions in Earth's systems.

feedback loop (73)
erosion (74)
geosphere (74)
lithosphere (74)
biosphere (74)
atmosphere (74)
hydrosphere (74)

LESSON 3 Earth's Spheres

- Earth's geosphere consists of the crust, the mantle, and the core.
- Earth's biosphere and atmosphere are the living Earth and the ocean of gases that supports and protects it.
- Water cycles through the lithosphere, biosphere, and atmosphere endlessly.

crust (76)	evaporation (81)
mantle (76)	transpiration (81)
core (76)	precipitation (81)
tectonic plate (77)	condensation (81)
landform (77)	aquifer (82)
deposition (77)	groundwater (82)

LESSON 4 Biogeochemical Cycles

- Nutrients cycle through the environment endlessly.
- Producers play vital roles in the cycling of carbon.
- Phosphorus availability is naturally low.
- The nitrogen cycle relies on bacteria that make nitrogen available to organisms and bacteria that can return it to the atmosphere.

law of conservation of matter (83)
nutrient (83)
biogeochemical cycle (83)
primary producer (84)
photosynthesis (84)
consumer (84)
decomposer (84)
cellular respiration (85)
eutrophication (86)
nitrogen fixation (88)

 GO ONLINE

INQUIRY LABS AND ACTIVITIES

- **Age the Islands**

  Use position, shape, and size of the volcanic Galápagos Islands to infer which are older or younger.

- **Effects of CO_2 on Plants**

  Do plants thrive or decline when atmospheric CO_2 levels increase? Graph a sample dataset to find out.

Chapter Assessment

  Defend Your Case

The Central Case in this chapter introduced the dead zone in the Gulf of Mexico. Scientists have evidence that farming practices and other human activities along the Mississippi River contribute to the dead zone. Based on what you have learned, how can the dead zone be reduced without hurting the livelihoods of the farmers upstream? Use examples from the Central Case and the lessons to provide evidence for your ideas.

Review Concepts and Terms

1. Which of the following are the basic units of matter?
   a. compounds
   b. solutions
   c. atoms
   d. macromolecules

2. The particles labeled with negative signs in the diagram at the right are
   a. elements.
   b. electrons.
   c. protons.
   d. neutrons.

3. Which of Earth's spheres encompasses all of Earth's water?
   a. the hydrosphere
   b. the atmosphere
   c. the asthenosphere
   d. the geosphere

4. The crust, mantle, asthenosphere, and core are all parts of Earth's
   a. atmosphere.
   b. biosphere.
   c. hydrosphere.
   d. geosphere.

5. Landforms include
   a. aquifers.
   b. tectonic plates.
   c. mountains.
   d. all of the above.

6. Matter that organisms require for their life processes are
   a. biogeochemical cycles.
   b. producers.
   c. nutrients.
   d. decomposers.

7. An organism that must get nutrients by eating other organisms is called a
   a. producer.
   b. consumer.
   c. decomposer.
   d. nitrifying bacterium.

8. The phosphorus cycle involves mainly the
   a. atmosphere and biosphere.
   b. lithosphere and hydrosphere.
   c. geosphere and biosphere.
   d. asthenosphere and hydrosphere.

9. Eutrophication of a body of water is often caused by the addition of
   a. carbon and/or proteins.
   b. lipids and/or hydrocarbons.
   c. carbon and/or phosphorus.
   d. phosphorus and/or nitrogen.

10. Nitrogen fixation can be accomplished naturally either by a lightning strike or by
    a. nitrogen-fixing bacteria.
    b. denitrifying bacteria.
    c. the Haber-Bosch process.
    d. burning fossil fuels.

Chapter Assessment

CHAPTER **3**

Modified True/False

Write true if the statement is true. If it is false, change the underlined word or words to make the statement true.

11. All material that has mass and occupies space is called <u>matter</u>.

12. Proteins, nucleic acids, carbohydrates, and lipids are all <u>macromolecules</u>.

13. The ever-worsening erosion of a patch of over-grazed land is an example of a <u>negative</u> feedback loop.

14. Most <u>decomposers</u> make their own food by photosynthesis.

15. Photosynthesis and <u>cellular respiration</u> can be considered the chemical reverse of each other.

Reading Comprehension

Read the following selection and answer the questions that follow.

Global climate change is occurring. Almost all environmental scientists agree that emissions of certain gases could be contributing to it. Carbon dioxide, methane, nitrous oxide, ozone, hydrochlorofluorocarbons, and water vapor are the main culprits. These "greenhouse gases" have increased dramatically in our atmosphere in the last 300 years. Human activities, especially the mining and burning of fossil fuels for transportation and industry, increase greenhouse gases in the atmosphere. And increasing industrial activity in developing nations will likely lead to rising emissions of those gases. If unchecked, carbon dioxide levels in the atmosphere could reach twice preindustrial levels by 2050 and double again by 2100. Computer models show that this rise in greenhouse gases could raise Earth's temperatures by as much as 10 degrees Fahrenheit.

16. Which of the following gases are considered greenhouse gases?
a. methane
b. carbon dioxide
c. ozone
d. all of the above

17. The primary human source of greenhouse gases in Earth's atmosphere is
a. photosynthesis.
b. the mining and burning of fossil fuels.
c. the use of aerosol sprays.
d. the removal of fossils.

18. How could an increase in industrial activity in developing nations contribute to global climate change?
a. Burning fossil fuels in industry increases greenhouse gases in the atmosphere.
b. Burning fossil fuels destroys the ozone layer.
c. Heat from industrial machines warms up the atmosphere.
d. Burning fossil fuels removes water vapor from the atmosphere.

Short Answer

19. What is the nucleus of an atom?
20. What particles are in the nucleus of an atom?
21. Give an example of each of three unusual properties of water.
22. What does pH describe?
23. What is erosion?
24. Briefly describe five of Earth's spheres.
25. Describe two ways in which Earth's biosphere and atmosphere interact.
26. What is the law of conservation of matter?

Critical Thinking

27. Classify Is pure water a solution? Explain.
28. Infer Describe how the process of convection is responsible for the movement of Earth's tectonic plates.
29. Sequence Briefly describe the water cycle using the terms *evaporation, transpiration, condensation,* and *precipitation.*
30. Explain How is understanding the law of conservation of matter important to understanding the biogeochemical cycles?

Analyze Data

A student took water samples from a small pond every three hours and measured their pH. The results are plotted on the graph. Use the graph to answer the questions.

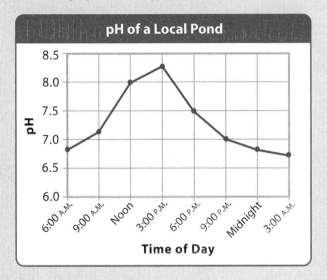

pH of a Local Pond

31. **Interpret Graphs** At which times of day is the pond most acidic?

32. **Analyze Data** How does the pH change from noon to 9:00 P.M.? How many times more acidic is the water at 9:00 P.M. than at noon?

33. **Form a Hypothesis** Form a hypothesis that could explain the data in the graph.

Write About It

34. **Explanation** Write a script for a one-minute announcement alerting people to the dangers of polluting groundwater.

35. **Explanation** Write a half-page explanation of the ways humans shift carbon to the atmosphere. Be sure to use the terms *atmosphere, lithosphere,* and *biosphere.*

36. **REVISIT INVESTIGATIVE** PHENOMENON
Suppose that you are a wildlife biologist. You have discovered many species of fish dying in a lake next to a large golf course. You have also observed that the lake looks greener than lakes farther away from the golf course. You suspect eutrophication. What are three questions you would ask the golf course manager as you try to find the cause of the problem?

Ecological Footprints

Read the information below. Copy the table into your notebook, and record your calculations. Then, answer the questions that follow.

In the United States, many homeowners aim for a green, weed-free lawn surrounding their house. As a result, there are about 60 million lawns in the nation. That adds up to about 20 million acres of lawn grass in the United States!

Fertilizer application	Number of lawns	Pounds of nitrogen
Your 1/3-acre lawn	1	15
The lawns of your classmates		
All the lawns in your town		
All the lawns in your state		
All the lawns in the United States	60,000,000	

1. Given what you have learned about nitrogen fixation, where do you think the nitrogen for large quantities of fertilizer comes from?

2. Calculate the number of lawns for your classmates, town, and state, and enter your results in the second column of the table. (*Hint:* For your town and state, assume that each household in your state has a lawn and that each household has three people.)

3. Using the completed row of the table as a model, calculate the total amount of nitrogen applied to lawns by each group in the table. Enter your results in the third column.

4. According to your calculations, how many pounds of nitrogen are used on lawns in the United States? What effects might the addition of this many pounds of fixed nitrogen have on the environment?

5. What two recommendations would you make to a homeowner who was concerned about her lawn fertilizer adding nitrogen to the environment?

ANCHORING PHENOMENON

These questions will help you apply what you have learned in this Unit to the Anchoring Phenomenon.

1. **Ask Questions** Research more information about harmful algal blooms (HABs). Suppose you plan to attend a public meeting about how your local or state government is working to reduce the environmental and economic impacts of HABs. Write a list of questions you would ask officials at the meeting.

2. **Develop and Use Models** Make models of the carbon cycle, the phosphorus cycle, and the nitrogen cycle to show both the short-term and long-term effects of excess nitrogen and phosphorus in runoff. How does making the model help you visualize the impacts of excess nutrients on ecosystems?

GO ONLINE

For activities that will give you an opportunity to demonstrate what you have learned.

CLAIM-EVIDENCE-REASONING Revisit your Anchoring Phenomenon CER with the information you have learned in this unit.

ANCHORING PHENOMENON PROJECT Design a solution to reduce external costs associated with excess nutrients in oceans and waterways.

Ecology

ANCHORING PHENOMENON

What is the impact of tourism on the environment?

CHAPTERS

GO ONLINE

To engage with real-world phenomena. Complete the Modeling worksheet and preview the anchoring phenomenon project.

CHAPTER 4

Population Ecology

How are changes in environmental conditions related to changes in population size?

Golden toads have not been seen since 1989 and are classified as extinct by the International Union for Conservation of Nature.

Lesson 1
Studying Ecology

Lesson 2
Describing Populations

Lesson 3
Population Growth

Finding Gold in a Costa Rican Cloud Forest

DURING A VISIT to Central America in 1963, biologist Jay Savage heard rumors of a brilliant golden toad living high in the mountains of Costa Rica. Local residents claimed that every year, at the early part of the first rainy season, countless tiny toads emerged from nowhere. They remained in view only briefly for mating season before disappearing again. No scientist had yet described them—Dr. Savage was determined to be the first.

The toads were rumored to live in Costa Rica's Monteverde region. *Monteverde* means "green mountain" in Spanish, and the name couldn't be more appropriate. The village of Monteverde sits beneath lush green slopes of the Cordillera de Tilarán mountains, which receive over 4 meters (13 feet) of rainfall per year. Some of the forests above Monteverde are known as *cloud forests* because they're often covered by slow-moving clouds that form as moist air blows inland from the Caribbean Sea. Monteverde's cloud forest is full of ferns, liverworts, mosses, clinging vines, orchids, and other organisms that thrive in cool, misty environments. Dr. Savage knew that such conditions create an ideal habitat for many toads and other amphibians.

In May of 1964, Savage organized an expedition into the muddy mountains above Monteverde to try to document the existence of the mysterious golden toad. Late on the afternoon of May 14, he and his colleagues found what they were looking for. Approaching the top of the mountain, they spotted bright orange patches on the forest's black floor. In one area that was only 5 meters (16.4 feet) in radius, they counted 200 golden toads. Savage gave the creature the scientific name *Bufo periglenes*, which means "the brilliant toad."

The discovery received international attention, making a celebrity of the tiny toad. The area became a travel destination. Researchers and

GO ONLINE
• Take It Local • 3-D Geo Tour

tourists flocked to see them. The government of Costa Rica protected the toads and their surroundings within the Monteverde Cloud Forest Reserve.

In 1987, twenty-three years after Dr. Savage first described the golden toad, biologist Martha Crump came to study them. Hundreds of the celebrated toads appeared during the mating season. Dr. Crump was delighted to see so many toads, but she noted that few tadpoles survived to maturity that year. She worried about the toad's future.

She had reason to worry. When Dr. Crump came back to the Monteverde forest two years later, there weren't hundreds of toads—there was just one. One single male toad. It was the last one anybody ever saw. Today, the golden toad is only a memory. The species has been declared extinct.

What happened to the golden toad? Why and how do population sizes change so quickly?

Studying Ecology

EVERYDAY PHENOMENON How do ecologists organize and study life?

Knowledge and Skills

- Describe the different levels of organization studied by ecologists.
- Explain the difference between biotic and abiotic factors.
- Discuss how an organism's habitat relates to its survival.

Reading Strategy and Vocabulary

✔ **Reading Strategy** Before you read, create a vocabulary word map for the following terms defined in the lesson: *species, population, community, ecosystem,* and *biosphere.* As you read, add details and adjust your definitions if necessary.

Vocabulary ecology, species, population, community, ecosystem, biosphere, biotic factor, abiotic factor, habitat, resource

HOW DO WE STUDY LIFE? If ecologists want to study something, such as a single plant, how do they do it? Should they separate the plant from its surroundings and isolate it in a lab? Is that the best way to try and understand it? Or, do they need to look not only at the plant, but also at how the soil it lives in, the other plants around it, the insects that pollinate it, and the animals that eat it all affect the plant during its life? Worms, bacteria, and insects break the plant down after it dies. Should they be included in the study? What about the weather patterns of the plant's environment? Where are the boundaries? If everything is connected, how do ecologists study anything?

Levels of Ecological Organization

When Dr. Savage hiked his way to the cloud-topped mountains of Costa Rica, he was surrounded by life. Life on Earth occurs in a hierarchy of levels. Different kinds of scientists study life at different levels—from single cells to entire forests. **Ecology** is the study of how organisms interact with each other and with their environments. The various levels of life ecologists study are shown in **Figure 1.**

 Connect to the Central Case

FIGURE 1 Ecological Organization
Ecologists study life at many levels, including individuals, populations, communities, ecosystems, and increasingly, the biosphere as a whole.
Apply Concepts
Do the students in your class make up a population or a community? Explain.

Individual   **Population**   **Community**   **Ecosystem**   **Biosphere**

Individuals You have probably learned that the cell is the basic unit of life. Most biology books describe cells, tissues, organs, and organ systems as the four levels of organization for a multicellular organism. Ecologists study life above these levels. The most basic level of study for an ecologist is an individual organism. At this level, the science of ecology involves describing relationships between individual organisms and their physical environments. Ecologists want to understand, for example, what aspects of the golden toad's environment were important to it, and why.

Populations Individual organisms are classified into species. The most common definition of a **species** is a group of individuals that interbreed and produce fertile offspring. Biologists recognize, however, that this definition can be problematic. For example, it does not work well for organisms, such as bacteria, that do not reproduce sexually. How to define *species* is a problem recognized as far back as the 1800s. Today, most biologists assign species on the basis of genetic similarity. Regardless of how they are defined, however, species are given a unique two-part scientific name. Modern humans are assigned the scientific name *Homo sapiens*. When Dr. Savage officially described the golden toad, he gave it the scientific name *Bufo periglenes*.

Members of a species that live in the same area at the same time make up a **population.** All of the golden toads that lived together in the Monteverde region of Costa Rica were members of the same population. All of the people living in your hometown make up a population. The fleas living on the neighborhood dog make up a population, too. *Population ecology* is the study of how individuals within a population interact with one another. At this level, ecologists seek to understand why populations of some species, such as the golden toad, decline while the sizes of other populations increase.

Communities All of the populations in a particular area make up a **community.** A population of golden toads together with all of the plant, animal, fungal, and microbial populations within the Monteverde Cloud Forest Reserve made up a single community. *Community ecology* is the study of interactions among species. These interactions can be simple, how a single bee pollinates a single flower, for example. Or, they can be complex, such as how entire herds of animals interact as they migrate across the African Serengeti. In the case of Monteverde, ecologists studied how the golden toad and other species of its cloud-forest community interacted, affecting each other's daily lives and long-term survival.

Ecosystems Unlike communities, ecosystems include, not only living things, but nonliving things as well. An **ecosystem** includes all of the living things and their physical environments within a particular area. Monteverde's cloud-forest ecosystem consists of all the organisms that live there plus the air, water, and nutrients they use.

FIND OUT MORE

What are the ecologists at your local college or university studying? Use the Internet to find their specialties, and then determine the level at which each studies ecology: individual, population, community, ecosystem, or biosphere.

Reading Checkpoint *What is the difference between a species and a population? Between a population and a community?*

Go Outside

Abiotic and Biotic Factors ⚠ 🔬

1. Make two cluster diagrams: one for biotic factors and one for abiotic factors. Brainstorm all of the biotic and abiotic factors you can think of in your school's ecosystem.

2. Following your teacher's instructions, find your designated observation spot.

3. For ten minutes, observe your surroundings. Note any abiotic and biotic factors you see. If you do not already have them on your cluster diagrams, add them. Be specific! Don't just write "trees;" try to describe the different trees you see.

4. Return to your classroom and compare cluster diagrams with a classmate.

Analyze and Conclude

1. **Observe** Did you find it easier to identify biotic factors or abiotic factors? Why?

2. **Conduct Peer Review** Did your classmate find any factors that you missed? Why do you think you missed them?

3. **Apply Concepts** Select three abiotic factors you observed and describe how each might affect some of the biotic factors you observed.

4. **Apply Concepts** Can biotic factors affect abiotic factors? Explain your reasoning.

Ecosystem ecology involves studying the living and nonliving components of a system together. Through their work, ecosystem ecologists often reveal patterns in energy or nutrient flow that may be controlled or changed by living or nonliving factors. An ecosystem ecologist studying the disappearance of the golden toad would consider the effects, not only of living things, but also of factors such as weather, climate, and water availability.

The Biosphere As technology advances, scientists are learning more about how natural systems behave on a global scale, expanding their studies beyond ecosystems to the biosphere as a whole. The **biosphere** includes all parts of Earth that host life, with all of its organisms and environments. Scientists who study ecology at this level might examine how energy and matter cycle throughout the biosphere and influence organisms worldwide.

Biotic and Abiotic Factors

To survive, organisms must interact with living and nonliving parts of their ecosystem. Most of the time it is obvious if something is living or not. Plants and animals are living. Air and water are nonliving. But what about a tree that has fallen down and is rotting? What is it then?

Biotic Factors Parts of an ecosystem that are living or used to be living are called **biotic factors.** A tree that has fallen down and is rotting on the forest floor is still considered a biotic factor, even though it is no longer living. Biotic factors in the golden toad's ecosystem included all of the organisms living in the cloud forest—from the smallest single-celled bacterium to the tallest tree. When Dr. Savage arrived to study the toads, he became a biotic factor in their ecosystem as well.

Abiotic Factors Parts of an ecosystem that have never been living are **abiotic factors.** Some abiotic factors are used or consumed by organisms. Plants require light to perform photosynthesis, for example. Organisms take in oxygen and use it to get energy from food. As described earlier, a dead organism is considered a biotic factor. However, we can now clarify that dead organisms are only considered biotic factors as long as their structure remains cellular. Once the cells break down, their components, such as oxygen, water, and carbon, become abiotic factors in the ecosystem. Other abiotic factors such as temperature, wind, and pH are not used or consumed by organisms but still affect their lives.

Habitat

The specific environment in which an organism lives is its **habitat.** A species' habitat consists of the biotic and abiotic elements around it. The golden toad lived in a habitat of cloud forest. The forest's soil, rocks, leaf litter, humidity, plant life, and seasonal pools of water were all parts of the toad's habitat. Habitats are similar to ecosystems but, unlike ecosystems, their boundaries are defined by the particular organism whose habitat it is. A tiny soil mite's habitat may be only one square meter of soil. A vulture's habitat, in contrast, may be several hundred square kilometers of hills and valleys that it easily crosses by air. So habitats may be a subset of an ecosystem or may include many ecosystems.

A habitat provides an organism with its resources. A **resource** is anything an organism needs, including nutrition, shelter, breeding sites, and mates. An organism's very survival depends on the availability of a suitable habitat and the resources it contains. As we'll see, the availability of resources plays a significant role in how populations grow and sometimes, like the golden toad, disappear.

 Connect to the Central Case

FIGURE 2 Biotic and Abiotic Factors A mix of biotic and abiotic factors made up the golden toad's ecosystem. **Classify** Was the leaf in the photo a biotic or abiotic factor in the golden toad's environment?

LESSON ① Assessment

1. **Apply Concepts** Would all the different kinds of organisms in a pond be considered a population or a community? Explain.

2. **Explain** In your own words, explain how an organism can be dead, yet still considered a biotic factor.

3. **Apply Concepts** Why do different organisms live in different habitats?

4. **REVISIT**
   INVESTIGATIVE PHENOMENON
   For each of the levels of ecological organization, state whether it contains only biotic factors, only abiotic factors, or both biotic and abiotic factors. Then, write a question that an ecologist might ask when studying life at each of the levels.

Describing Populations

EVERYDAY PHENOMENON What are the important characteristics of populations?

Knowledge and Skills

* Explain the usefulness of tracking population size.
* Define population density.
* Describe the three ways populations can be distributed.
* Explain what age structure diagrams tell you about a population.

Reading Strategy and Vocabulary

✔ **Reading Strategy** As you read, organize the lesson information using a T-chart. Be sure to note each key term and its definition.

Vocabulary population size, population density, population distribution, age structure, age structure diagram, sex ratio

Male resplendent quetzal

INDIVIDUALS OF THE SAME SPECIES living in a particular area make up a population. Species can consist of many populations that are geographically isolated from one another. This is the case with the resplendent quetzal *(Pharomachrus mocinno),* considered one of the world's most spectacular birds. These birds are characteristic of the Monteverde region. Although it ranges from southernmost Mexico to Panama, the resplendent quetzal lives only in high-elevation tropical forests. Today, the species exists in many separate populations scattered across Central America.

In contrast, humans have spread into nearly every corner of the planet. As a result, it is difficult to define a distinct human population on anything less than the global scale. Some would maintain that in the ecological sense of the word, all 7.8 billion of us make up one population.

Whether one is considering humans, or quetzals, or golden toads, all populations show characteristics that help population ecologists predict the future of that population. Population size, density, distribution, age structure, and sex ratio all help the ecologist understand how a population may grow or decline.

Population Size

Population size describes the number of individual organisms present in a given population at a given time. Population size may increase, decrease, undergo cyclical change, or remain the same over time. When population size increases or remains steady, it is often a sign of a healthy population. When population size declines quickly, however, it can mean extinction is coming. As late as 1987, scientists reported more than 1500 golden toads in the Monteverde population. In 1988, only 10 toads were reported. In 1989, scientists found only a single toad. By 1990, the species had disappeared.

The Decline of the Passenger Pigeon

The passenger pigeon (*Ectopistes migratorius*) illustrates the extremes of population size. As with the golden toad, dramatic and rapid changes in population size indicated trouble. Passenger pigeons, shown in **Figure 3,** were once the most abundant bird in North America. Huge flocks literally darkened the skies. In the early 1800s, an ornithologist (a scientist who studies birds) named Alexander Wilson described a flock of 2 billion individuals that formed a near-solid mass 390 kilometers (240 miles) long, took 5 hours to fly overhead, and sounded like a tornado.

Passenger pigeons nested and bred in the forests of the upper Midwest and southern Canada. Once people began cutting down the forests, however, hunters had easy access to the birds. Thousands of pigeons at a time were shot down and shipped to market as food. By the end of the 1800s, the population size was so small that the pigeons could not form the large colonies they needed to breed effectively. In 1914, the last passenger pigeon on Earth died in the Cincinnati Zoo in Ohio.

(a)

Determining Population Size

Do you think Alexander Wilson actually counted 2 billion passenger pigeons in the flock? Of course he didn't. While simply counting every individual in a population is the most direct way to determine population size, it is almost never possible. In nearly all situations, population size is estimated using sampling techniques. Here's how sampling works: Instead of counting every individual in a large area, ecologists count the number in a smaller sample area. Then, they use that information to estimate the number of individuals in the larger overall area. If there are 100 oak trees in one square kilometer of a large forest, for instance, it may be reasonable to estimate that there are about 1000 oak trees in ten square kilometers of the same forest. Sampling is particularly helpful for estimating the size of very large populations and populations that are widely spread out over an area.

Sometimes it is easier to find signs of organisms rather than the organisms themselves. For example, it can be very difficult to spot organisms that are rare or that simply prefer to remain hidden. For these creatures, such as jaguars, tigers, and tapirs, it is often easier to find and count animal tracks or droppings than the animals themselves.

(b)

FIGURE 3 Population Size (a) The passenger pigeon was once North America's most numerous bird. **(b)** However, habitat destruction and hunting drove the species to extinction within a few decades.

 Reading Checkpoint *When is sampling necessary?*

Population Density

The huge flocks and breeding colonies of passenger pigeons showed high population density. **Population density** describes the number of individuals within a population per unit area. For instance, the 1500 golden toads counted in 1987 were found within 4 square kilometers (988 acres). So their population density was 1500 toads/4 square kilometers, or 375 toads/square kilometer. In general, larger organisms, like lions and other big cats, have lower population densities because they require more resources, and thus more room, to survive.

Different Densities High population density can make it easier for organisms to group together and find mates. However, it can also lead to conflict as individuals compete for resources. Overcrowded organisms may also become more vulnerable to the predators that feed on them, and close contact among individuals can increase the transmission of infectious disease. In contrast, at low population densities, organisms benefit from more space and resources but may find it harder to locate mates and companions.

Density and the Harlequin Frog Overcrowding is thought to have doomed the harlequin frog *(Atelopus varius),* which disappeared from the Monteverde Reserve at the same time as the golden toad. The harlequin frog, shown in **Figure 4,** lived in very specific locations called "splash zones." Splash zones are areas alongside rivers and streams that receive spray from waterfalls and rapids. In the 1980s and 1990s, the Monteverde region of Costa Rica got warmer and drier. Water flow decreased and many streams dried up. Soon, there were only a few small splash zones left.

Scientists recorded frog population densities up to 4.4 times higher than normal around the remaining splash zones. Such overcrowding likely made the frogs vulnerable to disease transmission, predator attack, and assault from parasitic flies. From their field research, researchers concluded that these factors led to the harlequin frog's disappearance from Monteverde. A very small population is thought to remain outside the reserve, but scientists worry for its future.

FIGURE 4 Splashing No Longer
Harlequin frogs like this one are no longer found in the Monteverde Reserve. Scientists think that unusually high population densities, brought about by changes in climate, contributed to their decline.

Population Distribution

Another factor that contributed to the disappearance of harlequin frogs is how individuals were arranged within the Monteverde ecosystem. **Population distribution,** sometimes called population dispersion, describes how organisms are arranged within an area. Ecologists define three distribution types: random, uniform, and clumped, as shown in **Figure 5.**

▶ *Random Distribution* In a *random distribution,* individual organisms are arranged within a space in no particular pattern. This type of distribution can occur when the resources an organism needs are found throughout an area and other organisms do not strongly influence where members of a population settle.

▶ *Uniform Distribution* A *uniform distribution* is one in which individual organisms are evenly spaced throughout an area. This can occur when individuals hold territories or otherwise compete for space. In a desert, where there is little water, each plant needs a certain amount of room for its roots to gather adequate moisture. As a result, there tends to be roughly the same amount of space between individual plants.

▶ *Clumped Distribution* In a *clumped distribution,* individual organisms arrange themselves according to the availability of the resources they need to survive. This is the most common pattern in nature. For example, desert animals may live in patches around isolated sources of water. During their mating season, golden toads were found clumped at seasonal breeding pools. The harlequin frogs were clumped around splash zones. Humans, too, show clumped distribution; most people live and work near large urban centers.

Distributions can depend on the scale at which you're looking. For example, ants show a clumped distribution at a large scale; populations live together in colonies. Within the colony, however, individuals may be distributed more evenly.

 Reading Checkpoint *What is the difference between population density and distribution?*

(a) Random

(b) Uniform

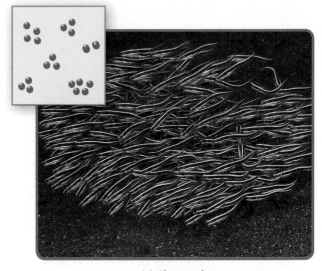

(c) Clumped

FIGURE 5 Population Distribution There are three fundamental population distribution patterns seen in nature: **(a)** random, **(b)** uniform, and **(c)** clumped.

Age Structure and Sex Ratios

Different populations have different mixes of ages. Likewise, populations can vary in the proportion of males and females present. These differences can affect how a population grows.

Age Structure Populations almost always include individuals of different ages. **Age structure,** or age distribution, describes the relative numbers of organisms of each age within a population. Age pyramids, or **age structure diagrams,** are visual tools scientists use to show the age structure of populations. As shown in **Figure 6,** the width of each horizontal bar in the diagram represents the relative size of each age group. Individuals capable of having offspring make up the reproductive group. Young individuals who have not yet reached the age where they can have offspring are called *pre-reproductive.* Older individuals past the age of having offspring are called *post-reproductive.*

Age structure diagrams can be effective tools when predicting population growth. A population with an even age distribution will likely remain stable as births keep pace with deaths. A population made up mostly of individuals past reproductive age will tend to decline over time. In contrast, a population of mostly reproductive or pre-reproductive individuals is likely to increase over time. Populations that are "bottom heavy" are capable of rapid growth. In this respect, the wide base of an age pyramid is like an oversized engine in a sports car—the bigger the engine, the faster it accelerates.

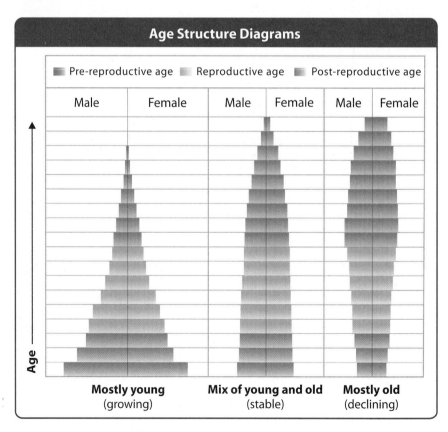

FIGURE 6 Age Structure Diagrams
A population's age structure diagram shows relative frequencies of males and females in different age groups. Populations with more young, pre-reproductive individuals tend to grow quickly. Populations with more older, post-reproductive individuals tend to decline.

Sex Ratios A population's **sex ratio** is its proportion of males to females. Notice that age structure diagrams also give information about sex ratio by providing the relative numbers of males and females in each age group. Sex ratio is an important characteristic for populations of organisms that reproduce sexually and have distinct male and female individuals. For example, in monogamous species (in which each sex takes a single mate), a 50:50 sex ratio is often ideal. If there are too many males or females, called an *unbalanced sex ratio,* many individuals would be left without a mate—making it much harder for any given individual to reproduce and pass on genes.

FIGURE 7 Sex Ratio The relative number of males and females determines a population's sex ratio. In this South African population of springboks, the ratio of males to females is about 50:50.

1. **Relate Cause and Effect** How is a population's size related to its well-being?

2. **Calculate** Which population of flamingos is more dense: 15 flamingos in a 5-square-meter area, or 40 flamingos in a 10-square-meter area?

3. **Apply Concepts** Describe the three patterns of population distribution. Which of these is the most common distribution in nature?

4. **Infer** Which of the populations shown in **Figure 6** do you think is most likely to get bigger in size? Explain your reasoning.

REVISIT

5. **INVESTIGATIVE** PHENOMENON

Paleontologists use fossils to study past life on Earth. Paleontologists have documented several times in Earth's history when massive numbers of species have declined and then disappeared from the fossil record all at once. Why do you think population ecologists studying living organisms might be interested in these mass extinction events?

Population Growth

EVERYDAY PHENOMENON What factors determine whether, and how, a population's size changes?

Knowledge and Skills

- Describe the factors that influence a population's growth rate.
- Explain exponential growth and logistic growth.
- Explain how limiting factors and biotic potential affect population growth.

Reading Strategy and Vocabulary

✅ **Reading Strategy** Create a KWL chart for each of the headings in this lesson. Before you read, fill in what you know and what you want to know. After reading, fill in what you learned.

Vocabulary survivorship curve, immigration, emigration, migration, exponential growth, limiting factor, carrying capacity, logistic growth, density-dependent factor, density-independent factor, biotic potential

WHY ARE THERE SO MANY BACTERIA and so few whales? Place a few bacteria on a nutrient-rich Petri dish, and a few hours later, each will have generated a colony of millions. But place a few whales in the middle of the ocean, and it takes a year or more for any new whales to be born. Why the difference?

Proteus bacteria colonies and two humpback whales

Factors That Determine Population Growth

In the simplest terms, populations *increase* in size when more individuals enter the population than leave it. Likewise, populations *decrease* in size when more individuals leave it than enter it. Two sets of factors influence the ratio of individuals entering and leaving a population: births and deaths, and immigration and emigration.

Birth- and Death Rates Population size, density, distribution, sex ratio, and age structure can all influence the rates at which individuals within a population are born and die. The rate at which individuals are born is called *natality*. The rate at which individuals die is called *mortality*. Natality and mortality are usually expressed as the number of births or deaths per 1000 individuals over a given time. All else being equal, when a population's birthrate is greater than its death rate, the population size increases. When its death rate is greater than its birthrate, the population size decreases.

▶ *Survivorship Curves* Individuals of different ages have different probabilites of dying. To show how the likelihood of death varies with age, population ecologists use graphs called **survivorship curves.** **Figure 8** shows the three basic types.

Organisms with a type I curve, such as humans, have higher mortality at older ages. Most individuals survive at young ages, and the likelihood of dying increases with age. If you were to follow a thousand 10-year-old and 80-year-old humans for a year, you would find that at year's end more 80-year-olds had died than 10-year-olds.

Amphibians such as the golden toad show a different survivorship pattern. Golden toads produced large numbers of young that suffered high death rates. This pattern, in which death is less likely (and survival more likely) at an older age than at a very young age, defines a type III survivorship curve. A type II survivorship curve indicates a population with equal mortality at all ages. Many bird species have type II curves.

▶ *Age Structure and Population Growth* Recall that a population's age structure describes the relative number of individuals within various age groups. The age structure of a population influences how relative birthrates and death rates affect its size. Consider a population following a type I survivorship curve. If the population is made up of mostly young, reproductive or pre-reproductive individuals, there will likely be more births than deaths, and the population size will increase. In a population of mostly older individuals, there are likely to be more deaths than births, and the population size will decrease. A population with an even age distribution will likely remain stable.

 Reading Checkpoint *Which type of survivorship curve describes populations whose mortality is highest at young ages?*

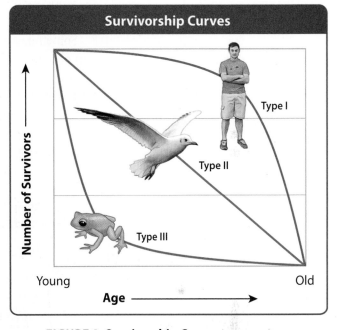

FIGURE 8 Survivorship Curves In a type I survivorship curve, individuals are most likely to die when they are old. In a type III survivorship curve, mortality is highest for young members of the population. In a type II survivorship curve, mortality remains constant throughout an individual's lifetime.

FIGURE 9 Seasonal Migration and Population Size The size of the turkey vulture population in Pennsylvania changes over the course of the year. Much of the change has to do with seasonal migration into and out of the area.

Immigration and Emigration In addition to births and deaths, population size can also change because of individuals moving into or out of a population. **Immigration** is the arrival of individuals from outside a given area. **Emigration** is the departure of individuals from a given area. Immigration and emigration can have dramatic effects on a population's size, especially when it comes to humans. Millions of people move around the world each year, driven by necessity, opportunity, or a desire to make new connections and see new places.

Sometimes, organisms make brief movements into and out of an area as part of a seasonal routine. **Migration** is a seasonal movement into and out of an area. Many animals, including fishes, mammals, and birds, migrate. Every year, for example, the turkey vulture population near Hawk Mountain Sanctuary in Kempton, Pennsylvania, increases in late summer and early autumn. Part of the population increase is due to local births. Most of the increase, however, is due to birds arriving from the north as part of their annual migration cycle. In the early winter, the entire local population leaves the area as the migration continues south. Then, in early spring, they come back. Some stay, and some continue to breeding grounds farther north. The cycle starts again when temperatures begin to drop.

Real Data

Turkey Vultures

Hawk Mountain Sanctuary in Kempton, Pennsylvania, is a protected area for birds of prey. Scientists at the sanctuary monitor bird populations by conducting roadside surveys. Scientists drive slowly along a set route and count the birds they spot. The graph at right shows the average number of turkey vultures surveyed along a 48-kilometer route near the sanctuary early and late month throughout the year.

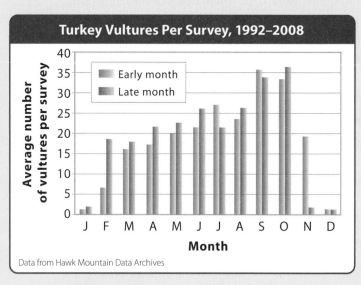

Turkey Vultures Per Survey, 1992–2008

Data from Hawk Mountain Data Archives

1. **Interpret Graphs** Describe the annual trend in turkey vulture sightings along the survey route.

2. **Apply Concepts** What factors might be increasing the vulture population's size? What factors decrease population size?

3. **Infer** Turkey vultures arrive from the north onto sanctuary lands and reside there for a while before migrating south. When do you think the vultures from the north arrive? When do you think they all leave?

4. **Perform Error Analysis** What is one potential source of error when conducting a roadside survey?

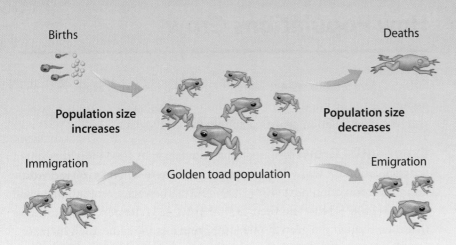

Births

Deaths

Population size increases

Population size decreases

Immigration

Golden toad population

Emigration

 Connect to the Central Case

FIGURE 10 The Population Growth Equation The balance of births, immigration, deaths, and emigration determines whether a population gets larger or smaller. **Draw Conclusions** Why were immigration and emigration not a factor in golden toad population growth? (*Hint:* How many different places did golden toads live?)

Calculating Population Growth As shown in **Figure 10,** births and immigration add individuals to a population. Deaths and emigration remove individuals from a population. A population's overall growth rate can therefore be expressed as follows:

(individuals added) – (individuals subtracted)

or

(birthrate + immigration rate) – (death rate + emigration rate)

The resulting number tells us the net change in a population's size. Shrinking populations have negative population growth. Positive population growth indicates the population is getting larger. Population growth is typically reported as a net change per 1000 individuals.

For example, suppose a population's annual birthrate is 18 per 1000. Its annual death rate is 10 per 1000. Its annual immigration rate is 5 per 1000. And its annual emigration rate is 7 per 1000. So, its overall annual growth rate would be calculated as follows:

(18 + 5) – (10 + 7) = 6

This population, growing at this rate over a year, will increase by 6 individuals for every 1000 in the population.

Population changes are often expressed as percentages, which we can calculate using the following formula:

Growth rate × 100%

 **MATH SUPPORT** For help with percentages, see the Math Handbook.

A growth rate of 6 individuals per 1000 expressed as a percentage is therefore:

(6/1000) × 100% = 0.006 × 100% = 0.6%

By measuring population growth in terms of percentages, scientists can compare increases and decreases in species that have different population sizes.

 Reading Checkpoint *What is the typical unit of measurement for population growth?*

How Populations Grow

Growth rates tend to change depending on the resources available to the organisms in the population. Population ecologists recognize two basic patterns of population growth: exponential and logistic.

Exponential Growth Based on a population of 1000 individuals, if the population grows by 10 percent per year, there will be 1100 individuals in the population next year (1000 + 100). The year after that, there will be 1210 (1100 + 110), and then 1331 (1210 + 121) the next year. Notice that even though the growth rate (10%) remains the same, each increase in population size is larger than the one before it. Only 100 individuals were added in the first year. But 110 were added in Year 2, and 121 were added in Year 3. Each year, a 10% increase means more and more individuals are added to the population. When a population increases by a fixed percentage each year, it is said to undergo **exponential growth.** Changes in population size are shown with population growth curves. The J-shaped curve in **Figure 11** shows exponential growth.

Normally, exponential growth occurs in nature only when the starting population is small and environmental conditions are ideal. Most often, these conditions occur when organisms are introduced to a new environment. Mold growing on a piece of bread and bacteria colonizing a recently dead animal are examples. But species of any size may show exponential growth under the right conditions. A population of the Scots pine (*Pinus sylvestris*) grew exponentially when it began colonizing the British Isles after the end of the last ice age. Receding glaciers had left conditions ideal for their expansion.

FIGURE 11 Exponential Growth
Populations growing by a fixed percent experience exponential growth. Every incremental increase in number is larger than the one before it. The Scots pine population grew exponentially in Great Britain following the last ice age.

Exponential Growth

Population Size

Time →

Logistic Growth When it happens, exponential growth rarely lasts long. After all, if a single species increased exponentially for many generations, it would take over the planet. Instead, most populations are eventually constrained by limiting factors. **Limiting factors** are characteristics of the environment that limit population growth. Limiting factors determine a population's carrying capacity. **Carrying capacity** is the largest population size a given environment can sustainably support.

Logistic growth describes how a population's initial exponential increase is slowed and finally stopped by limiting factors. **Figure 12** shows the S shape of logistic growth. Notice that the population size increases sharply at first, but then begins to level off as the effects of limiting factors become stronger. Eventually, population size stabilizes around its carrying capacity.

Population Growth in Nature The logistic curve is a simplified model, and real populations, like those shown in **Figure 13,** can behave differently. Some may fluctuate, or cycle, indefinitely above and below the carrying capacity. Others may rise quickly, overshoot the carrying capacity, and then crash.

Carrying capacities are not fixed. As limiting factors in an environment change, so does its carrying capacity. Plants in the understory of a dense forest, for example, may be limited by the amount of sunlight available. If a large tree dies, however, and sunlight pours in through a gap overhead, then the carrying capacity for understory plants in the area may increase.

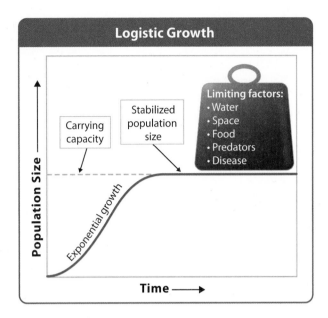

FIGURE 12 **Logistic Growth** The logistic growth curve shows how population size may increase rapidly at first, then grow more slowly, and finally stabilize at the carrying capacity.

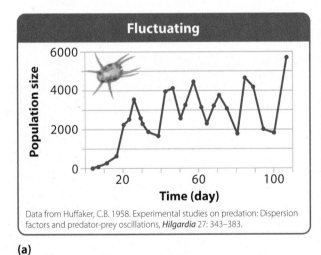

(a)

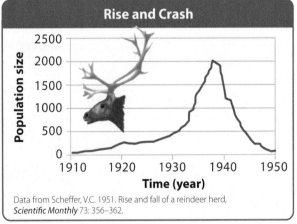

(b)

FIGURE 13 **Population Growth in Nature** Population growth in nature does not often follow an idealized logistic curve. **(a)** The population size of some organisms, such as mites, fluctuates around its carrying capacity. **(b)** Some populations grow rapidly and use resources too quickly, causing their numbers to crash suddenly. Reindeer introduced to the Bering Sea island of St. Paul showed this pattern.

Limiting Factors and Biotic Potential

Limiting factors slow population growth either by decreasing birthrates or immigration, increasing death rates or emigration, or some combination of these events. Some limiting factors have more of an effect in dense populations. Other limiting factors affect all populations in the same way.

Density-Dependent Factors Recall that high population density increases competition for resources such as food and water. Competition, as shown in **Figure 14,** is a density-dependent factor because its influence changes with population density. The higher the population density, the less food and water will be available per individual. In turn, this causes competition for those resources to intensify. Predation and disease are two other examples of density-dependent factors.

Density-Independent Factors Density-independent factors are limiting factors whose influence is not affected by population density. Catastrophic events such as floods, fires, and landslides are considered density-independent factors. It does not matter if the original population was dense or not. The result is always the same: a dramatic and sudden reduction in population size.

A change in the region's climate brought devastation to the golden toads of Monteverde. In the spring of 1987, unusually warm and dry conditions caused the breeding pools used by the toads to dry up almost completely. In the process, nearly all of the eggs and tadpoles within the pools were killed. This climate change was a density-independent factor that caused the golden toad population to crash. As you'll recall, by 1990, the toads were extinct.

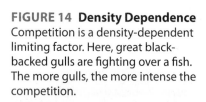

Reading Checkpoint *Why is severe weather considered a density-independent factor?*

FIGURE 14 Density Dependence Competition is a density-dependent limiting factor. Here, great black-backed gulls are fighting over a fish. The more gulls, the more intense the competition.

Biotic Potential Limiting factors from an organism's environment provide only half the story of population regulation. The other half comes from the characteristics of the organism itself. For example, organisms differ in their **biotic potential,** or maximum ability to produce offspring in ideal conditions.

Many factors influence biotic potential, including gestation and generation time. *Gestation time* is how long it takes for an embryo or fetus to develop and be "born." The span from an organism's birth to the time it has its own offspring is called *generation time.* Generation time is largely controlled by how long it takes an animal to reach sexual maturity. The number of offspring born at a time also affects biotic potential.

Cabezon, or "scorpion fish," and orangutans (**Figure 15**) vary greatly in their biotic potential. Once female cabezon are mature, at about 3 to 5 years old, they can release 50,000 to 100,000 eggs every year. Once fertilized, the eggs take just 12 to 16 days to hatch. Clearly, scorpion fish have a very high biotic potential. Orangutans, however, have a very low biotic potential. Females are not sexually mature until they are about 10 years old, and they give birth to a single baby only about once every 8 years. Populations of individuals with high biotic potential recover more quickly from declines than those of individuals with low biotic potential.

FIGURE 15 Biotic Potential
Organisms differ in their biotic potential. **(a)** Cabezon, like many fish species, have a very high biotic potential. In just one year, a female can release tens of thousands of eggs. **(b)** Female orangutans, however, usually only have three or four offspring in their lifetime.

LESSON ③ Assessment

1. **Calculate** A population has a birthrate of 10/1000, a death rate of 9/1000, an immigration rate of 3/1000, and an emigration rate of 7/1000. What is the population's growth rate? Is the population getting larger or smaller?

2. **Compare and Contrast** What is the difference between exponential growth and logistic growth? Which is more common over long terms in nature?

3. **Apply Concepts** In your own words, define *limiting factor* and *biotic potential.*

4. **THINK IT** *THROUGH* You are a population ecologist studying white-tailed deer populations in your state. Populations have been growing exponentially for some time, and food is becoming a limiting factor. Many deer are dying of starvation, and others are in bad health. What do you recommend to state officials? Should people intervene and try to limit deer populations through relocation or hunting? Or should they do nothing and wait for the population to regulate itself? Explain your reasoning.

THE CLOUDLESSFOREST

The last official sighting of a golden toad in the Monteverde region was in 1989, when Dr. Martha Crump visited the area and saw a single male toad. Since the disappearance of the toad, scientists have been trying to figure out what caused its rapid decline. Some scientists, including Dr. Crump, began to investigate the potential role of climate in the extinction of the golden toad and other cloud-forest species. They noted that the period from July 1986 to June 1987 was the driest on record at Monteverde. There were unusually high temperatures and record-low stream flows during that time. Could these conditions explain the golden toad's disappearance?

DRIER DAYS

By reviewing weather data, Dr. Crump and her colleague Dr. J. Alan Pounds found that it wasn't only dry from 1986 to 1987. The number of dry days in the Monteverde region had increased between 1973 and 1998. Dry conditions are particularly harmful to amphibians such as the golden toad because amphibians breathe and absorb moisture through their skin. Furthermore, like most other amphibians, golden toads released their eggs in shallow breeding pools. If the pools dried up, so did the eggs, and any tadpoles that had hatched died. Based on these facts, in 1994, the scientists hypothesized that hot, dry conditions were to blame for high adult mortality and breeding problems among golden toads and other amphibians.

Length of Dry Spells in Monteverde

Number of days in dry spells lasting 5 or more days

Year

Data from Pounds, J.A., et al. 1999. Biological response to climate change on a tropical mountain. *Nature* 398: 611–615.

▲ Evidence gathered over three decades showed an increase in the annual number of dry days since 1972.

Monteverde's cloud forest gets its name from clouds that sweep inland from the oceans. When ocean temperatures are cool, the clouds keep Monteverde moist. But as the ocean warms, clouds form at higher elevations passing over the mountains and drying out the forest.

Golden Toads

Researchers test an *Atelopus* toad for chytrid fungus in an Ecuadorian rain forest.

WARMING OCEANS

Around the same time, scientists worldwide were realizing that the atmosphere and oceans were warming. Warmer oceans, the researchers found, caused clouds to pass over at higher elevations, where they were no longer in contact with the trees. Once the cloud forest's moisture supply was pushed upward, out of reach of the mountaintops, the forest began to dry out. In a 1999 paper in the journal *Nature,* Pounds and two colleagues reported that higher clouds and decreasing moisture in the forest could explain the disappearance of not only the golden toad, but also the harlequin frog and 20 other species of frogs and toads from the Monteverde region.

WARMER NIGHTS

Pounds and his colleagues have recently fleshed out the story further. Although clouds had moved higher in the sky, the extra moisture evaporating from warming oceans was increasing cloud cover overall, blocking sunlight during the day and trapping heat at night. As a result, at Monteverde and other tropical locations, daytime and nighttime temperatures were becoming more similar. Such conditions are optimal for chytrid fungi, pathogens that can infect and kill amphibians.

Write About It What do you think caused the extinction of the golden toad—warm weather or dry conditions? Write a paragraph that defends your position.

LESSON 1 Studying Ecology

- Ecologists study life at many levels, including individual organisms, species, populations, communities, ecosystems, and the entire biosphere.
- Ecosystems include both biotic (living) and abiotic (non-living) factors.
- Organisms depend on resources provided by their habitat for survival.

ecology (100)
species (101)
population (101)
community (101)
ecosystem (101)
biosphere (102)
biotic factor (102)
abiotic factor (103)
habitat (103)
resource (103)

LESSON 2 Describing Populations

- The overall health of a population can often be monitored by tracking how its size changes.
- A population's density is a measure of how crowded the population is.
- Populations can be distributed randomly, uniformly, or in clumps. In a random distribution, individual organisms are arranged within a space in no particular pattern. A uniform distribution is one in which individual organisms are evenly spaced. In a clumped distribution, individual organisms arrange themselves according to the availability of resources they need to survive.
- Age structure diagrams show the number of males and females in different age groups within a population.

population size (104)
population density (106)
population distribution (107)
age structure (108)
age structure diagram (108)
sex ratio (109)

LESSON 3 Population Growth

- A population's growth rate is determined by births, deaths, immigration, and emigration.
- Populations can grow exponentially or logistically. Exponential growth rarely lasts long. The growth of most populations is held at a carrying capacity determined by limiting factors present in the environment.
- Limiting factors and biotic potential regulate a population's growth. Limiting factors can be density-dependent, or density-independent.

survivorship curve (111)
immigration (112)
emigration (112)
migration (112)
exponential growth (114)
limiting factor (115)
carrying capacity (115)
logistic growth (115)
density-dependent factor (116)
density-independent factor (116)
biotic potential (117)

 GO ONLINE

INQUIRY LABS AND ACTIVITIES

- **Using Mark-and-Recapture**
  Pull "population" samples from a cup of beans and calculate the total "population" in the cup.
- **Yeast Population Growth**
  Compare the sizes of yeast populations by counting cells. Then graph the growth and decline.
- **Migrating Populations**
  Find out when and where a local migration happens and how it affects the ecosystem.

Chapter Assessment

Defend Your Case

The Central Case in this chapter focused on the causes of the golden toad extinction. Most people view national parks as an excellent way to protect species and ecosystems. The golden toad, however, lived in a protected reserve and yet still became extinct. Use evidence from the Central Case and throughout the chapter to explain why the golden toad became extinct despite living on a reserve. Suggest other approaches that should be considered when trying to protect organisms.

Review Concepts and Terms

1. *A group of individuals that interbreed and produce fertile offspring* is a common definition for
   a. ecology.
   b. species.
   c. population.
   d. community.

2. An illustration of the Monteverde Cloud Forest is shown below. Which of the following is a biotic factor visible in the image?

   a. clouds   c. water
   b. golden toads   d. plants

3. Which of the following includes only biotic factors?
   a. ecosystem   c. biosphere
   b. habitat   d. population

4. Which of the following describes a population that is distributed evenly across an area?
   a. random   c. clumped
   b. uniform   d. crowded

5. Which of the following is NOT included in a typical age structure diagram?
   a. the population's sex ratio
   b. the relative numbers of people in different age groups
   c. the population's historical growth
   d. the proportion of reproductive-aged individuals

6. Which of the following terms describes seasonal movement of individuals into and out of a population?
   a. immigration
   b. emigration
   c. natality
   d. migration

7. Which of the following equations summarizes population growth?
   a. immigration – emigration
   b. (immigration + births) + (emigration + deaths)
   c. births – deaths
   d. (immigration + births) – (emigration + deaths)

8. The largest population size a given environment can sustainably support is known as its
   a. limiting capacity.   c. carrying capacity.
   b. logistic limit.   d. biotic potential.

9. A population that increases 5 percent every year is said to be experiencing
   a. exponential growth.   c. unlimited growth.
   b. logistic growth.   d. maximum growth.

Modified True/False

Write true if the statement is true. If it is false, change the underlined word or words to make the statement true.

10. The primary difference between a community and an ecosystem is that an ecosystem includes <u>biotic</u> factors.

11. A population's <u>distribution</u> describes how crowded it is.

12. A population of approximately equal numbers of males and females has a <u>balanced sex ratio.</u>

13. Exponential growth curves are generally <u>S shaped.</u>

14. Catastrophic events like floods are <u>density-dependent</u> factors that affect population growth.

Reading Comprehension

Read the following selection and answer the questions that follow.

In 1906, President Theodore Roosevelt established the Grand Canyon National Game Preserve on the Kaibab Plateau in northern Arizona. The preserve was created to protect deer from hunting and predation, which had reduced the population of Kaibab deer to only about 4000. Hunters were prohibited from shooting deer, but they were allowed to shoot the deer's predators, including cougars and coyotes. Between 1907 and 1923, over 600 cougars and 3000 coyotes were trapped or killed. As a result, the deer herd began to increase. By 1915, the deer were estimated at 25,000; by 1920, at 50,000; and by 1923, at approximately 100,000.

15. If you were to graph the population growth of the Kaibab deer from 1906 to 1923, what would you see?

   a. a straight line, showing a steady increase over time

   b. a J-shaped upward curve showing a very rapid increase

   c. an up-and-down, wavelike pattern

   d. an S-shaped curve that shows a smooth, rapid increase leveling off in 1923

16. Deer can live 10 to 25 years. Which of the following most likely describes an age structure diagram of the Kaibab deer population in 1923?

   a. an upside-down triangle, very wide at the top and narrow at the bottom

   b. a rectangle, almost the same size from bottom to top

   c. a narrow upside-down triangle, a little wider at the top than the bottom

   d. a triangle with a very wide base and narrow top

Short Answer

17. Name the different levels of ecological organization from largest to smallest.

18. Give an example of how an abiotic factor could affect organisms within an ecosystem.

19. Why is clumped distribution common in nature?

20. How do scientists calculate population density?

21. What is biotic potential?

Critical Thinking

22. **Pose Questions** Write a question that a population ecologist might ask about the photo below. Then, write a question that an ecosystem ecologist might ask. How are the questions different?

23. **Compare and Contrast** What is the difference between an organism's ecosystem and its habitat?

24. **Predict** A population of mice has a very bottom-heavy age structure diagram. Predict the growth of the population over the next several generations. Explain your prediction.

25. **Infer** If a population has random distribution, what can you infer about the availability of resources individuals need to survive?

26. **Compare and Contrast** What is the difference between a type I and type III survivorship curve?

27. **Apply Concepts** An ecologist is carrying out a population study on songbirds in your area. Over a three-year period, the songbird population increases. In that time, the population's birthrate was lower than its death rate. How can that be possible if the population size grew?

Analyze Data

An ecologist studying fruit flies records the following population size data. Use the data to answer the questions that follow.

Fruit Fly Population Growth	
Days	Number of Fruit Flies
5	10
10	50
15	100
20	200
25	300
30	310
35	320
40	320

28. Graph Make a graph of the data in the table. Be sure to label both axes.

29. Analyze Graphs What pattern of growth is demonstrated by this population of fruit flies?

30. Analyze Graphs What is the approximate carrying capacity in the fruit fly's current environment? On approximately which day did the population reach its carrying capacity?

31. Design an Experiment The ecologist thinks that either space or available food is the main limiting factor controlling population size in the fruit fly experiment. Describe a controlled experiment in which one could determine if food was the limiting factor.

Write About It

32. Description Write a paragraph that describes your habitat. Describe how you obtain the food, water, and shelter you need from your habitat. How does your habitat meet your needs in ways that other habitats do not?

33. Summary How do population ecologists describe populations? Briefly explain each of the characteristics of populations outlined in Lesson 2.

34. REVISIT INVESTIGATIVE PHENOMENON Differentiate between exponential and logistic growth curves. Give examples of the conditions under which each would occur. Finally, explain how changes to the limiting factors in a community can affect an organism's population size.

Ecological Footprints

Read the information below. Copy the table into your notebook and record your calculations. Then, answer the questions that follow.

Coffee is a very economically important crop. In fact, only petroleum is more valuable on the world market. Most coffee is grown in full sun on large tropical plantations where coffee plants are the only species present. Given that an average American consumes about 9 pounds of coffee per year, fill in the footprint table.

1. If about 15 billion pounds of coffee are produced every year, what percent is consumed by the United States?

2. Approximately 2 percent of coffee is *shade-grown*, meaning that it is grown in groves with many other species. Using your calculated data, approximately how many pounds of coffee consumed in the United States were shade-grown?

	Population	Pounds of Coffee Per Day	Pounds of Coffee Per Year
You (or the average American)			
Your class			
Your state			
United States			

Data from O'Brien, T.G., and M.F Kinnaird. 2003. Caffeine and conservation. *Science* 300: 587; and International Coffee Organization.

3. Shade-grown coffee helps protect tropical habitats because the land doesn't have to be cleared to grow the coffee plants. Assume that a pound of shade-grown coffee costs $1.50 more than a pound of traditional coffee, and that the added money goes to conservation efforts. If everyone in your state switched to shade-grown coffee for a year, how much money could be generated for conservation?

CHAPTER **5**

Evolution and Community Ecology

INVESTIGATIVE PHENOMENON

How do organisms affect the abiotic and biotic conditions in an environment?

Zebra mussels surrounding an underwater pipe

Lesson 1
Evolution

Lesson 2
Species Interactions

Lesson 3
Ecological
Communities

Lesson 4
Community Stability

Black and White, and Spread All Over

THINGS WERE REALLY LOOKING UP

on the Great Lakes. Once filled with pollution, the waters of Lake Erie and the other Great Lakes had become gradually cleaner in the years following passage of a federal clean water bill in 1972. With less waste and pollution in the water, aquatic organisms thrived once again, and visitors turned up in great numbers to swim, fish, and sail. Things were good.

Then the zebra mussel arrived. Black-and-white-striped shellfish the size of a dime, zebra mussels don't look like much. Zebra mussels (*Dreissena polymorpha*) are native to the Caspian Sea, Black Sea, and Azov Sea in western Asia and eastern Europe. By attaching themselves to the outsides of ships arriving from Europe, zebra mussels gained access to the Great Lakes. In 1988, the mussels were discovered in the Canadian waters of Lake St. Clair, which connects Lake Erie with Lake Huron.

Within just two years of their discovery in Lake St. Clair, zebra mussels had reached all five of the Great Lakes. The next year, they invaded New York's Hudson River to the east and the Illinois River to the west. From the Illinois River and its canals, they soon reached the Mississippi River, giving them access to a huge watershed covering more than 40 percent of the United States! By 2017, they had colonized waters in twenty-eight U.S. states and two Canadian provinces.

Zebra mussels directly and indirectly cost the U.S. economy hundreds of millions of dollars each year. They clog up water intake pipes at factories, power plants, municipal water supplies, and wastewater treatment facilities. Dense colonies of these organisms can damage boat engines, destroy docks, ruin fishing gear, and sink buoys that ships use for navigation.

The pesky mussels are also changing their own ecosystem. A few organisms seem to be thriving since the zebra mussel's arrival. For example, the smallmouth bass population in Lake St. Clair and

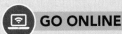

GO ONLINE
• Take It Local   • 3-D Geo Tour

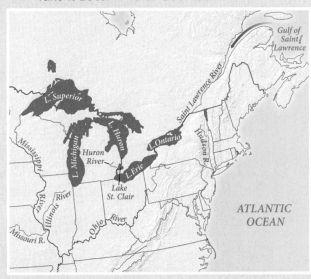

the Huron River has increased, making many fishers happy. But far more organisms, including native birds, fish, and mollusks, are struggling to survive since zebra mussels entered their waters.

Zebra mussels attach to almost any surface including native clams, mussels, and turtles. With zebra mussels attached to them, the animals may not survive. Scientists also think that animals higher up on the food chain, such as birds, are being poisoned by high concentrations of toxins naturally contained in the mussels.

As if this wasn't bad enough, the quagga mussel (*Dreissena bugensis*), a close relative of the zebra mussel from the Dneiper River in Ukraine, was introduced to the Great Lakes in 1989. It, too, rapidly spread—right on the heels of the zebra mussel. In some places, it even seems to have replaced the zebra mussel as the local pest.

How did the zebra and quagga mussels manage to spread so far so fast? And why did so many other populations collape while these mussels continue to thrive and spread—seemingly without bounds?

Evolution

EVERYDAY PHENOMENON What role does the environment play in an organism's survival and reproduction?

Knowledge and Skills

- Describe the four primary mechanisms of biological evolution.
- Describe how speciation and extinction affect the diversity of life on Earth.

Reading Strategy and Vocabulary

✔ **Reading Strategy** As you read, make a cause-and-effect diagram that summarizes the process of natural selection.

Vocabulary evolution, gene, mutation, genetic drift, natural selection, fitness, adaptation, artificial selection, speciation, extinction

THE ZEBRA MUSSEL IS JUST ONE of the 1.5 million to 1.8 million species described by scientists, and many more remain undiscovered or unnamed. Most estimates for the total number of species in the world range between 13 million and 20 million, most of which are thought to live in tropical rain forests. Tropical rain forests, however, are not the only places rich in life. Step outside anywhere on Earth, even in a major city, and you will find many species within easy reach.

Plants poke up from sidewalk cracks in every city in the world. Just a handful of backyard soil may contain an entire miniature world of life, including insects, mites, a millipede or two, worms, a few plant seeds, countless fungi, and millions upon millions of bacteria. Even Antarctic ice contains living microbes! Life is everywhere. But how did life come to be everywhere? That seemingly simple question and its answer form the foundation of modern biology.

Evolution and Natural Selection

Scientists today know that processes of evolution have acted to change a stark planet inhabited solely by single-celled organisms to a lush world of 1.5 million (and likely millions more) species. **Evolution,** as a general term, means "change over time." Specifically, biologists define *biological evolution* as a change in a population's gene pool over time. A *gene pool* includes all of the genes present in a population. A **gene** is a sequence of DNA that codes for a paticular trait. Often, biological evolution leads to changes in the frequency of an appearance or behavior from generation to generation. For example, if today 40 percent of mice in a population are brown and 60 percent are tan, and in the next generation, 28 percent are brown and 72 percent are tan, biological evolution has occurred.

Mechanisms of Biological Evolution

Envision a population of fish, such as those in **Figure 1a.** Genes control the pattern and color of the fish's scales. Any change to the fish's scales over generations indicates biological evolution has occurred, because pattern and color change means a change to the gene pool. There are four primary mechanisms, or processes, of biological evolution: mutation, migration, genetic drift, and natural selection.

▶ *Mutation* Mutations are changes in DNA. Mutations can give rise to genetic variation among individuals. In **Figure 1b,** a mutation causes some fish to be striped. If a mutation occurs in a sperm or egg cell, it may be passed on to the next generation and biological evolution has occurred.

▶ *Migration* Now envision a population in which half the fish are solid, and half the fish are striped, as shown in **Figure 1c.** Immigration into or emigration out of this population could cause a change in the proportion of solid to striped fish. Over generations, biological evolution occurs because the fish's gene pool has changed. This process is sometimes called *gene flow.*

▶ *Genetic Drift* Sometimes an unusual event, like a natural disaster or run-in with a fishing net (**Figure 1d**), kills or somehow separates all but a few individuals from a population. The next generation would therefore have a different gene pool from the original population just by chance. Biological evolution that occurs by chance is called **genetic drift.**

▶ *Natural Selection* If striped fish were more attractive to mates, or better able to avoid predation than solid fish (**Figure 1e**), natural selection could bring about biological evolution. **Natural selection** is the process by which traits that improve an organism's chances for survival and reproduction are passed on more frequently to future generations than those that do not.

In 1858, Charles Darwin and Alfred Russel Wallace each independently proposed the concept of natural selection as a mechanism for evolution and as a way to explain the great variety of living things. In 1859, Darwin published *On the Origin of Species* in which he presented decades worth of scientific evidence for natural selection that he had gathered. Thanks largely to the foundation Darwin built, natural selection is one of the best-supported theories in science today.

(a) Starting population

(b) Mutation

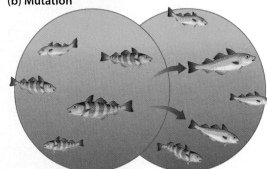

(c) Migration

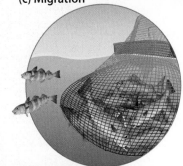

(d) Genetic drift

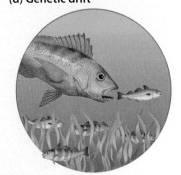

(e) Natural selection

FIGURE 1 **Biological Evolution (a)** A population of organisms can evolve in one of four major ways: **(b)** mutation, **(c)** migration, **(d)** genetic drift, and **(e)** natural selection.

Conditions of Natural Selection Natural selection is a simple concept that offers a powerful explanation for patterns seen in nature. At the core of the theory is the relationship between an organism and its environment. Natural selection follows from three straightforward conditions **Figure 2** summarizes the process of natural selection.

▶ *Condition 1: Organisms produce more offspring than can survive.*
Recall that if every individual in a population reproduced to its full biotic potential, the population would grow exponentially. However, in nature, limiting factors place restrictions on population size. There simply are not enough resources to support exponentially growing populations. So there is what Darwin described as a *struggle for existence* among organisms in their environment.

▶ *Condition 2: Individuals of a species vary in their characteristics.*
Not every member of a species is the same. Sure, all clownfish share the same basic characteristics that make them clownfish and not tunafish. But some clownfish have bigger fins than others. Some have better eyesight or swim faster. Some have fewer stripes and some females lay more eggs than others. **Figure 2** shows a hypothetical fish population in which some individuals have stripes and some do not. Although not known in Darwin's time, we now understand that variations among organisms are due to differences in both genes and the environments in which genes are expressed. Variations are described as *heritable* if they are passed from parent to offspring.

FIGURE 2 Natural Selection
Through natural selection, species evolve characteristics that lead to better reproductive success in a given environment.

❶ Organisms produce more offspring than can survive in a given environment. Fish can lay hundreds of eggs at a time. Very few will survive to adulthood. Offspring must compete for the resources they need.

❷ Organisms vary in their traits. Some of these traits, called adaptations, are heritable and increase an individual's fitness—its chance of surviving to adulthood and producing offspring.

► **Condition 3: Individuals vary in their fitness.** Most variations have little effect on an individual organism. Sometimes, however, variations can be harmful or helpful. Individuals with helpful variations are better suited to their environment than individuals without them. Fish with stripes, that hide in seaweed, might be harder for other fish to find and eat, for example. Organisms better suited to their environments are more likely to succeed. That is, they are more likely to survive and produce offspring. **Fitness** describes how reproductively successful an organism is in its environment. A heritable trait that increases an individual's fitness is called an **adaptation.**

► *Survival of the Fittest* An individual with high fitness, such as our striped fish, produces more offspring and therefore passes on its genes more frequently than an individual with low fitness. The next generation will therefore have a higher proportion of fitter striped individuals. In this way, organisms evolve in ways that maximize their success in a given environment. This is often described as *survival of the fittest.*

Note that fitness is defined in the context of an organism's environment. However, environments can change, and organisms may move to new places and encounter new conditions. In either case, a trait that is adaptive in one location or season may not be in another—that is, the organism that is "fittest" in one place and time may not be the fittest forever.

 Reading Checkpoint *What is the connection between adaptations and fitness?*

3 In this environment, having stripes is an adaptation that enables individuals to blend into their backgrounds and avoid predation. As a result, striped fish survive and reproduce more often than solid-colored fish.

4 Since adaptations are passed to offspring, the proportion of fitter individuals (striped fish) will increase in the next generation and the proportion of less-fit individuals (solid fish) will decrease.

Artificial Selection The results of natural selection are all around us, visible in every adaptation of every organism. In addition, countless lab experiments (mostly with fast-reproducing organisms, such as bacteria and fruit flies) have demonstrated rapid evolution of traits.

The evidence for selection that may be most familiar, however, is the selective breeding of domesticated animals and crops. Throughout recorded history, humans have chosen and bred animals and plants with traits we like instead of letting nature "select" what traits are best suited for a given environment. This process of selection conducted under human direction is termed **artificial selection.**

▶ *Artificial Selection and Dogs* Consider the great diversity of dog breeds, some of which are shown in **Figure 3a.** All dogs from the Great Dane to the Chihuahua are variations on a single species. Any two dogs can interbreed and produce offspring, and the DNA of any two dogs is very similar. Dog breeders maintain differences among varieties by allowing only *like* individuals to breed. That is, they breed Great Danes only with other Great Danes. They breed Chihuahuas only with other Chihuahuas.

▶ *Artificial Selection and Agriculture* Artificial selection has given us the many crop plants we depend on for food. In fact, our entire agricultural system is based on artificial selection. Humans have created corn with larger, sweeter kernels; wheat and rice with larger and more numerous grains; and apples, pears, and oranges with better taste. We have also diversified single plant species into many different crops. For instance, through selective breeding, the plant *Brassica oleracea* has given rise to broccoli, cauliflower, cabbage, and brussels sprouts, as shown in **Figure 3b.**

✔ **Reading Checkpoint** *What is the difference between artificial selection and natural selection?*

FIGURE 3 Artificial Selection
(a) Artificial selection has resulted in numerous breeds of dogs. The gray wolf *(Canis lupus)* is the ancestral species for all dog breeds. **(b)** Artificial selection has increased the variety of crops. Cabbage, brussels sprouts, broccoli, and cauliflower all evolved from a single plant.

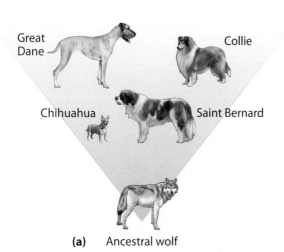

Great Dane

Collie

Chihuahua

Saint Bernard

(a) Ancestral wolf

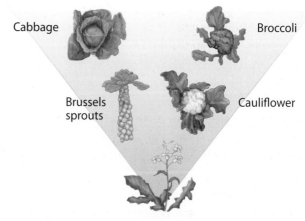

Cabbage

Broccoli

Brussels sprouts

Cauliflower

(b) Ancestral *Brassica oleracea* plant

Speciation and Extinction

How did Earth come to have so many species? Whether there are 1.5 million or 100 million, such large numbers require scientific explanation. On the other hand, scientists estimate that all of the species on Earth today represent only a tiny fraction of those that have ever lived.

Speciation The process by which new species are generated is called speciation. Speciation can occur in a number of ways. Biologists consider speciation caused by geographic separation of populations to be the most important. To understand this process, called *allopatric speciation,* begin by picturing a population of organisms, such as the squirrels in **Figure 4.** Individuals within the population mate with one another and share genetic information. However, if the population is somehow broken up into smaller isolated populations, individuals from one population cannot mate with individuals from the other populations.

Mutations that arise in the DNA of an organism in one of these isolated populations cannot spread to the other populations. Over time, genetic divergence occurs, meaning that each population develops its own set of mutations. Eventually, the populations may become different enough that their members can no longer mate with one another even if no longer separated. Once this has happened, there is no going back. The two populations have begun independent evolutionary paths.

The long-term geographic isolation of populations that can lead to allopatric speciation can occur in various ways. Glacial ice sheets may move across continents during ice ages and split populations in two. Major rivers may change course and do the same. A dry climate may partially evaporate lakes, subdividing them into multiple smaller bodies of water. Regardless of the mechanism of separation, for speciation to occur populations must remain isolated for a long time, generally thousands of generations. If the process that isolated the populations reverses itself—if the glacier recedes, the river returns to its old course, or dry climates turn wet again—then the populations can come back together. They will then either begin interbreeding, mixing their genes, or speciation will have occurred.

Through the speciation process, single species can generate multiple species, each of which can in turn generate more. Over millions, even billions of years, speciation events have resulted in every form of life known on Earth—today, and in the past.

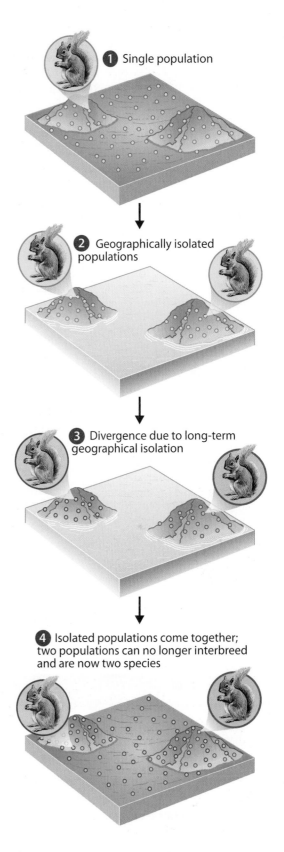

① Single population

② Geographically isolated populations

③ Divergence due to long-term geographical isolation

④ Isolated populations come together; two populations can no longer interbreed and are now two species

FIGURE 4 Allopatric Speciation Allopatric speciation has generated much of Earth's diversity. In this process, some kind of barrier splits a population.

FIGURE 5 **Mass Extinctions** There have been at least five worldwide mass extinctions in Earth's history. The Permo-Triassic extinction, about 250 million years ago, was the worst. Paleontologists estimate that 70% of land species and 90% of marine species went extinct at that time. Although there are many theories, scientists still do not know the exact cause. The Cretaceous-Tertiary extinction occurred 65 million years ago and killed off the dinosaurs.

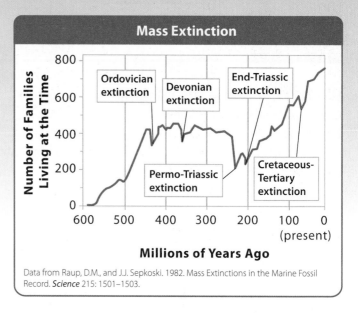

Mass Extinction

Data from Raup, D.M., and J.J. Sepkoski. 1982. Mass Extinctions in the Marine Fossil Record. *Science* 215: 1501–1503.

Extinction Scientists estimate that over 99% of all species that ever lived are now gone. The disappearance of a species from Earth is called **extinction.** From studying the fossil record, paleontologists calculate that the average time a species spends on Earth is 1 million to 10 million years. The number of species on Earth at any given time is equal to the number added through speciation minus the number removed by extinction.

In general, extinction occurs when environmental conditions change rapidly or severely enough that a species cannot adapt to the change. Natural selection simply does not have enough time to work. Most extinction occurs gradually, one species at a time. The rate at which this type of extinction occurs is referred to as the *background extinction rate*. However, Earth has seen five events of staggering proportions that killed off huge numbers of species at once. These episodes, called *mass extinctions,* have occurred at widely spaced intervals and have wiped out a large portion of our planet's species each time **(Figure 5).** The best-known mass extinction occurred 65 million years ago and brought an end to the dinosaurs—along with many other forms of life.

1. **Predict** Look back at **Figure 2.** Explain what would happen if conditions changed that causes the seaweed to die. Now striped fish stand out to predators more than solid fish. How could natural selection result in a change to relative numbers of solid and striped fish? What important concept does this illustrate about the connection between natural selection and the environment?

2. **Apply Concepts** Explain why an ecologist must consider both speciation and extinction when analyzing the diversity of life on Earth.

3. **REVISIT**
   INVESTIGATIVE PHENOMENON
   An organism's fitness describes how well it is adapted to its environment. The environment is made of biotic and abiotic factors. In the example shown in **Figure 2,** explain whether it is mostly the biotic or abiotic components of the fish's environment that are affecting their survival and reproductive success.

Species Interactions

EVERYDAY PHENOMENON How do species interact in nature?

Knowledge and Skills

- Discuss the factors that influence an organism's niche.
- Compare and contrast predation, parasitism, and herbivory.
- Describe mutualism and commensalism.

Reading Strategy and Vocabulary

✅ **Reading Strategy** As you read, complete a vocabulary word map for each of the boldface, highlighted words in the lesson.

Vocabulary niche, tolerance, resource partitioning, predation, coevolution, parasitism, symbiosis, herbivory, mutualism, commensalism

HOW MANY SPECIES do you interact with each day? At first, you might think the number is a low one. But if you really think about it, it is probably quite high. Did you eat any plants today? Accidentally step on any insects? Did you pet a dog or swat a fly? In nature, species interact all the time. Sometimes, they interact in ways that benefit both species. Other times, one species can harm the other. Species interactions form the structure of communities and ecosystems.

The Niche and Competition

Recall that an organism's habitat describes the general place it lives. Habitats provide organisms with all of the resources they need to survive. Together, habitat and resource use define the concept of niche.

Defining the Niche An organism's **niche** describes its use of resources and its functional role in a community. The niche includes not only the habitat where an organism lives, but also what food it eats, how and when it reproduces, and what other organisms it interacts with. The niche is therefore a kind of summary of everything an organism does and when and where it does it.

FIGURE 6 Niche A big part of a spider's role, or niche, is to prey on insects caught in its web.

Tolerance Where and how an organism lives is influenced by its tolerance. **Tolerance** is the ability to survive and reproduce under changing environmental conditions. Some organisms, such as panda bears, have very restricted tolerance ranges and are called *specialists*. Organisms with wide tolerance ranges, such as rats, are able to live in a wide array of habitats or use a wide array of resources. These organisms are called *generalists*.

Specialist and generalist strategies each have advantages and disadvantages. Specialists can be very successful in their niche by being extremely good at the things they do. However, they might not be able to adapt when conditions change. Generalists succeed by being able to live in many different places and variable weather conditions. However, they may not be as successful as specialists in a given situation.

Competition When multiple organisms seek the same limited resource, such as food, light, water, or space, they compete. Competing organisms do not always fight with one another directly and physically like the foxes in **Figure 7a.** Flowers in a field, for example, do not physically fight to attract pollinators, but they are still in competition for that valuable resource. Competitive interactions can take place among members of the same species, called *intraspecific competition*, or among members of two or more different species, called *interspecific competition*. Interspecific competition can give rise to different types of outcomes.

▶ *Competitive Exclusion* Direct competition between species often results in a winner and a loser. If one species is a very effective competitor, it may exclude another species from resource use entirely. This outcome, called *competitive exclusion*, can happen when two or more species try to occupy the exact same niche. In 1986, ecologists with the National Oceanic and Atmospheric Administration began monitoring mussel and clam populations in Lake St. Clair. The lake connects Lakes Erie and Huron. They found there were twenty native mussel species in Lake St. Clair. By 1997, they were all gone—only the invasive zebra mussel occupied the lake's waters. **Figure 7b** shows zebra mussels attached to a native clam on the shores of Lake Erie. When colonized by zebra mussels, shellfish cannot open their shells. They eventually suffocate or starve.

◆▶ **Connect to the Central Case**

FIGURE 7 **Competition** Competition can occur between members of **(a)** the same species or **(b)** different species. **Apply Concepts** What does it mean that zebra mussels have "outcompeted" native mussels in many ways?

(a)

(b)

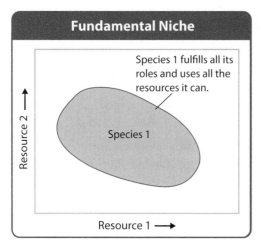

Fundamental Niche

Species 1 fulfills all its roles and uses all the resources it can.

Species 1

Resource 2 →

Resource 1 →

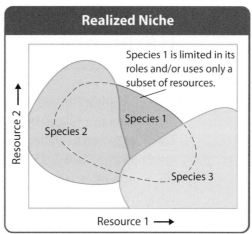

Realized Niche

Species 1 is limited in its roles and/or uses only a subset of resources.

Species 2

Species 1

Species 3

Resource 2 →

Resource 1 →

FIGURE 8 Fundamental and Realized Niche
(a) Without competitors, an organism can use its entire fundamental niche. **(b)** Competitors, however, limit an organism to a realized niche. The realized niche represents only a portion of what an organism can do and what resources it can use.

▶ *Fundamental and Realized Niche* The zebra mussel's total exclusion of its competitors in Lake St. Clair is unusual. Usually, neither competing species fully excludes the other. Instead, competing species tend to adjust to each other, minimizing competition. Individuals can do this by changing their behavior or using only a portion of the resources they are capable of using. In such cases, individuals do not fulfill their entire niche, as shown in **Figure 8.** The full niche of a species is called its *fundamental niche.* A niche restricted by competition is called a *realized niche.*

▶ *Resource Partitioning* Over time, competing species may evolve to occupy only their realized niches. In this way, they adapt to competition by using slightly different resources or their shared resources in different ways. If two bird species eat the same type of seeds, for example, one might come to specialize on larger seeds and the other to specialize on smaller seeds. Or one bird may become more active in the morning and the other more active in the evening. This process is called **resource partitioning** because the species partition, or divide, the resource they use in common by specializing in different ways, as shown in **Figure 9.**

▶ *Character Displacement* Sometimes, resource partitioning can lead to the evolution of physical characteristics among the competing species that reflect their specialized role in the environment. Ecologists call this *character displacement.* Through increased differences, two species can reduce competition. For example, through natural selection, birds that specialize in eating larger seeds may evolve larger bills that enable them to make the best use of the resource. Similarly, birds specializing in eating smaller seeds may evolve smaller bills. This is precisely what extensive research has revealed about the finches from the Galàpagos Islands that were first described by Charles Darwin.

✔ **Reading Checkpoint** *How does resource partitioning affect competition between species?*

FIGURE 9 Resource Partitioning
When species compete, they tend to divide resources. Many types of birds—including the woodpeckers, creeper, and nuthatch shown here—feed on insects from tree trunks. By each specializing in particular insects on particular parts of the tree, the birds minimize competition.

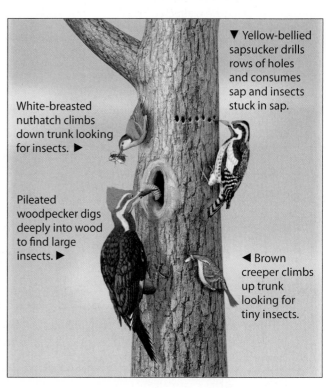

▼ Yellow-bellied sapsucker drills rows of holes and consumes sap and insects stuck in sap.

White-breasted nuthatch climbs down trunk looking for insects. ▶

Pileated woodpecker digs deeply into wood to find large insects. ▶

◀ Brown creeper climbs up trunk looking for tiny insects.

Evolution and Community Ecology **135**

Predation, Parasitism, and Herbivory

When organisms interact, they can affect each other in different ways. Throughout this lesson, the symbols "+", "–", and "0" are used to indicate how each interaction affects the success of the organisms involved. A "0" symbolizes a relationship in which there is no effect or the effect is neutral. Competition is a (–/–) relationship, because there is a negative effect on both organisms as each takes resources the other could have used. Other types of interactions are beneficial for one participant, but harmful for the other (+/–). Three examples of this type of species interaction are predation, parasitism, and herbivory.

Predation Every living thing needs food, and for many animals that means eating other living organisms. **Predation** is the process by which an individual of one species, a *predator*, hunts, captures, kills, and consumes an individual of another species, the *prey*. Interactions between predators and prey influence community structure by helping determine the relative numbers of predators and prey.

▶ *Population Cycles* Predation can sometimes cause cycles in population sizes. An increase in the population size of prey creates more food for predators, which may survive and reproduce more effectively as a result. As the predator population rises, additional predation drives down the population of prey. Less prey can then cause some predators to starve, so that the predator population declines. This allows the prey population to begin rising again, restarting the cycle. Most natural systems involve so many factors that such cycles don't last long, but in some cases, like the one shown in **Figure 10,** cycles can continue for a long time.

> ✔ **Reading Checkpoint** *Describe how predator and prey populations can affect each other.*

FIGURE 10 Predator-Prey Cycles Predator-prey systems sometimes show paired cycles. In this system, the number of moose is affected by the number of wolves and vice versa. Notice, too, that the wolf population was also affected by a disease outbreak.

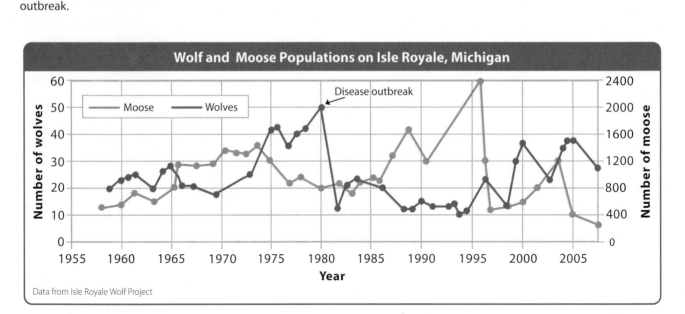

Wolf and Moose Populations on Isle Royale, Michigan

Data from Isle Royale Wolf Project

▶ *Predation and Evolution* Individual predators that are better at capturing prey will likely be more successful than less skilled predators. Thus, natural selection often leads to the evolution of adaptations that enable predators to be better hunters. Prey face an even stronger selective pressure—the risk of immediate death. In response to these pressures, prey organisms have evolved an elaborate array of defenses against being eaten, as shown in **Figure 11.**

▶ *Coevolution and Evolutionary "Arms Races"* Some predator–prey relationships are examples of coevolution. **Coevolution** is the process by which two species evolve in response to changes in each other. A change in one species, therefore, is usually followed by a change in the other. A newt, for example, might evolve toxins that kill animals that prey on it. Some predators, however, might evolve immunity to the toxins. Then, in turn, the newts evolve stronger toxins. Ecologists refer to this kind of coevolution as an *arms race.* Each species develops stronger and stronger "weapons" in response to the other.

Ecologists think that the rough-skinned newt, found on the west coast of the United States, and its predator, the common garter snake, have been locked in an arms race for a long time. Shown in **Figure 12,** the newt is one of the most poisonous animals in nature. A single newt has enough poison to kill more than 100 people. However, the common garter snake can still eat them! In this arms race, the newt's weapon is its toxin, and the predator's weapon is resistance to the toxin. As the newts evolved stronger toxins, the snakes evolved stronger resistance. It is important to remember, however, that natural selection does not produce adaptation *for* a purpose. The newts did not evolve toxins *to kill the snakes*, and the snakes did not evolve immunity *to respond to the newts*. Rather, these adaptations enabled the newts and snakes to better survive and reproduce in their environments.

FIGURE 11 Prey Defenses Natural selection to avoid predation has resulted in many dramatic adaptations. **(a)** Some prey hide from predators by camouflage, such as this leafy seadragon in the seaweed. **(b)** Other prey are brightly colored to warn predators that they are toxic or distasteful, such as this poisonous Sonoran coral snake. **(c)** Still others fool predators with mimicry—imitation of something else. This katydid does an excellent dead leaf impression.

FIND OUT MORE

your world • your turn

Have you heard about antibiotic resistance in the news? It's the result of an evolutionary arms race: bacteria vs. antibiotics. Look on the Internet or ask a doctor about antibiotic resistance in your area.

FIGURE 12 Fighting an Arms Race The rough-skinned newt has evolved incredible toxicity. Yet, the common garter snake can still make a meal out of it.

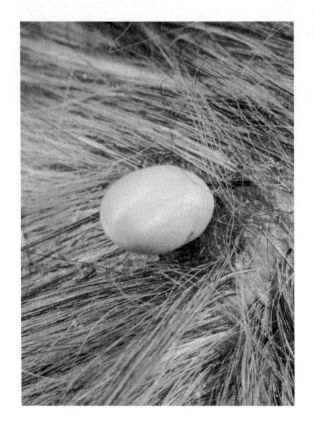

FIGURE 13 Parasitism A tick feeds on the blood of its host and may also carry disease-causing microorganisms.

Parasitism Parasitism is a relationship in which one organism, the *parasite*, depends on another, the *host*, for nourishment or some other benefit. In the process, the host is harmed. However, unlike predation, parasitism usually does not result in an organism's immediate death. Examples of parasites include tapeworms that live in the digestive tract of their host and ticks that attach themselves to their host's skin.

A close, long-term association between organisms—such as between a tapeworm and its host—is called symbiosis, literally "living together." Ecologists debate the exact definition of symbiosis. Some argue that symbiosis is any long-lasting relationship between species, regardless of distance. Further, some ecologists think that both organisms must benefit for a relationship to be considered symbiotic. Here, however, we define **symbiosis** as a long-lasting and physically close relationship in which at least one organism benefits.

Herbivory The interaction in which an animal feeds on a plant is called **herbivory.** Insects that feed on plants are the most common type of herbivore. In most cases, herbivory does not kill a plant directly but may affect its growth and reproduction. Because of natural selection, plants have evolved a wide array of defenses against the animals that feed on them. Many plants produce chemicals that are toxic or distasteful to herbivores. Others have thorns, spines, or irritating hairs. In response, herbivores may evolve ways to overcome these defenses.

FIGURE 14 Herbivory Herbivores like this giraffe get all of their nutrients and energy from plants.

Mutualism and Commensalism

Not every interaction between species results in one being harmed. Instead, both species can benefit. Or, one species can benefit without affecting the other one at all.

Mutualism A relationship in which two or more species benefit is called **mutualism** (+/+). Many mutualisms are symbiotic. For example, plant roots and some fungi together form symbiotic associations called mycorrhizae, shown in **Figure 15.** In these relationships, the plant provides energy and protection to the fungus, while the fungus assists the plant in absorbing nutrients from the soil.

Not all mutualists live in close proximity. One of the most important mutualisms, pollination, involves free-living organisms that may encounter each other only once in their lifetimes. Bees, birds, bats, and butterflies (**Figure 16**), transfer pollen (male sex cells) from one flower to another, fertilizing eggs that become embryos within seeds. Most pollinating animals visit flowers for their nectar, a reward the plant uses to attract them. The pollinators receive food, and the plants are pollinated and reproduce. Some plant-pollinator relationships are so close that they are examples of coevolving species.

One classic example of coevolution is that of orchid flowers and the African moths that pollinate them. The proboscis of the Darwin's hawk moth is an impressive 20–35 cm (8–14 in.) long—just long enough to reach the nectar at the bottom of the comet orchid's flower. Although not discovered and described until 1903, Darwin predicted the existence of the moth when he was shown the comet orchid in 1862. If such a flower exists, Darwin reasoned, so must an organism that pollinates it. There are many such seemingly perfect pairs of pollinators and plants in nature, each resulting from mutualistic, coevolutionary relationships.

 How do mycorrhizae fit the definition of a symbiotic relationship?

FIGURE 15 **Mutualism** Together, the hyphae of a fungus (white) and the roots of a strawberry tree (brown) form a mutualistic association known as a mycorrhiza. Both the fungus and the plant benefit from their association.

FIGURE 16 **Pollinators** Flowers that are pollinated by insects, such as butterflies, are brightly-colored and have strong scents and sticky pollen.

FIGURE 17 Commensalism Plants grow in the shady, moist, and nutrient-rich area beneath the palo verde "nurse" tree in the Sonoran Desert.

Commensalism Commensalism describes a relationship in which one species benefits and the other is unaffected (+/0). For instance, palo verde trees in the American Southwest's Sonoran Desert create shade and leaf litter that allow the soil beneath them to hold moisture. The area around palo verde trees becomes cooler and moister than the surrounding ground, making it easier for young plants to germinate and grow. Seedling cacti and other desert plants generally grow up directly beneath "nurse" trees such as palo verde, as shown in **Figure 17.**

② Assessment

1. **Relate Cause and Effect** Explain how competition can affect an organism's niche.

2. **Compare and Contrast** How are predation, parasitism, and herbivory similar? How are they different?

3. **Apply Concepts** The human digestive tract is filled with bacteria. The bacteria live in the body and get nutrients while helping to digest food. What kind of species interaction is this—mutualism or commensalism? Is it symbiotic? Explain.

REVISIT

4. **INVESTIGATIVE** PHENOMENON
   Copy the chart below into your notebook. For each species interaction, indicate whether it has a positive (+), negative (–), or neutral (0) effect on each species.

Interaction	Effect on Species A	Effect on Species B
Commensalism		
Competition		
Herbivory		
Mutualism		
Parasitism		
Predation		

Ecological Communities

EVERYDAY PHENOMENON How do energy and nutrients move through communities?

Knowledge and Skills

- Explain the difference between a producer and a consumer.
- Explain the effect of inefficient energy transfer on community structure.
- Describe how feeding relationships can have both direct and indirect effects on community members.

Reading Strategy and Vocabulary

✔ **Reading Strategy** As you read, generate a concept map using each of the boldface words highlighted in the lesson.

Vocabulary primary producer, photosynthesis, chemosynthesis, consumer, cellular respiration, herbivore, carnivore, omnivore, detritivore, decomposer, trophic level, biomass, food chain, food web, keystone species

LIFE REQUIRES ENERGY to organize matter into complex forms such as carbohydrates, to build and maintain cellular structures, to power interactions among species, and to power the geological forces that shape our planet. Energy is somehow involved in nearly every biological, chemical, and physical event. So, where does all this energy come from? And what, exactly, *is* energy?

Producers and Consumers

Energy is the ability to do work. It is energy that changes the position, composition, or temperature of matter. The first law of thermodynamics states that energy cannot be created or destroyed, only changed from one form to another. For example, solar energy is converted to thermal energy when absorbed by a sandy beach or a dark t-shirt. Just like matter, the total energy in the universe remains constant. However, unlike matter, energy is not recycled in the biosphere. It moves in a one-way stream, shaping communities in the process.

Primary Production Energy cannot be created or destroyed, but it has to enter an ecosystem somehow. Organisms called *autotrophs* or primary producers, like the plant shown in **Figure 18,** capture energy from the sun or from chemicals and store it in the bonds of sugars, making energy available to the rest of the community.

FIGURE 18 Primary Producers Green plants, like this spring pea, can capture radiant energy from the sun and store it in the bonds of sugar molecules.

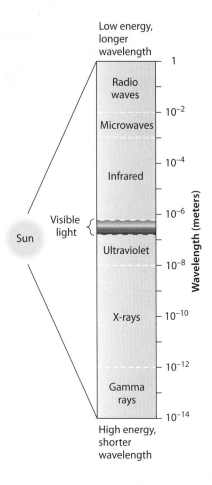

Low energy,
longer
wavelength

Radio
waves

Microwaves

Infrared

Visible
light

Ultraviolet

X-rays

Gamma
rays

Wavelength (meters)

1

10^{-2}

10^{-4}

10^{-6}

10^{-8}

10^{-10}

10^{-12}

10^{-14}

Sun

High energy,
shorter
wavelength

FIGURE 19 Energy From the Sun
The sun emits radiation from many
portions of the electromagnetic
spectrum. All photosynthesis is
powered by just a small portion of the
visible light that reaches Earth.

▶ *Energy From the Sun* For nearly all of Earth's ecological systems, the
sun is the ultimate source of energy. The sun releases radiation from large
portions of the electromagnetic spectrum, shown in **Figure 19.** Earth's
atmosphere filters much of this out, and we see only some of this radiation as visible light. Some primary producers, such as green plants, algae,
and cyanobacteria, can turn light energy from the sun into chemical
energy in a process called photosynthesis. **Photosynthesis** is the process
by which primary producers use sunlight to convert carbon dioxide and
water into sugars, releasing oxygen along the way. Photosynthesis is a
complex process, but the overall reaction can be summarized with the
following equation:

$$6CO_2 + 6H_2O + \text{the sun's energy} \rightarrow C_6H_{12}O_6 \text{ (sugar)} + 6O_2$$

▶ *Energy From Chemicals* Not all communities are powered by the sun's
energy. On the floor of the ocean, jets of water heated by magma under
Earth's crust gush into the icy-cold depths. In one of the more amazing
scientific discoveries of recent decades, scientists realized that these deep-
sea vents host entire communities of organisms. Deep-sea vents are deep
enough underwater that they completely lack sunlight. Instead, primary
producers such as bacteria use energy stored in the bonds of hydrogen
sulfide (H_2S) to convert carbon dioxide and water into sugars in a process
called **chemosynthesis.** Chemosynthesis can be summarized as:

$$6CO_2 + 6H_2O + 3H_2S \rightarrow C_6H_{12}O_6 \text{ (sugar)} + 3H_2SO_4$$

Photosynthesis and chemosynthesis use different energy sources, but
each uses water and carbon dioxide to produce sugars. Energy from
chemosynthesis supports many organisms including enormous clams and
tubeworms, and various species of mussels, shrimp, crabs, and fish. These
organisms have adaptations that enable them to live in the extreme high-
temperature, high-pressure conditions of deep-ocean vents.

✓ Reading
Checkpoint *What is the primary difference between photosynthesis and
chemosynthesis?*

Consumers Organisms that rely on other organisms for energy and
nutrients are called *heterotrophs,* or **consumers.** Consumers, like those in
Figure 20, make use of the chemical energy stored by photosynthesis or
chemosynthesis in a process called cellular respiration.

FIGURE 20 Consumers Most communities contain
many kinds of consumers, including a variety of herbivores,
carnivores, omnivores, detritivores, and decomposers.

(a) Herbivore

Cellular respiration is the process by which organisms use oxygen to release the chemical energy of sugars such as glucose, releasing carbon dioxide and water as a byproduct. The summary equation for cellular respiration is the exact opposite of that for photosynthesis:

$$C_6H_{12}O_6 \text{ (sugar)} + 6O_2 \rightarrow 6CO_2 + 6H_2O + \text{energy}$$

Cellular respiration does not only occur in consumers—primary producers also use cellular respiration to release energy and nutrients they themselves have stored. In fact, the term *autotroph* literally means "self feeder." *Heterotroph,* on the other hand, means "other feeder."

▶ *Herbivores, Carnivores, and Omnivores* Organisms that consume producers are known as *primary consumers.* Most primary consumers, such as deer and grasshoppers, eat plants and are called **herbivores.** Wolves that prey on deer are considered *secondary consumers,* as are rodents and birds that prey on grasshoppers. *Tertiary consumers* eat secondary consumers, and so on. Most secondary and tertiary consumers kill and eat other animals and are called **carnivores.** Animals that eat both plant and animal food are called **omnivores.**

▶ *Detritivores and Decomposers* Recall that nutrients, such as carbon, nitrogen, and phosphorus, are recycled in ecosystems. When animals eat plants, they break down plant tissues into their components. Then, the animals' bodies use the nutrients to build their own tissues. What happens when animals die? How do nutrients re-enter the ecosystem? Luckily, ecosystems have recyclers called detritivores and decomposers. **Detritivores,** such as millipedes and soil insects, consume detritus—nonliving organic matter including leaf litter, waste products, and the dead bodies of other community members. Large detritivores, like vultures, are often called *scavengers.* **Decomposers,** such as fungi and bacteria, break down nonliving matter into simpler parts that can then be taken up and reused by primary producers. If it were not for detritivores and decomposers, nutrients would be lost to an ecosystem when organisms die.

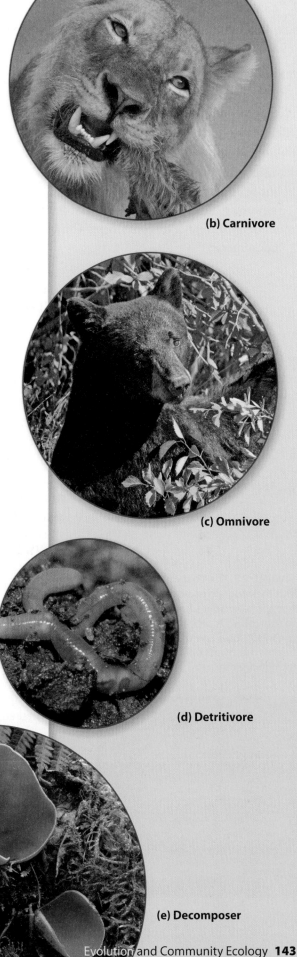

(b) Carnivore

(c) Omnivore

(d) Detritivore

(e) Decomposer

Energy Flow in Communities

Energy transfer from one trophic level to another in a community is only about 10% efficient. In addition to affecting community structure, this inefficiency affects our own "energy footprints."

1. **Calculate** If 1000 units of energy are available at the producer level of the energy pyramid, about how many units are available for first-level consumers? Second-level consumers? Third-level consumers?

2. **Infer** Use your answer to **Question 1** to explain why most communities have only about three or four trophic levels.

3. **Calculate** How many units of energy would there need to be in the first trophic level to end up with 1000 units of energy in the second? In the third? In the fourth?

4. **Apply Concepts** Use your answer to **Question 2** to explain why eating "down a food chain," vegetables instead of meat for example, is more energy efficient.

Energy and Biomass

As organisms feed on one another, matter and energy move through the community's trophic levels. An organism's **trophic level** is its rank in a feeding hierarchy. Primary producers always make up a community's first trophic level. Primary, secondary, and tertiary consumers make up the second, third, and fourth levels. In theory, a community can have any number of trophic levels. However, the relative amounts of energy and nutrients available at each trophic level put restrictions on a community's structure. Consequently, there are typically only three or four trophic levels in any community.

Energy in Communities Although the overall amount of energy is conserved in any process of energy transfer, the second law of thermodynamics states that energy tends to change from a more-ordered state to a less-ordered state. That is, systems tend to move toward increasing disorder, or *entropy*. The result of the second law of thermodynamics is that no process involving energy conversion is 100% efficient. When gasoline is burned in an automobile engine, for example, only about 14% of the energy is used to move the automobile down the road—most of the rest is converted to thermal energy and released as heat, as shown in **Figure 21.** Thermal energy has high entropy and is very hard to capture and convert to something else. In other words, thermal energy is generally "lost" when released as heat.

▶ *Energy Transfer in Communities* Organisms are not that different from car engines. They take in food through predation, herbivory, or parasitism, and "burn it" using cellular respiration. Energy needed for life activities is released, but in the process much of the original energy is lost as waste heat. Due mainly to heat loss, only a small amount of the energy consumed by an organism in one trophic level is available to be transferred to the next trophic level.

FIGURE 21 The Cost of Action
This thermogram of a car shows temperature ranges from hot (white) to cool (blue). A car engine, like an organism, loses energy in the form of heat as it converts energy from one form to another.

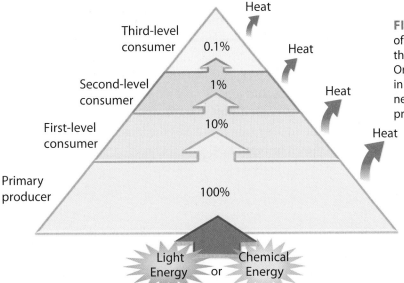

Heat

Heat

Heat

Heat

Third-level consumer — 0.1%

Second-level consumer — 1%

First-level consumer — 10%

Primary producer — 100%

Light Energy or Chemical Energy

FIGURE 22 Pyramid of Energy This pyramid of energy illustrates a rough rule of thumb for the way ecological communities are structured: Only about 10 percent of the energy contained in any given trophic level is transferred to the next highest level. The rest is used to power life processes or lost as heat.

▶ *The Ten Percent Rule* A general rule of thumb is that each trophic level contains just 10% of the energy of the trophic level below it, although the actual proportion can vary greatly. So, if the primary producers represent 100 calories of a community's energy, 10 calories (10% of 100 calories) will be available to level two, 1 calorie (10% of 10 calories) to level three, and 0.1 calories (10% of 1 calorie) to level four. Most communities, therefore, do not contain enough energy to support consumers above the third or fourth trophic level. Energy transfer in a community can be visualized as a pyramid, shown in **Figure 22.**

This pyramid-like pattern illustrates why eating at lower trophic levels—eating vegetables and fruit rather than meat, for instance—decreases a person's ecological footprint. When we eat meat, we are taking in the end product of far more energy consumption, per calorie of energy that we gain, than when we eat plant products.

Numbers and Biomass in Communities

Similar to the amount of available energy, there are generally fewer organisms at higher trophic levels than at lower ones. Look at **Figure 23.** A mouse eats many plants in its lifetime, a snake eats many mice, and a hawk eats many snakes. Thus, for every hawk in a community there must be many snakes, still more mice, and a huge number of plants. Because the difference in numbers of organisms among trophic levels tends to be large, the same pyramid-like relationship also often holds true for biomass. A trophic level's **biomass** is the total amount of living tissue it contains. So, although a snake weighs more than a mouse, the total snake biomass is much less than the total biomass of mice.

What happens to energy that is not passed from one trophic level to the next, or used to power life processes?

FIGURE 23 Pyramids of Numbers and Biomass Organisms at lower trophic levels generally exist in far greater numbers, with greater biomass, than organisms at higher trophic levels. The example shown here is generalized; the actual shape of any given pyramid may vary greatly.

Evolution and Community Ecology **145**

Food Webs and Keystone Species

As energy is transferred from species on lower trophic levels to species on higher trophic levels, it is said to pass up a food chain. A **food chain** is a linear series of feeding relationships. For example, a small fish eats algae, a larger fish eats the smaller fish, a bird eats the large fish, and an alligator eats the bird, as shown in **Figure 24.**

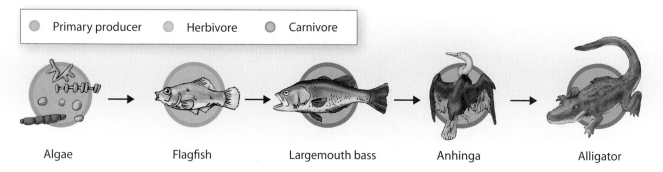

| ● Primary producer | ● Herbivore | ● Carnivore |

Algae → Flagfish → Largemouth bass → Anhinga → Alligator

FIGURE 24 Food Chains Food chains are a linear illustration of energy transfer through feeding relationships in a community.

One member of a community can have a direct effect on another, for example, when one organism eats another as part of a food chain. Organisms have indirect effects, too. Consider the zebra mussel's effects, shown in **Figure 25.** The mussels' waste products promote bacterial growth and disease pathogens that harm native mussels and clams. Zebra mussels can also contain high levels of toxic chemicals that can make animals at higher trophic levels sick. On the other hand, they provide nutrients that nourish crayfish and other invertebrate animals. The mussels also clarify the water by filtering out phytoplankton, which are photosynthetic algae that live in water. As a result, sunlight penetrates more deeply into the water and plants flourish.

Food Webs Thinking in terms of food chains can be useful, but in reality, ecological systems are far more complex than simple linear chains. For one thing, most organisms have more than one source of food! A more accurate representation of the feeding relationships in a community is a food web. A **food web** is a visual map of feeding relationships and energy flow, showing the many paths by which energy and nutrients pass among organisms as they consume one another. **Figure 26** shows a simplified food web from Florida's Everglades region. Note that even within this simplified diagram we can pick out a number of different food chains involving different sets of species.

 Reading Checkpoint *Why are most communities best represented with a food web instead of a food chain?*

◆ **Connect to the Central Case**

FIGURE 25 Indirect Effects Zebra mussels have many indirect effects on their community—some positive (green arrows) and some negative (red arrows). **Infer** How would the elimination of zebra mussels affect plants in this community?

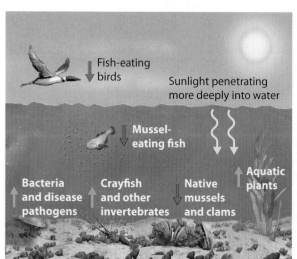

Fish-eating birds

Sunlight penetrating more deeply into water

Mussel-eating fish

Aquatic plants

Bacteria and disease pathogens

Crayfish and other invertebrates

Native mussels and clams

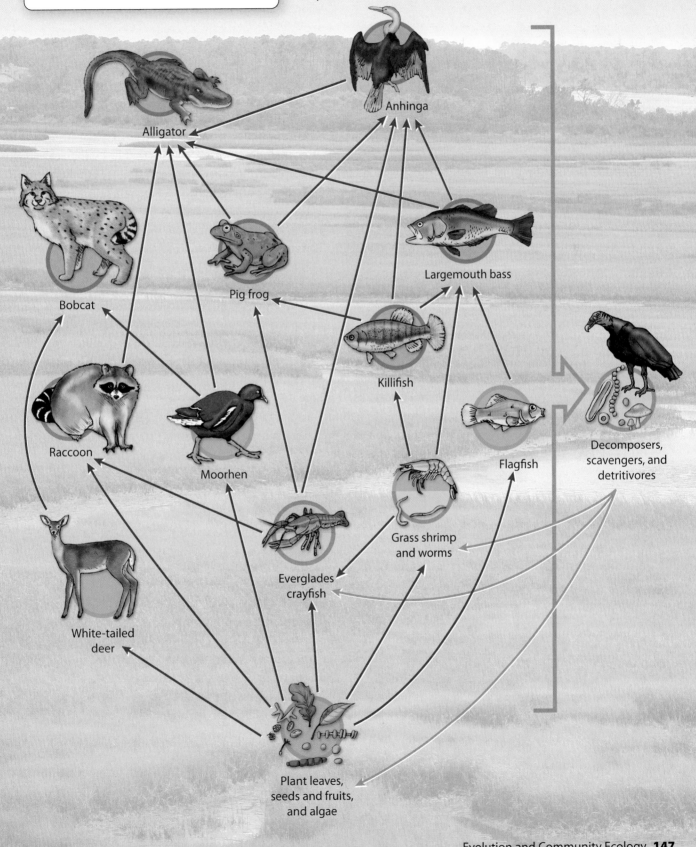

Decomposers, scavengers, and detritivores
Omnivore
Carnivore
Herbivore
Primary Producer

Alligator

Anhinga

Bobcat

Pig frog

Largemouth bass

Killifish

Raccoon

Moorhen

Decomposers, scavengers, and detritivores

Flagfish

Grass shrimp and worms

Everglades crayfish

White-tailed deer

Plant leaves, seeds and fruits, and algae

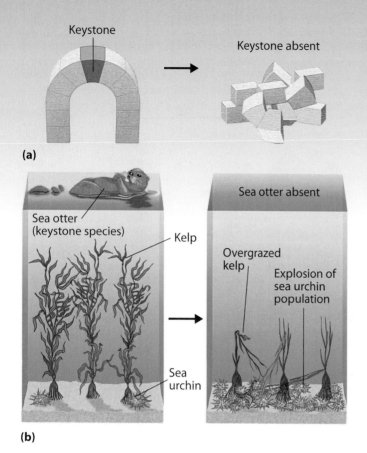

Keystone

Keystone absent

(a)

Sea otter absent

Sea otter (keystone species)

Kelp

Overgrazed kelp

Explosion of sea urchin population

Sea urchin

(b)

FIGURE 27 Keystone Species **(a)** A keystone is the stone that holds an arch together. **(b)** A keystone species, such as the sea otter, is one that greatly influences a community's composition and structure. Sea otters eat sea urchins that eat kelp in marine nearshore environments of the Pacific. When otters are present, they keep urchin numbers down, which allows forests of kelp to grow and provide habitat for many other species. When otters are absent, urchin populations increase and the kelp is devoured, destroying habitat and reducing species diversity.

Keystone Species Ecologists have found that in communities, some species exert greater influence than do others. A species that has strong or wide-reaching impact on a community is called a **keystone species.** Shown in **Figure 27a,** a keystone is the wedge-shaped stone at the top of an arch that holds the structure together. If the keystone is removed, the arch will collapse. In an ecological community, removal of a keystone species can alter a large portion of the food web.

Consider the ecosystem shown in **Figure 27b.** Sea otters, a keystone species, eat urchins, which in turn, eat kelp. In the 1990s, sea otter populations off the coast of Alaska declined when orcas (killer whales) ate large numbers of otters. Fewer otters meant more urchins. The increased urchin population caused a huge decline in the kelp "forests" offshore. The kelp had served as habitat for many animals and plants. This is an example of a *trophic cascade:* Predators at high trophic levels (sea otters) indirectly help organisms at low trophic levels (kelp) by limiting populations at intermediate trophic levels (urchins).

LESSON ③ Assessment

1. **Compare and Contrast** Explain the difference between a producer and a consumer. Then, explain the differences among an herbivore, carnivore, omnivore, detritivore, and decomposer.

2. **Calculate** If there are 1623 calories available at the first trophic level, approximately how many calories of energy would be available to a third-level consumer (fourth trophic level)?

3. **Infer** Describe three effects a sudden decrease of pig frogs have might have on the community structure shown in **Figure 26.** (*Hint:* Think about what pig frogs eat and what eats them.)

REVISIT

4. **INVESTIGATIVE** PHENOMENON
Identifying a community's keystone species is not always easy. In fact, some ecologists think that a community can have many keystone species or none at all. Ecologists all agree, however, that decomposers, as a category of consumers, have a huge impact on a community's structure. Write a paragraph in which you argue that decomposers are a "keystone group."

Community Stability

EVERYDAY PHENOMENON How do communities respond to a disturbance?

Knowledge and Skills

- Describe what happens to a community after a disturbance.
- Explain the conditions necessary for a species to become invasive.

Reading Strategy and Vocabulary

✅ **Reading Strategy** As you read, create a flowchart that summarizes the steps of both primary and secondary succession.

Vocabulary succession, primary succession, pioneer species, secondary succession, invasive species

DISTURBANCES ARE COMMON IN NATURE. A *disturbance* is any change in a community's environment, large or small. Over time, a given community may experience natural or human-caused disturbances ranging from gradual phenomena like climate changes to sudden events such as storms, floods, or fire. Disturbances can modify the composition, structure, or function of an ecological community. How communities respond to disturbances is a measure of their stability—or lack thereof.

Ecological Succession

A community described as being *in equilibrium* is generally stable and balanced. Normally, species interactions and limiting factors hold their populations at or around carrying capacity. Sometimes, however, disturbances throw a community into *disequilibrium*. Limiting factors shift, altering carrying capacities. Population sizes change, and the community enters a period of adjustment.

Some communities return to their original state following a disturbance, but other communities are changed permanently. Usually, permanent change happens in response to severe disturbances that eliminate all or most of the species in a community. When this occurs, a community experiences a somewhat predictable series of changes over time that ecologists call **succession.** Ecologists recognize two traditional types of succession: primary and secondary. Although usually described in terms of plant species, animals and other members of the community also change over the course of succession.

FIGURE 28 Disturbances A disturbance, such as a fire, can disrupt a community and start a series of changes called succession.

Primary Succession When a disturbance is so severe that no vegetation or soil life remains, **primary succession** occurs. In primary succession, a community is built essentially from scratch. Primary succession takes place after a bare expanse of rock, sand, or sediment is exposed for the first time. This can occur when glaciers retreat, lakes dry up, or volcanic lava or ash spreads across the landscape. Species that colonize the newly exposed land first are called **pioneer species.** Pioneer species are well adapted for colonization. For example, they often have spores or seeds that can travel long distances, helping them spread quickly across the land.

Lichens are particularly successful pioneers of bare rock. *Lichens* are formed by a mutualistic relationship between algae and fungi. The algae provide food and energy via photosynthesis, while the fungi take a firm hold on rock and capture the moisture that both organisms need to survive. As lichens grow, they release acids that break down the rock surface into the beginnings of soil. Once soil begins to form, small plants, insects, and worms can move in. As new organisms arrive, they change the environment by providing more nutrients and habitat for future arrivals. As time passes, larger plants establish themselves, the amount of vegetation increases, and species diversity increases. An example of primary succession is shown in **Figure 29.**

FIGURE 29 Primary Succession
When a glacier retreated from Glacier Bay, Alaska, barren rock was exposed. For more than 200 years, primary succession has been occurring. Today, a hemlock and spruce forest grows in the area.

| 15 years | 35 years | 80 years | 115+ years |

Time

Secondary Succession Secondary succession, unlike primary succession, begins when a disturbance, such as a fire, logging, or farming, dramatically alters an existing community but does not destroy all living things or all organic matter in the soil. In secondary succession, at least the soil from the previous ecosystem remains. As a result, secondary succession usually occurs faster than primary succession.

Consider the abandoned agricultural field in eastern North America, shown in **Figure 30.** In the first few years after farming ended, the site was colonized by grasses and herbs that were already in the area. (In comparison, it can take more than fifteen years for lichens to colonize bare rock in primary succession.) As time passes, shrubs and fast-growing trees such as aspens rose from the field. Pine trees then moved in, forming a pine-dominated forest. This pine forest developed an understory of hardwood trees that grow well under a canopy. Eventually, the hardwoods outgrew the pines, creating the hardwood forest that grows there today.

 Reading Checkpoint *Why does secondary succession usually happen faster than primary succession?*

FIGURE 30 Secondary Succession Secondary succession occurs after a disturbance, such as fire, flood, or farming, removes most—but not all—vegetation from an area. The typical series of changes in a plant community of eastern North America is shown here. Secondary succession began in many areas when farm fields were abandoned.

Time

3 years   5 years   40+ years

Quick Lab

Successful Succession? 🔧 🖐

① Obtain a clean jar with a cover and place a handful of dried plant material into the jar.

② Fill the jar with boiled pond water or sterile spring water.

③ Cover the jar and place it in an area that receives indirect light.

④ Examine the jar every day for the next few days.

⑤ When the jar appears cloudy, prepare microscope slides of water from various levels of the jar. Use a pipette to collect the samples.

⑥ View the slides under the low-power objective microscope and record your observations.

Analyze and Conclude

1. **Infer** Why did you use boiled or sterile water?

2. **Infer** Where did the organisms you saw come from?

3. **Draw Conclusions** Was ecological succession occurring? Give evidence to support your answer.

4. **Evaluate and Revise** Check your results against those of your classmates. Do they agree? Give possible explanations for any differences.

Succession in the Water Succession occurs in aquatic systems, too. Primary aquatic succession takes place when an area fills in with water for the first time. This can happen, for example, when glaciers retreat and leave depressions in the ground. Over time, aquatic communities become established as the water becomes richer in nutrients.

Disturbances to aquatic communities, such as floods or excess run-off, can lead to secondary succession. One classic example of secondary aquatic succession is shown in **Figure 31.** As algae, microbes, plants, and zooplankton (small floating animals) grow, reproduce, and die, they can gradually fill the pond with organic matter. Organic matter and nutrients may also enter the pond through streams and rivers. Eventually, the pond may fill in completely, and a terrestrial ecosystem can establish itself.

FIGURE 31 Aquatic Succession Secondary succession in lakes and ponds usually occurs over a number of years.

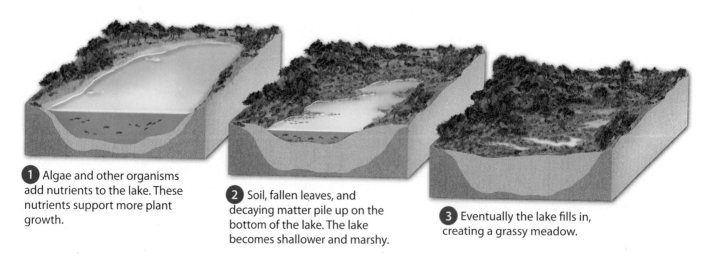

① Algae and other organisms add nutrients to the lake. These nutrients support more plant growth.

② Soil, fallen leaves, and decaying matter pile up on the bottom of the lake. The lake becomes shallower and marshy.

③ Eventually the lake fills in, creating a grassy meadow.

Climax Communities In the traditional view of succession that we have described, the transitions between stages of succession eventually lead to a climax community. A *climax community* is a stable community that "completes" the succession process. Ecologists used to think that each region had its own characteristic climax community determined by the region's climate. However, ecologists now know that not only climate but soil conditions and other factors influence a community's composition. Further, various conditions can promote or inhibit a community's progression between succession stages.

Many ecologists now view communities as temporary, ever-changing associations among individual species—not as cohesive and predetermined units. Once a climax community is disturbed, there is no guarantee that the community will ever return to that climax state. Though communities, such as the beech-maple forest in **Figure 32,** may appear stable over long periods, they are often not as uniform as they seem. Disturbances, small and large, are constantly affecting them.

FIGURE 32 Not So Stable?
Beech-maple forests , such as this one in Vermont, were once classic examples of stable climax communities. Ecologists now think that ecosystems such as this might not be as uniform nor as stable as once thought.

Invasive Species

Traditional concepts of succession involve sets of organisms native to an area. A pine forest, for example, would not grow in an area where pine trees don't usually live. But what if a new organism arrives from elsewhere? Sometimes these nonnative, or *exotic*, organisms can turn into invasive species. An **invasive species** is a nonnative organism that spreads widely in a community. Invasive species are one type of community disturbance and a major problem in many parts of the world. The zebra mussel is an example of an invasive species.

 What is an invasive species?

WHAT DO YOU THINK?

Are invasive species all bad? Some people have questioned the notion that all invasive species should be considered a problem. Is it always bad to change a native community? Does it make a difference whether the invasive species arrived on its own or through human intervention?

What Makes a Species Invasive? Not all exotic species turn invasive. Some exotic species may remain small and localized, eventually dying out. Others may simply exist without causing problems. Species only become invasive when such limiting factors as predators, parasites, or competitors are not present in their new environment. As a result, population growth of the exotic species is not held in check. The community is thrown out of balance as native species are eliminated through predation or herbivory, or simply out-competed for resources.

Examples of Invasive Species There are many examples of introduced species that have turned invasive and have had major ecological effects. As illustrated in the examples that follow, invasive species can be introduced to an area intentionally or by accident.

▶ *The Zebra Mussel* A wide variety of techniques to control the spread of zebra mussels has been tried, including removing them by hand, applying toxic chemicals, drying them out, introducing predators and diseases, and stressing them with heat, sound, electricity, carbon dioxide, or ultraviolet light. However, most of these are only short-term fixes that don't make a dent in the huge populations of the mussels in the Great Lakes.

▶ *The Cane Toad* The cane toad is a toxic organism native to Central and South America. In other parts of the world, notably in Australia, it's an invasive species. Cane toads were brought to Australia intentionally in 1935 to help rid sugar farms of the cane beetle pest. Unfortunately, the cane toad did not eat the cane beetle as predicted, but instead bred rapidly and began to spread. Without its native predators, like the black rat and water monitor, the cane toad population has been growing exponentially. Many native species have been out-competed by the toads, and their poisonous skin often kills animals that try to eat them.

✓ Reading Checkpoint   *Why was the cane toad introduced to Australia?*

FIGURE 33 Zebra mussels

FIGURE 34 Cane toads

▶ *Kudzu* Plants can be invasive, too. Kudzu was introduced to the United States from Japan in 1876. At the time, the United States government encouraged farmers in the Southeast to plant kudzu to prevent soil erosion. However, kudzu quickly became invasive. The lack of freezing temperatures and natural predators enabled kudzu to spread and literally cover the land from Texas to southern New Jersey.

▶ *The Honeybee* Not all invasive species are bad. The European honeybee is thought to have evolved in Africa, and then spread to Europe and Asia. Colonists to North America brought the bees with them, and they rapidly spread, becoming invasive. However, they are far from harmful! European honeybees pollinate most of America's commercial crops, providing billions of dollars to our economy.

What Can Be Done? Today, many ecologists think that invasive species are the second-greatest threat to species and natural systems, behind habitat destruction. In 1990 the U.S. Congress passed the Nonindigenous Aquatic Nuisance Prevention and Control Act, which, in 1996, became the National Invasive Species Act. Since then, funding has become widely available for the control of invasive species. However, in most cases, preventing the introduction of invasive species is a much better investment than trying to control them once they're here.

FIGURE 35 Kudzu

FIGURE 36 European honeybee

LESSON ④ Assessment

1. **Compare and Contrast** What are the major differences between primary and secondary succession?

2. **Infer** The cane toad was brought to Australia from the island of Hawaii. The toad had been introduced to Hawaii some time earlier, but has not had the same kind of destructive effects there as it has in Australia. What could explain why the toad has not become invasive in Hawaii as it did in Australia?

3. **THINK IT** *THROUGH* A federal agency has put you in charge of responding to the zebra mussel invasion. Based on what you've learned in this lesson, how would you try to control the mussel's spread and impact?

A BROKEN MUTUALISM?

In 1973, an ornithologist (a scientist who studies birds) named Stanley Temple realized that the tambalacoque tree, which lives only on the tropical island of Mauritius, was disappearing. He found only 13 trees, all older than 300 years. There were no young trees. Dr. Temple thought that tambalacoque seeds weren't sprouting because they were covered in a thick outer shell.

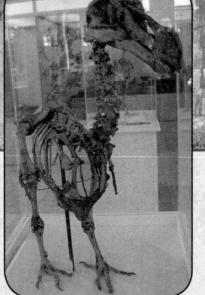

▶ A fossil (left) and artist's rendition (right) of the dodo bird. The dodo, which lived only on Mauritius, was driven to extinction by hunting and introduced species such as dogs and rats.

DODOS

Temple hypothesized that the dodo, a bird that became extinct on Mauritius in 1681, used to eat the tambalacoque seeds. The dodo had a strong gizzard that it used to help break down tough seeds and plants, which may have weakened the seed's shell and allowed it to sprout. Temple called this relationship an "obligatory mutualism," because he thought that without the dodo, there would not be enough new tambalacoque trees for the species to survive.

TURKEY TEST

Temple tested his hypothesis by feeding tambalacoque seeds to turkeys. After passing through the turkeys' digestive tracts, which are similar to the dodos', a few of the seeds sprouted. Temple took this as proof of his hypothesis, and he published his results in the prestigious journal *Science* in 1977. The story of the dodo-tambalacoque mutualism became popular and was taught in biology courses and textbooks.

DISAGREEMENT

However, Dr. Temple's theory may not have been as clear cut as it first appeared. Some botanists pointed out that tambalacoque seeds can actually sprout on their own, and that there are a few hundred young tamabalacoque trees on Mauritius—they are just difficult to find. Ecologists have also found that fruit bats and parrots feed on the fruit of the tambalacoque. However, Dr. Temple maintains that the only animals large enough to eat the *seeds* were the dodo and a species of giant tortoise that also went extinct on Mauritius. And even then, only the dodo had a gizzard strong enough to weaken the outer shell.

MANY MUTUALISMS?

Part of Temple's hypothesis is certainly well supported. Populations of tambalacoque trees are dwindling, in part because there are fewer animals to eat and spread their seeds. However, it isn't clear yet whether the tambalacoque and the dodo once had an obligatory mutualism. Only more research will reveal whether the tambalacoque needs the dodo to survive, or if the tambalacoque has formed many mutualisms with the many different types of animals that eat its fruit.

▼ **Tambalacoque seeds**

Write About It When using an experiment to answer a question such as *Why is the tambalacoque tree dying out?* it is important to test all the possible explanations. Describe an additional experiment you could run on Mauritius to see if tamabalacoque seeds must be eaten by a dodo bird before they can sprout.

Study Guide

How do organisms affect the abiotic and biotic conditions in an environment?

Lesson 1
What role does the environment play in an organism's survival and reproduction?

Lesson 4
How do communities respond to a disturbance?

Lesson 2
How do species interact in nature?

Lesson 3
How do energy and nutrients move through communities?

LESSON 1 Evolution

- Biological evolution can occur through mutation, migration, genetic drift, and natural selection. Evolution by natural selection occurs in a population when: (1) more organisms are born than can survive, (2) organisms differ in their characteristics, and (3) there is variable survival and reproduction among individuals.
- Two processes, speciation and extinction, combine to produce the diversity of life on Earth.

evolution (126)
gene (126)
mutation (127)
genetic drift (127)
natural selection (127)
fitness (129)
adaptation (129)
artificial selection (130)
speciation (131)
extinction (132)

LESSON 2 Species Interactions

- An organism's niche is affected by both its tolerance and competitive interactions.
- Predation, parasitism, and herbivory are interactions in which one species benefits, while the other is harmed.
- Mutualism and commensalism are relationships in which neither participant is harmed.

niche (133)
tolerance (134)
resource partitioning (135)
predation (136)
coevolution (137)
parasitism (138)
symbiosis (138)
herbivory (138)
mutualism (139)
commensalism (140)

LESSON 3 Ecological Communities

- Organisms are classified as either producers or consumers based on how they obtain energy and nutrients.
- Only about 10 percent of energy is transferred from one trophic level to the next. This inefficient energy transfer between organisms shapes the structure of a community.
- Feeding relationships have both direct and indirect effects on organisms in the community.

primary producer (141)
photosynthesis (142)
chemosynthesis (142)
consumer (142)
cellular respiration (143)
herbivore (143)
carnivore (143)
omnivore (143)

detritivore (143)
decomposer (143)
trophic level (144)
biomass (145)
food chain (146)
food web (146)
keystone species (148)

LESSON 4 Community Stability

- Following a disturbance, communities may undergo succession.
- Without limiting factors, species introduced to a new area can become invasive.

succession (149)
primary succession (150)
pioneer species (150)

secondary succession (151)
invasive species (153)

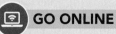 **GO ONLINE**

INQUIRY LABS AND ACTIVITIES

- **Simulating Adaptations**
  Use tools and a variety of materials to model how different bird beaks work. Then graph the results.
- **Life in a Drop of Pond Water**
  Even in a drop of water, organisms interact. Observe and sketch microscopic producers and consumers.
- **Invasive Organisms Near You**
  Research an invasive species in your area. What are its impacts? How is it managed?

Chapter Assessment

Defend Your Case

The Central Case in this chapter focused on the impact of invasive zebra mussels on the Great Lakes and beyond. How do you think the United States should address the problem of invasive species? Is it a local, national, or an international problem? Use evidence from the Central Case and throughout the chapter to support your answer.

Review Concepts and Terms

1. Which of the following is NOT a mechanism for biological evolution?
   a. mutation
   b. genetic drift
   c. inheritance of acquired characteristics
   d. natural selection

2. What is the term scientists use to describe how reproductively successful an organism is in its environment?
   a. adaptation
   b. fitness
   c. speciation
   d. evolution

3. "Everything an organism does and when it does it" describes an organism's
   a. tolerance.
   b. community.
   c. character displacement.
   d. niche.

4. Which of the following is an interaction in which one organism benefits and the other is harmed (+/−)?
   a. parasitism
   b. mutualism
   c. competition
   d. commensalism

5. Which of the following is an interaction in which both organisms are harmed (−/−)?
   a. parasitism   c. competition
   b. predation   d. commensalism

6. Which of the following types of organisms perform photosynthesis?
   a. a primary producer   c. a carnivore
   b. an herbivore   d. a detritivore

7. Which of the following organisms is a decomposer?
   a. a plant   c. a mushroom
   b. a tiger   d. a deer

8. A caterpillar eats some grass. A bird eats a caterpillar. A fox eats a bird. Which of the following food chains represents this series of feeding relationships?
   a. fox → bird → caterpillar → grass
   b. bird → fox → caterpillar → grass
   c. caterpillar → grass → bird → fox
   d. grass → caterpillar → bird → fox

9. Which of the following organisms is often a pioneer species?
   a. grasses   c. otters
   b. lichen   d. spruces

Modified True/False

Write true if the statement is true. If it is false, change the underlined word or words to make the statement true.

10. A trait that is passed to the next generations and promotes an individual's survival and reproduction is called an <u>adaptation</u>.

11. <u>Mass extinctions</u> occur gradually, one species at a time.

12. <u>Competition</u> describes an interaction in which both organisms benefit.

13. Photosynthesis is the process by which primary producers use sunlight to convert <u>oxygen</u> and water into sugars.

14. The organism below is a <u>primary consumer.</u>

Reading Comprehension

Read the following selection and answer the questions that follow.

Usually, large secondary or tertiary consumers near the top of a food web, such as wolves, sea stars, sharks, and sea otters, are considered keystone species. These predators control populations of herbivores, which, in the absence of the predators, could multiply and greatly change the plant community. However, other types of organisms also can exert strong community-wide effects. "Ecosystem engineers" physically modify the environment shared by community members. Beavers build dams and turn streams into ponds that flood acres of dry land and turn them to swamp. Small organisms and those toward the bottoms of food webs may have even greater impact. Remove the fungi that decompose dead matter or the insects that control plant growth, and a community may change very rapidly indeed.

15. From the passage, you can infer that organisms can be considered keystone species ONLY if they
    a. are predators.
    b. exert strong community-wide effects.
    c. eat plants.
    d. are at the bottom of a food web.

16. Which of the following would make the BEST title for this selection?
    a. "Keystone Species in Yellowstone Park"
    b. "Defining Trophic Levels"
    c. "Surprising Keystone Species"
    d. "Do Keystone Species Exist?"

Short Answer

17. What are the conditions of natural selection?
18. Describe the process of allopatric speciation.
19. What is symbiosis?
20. What is coevolution?
21. Why is energy transfer in a community best visualized as a pyramid?

22. Why does secondary succession proceed faster than primary succession?

Critical Thinking

23. **Compare and Contrast** What is the difference between commensalism and mutualism? Give an example of each.

24. **Use Analogies** Are decomposers and detritivores more like a manufacturing company or a recycling company? Explain your answer.

25. **Compare and Contrast** Compare the equations for photosynthesis and cellular respiration. How are they similar? In what ways are they different?

26. **Apply Concepts** Examine the food web below. Describe two food chains: one with the owl as a secondary consumer, and one showing the owl as a tertiary consumer.

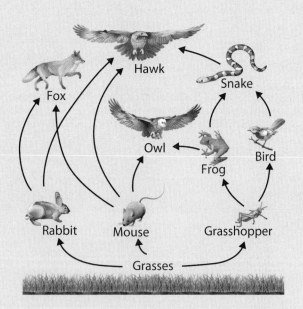

27. **Predict** A person vacationing on a tropical island discovers a plant that only grows on that island. He decides to bring it home and plant it in his New England garden. Do you think this plant will become invasive? Why or why not?

28. **Apply Concepts** What is a climax community? How have ecologists' views of climax communities changed?

Analyze Data

For nearly 100 years, scientists at the University of Toronto collected data for hare and lynx populations in Ontario, Canada. Their data are below. Use the graph to answer the questions that follow.

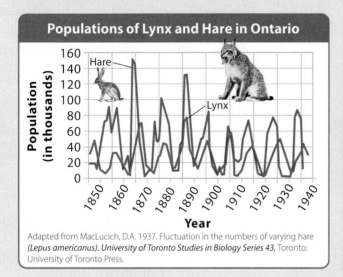

Populations of Lynx and Hare in Ontario

Adapted from MacLucich, D.A. 1937. Fluctuation in the numbers of varying hare *(Lepus americanus). University of Toronto Studies in Biology Series 43,* Toronto: University of Toronto Press.

29. Interpret Graphs Describe the general pattern of the population curves. What kind of relationship do they show?

30. Infer Do you think sampling techniques were used to collect this population data? Explain your reasoning.

31. Predict Suppose a viral infection killed off most of the lynx around 1910. How would the hare population curve differ from the one shown?

32. Analyze Graphs Using only the information in the graph, what caused the drop in the hare population between 1865 and 1870?

Write About It

33. Creative Writing The local aquarium wants your help explaining to the public the importance of sea otters in kelp forest ecosystems. Use illustrations and words to make a sign that could be placed in front of the sea otter exhibit. Explain the concept of "keystone species" and describe the role sea otters play in nature.

34. REVISIT INVESTIGATIVE PHENOMENON You have learned that competition can have big effects on organisms. Write a paragraph in which you describe a situation in which competition, through the process of natural selection, leads to a change in the behavior or physical appearance of an organism.

Ecological Footprints

Read the information below. Copy the table into your notebook and record your calculations. Then, answer the questions that follow.

In 2003, scientist David Pimentel reviewed available data on the ecological and economic costs of invasive species in the United States. He estimated that the cost of controlling just the aquatic invasive species was about $9 billion a year. He also estimated that 50,000 species had been introduced to the United States in the proportions shown in the table. Use this information to fill in the table.

1. About how many more invasive species in the United States are plants than mammals?

2. If zebra and quagga mussels represent 11% of the cost to control aquatic invaders, about how much money per year is spent on them?

3. Why do you think there are so many more invasive plants than invasive mammals and birds?

	Percentage of Total Introduced	Number of Species Introduced
Plants	30.00	
Mammals	0.04	
Birds	0.19	
Mollusks	0.18	
Arthropods	9.00	
Microbes	40.00	
Other	20.59	

Source: Pimentel, D., 2003. Economic and ecological costs associated with aquatic invasive species. *Proceedings of the Aquatic Invaders of the Delaware Estuary Symposium,* Malvern, Pennsylvania, May 20, 2003.

 MATH SUPPORT For help multiplying with percentages, see the Math Handbook.

CHAPTER 6

Biomes and Aquatic Ecosystems

How do organisms interact with the environment?

African elephants are protected in Hwange National Park in Zimbabwe, Africa.

Lesson 1
Defining Biomes

Lesson 2
Biomes

Lesson 3
Aquatic Ecosystems

Too Much of a Good Thing?

CAN YOU EVER have too much of a good thing? It seems strange, but there are many people who think that Africa has too much of a very good thing—elephants.

Historically, millions of elephants roamed across sub-Saharan (mostly nondesert) Africa. Throughout the nineteenth century, however, hunters seeking ivory tusks decimated the elephant population. Thanks to nature preserves and hunting regulations, elephants have since made an impressive comeback. For example, Hwange National Park was established in present-day Zimbabwe in 1928 to protect the country's remaining 1000–2500 elephants. Today, the park is home to about 53,000 elephants. South Africa's Addo Elephant National Park was established in 1931 with 11 elephants. Around 600 live there today.

African elephants are the largest land animals on Earth. To sustain their bulk, elephants must eat hundreds of kilograms of leaves, twigs, bark, fruits, and roots every day. In search of food, elephants are always on the move. As they roam, trampling the ground, shaking trees, and digging dirt, elephants create open spaces that allow new kinds of plants to flourish in their wake. Forests are converted to shrubland, and shrubland to grassland.

These disturbances used to occur relatively infrequently as elephants made their way over huge expanses of land. As such, they tended to increase an area's biodiversity. Unfortunately, elephants today are mostly confined to parks and nature reserves that are running out of room. Experts recommend an elephant density of less than one elephant (0.6) per square kilometer. Elephant density in Hwange National Park is more than six times that. Such a dense population of such a large animal is bound to cause problems—and it has.

Instead of increasing biodiversity, elephants are decreasing it in some areas. Habitats used

GO ONLINE
• Take It Local   • 3-D Geo Tour

by other organisms are being destroyed, and elephants are out-competing some species for food and water. Elephants are also colliding with the human world, wandering off protected areas and eating crops, trampling farmland, and digging up water pipes.

Limited resources can bring issues related to the population density of elephants in the park to the forefront. In 2019, about 200 elephants in the park died as a result of a severe drought in Zimbabwe. Park officials responded by moving 600 elephants to other parks that were not as crowded. Other efforts to control elephant populations include injecting them with proteins that prevent pregnancies, and, most controversially, shooting herds from helicopters, a practice called culling.

Elephants can't help but alter their habitat—they've been doing it for millions of years. Can the need to protect the elephant's environment be balanced with the need to protect the elephant?

Defining Biomes

EVERYDAY PHENOMENON What makes Zimbabwe a suitable place for elephants to live?

Knowledge and Skills

- Explain how biomes are characterized.
- Describe how net primary production varies among biomes.

Reading Strategy and Vocabulary

✅ **Reading Strategy** As you read the lesson, make a concept map. Begin with a circle for *biome* and then use linking words to connect "biome" to each of the other vocabulary words for the lesson.

Vocabulary biome, climate, weather, climatograph, net primary production

WHAT SHOULD OUR PLANET LOOK LIKE? In North America, fossil evidence suggests that when woolly mammoths and other great mammals of the last ice age went extinct, a dramatic ecological shift occurred. Over time, open grasslands gave way to vast areas of forest. Does that mean that North America is "supposed" to be forested? Would the ecosystems of southern Africa return to a "normal" state without their dense populations of elephants? What determines what plants and animals are native to an area? In other words, what makes a natural community *natural*?

What Is a Biome?

South Africa's Addo Elephant National Park is facing a difficult situation: The reserve was established within a rare ecosystem known as succulent thicket, and the 600 resident elephants are having negative effects on its biodiversity. Recall that an ecosystem includes all of the living things in a particular area plus their physical environments. Across the world, each continent has many ecosystems with different sets of specific abiotic and biotic conditions. However, ecosystems in places scattered around the globe can share similarities in their structure and function.

Earth's Major Biomes Ecologists use similarities among ecosystems to classify them into broad categories called biomes. A **biome** is a group of ecosystems that share similar abiotic and biotic conditions. Although there are several different ways to categorize biomes, each varying slightly in the details, biomes are always primarily defined by their climate and typical plant and animal life. The world contains many biomes, each covering large areas. The major biomes discussed in this text are shown in **Figure 1.** The three main biomes in Southern Africa are desert, savanna, and chaparral. Succulent thicket is one of the ecosystems that makes up the chaparral biome. Succulent thicket is characterized by grasses and short fleshy plants.

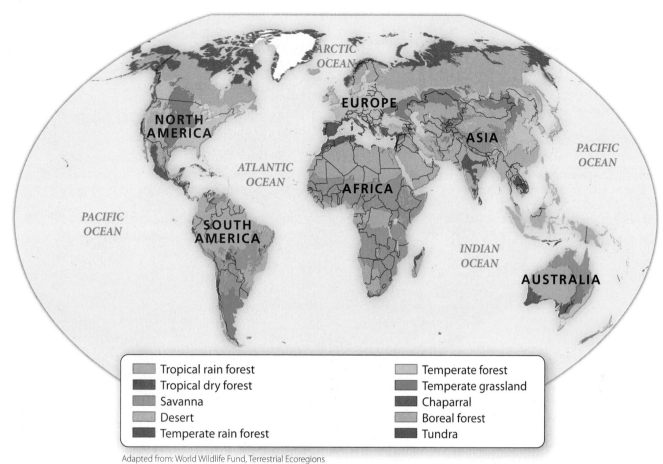

Tropical rain forest | Temperate forest
Tropical dry forest | Temperate grassland
Savanna | Chaparral
Desert | Boreal forest
Temperate rain forest | Tundra

Adapted from: World Wildlife Fund, Terrestrial Ecoregions

FIGURE 1 Major Biomes This map shows the locations of Earth's major biomes. Biomes are characterized by their climate and typical plant and animal life.

Biomes and Climate A region's climate largely determines which biome covers any particular portion of the planet. **Climate** describes the average conditions, including temperature and precipitation, over long periods in a given area. Climate is different from **weather,** the day-to-day conditions in Earth's atmosphere like "sunny and humid" or "cold and snowy." Scientists often use climate diagrams, or **climatographs,** to describe the conditions in a biome. A typical climatograph is shown in **Figure 2.** You will see many examples of climatographs in the next lesson.

 Reading Checkpoint *What's the difference between an ecosystem and a biome?*

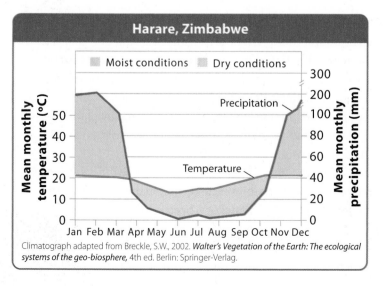

Climatograph adapted from Breckle, S.W., 2002. *Walter's Vegetation of the Earth: The ecological systems of the geo-biosphere,* 4th ed. Berlin: Springer-Verlag.

FIGURE 2 Climatograph Scientists use climate diagrams to illustrate an area's average monthly precipitation and temperature. The twin curves plotted on a climate diagram indicate trends in precipitation (blue) and in temperature (orange) from month to month. When the precipitation curve lies above the temperature curve, the region experiences relatively "moist" conditions, which we indicate with blue shading. Orange shading indicates relatively dry conditions.

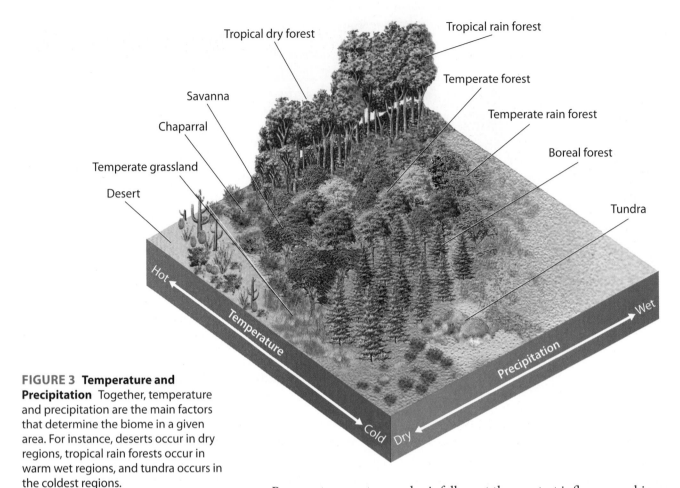

Tropical dry forest

Tropical rain forest

Temperate forest

Savanna

Temperate rain forest

Chaparral

Boreal forest

Temperate grassland

Tundra

Desert

Hot

Wet

Temperature

Precipitation

Cold   Dry

FIGURE 3 Temperature and Precipitation Together, temperature and precipitation are the main factors that determine the biome in a given area. For instance, deserts occur in dry regions, tropical rain forests occur in warm wet regions, and tundra occurs in the coldest regions.

Because temperature and rainfall exert the greatest influence on biome classification, we can "plot" biomes according to these factors, as seen in **Figure 3.** Global climate patterns cause biomes to occur in large patches in different parts of the world. For instance, temperate forest is found in North America, north-central Europe, and eastern China. Note on the biome map that patches representing the same biome tend to occur at similar latitudes. This is due to the north–south gradient in temperature (temperatures get warmer toward the equator) and to atmospheric circulation patterns. You will learn more about these climate factors in a later chapter.

Biomes and Organisms Remember that natural selection results in the survival and reproduction of organisms best suited to their current environment. Although some organisms can thrive in a variety of conditions, each biome tends to have a suite of characteristic organisms adapted to its particular set of conditions. After all, organisms that thrive in the desert are not likely to do as well in the tropical rain forest! However, within any biome, there is some degree of variation among plant and animal communities.

The chaparral biome, for example, consists of a few different ecosystems, including the succulent thicket. Likewise, many different types of temperate forest, such as oak–hickory, beech–maple, and pine–oak forests, make up the temperate forest biome that covers most of the eastern United States. These variations within biomes can be caused by local differences such as soil type, elevation, or wind exposure.

FIND OUT MORE

your world • your turn

Use the Internet or other references to find the average monthly temperature and precipitation last year for your hometown or nearest large city. Plot both sets of data. In the next lesson, you can see if your graphs match the climatograph for your biome.

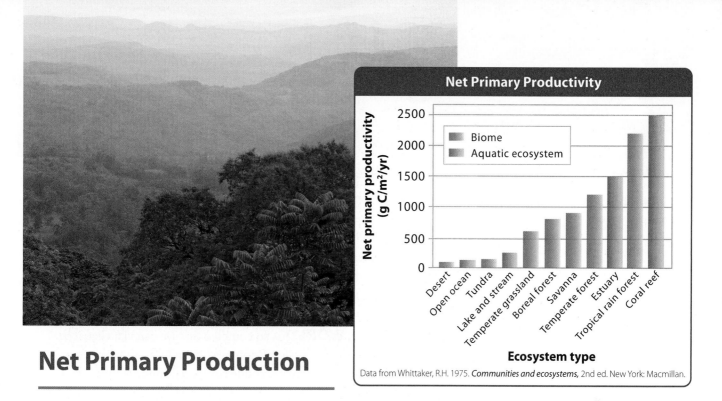

Net Primary Production

Net Primary Productivity

Data from Whittaker, R.H. 1975. *Communities and ecosystems,* 2nd ed. New York: Macmillan.

Ecologists compare biomes not only based on their climates and typical organisms, but also on how productive they are; that is, how much new organic matter they generate. Plants and other primary producers convert solar or chemical energy into energy stored in the bonds of organic sugars. Over a given unit of time, the rate at which primary producers carry out this conversion of energy is called *gross primary production*. Primary producers use a portion of this production to carry out their own life functions through cellular respiration. **Net primary production** is the organic matter, or biomass, that remains after cellular respiration.

Ecosystems vary in their *net primary productivity,* which is the rate at which primary producers convert energy to biomass. The annual net primary productivity for some of the major biomes and aquatic ecosystems is shown in **Figure 4.** Notice that, in general, warmer and wetter biomes have higher net primary productivity than colder and drier biomes. This trend should make sense, since plants require sunlight, water, and warm enough temperatures to grow. In aquatic ecosystems, net primary production is limited by the sunlight and nutrients that are available.

FIGURE 4 Primary Productivity On land, net primary productivity varies geographically with temperature and precipitation. In general, warm and wet biomes, such as the rain forest seen here in Brazil, have higher primary productivity than cold, dry biomes. Net primary productivity in aquatic ecosystems is related to available sunlight and nutrients.

LESSON ① Assessment

1. **Interpret Visuals** Locate tropical rain forests and tundra in both **Figure 1** and **Figure 3.** Describe the general climate and global location of both biomes.

2. **Explain** What is net primary productivity? Which biome has higher net primary productivity: tropical rain forest or tundra? Does this make sense based on your answer to Question 1 above?

3. REVISIT
   INVESTIGATIVE PHENOMENON
   You have learned that the environment influences organisms through natural selection. What kinds of adaptations would you expect the plants and animals in a desert to have?

Biomes

EVERYDAY PHENOMENON Why are vines more likely to grow in a rain forest than in a desert?

Knowledge and Skills

- Explain how organisms are adapted to the conditions of their biomes.

Reading Strategy and Vocabulary

✔ **Reading Strategy** As you read the lesson, make a compare/contrast table that summarizes the abiotic and biotic characteristics of each major biome.

Vocabulary canopy, emergent layer, understory, epiphyte, deciduous, estivation, coniferous, hibernation, permafrost

THE NATURAL WORLD is so complex that we can visualize it in many ways and at various scales. Zoom way in and find differences in the organisms living on the shaded side compared to the sunny side of a tree. Zoom out and find differences between the forests of New York and the forests of Virginia. Zoom even farther out, and find the differences between biomes.

Tropical Rain Forest

Tropical rain forests are found in Central America, South America, Southeast Asia, West Africa, and other tropical regions. Tropical regions are located close to the equator and are characterized by year-round warm temperatures and near constant 12-hour days. Tropical rain forests receive more rain than any other biome—at least 2 meters (6.6 feet) per year. Nearly all nutrients present in this biome are contained in the trees, vines, and other plants—not in the soil. Any available organic material is quickly recycled by decomposers and taken up by plants. As a result, many tropical rain forests cleared for farming leave behind nutrient-poor soils that can only support crops for a short time.

Intact tropical rain forests contain an astonishing variety of plant life. A single square kilometer can host hundreds of tree species. Tall trees form a dense covering, called the **canopy,** that towers 50 to 80 meters above the ground. The tallest trees pop through the canopy and make up the top layer of the rain forest, known as the **emergent layer.** The canopy keeps the forest dark and damp. Shorter trees and plants that make up the **understory** compete for available light. Large, flat leaves are typical of understory plants as they allow maximum surface for light absorption. In addition, rainforest plants tend to have shallow roots that maximize their absorption of what little nutrients are available in the uppermost soil layers.

Bumblebee dart frog

Rainforest plants display a variety of adaptations that enable them to survive in a place where nutrients and light are in short supply. For example, pitcher plants and other predatory plant life trap curious animals and dissolve them, gaining nutrients in the process. **Epiphytes** are plants that grow on other plants instead of in soil. These plants, such as orchids, take advantage of their hosts' height to gain access to sunlight.

While tall plants may have an advantage competing for light, they require support to stay upright, especially when draped with vines and loaded with epiphytes. Buttresses, large aboveground roots, provide stability in the shallow rainforest soil. Another challenge for plants is reproduction. Because there is little wind to help spread pollen, many rainforest plants grow bright, attractive flowers to lure potential pollinators, such as butterflies.

In addition to their dizzying variety of plants, tropical rain forests support far more animal species than any other biome. Rainforest birds, insects, amphibians, and other animals tend to be highly specialized, feeding on a particular kind of food or living on a particular sort of plant. Millions of years of evolution have resulted in animals finely tuned for life in the tropical rain forest. Monkeys, for example, have long limbs and a grasping, prehensile tail that enable them to swing easily through the canopy trees.

Reading Checkpoint *What are the major layers of the rain forest?*

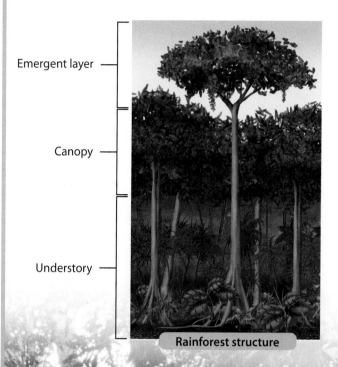

Emergent layer

Canopy

Understory

Rainforest structure

TROPICAL RAIN FORESTS, famed for their biodiversity, grow where there are constant warm temperatures and a great deal of rain.

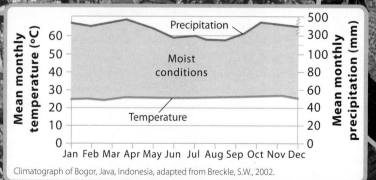

Climatograph of Bogor, Java, Indonesia, adapted from Breckle, S.W., 2002.

Precipitation

Moist conditions

Temperature

Wild orchid

Tropical rain forest, Sarawak, Malaysia

Tropical Dry Forest

Tropical areas that are warm year-round but where rainfall is highly seasonal give rise to tropical dry forest, or tropical deciduous forest. Tropical dry forests are widespread in India, southern North America, Central America, South America, and southeast Asia. Wet and dry seasons each span about half a year. Precipitation during the wet season can be extremely heavy. Across the globe, people have converted a great deal of tropical dry forest for agriculture. Clearing the land for farming or ranching is relatively easy because vegetation is much shorter and canopies less dense than in a tropical rain forest.

Organisms that inhabit tropical dry forests have adapted to seasonal fluctuations in precipitation and temperature. For instance, most trees are deciduous. **Deciduous** trees lose their leaves and stop photosynthesis during part of the year. Seasonal loss of leaves is beneficial in dry climates because it enables plants to seal off the area between the leaf stem and trunk, preventing water loss. Trees survive by consuming food stored in their tissues. Some plants, like the "striking green giant" shown here, have the ability to maintain photosynthesis even after they drop their leaves because their bark contains chlorophyll. Many plants that keep their leaves year-round have an extra coating of wax on their leaves to prevent water loss during the dry season. Roots tend to be deeper here than in a tropical rain forest, which enables trees to seek water deeper in the soil. Some plants store water in their tissues for use during the dry season. Thick bark protects trees from occasional fires.

Animals, too, must cope with the lack of water during much of the year. When conditions are dry, some animals enter a deep, sleeplike period of dormancy called **estivation.** Animals that do not enter dormancy, including most bird species, may migrate to areas where water is more plentiful.

✓ **Reading Checkpoint** *How do the plants and animals of the tropical dry forest cope with the dry season?*

TROPICAL DRY FORESTS experience significant seasonal variations in precipitation and relatively stable warm temperatures.

Indian pitta

Ceibo tree, "striking green giant"

Climatograph of Darwin, Australia, adapted from Breckle, S.W., 2002.

Tropical dry forest, Madhya Pradesh, India

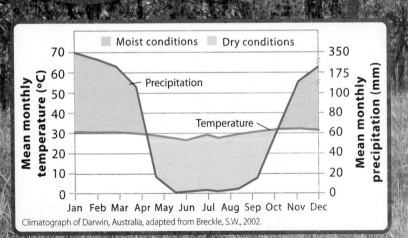

| Savanna | Tropical regions with less rain than tropical dry forests, but more rain than deserts, are called savannas, or tropical grasslands. Here, grasses are interspersed with clusters of acacias or other trees. Frequent fires and strong winds discourage much tree growth. The savanna biome is found today across stretches of Africa, South America, Australia, India, and other dry, tropical regions. Precipitation in savannas usually arrives during distinct rainy seasons. Savanna soil is very porous, so water drains through it quickly, making it even more difficult for organisms to find water during the dry season.

To cope with the frequent dry periods, savanna plants tend to be deciduous and extra waxy coatings are common. Plants here also tend to grow quickly, enabling them to recover quickly from fire damage and to make the most of available water. Deep roots help plants access water, and thick bark protects plant tissues from fire. Some plants, like the baobab tree, or "tree of life," store water for the dry season. As protection against herbivory, some plants develop bitter tastes, rough texture, or thorns that make them less appetizing.

Elephants drink 100–200 liters (30–50 gallons) of water every day. When water is scarce, they dig for water using their massive ivory tusks. Elephants cause significant damage to baobob trees by using their tusks to reach the water stored in the trunks. Grazing animals, such as zebras, wildebeest, gazelles, and giraffes migrate in search of water and usually gather near widely spaced water holes. Predators such as lions, hyenas, and leopards follow their migrating prey. Some small animals burrow to avoid predation and remain dormant during the dry season. Many animals give birth only in the rainy season, when food and water are abundant.

Reading Checkpoint *Why is migration so common in the savanna?*

 Connect to the Central Case

SAVANNAS are grasslands with clusters of trees. They experience slight seasonal variation in temperature but significant variation in rainfall. **Interpret Graphs** According to the graph below, when is Zimbabwe's rainy season?

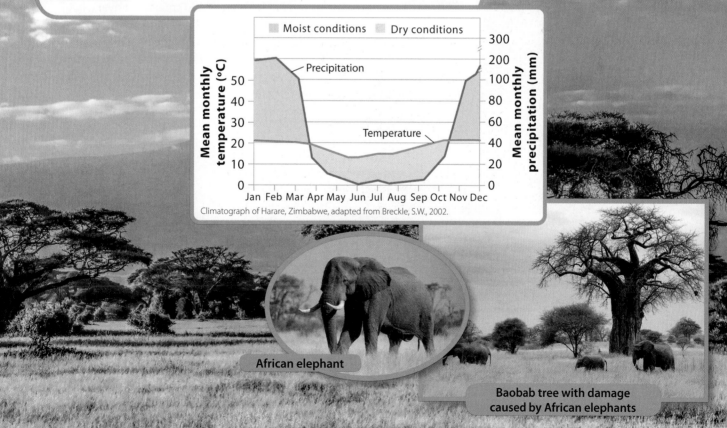

Climatograph of Harare, Zimbabwe, adapted from Breckle, S.W., 2002.

African elephant

Baobab tree with damage caused by African elephants

Savanna, near Mount Kenya, Kenya

Desert

Deserts are the driest biome on Earth. Most deserts receive well under 25 centimeters (9.8 inches) of precipitation per year, much of it during isolated storms that occur months or even years apart. Depending on rainfall, deserts vary greatly in the amount of vegetation they support. Some, such as the Sahara and Namib deserts of Africa, are mostly bare sand dunes; others, such as the Sonoran Desert of Arizona and northwest Mexico, are home to a great diversity of plants. Without a lot of water, desert air tends to be very dry. Sunlight quickly heats up dry air in the daytime, but the heat is quickly lost at night. As a result, temperatures vary widely from day to night and across seasons of the year. Because there is not very much plant life in the desert, soils here contain very little organic matter.

Desert animals and plants have many adaptations that enable them to survive their harsh climate. Desert animals get most of the water they need from the food they eat, and they tend to release very concentrated urine, to conserve water. Many desert animals are *nocturnal,* meaning they are active only in the cool of night. Gila monsters can spend days at a time in their cool, underground burrows. Desert mammals, like the kangaroo rat, tend to be small. Exaggerated appendages, such as large ears, help them get rid of excess body heat. Many Australian desert birds are nomadic, wandering long distances to find areas of recent rainfall and plant growth.

Desert plants tend to have thick, leathery leaves to reduce water loss. Many desert plants, called *succulents,* store water in their tissues. Cacti and aloe vera are examples of succulents. The sharp, tough spines of cacti are modified leaves that discourage herbivores desperate for the precious water contained within their tissues. Cacti and many other desert plants have green stems and trunks that enable the plants to perform photosynthesis without broad leaves.

The roots of desert plants tend to be shallow and spread out over a large area, enabling the plant to quickly gather any available water. Plants such as the mesquite tree, however, take advantage of water deep underground. Although they also have roots near the surface, mesquite trees send taproots deep into the ground in search of water. Scientists discovered one mesquite tree with roots stretching 50 meters (164 feet) below ground.

Reading Checkpoint *How much precipitation do deserts receive in a year?*

DESERTS are dry year-round, but they are not always hot. Precipitation can arrive in intense, widely spaced storm events.

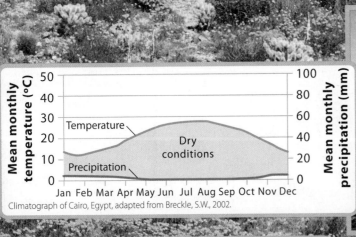

Climatograph of Cairo, Egypt, adapted from Breckle, S.W., 2002.

Desert, Arizona, United States

Aloe vera

Gila monster

Temperate Rain Forest

Temperate rain forests occur in regions with heavy rainfall and year-round moderate temperatures. The largest extent of this biome occurs in the Pacific Northwest coast of the United States. However, small bits (too small to show up on our biome map) can be found in South America and Asia.

Cedars, spruces, hemlocks, and Douglas fir trees grow very tall in the temperate rain forest. These types of trees are called *evergreen* trees because they do not annually lose their leaves. Many evergreen species in the temperate rainforest are **coniferous** trees, trees that produce seed-bearing cones. Coniferous trees, also known as *conifers*, have needlelike leaves that are coated in a thick, waxy substance that helps minimize moisture loss. Coniferous trees are so common in this biome that it is sometimes called the northwestern coniferous forest. Plants in the temperate forest compete for sunlight, so being tall is an advantage. Indeed, trees here are among the world's tallest. Temperate rain forests can produce large volumes of commercially important forest products, such as lumber and paper.

The abundance of rainfall and tall trees causes the forest interior to be shaded and damp. These are perfect conditions for moss, which blankets most of the forest floor. Moisture-loving animals such as the bright yellow banana slug and numerous amphibian species are common. Squirrels, deer, elk, and birds have varied diets that enable them to eat whatever food is available.

✓ **Reading Checkpoint** *What is the difference between an evergreen and deciduous tree?*

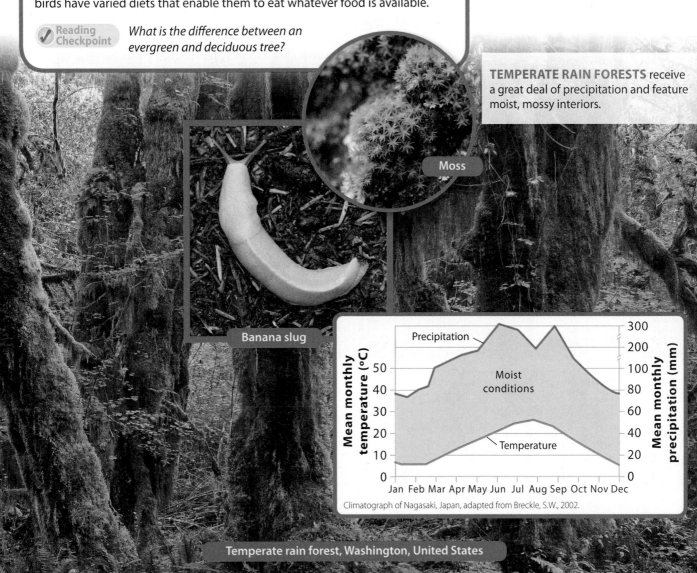

TEMPERATE RAIN FORESTS receive a great deal of precipitation and feature moist, mossy interiors.

Moss

Banana slug

Climatograph of Nagasaki, Japan, adapted from Breckle, S.W., 2002.

Temperate rain forest, Washington, United States

Temperate Forest   Broad-leafed deciduous trees characterize the temperate forests that cover most of Europe, eastern Asia, and the eastern United States. Seasonal loss of leaves enables plants to avoid damage during harsh winter freezes. When longer days and warmer temperatures return, leaves regrow and plants resume photosynthesis. Oaks, beeches, and maples are a few of the most abundant types of deciduous trees in these forests. Annual leaf drop enriches the soil of the deciduous forest with nutrients through decomposition.

Temperate forests occur in areas where precipitation is spread relatively evenly throughout the year. Organisms that live in the temperate forest experience a range of temperature conditions throughout the seasons, from quite hot in the summer to very cold in the winter. Temperate forest animals have a variety of adaptations that enable them to deal with the shifting temperatures. Some animals, like most birds, migrate to warmer areas until the winter passes. Instead of moving to avoid the winter, some animals, like black bears and some snake species, hibernate. **Hibernation** is a deep, sleeplike state that an animal enters for most of the winter. Note the similarity between estivation and hibernation. The only difference is the type of condition that triggers the period of inactivity: lack of water for estivation, and cold for hibernation. By hibernating, animals avoid expending energy looking for food in the coldest months. Instead, they live off stored fat.

Animals that remain active all winter, like deer mice and eastern chipmunks, prepare for food shortages in the winter by building up their own fat reserves and hiding food for later consumption. Others, such as white-tailed deer and eastern cottontail rabbits, survive in the winter by eating the little food that is available, such as moss and tree bark. Camouflage helps animals that are active in the winter avoid predation when the lack of leaves makes them more exposed.

✔ **Reading Checkpoint**   *Why do animals hibernate?*

TEMPERATE FORESTS experience relatively stable seasonal precipitation but more varied seasonal temperatures.

Maple leaves

American black bear

Mean monthly temperature (°C) — Precipitation — Moist conditions — Temperature — Mean monthly precipitation (mm)

Jan Feb Mar Apr May Jun Jul Aug Sep Oct Nov Dec

Climatograph of Washington, D.C., USA, adapted from Breckle, S.W., 2002.

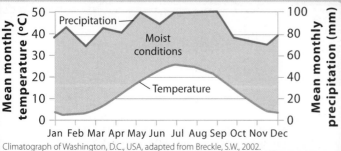

Temperate forest, Connecticut, United States

Temperate Grassland

Temperate grasslands, sometimes called prairies or steppes, occur in areas with moderate seasonal precipitation, but not enough precipitation to support the large trees common in temperate forests. Temperatures in the grassland also tend to be more extreme than the temperate forest. Periodic fires and droughts are common here.

Temperate grasslands used to cover most of the central and midwestern United States. However, like most of the world's temperate grasslands, this region has been almost entirely converted for agriculture to take advantage of the rich, fertile soil. The soil's fertility comes from the tendency for grassland plants to die in the winter. While roots remain, the bulk of the plant dies off, contributing its organic content to the soil.

Grasses have many adaptations that enable them to thrive in temperate grasslands. In fact, they are so successful and common that they give the biome its name! Grasses, unlike most plants, grow from their bases, not their tips. This enables grasses to continue growing after being grazed by wildlife or harmed by drought or fire. The roots of grasses also form thick mats that help capture moisture and nutrients and avoid damage in harsh conditions. Like most grassland plants, grasses use wind to disperse their seeds. On the open plains, strong winds that could damage tall trees do not harm grassland grasses and shrubs.

Without trees and taller vegetation, animals in the temperate grassland have few places to hide. Some animals, such as the prairie dog, burrow underground to limit their exposure to predators such as owls, coyotes, and foxes. Some animals survive by being the biggest thing around. Not much bothers the herds of great American bison, for example, that migrate south in the winter in search of exposed grass.

Reading Checkpoint *Why has so much grassland been converted for agriculture?*

TEMPERATE GRASSLANDS experience temperature variations throughout the year and too little precipitation for many trees to grow.

Grass, showing roots

Coyote

Moist conditions Dry conditions

Precipitation Temperature

Mean monthly temperature (°C): 40, 30, 20, 10, 0, −10

Mean monthly precipitation (mm): 60, 40, 20, 0

Jan Feb Mar Apr May Jun Jul Aug Sep Oct Nov Dec

Climatograph of Odessa, Ukraine, adapted from Breckle, S.W., 2002.

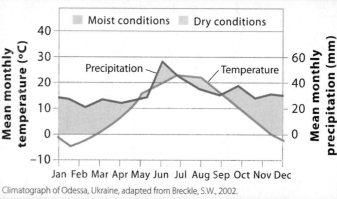

Temperate grassland, Wisconsin, United States

Chaparral

Conditions in the chaparral biome are highly seasonal, with mild, wet winters and warm, dry summers. This type of climate is common near oceans and is found around the Mediterranean Sea in Europe and Africa (in fact, chaparral is sometimes described as the "Mediterranean biome"). Chaparral is also located along the coasts of California, Chile, southern Australia, and southern Africa. Soils in the chaparral are often thin and not rich in nutrients.

Plant life in the chaparral must be able to withstand periods of drought. The most common types of vegetation are shrubs, such as the common sagebrush, and small trees, such as olive trees and blue oaks. Most plants have thick waxy leaves that help prevent water loss during the lengthy dry season. Some chaparral plants have hairs on their leaves that help gather moisture. South Africa's succulent thicket ecosystem, found in Addo Elephant National Park, features a number of succulent plants that withstand the dry season by holding water in their tissues. Succulents make up a little more than 10 percent of a typical elephant's diet within the reserve.

Chaparral communities experience frequent fire due to prolonged periods of hot temperatures and dry conditions. Plant species here are adapted to live with, or resist, fire. Many have thick bark and deep roots that can survive fire exposure, while a few plant species actually benefit from it. For these species, fire can help seeds to germinate, clear away dead vegetation, or help recycle nutrients. Some plants of the chaparral, such as sage, eucalyptus, and thyme, contain oily, flammable compounds that deter herbivores, but also encourage the spread of fire.

Animals living in the chaparral also need to cope with hot, dry conditions. Many animals, such as the pocket mouse or Mediterranean gecko, are nocturnal, which enables them to avoid the hottest temperatures of the day. Burrowing is a common behavior here, as it enables animals to avoid daytime heat and times of fire. Some animals, such as jackrabbits, have long legs and ears that help them to regulate their body temperature. African elephants lack sweat glands, so heat regulation would be a real problem if it weren't for their oversized ears that radiate excess heat.

Reading Checkpoint *How does fire help some chaparral plants?*

Connect to the Central Case

CHAPARRAL is a highly seasonal biome dominated by shrubs, influenced by marine weather, and dependent on fire. In many ways, the chaparral climate is similar to that of the savanna though the vegetation types are different. As elephants disrupt the landscape, grassland plants may move in to areas of chaparral before eventually giving way to shrubs again. **Infer** How might elephants alter chaparral landscapes?

Jackrabbit

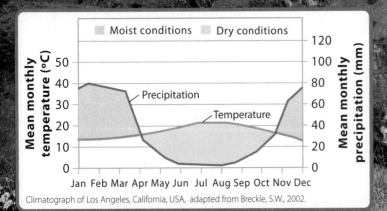

Sagebrush with forget-me-not flower

Climatograph of Los Angeles, California, USA, adapted from Breckle, S.W., 2002.

Chaparral, California, United States

Boreal Forest

The boreal forest, or taiga, stretches in a broad band across much of Canada, Alaska, Russia, and Scandinavia. These forests develop in cooler, drier regions than do temperate forests. They experience long, cold winters and short, cool summers. Soils are typically nutrient-poor and somewhat acidic.

Species diversity is low in the boreal forest. Huge stretches of forest may consist of just a few species of coniferous trees, such as black spruce. Conifers are well adapted to the harsh boreal-forest climate. Their conical shape sheds snow so it does not pile up on tree branches. Waxy needles avoid excess water loss, which is important when the ground is frozen and the trees' roots cannot take up water. Since they do not shed their needles all at once, conifers can undergo photosynthesis as soon as conditions allow. There is no waiting period while leaves regrow. Many conifers have symbiotic relationships with fungi that enable them to make use of scarce nutrients.

As a result of the strong seasonal variation in day length, temperature, and precipitation, many animals compress a year's worth of feeding, breeding, and rearing of young into the few warm, wet months. Year-round residents of boreal forests include mammals such as moose, wolves, bears, lynx, and many burrowing rodents. Boreal forest animals tend to have small extremities and thick insulation (such as fat, fur, or feathers) to avoid losing heat. Some boreal forest dwellers change color to avoid predation in the winter. Snowshoe hares and ermines, for example, grow white coats when cold temperatures bring the snow, but are mostly covered in brown fur during the summer.

Other animals come to the boreal forest only for the short, mild summer. Many insect-eating birds, for example, migrate from the tropics to breed in the boreal forest once warm temperatures bring about an influx of insects to feed on. When temperatures drop again, however, they return to warmer climates in the tropics.

Reading Checkpoint *Explain how conifers are well adapted to the boreal-forest environment.*

BOREAL FOREST is characterized by long, cold winters, relatively cool summers, and moderate precipitation.

Black spruce

Ermine, in winter coat

Climatograph of Archangelsk, Russia, adapted from Breckle, S.W., 2002.

Boreal forest, Newfoundland, Canada

Tundra

Nearly as dry as a desert, tundra occurs at very high latitudes along the northern edges of Alaska, Canada, Scandinavia, and Russia. Due to its position near the North Pole, extremely cold, dark winters and moderately cool, bright summers characterize this biome's climate. In the winter, when this part of Earth is angled away from the sun, days are short and temperatures very cold. When it is angled toward the sun in the summer, days are long and temperatures relatively mild.

Harsh winds, nutrient-poor soils, and freezing temperatures limit plant growth. Tundra supports no tall trees, only low, scrubby vegetation and ground-hugging mosses and lichens. Some trees, such as willows, have dwarf forms that grow close to the ground. Most seed dispersal happens by wind. Some plants have symbiotic relationships with bacteria on their roots that enable them to gain additional nutrients.

Because of the cold climate, underground soil remains frozen year-round, and is called **permafrost.** During the long, cold winters, the surface soils freeze as well. When the weather warms, the ice in the soil melts and produces seasonal accumulations of surface water that make ideal habitats for mosquitoes and other biting insects. The swarms of insects benefit bird species that migrate long distances to breed during the brief but productive summer. Every year, thousands of caribou migrate to the tundra to breed, feeding on vast fields of lichens. Caribou are well adapted to the cold tundra. They have thick coats packed with insulating air spaces and wide hooves that enable them to move easily across mud and snow. Even caribou, however, leave this harsh environment for the winter. Only a few animals, such as polar bears and musk oxen, can survive year-round in this extreme climate.

✓ **Reading Checkpoint** *Why do plants of the tundra tend to be short?*

TUNDRA is a cold, damp biome found near the poles and atop high mountains at lower latitudes.

Dwarf willow

Musk oxen

Mean monthly temperature (°C)

Mean monthly precipitation (mm)

Moist conditions

Precipitation

Temperature

Jan Feb Mar Apr May Jun Jul Aug Sep Oct Nov Dec

Climatograph of Vaigach, Russia, adapted from Breckle, S.W., 2002.

Tundra, Yukon Territory, Canada

Which Biome?

Average monthly temperature data from two different biomes are shown in the graph. Location *A* has a total annual precipitation of 13.5 cm. Location *B* has a total annual precipitation of 69.1 cm. Use this information and the graph to answer the questions that follow.

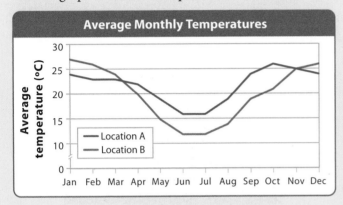

Average Monthly Temperatures

Average temperature (°C)

Jan Feb Mar Apr May Jun Jul Aug Sep Oct Nov Dec

— Location A
— Location B

1. **Interpret Graphs** Describe the annual temperature trends in both locations included in the graph.
2. **Interpret Graphs** Based only on the graph, it is obvious that Locations *A* and *B* are both in the Southern Hemisphere. Why?
3. **Infer** Both Location *A* and Location *B* are cities in Africa. One of them is a city near a large elephant reserve. Given the data in the graph and the annual precipitation at each location, which location do you think is near the elephant reserve? Explain your reasoning.

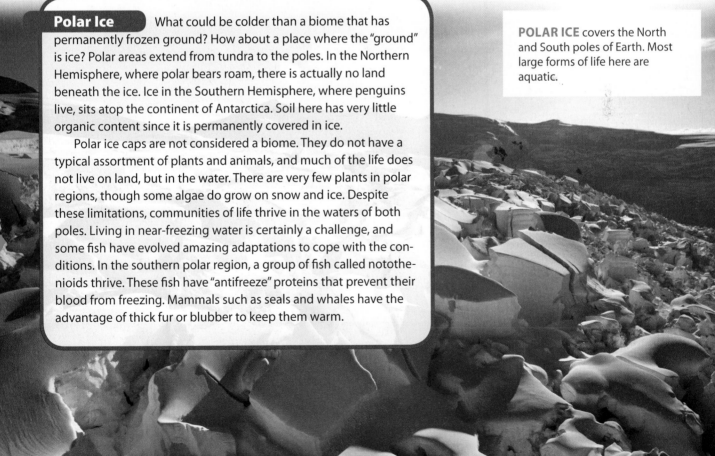

Polar Ice What could be colder than a biome that has permanently frozen ground? How about a place where the "ground" is ice? Polar areas extend from tundra to the poles. In the Northern Hemisphere, where polar bears roam, there is actually no land beneath the ice. Ice in the Southern Hemisphere, where penguins live, sits atop the continent of Antarctica. Soil here has very little organic content since it is permanently covered in ice.

Polar ice caps are not considered a biome. They do not have a typical assortment of plants and animals, and much of the life does not live on land, but in the water. There are very few plants in polar regions, though some algae do grow on snow and ice. Despite these limitations, communities of life thrive in the waters of both poles. Living in near-freezing water is certainly a challenge, and some fish have evolved amazing adaptations to cope with the conditions. In the southern polar region, a group of fish called notothenioids thrive. These fish have "antifreeze" proteins that prevent their blood from freezing. Mammals such as seals and whales have the advantage of thick fur or blubber to keep them warm.

POLAR ICE covers the North and South poles of Earth. Most large forms of life here are aquatic.

Mountains   As any hiker or skier knows, climbing in elevation causes a much more rapid change in climate than moving the same distance on flat ground. Like the climate, plant communities change along mountain slopes. It is often said that hiking up a mountain in the southwestern United States is like walking from Mexico to Canada. A hiker climbing up one of southern Arizona's higher mountains would begin in the Sonoran Desert or desert grassland and proceed through oak woodland, pine forest, and finally spruce–fir forest—the equivalent of passing through several biomes. A hiker scaling one of the great peaks of the Andes in Ecuador could begin in tropical rain forest and end amid glaciers in alpine tundra!

✔ **Reading Checkpoint**   *Why do you think mountains are not typically classified as a biome?*

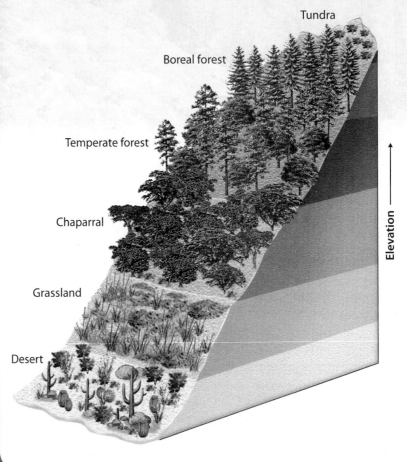

MOUNTAINS host a variety of communities. As altitude increases, vegetation changes in ways similar to the ways it changes as one moves toward the poles. Climbing a mountain in southern Arizona, as pictured here, takes the hiker through the local equivalent of several biomes.

Tundra
Boreal forest
Temperate forest
Chaparral
Grassland
Desert
Elevation

---

② Assessment

1. **Apply Concepts** Select any three of the major biomes and describe their climates. Then, give an example of a plant adaptation and an animal adaptation found in each, and explain how the adaptation benefits the organism.

2. **Compare and Contrast** Explain how climbing a mountain is similar to hiking from the equator to one of the poles.

REVISIT

3. **INVESTIGATIVE** PHENOMENON
   Tundra and deserts both receive very little annual precipitation. Explain why the organisms in these biomes are so different.

Aquatic Ecosystems

EVERYDAY PHENOMENON What conditions and organisms characterize the areas where rivers meet oceans?

Knowledge and Skills

- Describe the criteria ecologists use to classify aquatic ecosystems.
- List the major categories of freshwater ecosystems.
- Explain the ecological importance of estuaries.
- List the three major zones of the ocean.

Reading Strategy and Vocabulary

✓ **Reading Strategy** As you read the lesson, make a cluster diagram for each aquatic ecosystem. Place the ecosystem's name in the center circle, and connect it to words, phrases, or illustrations that describe it.

Vocabulary salinity, photic zone, aphotic zone, benthic zone, littoral zone, limnetic zone, wetland, flood plain, estuary, upwelling

TRADITIONALLY, THE BIOME CONCEPT has been limited to terrestrial (land-based) ecosystems. However, about 75 percent of Earth's surface is covered in water, not land. What characteristics define aquatic environments, and how do ecologists group similar ecosystems into biome-like categories?

Describing Aquatic Ecosystems

Biomes are described by patterns in temperature and precipitation, but there aren't really hot summers or rainy seasons in the deep ocean. While terrestrial biomes are shaped by air temperature and precipitation, aquatic systems are characterized by factors such as water salinity, depth, and whether the water is moving or standing.

Salinity Salinity measures the amount of salts dissolved in water. A straightforward measurement of salinity is parts per thousand (ppt), meaning the number of units of salt dissolved in 1000 units of water. "Salt water" generally has a salinity between 30 and 50 ppt. The oceans have an average salinity of 35 ppt. Water is considered "fresh" if it has a salinity of a 0.5 ppt or less. The aquatic ecosystems with salinity between 0.5 and 30 ppt are called *brackish*.

The salinity of water has direct effects on an aquatic organism's survival. Adaptations enable organisms to maintain careful water and salt balance with their surroundings. Water moves from areas of high concentration (low salinity) to areas of low concentration (high salinity). As such, a freshwater fish placed in salt water would die from water loss, as water moves from an area of higher concentration (the fish) to an area of lower concentration (the salt water). A saltwater fish moved to fresh water would fare no better. The fish would swell and die as water rushed from an area of higher concentration (the fresh water) to an area of lower concentration (the fish).

Depth In most terrestrial environments, primary production is limited by temperature and precipitation. Under water, however, photosynthesis by aquatic plants and phytoplankton is mostly limited by available light. In aquatic ecosystems, light availability is largely a function of water depth.

▶ *Aquatic Layers* The uppermost layer of an aquatic ecosystem, where there is enough sunlight for photosynthesis, is called the **photic zone.** The depth of the photic zone depends on how clear the water is. In some crystal-clear tropical seas, the photic zone may extend over 200 meters (650 feet), but in muddy streams it could be a meter or less. Below the photic zone is the **aphotic zone,** where no sunlight penetrates and photosynthesis cannot occur. The very bottom of a body of water is called the **benthic zone.** Depending on the depth and clarity of the water, benthic zones can be sunlit or pitch dark.

▶ *Depth and Life* Consumers on land rely on oxygen in the air to breathe. Some aquatic consumers, such as sea turtles and whales, breathe in air by periodically rising to the top of the water. Most aquatic consumers, however, do not breathe air. Instead, they obtain the oxygen they need to carry out cellular respiration from water taken in through gills. Dissolved oxygen in the water comes from aquatic photosynthetic organisms that release oxygen during photosynthesis. The photic zone, where photosynthesis can take place, has much more dissolved oxygen than the aphotic zone. Therefore, there tends to be more life—both producers and consumers—in this upper portion of any aquatic ecosystem.

▶ *Depth and Temperature* The presence of sunlight also causes warmer temperatures. Upper layers of aquatic ecosystems tend to be warmer than deeper layers. Temperature shifts can occur, however, brought on by seasonal temperature changes or shifting currents.

Flowing and Standing Water Aquatic ecosystems are sometimes divided into flowing-water and standing-water categories. Flowing-water ecosystems contain water that is in near-constant motion, such as in a river. Standing-water ecosystems contain water that does not move, or moves slowly, such as in a pond or wetland.

FIGURE 5 Light and Dark The photic zone is the area of an aquatic ecosystem that receives sunlight. The depth of the photic zone differs depending on the clarity of the water.

Freshwater Ecosystems

Freshwater ecosystems have very low salinity, less than 0.5 ppt. These ecosystems vary in depth from a few meters to several hundred meters. They can be either standing or flowing.

Ponds, Lakes, and Inland Seas

Ponds and lakes are bodies of open standing water that collect in depressions on Earth's surface. Typically, smaller and shallower bodies of standing water are called ponds and larger, deeper ones are called lakes—though, beyond size and depth, there is no real difference between the two. Some lakes, however, are so large that they differ substantially in their characteristics from smaller lakes. These large lakes are sometimes known as *inland seas*. North America's Great Lakes are prime examples. Because they hold so much water, most of their organisms are adapted for life in open water. The range in size among these freshwater bodies is considerable. Backyard ponds may be only a few square meters while the world's largest inland sea, the Caspian Sea in central Asia, has an area of 371,000 square kilometers (143,000 square miles). Lakes and ponds also vary greatly in their nutrient content. Some may have little to no nutrients at all, whereas others may be so full of nutrients that they literally fill in and become a terrestrial ecosystem through secondary succession.

As shown in **Figure 6,** ecologists tend to divide the photic zone of lakes and ponds based on distance from the shore. The shallow near-shore portion of the photic zone is named the **littoral zone.** Here the water is shallow enough that aquatic plants grow from the mud and reach above the water's surface. The **limnetic zone** is farther from the shore, where there are no rooted plants. The nutrients and plant growth of the littoral zone make it rich in invertebrates—such as insect larvae, snails, and crayfish—on which fish, birds, turtles, and amphibians feed.

Go Outside

Who's in the Water?

❶ Obtain several small, clean jars with lids.

❷ Collect samples of fresh water near your school or home. Samples can come from puddles, ponds, lakes, or rivers. Be sure to label all jars carefully with the location of the sample. If possible, take samples from different water sources and depths.

❸ Examine each sample with a microscope or hand lens.

❹ Use reference materials to identify the organisms you see.

Analyze and Conclude

1. **Compare and Contrast** Which of your samples contained the most life? The least?

2. **Propose a Hypothesis** Explain your findings with a hypothesis that relates to abiotic conditions for life in fresh water.

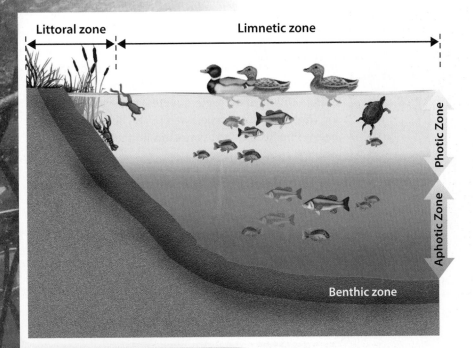

FIGURE 6 Freshwater Zones The photic zone in a pond, lake, or inland sea is divided into the near-shore littoral zone and open limnetic zone.

FIGURE 7 Wetlands Wetlands provide many benefits, such as preventing flooding, purifying water, and serving as home for many commercially important fish species. Three of the four types of wetlands are shown: **(a)** a freshwater marsh, **(b)** a swamp, and **(c)** a bog.

Wetlands Systems that combine elements of fresh water and dry land are enormously rich and productive. Wetlands are areas of land that are flooded with water at least part of the year. Water can either flow slowly through wetlands and into other bodies of water, or can remain year-round. There are four types of freshwater wetlands: marshes, swamps, bogs, and fens (**Figure 7**).

The Ecological Importance of Wetlands

Wetlands are extremely important habitats. They help prevent flooding by absorbing excess water—much like a sponge. Wetlands recharge aquifers and filter pollutants and sediment. Recreational activities like bird-watching and photography also depend on healthy wetlands. Finally, wetlands provide habitats for many species of commercially valuable fish.

Despite these vital roles, many wetlands have been drained and filled for agriculture or development. Wetlands accumulate organic material, so they tend to be nutrient-rich—and therefore ideal for farming. It is estimated that southern Canada and the United States have lost well over half their wetlands since European colonization. In recent years, however, people have come to recognize the importance of wetlands, and many conservation groups have worked toward their restoration. Further, many artificial wetlands have been built for their ecological benefits.

Freshwater Marshes Freshwater marshes are shallow-water wetlands typified by tall, grasslike plants. The shallow water allows plants, such as cattails and bulrushes, to grow above the water surface.

Swamps Swamps also consist of shallow water rich in vegetation, but they are typified by woody shrubs and trees, not grasses. The cypress swamps of the southeastern United States, where cypress trees grow in standing water, are an example. Swamps can be created when beavers build dams across streams from trees, flooding wooded areas upstream.

Bogs and Fens Bogs are wetlands characterized by low nutrients, acidic water, and thick, floating mats of vegetation, usually a type of moss. Bogs form either in depressions where water can collect or through secondary succession. Secondary succession can occur when ponds are filled in with nutrients or when moss covers land and traps water underneath. Fens are similar to bogs, but are connected to a source of groundwater. They tend to be less acidic and more nutrient-rich ecosystems.

Rivers and Streams

Water from rain, snowmelt, or springs runs downhill and converges where the land dips, forming streams, creeks, or brooks. These watercourses merge into rivers, whose water eventually reaches either the ocean or a landlocked water body. A smaller river flowing into a larger one is called a *tributary,* and the area of land drained by a river and all of its tributaries is called a *watershed.*

A River's Course Rivers shape the landscape through which they run, as shown in **Figure 8.** The *source,* or beginning, of most rivers is high in the mountains, where melting snow collects and runs downhill due to gravity. Water near a river's source tends to be cold and full of oxygen. Few organisms can live here, however, as the water moves too swiftly. Because water moves so fast near the source, it tends to cut a relatively deep and straight path through the earth.

Downstream, where the slope is gentler, rivers slow down and are warmed by the sun. Nutrients and sediment collected by the running water begin to build up in the benthic zone. Plants can then take root, providing food for consumers. Water here contains less dissolved oxygen, as organisms are constantly using it for cellular respiration. When water flows slowly, it creates wide, curvy paths called *meanders* through the earth. Eventually, a bend may become such an extreme loop that water erodes a shortcut from one end of the loop to the other. The bend is cut off and remains as an isolated, U-shaped water body called an *oxbow lake.*

Over thousands or millions of years, a river may shift from one course to another, back and forth over a large area, carving out a flat valley. Areas nearest a river's course that are flooded periodically are said to be within the river's **flood plain.** Frequent deposition of silt from flooding makes flood plain soils especially fertile. Rivers empty into larger bodies of water, such as an ocean, at their *mouth.*

River Organisms Rivers and streams host diverse ecological communities. Nearer the river's source, organisms have adaptations that enable them to avoid being carried away by swift currents. Mosses cling to rocks, and fish may attach themselves to a rock on the riverbed with suckerlike mouths. Fish living in the swifter parts of a river, such as trout, must have strong, sleek bodies that enable them to swim against the current.

FIGURE 8 The Path of a River Rivers and streams flow downhill, shaping landscapes as they go.

Estuaries

Estuaries are bodies of water, partly enclosed by land, that occur where fresh water from land drainage meets the water of an ocean or inland sea. Organisms living in coastal estuaries, where fresh and salt water mix to form brackish ecosystems, must be able to tolerate a wide range of temperature and salinity conditions. For fishes such as salmon that spawn in fresh water and mature in salt water, estuaries provide a transitional zone where young fish make the passage from fresh water to salt water. Years later, when the fish return to their hatching grounds to spawn, estuaries provide the transitional zone in the opposite direction—from salt to fresh water. Some estuaries involve only fresh water, for example, where rivers empty into inland seas such as the Great Lakes. Although there is no change in salinity in these freshwater estuaries, they tend to be diverse ecosystems with a mix of river and lake organisms.

Because river water constantly supplies nutrients to estuaries, they tend to be extremely productive. In fact, coastal estuaries are often home to two of the most productive ecosystems on Earth: salt marshes and mangrove forests.

FIGURE 9 Marshes and Mangroves
(a) Chesapeake Bay is home to enormous stretches of salt marsh that extend along more than 300 kilometers of coastline from Maryland to Virginia. **(b)** Mangrove trees, such as these in Florida's Everglades National Park, show specialized adaptations for growing in changeable coastal conditions. The trees provide habitats for many types of fishes, birds, crabs, and other animals.

Salt Marshes   Along many of the world's coasts at temperate latitudes, salt marshes occur. Salt marshes are grassy ecosystems that are regularly flooded by bordering bodies of water. Salt marshes boast very high primary productivity and provide critical habitat for shorebirds, waterfowl, and the adults and young of many commercially important fish and shellfish species. They also filter out pollution and stabilize shorelines against storm surges. Chesapeake Bay, off the coasts of Maryland and Virginia, contains some of the most extensive areas of salt marsh in the United States.

Mangrove Forests   In tropical and subtropical latitudes, mangrove forests grow along gently sloping sandy and silty coasts. Mangroves are specialized trees and shrubs with roots that curve upward, out of the ground, to attain oxygen lacking in the mud or that curve downward like stilts to support the tree in changing water levels. Fish, shellfish, crabs, snakes, and other organisms thrive among the root networks, and birds feed and nest in the dense foliage of these coastal forests. Besides serving as nurseries for fish and shellfish that people harvest, mangroves also provide materials that people use for food, medicine, tools, and construction. The largest mangrove forests in America are in Florida's Everglades region.

(a)

(b)

The Ecological Importance of Estuaries Estuary ecosystems provide many benefits. Like freshwater wetlands, salt marshes and mangrove forests help prevent soil erosion and flooding. They also act as a protective barrier between the sea and land. However, people want to live along coasts, and coastal sites are desirable for commerce. As a result, vast expanses of coastal estuaries worldwide have been destroyed to make way for coastal development.

Unfortunately, we have suffered for their loss. When a tsunami struck areas along the Indian Ocean in 2004, it devastated coasts where mangrove forests had been removed but caused less damage where the forests were intact. In Florida, researchers found that in counties where mangroves grow there was 25% less damage from Hurricane Irma in 2017 than in counties where they were absent. Mangroves protected over 500,000 people and prevented $1.5 billion dollars in flood damage during just that one storm.

The Oceans

We generally speak of the world's oceans in the plural, giving each major basin a name: Pacific, Atlantic, Indian, Arctic, and Southern. However, all of these oceans are connected, forming a single, vast body of water. This one "world ocean" covers 71% of Earth's surface and contains 97.5% of its water. The world's oceans touch and are touched by virtually every environmental system and every human endeavor.

Ocean Structure Salts in ocean water are carried from land by wind and water. If we were able to evaporate all the water from the oceans, the empty basins would be covered with a layer of salt roughly 60 meters (200 feet) thick. Salt content and temperature have an effect on water density. Water density increases as salinity rises and as temperature falls. These relationships give rise to different layers of water. Heavier (colder and saltier) water sinks, and lighter (warmer and less salty) water remains nearer the surface.

▶ *Ocean Currents* Earth's ocean is composed of many riverlike flows driven by heating and cooling, gravity, wind, and differences in water density. These currents, shown in **Figure 10,** flow horizontally and for great distances. Some currents are very slow. Others, like the Gulf Stream, are rapid and powerful. From the Gulf of Mexico, the Gulf Stream moves up along the Atlantic coast at a rate of 160 kilometers per day (over 4.1 miles per hour). Averaging 70 kilometers (43 miles) across, the Gulf Stream continues across the North Atlantic, bringing warm water to Europe and moderating that continent's climate, which otherwise would be much colder.

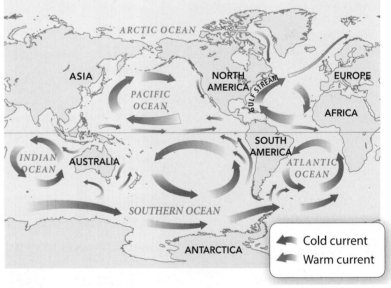

FIGURE 10 Ocean Currents The upper waters of the oceans flow in currents, which are long-lasting and predictable global patterns of water movement. Warm- and cold-water currents interact with the planet's climate system, and people have used them for centuries to navigate the oceans.

▶ **Upwelling and Downwelling** Surface winds and heating create vertical currents in seawater that move nutrients and oxygen through the ocean's layers. **Upwelling,** the vertical flow of cold, nutrient-rich water toward the surface, occurs where horizontal currents diverge, or flow away from one another. In areas where surface currents converge, or come together, surface water sinks in a process called *downwelling.* Downwelling transports warm water rich in dissolved gases from the surface into the ocean depths.

▶ **Ocean Zones** Ecologists typically break the ocean into zones defined by water depth and distance from shore. As shown in **Figure 11,** the ocean is divided vertically into the sunlit photic zone, the vast and dark aphotic zone, and the mysterious benthic zone along the ocean floor. In most places, the photic zone extends about 200 meters (660 feet) down. The photic zone is further divided into three major zones: the intertidal zone, the neritic zone, and the open-ocean zone.

Ocean Ecosystems Most ocean ecosystems are powered by solar energy, with sunlight driving photosynthesis by phytoplankton in the photic zone. Yet, even the darkest ocean depths host life.

FIGURE 11 **Ocean Zones** Ecologists divide the ocean into zones based on depth and distance from the shore. By far, the largest zone is the aphotic zone. The most productive zones, however, are shallower and closer to shore.

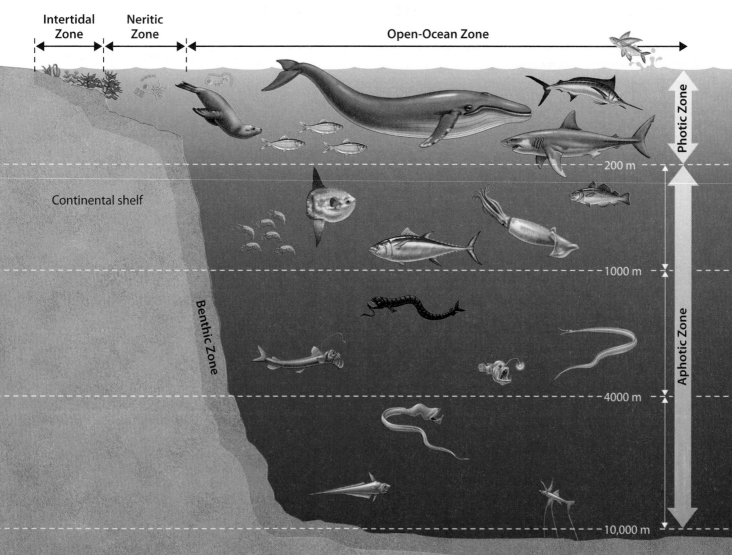

Intertidal Zone   Neritic Zone   Open-Ocean Zone

Continental shelf

Benthic Zone

Photic Zone

Aphotic Zone

200 m

1000 m

4000 m

10,000 m

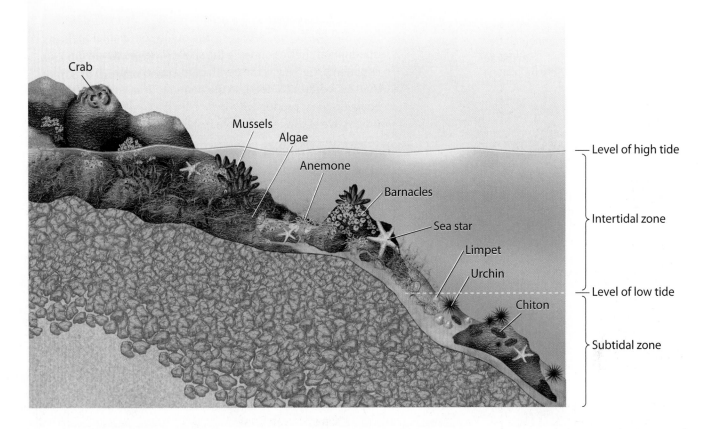

Crab

Mussels

Algae

Anemone

Barnacles

Sea star

Limpet

Urchin

Chiton

Level of high tide

Intertidal zone

Level of low tide

Subtidal zone

Intertidal Ecosystems Where ocean meets land, *intertidal* ecosystems spread between the uppermost reach of the high tide and the lowest limit of the low tide. Tides are the periodic rising and falling of the ocean's height at a given location, caused by the gravitational pull of the moon and sun. In most places, high and low tides occur roughly 6 hours apart, so intertidal organisms spend part of each day submerged in water, part of the day exposed to the air and sun, and part of the day being lashed by waves. Subject to tremendous extremes in temperature, moisture, sun exposure, and salinity, these creatures must also protect themselves from marine predators at high tide and terrestrial predators at low tide.

The intertidal environment is a tough place to make a living, but it is home to a remarkable diversity of organisms. Nutrient content is generally high, and ample sunlight fuels a variety of primary producers. On a rocky shore, animals such as anemones, mussels, and barnacles live attached to rocks, filter-feeding on plankton in the water that washes over them. Urchins, chitons, and limpets eat intertidal algae or scrape food from the rocks. Sea stars creep slowly along, preying on the filter feeders and herbivores at high tide. Crabs clamber around the rocks, scavenging detritus. Sandy intertidal areas, such as those of Cape Cod in Massachusetts, host less biodiversity, yet plenty of organisms burrow into the sand at low tide to await the return of high tide, when they emerge to feed.

FIGURE 12 The Intertidal Zone
The rocky intertidal zone is rich in biodiversity, typically containing large invertebrates such as sea stars, barnacles, crabs, sea anemones, limpets, chitons, mussels, and sea urchins. Areas higher on the shoreline are exposed to the air more frequently and for longer periods, so organisms that can tolerate exposure best specialize in the upper intertidal zone. The lower intertidal zone is exposed less frequently and for shorter periods, so organisms less able to tolerate exposure thrive in this zone.

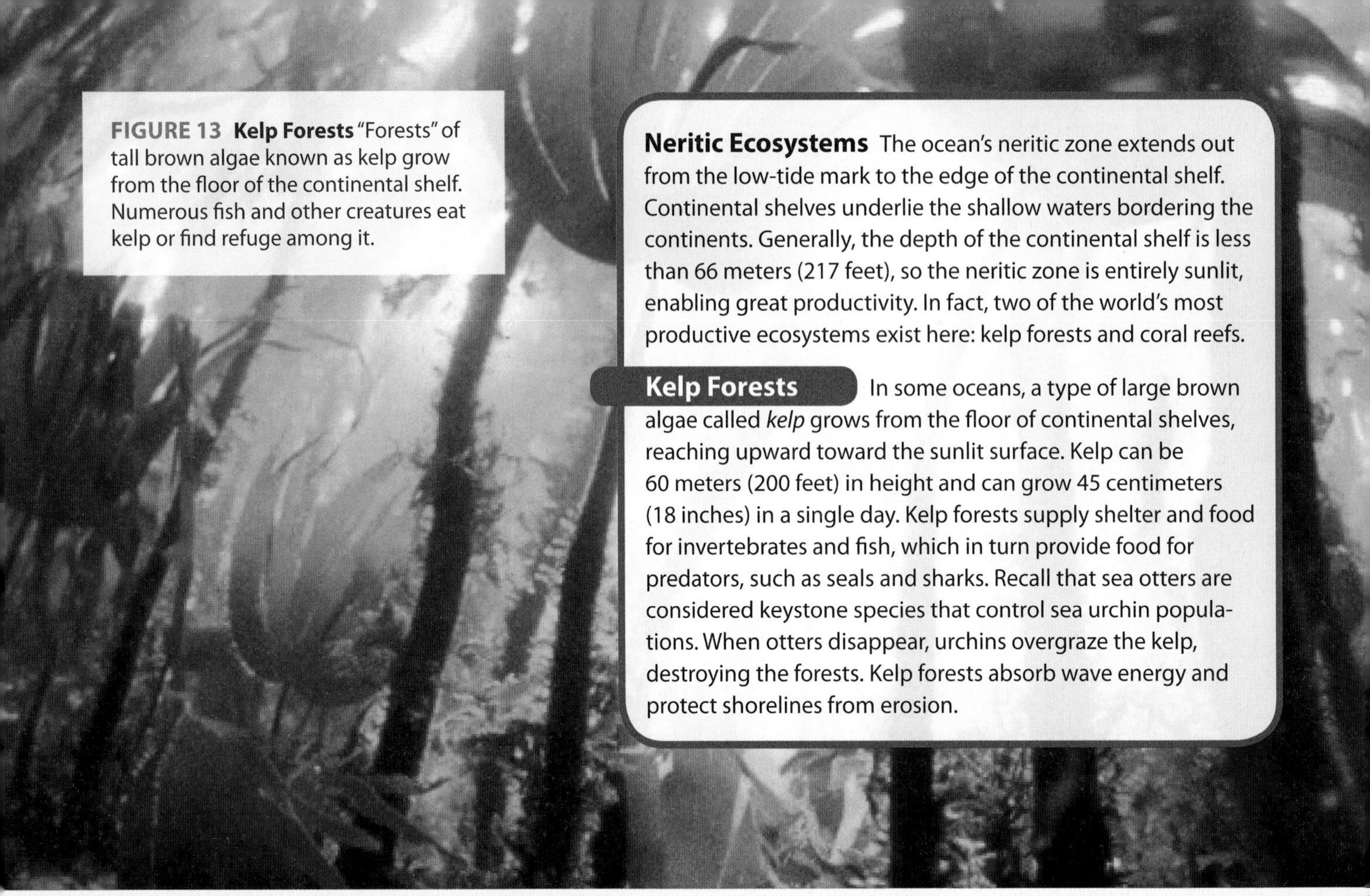

FIGURE 13 Kelp Forests "Forests" of tall brown algae known as kelp grow from the floor of the continental shelf. Numerous fish and other creatures eat kelp or find refuge among it.

Neritic Ecosystems The ocean's neritic zone extends out from the low-tide mark to the edge of the continental shelf. Continental shelves underlie the shallow waters bordering the continents. Generally, the depth of the continental shelf is less than 66 meters (217 feet), so the neritic zone is entirely sunlit, enabling great productivity. In fact, two of the world's most productive ecosystems exist here: kelp forests and coral reefs.

Kelp Forests In some oceans, a type of large brown algae called *kelp* grows from the floor of continental shelves, reaching upward toward the sunlit surface. Kelp can be 60 meters (200 feet) in height and can grow 45 centimeters (18 inches) in a single day. Kelp forests supply shelter and food for invertebrates and fish, which in turn provide food for predators, such as seals and sharks. Recall that sea otters are considered keystone species that control sea urchin populations. When otters disappear, urchins overgraze the kelp, destroying the forests. Kelp forests absorb wave energy and protect shorelines from erosion.

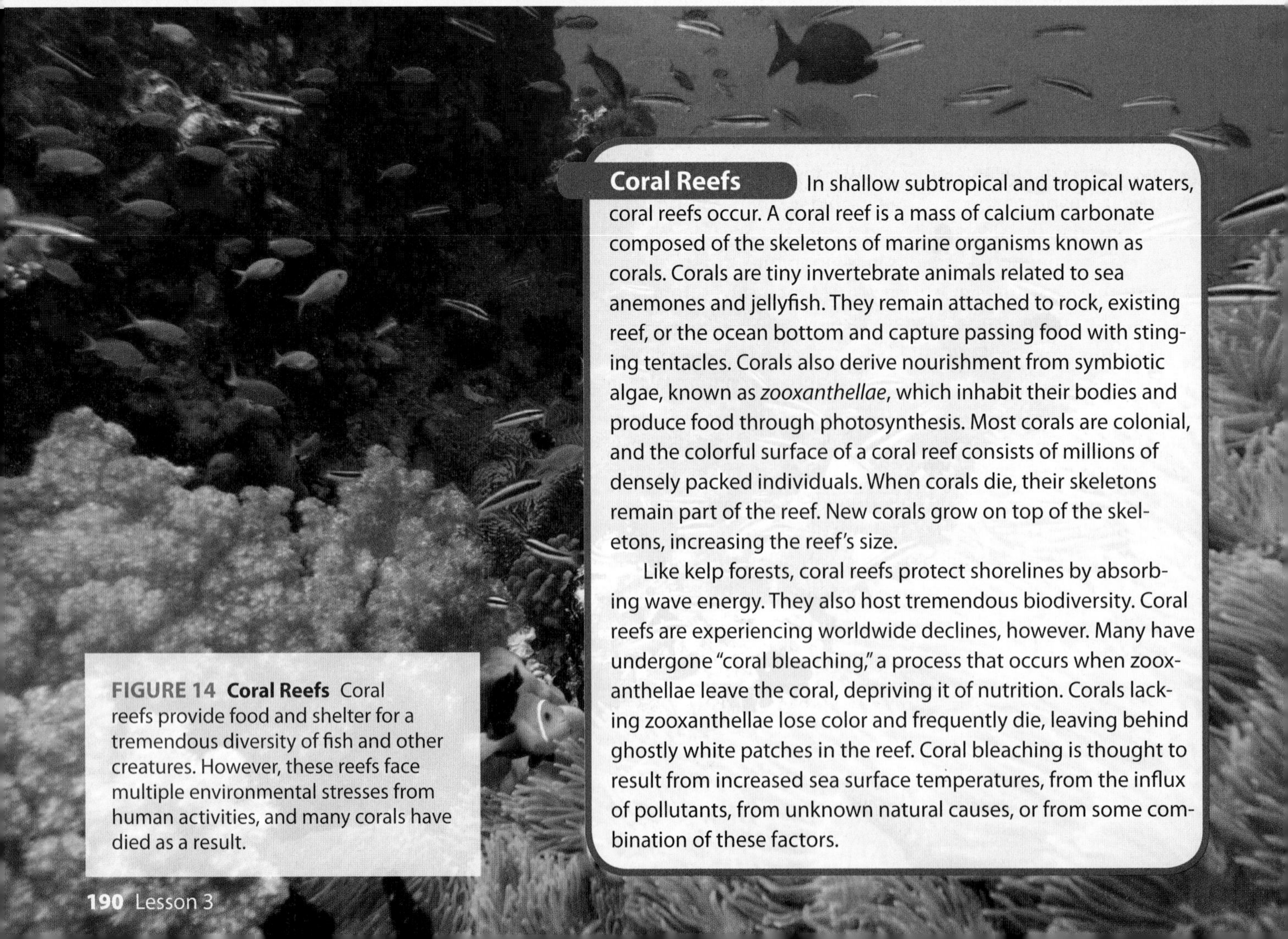

FIGURE 14 Coral Reefs Coral reefs provide food and shelter for a tremendous diversity of fish and other creatures. However, these reefs face multiple environmental stresses from human activities, and many corals have died as a result.

Coral Reefs In shallow subtropical and tropical waters, coral reefs occur. A coral reef is a mass of calcium carbonate composed of the skeletons of marine organisms known as corals. Corals are tiny invertebrate animals related to sea anemones and jellyfish. They remain attached to rock, existing reef, or the ocean bottom and capture passing food with stinging tentacles. Corals also derive nourishment from symbiotic algae, known as *zooxanthellae*, which inhabit their bodies and produce food through photosynthesis. Most corals are colonial, and the colorful surface of a coral reef consists of millions of densely packed individuals. When corals die, their skeletons remain part of the reef. New corals grow on top of the skeletons, increasing the reef's size.

Like kelp forests, coral reefs protect shorelines by absorbing wave energy. They also host tremendous biodiversity. Coral reefs are experiencing worldwide declines, however. Many have undergone "coral bleaching," a process that occurs when zooxanthellae leave the coral, depriving it of nutrition. Corals lacking zooxanthellae lose color and frequently die, leaving behind ghostly white patches in the reef. Coral bleaching is thought to result from increased sea surface temperatures, from the influx of pollutants, from unknown natural causes, or from some combination of these factors.

Open-Ocean Ecosystems The open ocean begins at the edge of the continental shelf. It contains the majority of Earth's ocean water—over 90 percent of it! However, it is among the least productive ecosystems because most of it is dark and incapable of productivity by photosynthesis. Even in the sunlit photic zone, photosynthesis is often limited because not enough nutrients make their way into the open ocean from land. As a result, primary productivity and animal life near the surface are concentrated in regions of nutrient-rich upwelling.

Microscopic phytoplankton make up the base of food chains in the open ocean, where water is too deep for rooted plants. Phytoplankton are a source of food for zooplankton, which in turn become food for fish, jellyfish, whales, and other free-swimming animals. Predators at higher trophic levels include larger fish, sea turtles, sharks, and fish-eating birds that nest on islands and coastlines.

In the aphotic open-ocean zone, animals have adaptations that enable them to live in the dark without food from plants. Some of these often bizarre-looking creatures scavenge carcasses or organic detritus that falls from above. Others, like the frilled shark in **Figure 15,** are predators, and still others obtain food from symbiotic mutualistic bacteria. Some species carry bacteria that produce light chemically with bioluminescence.

Benthic ecosystems that occur around hydrothermal vents, where heated water spurts from the seafloor, host some of the stranger forms of ocean life. Tubeworms, shrimp, and other creatures in these recently discovered systems use symbiotic bacteria to derive their energy from chemicals in the heated water rather than from sunlight. They manage to thrive here, kilometers below the surface, despite enormous pressure caused by the weight of the water above.

FIGURE 15 Creatures From the Deep Frilled sharks are uncommon deep ocean fish that are occasionally caught in deep-sea fishing nets. They feed on squid and other fish, possibly swallowing their prey whole. They can grow up to 2 m long and move through the water like an eel.

LESSON 3 Assessment

1. **Apply Concepts** How do ecologists classify aquatic ecosystems?

2. **Compare and Contrast** What are the similarities and differences among a lake, wetland, and river?

3. **Predict** Dams are obstructions placed in a river or stream to block its flow. In addition to water, sediment builds up behind the dam. How might a dam placed upriver affect the productivity of an estuary at the river's mouth?

4. **Apply Concepts** What kinds of conditions do organisms need to be adapted for in the intertidal zone of the ocean?

5. **THINK IT** *THROUGH* Scientists use deep-sea submarines to explore the ocean's benthic zone. However, it is extremely difficult to bring deep-sea organisms to the surface alive without expensive and specialized equipment. Use what you know about the conditions in the deepest ocean to explain why deep-sea organisms cannot survive in conditions closer to the ocean's surface.

SHOULD ELEPHANT CULLING BE ALLOWED?

Since agriculture began some 10,000 years ago, people have needed to defend their growing crops from wildlife, such as deer, rabbits, moles, or other pests. In Africa, one pest in particular is stirring up a worldwide debate. It is much larger than a deer and brings about far more sympathy than a mole. What is it? The elephant.

Elephants in sub-Saharan Africa have made a remarkable comeback since international law has halted the trade of ivory. Protected from poaching, elephants have reproduced in great numbers and family groups roam in protected land reserves.

However, not everyone is convinced that so many elephants—24,000 in South Africa alone, about 415,000 across all of Africa—is a good thing. In 2008, the South African government announced that it was going to allow elephant culling as a last-resort measure to control elephant populations. Culling, is the process of removing animals in order to control overcrowded populations. It is a highly controversial practice that has government officials, scientists, and activists all talking.

THE OPINIONS

Ivory products for sale in China—where demand for ivory is particularly high

VIEWPOINT 1
Elephant culling should not be allowed.

Anti-culling groups, including the International Fund for Animal Welfare, maintain that there is not enough evidence to support the idea that there are "too many" elephants. There are no reliable statistics on damage done to private property and farmland. Furthermore, there is not adequate research linking elephants to reduced biodiversity. On the contrary, there *is* research that shows some protected areas have maintained their biodiversity in spite of dense elephant populations.

Beyond the scientific arguments, the morals and ethics of culling should be considered. Scientists are sure that elephants have a level of self-awareness similar to that of humans and dolphins. They form strong family ties and are known to grieve their dead. Finally, if the selling and trading of culled elephant parts were legal, it seems inevitable that poaching would increase. If that happens, there is no telling how many elephants would be lost.

VIEWPOINT 2
Elephant culling should be allowed.

South Africa National Parks (SANParks) is an independent board that recommended in 2005 that culling be approved by the government as one method to control elephant populations. SANParks notes in its report that biodiversity in the succulent thicket ecosystem of Addo Elephant National Park has declined as elephant populations have risen. Moreover, elephants are increasingly wandering off reservations and eating crops on neighboring farms. While some may wonder if it is ethical to kill elephants, pro-culling groups counter that it is no more ethical to allow elephants to degrade the landscape or threaten the livelihood of local farmers.

Another moral issue to consider is what will happen to the elephants if their numbers continue to rise. It seems inevitable that disease and starvation will increase, causing suffering among the elephants. Finally, there are economic incentives to culling. Should culling be allowed, money generated by selling elephant meat and other products could support local communities—most of which are extremely poor.

Elephants run away while being pursued by helicopter.

Write About It Think of at least three groups that might be affected by elephant populations in Africa. Which viewpoint would each group support? Why? As best you can, design a solution that is a compromise between the groups and describe it in a paragraph.

INVESTIGATIVE PHENOMENON

How do organisms interact with the environment?

Lesson 1
What makes Zimbabwe a suitable place for elephants to live?

Lesson 3
What conditions and organisms characterize the areas where rivers meet oceans?

Lesson 2
Why are vines more likely to grow in a rain forest than in a desert?

LESSON 1 Defining Biomes

- Biomes are characterized by their climates as well as typical plant and animal life.
- Ecologists use climatographs to show annual temperature and rainfall patterns.
- Biomes vary in their rates of net primary production. Warm and wet biomes have the highest net primary production, and cold, dry biomes have the lowest.

biome (164)
climate (165)
weather (165)
climatograph (165)
net primary production (167)

LESSON 2 Biomes

- There are ten major biomes: tropical rain forest, tropical dry forest, savanna, desert, temperate rain forest, temperate forest, temperate grassland, chaparral, boreal forest, and tundra. Organisms in these biomes show adaptations to their environments.
- Polar ice and mountains are not usually classified as biomes. Most life in polar regions is aquatic, and conditions on mountains change dramatically with altitude.

canopy (168)
emergent layer (168)
understory (168)
epiphyte (169)
deciduous (170)
estivation (170)
coniferous (173)
hibernation (174)
permafrost (178)

LESSON 3 Aquatic Ecosystems

- Ecologists classify aquatic ecosystems according to criteria such as salinity, depth, and whether the water is flowing or standing.
- Standing freshwater ecosystems include ponds, lakes, inland seas, and wetlands. Flowing freshwater ecosystems include rivers and streams.
- Estuaries are home to diverse ecosystems that protect coastal environments from soil erosion and flooding.
- The ocean can be divided into three zones based on their distance from shore: intertidal, neritic, and open ocean.

salinity (181)
photic zone (182)
aphotic zone (182)
benthic zone (182)
littoral zone (183)
limnetic zone (183)
wetland (184)
flood plain (185)
estuary (186)
upwelling (188)

 GO ONLINE

INQUIRY LABS AND ACTIVITIES

- **Collecting Climate Data**
  Take temperature readings daily and collect precipitation data. How close is your data to the climate data for your biome?
- **Mapping Kelp Forests**
  Use maps of sea surface temperatures and ocean currents to identify where kelp forests are located.

Chapter Assessment

Defend Your Case

The Central Case in this chapter explored the relationship between African elephants and their environments. Use evidence from the Central Case and the chapter to explain the major effects elephants have on Africa's ecosystems and biomes. How do you think African nations should handle elephant overpopulation, if at all?

Review Concepts and Terms

1. Climatographs are useful tools in describing a biome's climate. They typically show patterns in annual
   a. rainfall and snowfall.
   b. precipitation and humidity.
   c. precipitation and temperature.
   d. temperature and sunlight.

2. Which of the following terms describes the net amount of organic matter that an ecosystem or biome produces?
   a. gross production
   b. net productivity
   c. photosynthetic mass
   d. net primary production

3. Nearly all nutrients present in tropical rain forests are contained in the
   a. soil.
   b. epiphytes.
   c. emergent layer.
   d. trees, vines, and other plants.

4. What is the extended period of deep, sleeplike inactivity that an animal enters for the winter?
   a. hibernation   **c.** drought
   b. estivation   **d.** emigration

5. Which of the following types of organisms experience seasonal loss of leaves as an adaptation to their climate?
   a. coniferous trees   **c.** deciduous trees
   b. succulent plants   **d.** grasses

6. Which of the following describes the frozen underground soil that is found in the tundra?
   a. polar ice   **c.** permafrost
   b. hard frost   **d.** emergent layer

7. Life underwater is greatly affected by light availability, which is directly related to
   a. water quality.   **c.** salinity.
   b. water depth.   **d.** temperature.

8. In which of the ocean's zones would you expect to find the ecosystem seen below?
   a. the intertidal zone **c.** the open ocean zone
   b. the neritic zone   **d.** the benthic zone

9. Which of the following aquatic ecosystems is NOT a type of wetland?
   a. swamp
   b. bog
   c. stream
   d. freshwater marsh

10. The vertical movement of cold, nutrient-rich water from the ocean depths to its surface is called
    a. upwelling.
    b. downwelling.
    c. tides.
    d. surface currents.

Modified True/False

Write true if the statement is true. If it is false, change the underlined word or words to make the statement true.

11. <u>Weather</u> describes the average conditions of an area over long periods of time.

12. The mud and muck at the very bottom of any body of water is called the <u>aphotic zone</u>.

13. High in the mountains, near a river's source, water tends to be <u>cold and oxygen-rich</u>.

14. <u>Bogs</u> are brackish ecosystems that occur where rivers flow into the ocean.

Reading Comprehension

Read the following selection and answer the questions that follow.

Despite the daily heating and cooling of surface waters, ocean temperatures are much more stable than temperatures on land. Midlatitude oceans experience maximum yearly temperature variation of only around 10°C (equivalent to a variation of around 18°F), and tropical and polar oceans are still more stable. The reason for this stability is that water has a very high *heat capacity*, a measure of the energy required to increase temperature by a given amount. It takes much more energy to increase the temperature of water than it does to increase the temperature of air by the same amount. High heat capacity enables the oceans to absorb a tremendous amount of energy from the atmosphere. In fact, the energy content of the entire atmosphere is equal to that of just the top 2.6 meters of the oceans. By absorbing thermal energy and releasing it to the atmosphere, the oceans help regulate Earth's climate.

15. According to the passage, which of the following will experience the LEAST amount of temperature variation?

    a. a coastal city   **c.** a midlatitude ocean

    b. an inland pond   **d.** a tropical ocean

16. A material, like water, that requires a large amount of energy to raise its temperature has a

    a. high heat capacity.   **c.** high heat absorption.

    b. low heat capacity.   **d.** stable temperature.

Short Answer

17. What is the difference between climate and weather?

18. Why do the same biomes tend to occur at similar latitudes?

19. Why do warmer and wetter biomes have higher net primary productivity?

20. What is estivation? How is it similar to hibernation?

21. Why are there no rooted plants in the limnetic zone of a lake or pond?

22. How has the succulent plant seen here adapted to the conditions of its desert environment?

Critical Thinking

23. **Apply Concepts** An organism that thrives in the desert does not do well in a tropical rain forest. When there is plenty of water, shouldn't the organism do even better? Explain.

24. **Relate Cause and Effect** Farms built on cleared grassland tend to be very productive. Farms built on cleared rain forest, however, tend not to do well. Explain the difference.

25. **Infer** There is very little rainfall in the tundra, but the ground is very wet during the summer. Why?

26. **Compare and Contrast** Wetlands and estuaries are both ecologically important. Describe both ecosystems, pointing out their similarities and differences. Then, explain their importance.

27. **Infer** The open ocean is among the least productive ecosystems on Earth. However, it contributes greatly to the overall productivity of the biosphere. How can you explain this paradox?

Analyze Data

The graph below shows the relationship between ocean depth and temperature. Use the data to answer the questions.

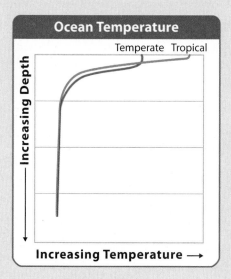

28. Interpret Graphs Describe the basic relationship between ocean depth and temperature seen in the graph.

29. Infer Why does the tropical ocean have a greater temperature range than the temperate ocean?

30. Infer What do you think the data line for polar oceans would look like? Explain your answer.

Write About It

31. Explanation How does your biome affect how you live? If you had to move, would you select a similar biome or a different one? Explain.

32. Persuasion The owners of a large tropical resort are considering a plan to destroy a large coral reef just offshore. They reason that, if the reef is gone, cruise ships will be able to dock closer to their resort and they will gain business. Write a letter to the resort's owners explaining how they might benefit more by preserving the reef instead.

33. REVISIT INVESTIGATIVE PHENOMENON Organisms evolve, through the process of natural selection, in ways that enable them to live successfully in their environments. Choose three biomes or aquatic ecosystems and describe how abiotic factors have influenced the organisms that live there.

Ecological Footprints

Read the information below. Copy the table into your notebook and record your calculations. Then, answer the questions that follow.

Commercial fishing has had a huge negative impact on the health of Earth's oceans. On average, every person consumes 20.2 kilograms of food from the ocean per year. In North America, we consume more from the oceans than the world average—about 21.6 kilograms per year. Use this information to fill in the footprint table.

Consumer Group	Population	North America (21.6 kg Per Person)	World (20.2 kg Per Person)
You			
Your class			
Your state			
United States			
World			

Data from U.N. Food and Agriculture Organization (FAO), Fisheries Department. 2018. *The state of world fisheries and aquaculture: 2018.* Data are for 2015, the most recent year for which comparative data are available.

1. How might commercial fishing affect ocean ecosystems?

2. If everyone in the world ate as much food from the ocean as a person from North America, how much more food from the ocean would be consumed per year?

3. The population of North America represents about 5% of the world's population. Does North America consume more or less than 5% of all the food from the ocean? (Hint: Your first step should be to calculate the population of North America.)

MATH SUPPORT For help multiplying with percentages, see the Math Handbook.

CHAPTER 7

Biodiversity and Conservation

INVESTIGATIVE PHENOMENON Why is it important to measure and protect biodiversity?

There are less than 300
Malayan tigers in the wild.

Lesson 1
Our Planet of Life

Lesson 2
Extinction and
Biodiversity Loss

Lesson 3
Protecting Biodiversity

Saving the Siberian Tiger

WHAT COMES TO MIND when someone says "tiger"? Adjectives like *powerful*, *beautiful*, and *deadly* are certainly fitting, but chances are you also thought of something like *endangered* or *rare*. It wasn't always this way. Tigers (scientific name *Panthera tigris*) used to roam all over Asia, from Turkey to northeast Russia to Indonesia. Within the past 200 years, however, humans have driven tigers from most of their historic range. Three subspecies have already been lost forever; the remaining five subspecies are in danger of following them to extinction.

The largest surviving tiger subspecies is the Siberian tiger *(Panthera tigris altaica)*, also known as the Amur tiger after the river that runs through their habitat. Males of this variety can reach 3.7 meters (12 feet) in length and weigh up to 360 kilograms (800 pounds). Siberian tigers live in the remote forests of the Sikhote-Alin Mountains in easternmost Russia. For thousands of years, Siberian tigers coexisted with the region's native people. Called "Old Man" or "Grandfather," Siberian tigers were viewed as guardians of the mountains and forests, and were only killed when they had preyed on a person.

Settlers to the region in the early twentieth century, however, had no such cultural traditions. They hunted tigers for sport and hides. Soon, there was a market for tiger skins, bones, and meat—especially in China and other Asian countries where tiger parts are used in traditional forms of medicine. Suddenly, dead tigers were worth a lot of money. At the same time, road building, logging, and agriculture fragmented the tiger's habitat and provided easy access for hunters. The wild Siberian tiger population plummeted to just 20–30 animals.

Eventually, international conservation groups got involved, working with Russian biologists to save the remaining tigers. Today, biologists use radio collars to track tigers, monitor their health,

GO ONLINE

• Take It Local   • 3-D Geo Tour

KEY

Current Siberian
tiger range

| 0 | | 300 mi |
| 0 | 300 km | |

and determine causes of death when they die. They also provide funding for local wildlife officials to protect the tigers from hunters. Although Siberian tigers are still endangered, thanks to conservation efforts, there are about 500 of them in the wild today.

Like the Siberian tiger, all five of the other subspecies of tigers are endangered. Two are critically endangered. Sumatran tigers are found only on the island of Sumatra and it is estimated that there are less than 400 left. Threats to these tigers include deforestation and poaching. Conservation efforts are focused on preserving habitat and enforcing anti-poaching laws. On the Malay Peninsula and a small area on mainland Thailand, less than 300 Malayan tigers are still in the wild. Habitat loss and poaching are the biggest threats to these tigers. Conservation efforts include educating the public, decreasing poaching, and collecting data on the remaining tigers.

Our Planet of Life

EVERYDAY PHENOMENON Why is maintaining biodiversity important?

Knowledge and Skills

- Differentiate the components of biodiversity.
- Explain two ways in which biodiversity varies across groups or geography.
- Describe the economic benefits of biodiversity.

Reading Strategy and Vocabulary

✔ **Reading Strategy** Before you read, set up a main idea and details chart for this lesson. Use the blue headings for main ideas. As you read, fill in supporting details from the text.

Vocabulary biodiversity, species diversity, genetic diversity, ecosystem diversity

SCIENTISTS WORLDWIDE are confirming what most people have suspected for a long time: many once-thriving species are disappearing. This suggests the question, "Does it matter?" There are a number of ways to answer that—from the practical to the ethical. To formulate your own answer, it is important to understand just how much life there is on our planet and what might happen if it is lost forever.

Biodiversity

From tigers to tiger beetles, Earth is full of life. The variety of life across all levels of ecological organization is called **biodiversity.** Overall biodiversity, whether of an isolated population of organisms or the entire biosphere, includes genetic diversity, species diversity, and ecosystem diversity, as seen in **Figure 1.** Of these levels of biodiversity, the most commonly used and easiest to visualize is species diversity.

Genetic diversity Genetic diversity describes the differences in DNA among individuals of a population or species.

Species diversity The number or variety of species in a given area is known as species diversity.

Ecosystem diversity An area's ecosystem diversity refers to its variety of ecosystems, communities, or habitats.

FIGURE 1 Levels of Biodiversity The concept of biodiversity encompasses several levels in the hierarchy of life.

Species Diversity Recall that members of a species share certain characteristics, including similar DNA, and can breed with one another to produce fertile offspring. **Species diversity** is the number or variety of species in a particular region. There is currently a massive project underway, called the *Encyclopedia of Life*, that is attempting to provide an accessible online library of worldwide species diversity.

Speciation generates new species, adding to species diversity, whereas extinction decreases species diversity. Although immigration and emigration may increase or decrease species diversity locally, only speciation and extinction change it globally.

▶ *Classifying Species* *Taxonomists,* the scientists who classify species, use an organism's physical appearance and genetic makeup to determine its species. Species are then placed within a hierarchy of categories, called *taxonomic groups,* that reflect evolutionary relationships. Closely related species are grouped together into *genera* (singular, *genus*). In traditional classification, there are five taxonomic groups above the level of genus: family, order, class, phylum, and kingdom. As our knowledge of evolutionary relationships increases, however, there have been some changes to the system. For example, many scientists now use a taxonomic group even larger than the kingdom, called the domain, to classify phyla.

Every species is given a two-part scientific name denoting its genus and species. The tiger, *Panthera tigris,* differs from the world's other species of large cats, such as the jaguar (*Panthera onca*), the leopard (*Panthera pardus*), and the African lion (*Panthera leo*). These four species are closely related in evolutionary terms, as indicated by the genus name they share, *Panthera.* They are more distantly related to cats in other genera such as the cheetah (*Acinonyx jubatus*) and the bobcat (*Felis rufus*), although all cats are classified together in the family Felidae.

▶ *Classification Below the Species Level* Below the species level organisms may be classified into subspecies. A *subspecies* is a population of organisms that has genetically based characteristics, such as size or color, that differ from members of the same species in a different area. Subspecies are formed by the same processes that drive speciation. However, divergences stop short of producing separate species. Scientists denote subspecies with a third part of the scientific name. The Siberian tiger, *Panthera tigris altaica,* is one of six subspecies of tiger still surviving. As shown in **Figure 15,** tiger subspecies differ in color, coat thickness, stripe patterns, and size, but could interbreed if they lived together.

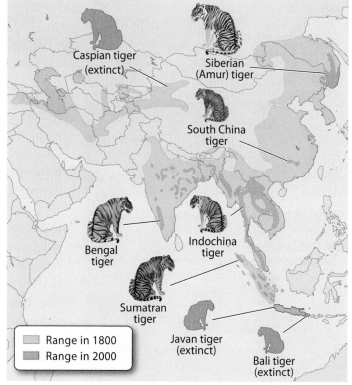

Data from the Tiger Information Center.

◆ **Connect to the Central Case**

FIGURE 2 **Subspecies** Deforestation, hunting, and other pressures have caused tigers to disappear from most of the geographic range they historically occupied. This map contrasts the ranges of eight tiger subspecies in the years 1800 (yellow) and 2000 (orange). **Interpret Maps** Which tiger subspecies shown here are extinct?

 What is a subspecies?

(a)

(b)

FIGURE 3 Ecosystem Diversity
Ecosystem diversity is not uniform.
(a) This area of coastline in Big Sur, California, clearly shows more ecosystem diversity than **(b)** this farmland in Tuscany, Italy.

Genetic Diversity Scientists designate subspecies when they recognize major, genetically based differences among individuals of the same species but different populations. However, within each species, all individuals vary genetically to some degree. **Genetic diversity** describes the differences in DNA among individuals within species and populations.

Genetic diversity provides the raw material for adaptation to local conditions. For example, different genes for coat thickness in tigers allowed natural selection to favor genes for thin coats of fur in Bengal tigers living in warm regions, and genes for thick coats of fur for Siberian tigers living in cold regions. In the long term, populations with more genetic diversity may stand better chances of survival, because their variation enables them to cope better with environmental change. Populations with little biodiversity, therefore, may have a reduced ability to withstand environmental change. In addition, these populations may be more vulnerable to disease and produce weak or defective offspring.

Ecosystem Diversity Biodiversity above the species level is referred to as **ecosystem diversity**, the number and variety of ecosystems within a given area. For example, a seashore of rocky and sandy beaches, forested cliffs, and ocean waters would hold far more biodiversity than the same amount of area of farmland, as shown in **Figure 3.** Sometimes, scientists look at the diversity not just of ecosystems, but of community types and habitats within the ecosystem.

Biodiversity Distribution

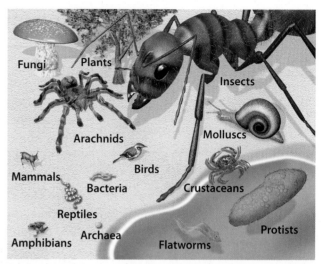

Coming up with precise ways to express a region's biodiversity is difficult. Scientists often express biodiversity in terms of its most easily measured component, species diversity. But counting species is a lot harder than it sounds, and scientists still can only estimate the total species richness of our planet.

Measuring Biodiversity Species are not evenly distributed among taxonomic groups. Although most insects are small, in terms of number of known and described species, they dwarf all other forms of life, as shown in **Figure 4.** Among known insects, about 40 percent are beetles. A scientist from the Smithsonian Institution named Terry Erwin fogged rainforest trees in Central America with clouds of insecticide and then collected organisms as they died and fell from the treetops. His results, published in 1982, include finding 1200 species of beetle living on 19 trees of the same species. Of those, he concluded that 163 of the beetle species lived *only* on that particular species of tree.

So far, scientists have identified and described 1.7 million to 2 million species of plants, animals, fungi, and microorganisms. However, using a variety of methods, including tree fogging, scientists estimate the total number of species that actually exists is far greater. Most estimates are in the range of 3 million to 100 million, with best-educated guesses spanning from 5 million to 30 million. Why do these estimates vary so much? First, some areas of Earth, such as the deepest ocean, remain relatively unexplored. Second, many species, such as bacteria and many fungi, are tiny and easily overlooked. Third, many organisms are extremely difficult to identify and tell apart from other species. This is frequently the case with microbes, fungi, and small insects, but also sometimes with organisms as large as birds, trees, and whales.

Patterns of Biodiversity In addition to being unevenly distributed across organism groups, living things are also unevenly distributed across our planet. For example, there is a general increase in species richness toward the equator. This pattern of variation with latitude, called the *latitudinal gradient,* is one of the most obvious and striking patterns in ecology.

At smaller scales, diversity patterns vary with habitat type. Generally, habitats that are structurally diverse have more ecological niches and support greater species richness. For instance, forests usually support greater diversity than grasslands. For any given geographic area, species diversity tends to increase with diversity of habitats because each habitat supports a somewhat different community of organisms.

Data from Groombridge, B., and M.D. Jenkins, 2002. *Global biodiversity: Earth's living resources in the 21st century.* UNEP-World Conservation Monitoring Centre. Cambridge, U.K.: Hoechst Foundation.

FIGURE 4 Where Insects Are King
This illustration shows organisms scaled in size to the number of species known in several major groups, giving a visual sense of the difference in their species diversity. However, scientists think that many species have not been described or even discovered. So, some groups (such as bacteria, archaea, insects, flatworms, protists, fungi, and others) most likely contain far more species than we now know about.

 Reading Checkpoint *Why don't scientists know exactly how many species there are on Earth?*

Benefits of Biodiversity

Contrary to popular opinion, some things in life can indeed be free. Intact ecosystems provide valuable processes, known as *ecosystem services,* for all of us free of charge. The United Nations Environment Programme (UNEP) identifies ecosystem services provided by biodiversity, including purification of air and water, control of pests and diseases, and decomposition of wastes. Biodiversity also provides food, fuel, and fiber. One 1997 study published in the journal *Nature* estimated that Earth's ecosystems, such as the wetland in **Figure 5,** provide at least $33 trillion worth of ecosystem services a year.

Biodiversity and Ecosystem Function Functioning ecosystems are clearly important, but what does biodiversity have to do with it? Ecologists are finding that high levels of biodiversity tend to increase the stability of communities and ecosystems. An ecosystem is considered stable if it is both resistant and resilient. *Resistant* ecosystems can resist environmental change without losing function. *Resilient* ecosystems are affected by change but can bounce back and regain function. Most of the research on ecosystem stability has dealt with species diversity, but new work is finding that high genetic diversity can also have a stabilizing effect on ecosystems. Thus, a loss of biodiversity at any level could decrease a natural system's ability to function and provide services to our society.

What about the extinction of individual species? Ecological research suggests that this depends on which species are removed. Ecosystems are complex, and it is difficult to predict which particular species may be important. Removing a species that can be replaced by others—one grazing herbivore for another grazing herbivore, for example—may make little difference. Recall, however, that removal of a keystone species results in significant changes in an ecological system.

FIGURE 5 Ecosystem Goods and Services This wetland in Georgia naturally purifies the water that flows through it—just one of the many ecosystem services it provides.

Top predators, such as tigers, are often considered keystone species because a single individual may prey on many other carnivores, each of which may prey on many herbivores. In turn, each herbivore may consume many plants. Thus the removal of a top predator produces effects that multiply as they cascade down the food web, ultimately changing how the ecosystem functions. Similarly, removal of a species at the base of a food web can set huge changes in motion. In Antarctica, almost all life is indirectly dependent upon microscopic, photosynthetic algae that grow beneath the ice—without them, the whole food web collapses.

Biodiversity and Agriculture Biodiversity, especially genetic diversity, benefits agriculture. Wild strains can be cross-bred with their crop plant relatives, passing on traits such as pest resistance in the process. During the 1970s, for example, a researcher discovered a maize species in Mexico known as *Zea diploperennis*. This maize is highly resistant to disease, and it is a perennial, meaning it will grow back year after year without being replanted. Plant breeders can cross-breed *Zea diploperennis* with other maize species to create a variety of disease-resistant, perennial hybrids. In addition, scientists continue to discover new plants that have potential for widespread use. The babassu palm *(Orbignya phalerata)* in **Figure 6a,** for example, yields more vegetable oil than either coconut or palm nuts. The oil, similar to coconut oil, can be used for cooking, fuel, and many industrial processes.

Biodiversity and Medicine Every species that goes extinct represents a lost opportunity to find a cure for a disease. The rosy periwinkle *(Catharanthus roseus)* in **Figure 6b,** for example, produces compounds that treat Hodgkin's lymphoma and a particularly deadly form of leukemia. Had this native plant of Madagascar become extinct before its discovery by medical researchers, these deadly diseases would have claimed far more lives. Many other common medicines come from plants, such as the cancer drugs colchicine and paclitaxel, the heart medicine digitoxin, and the antimalarial drug quinine. About half of medications approved in the last three decades originate from nature, not from labs.

FIGURE 6 Biodiversity's Benefits
Nature provides us with a variety of resources—some we have only begun to use. **(a)** The fruit of the babassu palm produces large quantities of oil that can be used for everything from cooking to fuel. **(b)** Medicines derived from the rosy periwinkle are used to treat two forms of life-threatening cancer.

 Reading Checkpoint *How can the extinction of a single species affect how an ecosystem functions?*

Biodiversity, Tourism, and Recreation

Besides providing for our food and health, biodiversity can be a direct source of income. *Ecotourism* describes environmentally responsible travel to protected natural areas for the purpose of appreciating nature, promoting conservation, and providing economic benefits to local peoples. Ecotourism is different from tourism because it emphasizes conservation, education, sustainability, and community participation.

Ecotourism has become a vital source of income for nations such as Costa Rica, with its rain forests; Australia, with its Great Barrier Reef; Belize, with its reefs, caves, and rain forests; and Kenya and Tanzania, with their savanna wildlife. The United States, too, benefits from ecotourism. American national parks, for example, draw millions of visitors each year from around the world.

Money from ecotourism provides a good reason for nations, states, and local communities to preserve natural areas and species. However, critics have warned that too many visitors to natural areas can disturb and harm wildlife. As ecotourism continues to increase, so will debate over its costs and benefits for local communities and for biodiversity.

FIGURE 7 Ecotourism Ecotourism can bring millions of dollars into a nation's economy. Here, a tourist is photographing cheetahs on the Masai Mara Game Reserve in Kenya.

LESSON ① Assessment

1. **Contrast** Explain the differences among genetic diversity, species diversity, and ecosystem diversity.

2. **Apply Concepts** Do the location and general biodiversity of tropical rain forests and boreal forests agree with what you would predict according to the latitudinal gradient pattern? Explain your answer. (*Hint:* You may want to refer to the biome map in the previous chapter.)

3. **Form an Opinion** You are trying to convince a friend about the importance of protecting biodiversity. Which one of the economic benefits discussed (ecosystem function, agricultural, medical, recreational) makes the strongest argument? Why?

REVISIT

4. **INVESTIGATIVE** PHENOMENON
Scientists are worried about the future of some species that have experienced extreme decreases in both population size and genetic diversity, including cheetahs, bison, and elephant seals. Using the concept of genetic diversity, explain why these animals may be in trouble even if their population sizes have increased in recent years.

Extinction and Biodiversity Loss

EVERYDAY PHENOMENON Why is global biodiversity decreasing?

Knowledge and Skills

- Describe how biodiversity is monitored and explain current biodiversity trends.
- List the major causes of biodiversity loss.

Reading Strategy and Vocabulary

✔ **Reading Strategy** As you read this lesson, fill out a cause-and-effect diagram for biodiversity loss. Remember that one cause can have multiple effects.

Vocabulary extirpation, endangered species, threatened species, habitat fragmentation, poaching

BIODIVERSITY LOSSES caused by humans are common throughout history. Archaeological evidence shows that waves of extinctions tend to follow whenever people colonize islands and continents. After the Polynesians reached Hawaii, for example, half its birds went extinct. Birds, mammals, and reptiles vanished following the colonization of New Zealand and Madagascar. Dozens of species of large vertebrates died off in Australia after the Aborigines arrived roughly 50,000 years ago. North America lost 33 genera of large mammals after people arrived on the continent 10,000 years ago. Why does human settlement seem to mean extinction for other organisms? And, more important, is there anything we can do about it?

Biodiversity at Risk

Once extinct, a species can never return. Recall that extinction occurs when the last member of a species dies. The disappearance of a particular population from a given area, but not of the entire species globally, is called **extirpation.** The tiger has been extirpated from most of its historic range, but it is not yet extinct. However, as populations become extirpated, the species as a whole is pushed closer and closer to extinction.

Natural Biodiversity Loss If organisms did not naturally go extinct, dinosaurs might be the main attraction at your local zoo. Extinctions usually occur one by one at a pace that paleontologists and other scientists refer to as the *background rate of extinction.* Before modern humans evolved, for example, the fossil record indicates that about one of every 1000 mammal species would typically go extinct every 1000–10,000 years. This means that, before humans, approximately one mammal species out of every 1 million to 10 million went extinct per year.

There have been times, however, when extinction rates have been far above the normal background rate. These events, called *mass extinctions,* have occurred at least five times in Earth's history. Each time more than one fifth of all families and half of all species have gone extinct.

A Sixth Mass Extinction? If current trends continue, the modern geologic era, known as the Quaternary period, may see the extinction of more than half of all species. Today, species loss seems to be accelerating as human population growth puts an increasing strain on habitats and wildlife. In 2005, scientists with the *Millennium Ecosystem Assessment* calculated that the current global extinction rate is 100 to 1000 times greater than the usual background rate. Moreover, they projected that the rate will be 10 times as high in future decades. These trends and predictions have caused some scientists to claim that we are in the middle of Earth's sixth mass extinction.

▶ *Categorizing Risk* To help track biodiversity trends, scientists classify at-risk species as either endangered or threatened. An **endangered species** is one that is at serious risk of extinction. A **threatened species,** or vulnerable species, is one that is likely to become endangered soon throughout all or part of its range. As of March 2020, there were 1661 species in the United States officially classified as "endangered" or "threatened." The International Union for the Conservation of Nature (IUCN) maintains the IUCN Red List of Threatened Species™, a global list of species facing high risk of extinction. As of early 2020, the Red List reported that 25 percent of mammal species worldwide, including all remaining subspecies of tiger, are threatened or endangered.

▶ *Tracking Decline* Scientists at the World Wildlife Fund (WWF) and the United Nations Environment Programme (UNEP) developed a metric called the Living Planet Index to track species decline. This index summarizes population trends for a set number of terrestrial, freshwater, and marine species that are closely monitored and provide reliable data. As seen in **Figure 8,** between 1970 and 2005, the Living Planet Index fell by nearly 30 percent.

Reading Checkpoint *What is the difference between an endangered and a threatened species?*

FIGURE 8 The Living Planet Index
Tigers are one of the more than 1600 vertebrate species whose population trends are summarized by the Living Planet Index. Biodiversity in 1970 is 1.0 on the graph. Between 1970 and 2005, the index fell by roughly 28%. The index for terrestrial species fell by 33%; for freshwater species, 35%; and for marine species, 14%.

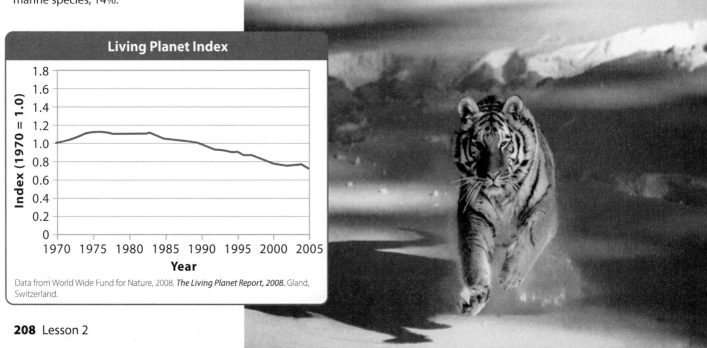

Living Planet Index

Index (1970 = 1.0) vs. Year (1970–2005)

Data from World Wide Fund for Nature, 2008. *The Living Planet Report, 2008.* Gland, Switzerland.

Causes of Biodiversity Loss

Reasons for the decline of any given species are often complex and difficult to determine. Moreover, more than one factor is often to blame. Overall, scientists have identified four primary causes of population decline and species extinction: habitat change and loss, invasive species, pollution, and overharvesting. Many scientists think global climate change will become a greater factor in the future.

Habitat Change and Loss Because organisms are adapted to the places in which they live, any major change in their habitat is likely to make it less suitable. Clearing forests for logging or road building, for example, removes the food, shelter, and other resources that forest-dwelling organisms need to survive. Thus, organisms can be caught in "habitat islands," or patches of suitable habitat type surrounded by "seas" of unsuitable habitat. This pattern, shown in **Figure 9,** is called **habitat fragmentation.** The Sikhote-Alin Mountains, home of the Siberian tiger, is a habitat fragment. The tigers are trapped on the mountains, separated from other regions of suitable forested habitat by unsuitable populated areas.

Scientists have developed models that can predict the species diversity of a habitat fragment based on its size. In general, the larger the fragment, the more species it can support. Studies of oceanic islands have found that the number of species living on an island roughly doubles as island size increases tenfold. This is partly because large islands tend to have more habitats than smaller islands, providing suitable environments for a wider variety of arriving species. The pattern holds up for habitat fragments—the smaller the habitat island, the faster it tends to lose biodiversity.

Habitat change and loss is by far the greatest cause of biodiversity loss today. It is the primary source of population declines for 83% of threatened mammals and 85% of threatened birds, according to UNEP data. As one example, less than 1% of the prairies native to North America's Great Plains remain. The rest have been converted to farmland. As a result, grassland bird populations have declined by an estimated 82–90%. Of course, human-induced habitat change may benefit some species. Animals such as house sparrows, pigeons, gray squirrels, and cockroaches, for example, do very well in urban and suburban environments. However, the number of species that benefit are relatively few, and these species tend to be generalists that have the potential to become pests.

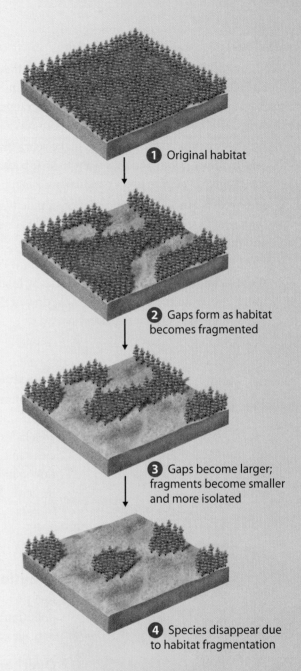

1 Original habitat

2 Gaps form as habitat becomes fragmented

3 Gaps become larger; fragments become smaller and more isolated

4 Species disappear due to habitat fragmentation

FIGURE 9 Habitat Loss Forest clearing, farming, road building, and other types of human land use and development can fragment natural habitats. As a habitat becomes fragmented, the number of species in the fragments decreases.

Map it

Invading Mussels

Zebra mussels were accidentally introduced to the Great Lakes from European and Asian cargo ships. The map at right shows the extent of the mussels' range as of early 2020.

1. **Apply Concepts** What qualities make zebra mussels invasive? (*Hint:* You may want to look back to the chapter *Evolution and Community Ecology*.)

2. **Interpret Maps** What is the relationship between the major rivers shown on the map (by blue lines) and the spread of zebra mussels?

3. **Infer** Notice the black dots on the map. Some of these locations appear to be inaccessible by inland waterways from the Great Lakes. How do you think zebra mussels got to these places?

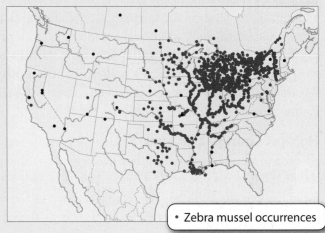

• Zebra mussel occurrences

Source: U.S. Geological Survey. [2020]. Nonindigenous Aquatic Species Database.

FIGURE 10 A Sticky Situation
Pollution, as from an oil spill, can poison humans and other living things. Here, a seabird is getting a bath to wash away oil leaked from a damaged ship in 2007 off the coast of England.

Invasive Species The introduction of non-native species to new environments can sometimes push native species toward extinction. Most organisms introduced to new areas do not survive long because the new area lacks certain conditions necessary for survival. However, some species can survive *too well*. Once released from the limiting factors of predation, parasitism, and competition, an introduced species may become invasive. Non-native species are considered invasive if their populations increase rapidly, spread, and displace native species. Invasive species, such as the zebra mussel, cause billions of dollars in economic damage each year. Very few, such as the honeybee, are beneficial.

Pollution Heavy metals, fertilizers, pesticides, and the toxic chemicals that pollute the air and water can poison people and wildlife. Although pollution is a substantial threat, it tends to be less significant than the damage caused by habitat loss or invasive species.

Overharvesting For most species, hunting or harvesting by humans does not pose a threat of extinction, but there are exceptions. Overharvesting occurs when humans hunt, fish, or harvest a species faster than it can replenish its population. Some species of fish, for example, are facing extinction because of overfishing. Likewise much of the Siberian tiger's population decline is due to overharvesting. Large, few in number, long-lived, and raising few young in its lifetime, the Siberian tiger is just the type of animal that is vulnerable to population reduction by hunting.

 Reading Checkpoint *How do invasive species affect biodiversity?*

Hunting nearly drove Siberian tigers to extinction in the early twentieth century. Then after World War II, a decrease in hunting allowed the population to increase to about 250 individuals. The early 1990s, however, brought a boom in **poaching,** the illegal capture or killing of an organism. Organisms are often poached when their parts can be sold illegally. The parts from one tiger, for example, can be sold for about $15,000 in today's black market, which is a lot of money for poachers in poor regions.

Climate Change Habitat loss, invasive species, pollution, and overharvesting usually affect biodiversity only in certain places and at certain times. In contrast, recent changes to Earth's climate system are beginning to have *global* effects on biodiversity. Extreme weather events such as droughts increase stress on populations. Warming temperatures are causing organisms to move toward the poles and higher altitudes where the climate is cooler. Some species will be able to adapt, but others will not. In the Arctic, where warming has been greatest, polar bears are struggling as the ice they live and hunt on thins and melts (**Figure 11**). Unfortunately for the bears, there is nowhere colder for them to go and their future looks grim. One recent study found that about 50 percent of plant and animal species in the world's most diverse areas could become extinct if global temperatures continue to increase.

FIGURE 11 On Thin Ice The long-term survival of polar bears *(Ursus maritimus)* is threatened by climate change as Arctic warming melts the sea ice. The bears hunt seals from the icy surface. Less ice means they have to swim farther for food, sometimes drowning in the process.

LESSON ② Assessment

1. **Explain** What is the Living Planet Index and what does it suggest about current biodiversity trends?

2. **Apply Concepts** What are the major factors affecting biodiversity today? Which one currently has the greatest overall effect? How is climate change different from the other factors?

3. **THINK IT** *THROUGH* Suppose someone tells you that human development increases biodiversity. When a forest is fragmented, he or she argues, new habitats, such as grassy lots and gardens, may be introduced to an area and allow additional species to live there. How would you respond to this claim? Do you agree? Explain your answer.

Protecting Biodiversity

EVERYDAY PHENOMENON How can we protect and preserve biodiversity?

Knowledge and Skills

- Explain legal actions nations can take to protect biodiversity.
- Explain the goal of Species Survival Plans.
- Describe three strategies for managing whole ecosystems and habitats.

Reading Strategy and Vocabulary

Reading Strategy Before you read, set up a T-chart. Label the left column "Ways to Protect Biodiversity" and the right column "Details." As you read, fill in both columns. You may choose to use the blue headings to fill in the left column.

Vocabulary Endangered Species Act (ESA), captive breeding, Species Survival Plan (SSP), biodiversity hotspot, endemic

TODAY, MORE AND MORE SCIENTISTS and citizens see a need to do something about the loss of biodiversity. In his 1994 autobiography, *Naturalist*, E. O. Wilson writes: "When the [20th] century began, people still thought of the planet as infinite in its bounty. The highest mountains were still unclimbed, the ocean depths never visited, and vast wildernesses stretched across the equatorial continents." But, since then, extinction rates have increased, and what was once seemingly endless wilderness is now threatened. So, Wilson writes, "Troubled by what we have wrought, we have begun to turn in our role from local conqueror to global steward." Is Wilson right? Are we changing roles from conqueror to steward? And are we doing enough to protect remaining biodiversity?

Legal Efforts

Biodiversity can be protected by law. In the United States, the major law that protects biodiversity is the **Endangered Species Act (ESA).** Passed in 1973, the ESA has three major parts. First, it forbids the government and private citizens from harming listed endangered and threatened species or their habitats. Harmful actions could be direct, such as cutting down protected tree species, or indirect, like funding such a project. Second, the ESA forbids trade in products made from species that are on the list. Finally, it requires the U.S. Fish and Wildlife Service to maintain the official list of endangered and threatened organisms, and to develop recovery plans for each protected species. The goal of the law is to prevent extinctions by protecting at-risk species from natural or artificial threats, such as pollution, predation, disease, and habitat destruction. The hope is that with protection, declining populations can stabilize and eventually recover.

 What does the Endangered Species Act do for protected species?

(a) Peregrine Falcon

(b) Spotted Owl

FIGURE 12 Protection Under Law (a) The peregrine falcon *(Falco peregrinus)* owes its recovery to careful management under the ESA. **(b)** ESA protection for the northern spotted owl *(Strix occidentalis caurina)* caused some controversy in the Pacific Northwest when loggers lost their jobs.

Benefits and Costs of the ESA The ESA has had a number of notable successes. For example, the peregrine falcon **(Figure 12a),** brown pelican, bald eagle, and other birds affected by the pesticide DDT are no longer listed as endangered. Other species, such as the red-cockaded woodpecker, are still endangered, but have stopped declining thanks to careful management under the ESA. In fact, roughly 40 percent of once-declining populations in the United States are now stable.

Polls repeatedly show that most Americans support the idea of protecting endangered species. However, some feel that species preservation under the ESA comes at too high a price. In the 1990s, part of the species recovery plan for the northern spotted owl **(Figure 12b)** in the Pacific Northwest, for example, protected large areas of old-growth forest. During the decline in timber harvesting that followed, many loggers lost their jobs. In addition, some landowners worry that use of their private land could be restricted if threatened or endangered species are found on it. Supporters, however, point out that parts of the ESA promote cooperation and trade-offs with landowners and developers.

International Cooperation At the international level, the United Nations has facilitated several treaties to protect biodiversity. A treaty is an agreement under international law. When nations ratify a treaty, they promise to uphold the laws that are described. One important biodiversity treaty is the 1975 Convention on International Trade in Endangered Species of Wild Fauna and Flora (CITES). CITES protects endangered species by banning the international transport of their body parts. When enforced by the 175 member nations, CITES can protect tigers and other rare species whose body parts are traded internationally.

In 1992, leaders of many nations met in Rio de Janeiro, Brazil, and agreed to the Convention on Biological Diversity, sometimes called the biodiversity treaty. The treaty has three goals: to conserve biodiversity, to use biodiversity in a sustainable manner, and to ensure the fair distribution of biodiversity's benefits. The treaty has already had many accomplishments. It has helped increase global markets for "shade-grown" coffee and other crops grown without removing forests, for example. As of 2016, close to 200 nations have joined the Convention on Biological Diversity. The United States has signed the treaty, but has not ratified it, meaning that the treaty is not yet enforced by U.S. law.

MAKE A DIFFERENCE

your world • your turn

Do you think the United States should ratify the biodiversity treaty? Write a letter to your state or federal legislator explaining why you think it is or is not important that the United States enforce the regulations of the treaty.

Single-Species Approaches

Conservation biologists use field data, lab data, theory, and experiments to study the effects of people on other organisms. In protecting biodiversity, conservation programs can target specific, single species, or can try to protect whole habitats and ecosystems. Captive breeding and cloning are examples of single-species approaches.

Captive Breeding Programs In the effort to save threatened and endangered species, zoos and botanical gardens have become centers for captive breeding. **Captive breeding** is the process of breeding and raising organisms in controlled conditions. In modern zoos and aquariums, captive breeding is part of an overall program to protect the species called a **Species Survival Plan (SSP)**.

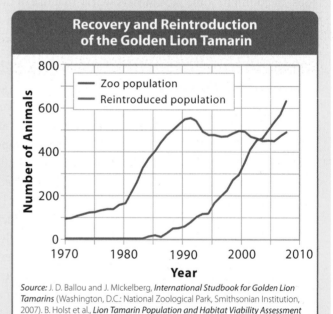

Golden Lion Tamarin

Golden Lion Tamarin

Species Survival Plans, or SSPs, are efforts to protect and manage captive populations of specific organisms. These plans are coordinated by zoos and aquariums with the ultimate goal of reintroducing healthy individuals to the wild. Since the early 1980s, Dr. Jonathan Ballou at the Smithsonian Institution's National Zoo in Washington, D.C., has been tracking and managing the captive population of golden lion tamarins around the world. Some of his data are shown at right.

1. **Calculate** By approximately what percent has the zoo population of tamarins in this SSP increased since 1970?

2. **Analyze Data** Reintroduction typically begins once a captive population has reached a certain "target size." Based on the graph, what is the approximate target captive population size for the golden lion tamarin?

3. **Infer** According to Dr. Ballou's data, 153 golden lion tamarins have been reintroduced to the wild from captivity. However, according to the graph, the reintroduced population includes about 650 individuals. Where did the other 497 tamarins come from?

Recovery and Reintroduction of the Golden Lion Tamarin

Source: J. D. Ballou and J. Mickelberg, *International Studbook for Golden Lion Tamarins* (Washington, D.C.: National Zoological Park, Smithsonian Institution, 2007). B. Holst et al., *Lion Tamarin Population and Habitat Viability Assessment Workshop 2005, Final Report* (Apple Valley, MN: IUCN/SSC Conservation Breeding Specialist Group, 2006).

4. **Form an Opinion** Do you think it is ever okay to remove animals from the wild and bring them into captivity? Why or why not?

In North America, the Association of Zoos and Aquariums (AZA) currently oversees SSPs for almost 500 species. Captive breeding as part of an SSP is carefully managed to ensure the greatest possible genetic diversity. One goal of SSPs is for captive-bred organisms to be reintroduced into the wild. SSPs also involve education, outreach, and research.

One example of a successful SSP is the program to save the golden lion tamarin *(Leontopithecus rosalia)*. Golden lion tamarins are primates native to the coastal forests of Brazil. By the early 1970s, habitat fragmentation had caused a dramatic population decline—only 200 or so were left in the wild. The SSP for golden lion tamarins started with just 91 individuals in 26 zoos. As of 2020, there were nearly 500 golden lion tamarins in 150 participating zoos worldwide. And best of all, more than 150 tamarins cared for in captivity have been reintroduced to the wild.

Cloning The newest idea for saving species from extinction is to make more individuals through cloning. In this technique, DNA from an endangered species is inserted into a cultured egg cell that has had its nucleus removed. The egg is then implanted into a closely related species that can act as a surrogate mother. Even if cloning can succeed from a technical standpoint, most biologists agree that cloning won't really help prevent biodiversity loss. Without ample habitat and protection in the wild, most scientists think having cloned animals in a zoo does little good.

Ecosystem and Habitat Approaches

Most laws, including the Endangered Species Act, do not specifically provide protection for whole habitats and ecosystems, only individual species. However, many conservation biologists recognize the need to move beyond single-species approaches.

Biodiversity Hotspots One effort oriented around geographic regions, rather than single species, is the mapping of biodiversity hotspots. A **biodiversity hotspot** is an area that both supports an especially high number of endemic species and is rapidly losing biodiversity. A species is **endemic** to an area if it is found nowhere else in the world. To qualify as a hotspot, a location must harbor at least 1500 endemic plant species, or 0.5% of the world total. In addition, a hotspot must have already lost 70% of its habitat as a result of human actions and be in danger of losing more. Hotspots are seen as areas critical to global biodiversity.

 Reading Checkpoint *What is an endemic species?*

FIGURE 13 Endemic Species This enormous tree is a coastal redwood *(Sequoia sempervirens)*, a species found only in a thin strip of land from central California to Oregon. It is one of the species endemic to the biodiversity hotspot known as the California Floristic Province.

FIGURE 14 Biodiversity Hotspots Some areas of the world possess exceptionally high numbers of species found nowhere else. Many conservation biologists have supported prioritizing habitat preservation in these areas, called biodiversity hotspots. Shown in red are the 36 biodiversity hotspots mapped by Conservation International.

The nonprofit group Conservation International maintains a list of 36 biodiversity hotspots, shown in **Figure 14.** Together, these areas once covered 16.7% of the planet's land surface. Today, however, they cover only 2.4%. This small amount of land is the exclusive home to more than 50% of the world's plant species and 43% of all terrestrial vertebrate species. The hotspot concept helps conservation biologists focus on these areas, where the greatest number of unique species can be protected with the least amount of effort.

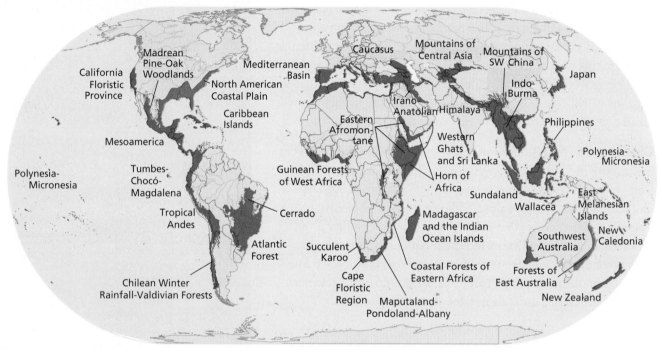

Adapted from *Hotspot map,* Conservation International, 2020.

Economic Approaches Many of today's conservation efforts attempt to protect not only land and wildlife, but the economic interests of the local people as well. Wisconsin-based Community Conservation, for example, has set up a number of community-based conservation projects in the small Central American nation of Belize. These projects not only protect wildlife, but also bring in money from researchers and ecotourists.

A more direct economic approach is the *debt-for-nature swap.* Here, a conservation organization raises money and offers to pay off a portion of a developing nation's international debt in exchange for a promise by the nation to set aside reserves, fund environmental education, and better manage protected areas.

A newer economic strategy that Conservation International has pioneered is called the *conservation concession.* Governments often sell concessions, or rights, to corporations allowing them to extract resources. A nation can, for example, earn money by selling the right to log its forests. Conservation International has started paying countries for the right to conserve its resources, not extract them. The South American nation of Suriname, which has extensive areas of untouched rain forest, entered into such an agreement. As a result, Suriname has made about $15 million and logging in the rain forest has been significantly reduced.

 Reading Checkpoint *How do conservation concessions work?*

FIGURE 15 Safe Passage The southern cassowary (left) is a large flightless bird closely related to the emu and ostrich. Only 1200–1500 individuals remain in Australia. Conservation biologists hope that when completed, the corridor (right) will enable isolated cassowary populations to interbreed. Above, volunteers are planting trees that will form part of the corridor.

Wildlife Corridors Recall that population sizes often decline when habitat is fragmented. One way to increase fragment size is to establish *wildlife corridors* that connect habitat fragments. A major benefit of wildlife corridors is that they enable once-isolated populations of organisms to interbreed, thus increasing genetic diversity.

There are currently several corridor initiatives at work in Southeast Asia to help rejoin fragments of tiger habitat. The most ambitious is a proposal made in 2008, by the Wildlife Conservation Society and the Panthera Foundation. They hope to someday establish an 8000-km (5000-mi)-long corridor across eight southeast Asian countries. The Australian Rainforest Foundation is in the midst of a similar project called "Operation Big Bird." The foundation is building a 250-km (150-mi)-long corridor of rainforest habitat for the endangered southern cassowary (*Casuarius casuarius*). With luck, the corridor will help the declining population of this unusual "big bird" to recover.

LESSON ③ Assessment

1. **Explain** What are the major benefits and costs of the Endangered Species Act?

2. **Apply Concepts** In what ways has the golden lion tamarin SSP been successful?

3. **Compare** What do the hotspot mapping project, conservation concession programs, and wildlife corridors have in common?

REVISIT

4. **INVESTIGATIVE** PHENOMENON

What are some of the advantages to focusing on the conservation of a single species versus trying to conserve ecosystems or habitats? What might be some of the disadvantages? Which do you think is the better approach, or should we use both?

A COUPLE OF **BIRDS** MAKE
BIG COMEBACKS

Biodiversity faces many threats. Habitat loss, invasive species, pollution, overharvesting, and climate change are all negatively affecting wildlife around the globe. There are, however, people working tirelessly to help reverse the trend. Here are two examples of species recovering from near-extinction thanks to the efforts of conservation scientists ... and a little luck.

CALIFORNIA CONDORS

The California condor is North America's largest bird. Sadly, collisions with electrical wires and lead poisoning (caused by scavenging carcasses of animals killed with lead ammunition) devastated condor populations. By 1982, only 22 condors remained. Biologists decided to take all the birds into captivity in hopes of boosting their numbers and then releasing them to the wild. The program is succeeding. In order to sustain growth in the population, the plan is to have two self-sustaining populations—one in California and one in Arizona—each with at least 150 condors. In addition, there will be 15 breeding pairs kept in captivity. One positive note has been that a few of the released pairs have begun nesting and hatching wild chicks.

Condors mate for life and lay only one egg per year. However, if the egg is lost, they will lay another one to replace it. Wildlife ecologists increase hatchings by taking eggs from nests and placing them with surrogate condor parents to hatch. The nonprofit group Ventana Wildlife Society has been tracking the success of reintroduced California condors since 1997. Through its work, interested people can track the progress of their favorite condors, report sightings, and even watch videos of condors caught on their many motion-sensitive "critter cams."

Scientists use lifelike condor hand puppets to minimize the impact of human interaction during captivity.

CHATHAM ISLAND BLACK ROBINS

The management of the condor population is both similar to and different from another successful story of an avian comeback—that of the Chatham Island black robin. These small, sparrow-sized birds are native to the Chatham Islands east of New Zealand. They evolved in an environment free of predators. When humans came to the islands in 1900, the birds faced something they never had before—rats and cats. The birds' eggs and chicks are a favorite snacks of rats, and because even adult black robins are not very good fliers, they are caught easily by predatory cats. Before long, the entire population on the main island was completely wiped out. By 1976, there were only seven birds left on the tiny island of Little Mangere.

Instead of bringing the remaining birds into captivity, as with the condors, wildlife conservationists relocated them to an area of protected habitat and let them loose. Success was not immediate. Four years later, two birds had died and no new chicks were hatched. There was just one breeding pair left, a female called "Old Blue" and her mate "Old Yellow." Like California condors, Chatham Island black robins mate for life. They produce one clutch of two eggs per year. Also like condors, black robins lay more eggs if their eggs are lost.

So, scientists gave robin eggs to surrogates for hatching—though this time, the surrogates were of a different species because there were no additional black robin females to place them with. This unusual program has worked. As of October 2016, there were about 230 mature robins, all descended from "Old Blue" and "Old Yellow," living in protected, predator-free refuges on two of the Chatham Islands. Despite low genetic diversity and severe habitat fragmentation, the population seems healthy and continues to increase slowly.

CAREER **Animal Conservationist** Animal conservationists work to protect and preserve the animal species and their environment. Depending on your interests you could work in wildlife rescue, rehabilitation, in zoos, aquariums, or wildlife sanctuaries. Go Online and research careers in animal conservation. Write a brief summary of your findings.

INVESTIGATIVE PHENOMENON

Why is it important to measure and protect biodiversity?

Lesson 1
Why is maintaining biodiversity important?

Lesson 2
Why is global biodiversity decreasing?

Lesson 3
How can we protect and preserve biodiversity?

LESSON 1 Our Planet of Life

- Ecologists break down an area's overall biodiversity into three major categories: species diversity, genetic diversity, and ecosystem diversity. Species diversity is the number or variety of species in a particular area. Genetic diversity describes the differences in DNA among individuals of a population or species. Ecosystem diversity refers to an area's variety of ecosystems, communities, or habitats.
- Biodiversity varies among taxonomic groups and geographic regions.
- Biodiversity enables ecosystems to provide economically valuable services and products, such as clean water, food crops, medicines, and recreation areas.

biodiversity (200)
species diversity (201)
genetic diversity (202)
ecosystem diversity (202)

LESSON 2 Extinction and Biodiversity Loss

- Scientists monitor biodiversity closely and have noticed significantly higher than normal extinction rates in recent decades. Endangered species are at serious risk of extinction. Threatened species are likely to become endangered soon throughout all or part of their range.
- Habitat change and loss, invasive species, pollution, and overharvesting are the major causes of biodiversity loss. Climate change is also a factor and may become a greater one in the future.

extirpation (207)
endangered species (208)
threatened species (208)
habitat fragmentation (209)
poaching (211)

LESSON 3 Protecting Biodiversity

- Nations can pass laws (such as the Endangered Species Act) and sign international treaties (such as CITES) that protect biodiversity.
- Species Survival Plans manage, protect, and reintroduce threatened and endangered species.
- Strategies that manage whole ecosystems and habitats, such as the hotspot approach, conservation concessions, and wildlife corridors, protect many species at once. The hotspot approach involves focusing conservation efforts on areas with especially high numbers of endemic species that are rapidly losing biodiversity. Conservation concessions are agreements in which countries are paid to protect their natural resources. Wildlife corridors connect habitat fragments, enabling populations to interbreed.

Endangered Species Act (ESA) (212)
captive breeding (214)
Species Survival Plan (SSP) (214)
biodiversity hotspot (215)
endemic (215)

 GO ONLINE

INQUIRY LABS AND ACTIVITIES

- **Exploring Plant Diversity**
  Mark an outdoor area and classify the variety of plant life there. Then calculate the plant diversity of the area.
- **Overharvesting**
  Using a method of scooping beans that models trawling, try to catch your "target fish species" without harming the "protected species."
- **Endangered Species**
  Is there a species near you that is endangered? Find out what's being done to increase the current population.

Chapter Assessment

Defend Your Case

The Central Case in this chapter explored efforts that brought the Siberian tiger back from the brink of extinction. All over the world, scientists are trying to slow the loss of our planet's biological diversity. Based on what you have learned, do you think that all nations should be responsible for protecting biodiversity? Explain. Use evidence from the Central Case and throughout the chapter to support your answer.

Review Concepts and Terms

1. Which of the following is NOT part of overall biodiversity?
   a. species diversity
   c. individual diversity
   b. genetic diversity
   d. ecosystem diversity

2. The tiger (*Panthera tigris*), jaguar (*Panthera onca*), and lion (*Panthera leo*) are all members of the same
   a. subspecies.
   c. genus.
   b. species.
   d. ecosystem.

3. What provides the raw material for adaptation to local conditions?
   a. ecosystem diversity
   c. extirpation
   b. species diversity
   d. genetic diversity

4. Which of the following increases species diversity?
   a. extirpation
   c. extinction
   b. speciation
   d. poaching

5. The disappearance of a particular population from a given area, but not of the entire species globally, is called
   a. extinction.
   c. extirpation.
   b. immigration.
   d. speciation.

6. Globally, the leading cause of biodiversity loss is
   a. invasive species.
   b. poaching and overharvesting.
   c. pollution.
   d. habitat change and loss.

7. The illegal capture or killing of an organism, often for money, is called
   a. poaching.
   c. fragmentation.
   b. harvesting.
   d. extinction.

8. Which of the following forbids the U.S. government and its citizens from harming endangered or threatened species and their habitats?
   a. the Environmental Protection Agency
   b. Species Survival Plan
   c. the Endangered Species Act
   d. the Convention on International Trade in Endangered Species

9. Some conservation biologists focus on areas where the greatest number of unique species can be protected with the least amount of effort. These areas are called
   a. wildlife corridors.
   b. habitat fragments.
   c. biodiversity hotspots.
   d. conservation concessions.

10. The eastern long-beaked echidna, shown here, is an egg-laying mammal found only in New Guinea. Which of the following terms describes an organism such as the echidna that is found in one place and nowhere else in the world?
    a. endemic
    c. endangered
    b. threatened
    d. conserved

Modified True/False

Write true if the statement is true. If it is false, change the underlined word or words to make the statement true.

11. Biodiversity tends to <u>decrease</u> nearer the equator.

12. <u>Threatened species</u> are at the highest risk of extinction.

13. <u>Climate change</u> can have *global*, not just local, impacts on biodiversity.

14. The process of breeding and raising organisms in controlled conditions is called <u>cloning</u>.

Reading Comprehension

Read the following selection and answer the questions that follow.

The latitudinal gradient influences the species diversity of Earth's biomes. Tropical dry forests and rain forests tend to support far more species than tundra and boreal forests, for instance. It seems likely that plant productivity and climate stability are at least partially responsible for this pattern. Greater amounts of solar energy, heat, and humidity at tropical latitudes lead to more plant growth, making areas nearer the equator more productive and able to support larger numbers of animals. Further, the relatively stable temperatures and rainfall of equatorial regions favor organisms with specialized niches that do particular things very well. Thus, many species can divide up resources and coexist in tropical areas.

15. An appropriate title for this passage might be
a. "Describing Biomes"
b. "Is There a Latitudinal Gradient?"
c. "Explaining the Latitudinal Gradient"
d. "Why Is Biodiversity Decreasing?"

16. From the passage, it is possible to infer that
a. rain forests are found closer to the equator than boreal forests.
b. boreal forest has the lowest biodiversity of any biome.
c. rainforest animals are larger than animals that live in boreal forests.
d. boreal forest animals never divide resources.

Analyze Data

The graph below shows the potential loss or gain of habitat in terrestrial biomes by 2050. The percentage of potential losses are in purple. The percentage of potential gains are shown in orange. Use the data to answer the questions.

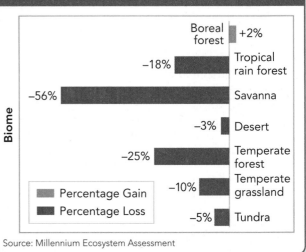

Source: Millennium Ecosystem Assessment

17. **Interpret Graphs** Which biome(s) are predicted to lose over 40 percent of their habitat by 2050?

18. **Interpret Graphs** Which biome(s) are predicted to gain habitat by 2050?

19. **Infer** Why do you think that some biomes will lose habitat, while others will gain habitat?

20. **Infer** How do you think the predicted changes will affect biodiversity? How will they affect human activities, such as agriculture and other land use?

Short Answer

21. What is biodiversity?

22. What are ecosystem services? Give two examples.

23. What is the difference between ecotourism and tourism?

24. What are mass extinctions?

25. Are all non-native species invasive? What makes a species invasive?

26. What is a biodiversity hotspot? How does an area qualify to be a hotspot?

Critical Thinking

27. **Form an Opinion** Ecotourism can have both beneficial and harmful effects on an area. Describe these effects, and then explain whether you would support ecotourism in your area.

28. **Apply Concepts** Some scientists think that we are in the middle of the "sixth mass extinction." What does that mean? What evidence do they use to support that claim?

29. **Relate Cause and Effect** What is the relationship between biodiversity loss, medicine, and agriculture?

30. **Explain** What happens when a top predator, such as the Siberian tiger, is removed from an ecological system?

31. **Apply Concepts** How does the Endangered Species Act protect biodiversity?

32. **Propose a Solution** Suppose you are a town planner. There has been huge growth recently. Several new housing subdivisions are sprouting up at the edge of town where there was once forest. What suggestions can you make to ensure minimal impact on the local species?

Write About It

33. **Creative Writing** What could happen if more nations do not take steps to prevent habitat loss? Write a letter from the future. Describe what has become of some of the world's species and ecosystems.

34. **REVISIT INVESTIGATIVE PHENOMENON** Most scientists think there is a strong connection between biodiversity loss and increasing human population size. How do you think an increased number of people affect biodiversity in your area? Consider each of the major causes of biodiversity loss in your answer.

Ecological Footprints

Read the information below. Copy the table into your notebook, and record your calculations. Then, answer the questions that follow.

Habitat loss is a leading cause of biodiversity loss today. The World Wildlife Fund, Zoological Society of London, and Global Footprint Network released their *Living Planet Report* in 2008. According to the report, the American ecological footprint was 9.5 hectares (23.5 acres) per person in 2005. Of that, approximately 1.02 hectares (2.5 acres) were forest. Given this information, fill in the footprint table.

	Population	Total Hectares of Land Used	Hectares of Forest Used
You			
Your class			
Your hometown			
Your state			
United States			

Data from **Living Planet Index**. 2008. World Wildlife Fund International, Switzerland.

1. Other ecological footprint categories noted by the *Living Planet Report* include cropland and grazing land. They calculate that 1.38 hectares of cropland and 0.30 hectare of grazing land are required to support the average American. How many total hectares of cropland and grazing land does that add up to for the current population of the United States?

2. The uses for cropland and grazing land are obvious—they provide food. But what about forest? One of the largest uses for forest is timber for housing. What are some other uses for forest?

3. Today, in the United States there are about 302 million hectares of forests. That is about 33 percent of the total land area. If the population of the United States remains stable, and if we do not regrow any forest we cut down, how many generations will it take to completely use up our forested land?

4. What is the connection between land use and biodiversity?

ANCHORING PHENOMENON

These questions will help you apply what you have learned in this Unit to the Anchoring Phenomenon.

1. **Develop and Use Models** Make a model to show how tourism could positively or negatively impact abiotic and biotic factors in an ecosystem.

2. **Obtain, Evaluate, and Communicate Information** Use evidence from your textbook and other sources to identify an ecosystem that may be vulnerable even to ecotourism. Write a short report summarizing your findings.

3. **Engage in Argument from Evidence** Recall the causes of biodiversity loss. Make an argument that ecotourism could be more of a risk than a benefit to an endangered species. Research and use evidence to support your argument.

GO ONLINE

For activities that will give you an opportunity to demonstrate what you have learned.

MODELING Revisit your Anchoring Phenomenon Modeling worksheet with the information you have learned in this unit.

ANCHORING PHENOMENON PROJECT Design a solution to increase the benefits and decrease the costs of ecotourism.

Humans and the Environment

ANCHORING PHENOMENON

What is the impact of population size during an environmental hazard, such as a global pandemic?

CHAPTERS

8 Human Population

9 Environmental Health

10 Urbanization

GO ONLINE

To engage with real-world phenomena. Complete the CER worksheet and preview the anchoring phenomenon project.

CHAPTER 8

Human Population

Tourists and residents alike crowd the streets of the Shichahai hutong old town area in Beijing, China.

Lesson 1
Trends in Human
Population Growth

Lesson 2
Predicting Population
Growth

Lesson 3
People and Their
Environments

China's Changing Population Needs

SIXTY YEARS AGO, about 540 million people lived in a mostly rural, war-torn China. Then, a new leader, Mao Zedong, took charge. Under his leadership, China grew and changed. Although the start of this change was tumultuous, eventually people had greater access to food, and public health improved. By 1970, China's population had grown to about 790 million people. At that time, each Chinese woman had an average of about 5.9 children in her lifetime.

But China's population growth was taking a toll on the environment. Soils were eroding. Forests and water supplies were diminishing. The air was becoming more and more polluted. Chinese leaders realized that the nation might not be able to feed its people if the population kept growing as rapidly. To prevent a catastrophic strain on the nation's resources, the government started a population-control program.

The program began with education and outreach that encouraged people to marry at an older age and have fewer children. But these initial efforts didn't meet the government's goals. In 1979, the government set up a new system. It used rewards and punishments to enforce a one-child limit. Families with one child received access to better schools, medical care, housing, and government jobs. Mothers of a single child were given longer maternity leaves. Couples with more than one child, meanwhile, were fined. In some cases, the fines were more than half of what the couple earned in a year! Socially, these families were scorned and ridiculed.

In enforcing its policies, China ultimately conducted one of the largest and most controversial social experiments in history. Sons are traditionally favored in China, because they provide support for their parents as they age. Enforcing a one-child policy led to an unbalanced ratio of males and females. In 2005, there were 32 million more males in China under the age of 20 than females.

🖥 **GO ONLINE**
• Take It Local • 3-D Geo Tour

Today, the policy has been loosened to a two-child policy in an effort to bolster the decreasing population and rectify the skewed male to female ratio. So far this policy hasn't worked to encourage parents to have more children. One reason for this is increased educational standards and job opportunities for women. In addition, the high costs of raising children is also limiting the number of children being born.

By 2050, it is estimated that one-third of the nation's population will be over the age of 60. Concerns now are how younger generations will be able to support their aging relatives and how to deal with a shrinking workforce.

China is not alone in worrying about the population size of its citizens. Other nations are also facing the challenge of populations that are increasing at a fast rate or having fewer young citizens to care for its aging population. How, and to what extent, these nations control their growth is an uncertain but critical question for future generations.

Human Population **227**

Trends in Human Population Growth

LESSON 1

EVERYDAY PHENOMENON What social and environmental factors affect human population size?

Knowledge and Skills

- Describe how technological advances have contributed to human population growth.
- Explain recent trends in population growth.
- Identify characteristics of human population that are studied by demographers.

Reading Strategy and Vocabulary

✓ **Reading Strategy** Before reading, scan the lesson. Write a few sentences that predict what you think the lesson is about. When you finish reading, rewrite your sentences to better summarize the lesson.

Vocabulary Industrial Revolution, infant mortality, life expectancy, growth rate, demography

ABOUT 7.8 BILLION … and counting. That is the approximate size of the human population as of 2020. Just how great a number is 7.8 billion? Even the number 1 billion is difficult to picture. If you started to count once each second without ever stopping to sleep, it would take you more than 30 years to reach just 1 billion.

Although the rate of human population growth is slowing, actual growth does continue. Every person who is born needs food, water, and space. How long will population growth continue? How much food, water, and space can Earth provide? These are questions that some environmental scientists seek to answer.

History of Human Population Growth

Over just the past 300 years, the human population has undergone tremendous growth that dwarfs all previous growth during our 200,000 years of existence. The population didn't reach 1 billion people until about 1800. Yet, there are now about 7.8 billion people. Advances in agriculture and industry gave the human population the means to expand so quickly over a relatively short period of time.

Development of Agriculture About 10,000 years ago, many human societies changed from roaming hunter-gatherers to settled farmers. As people began to grow crops and raise domestic animals, they met their nutritional needs more easily. As a result, people lived longer and more children survived to adulthood. Eventually, some people began trading and purchasing food from other people. Because their time was freed from growing food, they could pursue crafts and trades. As shown in **Figure 1,** the size of the human population began to slowly increase. Diseases such as smallpox and plague still claimed many lives.

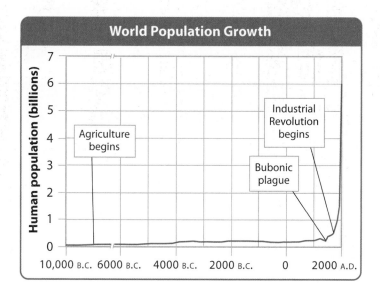

World Population Growth

Human population (billions)

Agriculture begins

Industrial Revolution begins

Bubonic plague

10,000 B.C. 6000 B.C. 4000 B.C. 2000 B.C. 0 2000 A.D.

FIGURE 1 Human Population Size For a great part of human history, the population was small and fairly stable. Widespread agriculture and, especially, the Industrial Revolution caused it to skyrocket to 6 billion by the year 2000.

Industrial Revolution During the **Industrial Revolution,** which began in the mid-1700s, many societies started to shift from a rural life focused on agriculture and goods made by craftspeople to urban societies powered by fossil fuels. Besides changing daily life, the Industrial Revolution led to improvements in sanitation, medical technology, and the ability to mass produce food that contributed to the human population explosion.

▶ *Sanitation* During the time of the Industrial Revolution, Louis Pasteur and other scientists developed the germ theory of disease. People began to understand that many deadly diseases are caused by organisms (germs) that spread from person to person. Previously acceptable behaviors, such as throwing garbage and human waste into public waterways, were no longer tolerated. As a result, living conditions in cities became cleaner. Also, doctors began washing their hands before moving from one patient to the next. This greatly reduced deaths from infections, especially deaths related to childbirth. Mass production of soap and cotton clothes, which were less likely than woolen clothes to attract body lice and fleas, also helped slow the spread of disease.

▶ *Medical Technology* The advances in industry made it possible to mass produce medical instruments and, most important of all, medicines such as antibiotics and vaccines. Antibiotics treat bacterial infections and vaccines help to prevent or reduce the severity of both viral and bacterial infections. In less than a hundred years, these developments have saved millions of lives.

▶ *Changes in Agriculture* How was it possible to feed this quickly expanding population while fewer people were devoting their lives to growing food? The Industrial Revolution led to the invention of large fossil-fueled machines that made it possible to plant and harvest food in mass quantities. Pesticides were developed which reduced competition from weeds and killed insects that destroy crops. Synthetic fertilizers were also invented that enabled farmers to grow more food from the same amount of soil.

FIGURE 2 Sanitation Improvements Products of the Industrial Revolution, such as cheap soap, contributed to more sanitary conditions.

Real Data

Population Growth Rates

Not every nation's population is growing at the same rate, or growing at all. In fact, some are increasing quickly, while others are actually decreasing. The table shows 2020 estimates of growth rates and population sizes for several nations and the world.

1. **Interpret Data** Which nation is growing the fastest? Explain your answer.

2. **Infer** What is happening to Hungary's population size?

3. **Calculate** Which nation will likely add the most people to the world over the course of a year?

4. **Infer** In 1970, China's population growth rate was 2.8 percent. Do you think China's population control policies have been effective? Why or why not?

Population Growth Rate of Selected Nations and World, 2020		
	Annual Population Growth Rate	**Population Size (millions)**
China	0.3%	1394.2
Hungary	−0.3%	9.8
India	1.1%	1326.1
Madagascar	2.4%	27.0
United States	0.7%	332.6
World	1.0%	7694.3
Data: CIA		

Recent Trends in Human Population Growth

Results of the Industrial Revolution such as more food and fewer deaths from disease led to decreased infant mortality and increased life expectancy. **Infant mortality** is the number of babies out of 1000 that die during their first year of life. **Life expectancy** is the average number of years an individual is expected to live. When babies have a greater chance of survival and adults live longer, a population is likely to grow ... and possibly grow quickly. Understanding human population growth is important for many reasons. This knowledge helps us understand how differences in populations affect human communities and environments.

FIGURE 3 Fast-Growing India
Indian women wait in line for immunizations for their babies. India is on course to surpass China as the world's most populous nation.

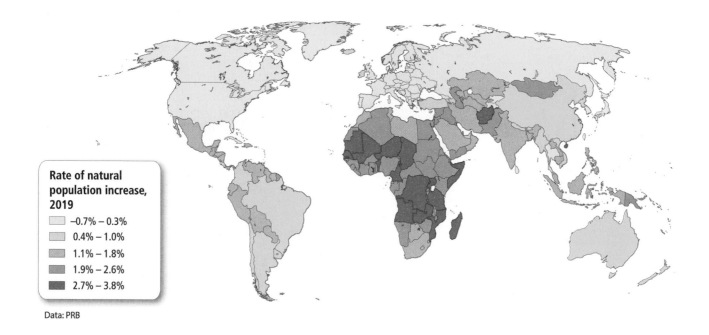

Rate of natural population increase, 2019

- −0.7% – 0.3%
- 0.4% – 1.0%
- 1.1% – 1.8%
- 1.9% – 2.6%
- 2.7% – 3.8%

Data: PRB

Growth Rate Has Slowed For much of the twentieth century, the human population growth rate rose from year to year. **Growth rate** refers to how a population changes in size during a specific period of time. Recently, it has started to decline. During the 1960s, the growth rate peaked at 2.1 percent. Since then, it has slowed to about 1 percent. To put these rates into perspective, at 2.1 percent, it takes 33 years for a population to double. At 1 percent, it takes 70 years for it to double. To estimate how long it would take any population to double, divide the number 70 by the annual percentage growth rate.

Growth Rates Vary by Region As shown in **Figure 4,** annual growth rates differ greatly around the globe. Some nations, like Germany and Russia, have a negative population growth rate. That is, their populations are decreasing. Other populations continue to increase at rates much greater than the average global rate. In the next lesson, you'll read about the factors that contribute to these variations among regions.

How Long Will Growth Continue? We have technology that allows us to manipulate our environment in ways that other species cannot. For example, the abilities to build shelters that can be heated and to transport food and water mean we can live comfortably just about anywhere. Such advances have allowed people to temporarily increase the species' *carrying capacity*—the number of organisms that an environment can support.

Technology has taken people a long way, but at some point, environmental factors such as food, water, and land will limit human population growth. Recall that when a species reaches carrying capacity, the population neither increases nor decreases. Growth rate becomes zero. No one knows what the maximum population size will be before the growth rate is zero. However, we do know that the population cannot grow forever.

FIGURE 4 Population Growth Rates Vary Population growth rates vary greatly from place to place. Shown here are rates of population change due to births and deaths. The data do not include increases from immigration or decreases from emigration.

 Reading Checkpoint *What is the relationship between carrying capacity and population growth?*

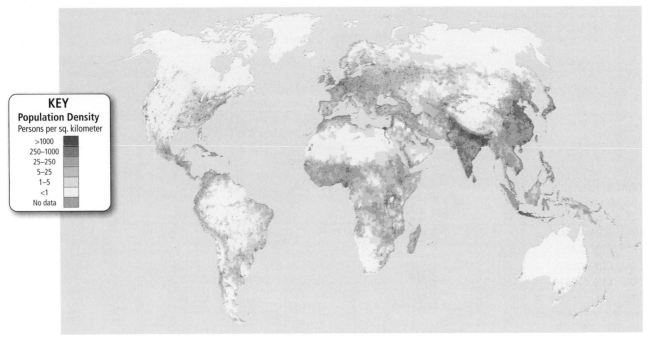

FIGURE 5 Population Density
Human population density varies greatly from one region to another. Tundra and desert regions have the lowest population densities, whereas India, Bangladesh, and eastern China—areas of temperate climate—have the highest.

Describing the Human Population

The study of human population statistics is called **demography.** *Demographers*, people who study demography, apply the principles of population ecology to humans. For example, they study human population size, population density, and distribution, just as ecologists study these characteristics in other types of populations. The data that demographers collect help them to predict changes in human population and the environmental impacts that can result.

Population Size The human population size is roughly 7.8 billion, but the exact number changes every second. In the time it took you to read the last sentence, people were born and people died—although it is likely that more people were born than died. The size of the human population does not tell the whole story of how the human population affects the environment, however. Demographers also look at where people live and the concentration of people in specific areas.

Population Density Population density describes how many people live per square mile or square kilometer. At the global scale, population density is highest in regions with temperate and tropical climates such as China, Europe, Mexico, and India **(Figure 5).** Population density is lowest in regions with extreme climates such as deserts and tundra. More people live in areas by seacoasts and rivers than in locations far from water. Regionally, populations are dense in cities and suburbs and are spread more thinly across rural areas. Locally, people are grouped in certain neighborhoods and within households.

 Reading Checkpoint *Egypt is the northeasternmost nation in Africa. How can* **Figure 5** *help you determine where the Nile River flows through Egypt?*

(a)

(b)

FIGURE 6 Population Distribution
(a) Clusters of people tend to live along waterways, as shown in this photograph of Bosa, a small city in Italy. **(b)** The population may be more spread out in dry areas, as shown in this photograph taken in Rajasthan, India.

Population Distribution In ecological terms, the human population distribution is clumped, rather than random or uniform. This uneven distribution means that some areas bear more of an environmental impact than others. Major rivers such as the Yellow River in China and the Mississippi River have been negatively affected by clustered human populations and the pollution that comes with them.

The environment can also be harmed when people live in areas that really cannot support them. For example, deserts are easily affected by development that overtakes a large share of limited water supplies. In parts of the Middle East, China, and the United States, some grasslands have been so overfarmed that they have become deserts.

Population size, density, and distribution statistics are like snapshots. They give demographers a "picture" of what the human population looks like at a particular moment in time. Other statistics you will learn about in the next lesson, such as fertility rates, age structure, and sex ratio, give demographers information to predict the future of human populations in different areas of the world.

LESSON ① Assessment

1. **Explain** Describe the main factors that led to a boom in the human population size in the last 300 years.

2. **Calculate** Population *A* contains 450,000 people and has a 3.3 percent annual growth rate. Population *B* has 900,000 people and a 1.8 percent annual growth rate. Which population would increase by more people in one year? Explain.

3. **Compare and Contrast** Describe the relationship between population density and population distribution.

   REVISIT

4. **INVESTIGATIVE** PHENOMENON
   As people become more concentrated in cities, some pressure on ecosystems in areas that are now less populated eases. Why do you think this is the case?

Predicting Population Growth

EVERYDAY PHENOMENON How do human population growth trends differ between developed nations and developing nations?

Knowledge and Skills

- Describe total fertility rates and replacement fertility.
- Explain how the age structure and sex ratio of a population define its potential for growth.
- Describe the demographic transition.
- Discuss social factors that affect population growth.

Reading Strategy and Vocabulary

✅ **Reading Strategy** Before you read, make an outline using the blue and green headings in this lesson. As you read, fill in key phrases or sentences about each heading.

Vocabulary total fertility rate, replacement fertility, demographic transition

THE NUMBER OF PEOPLE sharing Earth and its resources is getting bigger and bigger by the minute. Right now, assuming moderate population growth, scientists project that the human population may increase to more than 9 billion people by 2050. Some scientists project that it could reach 10.5 billion people by then! That's a lot of people—and a big difference in projections. So, what information do demographers use to make these predictions?

Fertility Rate

At the most basic level, the factors that affect human population growth are the same as those that affect the populations of other organisms. Births add individuals to the global population and deaths remove them. Immigration and emigration affect the population size of particular regions. To get a clear picture of a population's potential for growth, demographers look at many characteristics of a particular population.

FIGURE 7 Collecting Data
Around the world, demographers collect data in similar ways, such as these census workers in Ecuador **(a)** and the United States **(b).**

Trends in China's Population Growth					
Measure	1950	1970	1990	2007	2019
Total fertility rate	5.8	5.8	2.2	1.6	1.6
Rate of natural population increase (% per year)	1.9	2.6	1.4	0.5	0.4
Doubling time (years)	37	27	50	140	166
Population (billions)	0.55	0.83	1.14	1.32	1.40

Data from China Population Information and Research Center; and Population Reference Bureau. 2019. *2019 World population data sheet.*

 Connect to the Central Case

FIGURE 8 Trends in China The data show that the population growth rate in China has declined since the establishment of the one-child policy. Natural population increase refers to the balance of births and deaths, but does not include changes due to immigration or emigration. **Interpret Tables** Do the data in this table indicate that China's population size is decreasing?

Total Fertility Rate One key statistic that demographers examine is total fertility rate. The average number of children a female member of a population has during her lifetime is the population's **total fertility rate.**

Various factors influence total fertility rate. Historically, people tended to have many children to ensure that at least some would survive childhood. On farms, people also had more children so that they had help with farm work. And, as parents got older, they could rely on their children to support them.

Recently, total fertility rates have started to drop in many nations, which indicates that most women are having fewer children. There are many reasons for this trend. In China the trend can be partly attributed to the one-child policy **(Figure 8).** In many other nations, parents feel less pressure to have many children because almost all children survive childhood. Also, many governments now have programs to help support older adults. Because every child requires food, clothing, and shelter, parents may feel that they can better provide for smaller families. However, although fertility rates are dropping, it's important to remember that the human population is still increasing.

Replacement Fertility The total fertility rate for a nation that would keep its population size stable is called **replacement fertility.** This rate differs from nation to nation depending on its death rate. In many nations, the replacement fertility is about 2.1. If a nation's total fertility rate climbs above 2.1, then the population will most likely increase over time. If it falls below 2.1, then the population will most likely decrease over time. Almost half of the world's populations live in nations that have a total fertility rate of 2.1 or lower. In nations that have a higher than average death rate, replacement fertility is greater than 2.1.

Age Structure and Sex Ratios

Total fertility rate helps demographers predict if a population's size will increase, decrease, or stay the same. But the statistic does not tell the whole story. Age structure and sex ratios can also help demographers predict how a population might change.

WHAT DO YOU THINK?

In the United States, Canada, and many European nations, the total fertility rate has fallen below the replacement rate. What economic and social consequences do you think might result from below-replacement fertility rates?

Age Structure Populations consist of individuals of different ages. *Age structure* describes the relative numbers of organisms of each age within a population and is often represented by a graph called an age structure diagram. Age structure diagrams also show how many males and females there are in each age group.

Age structure shows the proportion of individuals currently of reproductive age, and those who could reproduce in the future. This information helps demographers predict how the size of a population will change over time. A population with many young people compared to older people could likely experience rapid population growth as the young people mature and have children. A population with fewer younger people will likely decrease in the future.

Look at the age structure diagrams for Canada and Madagascar shown in **Figure 9**. The pyramid shape of Madagascar's diagram indicates that it has a greater population growth rate than Canada. In fact, its annual growth rate is 2.7 percent, while Canada's is only 1.2 percent.

The pattern of population aging seen in Canada is occurring in many nations, including the United States. Older populations present new challenges for many nations, as increasing numbers of older people require the care and financial assistance of relatively fewer working-age citizens. But, healthy older citizens can also be very productive as volunteers in their communities and caregivers to grandchildren. Nations undergoing rapid growth, such as Madagascar, face different challenges as they try to provide education, roads, and other resources to support a rapidly growing population.

FIGURE 9 Age Structure Diagrams
Canada's age structure is relatively balanced. This indicates that there will be fewer people of reproductive age in future decades than there are now. In Madagascar, however, there are many more young people than older people.

GO ONLINE

- **Graph It** Age Pyramids and Population Growth

Reading Checkpoint *Do you think that an age structure diagram representing China's population would look more like Canada's or more like Madagascar's? Explain.*

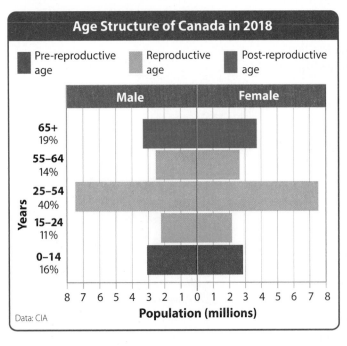

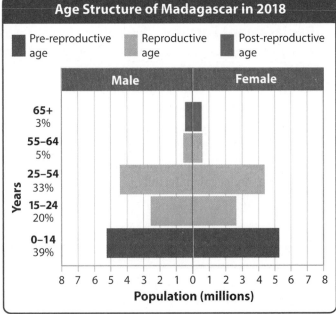

Quick Lab

Build and Compare Age Structure Diagrams

Although the United States' population as a whole is aging, not every subset of the population is following the same pattern. The data in the table are from the U.S. Census Bureau. Use the data to make age structure diagrams for these two populations. Then use the diagrams to answer the questions.

1. **Predict** Which of these two populations will likely grow at the greater rate over the next thirty years? Explain.

2. **Interpret Diagrams** Could you use age structure diagrams to compare total fertility rates of two populations? Explain.

3. **Calculate** Calculate the percentage of the white population and the Hispanic or Latino population that was younger than 20 years old. Does your answer follow the prediction you made in **Question 1**? Explain.

   % MATH SUPPORT For help calculating with percentages, see the Math Handbook.

Population Size of Two Subgroups in the U.S.				
Age	White Male	White Female	Hispanic or Latino Male	Hispanic or Latina Female
Under 5	7,672,000	7,329,000	2,628,000	2,527,000
5–14	16,013,000	15,254,000	4,959,000	4,760,000
15–24	17,118,000	16,176,000	4,784,000	4,382,000
25–34	16,594,000	15,893,000	4,579,000	4,092,000
35–44	15,882,000	15,573,000	3,919,000	3,730,000
45–54	17,701,000	17,853,000	2,967,000	2,922,000
55–64	15,549,000	16,340,000	1,747,000	1,888,000
65–74	9,667,000	10,809,000	840,000	1,029,000
75–84	4,977,000	6,576,000	389,000	557,000
85 +	1,766,000	3,485,000	116,000	213,000
Total	122,937,000	125,287,000	26,930,000	26,098,000

Data: U.S. Census Bureau

Sex Ratios Age structure diagrams also show the sex ratio for each age group. *Sex ratio* is the number of males compared to females in a population. At birth, the naturally occurring sex ratio of humans has slightly more males. For every 100 females born, about 105 males are born (sex ratio of 1.05 to 1). This phenomenon may be an evolutionary adaptation because males are slightly more likely to die during any given year of life. Therefore, having more male children in a population tends to ensure that the sex ratio is about equal when they reach reproductive age.

Human activities can skew the sex ratio one way or another. Some regions may have more females than males because many males emigrate to find work. Other areas may have more males than females. For example, in a culture that values sons more than daughters, daughters may not be given the same quality of care.

The Demographic Transition

In nations with good sanitation, effective healthcare, and reliable food supplies, people are living longer lives. In fact, over the past half-century, worldwide average life expectancy has increased from 46 to 68 years. Also, infant mortality rates have fallen in many regions. Societies going through these changes are generally those that have undergone the shift from rural life to urban life and industrialization, and that have generated personal wealth for their citizens.

To make sense of these trends, demographers use a concept called the demographic transition. The **demographic transition** is a model that explains the change from high birthrates and death rates to a condition of low birthrates and death rates. A demographic transition is the result of economic growth that has led to social changes. As shown in **Figure 10,** the demographic transition is a four-stage process.

FIGURE 10 Demographic Transition During the demographic transition, birthrates and death rates start high. Death rates fall first, followed by birthrates.

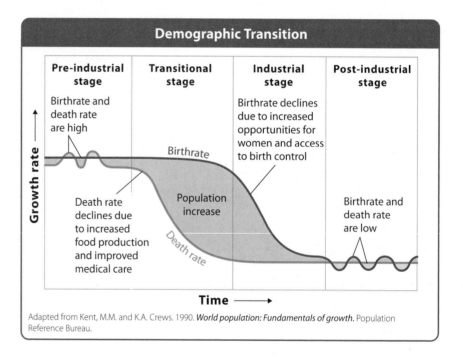

The Pre-Industrial Stage The first stage, or the *pre-industrial stage,* is characterized by conditions that have defined most of human history. For pre-industrial societies, both death rates and birthrates are high. Death rates are high because of widespread disease, poor medical care, and unreliable food and water supplies. Birthrates are high because people want larger families or they don't have access to family planning methods. Infant mortality is likely to be high during this stage, and having many children increases the chance that some of them will survive. Populations in the pre-industrial stage are not likely to experience much growth. This may explain why the human population was relatively stable until the Industrial Revolution.

The Transitional Stage Industrialization starts the *transitional stage* of the demographic transition. In this stage, death rates decline as food production increases and medical care improves. Because people have not adjusted to the new economic and social conditions, birthrates remain high. Population growth increases because births exceed deaths.

The Industrial Stage The third stage in the demographic transition is the *industrial stage*. Industrialization increases job opportunities outside the home, particularly for women. Couples may choose to have fewer children in part because there is less fear of losing them to disease or famine. Birthrates fall, closing the gap with death rates. In turn, the rate of population growth also falls.

The Post-Industrial Stage In the final stage, the *post-industrial stage*, both birthrates and death rates fall to low and stable levels. Population sizes stabilize or decline slightly but are much higher than they were at the pre-industrial stage. The society enjoys the benefits of industrialization without the threat of runaway population growth.

The demographic transition has occurred in many nations over the past 200 to 300 years. For example, many European nations, the United States, Canada, and Japan have all undergone this transition. But social scientists cannot predict whether every nation will eventually follow the same pattern.

 Reading Checkpoint *Briefly describe the four stages of the demographic transition.*

(a)

(b)

FIGURE 11 Japan and India
(a) Japan has already gone through the demographic transition, which means that many couples have only one or two children. **(b)** No one knows if population growth in other nations, such as India, will follow the demographic transition pattern.

Social Factors

Predicting population growth is not just a numbers game. People live in complex societies that influence population growth and their impact on the environment. Factors such as poverty, wealth, and education levels affect population size.

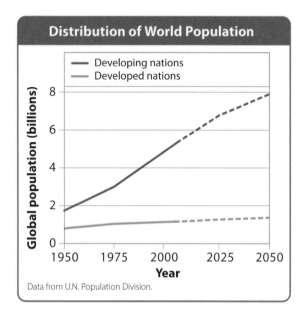

Distribution of World Population

FIGURE 12 **Distribution of Future Growth** Almost all of the next 1 billion people added to Earth's population will reside in less developed, poorer parts of the world. The dashed lines indicate projected future trends.

Developing Nations The term *developing nation* refers to nations with moderate or low income and includes China and Mexico as well as all the nations of Africa, Central America, South America, Indonesia, and eastern Europe. Worldwide, more people live in developing nations than live in developed nations. *Developed nations* are high-income nations including the United States, Canada, western European nations, Australia, New Zealand, Japan, and some Arab states.

Compared to developed nations, developing nations tend to have higher fertility rates, infant mortality rates, and death rates. Life expectancy is also typically lower. In some areas, crowded conditions, poor sanitation, poor nutrition, and lack of health education lead to higher frequency of diseases such as AIDS and tuberculosis that can spread from person to person.

Despite these difficulties, the population growth of developing nations as a whole surpasses population growth in developed nations as shown in **Figure 12.** This affects the distribution of people on the planet. In 1950, 68 percent of the world's population lived in developing nations. By 2009, 82 percent of the world's population lived in these nations. Population growth in developing regions presents many challenges. Will there be enough jobs for people to support themselves? Will there be enough resources to support a quickly growing population?

▶ *National Policies* Many developing nations experiencing rapid population growth have programs to encourage citizens to have smaller families. China's program was an extreme example. Other rapidly growing nations have implemented less restrictive programs. For example, Thailand relies on an education-based approach to family planning. In the 1960s, Thailand's growth rate was about 3 percent. Now it is about 0.3 percent.

In 1994, the United Nations hosted a conference in Cairo on population and development. The conference urged governments to offer better education and healthcare and to address social needs that influence population size. Since then Brazil, Mexico, Iran, Cuba, and other nations have instituted programs that involve economic incentives, education, free contraception, and reproductive healthcare.

FIGURE 13 Uneven Consumption Rates The amount of resources needed to supply a food market is a sign of uneven consumption rates. **(a)** The U.S. market needs fossil fuels for shipping, materials for packaging, and electricity that the **(b)** Sengalese market does not.

▶ *Empowering Women* Better educational opportunities for women are closely tied to declining fertility rates. Studies show that in societies in which women are freer to decide whether and when to have children, fertility rates fall. Many social scientists and policymakers recognize that for population growth to slow and stabilize, women need to achieve equal education and power with men. But there is a long way to go. Over two thirds of the world's people who cannot read and 60 percent of those living in poverty are women.

Developed Nations Beyond the actual number of people, it's also important to consider the amount of resources a particular population uses and the amount of waste it produces. Just as population size is distributed unevenly around the globe, so are wealth and rate of resource consumption. As explained in **Figure 13,** people in nations such as the United States typically use far more resources compared to people in developing nations. In this sense, the addition of one American has as much environmental impact as the addition of five Chinese or thirteen Pakistanis. As more and more nations become industrialized, whether or not they go through the demographic transition, their consumption rates will also rise.

LESSON ② Assessment

1. **Infer** Assuming there is no emigration, would you expect the total fertility rate of a declining population to be more or less than 2.1? . Explain.

2. **Explain** How does age structure help us predict population growth?

3. **Apply Concepts** A population that is industrialized is experiencing a drop in death rates. However, the birthrate remains high. Could it be undergoing the demographic transition? Explain.

4. **Review** How does population growth compare between poorer and wealthier societies?

5. **THINK IT** *THROUGH* A nation has a total fertility rate of 2.5. The age structure of this population is fairly balanced. Recently people from a neighboring nation have been arriving in masses to escape a civil war. Do you think this population will likely increase or decrease in the near future? Explain your answer.

People and Their Environments

Knowledge and Skills

- Describe how humans impact their environments.
- Discuss the negative and positive impacts of technology.

Reading Strategy and Vocabulary

✓ **Reading Strategy** Create a three-column KWL chart. In the first column, write what you know about how humans impact their environment. In the second column, write what you want to know more about. After you read the lesson, write in the last column what you learned.

Vocabulary wealth gap

WHAT WILL THE EARTH of tomorrow look like? Will open plains, deep-green forests, and other areas to roam still exist? Or will human population growth reach the point where human development affects every nook and cranny of the planet? So far, this chapter has focused primarily on the human population—in particular its potential for growth. But, we also need to understand how this growing population affects Earth. After all, our actions today impact Earth's tomorrow.

Impacts of Population

The Industrial Revolution may have changed how people live in many positive ways, but it also has caused ever-increasing resource consumption and pollution. As the population grows in size and as more nations become industrialized, our impact on the environment will also increase unless more sustainable ways of living become commonplace. Currently, the type of environmental impact varies greatly among societies.

Affluent Societies The environmental impact of humans depends on the way people live. When people have more money, they tend to consume more food, purchase more items, produce more wastes, and live in larger homes that use more energy. Much of the materials required to make the products affluent societies purchase don't come from their lands, but from far-off places. Natural resources also are required to ship the products to the consumers.

The relationship between affluence and environmental impact is linked directly to the concept of ecological footprints. Recall that an ecological footprint is the amount of land needed to provide a person (or population) with the resources he or she consumes and to handle his or her wastes. Although the population growth rate is usually lower in affluent societies, individuals from affluent societies tend to have larger ecological footprints than those from poor societies (**Figure 14**). Therefore, the addition of a person in an affluent society has a greater impact on the environment than the addition of a person in a poorer society.

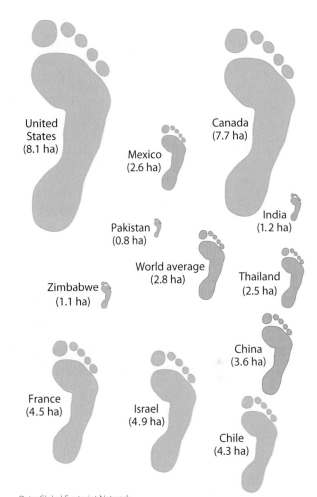

◆ **Connect to the Central Case**

FIGURE 14 Ecological Footprints The average ecological footprint of a person in each nation can vary greatly. Shown here are average footprints for several developed (green) and developing (blue) nations. The world average is also shown (brown). Note that *ha* stands for hectare.

Apply Concepts Explain why the average footprint of someone in China is smaller than the average footprint of an American, even though China's population is much larger.

United States (8.1 ha)
Canada (7.7 ha)
Mexico (2.6 ha)
India (1.2 ha)
Pakistan (0.8 ha)
World average (2.8 ha)
Thailand (2.5 ha)
Zimbabwe (1.1 ha)
France (4.5 ha)
Israel (4.9 ha)
China (3.6 ha)
Chile (4.3 ha)

Data: Global Footprint Network

Poor Societies When people live in poverty, they place different types of strains on their environment than people in affluent societies. Many of these strains are related to population growth and survival.

▶ *Overwhelmed Governments* As you learned in the last lesson, poverty is strongly correlated with population growth. When more people are added to a given area, the impact on the environment increases. In some nations where population growth is outpacing the nation's economic growth, governments are so overwhelmed they cannot provide infrastructure that protects people and the environment, such as adequate sewage treatment facilities.

▶ *Land Overuse* Poverty may also force people to engage in environmentally harmful activities just to survive. For example, people who depend on agriculture in a region of poor farmland may continue to farm heavily, even if it destroys the soil. They may also try to raise more grazing animals than the land can support. This is largely why some land in Africa's once-productive Sahel region turned to desert **(Figure 15).**

FIGURE 15 Land Overuse In the semiarid Sahel region of Africa, where population is increasing beyond the land's ability to handle it, drought and dependence on grazing and agriculture led to poor soil conditions.

Human Population **243**

▶ **Land Clearing** The ever-increasing need for more farmland, land to raise livestock, and wood contributes to deforestation. Loss of forests can lead to flooding in areas that did not have flooding problems before. Flooding causes property damage, lost crops, and disease, which increase the level of poverty in the area.

As people continue to expand their territory, they come into closer contact with animals that they generally did not come into close contact with before. Many new diseases, sometimes called *emerging diseases,* that could become threats to the human population as a whole have arisen because human and animal habitats have merged. A recent example of this is COVID-19, a global pandemic so named because it was caused by a coronavirus that was first identified in 2019. Human takeover of habitat has also led to an increased rate of species extinction.

Many international agencies have introduced programs to help people in poorer nations earn a living, while conserving their land and other resources. Many efforts concentrate on introducing sustainable farming techniques and gaining access to renewable energy sources.

FIGURE 16 Wealth Gap The graph reveals the wealth gap among different regions of the world. **(a)** The number of cars on American roads is one sign of the wealth gap. In 2002, there were 812 cars per 1000 people in the United States. **(b)** In India, in the same year, there were 17 cars per 1000 people.

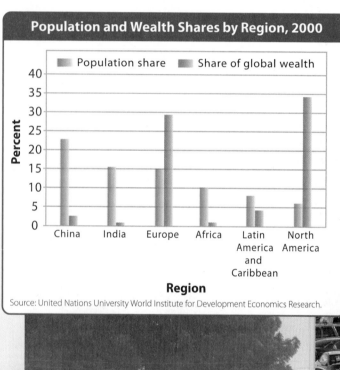

Population and Wealth Shares by Region, 2000

Source: United Nations University World Institute for Development Economics Research.

The Wealth Gap All societies affect their environment in some way. To move toward a sustainable future, we will have to address the environmental issues of both developed and developing nations. But the stark contrast between affluent and poor societies in today's world is the cause of social as well as environmental stress. This contrast is often called the **wealth gap,** which refers to the difference in assets and income between individuals in a society or between nations.

(a)

(b)

As **Figure 16** indicates, the regions of the world with the greatest population sizes have a much smaller percentage of global wealth. In 2012, more than 900 million people live below the internationally defined poverty line of U.S. $1.90 per day. Another 2.6 billion live on less than $2 a day. The richest one fifth of the world's people uses 86 percent of the world's resources. Many of these resources are actually imported from developing nations, leaving these nations with fewer resources to support their own populations. That leaves only 14 percent of global resources—energy, food, water, and other essentials—for four fifths of the world's people. It seems reasonable that at some point, four fifths of the world will demand a more equal share of resources.

 Reading Checkpoint *Which region shown in **Figure 16** has the smallest share of global wealth?*

FIGURE 17 Resource Strain
As China's population has increased and become wealthier, larger demands have been placed on its natural resources. For example, a combination of drought and excessive water use has greatly depleted the Yellow River in some areas.

When Developing Nations Develop As developing nations develop, they may encounter new sets of problems. For example, consider China's immense economic growth over the past few decades. While millions of Chinese are increasing their material wealth and their consumption of resources, the nation is battling environmental challenges brought on by this rapid economic growth. People are purchasing more food, which has forced agriculture to expand westward out of the moist rice-growing areas. Poorer farmland is eroding and literally blowing away. A similar situation occurred in the United States during the 1930s, when parts of the Great Plains became known as the Dust Bowl.

China has overpumped many of its underground water supplies and has drawn so much water for irrigation from the Yellow River that the once-mighty waterway now dries up in many stretches, as shown in **Figure 17.** Although China is reducing air pollution from industry and charcoal-burning homes, the nation faces new urban pollution and congestion threats from rapidly increasing numbers of cars. As the world's developing nations try to attain the level of material prosperity that industrialized nations enjoy, China provides a glimpse of what much of the rest of the world could soon become.

WHAT DO YOU THINK?

Consider your own city or town. Can you find examples of how population, affluence, and technology affect your own environment? How might your city reduce negative effects on the environment?

Quality of Life The impact that human populations have on the environment not only affects ecosystems, but it affects quality of life. *Quality of life* refers to how well an individual lives. It includes having basic life necessities such as a reliable food and water supply and space to live. Quality of life also includes less tangible, but life-affecting elements. For example, it includes a person's feeling of safety, access to healthcare and education, and available time for recreation.

Of course, quality of life is a relative term that depends greatly on the areas where people live, their likes and dislikes, and their culture. But in general, for humankind to experience the most basic quality of life in the future, the availability and quality of resources need to keep pace with population growth and resource consumption.

Impacts of Technology

Without the technology that has brought about modern life, it's unlikely that the human population ever would have experienced the ongoing exponential growth of the past couple of hundred years. We have developed technology time and again to fight diseases, reduce our strain on resources, and allow us to further expand our population size. For example, technology has allowed global agricultural production to grow faster than our population has grown. Because of such technologies, many people live longer, healthier, and often more comfortable lives. But to the rest of the biosphere, human technology has brought a mix of both negative and positive effects (**Figure 19**).

FIGURE 18 Limited Space Space is a limited resource. We cannot expand Earth like a balloon to increase its surface area. In cities such as Bangkok, Thailand, people make the most of limited space by building giant skyscrapers.

(a)

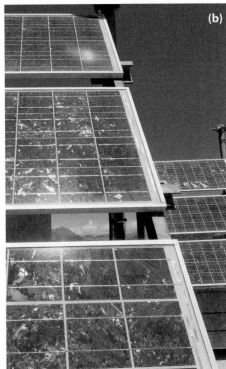
(b)

FIGURE 19 **Impacts of Technology** Much of human technology over the past few centuries has had negative effects on the environment. **(a)** Mining for fossil fuels can be particularly destructive. This mountaintop in West Virginia was blasted off to mine coal. **(b)** The focus of new technologies, such as solar energy, is to provide people with the energy they need at less cost to the environment.

Negative Impacts The environment has often paid the price for human achievements because many of these technologies have involved exploitation of resources such as soil, minerals, fossil fuels, old-growth forests, and the oceans. The short-sighted use of technology that has occurred for the past several hundred years has caused many problems. We are currently witnessing some of these problems in the form of pollution and loss of biodiversity. Other problems, for example the ongoing effects of climate change, can only be predicted.

In recent years, the use of technology has intensified the environmental impact of developing nations. Often the same industrial technologies from the developed world that have caused such harm are exported to poorer nations that are eager to become industrialized.

Positive Impacts In recent years less harmful technologies have begun reducing environmental impact. For example, recycling programs and advances in wastewater treatment are helping reduce waste output. Solar, wind, and geothermal energy technologies are producing cheaper and cleaner renewable energy. Ensuring that these technologies become equally available and implemented in developing nations is a goal of many international agencies.

LESSON (3) **Assessment**

1. **Explain** Explain the relationship between wealth and poverty, and impact on the environment.

2. **Describe** How has technology had both a negative and positive impact on the environment?

REVISIT

3. **INVESTIGATIVE** PHENOMENON

As developed nations implement ways that reduce their effect on the environment, do you think this will affect quality of life throughout the world? Explain.

A CLOSER LOOK

The United States CENSUS

Every 10 years, since it began in 1790, the U.S. Census Bureau has counted the nation's population. The 2020 census is currently in progress. The U.S. Census was created to determine how many representatives should be sent to Congress from each region. Over the years, however, the census has come to be about more than just determining representation in the federal government. Now, the census is also a key factor in determining how federal funding is distributed to states for projects such as new hospitals and schools.

HOW DOES THE CENSUS COUNT EVERYONE?

The census aims to actually count every single person living in the United States, which is no easy task in a nation of more than 331 million people. It provides a record of how many people live where, as well as their age and race.

At the start of the 10-year census, the Census Bureau mails census forms to every recorded address in the country. Census workers hand-deliver forms to homes without mail service, sometimes riding motorboats and snowmobiles to get there. Residents are asked to answer the questions on the census form and mail it back or complete the questionnaire online.

The Census Bureau hires millions of workers to visit all the addresses that don't return the forms. Workers also visit homeless shelters and soup kitchens to find people who may not live in traditional homes.

HOW IS THE CENSUS USED?

The census results are available to the public. Many groups, from local governments to nonprofit organizations, use census data to improve their communities. For example, information on how fast communities are expanding can help city planners know where to build new homes, and where to place roads and services. Census data have helped city planners create "smart growth" communities, which are designed to have stores, workplaces, and schools within walking distance of people's homes. By using census data on how many people use public transportation and own cars, communities can also figure out how to best improve access to public transportation.

Census data can also help nonprofit and state environmental organizations protect natural lands from development. For example, environmental organizations used census data on rapid development along the Florida coast to petition the state government to expand manatee protection laws.

▲ Walking paths connect public transportation to metropolitan areas.

CAREER **Demographer** Demographers study statistics relating to human populations. They study why populations increase or decrease, and analyze the data to predict future changes in population. Go Online and research careers in demography and population studies. Write a brief summary of your findings.

Lesson 1
What social and environmental factors affect human population size?

Lesson 2
How do human population growth trends differ between developed nations and developing nations?

Lesson 3
How does a nation's wealth relate to its consumption of resources?

LESSON 1 Trends in Human Population Growth

- Technological advances of the Industrial Revolution, especially in agriculture and industry, changed the ways people lived and triggered remarkable increases in population size. Improvements in sanitation and medical technology led to lower death rates.
- The human population's growth rate has decreased over the past several decades, but the population still continues to grow.
- Demographers study the size, density, and distribution of human populations. Density describes how many people live in a square mile or square kilometer, and distribution describes how and where the human population is clustered.

Industrial Revolution (229)
infant mortality (230)
life expectancy (230)
growth rate (231)
demography (232)

LESSON 2 Predicting Population Growth

- Fertility rate helps demographers predict the rates at which populations will grow in the future. Total fertility rate is the average number of children a woman has during her lifetime. Replacement fertility is the total fertility rate required to keep a population size stable.
- Age structure and sex ratios define a population's potential for growth.
- The demographic transition may explain the reason that some industrialized nations have experienced a large drop in birthrates and death rates.
- Social factors, such as wealth and education, affect a nation's population growth and its resource use. Population growth rates in developing nations are usually higher than in developed nations.

total fertility rate (235)
replacement fertility (235)
demographic transition (238)

LESSON 3 People and Their Environments

- People have an enormous impact on their environment, but the types of impacts can differ based on the characteristics of a particular society. Affluent societies consume a lot of resources. Poor societies may place great demands on fragile environments to meet their needs for food, water, and other resources.
- Technology can have both negative and positive impacts on the environment. Many modern-day technologies have involved short-sighted exploitation of resources such as soil, fossil fuels, forests, and oceans. A new trend is to use technologies that take advantage of solar, wind, and geothermal energy to produce cheaper, cleaner, renewable energy.

wealth gap (244)

 GO ONLINE

INQUIRY LABS AND ACTIVITIES

- **Longevity**
  How do local obituaries compare to national figures on life expectancy? Graph the two to find out.
- **Using Census Data**
  Find census data on age structure for your town, and compare it with national and historical data.
- **Interpreting Age Structure**
  Read age structure diagrams for Haiti and Japan to compare trends in population growth.

Chapter Assessment

Defend Your Case

Consider both the benefits and costs associated with China's population policies. Do you think governments should be able to enforce policies like China's? If you think they should, explain why. If not, explain other ways a government might deal with the resource demands of a quickly growing population.

Review Concepts and Terms

1. The human population today is approximately
   a. 300 million.
   b. 1.3 billion.
   c. 7.8 billion.
   d. 10 billion.

2. For most of human history, the population has been relatively
   a. small and stable.
   b. small and rapidly growing.
   c. large and shrinking.
   d. large and rapidly growing.

3. Recently, the size of the human population has been
   a. decreasing slowly.
   b. decreasing exponentially.
   c. increasing slowly.
   d. increasing exponentially.

4. Which fertility rate keeps the population size stable?
   a. replacement fertility
   b. stable fertility
   c. balanced sex ratio
   d. total fertility rate

5. How individuals of different ages are distributed in a population is called the population's
   a. age ratio.
   b. age structure.
   c. sex ratio.
   d. sex structure.

6. The model that describes how industrialized nations undergo a large drop in birthrates and death rates is called
   a. life expectancy.
   b. demography.
   c. the fertility rate transition.
   d. the demographic transition.

7. Which of these factors does NOT affect population growth?
   a. educating women
   b. poverty
   c. statistics
   d. policy

8. Regions of the world with the largest populations tend to
   a. have the largest share of global wealth.
   b. have a smaller share of global wealth.
   c. use the most resources per person.
   d. have the largest ecological footprints.

9. Which of the following does NOT affect a person's quality of life?
   a. replacement fertility
   b. access to education
   c. available living space
   d. food supply

10. How can technology affect human impact on the environment?
    a. It can both increase and reduce human impact.
    b. It always increases human impact.
    c. It always reduces human impact.
    d. It rarely affects human impact.

Modified True/False

Write true if the statement is true. If it is false change the underlined word or words to make the statement true.

11. The study of human populations is called <u>demography</u>.

12. Population <u>size</u> describes how a population is clumped, spatially.

13. A population's <u>total fertility rate</u> is the average number of children a female member of the population has during her lifetime.

14. The number of males compared to females in a population is the population's <u>age structure</u>.

15. Affluent individuals tend to consume <u>more</u> resources than those from poorer societies.

Reading Comprehension

Read the following selection and answer the questions that follow.

Everywhere in sub-Saharan Africa, AIDS is undermining the ability of developing nations to make the transition to modern technologies because it is removing many of the most productive members of society—young adults. In 1999 Zambia lost 600 teachers to AIDS, and only 300 new teachers graduated to replace them. Despite medical advances there were almost 21 million people with HIV (57%) in southern and eastern Africa in 2018, and 5 million (13%) in central and western Africa.

The result is a slow economy with high unemployment, a shortage of trained workers, and a high level of poverty. The loss of productive household members to AIDS causes families and communities to break down as income and food production decline, while medical expenses and debt skyrocket.

16. What do you think has happened to estimated life expectancy in parts of sub-Saharan Africa?

   a. It has fallen dramatically in the past few decades.

   b. It is just starting to fall.

   c. It is on the rise.

   d. It has stabilized.

17. According to the selection, what is one way that the AIDS epidemic has affected education in sub-Saharan Africa?

   a. More people are enrolling in training programs.

   b. Teachers have been lost to the epidemic faster than they can be replaced.

   c. There aren't enough children to keep schools open.

   d. There isn't enough food for schools to operate.

Short Answer

18. What is the difference between population density and population distribution?

19. Explain why even though the global human population's growth rate is declining, the human population is growing.

20. What does replacement fertility mean?

21. What might the age structure diagram of a rapidly growing population look like?

22. What is one hypothesis proposed to explain why the naturally occurring human sex ratio has slightly more males than females?

23. What is the demographic transition model used to explain?

24. How does an increase in population size affect the impact of that population on the environment?

25. Describe two factors that affect a person's quality of life.

Critical Thinking

26. Synthesize Why does examining population size, density, and distribution together give you a better understanding of a population than looking at these characteristics separately?

27. Form an Opinion Do you think human population growth is a problem? Why or why not?

28. Infer Why do you think the human replacement fertility in many nations is 2.1 rather than 2.0?

29. Explain How does the demographic transition explain the increase in population growth rates in recent centuries in some nations? How does it explain the decrease in population growth rates in recent decades in some nations?

30. Form an Opinion Do you think that all of today's developing nations will complete the demographic transition? Why or why not?

31. Review Explain how both poverty and affluence affect the environment in different ways.

32. Form an Opinion When forming population-control policies, do you think it is important for governments to consider quality of life issues? Why or why not?

Analyze Data

As the population of the United States has increased, the average number of people per household has also changed. The graph shows the percentage of U.S. households of different sizes in 1970, 2000, and 2019. Use the graph to answer Questions 33 and 34.

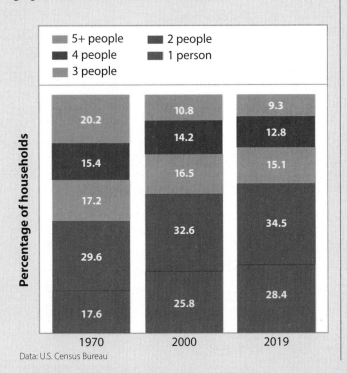

Data: U.S. Census Bureau

33. Interpret Graphs Did household sizes generally increase, decrease, or stay the same from 1970 to 2019?

34. Draw Conclusions How do you think these changes in household size may have affected resource consumption?

Write About It

35. Review Describe how the human population has grown over time.

36. Compare and Contrast Define the term *ecological footprint*. Describe how the ecological footprint of an average American differs from that of a person living in a developing nation.

37. Explain Why do environmental scientists consider limitless human population growth a problem?

38. REVISIT INVESTIGATIVE PHENOMENON
Suppose you are living in the year 3000. You are a reporter writing an article about the quality of life of the average person. Write two versions of the article. In one article, you are living in a global population that has continued to grow. In the other article, you are living in a global population that has leveled off at the current population size.

Ecological Footprints

Read the information below. Copy the table in your notebook and record your calculations. Then, answer the questions that follow.

Population size and affluence each affect a nation's environmental impact. The data (from 2006) in the table will help you to explore how population, affluence, and impact are related.

1. Calculate the total ecological footprint for each nation. (*Hint:* Multiply the population size by the personal ecological footprint of each person.)

2. Look at the affluence and personal ecological footprints of people in each nation. Do you observe a relationship between these two factors? Explain.

Nation	Affluence (per person income)	Population (millions of people)	Personal Ecological Footprint (ha/person)	Total Ecological Footprint (millions of ha)
Brazil	$8230	186.8	2.1	392.3
Ethiopia	$1000	74.8	0.8	
Japan	$31,410	127.8	4.4	
Mexico	$10,030	108.3	2.6	
Russia	$10,640	142.3	4.4	
United States	$41,950	299.1	9.6	2871.4

Data sources: Population Reference Bureau. 2006. *World population data sheet* 2006; and WWF–World Wide Fund for Nature, 2006. *Living planet report.* Gland, Switzerland: WWF.

INVESTIGATIVE PHENOMENON How do we balance the relationship between our own health and the health of the environment?

The inside of a house in Africa is sprayed with insecticide to help reduce the incidence of malaria.

Lesson 1
An Overview of
Environmental Health

Lesson 2
Biological and
Social Hazards

Lesson 3
Toxic Substances in
the Environment

Lesson 4
Natural Disasters

The Rise and Fall of DDT

In its short history, dichloro-diphenyl-trichloroethane, or DDT, has been viewed as both a miracle worker and a villain. Its use led to the eradication of malaria, a deadly disease spread by mosquitoes, in some countries. However, DDT remains in the environment and animal tissues for many years. These changing faces of DDT clearly show us the difficulty that policymakers and scientists must face when weighing the costs and benefits of using synthetic pesticides.

In the case of DDT, we know it can negatively affect ecosystems. On the other hand, malaria is a devastating mosquito-borne disease that kills millions of people every year. DDT is an inexpensive and easy way to kill mosquitoes. And so, we are forced to choose the lesser of two evils—which shows that when it comes to human health and the environment, there are very few easy answers.

DDT was first made in the 1870s, but it wasn't until 1939 that Swiss chemist Paul Müller noticed it killed flies on contact. Even small amounts killed the flies. But the DDT did not appear to harm Müller or other animals. Effective and stable, DDT seemed a perfect insecticide.

Müller's company sold DDT to the United States military during World War II. The military sprayed DDT on soldiers and prisoners to kill lice that carried the disease typhus. They also sprayed DDT near swamps to kill mosquitoes that carried malaria. In fact, with DDT's help, the United States eradicated malaria inside the nation by 1951.

DDT's success helped it spread rapidly. Other nations eradicated malaria, while farmers sprayed DDT on their crops to protect them from pests. By 1962, Americans were using about 40,000 tons of DDT a year; the rest of the world consumed even more.

That same year, the glory of DDT began to fade. Fish were dying. Bald eagles were disappearing. Marine biologist Rachel Carson made the public aware of the consequences of DDT in her book *Silent Spring.* DDT was linked

GO ONLINE
• Take It Local   • 3-D Geo Tour

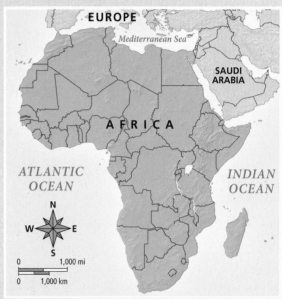

to liver damage, cancer, and convulsions. Clearly, DDT was not perfect. Throughout the 1970s, the United States and other nations banned its use.

Malaria remains a public health threat. In 2018, there were over 200 million cases of malaria worldwide and about 400,000 people died from the disease. Over 90 percent of cases and deaths occurred across Africa. Nations and health organizations are working together to eliminate malaria. This partnership has found two effective ways of reducing exposure to malaria. These methods include mosquito nets sprayed with insecticide and indoor residual spraying (IRS). IRS involves spraying small amounts of DDT or other insecticides inside homes. However, due to an increase in insecticide resistance, alternative methods for malaria prevention are being explored.

The story of DDT is not unique. How do we view the use of chemicals that benefit humans in an immediate time frame versus long term damage to ecosystems?

An Overview of Environmental Health

EVERYDAY PHENOMENON What is environmental health?

Knowledge and Skills

- List the types of environmental health hazards.
- Compare and contrast epidemiology and toxicology.
- Describe the reasons why individuals respond differently to the same environmental hazards.
- Discuss risk assessment.

Reading Strategy and Vocabulary

✔ **Reading Strategy** Create a main ideas and details chart for the lesson. As you read, write down the main ideas of the lesson. Fill in important details about each main idea.

Vocabulary environmental health, hazard, pathogen, epidemiology, toxicology, toxicity, dose, response, dose-response relationship, risk, risk assessment

A LEAKY SEWER pipe can threaten your health in more ways than you can imagine. It pollutes the soil you walk on. It could pollute the water supply. Obvious health concerns like these, however, are only a small fraction of the environmental factors that affect your health every day. Your home, your neighborhood, and even the sun can pose health risks. Because of this, many scientists are trying to figure out just exactly how the environment affects our health and how we can stay healthy in our environment.

Types of Hazards

The study of how environmental factors affect human health and our quality of life is called **environmental health**. Environmental factors include natural ones, such as hurricanes and the sun's rays. They also include human-made factors, such as car exhaust and some liquid detergents. Factors that threaten or are harmful to human health are called **hazards**. Environmental hazards can be biological, social, chemical, or physical, as shown in **Figure 1.**

Biological Hazards Viruses, bacteria, and other organisms in the environment that harm human health are classified as biological hazards. These disease-causing agents, or **pathogens**, infect humans and make us sick. Examples of biological hazards include the flu virus, the bacterium that causes strep throat, and even pet dander that may cause allergies.

Social Hazards Hazards that result from where we live, our jobs, or our lifestyle choices are social hazards. For example, smoking cigarettes is a lifestyle choice. If you choose to smoke, you increase your risk of developing lung cancer. On the other hand, living next to a factory that is illegally releasing harmful chemicals into the air is a social hazard that you do not have control over.

Chemical Hazards Chemicals in the environment that harm human health are called chemical hazards. These include both synthetic chemicals and hazardous chemicals produced by organisms. For example, some disinfectants you may use to clean your kitchen and bathroom can be chemical hazards.

Physical Hazards Physical processes that pose health hazards include natural disasters. Earthquakes, fires, tornadoes, and droughts are all physical hazards. Physical hazards also include ongoing natural phenomena, such as ultraviolet (UV) radiation from sunlight. Ultraviolet radiation damages DNA and has been linked to skin cancer.

FIGURE 1 Environmental Hazards Environmental hazards include physical hazards, such as fire **(a)**; social hazards, such as smoking **(b)**; biological hazards, such as the bacterium that causes tuberculosis **(c)**; and chemical hazards, such as the products you may use to clean your home **(d)**.

Epidemiology and Toxicology

Identifying hazards in our environment is just one part of environmental health. Scientists also want to understand how these hazards affect people. Epidemiology and toxicology are two scientific fields that help us understand how, where, and to what extent environmental hazards affect our health.

Epidemiology The study of disease in human populations is called **epidemiology**. Epidemiologists are scientists who study how and where diseases occur, as well as how to control them. For example, epidemiologists might try to find out why there are unusually large numbers of cancer cases in a town. Or, they may try to determine how diseases spread through a population.

Epidemiological studies often involve studying large groups of people over long periods of time. In many studies, a group of people that has been exposed to a hazard is compared to a control group, or one that has not been exposed. Epidemiologists then track both groups and measure the rate at which death, disease, or other health problems occur in each group. They then analyze the data, looking for statistical differences between the groups. Note that epidemiological studies find statistical associations between a health hazard and an effect. However, they do not confirm that the hazard causes the effect.

Toxicology The study of how poisonous substances affect an organism's health is called **toxicology**. A substance's **toxicity** determines how harmful a substance is to an organism. Toxicity depends on two things: (1) what the substance is, and (2) how much of the substance is needed to cause harm.

▶ *Dose-Response Relationship* Toxicologists determine toxicity by measuring the response a substance produces at different doses. A **dose** is the amount of a substance an organism is exposed to. This includes both the concentration of the substance and the length of time the organism was exposed. The **response** is the effect an organism shows as a result of exposure. For example, if an organism is exposed to an extremely high dose of radiation, the response can be death. If the dose is lower, the organism may get sick, but not die. This relationship between the different doses and the responses they generate is known as a **dose-response relationship**.

Sometimes responses occur only above a certain dose. This is called a *threshold dose*. At doses below the threshold dose, the body's organs are able to break down the substance. But at the threshold dose or above, the body becomes overwhelmed.

▶ *Determining Dose-Response Relationships* Determining a dose-response relationship in humans is difficult. For people who have been accidentally exposed to a hazard, it is often hard to determine the exact doses they may have received. In addition, people are exposed to different environmental hazards daily. How much of and when a person has been exposed to one particular hazard is usually difficult to figure out. Because of this, scientists often use animals as subjects when they study dose-response relationships. Scientists expose animals to different doses of a substance. Then, they observe any health effects the amounts may cause. This data can then be graphed as a dose-response curve, shown in **Figure 2**.

FIGURE 2 Dose-Response Curve
Dose-response curves show how an organism's response changes with increasing doses of a toxicant. This is a typical dose-response curve. Dose-response curves vary in shape depending on the substance.

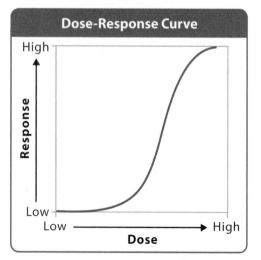

 Reading Checkpoint *Will an organism always have the same response to a chemical regardless of the dose it is exposed to? Explain.*

The Role of the Individual

Every person is different. In fact, two people can respond very differently to exactly the same hazard. For example, drinking from a contaminated well might make one person sick, while another person may not be affected. Therefore, while scientists try to understand how hazards affect human health, they cannot always predict with certainty how a hazard may affect a particular person.

Sensitivity People with health issues such as asthma and compromised immune systems are often more sensitive to biological and chemical hazards than healthy people. That is, they are more likely to feel the effects of these hazards. Sensitivity can also vary with sex, age, and weight. Fetuses, infants, and young children tend to be more sensitive to harmful chemicals than adults. This is because they are smaller and their organ systems are still developing. For example, fetuses are more sensitive to alcohol than adults. Exposing a fetus to alcohol can cause mental retardation and birth defects **(Figure 3)**.

Genetics Many diseases have both genetic and environmental factors. In other words, both a person's genes and the environment he or she lives in can affect the individual's chances of suffering from the disease. For example, certain genetic mutations make it more likely for some women to develop breast cancer than others. But environmental factors can increase the risk of getting breast cancer. If a young girl is exposed to ionizing radiation, her chances of developing breast cancer later in life increases.

FIGURE 3 Environmental Hazards and Sensitivity Environmental hazards are particularly dangerous to fetuses, infants, and young children. When fetuses are exposed to alcohol during development, they may be born with fetal alcohol syndrome.

FIGURE 4 Genetics and Environmental Hazards Breast cancer is one disease that has been traced to genetic factors as well as environmental hazards. If caught early, breast cancer is often curable.

Common Hazards	
Hazard	Annual Risk of Death per 100,000 People
Heart Disease	198.8
Illegal Drugs	21.6
Motor Vehicle Accident	12.0
Falls	6.0
Rail Trespassing Accidents	0.15
Being Hit by a Meteorite	0.04
Lightning	0.008

FIGURE 5 Common Hazards Many activities have risks associated with them. Knowing these risks can help people make informed decisions about how they live their lives.

Risk Assessment

Exposure to an environmental hazard does not always produce a response. Given this, scientists try to determine how likely it is that a given hazard will cause harm. This is called **risk**, or the probability that a hazard will cause a harmful response, such as death or disease. One way to express risk of various activities is to calculate and compare the probability of dying from these hazards. **Figure 5** shows the risks of some common hazards.

The process of measuring risk is called **risk assessment**. To assess risk, scientists need to take many factors into account. These include what the hazard is, how often humans will be exposed to it, and how sensitive individuals are to the hazard.

Risk assessment for a chemical hazard involves several steps. First, scientists identify the potentially hazardous chemical. Then, they determine its toxicity and the extent that humans will be exposed to it. For example, to determine toxicity, scientists may use animal testing to establish a dose-response relationship. To assess exposure, scientists may investigate how often humans have contact with the substance, what concentration of the chemical they will likely encounter, and the length of time people will be exposed.

Scientists use risk assessments to help them make decisions about which hazards may be harmful. Policymakers can use risk assessments to help them shape policies that protect both people and the environment.

LESSON ① Assessment

1. **Classify** List the four types of environmental health hazards.

2. **Compare and Contrast** How are epidemiology and toxicology similar? How are they different?

3. **Infer** Suppose two people smoke five cigarettes a day for 20 years. One develops lung cancer. Will the other person definitely develop lung cancer as well? Explain.

4. **Explain** What is risk assessment?

5. **THINK IT** *THROUGH* Both a father and his child drink water that has flowed through lead pipes. There is also lead-based paint on the walls of their home. Over time, the child shows the effects of lead poisoning. The father does not. Explain how this could be possible.

Biological and Social Hazards

EVERYDAY PHENOMENON How do biological and social factors in the environment affect human health?

Knowledge and Skills

- Describe how infectious diseases spread.
- Explain why emerging diseases are important to monitor and control.
- Differentiate between social hazards that are lifestyle choices and those that cannot be controlled.

Reading Strategy and Vocabulary

✓ **Reading Strategy** As you read each section under a large blue heading, jot down the key points. Using the key points, write in your notebook a summary of what you have read.

Vocabulary infectious disease, emerging disease

YOU ENCOUNTER biological hazards every day. They are in the air you breathe, the food you eat, and the water you drink. Your body is constantly working to fight these pathogens off. Usually, your body wins—but not always. In fact, diseases caused by biological hazards are the second-leading cause of death worldwide. Because of this, scientists around the globe are working on ways to identify, treat, and prevent these diseases.

Infectious Disease

Infectious diseases are diseases caused by a pathogen, such as a virus or a bacterium. Pathogens are biological hazards. Globally, infectious diseases are the leading cause of death. In 2016, lower respiratory infections, diarrheal diseases, and tuberculosis all made the top ten list of causes of death worldwide. **Figure 6** lists these diseases and the estimated number of deaths they caused in 2017.

Disease Transmission Infectious diseases spread through the human population in different ways. For example, pathogens can be spread by humans, water or food, or by other organisms.

▶ *Humans* Some diseases are spread directly from one human to another. For example, touching, biting, sexual intercourse, contact with bodily fluids, and inhaling expelled droplets can all spread disease. HIV—the virus that causes AIDS—can be transmitted when a person comes into contact with the blood or body fluids of an infected person. Tuberculosis (TB) is spread through droplets in the air. People who are infected with TB release bacteria-laden droplets when they cough, sneeze, speak, and spit. If a person nearby breathes in the droplets, he or she may become infected with TB.

FIGURE 6 Global Infectious Disease The five types of diseases listed killed an estimated 6.9 million people in 2017.

Global Deaths by Infectious Diseases

Disease	Deaths (in millions)
Lower Respiratory Infections	2.6
Diarrheal Diseases	1.6
Tuberculosis	1.2
HIV	0.9
Malaria	0.6

Source: World Health Organization. WHO global burden of disease (GBD) 2017 estimates (revised).

◆ **Connect to the Central Case**

FIGURE 7 Animal Vectors Female *Anopheles* mosquitoes can transmit the malaria pathogen when they bite. **Form an Opinion** DDT kills *Anopheles* mosquitoes. Does this fact justify spraying DDT in Africa?

▶ *Water or Food* Some pathogens spread when people consume contaminated water or food. For example, *Vibrio cholerae*, the bacterium that causes cholera, is a waterborne pathogen. Human feces that contain *Vibrio cholerae* contaminate water supplies. When a person drinks contaminated water, he or she may experience intense diarrhea and vomiting. These symptoms can lead to dehydration and even death.

▶ *Other Organisms* Disease can also be spread by other organisms. In these cases, the organism carries the pathogen and passes it to a person. These disease-carrying organisms, or *vectors*, usually do not suffer from the disease themselves. Some vectors, such as ticks and mosquitoes, transmit pathogens when they bite humans. For example, female mosquitoes in the genus *Anopheles* carry pathogens that cause malaria. A mosquito picks up the pathogen when it bites an infected person and transmits it when it bites a non-infected person (**Figure 7**).

Reducing Risk Infectious diseases account for almost half of all deaths in developing nations. But, in developed nations, infectious disease is less of a threat because of public health measures, such as better sanitation and access to medicine. For example, developed nations often have effective water treatment facilities. Public water supplies are closely monitored and treated so that high levels of pathogens do not contaminate the water. In addition, developed nations often have adequate wastewater treatment plants. These facilities accept and treat sewage so that human wastes are not released directly into the environment.

FIGURE 8 Clean Water Supplies Clean water is a critical step toward reducing infectious diseases worldwide. Lack of clean water and basic sanitation kills nearly 2 million young children each year (nearly 5000 per day). In the inset photo, young African children collect water to bring home, unaware that it could be contaminated with cholera.

Quick Lab

How Do Diseases Spread?

1. Your teacher has placed a fluorescent material in the classroom to simulate a virus. Keep track of the people and objects you touch. Then, use a UV flashlight to check for the "virus" on your hands, objects, and people you have touched since entering the classroom. **CAUTION:** *Do not look directly at the UV light.*

2. Exchange results with your classmates to determine how the "virus" spread throughout the classroom. Wash your hands with soap and warm water before leaving your classroom.

Analyze and Conclude

1. **Infer** What can you infer about how the "virus" spread through the classroom?

2. **Apply Concepts** How does thorough hand washing help prevent the spread of diseases?

3. **Design an Experiment** Suggest a way to model the spread of a vector-borne disease.

Cholera is a good example of how wastewater treatment plants help reduce the spread of disease. Because *Vibrio cholerae* gets into waterways through human feces, sewage contamination can lead to cholera epidemics. Treating sewage, therefore, helps reduce the incidence of cholera.

There are many ways you can reduce your risk of catching and spreading infectious diseases. For example, you should cover your nose and mouth with your sleeve or a tissue when you cough or sneeze. Then, throw the tissue in the garbage. You should wash your hands often with soap and warm water. If soap is not available, use an alcohol-based hand sanitizer. And if you are sick, stay home from school to avoid spreading the disease.

 Reading Checkpoint *Describe how pathogens can spread directly from one person to another.*

Emerging Diseases

Despite our attempts to reduce and avoid disease, we are constantly battling new diseases. An **emerging disease** is a disease that has appeared in the human population for the first time, or that has existed for a while but is increasing rapidly or spreading around the world.

The pathogens that cause emerging disease are particularly dangerous because humans have developed little or no resistance to them. In addition, methods of controlling emerging diseases, such as vaccines, have not been developed.

One good example of an emerging disease is the Zika virus. The virus was first identified in 1947. In March 2015 an outbreak began in Brazil and spread to more than 85 nations and territories, with millions of people infected. In February 2016, the World Health Organization (WHO) declared it a global pandemic. A *pandemic* is an outbreak that becomes widespread and affects a whole region, continent, or the world. COVID-19 is another example of a pandemic.

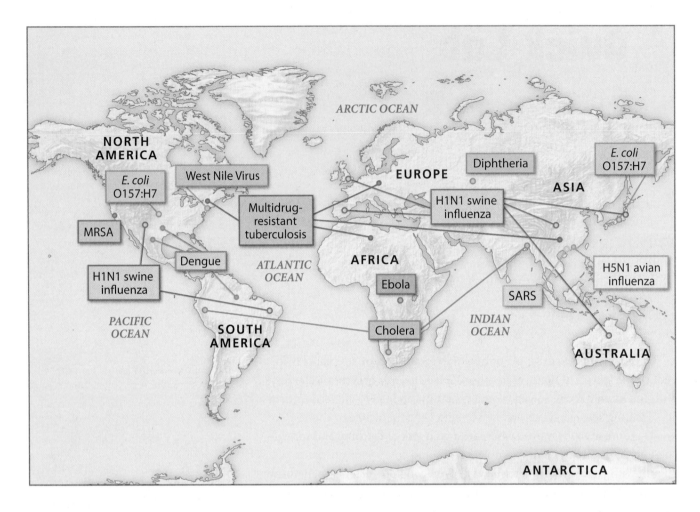

FIGURE 9 Emerging Diseases The map shows where some emerging diseases have recently appeared. Some of these diseases, such as cholera and diphtheria, are not new, but have appeared in new areas. Others, like SARS and MRSA are more recent threats.

The Spread of Emerging Diseases Emerging diseases may quickly spread to new regions or population centers. Therefore, it is important to understand some of the ways diseases emerge and spread.

▶ *Increasing Mobility* Many diseases are spreading as people become more mobile. A virus for influenza can move across continents in just a few hours if an infected person takes a long airplane flight. Whenever people or other animals move around Earth, they may be taking pathogens along with them.

▶ *Antibiotic Resistance* Other diseases, such as tuberculosis, are becoming resistant to our antibiotics. That is, they can survive and grow even when we take medicines that have previously killed them. Antibiotic resistance is a result of natural selection. If a few pathogens in a population are either naturally resistant or develop resistance to an antibiotic, they will survive when exposed to the drug. The rest of the population will die, but a few resistant organisms may then reproduce and create new populations of resistant pathogens.

▶ *A Changing Environment* By altering their environment, people may spread emerging diseases. For example, when people cut down forests, they may come into contact with animals that carry pathogens. These animals, and their pathogens, may have been previously contained inside the forest environment.

Climate change is another way our changing environment may encourage the spread of disease. If global temperatures continue to rise, tropical diseases such as malaria and cholera could expand into new, formerly cooler areas.

Responding to Emerging Diseases Emerging diseases can surface and spread quickly. As a result, having a reliable response system in place is a necessary step toward maintaining global health. Currently, international and government agencies and organizations work together to help monitor, respond to, and control the spread of emerging diseases.

▶ *International Response* The World Health Organization (WHO) is an international group that helps respond to emerging diseases. It has networks of organizations, agencies, labs, and medical centers that monitor world health events. When an emerging disease is identified, WHO posts the information on the World Wide Web. Within 24 hours, a team goes to the site to assess the situation. If needed, WHO will then help coordinate an international response.

▶ *National Response* Individual nations also help respond to emerging diseases. In the United States, the Centers for Disease Control and Prevention (CDC) is the primary national center for responding to emerging diseases. It works with international as well as other federal, state, and local organizations to develop and apply disease prevention and control measures.

For example, the CDC worked to identify cases of Zika virus during the 2015-2016 outbreak, as well as to develop a rapid test to detect Zika virus in patients. The CDC also worked with local health departments to educate the public, especially pregnant women, about the disease. Today, the CDC has a system for tracking cases. In 2018 and 2019, there were no confirmed cases of Zika virus in the United States.

✓ Reading Checkpoint *What are three factors that influence the spread of emerging diseases?*

FIGURE 10 **Response to Emerging Disease** Researchers work with the Zika virus at a CDC lab in Puerto Rico. The inset shows a colorized micrograph of the Zika virus (red).

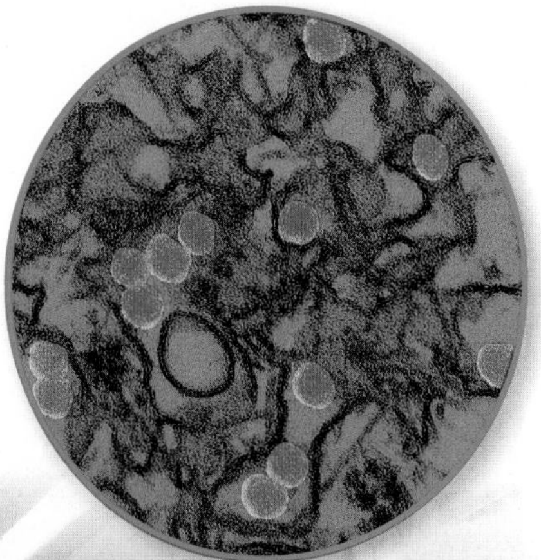

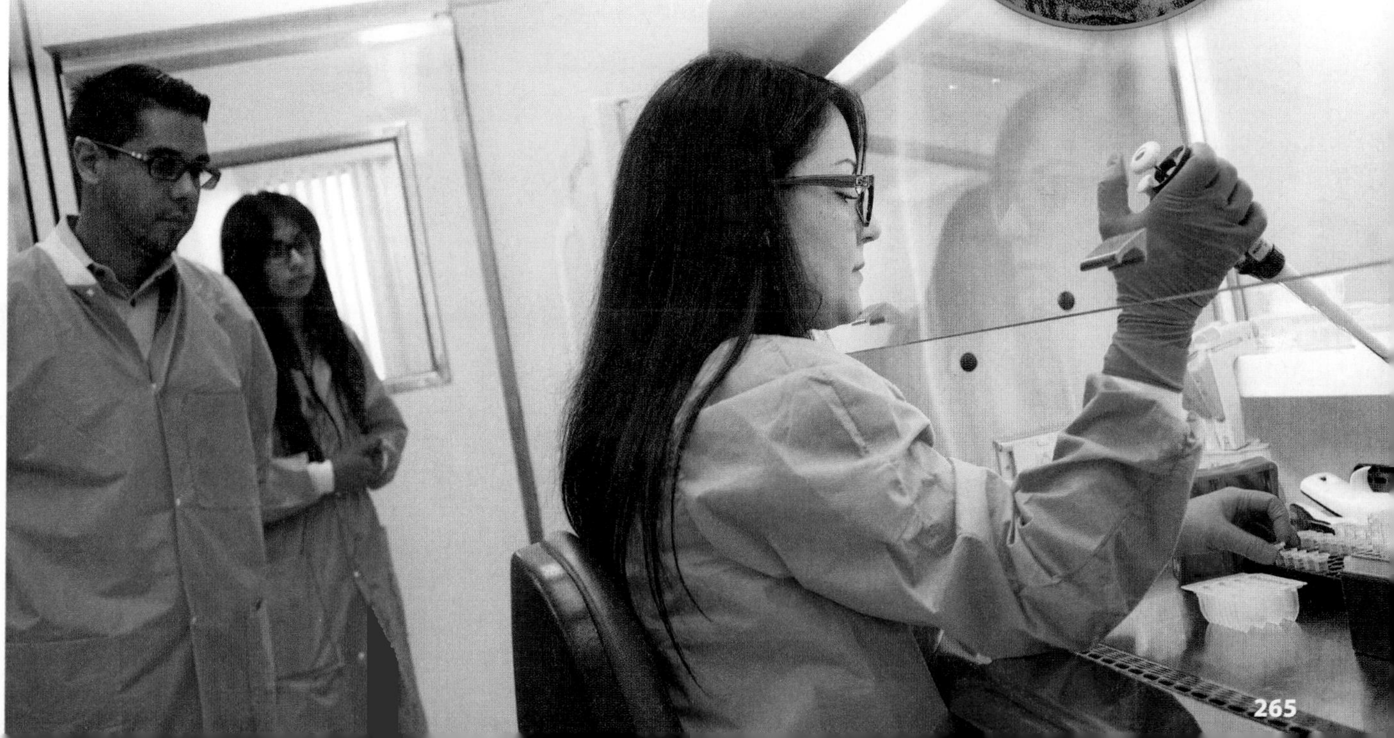

Social Hazards

Where you live, your job, and the choices you make every day affect your health. When these factors harm your health, they are called social hazards. Some social hazards can be easily avoided, while others are more difficult. For example, you might live near an old toxic waste site that is leaking harmful chemicals into the soil. Or your job could put you into contact with harmful chemicals.

Smoking is a social hazard that can cause lung cancer. A person can avoid this risk by not smoking. Cigarette smoke irritates a person's eyes, nose, and throat and can make asthma worse. But tobacco smoke can also affect the health of a nonsmoker when he or she breathes in secondhand smoke. Secondhand smoke is the exhaled smoke from nearby smokers mixed with smoke from a burning cigarette, pipe, or cigar. Secondhand smoke exposure has been linked to lung cancer and respiratory tract infections. While you can choose not to smoke, how much secondhand smoke you breathe in may be difficult to control, especially if you live with a smoker.

You may not think of potato chips as a hazard. But if your diet consists primarily of fatty foods, this is considered a social hazard. A high-fat diet can put you at risk for heart attack and stroke. The good news is that diet, along with many other social hazards, can be reduced simply by changing your behavior. You can choose to eat healthful foods. You can also choose to stay active by exercising regularly. By staying active, and eating healthfully, you may be able to avoid obesity, heart disease, and high blood pressure.

FIGURE 11 Healthy Lifestyle Choices You can exercise regularly to avoid the dangers of a sedentary lifestyle.

LESSON 2 Assessment

1. **Review** Describe one way pathogens can spread through the environment.

2. **Explain** Why is it important to have an international organization such as WHO coordinating responses to emerging diseases?

3. **Apply Concepts** Describe three social hazards that are a result of choices you make every day.

REVISIT

4. **INVESTIGATIVE** PHENOMENON Do you think that modern medicine will ever eliminate biological hazards from Earth? Why or why not?

Toxic Substances in the Environment

EVERYDAY PHENOMENON How do chemicals in our environment affect our health?

Knowledge and Skills

- Explain what makes chemicals hazardous.
- Discuss how chemical hazards affect human health.
- List some indoor chemical hazards.
- Discuss where chemical hazards can be found in the environment.
- Describe biomagnification.

Reading Strategy and Vocabulary

✓ **Reading Strategy** Before you read, create a KWL chart. In the first column write down everything you already know about toxic chemicals. In the second column, list what you want to know. After you read the lesson, write down what you have learned in the third column.

Vocabulary pollution, carcinogen, teratogen, neurotoxin, asbestos, radon, bioaccumulation, biomagnification

FROM THE SALT on your table to the cleaners in your cabinets, chemicals surround you. Many of them are harmless in small amounts, but some are toxic at low concentrations. Because of this, it is important to know what the harmful chemicals are—and how and when you might encounter them in your daily life.

Chemical Hazards

A chemical hazard, or toxic substance, is any chemical that may harm human health. It's important to remember that any chemical can be harmful in large enough amounts. For example, a person can die from drinking too much water, too quickly. In moderate amounts though, water is not only harmless, but necessary for human survival. Other chemicals, such as methylmercury that can accumulate in fish tissue, are toxic in small amounts. In essence, "the dose makes the poison."

As you learned in the first lesson, a substance's toxicity depends not just on what it is, but on how much of it a person is exposed to. This lesson focuses on chemicals that may be present in the environment at levels that could harm human health.

You may be tempted to think of chemical hazards as simply another term for pollution—but this is not completely true. **Pollution** is matter or energy that is released into the environment, causing negative effects that impact people, wildlife, and other aspects of the environment. While some pollutants, such as methylmercury, are chemicals, there are other forms of pollution that are not. Similarly, chemical hazards include chemicals that are not pollutants. For example, an oil found in the tissues of poison ivy plants can cause itchy, blistering rashes on human skin (**Figure 12**). This oil is considered a chemical hazard because it harms human health, but it is not a pollutant because it doesn't harm the environment.

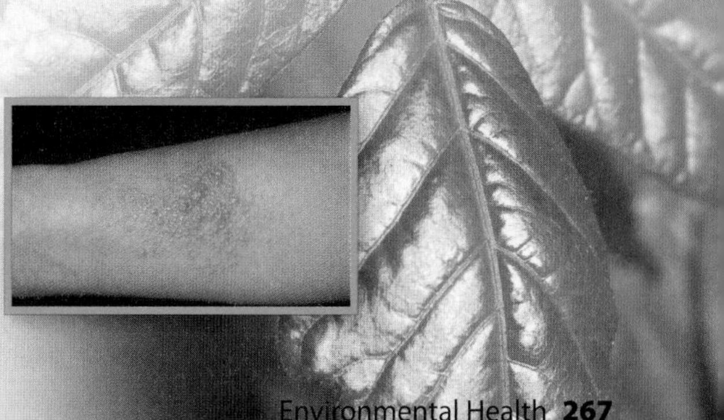

FIGURE 12 Chemical Hazards
When you brush up against a poison ivy plant, you may get oil on your skin. Even if you don't notice when you touch it, later you might feel its effects!

Types of Chemical Hazards

Not every chemical affects human health in the same way. In fact, chemical hazards can be classified by how they affect people. Some chemicals cause cancer. Others cause birth defects. Still others harm the nervous system. Common groups of chemical hazards are carcinogens, chemical mutagens, teratogens, neurotoxins, allergens, and endocrine disruptors.

Carcinogens Chemicals that cause cancer are known as **carcinogens.** Cancer is a disorder in which some of the body's cells lose the ability to control growth. As a result, the cells grow uncontrollably, forming tumors, damaging the body's functioning, and often leading to death. Cancer often has a genetic component, but a wide variety of environmental factors are thought to increase the risk of cancer. In our society today, nearly one third of cancer cases are thought to result from carcinogens contained in cigarette smoke. Carcinogens can be difficult to identify because there may be a long lag time between exposure to the agent and the detectable onset of cancer. Cancer is a leading cause of death that kills millions and leaves few families untouched. As a result, the study of carcinogens has influenced the way that toxicologists pursue their work.

Chemical Mutagens Chemical mutagens are substances that cause genetic changes, or mutations, in the DNA of an organism. Although most mutations have little or no effect, some can lead to severe problems, including cancer. If a harmful mutation occurs in an individual's sperm or egg cells, then the individual's offspring will suffer the effects.

Teratogens Chemicals that harm embryos and fetuses are called **teratogens.** Teratogens that affect the development of human embryos and fetuses can cause birth defects. One example involves the drug thalidomide, developed in the 1950s as a sleeping pill and to prevent nausea during pregnancy. Tragically, the drug turned out to be a powerful teratogen, and its use caused birth defects in thousands of babies. Even a single dose during pregnancy could result in limb deformities (**Figure 13**) and organ defects. Thalidomide was banned in the 1960s once scientists recognized its connection with birth defects. Ironically, today the drug shows promise in treating a wide range of diseases, including Alzheimer's disease, AIDS, and various types of cancer.

Neurotoxins Chemicals that affect the nervous system are called **neurotoxins.** Neurotoxins include various heavy metals such as lead, mercury, and cadmium, as well as pesticides and some chemical weapons developed for use in war. A famous case of neurotoxin poisoning occurred in Japan, where a chemical factory dumped mercury waste into Minamata Bay from the 1930s to the 1960s. Thousands of people near the bay ate fish contaminated with the mercury, and soon started showing signs of mercury poisoning, including slurred speech, loss of muscle control, and in some cases death.

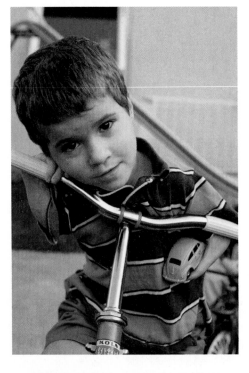

FIGURE 13 Result of Teratogens Thalidomide, a powerful teratogen, caused thousands of children to be born with birth defects, including missing or shortened limbs.

In 1968, the Japanese government confirmed that the dumping was causing the mercury poisoning and ordered the company to stop the dumping. Today, the bay has been cleaned up and reopened for fishing.

Allergens The human immune system protects our bodies from disease. Some substances weaken the immune system, reducing the body's ability to defend itself. Other substances, called *allergens*, overactivate the immune system, causing an immune response when one is not necessary. Some common chemical allergens include animal proteins, tobacco smoke, and certain antibiotics. Living organisms, such as mold and bacteria, can also be allergens. Symptoms of an allergic reaction include hives, skin rashes, itchy skin and eyes, swelling, and wheezing. Allergens are not considered to be toxic substances, however, because they affect some people but not others.

Asthma, an inflammation of the respiratory system, is a major health problem in the United States. In fact, it has become the most common chronic childhood disease, afflicting 7 million American children in 2008. One hypothesis for the increase in asthma occurrences is that allergenic synthetic chemicals are more prevalent in our environment.

Endocrine Disruptors Another type of chemical hazard, endocrine disruptors, interferes with the endocrine system. The endocrine system is the body system that sends and receives chemical signals, called hormones. It regulates body functions such as growth, development, and sexual maturity. The endocrine system also regulates brain function, appetite, and many other aspects of our physiology and behavior. Some hormone-disrupting substances can affect an animal's endocrine system by blocking the action of hormones or accelerating their breakdown. Others are so similar to certain hormones in their molecular structure and chemistry that they "mimic" the hormone by interacting with receptor molecules just as the actual hormone would. Because endocrine disruptors affect the development of the body's organs and endocrine system, fetuses, infants, and small children are at the greatest risk.

FIGURE 14 Chemical Hazards
Different types of chemical hazards affect the human body in different ways.

Chemical Hazards			
Type of Chemical Hazard	**Example**	**Found In**	**Effects on Humans**
Carcinogen	Tobacco smoke	Burning tobacco products	Lung cancer and chronic respiratory ailments
Chemical mutagen	Benzene	Secondhand smoke, gasoline, air pollution	Lowers white blood cell count and can cause leukemia
Teratogen	Alcohol	Alcoholic beverages	Mental retardation and birth defects in developing embryos and fetuses
Neurotoxin	Methylmercury	Contaminated fish tissues	Speech, hearing, vision, and walking impairments; skin tingling; movement coordination loss; muscle weakness; impaired nervous system development in fetuses
Allergen	Animal skin and saliva proteins	Cats, dogs, and other animals	Itchy eyes, sneezing, runny nose, congestion, postnasal drip, cough
Endocrine disruptor	PCBs	Fish tissues, soil, contaminated water	Altered thyroid hormone levels

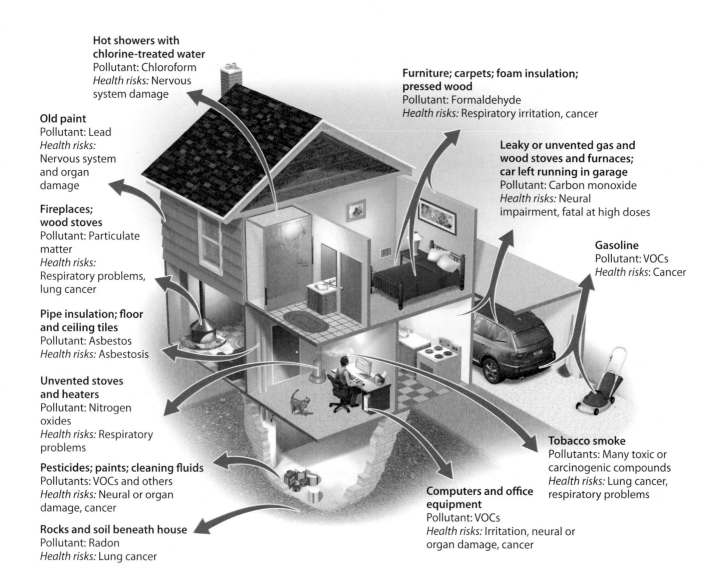

Hot showers with chlorine-treated water
Pollutant: Chloroform
Health risks: Nervous system damage

Old paint
Pollutant: Lead
Health risks: Nervous system and organ damage

Fireplaces; wood stoves
Pollutant: Particulate matter
Health risks: Respiratory problems, lung cancer

Pipe insulation; floor and ceiling tiles
Pollutant: Asbestos
Health risks: Asbestosis

Unvented stoves and heaters
Pollutant: Nitrogen oxides
Health risks: Respiratory problems

Pesticides; paints; cleaning fluids
Pollutants: VOCs and others
Health risks: Neural or organ damage, cancer

Rocks and soil beneath house
Pollutant: Radon
Health risks: Lung cancer

Furniture; carpets; foam insulation; pressed wood
Pollutant: Formaldehyde
Health risks: Respiratory irritation, cancer

Leaky or unvented gas and wood stoves and furnaces; car left running in garage
Pollutant: Carbon monoxide
Health risks: Neural impairment, fatal at high doses

Gasoline
Pollutant: VOCs
Health risks: Cancer

Tobacco smoke
Pollutants: Many toxic or carcinogenic compounds
Health risks: Lung cancer, respiratory problems

Computers and office equipment
Pollutant: VOCs
Health risks: Irritation, neural or organ damage, cancer

FIGURE 15 Indoor Chemical Hazards Houses can have many potential sources of chemical hazards. Some of the most common sources and their possible health effects are shown.

Indoor Chemical Hazards

Many of the most obvious chemical hazards are outdoors—oil spills, toxic waste dumps, and smoke-filled air. However, significant amounts of chemical hazards are also found indoors. Since many Americans spend most of their day indoors, it is important to consider how these hazards may affect our health.

Indoor Air Pollution The air inside homes and buildings can contain chemical hazards. Sometimes, these hazards are not easy to detect. However, they can have noticeable effects on human health. Asbestos, radon, and volatile organic compounds (VOCs) are just a few examples of indoor air pollutants.

▶ **Asbestos** Asbestos is a mineral that forms long, thin microscopic fibers as shown in the inset of **Figure 16.** This structure allows asbestos to insulate heat, muffle sound, and resist fire. Because of these qualities, asbestos was used widely as insulation in buildings and in many products.

When disturbed, asbestos-containing insulation and products can release the fibers into the air. These fibers can then be inhaled and may lodge in lung tissue. Fibers embedded in the lung tissue may cause serious lung diseases, including cancer and asbestosis.

Because of these risks, asbestos has been removed from many schools and offices. However, removing asbestos may sometimes be more dangerous than leaving it in place because improper removal of asbestos increases airborne exposure.

▶ **Radon** Another indoor hazard is radon. Radon is a colorless, odorless, highly toxic radioactive gas. It is made and released naturally when uranium in rock, soil, and water decays. It can seep up from the ground and build up inside basements and homes with poor air circulation. The U.S. EPA estimates that slightly less than 1 person in 1000 may contract lung cancer as a result of a lifetime of radon exposure at average levels.

The level of radon exposure a person might experience depends in part upon the geology of the place he or she lives. Certain areas have a higher risk for radon exposure than others. **Figure 17** shows the relative risk of radon exposure for different locations in the United States.

Radon is detected using special kits. If high levels of radon are found in your home, there are ways to reduce your exposure. For example, a technique called soil suction involves installing one or more pipes under your home. Radon is then vented above ground through the pipe.

FIGURE 16 Asbestos The long, thin fibers of asbestos (inset) make it a good insulator, but when inhaled they can cause lung disease. Only trained personnel wearing protective gear should remove asbestos.

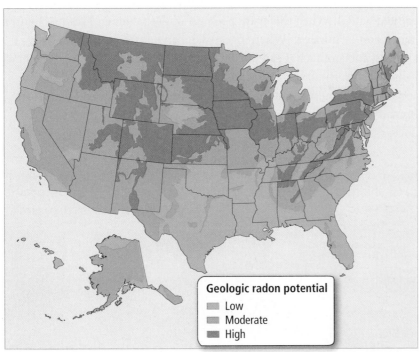

Geologic radon potential
■ Low
■ Moderate
■ High

Data from U.S. Geological Survey. 1993. Generalized geological radon potential of the United States, 1993.

FIGURE 17 Radon Risk in the United States This map shows U.S. regions that, due to their geology, have low, moderate, and high levels of radon risk.

Make a Difference

your world • your turn •

Check around your school for possible sources of indoor air pollution. Make a list of these sources. Discuss ways to reduce your exposure with your teacher. If possible, implement some of these solutions.

▶ ***Volatile Organic Compounds (VOCs)*** The most diverse group of indoor air pollutants are volatile organic compounds (VOCs). These carbon-containing compounds are released into the air by many products including plastics, perfumes, and pesticides. Although we are surrounded by products that give off VOCs, volatile organic compounds tend to be released in very small amounts.

Since there are so many different types of VOCs, and we are exposed to them at such low levels, it is difficult to determine exactly how VOC exposure may affect our health. An exception is formaldehyde, which has known health impacts. Formaldehyde is a VOC used in pressed wood and insulation, among other products. Exposure to formaldehyde can irritate the eyes, nose, throat, and skin.

Carbon Monoxide A colorless and odorless gas, carbon monoxide can be difficult to detect without special equipment. At low levels, carbon monoxide can cause headaches, dizziness, nausea, and fatigue. With higher exposure, impaired vision, chest pain, lowered brain function, and death can occur.

Sources of carbon monoxide include leaky or unvented stoves, car exhaust, and tobacco smoke. One way to protect yourself against carbon monoxide poisoning is to install a carbon monoxide detector in your home. If your carbon monoxide alarm goes off, leave your house immediately. Then, call your local emergency number.

Lead Another indoor health hazard is lead. People can be exposed to lead through the air, drinking water, contaminated soil, lead-based paint, and dust. Lead poisoning can result from drinking water that has passed through lead pipes or pipes that have been joined with lead solder. Lead paint is another dangerous source of lead, especially for young children. Until 1978, most paints contained lead and the walls of many houses were painted with it. When this paint peels off walls, babies and young children may ingest or inhale it. When ingested, it can damage the brain, liver, kidneys, and stomach. Lead poisoning can also lead to learning problems, behavior abnormalities, anemia, hearing loss, and even death. Today, about 2.5 percent of children under age 6 are affected by lead poisoning. In many states, young children are now tested for lead at their yearly doctor's appointments.

FIGURE 18 Lead Poisoning In many older homes and apartments, lead-based paint covers the walls both inside and out. Unfortunately, curious young children may eat this peeling paint. Over time, lead poisoning could result.

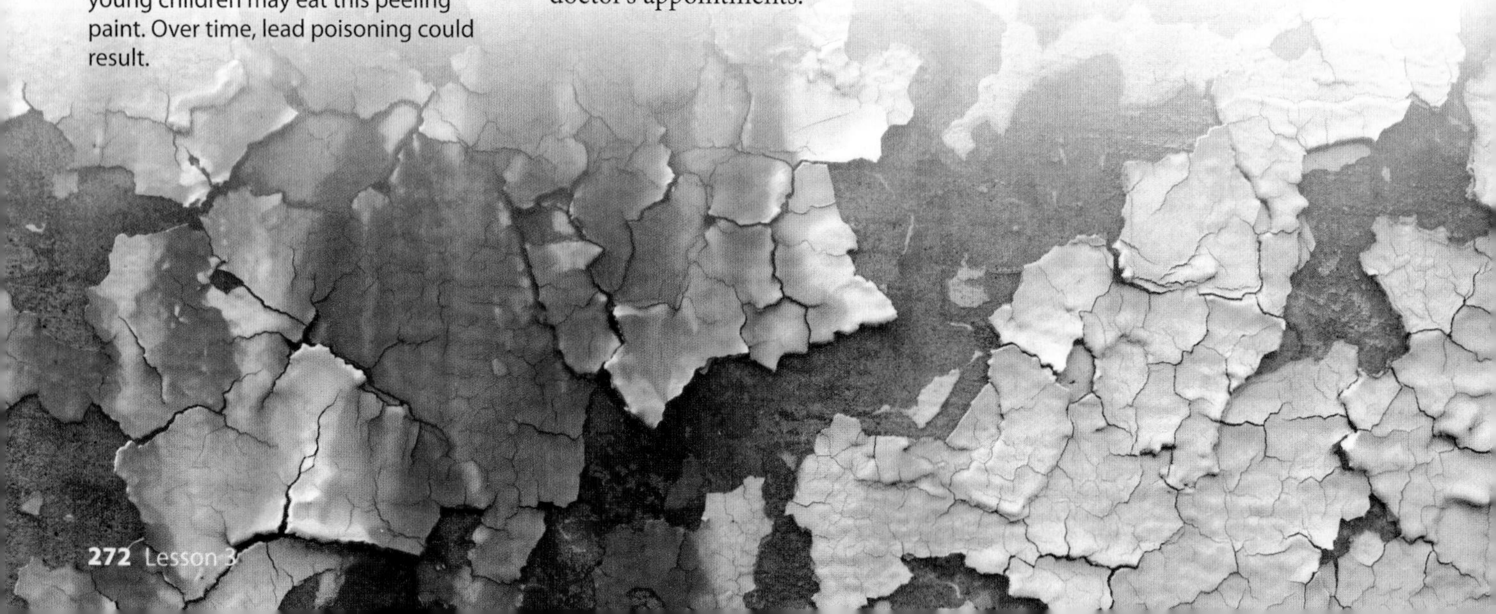

Outdoor Chemical Hazards

FIGURE 19 Outdoor Air Pollution
Outdoor air pollution contributes to millions of premature deaths each year. Tough laws have been passed to reduce some of the harmful emissions.

Thousands of chemicals have found their way into the air, land, and water. A 2002 study found that one or more of 82 wastewater contaminants was found in 80 percent of streams in the United States. These contaminants include antibiotics, detergents, drugs, disinfectants, solvents, perfumes, and other substances.

Chemical Hazards in Air Chemical hazards in air come from both natural sources and human activity. For example, volcanic eruptions can release huge amounts of small particles, sulfur dioxide, and other gases. Human activities also release chemical hazards, such as carbon monoxide, sulfur dioxide, nitrogen dioxide, ozone, and lead into the air.

Understanding what chemical hazards exist in the air is especially important because winds can carry chemicals far away from their original source. As a result, chemicals released into the air at one site can affect people and other organisms far away. Airborne transport of pesticides is sometimes called *pesticide drift*. The Central Valley of California is widely considered the most productive agricultural region in the world. But because it is a naturally arid area, food production depends on intensive use of irrigation, fertilizers, and pesticides. The region's frequent winds often blow the airborne spray—and dust particles containing pesticide residue—for long distances. In the mountains of the Sierra Nevada, research has associated pesticide drift from the Central Valley with population declines in four species of frogs. Families living in towns in the Central Valley have suffered health impacts, and activists for farm workers maintain that hundreds of thousands of the state's residents are at risk.

Chemical Hazards on Land Land can also become contaminated with chemical hazards. Chemical hazards get into the soil in many ways. For example, when you use pesticides or improperly dispose of electronic equipment, you may be adding chemical hazards to the ground. Some common soil toxicants include pesticides and heavy metals such as lead.

Chemical hazards on or in land can affect both human and ecosystem health. People can inhale them, absorb them by touching contaminated soils, or ingest them while working with soil or eating produce grown in the area. In addition, soil toxicants can also be picked up by water that runs off of land.

Chemical Hazards in Water Many chemicals are soluble in water and enter organisms' tissues through drinking or absorption. For this reason, aquatic animals such as fish, frogs, and stream invertebrates are effective indicators of pollution. When aquatic organisms become sick, we can take it as an early warning that something is amiss. This is why many scientists see findings that show the effects of low concentrations of pesticides on frogs, fish, and invertebrates as a warning that humans could be next. The contaminants that wash into streams and rivers also flow and seep into the water we drink and drift through the air we breathe.

Chemicals get into our waterways in many different ways. For example, water can pick up toxic substances when it runs off land. If a car leaks oil onto a road, this oil may wash off the road during a rainstorm. The runoff, carrying the oil with it, may eventually find its way into a nearby river. Runoff is of particular concern to environmental scientists because it carries toxic substances from large areas of land and concentrates them in small amounts of surface water. In addition, chemical hazards may drain directly into a waterway from a specific source, such as a storm drain, as shown in **Figure 20.**

FIGURE 20 Chemical Hazards in Water Runoff carries many pollutants into waterways.

Biomagnification

Of the toxic substances that organisms absorb, breathe, or consume, some are quickly excreted. Others are broken down into harmless products. Still others can last for months or years. How long a chemical lasts, or persists, can be a major concern for environmental scientists.

Bioaccumulation Organisms absorb, breathe, and ingest toxic substances from their environments. If these chemicals are persistent, or last a long time, organisms may end up storing them in their bodies. Eventually, organisms can build up large concentrations of toxic substances in their bodies, through a process called **bioaccumulation.** For example, DDT can accumulate in fatty tissues. Methylmercury can be stored in muscle tissue.

The Process of Biomagnification Toxic substances that bioaccumulate in the tissues of one organism may be transferred to other organisms as predators consume prey. When one organism consumes another, it takes in any stored toxic substances and stores them itself, along with the toxic substances it has received from eating other prey. Thus with each step up the food chain, from producers to primary consumer to secondary consumer and so on, concentrations of toxic substances can be greatly magnified, in a process called **biomagnification.**

The biomagnification of DDT is a good example of this process. In the 1940s through 1960s, DDT was a commonly used pesticide. However, it ran off land into waterways and was taken up by aquatic producers called phytoplankton. Zooplankton then fed on the phytoplankton and accumulated an increased concentration of DDT in their bodies. When small fish ate the zooplankton, they accumulated an even higher concentration of DDT in their tissues. Larger fish fed on smaller fish and fish-eating birds fed on larger fish. At each step up the food chain, the concentration of DDT was further increased in organisms' bodies. Eventually, DDT concentrations were so high in bird tissues that it affected their ability to reproduce. Their eggshells became so thin they broke in the nest. Osprey populations started declining, and peregrine falcons were nearly wiped out. **Figure 21** shows how DDT can be biomagnified up an aquatic food chain.

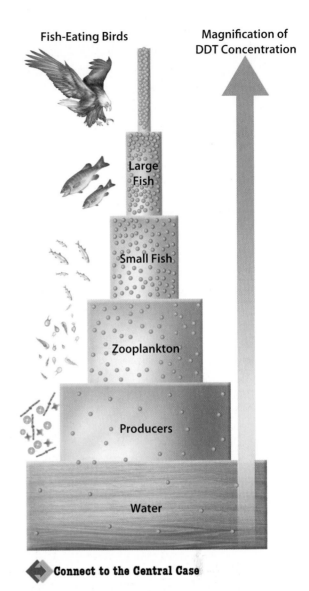

Fish-Eating Birds

Magnification of DDT Concentration

Large Fish

Small Fish

Zooplankton

Producers

Water

◆ **Connect to the Central Case**

FIGURE 21 Biomagnification DDT becomes more concentrated in the tissues of organisms at each step up the food chain.

The "Dirty Dozen" Persistent Organic Pollutants (POPs)	
Toxicant	**Description**
Aldrin	Pesticide
Chlordane	Pesticide
DDT	Pesticide
Dieldrin	Pesticide
Dioxins	Unintentional byproduct
Endrin	Pesticide
Furans	Unintentional byproduct
Heptachlor	Pesticide
Hexachlorobenzene	Pesticide
Mirex	Pesticide
PCBs	Industrial chemical
Toxaphene	Pesticide

Data from United Nations Environment Programme (UNEP), 2001.

FIGURE 22 The Dirty Dozen The original goal of the Stockholm Convention was to end the use of these twelve dangerous POPs. Since then, eighteen more chemicals have been added to the list.

Persistent Organic Pollutants (POPs) Some toxic chemicals persist in the environment, biomagnify through the food web, and cause adverse effects to human health and the environment. These chemicals are called persistent organic pollutants (POPs). DDT is a persistent organic pollutant, as are PCBs (polychlorinated biphenyls).

POPs can be carried long distances by water and wind. This means that POPs released in one place can accumulate in locations far away. Because contaminants often cross international boundaries, an international treaty seemed the best way of dealing fairly with such transboundary pollution. The global nature of addressing POPs has led to an international response. For example, the *Stockholm Convention on Persistent Organic Pollutants* came into force in 2004 and was ratified by roughly 140 nations. The Stockholm Convention's inital goal is to end the use and release of 12 of the most dangerous POPs, a group nicknamed the "dirty dozen" **(Figure 22)**. It sets guidelines for phasing out these chemicals and encourages transition to safer alternatives. As of March 2020, a total of 152 countries had signed the treaty, including the United States.

Many of the POPs included in the Stockholm Convention are no longer produced in the United States. However, people and ecosystems can still be at risk from those that persist in the environment, or those that travel from elsewhere by wind or water.

LESSON ③ Assessment

1. **Review** Explain the phrase "The dose makes the poison."

2. **Classify** List two types of chemical hazards that affect human health.

3. **Review** Name one indoor chemical hazard and describe how it can affect human health.

4. **Apply Concepts** A pollutant released on one continent is found concentrated in the tissues of organisms on another continent. Is this likely an air, land, or water pollutant? Explain.

5. **Explain** Describe the process of biomagnification.

6. **THINK IT** *THROUGH* A farmer decides to use a new pesticide on her fields to combat some new pests. She continues to apply it for several years. Over time, a neighbor notices that there are fewer and fewer big fish in a nearby pond. She can't think of any explanation, so she notifies scientists at a local university. The scientists look into the issue and find that high levels of the pesticide have accumulated in the fishes' tissues. Describe how this might have occurred.

Natural Disasters

EVERYDAY PHENOMENON How can physical events in the environment affect our health?

Knowledge and Skills

- Discuss how earthquakes affect structures on Earth's surface.
- Discuss how volcanoes affect human lives and property.
- Describe tornadoes, hurricanes, and thunderstorms.
- Discuss the dangers of avalanches.

Reading Strategy and Vocabulary

✓ **Reading Strategy** Create a three-column table. Label the first column Hazard, the second column Damages, and the third column Safety and Preparation. As you read the lesson, fill in the first column with each physical hazard discussed. Take notes on the damage each causes and how to prepare for and stay safe during each.

Vocabulary earthquake, landslide, tsunami, volcano, tornado, hurricane, thunderstorm, avalanche

ON SEPTEMBER 28, 2018, an earthquake with a magnitude of 7.5 shook the Indonesian island of Sulawesi. Homes and buildings collapsed and thousands of people were either killed or injured. The earthquake also generated a tsunami that further devastated the region.

Earthquakes are just one example of how the forces of Earth, wind, and water can quickly and completely disrupt our lives. Other examples of physical hazards that occur naturally in the environment and pose health hazards include volcanic eruptions and violent storms, including hurricanes and tornadoes. We can do little to predict the timing of a natural disaster such as an earthquake, and nothing to prevent one. However, scientists can map geologic faults to determine areas at risk of earthquakes, engineers can design buildings in ways that help them resist damage, and citizens and governments can take steps to prepare for the aftermath of a severe quake.

Some common practices increase our vulnerability to certain physical hazards. Deforesting slopes makes landslides more likely, for instance, and damming rivers makes flooding more likely in some areas while preventing flooding in others. We can reduce risk from such hazards by improving our forestry and flood control practices and by choosing not to build in areas prone to floods, landslides, fires, and coastal waves.

Earthquakes

The forces that move mountains are also the ones that create earthquakes. Earth's crust is broken into several large sections called tectonic plates. These hard plates "float" on a layer of hot, soft rock. As plates scrape against each other, sometimes they get stuck and the stress builds up. When the plates finally move, energy is released. This energy causes the earth to shake, a phenomenon called an **earthquake.**

FIGURE 23 Damage from the March 2011 earthquake and tsunami in Japan

Surface Effects Depending on where they occur, how much energy is released, and how long the earth shakes, earthquakes can have extensive effects on Earth's surface. For example, earthquakes can cause the ground to sink and soil to liquefy. Earthquakes can set off landslides and mudslides. Landslides occur when rock and soil slide down a slope. When an earthquake triggers a landslide, it can be a very dangerous event for people nearby. In 2018, an earthquake in Japan set off hundreds of landslides, killing 36 people.

When an earthquake occurs at the bottom of the ocean, it can set off a tsunami. A tsunami is a large ocean wave. When tsunamis hit coastal towns, they can cause massive damage and loss of life. In March 2011, a 9.1 magnitude earthquake off the coast of Japan generated a tsunami with waves as high as 10 m. Over 22,000 people were killed and the Fukushima Daiichi nuclear plant was unable to contain radiation from the reactors.

Earthquake Damage Earthquakes can be incredibly costly events, both in terms of structural damage (**Figure 23**) and human life. For example, it is estimated that the cost of cleaning up and rebuilding as a result of the 2011 earthquake in Japan is over $200 billion.

Earthquake Safety Scientists cannot predict when earthquakes might occur. There are places, however, where earthquakes are more likely to occur than others. In the United States, Alaska and California have the most earthquakes (**Figure 24**). People who live in high-risk areas can take precautions to help them survive if an earthquake occurs.

If an earthquake occurs, take cover under something sturdy. Cover your face and head. Keep clear of anything that may fall or break on you, such as hanging lights and windows. Stay away from buildings, power lines, and streetlights.

Map it

Predicting Earthquakes

Figure 24 shows where the major earthquakes occurred between 1980 and 1990. The red dots indicate locations of the earthquakes. The orange lines are the boundaries of the tectonic plates. Study the map and answer the following questions.

1. **Observe** What general pattern do you observe between the location of earthquakes and the location of the tectonic plates?

2. **Interpret Maps** Do most earthquakes take place in the interiors of the continents or along the coastlines?

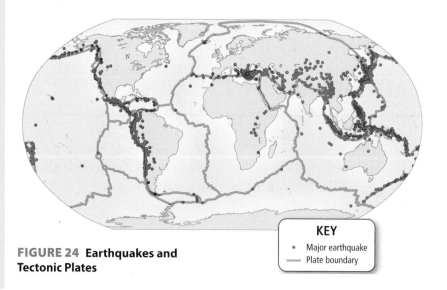

FIGURE 24 Earthquakes and Tectonic Plates

KEY
- Major earthquake
- Plate boundary

Volcanoes

A **volcano** is an opening in Earth's crust through which lava, ash, and gases are ejected. When molten rock inside Earth comes to the surface, it is called a volcanic eruption. In an eruption, rock may seep quietly out of the land or it may explode. Eventually, the rock hardens and forms a new rock layer on Earth's surface.

Damage From Volcanic Eruptions The molten rock, or lava, that surfaces in a volcanic eruption can cover large areas of land, destroying what was once there. Volcanoes can also spew clouds of gas, ash, and cinders into the atmosphere. In 2010, a volcanic eruption in Iceland sent so much ash into the atmosphere that air traffic between Europe and the rest of the world was severely disrupted for about 10 days **(Figure 25)**. Clouds from extreme volcanic eruptions can block the sun's rays and cause global temperatures to drop. Eruptions can also trigger landslides and mudflows. *Mudflows* are large masses of liquid soil and rock, sliding down a slope. Mudflows are also called mudslides.

The 1991 eruption of Mount Pinatubo in the Philippines is a powerful example of the destructive potential of volcanoes. The valleys surrounding the mountain filled with thick deposits of volcanic material. Deposits in some areas were over 180 meters (600 feet) thick! The eruption set off mudflows and sent up a massive ash cloud about 35 kilometers (22 miles) into the air. Some of the ash settled onto nearby roofs and mixed with rain. This heavy mix caused roof collapses that killed most of the 300 people who died from the eruption.

Preparing for a Volcanic Eruption Like earthquakes, many volcanoes are located near the edges of tectonic plates. Scientists monitor volcanoes to try to predict when they will erupt. They cannot tell for certain the size of an eruption or predict far in the future when one might occur. However, scientists can sometimes warn people in time to evacuate. Before Mount Pinatubo erupted, scientists warned people far enough in advance that more than 70,000 people were evacuated.

Ash trail

(a)

FIGURE 25 Eyjafjallajokull and Mount Pinatubo (a) The ash trail from Eyjafjallajokull volcano in Iceland extended from Iceland to western Europe disrupting air traffic for days. **(b)** Ash from the eruption of Mount Pinatubo in the Philippines remained in the air for days, **(c)** coating villagers as they left the affected area.

(c)

(b)

FIGURE 26 Tornadoes
A tornado often destroys anything in its path.

Storms

Geologic forces are not the only physical hazards powerful enough to devastate towns and cities. Storms, such as tornadoes and hurricanes, can also claim lives and homes.

Tornadoes A tornado is a type of windstorm in which a funnel of rotating air drops down from a storm cloud and touches Earth's surface. Funnel wind speeds can reach over 400 kilometers (250 miles) per hour.

▶ *Tornado Damage* Tornadoes can cause incredible damage where they touch down. Tornadoes can flatten houses, lift cars, and tear the bark off trees. They can also be deadly. In 2019, forty-one Americans were killed by tornadoes. The majority of people who die in a tornado are struck by flying objects that have been picked up by the strong winds.

▶ *Tornado Safety* If you are indoors, seek shelter in the lowest floor of the building, such as the basement. If you are in a vehicle or mobile home, get out and find the nearest sturdy building for shelter. If you are stuck outside, try to find a ditch or a low point and lie face down in it. Try to protect your head as best as possible.

Hurricanes A hurricane is a powerful storm that forms over the ocean in the tropics. Hurricanes produce winds that are at least 119 kilometers (74 miles) per hour. When a hurricane strikes land, it brings high winds, heavy rain, and a storm surge along with it. A *storm surge* is a dome of water that crashes along the coast where the hurricane hits.

 ✔ Reading Checkpoint   *What is the difference between a tsunami and a storm surge?*

▶ *Hurricane Damage* Hurricanes can destroy buildings, wash away beaches, and blow away trees. They can also cause severe flooding. Hurricane Harvey is one example of the destructive power of hurricanes. In August 2017, Hurricane Harvey struck land near Corpus Christi, Texas. As a Category 4 hurricane, it had winds of about 209 kilometers/hour (130 miles/hour) and brought a record-setting 152 cm (60 inches) of rain to parts of Texas. The storm surge generated waves over 4 meters (12 feet) high. High winds and flooding caused about 125 billion dollars in damage and killed at least 68 people.

▶ *Hurricane Safety* To prepare for a hurricane, secure your home before it hits. For example, close storm shutters and clear rain gutters. If local authorities tell you to evacuate, do so. During the hurricane, try to stay away from windows. If necessary, take shelter in an interior room under a sturdy object.

FIGURE 27 Hurricane Harvey On August 25, 2017, Hurricane Harvey made landfall in southeastern Texas. Cities, such as Houston, were flooded by heavy rains.

Thunderstorms A thunderstorm is a storm that produces both lightning and thunder. Thunderstorms also usually produce heavy rain and sometimes hail. Thunderstorms are common events. At this very moment, there are probably about 2000 thunderstorms in progress around the globe. But just because they are common does not mean that thunderstorms are harmless.

▶ *Thunderstorm Damage* Heavy rain from thunderstorms can cause flooding. Strong winds can take down power lines and trees. If a severe thunderstorm generates large hail, it can damage crops and property. And, lightning can start fires and kill people when it strikes. In 2019, twenty Americans were struck and killed by lightning.

▶ *Thunderstorm Safety* The best way to stay safe in a thunderstorm is to stay indoors. If you are outside, stay away from tall objects such as trees and poles. Squat down and keep your head low.

Avalanches

An avalanche is a mass of snow sliding down a slope. In North America, a big avalanche might send 300,000 cubic yards of snow crashing down a mountain. This is roughly equal to 20 football fields, each filled with snow that is about 3 meters (10 feet) deep.

Avalanche Conditions There are certain conditions that create the potential for avalanches. Avalanches usually occur on slopes that are greater than 30 degrees. Another factor is the snowpack, or the layers of snow on the slope. Unstable snowpacks create the potential for an avalanche. A snowpack is unstable when a layer of hard, strong snow sits on top of soft, weak snow. If the weak layer gives, the snowpack can break apart and send a mass of snow sliding down the slope.

Weather is another significant factor for avalanches. Heavy snowfall adds weight to the snow pack and can trigger an avalanche. Warm temperatures can also influence snowpack stability. Initially, warm temperatures can melt the top of the snowpack and increase the potential for an avalanche. However, if periods of melting and re-freezing occur, the snowpack can actually become more stable.

Avalanche Damage Avalanches can bury both people and places in large masses of snow. In 2018 and 2019, 25 people died in avalanches in the United States. Avalanches can block roads and railroad tracks as well as damage phone lines and bridges.

Lightning Bolts

Avalanche Safety Most Americans who die in avalanches are on the slopes for recreation, skiing, snowboarding, or hiking. The best way to stay safe while participating in one of these activities is to avoid risky slopes altogether. If you do get caught and buried by an avalanche, try to stay near the surface. Swim up through the sliding snow as best you can. Stay calm and try to conserve any air you have.

FIGURE 28 Avalanche Damage This road and bridge have been completely destroyed by an avalanche.

_{LESSON} **④ Assessment**

1. **Review** What is a landslide?
2. **Explain** Name some ways a volcanic eruption can damage property.
3. **Compare and Contrast** How are hurricanes and tornadoes similar? How are they different?
4. **Apply Concepts** Why do you think it is important to stay calm if you are caught in an avalanche?

5. **THINK IT** *THROUGH* Suppose you are in a car driving through a new town. The national weather service issues a tornado warning for this area. At the same time, you notice the weather looks threatening. What might you do?

SHOULD BPA BE REGULATED?

If you've had a drink from a reusable water bottle or eaten canned food, chances are you've swallowed a little bit of Bisphenol-A (BPA). BPA is an important chemical building block in polycarbonate plastic, which is a clear, nearly shatter-proof plastic used to make water bottles and baby bottles. BPA is also part of plastic films used to line food and soft drink cans. Over time, BPA can leach out of plastic and be consumed along with foods and drinks. Most people have some BPA in their bodies—of thousands of Americans tested, 95 percent had traces of BPA in their urine.

In the late 1990s, some scientists became concerned that BPA may be toxic. Many people have stopped buying bottles made of polycarbonate plastic because they are concerned about the effects of BPA on their health. But other groups, including government agencies, have claimed that the health risks of BPA are low and the public is overreacting. The debate about whether the health risks of BPA are real or not rages on.

VIEWPOINT 1

BPA is dangerous to everyone.

Many environmental and public health groups are concerned about BPA because they think that even small amounts are toxic to humans. They want the Federal Food and Drug Administration (FDA) to limit the amount of BPA allowed in cans and bottles.

BPA mimics the activity of the hormone estrogen, which means it can cause problems with development and reproduction. Dr. Patricia Hunt was one of the first researchers to discover that BPA can cause birth defects in mouse embryos when mice she was studying were exposed to BPA in their plastic cages. Other tests on rats and mice have shown that doses of BPA as low as 10 µg/kg, just ten millionths of a gram per kilogram of body weight, can increase the risk of prostate and breast cancer, obesity, and reproductive problems. A 2007 university panel concluded that most Americans' BPA levels are over 10 µg/kg.

VIEWPOINT 2

BPA is completely safe.

Companies that use BPA argue that the majority of people only consume very small amounts of the chemical, and this is quickly metabolized and flushed out of the body before it can cause harm. Furthermore, BPA has been used since the 1960s and there is no conclusive evidence that it has had a harmful effect on humans—most studies on the health risks of BPA have only been done on mice and rats.

There are, however, studies that suggest BPA is safe. In 2008, the European Food Safety Authority concluded that BPA is safe for all types of plastic liners and containers. Several European studies have confirmed the safety of BPA for humans, including one French study that found that there were no health risks for babies fed out of polycarbonate bottles.

VIEWPOINT 3

BPA is only dangerous for children.

Most government agencies have only found serious health risks for BPA in children, not adults. Based on animal studies, the National Institute of Health (NIH) concluded that BPA has negative effects on brain development and behavior in fetuses and young children. However, the NIH concluded that levels of BPA found in the average American are too low to pose any health risks for adults.

Because of the potential threats to infants, some nations and states, including Canada, Minnesota, Connecticut, and California, have already decided to regulate BPA in products intended for children. In 2012, the FDA announced that baby bottles and children's drinking cups could not contain BPA.

In 1999, Dr. Patricia Hunt discovered that BPA caused birth defects in mouse embryos when pregnant mice were exposed to BPA from their plastic cages and water bottles.

Some companies have started making BPA-free bottles.

21st Century Skills

Social Responsibility Imagine you and your classmates are employees of a company that makes polycarbonate plastic water and baby bottles. Decide as a group what your company should do about BPA. Then design a one-page article for the company's Web site announcing your decision to your customers. Explain what steps the company plans to take, if any, and what facts led you to this decision.

CHAPTER 9 — Study Guide

INVESTIGATIVE PHENOMENON
How do we balance the relationship between our own health and the health of the environment?

Lesson 1
What is environmental health?

Lesson 2
How do biological and social factors in the environment affect human health?

Lesson 3
How do chemicals in our environment affect our health?

Lesson 4
How can physical events in the environment affect our health?

LESSON 1 An Overview of Environmental Health
- Environmental health hazards can be biological, social, chemical, or physical.
- Epidemiology is the study of disease in human populations. Toxicology is the study of how poisonous substances affect the health of humans and other organisms.
- People respond differently to environmental hazards due to individual differences such as age, sex, weight, health issues, and genetic makeup.
- Risk assessment is the process of measuring the chance that an environmental hazard will cause harm.

environmental health (256)	dose (258)
hazard (256)	response (258)
pathogen (256)	dose-response relationship (258)
epidemiology (258)	risk (260)
toxicology (258)	risk assessment (260)
toxicity (258)	

LESSON 2 Biological and Social Hazards
- Infectious diseases are spread by direct human contact through contaminated food and water, and by animals.
- Since new diseases are continually emerging, it is important to know how, where, and to what extent they are spreading.
- Some social hazards result from lifestyle choices a person makes, while other social hazards cannot be controlled.

infectious disease (261)	emerging disease (263)

LESSON 3 Toxic Substances in the Environment
- All chemicals can be hazardous in large enough quantities.
- Chemical hazards can cause cancer, birth defects, and improper functioning of human body systems.
- Our homes and buildings may contain chemical hazards including asbestos, radon, volatile organic compounds, carbon monoxide, and lead.
- Chemical hazards can be found in the air, on land, and in the water.

- Toxic chemicals accumulate in organisms and increase through biomagnification as they feed on one another.

pollution (267)	asbestos (271)
carcinogen (268)	radon (271)
teratogen (268)	bioaccumulation (275)
neurotoxin (269)	biomagnification (275)

LESSON 4 Natural Disasters
- Earthquakes occur as Earth's plates scrape against each other. Earthquakes can destroy natural landforms as well as human-made structures.
- The molten rock, gas, ash, and cinders released during a volcanic eruption can cause significant damage and loss of life in nearby cities and towns.
- Tornadoes, hurricanes, and thunderstorms are powerful weather events that can damage property and threaten human lives.
- An avalanche is a mass of sliding snow that can bury people and places in its path.

earthquake (277)	tornado (280)
landslide (278)	hurricane (280)
tsunami (278)	thunderstorm (282)
volcano (279)	avalanche (282)

GO ONLINE

INQUIRY LABS AND ACTIVITIES
- **Tracking an Outbreak**
  Find the source of a mysterious cholera outbreak. Use the same clues a detective uses.
- **Home Hazmat Survey**
  Find out which products in your home are classified as "hazardous materials" and why.
- **Testing for Lead**
  Use a lead-testing kit to find out whether common household items may contain lead.

Chapter Assessment

Defend Your Case

The Central Case in this chapter explored the costs and benefits of using the pesticide DDT. In some African nations, governments use DDT to battle disease-carrying mosquitoes. Based on what you have learned, would you support continued use of DDT? Use evidence from the Central Case and the lessons to support your stand.

Review Concepts and Terms

1. What type of environmental hazard is shown below?

   a. social hazard   c. chemical hazard

   b. physical hazard   d. biological hazard

2. The study of disease in human populations is

   a. epidemiology.

   b. toxicology.

   c. a dose-response relationship.

   d. risk assessment.

3. A person's age, sex, weight, health issues, and genetic makeup influence how he or she responds to

   a. risk assessment.

   b. natural disasters.

   c. antibiotic resistance.

   d. environmental hazards.

4. Infectious diseases can be spread by

   a. contaminated water.   c. animals.

   b. human contact.   d. all of the above.

5. Chemicals that cause cancer are called

   a. teratogens.   c. neurotoxins.

   b. carcinogens.   d. endocrine disruptors.

6. A colorless, toxic, radioactive gas is

   a. asbestos.   c. carbon monoxide.

   b. radon.   d. lead.

7. In the United States, which agency takes the lead for responding to emerging diseases?

   a. Centers for Disease Control and Prevention (CDC)

   b. Environmental Protection Agency (EPA)

   c. World Health Organization (WHO)

   d. Federal Emergency Management Agency (FEMA)

8. The process through which pollutants get increasingly more concentrated at each step up the food chain is

   a. biomagnification.   c. toxicity.

   b. anaphylaxis.   d. bioaccumulation.

9. A large ocean wave often created by an ocean floor earthquake is a (an)

   a. avalanche.   c. tsunami.

   b. tornado.   d. mudslide.

10. A powerful storm that forms over the ocean in the tropics is called a (an)

   a. earthquake.   c. tsunami.

   b. tornado.   d. hurricane.

Modified True/False

Write true if the statement is true. If it is false, change the underlined word or words to make the statement true.

11. The relationship between different doses of chemicals and the responses they generate is called a <u>risk assessment</u>.

12. <u>Infectious diseases</u> are caused by a pathogen, such as a virus or a bacterium.

13. Chemicals that harm embryos and fetuses, thus causing birth defects, are known as <u>pathogens</u>.

14. <u>Biomagnification</u> begins when organisms begin to bioaccumulate pollutants in their tissues and cells.

15. A mass of snow sliding down a slope is <u>a mudslide</u>.

Chapter Assessment

Reading Comprehension

Read the following selection and answer the questions that follow.

Mercury is a heavy metal. It occurs naturally in minerals and rocks. Throughout most of human history, natural sources released mercury into the air at a constant rate. More recently, however, human activity has accelerated the release of mercury.

Burning fossil fuels such as coal releases mercury into the air. Eventually, it ends up in soils or in surface water. Microbes in the water convert mercury into methylmercury. The mercury gets concentrated in the tissues of predatory fish such as shark and swordfish. Large fish typically concentrate more mercury than small fish.

People who eat fish with high methylmercury concentrations can suffer from muscle tremors, deafness, and poor concentration. Pregnant women and children are especially sensitive to its toxic effects. Learning disabilities and developmental delays are common in children who have been exposed to significant levels of methylmercury during development.

16. Based on the health effects described above, methylmercury would be best classified as a(n)
   a. carcinogen.
   b. endocrine disruptor.
   c. neurotoxin.
   d. allergen.

17. Concentrations of methylmercury are higher in large fish compared to concentrations in the water. This is best described as
   a. bioaccumulation.
   b. biomagnification.
   c. synergism.
   d. toxicology.

Short Answer

18. What sort of chemical hazard is thalidomide?

19. What's the difference between a landslide and an avalanche?

20. Do all social hazards result from an individual's lifestyle choice? Explain.

21. Do all vectors, or disease-carrying organisms, suffer from the disease they carry?

22. What sort of biological hazards spread through contaminated food and water or by direct human contact?

23. Describe and give an example of an indoor chemical hazard and an outdoor chemical hazard.

24. Explain the process of biomagnification.

Critical Thinking

25. **Apply Concepts** During flu season, there are constant reminders to wash your hands. Why is this important? Can you suggest something else people should do to prevent infection?

26. **Infer** What is the relationship between human population growth and the spread of diseases?

27. **Infer** Do you think it is possible that climate change contributes to environmental hazards? Explain.

28. **Explain** What are carcinogens and why are they difficult to identify?

29. **Apply Concepts** What happens when we build office buildings or schools with windows that are sealed and cannot be opened? What sort of chemical hazards build up?

Analyze Data

Over the past several decades, the incidence of some deadly cancers, such as lung cancer, has decreased. During the same time period, the incidence of melanoma (a type of skin cancer) increased. The incidence of both lung cancer and melanoma increases with age. But melanoma is one of the most common cancers in young adults. Although both forms of cancer are social hazards, you can control some of the risk factors attributed to them.

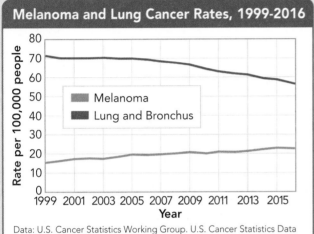

Melanoma and Lung Cancer Rates, 1999-2016

Data: U.S. Cancer Statistics Working Group. U.S. Cancer Statistics Data Visualizations Tool, based on November 2018 submission data (1999-2016): U.S. Department of Health and Human Services, Centers for Disease Control and Prevention and National Cancer Institute

30. **Interpret Graphs** Describe the trends shown in this graph for the incidence of lung cancer and melanoma from 1999 to 2016.

31. **Predict** The data are for all age groups. If you were to look at similar data for the specific group of people aged 20–24, how do you think the graph would differ? Explain.

32. **Infer** How do you think increased education and improvements in treatments could affect the rate of each cancer in the next ten years?

Write About It

33. **Creative Writing** What have you learned about environmental hazards, from this textbook and from your own experiences in life? Reflect on that question. Then, in response, write a poem, a rap song, a short story, or a personal account about environmental hazards.

34. **Persuasion** Write a short video script to convince others to protect environmental health. Keep your message brief and compelling.

35. **REVISIT INVESTIGATIVE PHENOMENON** Write a short summary that explains the relationship between environmental health and our own health.

Ecological Footprints

Read the information below. Copy the table into your notebook and record your calculations. Then, answer the questions that follow.

In 2001, the population of the United States was about 285 million (0.285 billion). The world's population was about 6.1 billion. At the same time, annual pesticide use in the United States was around 1.20 billion pounds. World pesticide use was around 5.05 billion pounds. Finish filling in the table. Then, answer the questions.

	Population	Annual pesticide use (pounds of active ingredient)
You	1	4.21
Your class		
Your state		
United States		
World (total)		
World (per capita)		

1. What is your annual pesticide use?

2. What is the world average annual pesticide use per person?

3. What factors might contribute to this difference?

How can we balance the ways we use land with the needs of the environment?

Green roofs are another way Portland, Oregon has remained an eco-friendly city.

Lesson 1
Land Use and
Urbanization

Lesson 2
Sprawl

Lesson 3
Sustainable Cities

 # Growing Pains in Portland, Oregon

IN 1973, Oregon governor Tom McCall challenged his state's legislature to take action against runaway development. McCall echoed the growing concerns of many state residents that farms, forests, and open spaces on the boundaries of cities were being devoured by development that was growing ever outward from cities. So Oregon's state legislature acted. They passed Senate Bill 100, a sweeping land use law. For years afterward, it was the focus of praise, criticism, and scrutiny by other states and communities trying to manage growth. Senate Bill 100 required every city and county in Oregon to draw up a land use plan. As part of its plan, boundaries had to be established around each city. Development for housing, businesses, and industry would be encouraged within these boundaries but severely restricted beyond them. The intent was to revitalize city centers and to protect farmland, forests, and other open areas from being consumed by suburban development.

Residents of the Portland area established a new regional government to help plan land use in the region. The Metropolitan Service District adopted the Portland-area boundary in 1979. The boundary largely worked as intended. Portland's downtown and older neighborhoods thrived, regional city centers became denser and more community oriented, mass transit improved, and the countryside outside the boundary was protected.

Many Portlanders, both within and beyond the boundary, began to feel that it was the key to maintaining livability in the area. To its critics, however, the boundary was an intrusive government tool. Still, most citizens had supported land use rules for 25 years. So many observers were surprised when, in November 2004, Oregon voters approved a ballot measure that threatened to destroy those rules. Measure 37 required the state to pay certain landowners if laws had decreased the value of their land. For example, laws prevented landowners outside the established boundaries from selling off parts of their property for housing development.

GO ONLINE

• Take It Local   • 3-D Geo Tour

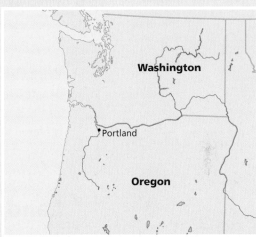

Under Measure 37, the state either had to pay landowners to make up for income lost because they were not allowed to sell their property or waive the rules and allow them to sell it. Eventually, more than 7500 landowners, mostly real-estate developers, filed claims. Because the state did not have enough money to pay them, owners of land outside the boundary would have been allowed to develop it. Measure 37 would have basically canceled out the 30-year-old land use rules that had helped make Portland a livable city. So the state legislature, under pressure from both supporters and opponents of Measure 37, decided the voters would have another chance to speak. They would vote on Measure 49, which would modify many of the policies in Measure 37 and protect the rights of small landowners. In November 2007, Measure 49 passed easily. Many landowners outside the boundary are once again prevented from selling their land for residential development.

The long, complicated, and unpredictable story of Portland's struggles with growth will continue. And Portland is only one of many cities with that challenge. The stories that unfold in these cities will tell us much about the future of our cities and landscapes.

Land Use and Urbanization

EVERYDAY PHENOMENON How do we use the land we live on?

Knowledge and Skills

- Differentiate between land cover and land use, and describe how people affect both.
- Explain how and where urbanization occurs.
- Describe the environmental impacts of urbanization.

Reading Strategy and Vocabulary

✔ **Reading Strategy** As you read, fill in a main ideas and details chart. List the main ideas of this lesson in the left column. To the right of each, note important details.

Vocabulary land cover, land use, urban area, rural area, urbanization, infrastructure, heat island

WE LIVE AT a turning point. For the first time in human history, more people live in cities than in the countryside. Our growing population is also consuming more and more resources. As we design our new city-centered world, the ways we use land and manage natural resources will become critical for our future quality of life.

Land Cover and Land Use

Land cover refers to the vegetation and manufactured structures that cover land. Examples of land cover include trees, grass, crops, wetlands, water, buildings, and pavement. The U.S. Geological Survey (USGS) researches rangeland, forest land, cropland, parks and preserves, wetlands, mountains, deserts, and urban land.

Human activities that occur on land and are directly related to the land are called **land use.** Examples of land use include farming, grazing, logging, mining, residential and industrial development, and recreation. You can see a description of some major categories of land cover and land use in **Figure 1.** As you might expect, land use depends on land cover. You wouldn't have much success grazing your cattle on a city street!

Land Cover and Land Use	
Land cover type	**Human uses of land**
Rangeland	Grazing livestock
Forest land	Harvesting wood, wildlife, fish, nuts, and other resources
Cropland	Growing plants for food and fiber
Parks and preserves	Recreation; preservation of native animal and plant communities and ecosystems
Wetlands, mountains, deserts, and others	Preservation of native animal and plant communities and ecosystems
Urban land	Residences, other buildings, and roads

FIGURE 1 Land Use The environmental scientists of the USGS study several different types of land cover and land use and the ways that people change both.

Land Cover and Environmental Science The land cover of an area may change as people settle there and begin to use the land. The vast grasslands that once covered the middle of North America have mainly been replaced by rangeland and cropland. The deciduous forest lands of the Northeast have been replaced mainly by cities and industrial areas. You can see the proportions of different types of U.S. land cover in **Figure 2.**

The USGS studies land cover and land use changes and assesses their environmental impact. Land cover scientists observe land cover and monitor how—and how rapidly—land cover changes. They also study the economic impacts of land cover change as well as its effects on water quality, the spread of invasive species, habitat and biodiversity loss, climate change, and other environmental factors. Scientists require up-to-date land cover information to accurately understand current conditions and to assess the extent and impact of land cover change on Earth's ecosystems.

Urban Areas *Urban area* is a category of land cover and land use. An **urban area** is mostly developed land covered mainly with buildings and roads that has a human population of 2500 or more. We often call these areas towns or cities. Suburbs are smaller towns or cities that are outside a large city but still within the urban area. (In this chapter, the term *urban area* refers both to the larger town or city and any suburbs around it.) The USGS studies the land cover and land use of urban areas just as it does other types of land. Generally, any other type of land use or land cover is considered **rural area.** You may hear people refer to sparsely populated rural areas as "the country."

Urbanization

Cities are not a new idea; people built cities thousands of years ago. The great Chinese dynasties and the Mayan and Incan empires of Central America had sophisticated and powerful cities. But the enormous size of today's cities *is* new. Today, 33 cities have more than 10 million residents. You can see a list of the five most populous cities in **Figure 3**. The urban area of Tokyo, Japan, is home to around 37 million people. Several cities have around 22 million people. Most urban dwellers, however, live in smaller cities, such as Portland, Oregon; Orlando, Florida; Austin, Texas; and their suburbs. What encourages people to build—or move to—huge cities?

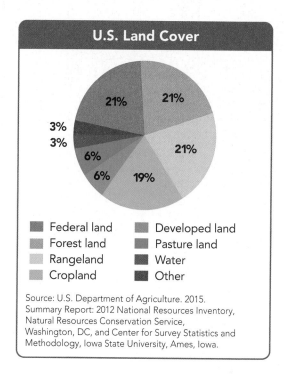

U.S. Land Cover

21% 21%

3% 3% 21%

6% 6% 19%

21%

- Federal land
- Forest land
- Rangeland
- Cropland
- Developed land
- Pasture land
- Water
- Other

Source: U.S. Department of Agriculture. 2015. Summary Report: 2012 National Resources Inventory, Natural Resources Conservation Service, Washington, DC, and Center for Survey Statistics and Methodology, Iowa State University, Ames, Iowa.

FIGURE 2 Land Cover in the United States The graph shows the distribution of land cover types in the United States.

FIGURE 3 Five Most Populous Cities Today's urban areas are highly populated (table). Tokyo is home to about 37 million people (photo).

Five Most Populous Urban Areas	
Urban Area	**2018 Population (millions)**
Tokyo, Japan	37
New Delhi, India	29
Shanghai, China	26
Mexico City, Mexico	22
Sao Paulo, Brazil	22

Data: United Nations, Department of Economic and Social Affairs, Population Division (2018)

FIND OUT MORE

Consider the town or city in which you live, or the nearest big city. Research its growth online or through your City Hall or other city resources. What geographical, social, or political factors helped it grow?

Continuing Urbanization Since 1950, the world's urban population has more than quadrupled. The United Nations now projects that the world's urban population will double again by 2050. So the world's population is still moving toward cities. Urban populations are growing both because the overall human population is growing, and because more people are moving from farms to cities than are moving from cities to farms. This shift of population from the countryside to urban areas is called **urbanization.** The shift from country to city began hundreds of years ago. Around the time of the Industrial Revolution, farms started to produce surplus food. This allowed a proportion of the population to stop farming. At the same time, technological advances of the Industrial Revolution created jobs in cities for these former farmers. So these farmers and their families moved to cities.

Like most developed nations, the United States has a population that is more urbanized than the world average. In the United States in 1950, about 65 percent of the population was urban (including the suburbs). The U.S. urban population now stands at about 80 percent, including the 50 percent of the population that lives in suburbs.

Transportation and Urbanization But how did cities end up where they are? Location is essential to the growth of an urban area. A moderate climate, central geography, and ease of transportation all help a small town grow into a large city. A location near a transportation route is especially important. Think of any major city. Chances are it grew near a large body of water, railroad, or highway on which goods and people could travel to it and from it. Chicago, which you see in **Figure 4,** is a good example. Because of the ease of transportation to and from Chicago, via waterways and later, railroads, and its location between the natural resources of the West and the big industrial cities of the East, it was able to grow into a large city.

FIGURE 4 Growth of a City Chicago's location on waterways and other transport routes and its location between the West's natural resources and the East's industrial centers helped it to become a large, prosperous city.

Urban Environmental Impacts

Urban centers affect the environment both negatively and positively. The type of impact depends on how we use resources, produce goods, transport materials, and deal with waste. You might guess that urban living, overall, has a more negative environmental impact than rural living. The reality, however, is not that simple.

Pollution Urban areas export wastes, passively through pollution, or they export wastes actively through trade such as paying another area to take their garbage. In so doing, urban areas transfer the environmental costs of their activities to other regions—and mask the costs to their own residents. Citizens of a big city may not realize how much garbage their city produces if it is shipped away for disposal—or how much it costs to do so.

Not all waste and pollution leave a city, however. Urban residents are exposed to heavy metals, chemical byproducts of industrial processes, and chemicals from motor-vehicle engines and manufactured products. Airborne pollutants from industrial processes and motor vehicles cause smog and acid precipitation. Fossil fuel combustion releases carbon dioxide and other pollutants, which lead to climate change as well as pollution.

Urban residents also suffer noise pollution and light pollution. *Noise pollution* consists of undesired background noise, such as a jackhammer on a city street or the constant sound of traffic. *Light pollution*, as seen in the top photo in **Figure 5,** describes the way that city lights brighten the night sky, obscuring the stars and planets.

Pollution and the health threats it poses are not evenly shared among urban residents. Unfortunately, the poor typically live in more polluted areas because they cannot afford to live in cleaner areas. A disproportionate number of people living near, downstream from, or downwind from polluting factories, power plants, and other facilities are poor or otherwise disadvantaged. This is a major concern of those who work for environmental justice.

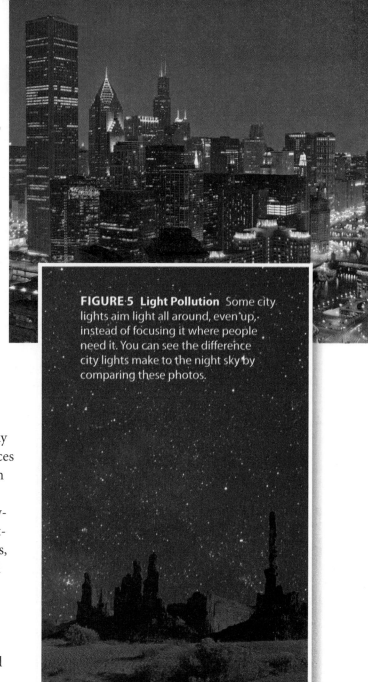

FIGURE·5 Light Pollution Some city lights aim light all around, even up, instead of focusing it where people need it. You can see the difference city lights make to the night sky by comparing these photos.

 Reading Checkpoint *Give one example of a waste that urban areas export passively and one example of a waste that urban areas export actively.*

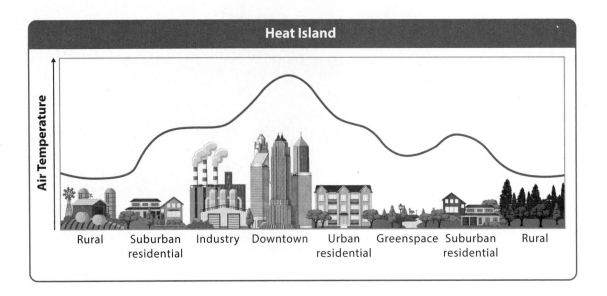

Heat Island

FIGURE 6 **Heat Island** The diagram shows how air temperature varies from a city center to outlying areas at the hottest part of a summer afternoon. The hot air hovering over the downtown area is a heat island caused by the heat absorbed by pavement and structures such as dark roofs.

Heat Islands When people move into an area, they usually create an infrastructure. **Infrastructure** is made up of the facilities, services, and installations needed for the functioning of a community—transportation, communications systems, water, power, and schools, for example. The building of infrastructure makes surfaces that were moist and permeable, such as grasslands, into dry and impermeable surfaces, such as pavement. As a result, a phenomenon called a heat island occurs. A **heat island** is an area in which the temperature is several degrees higher than that of the surrounding area. As **Figure 6** shows, it is like an "island" of hot air hovering over a city. Heat islands occur because the sun-heated pavement and structures of a city can be a blistering 27–50°C hotter than the surrounding air. They heat the air, which then rises over the city. Heat islands can affect local weather in other ways as well. They can cause more rain in a city, for example, since they produce rain clouds as heated air rises and cools. Because of the way hot air rises, heat islands can also collect polluting substances over a city, such as the ozone that can form smog. The heat island effect can be lessened by planting shade trees in a city and installing roofs that reflect, rather than absorb, heat.

Imported Resources Cities have to import nearly all the resources their residents and business owners need from areas outside the city. Urban areas rely on rural areas to supply resources such as food, water, building materials, and fuels. For example, major cities such as New York and San Francisco may rely on water from watersheds that are more than 160 kilometers (100 miles) away. Urban centers also need areas of natural land to provide ecosystem services, including purification of water and air, matter cycling, and waste treatment.

This long-distance transportation of resources and goods to and from urban areas requires a great deal of fossil fuel. Heavy use of fossil fuel is often bad news for the environment. But what if the world's 3.3 billion urban residents were spread evenly across the landscape? Resources and goods would have to be delivered to people in all those scattered locations. A world without cities would probably require *more* fossil fuel to allow people the same access to resources and goods they now have.

FIGURE 7 Efficiency of Cities In cities with dense populations, delivery of goods and services, such as the mail, is more energy- and time-efficient than it is in rural areas.

Efficiency Once resources have arrived in a city, the city should be able to minimize per capita, or per person, resource consumption. People in a city live close together, which reduces the amount of fuel and other resources needed to deliver resources and goods. For example, delivering mail to urban houses built close together is more efficient than delivering it to houses widely scattered throughout the countryside, as **Figure 7** shows. The high population density of cities allows for the efficient distribution of many other services as well, including healthcare, education, power, water and sewer systems, waste disposal, and public transportation.

 Reading Checkpoint *How is it more efficient to deliver goods and services to people in a city than to people in sparsely populated rural areas?*

Ecological Footprints Because cities draw most of their resources from far away, their ecological footprints are much greater than their actual land areas. An ecological footprint is more meaningful when you consider its size for a *person*, however. So, in asking whether urbanization causes increased resource consumption, we must ask whether the average urban resident has a larger footprint than the average rural resident. The answer is yes. This may simply reflect the fact that urban and suburban residents tend to be wealthier than rural residents. Because wealth and resource consumption are closely related, the wealth of urban and suburban residents results in a larger ecological footprint for them.

But the ecological impact of cities is not all negative. Cities often have universities and other research centers. And the proximity of diverse people to each other in cities can lead to a stimulating, innovative environment. The education and innovation that urbanization promotes can lead to ideas that reduce negative environmental impacts. For example, research into renewable energy sources is helping us develop ways to replace fossil fuels, and technological advances have helped us reduce pollution and recycle resources more effectively. Much of this research is done by organizations in and near cities. Wealthy and educated urban residents also buy more organic foods and other goods that have less-negative environmental impacts than their counterparts. All these benefits grow from the education and innovation that are part of urban culture.

Bobolinks require at least 2 hectares (5 acres) of moist grasslands for successful nesting.

Mountain lion territories can be as large as 1000 square kilometers (386 square miles).

An American alligator needs a swampy area of 1 hectare (2.5 acres) or more.

FIGURE 8 Cities Preserve Land
The concentration of people and businesses in cities allows for more wildlife habitat outside cities.

Land Preservation The ecological footprints of urban areas are large, but because people are packed densely together in cities, more land outside cities is left undeveloped. If cities did not exist, and all 7.8 billion of us were evenly spread across Earth's land area, we would have much less room for agriculture, wilderness, biodiversity, and privacy. Houses would be everywhere. There would be no large blocks of unfragmented habitat for wildlife, such as the alligator, mountain lion, and bobolink in **Figure 8.** The fact that half the human population lives in densely populated cities helps natural ecosystems maintain themselves and continue providing the ecosystem services on which all of us, urban and rural, depend.

LESSON ① Assessment

1. **Compare and Contrast** Compare land cover and land use, explaining how they are related and describing one way that humans can affect that relationship.

2. **Describe** How does urbanization typically occur?

3. **Draw Conclusions** Is the environmental impact of big cities all positive, all negative, or neither? Explain.

4. **THINK IT *THROUGH*** In which of the following places would you choose to live: a high-rise apartment in a big city or a 40-acre ranch bordering a national forest? Why? What factors would play a part in your decision?

Sprawl

EVERYDAY PHENOMENON How can the effects of urbanization lead to sprawl?

Knowledge and Skills

- Describe the contributors to sprawl and its patterns.
- Explain the impacts sprawl has on an area.

Reading Strategy and Vocabulary

✔ **Reading Strategy** Before you read, preview **Figure 11.** As you read, consider the effects of each pattern of sprawl.

Vocabulary sprawl

IN THE UNITED STATES in the mid-1900s, many factors encouraged people to move out of cities and into the suburbs. Government programs like the National Housing Act of 1934 made land and housing outside cities cheaper and easier to buy. In addition, automobiles became more affordable in the manufacturing boom after World War II, and the 1956 Federal-Aid Highway Act built and improved roads between cities and suburbs. Though the new suburbanites now had to drive to work, they considered it a fair tradeoff for additional space and privacy, cheaper real estate, cleaner neighborhoods, less crime, and better schools. As people moved out of cities, however, fewer people were left to invest in them. Inner cities became poorer, and unemployment and crime began to rise. These factors caused even more people to move out of cities.

FIGURE 9 Megalopolis Several large cities that sprawl together can be called a *megalopolis.* "Bos-Wash" is the name some people use for the megalopolis that runs from Boston south through New York City to Washington, D.C. Bos-Wash is shown here at night from space.

How Sprawl Occurs

Because suburbs allow more space per person than cities do, in most cases the growth of suburban areas has outpaced their population growth. Natural areas and farms have disappeared as they have been cleared for housing developments and roads. In some cases, the expanding rings of suburbs surrounding cities have grown larger than the cities themselves, and urban areas sometimes run into one another, as you can see in the photo of the eastern United States in **Figure 9.** These aspects of suburban growth have inspired the term *sprawl.*

Sprawl means different things to different people. To some, the word brings to mind strip malls, ugly industrial buildings, and rows of similar-looking, small houses that have replaced woods and farms. It suggests traffic jams, destruction of wildlife habitat, and loss of natural lands. To other people, sprawl just represents the collective result of choices made by millions of well-meaning people trying to make a better life for themselves and their families. In this view, those who criticize sprawl fail to appreciate the good things about suburban life. In this book, we give sprawl a simple, nonjudgmental definition: the spread of low-density urban or suburban development outward from an urban center.

Contributors to Sprawl Two primary factors contribute to sprawl. One is population growth. The other is increased per capita land consumption—each person is living on more land. The degree of sprawl is a function of the increase in the population of an area multiplied by the amount of land the average person lives on. A study of the 100 major metropolitan areas of the United States between 1970 and 1990 found that population growth and increased per capita land consumption each contribute about equally to sprawl. In any given city, however, either factor may be more important. For example, the Los Angeles urban area grew in size by 1021 square kilometers (394 square miles) between 1970 and 1990. In addition, the city's population density grew by 9 percent, making Los Angeles the nation's most densely populated urban area. So the area of Los Angeles grew even though the per capita land consumption decreased. These factors indicate that population growth was driving sprawl in Los Angeles. In contrast, the Detroit urban area lost 7 percent of its population between 1970 and 1990, yet it expanded in area by 28 percent. Clearly population growth was not the issue in Detroit; rather, sprawl was caused solely by increased per capita land consumption. You can see how sprawl progressed in another major city, Las Vegas, in **Figure 10.**

Why has per capita land consumption increased in some areas? The primary reason is that most people like having some space and privacy and dislike congestion. In addition, interstate highways and technologies such as telecommunications and the Internet have freed businesses from dependence on the centralized infrastructure a major city provides. Highways and telecommunications also allow workers greater flexibility to live farther from their jobs.

 Reading Checkpoint *Explain per capita land consumption in your own words.*

FIGURE 10 Sprawl From Space Satellite images show sprawl in Las Vegas, Nevada, one of the fastest-growing cities in North America. Between 1984 **(a)** and 2011 **(b),** the population of Las Vegas increased more than three times.

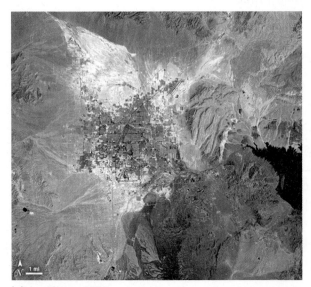

(a) Las Vegas, 1984

(b) Las Vegas, 2011

Patterns of Sprawl Several development approaches lead to sprawl. As you can see in **Figure 11,** uncentered commercial (strip) development; low-density single-use development; scattered, or leapfrog, development; and sparse street networks all lead to sprawl.

FIGURE 11 Sprawling Development Several approaches to development can result in sprawl. All these approaches rely on automobile use.

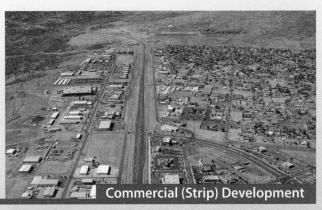

Commercial (Strip) Development

(a) In *uncentered commercial (strip) development,* businesses are arranged in a long strip along a roadway, with no central community.

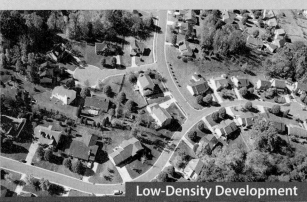

Low-Density Development

(b) In *low-density single-use residential development,* homes are located on large lots in residential areas far from businesses.

Scattered Development

(c) In *scattered,* or *leapfrog, development,* residential developments are built far from a city center and are not integrated with one another.

Sparse Street Network

(d) In developments with a *sparse street network,* roads are far enough apart that areas remain undeveloped, but not far enough apart for these areas to function as natural areas or recreational areas.

Real Data

Population Density and Carbon Emissions

In the accompanying graph, urban population density is used as an indicator of sprawl (lower density = more sprawl). Carbon emissions per person per year for transportation represents the environmental impact of the transportation system or preferences for each of the cities represented.

1. **Describe** What relationship between population density and carbon emissions for transportation does the graph show?

2. **Form a Hypothesis** Assuming that the rate of car ownership is similar in these cities, how would you explain the relationship in **Question 1**?

3. **Predict** If Houston were to pass laws limiting sprawl, resulting in a doubling of its population density, how would you predict its data would change?

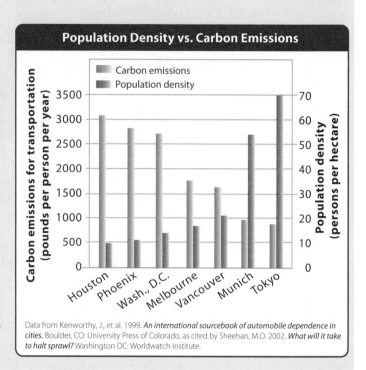

Population Density vs. Carbon Emissions

Data from Kenworthy, J., et al. 1999. *An international sourcebook of automobile dependence in cities.* Boulder, CO: University Press of Colorado, as cited by Sheehan, M.O. 2002. *What will it take to halt sprawl?* Washington DC: Worldwatch Institute.

Impacts of Sprawl

Economists and city politicians have almost unanimously encouraged the unlimited expansion of cities and suburbs. Their assumption has been that all growth is good and that attracting business, industry, and residents will always increase a community's economic well-being, political power, and cultural influence. The negative effects of sprawl, however, challenge this assumption. Growing numbers of people have begun to question the philosophy that all growth is good.

Transportation Most studies show that sprawl limits transportation options. A lack of mass transit options on the outskirts of cities means that people are essentially forced to buy and drive cars. This results in more traffic accidents and greater use of fossil fuels. As sprawl has increased across the United States, the average person's commute to work has risen to 27 minutes one-way. The total miles driven in the nation increased at more than twice the rate of population growth.

Pollution Sprawl's effects on transportation give rise to increased pollution. Carbon dioxide emissions from vehicles contribute to air pollution and global climate change. Motor oil and road salt from roads and parking lots pollute waterways, posing risks to ecosystems and human health. In fact, runoff of polluted water from paved areas is about 16 times greater than runoff from naturally vegetated areas.

Public Health In addition to the health impacts of pollution caused by sprawl, some research suggests that sprawl promotes physical inactivity. For example, in sprawling areas, people must drive cars to do errands, as opposed to walking or biking, which people in urban areas can often do **(Figure 12)**. Physical inactivity increases the risk of obesity and high blood pressure, which can lead to other ailments. A 2003 study found that people from the most-sprawling U.S. counties weighed about 2.7 kilograms (6 pounds) more for their height than people from the least-sprawling U.S. counties. In addition, slightly more people from the most-sprawling counties have high blood pressure.

FIGURE 12 Sprawl and Public Health People who walk to do their errands tend to have fewer illnesses linked to obesity.

Land Use The spread of low-density development means that more land is used for buildings and roads while less is left as forests, fields, farmland, or ranchland. Of the estimated 1 million hectares (2.5 million acres) of U.S. land converted from rural area to urban area each year, roughly 60 percent is agricultural land and 40 percent is forest. Farms and forests provide vital resources, aesthetic beauty, habitat for wildlife, cleansing of water, recreation, and many other ecosystem services. Sprawl destroys or degrades these areas and the ecosystem services they provide, and city residents end up paying higher taxes to build facilities to replace these lost services.

 Reading Checkpoint *Give one example of the effect of sprawl on people's health.*

FIGURE 13 **Sprawl and Infrastructure** Cities that have lost residents to the suburbs often cannot afford to repair infrastructure, such as this bridge with exposed, rusting supports.

Economics When people move out of city centers, they take their tax money with them. The money they would give the city in real-estate taxes goes instead to the sprawling communities on the outskirts of the city. And since it is usually the wealthier residents who move out, declining cities often end up populated by citizens who are least able to provide the revenue the city needs for its infrastructure. Money that could have been spent maintaining and improving city centers is instead spent on new infrastructure in outlying communities. You can see an example of badly declining infrastructure in **Figure 13.**

For example, one study calculated that sprawling development in Virginia Beach, Virginia, would require 81 percent more in infrastructure costs and would take 3.7 times more money from the community's general fund each year than compact urban development would. Advocates for sprawling development argue that taxes on that development eventually pay back a town's taxpayers for their investment in the new infrastructure. Studies, however, have found that in most cases taxpayers continue to pay for new infrastructure unless cities pass on the costs to real-estate developers.

 Reading Checkpoint *Make a cycle diagram showing how people moving out of cities leads to the decline of those cities.*

(2) Assessment

1. **Explain** Define *sprawl*. What two factors contribute to it?

2. **Relate Cause and Effect** Briefly describe the effect of sprawl on each of the following aspects of a region: transportation, pollution, public health, land use, and economics.

3. **THINK IT** *THROUGH* Suppose you were offered a well-paying, interesting job with three choices of where to live. One choice is a densely populated city where you could walk to your office. The second is in a suburb where you would have more space, but you would spend an hour each day driving back and forth to work. The third is a quiet, rural area with plenty of space, but you would have to spend three hours each day driving back and forth to work. Where would you choose to live? Why?

Sustainable Cities

EVERYDAY PHENOMENON What are the characteristics of a sustainable city?

Knowledge and Skills

- Describe four different components of city planning.
- Explain the importance of mass transit options to a city and its residents.
- Explain the importance of open space to a livable city.
- Differentiate green buildings from conventional buildings.
- Discuss the progress toward sustainability some cities have made and its importance to the world.

Reading Strategy and Vocabulary

✔ **Reading Strategy** As you read, draw a cluster diagram that relates city planning, mass transit options, and open space to the sustainability of a city.

Vocabulary city planning, geographic information system (GIS), zoning, urban growth boundary (UGB), smart growth, ecological restoration, greenway

ARCHITECTS, PLANNERS, DEVELOPERS, and policymakers today are all responding to the challenges of urban sprawl. Their goals are to plan and manage urbanization so that the cities that develop are sustainable. What makes a city sustainable? The same characteristic that makes forestry or farming sustainable—its ability to continue without depleting or destroying the resources that support it.

City Planning

City planning is the attempt to design cities so as to maximize their functionality and beauty. City planning grew in importance throughout the 1900s as urban populations grew beyond the available jobs and wealthier residents fled to the suburbs, as you recall from Lesson 2. City planners advise city policymakers on development options, transportation needs, public parks, and other matters. City planners may use several tools and strategies in their work, including zoning, urban growth boundaries, the ideals of smart growth, and concepts of new urbanism. Technology helps with every aspect of the process.

City planners often have sophisticated technology at their disposal. A **geographic information system (GIS)** is a computerized system for storing, manipulating, and viewing geographic data. When planners enter data in a GIS, such as locations of roads, parks, bodies of water, or sewer lines, they can see maps of them. The GIS can then layer multiple maps so city planners can see a combined map with all the different types of information. By using a GIS, planners can see conflicts between proposed uses of land. For example, a GIS can reveal whether a proposed chemical processing plant is close to a school.

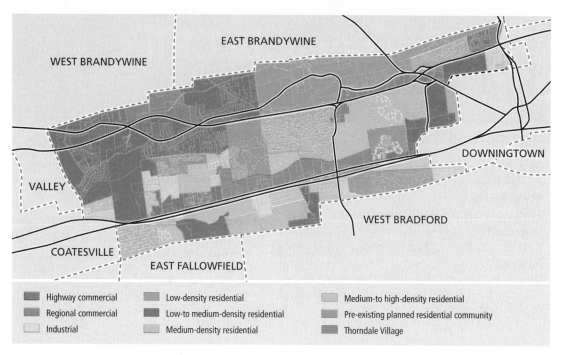

FIGURE 14 Zoning Map Zoning allows planners to guide how a community develops. This zoning map for Caln Township, Pennsylvania, shows several common zoning patterns. Industrial properties are clustered away from most residential areas, commercial properties are clustered along roadways, and residential zones are in the center of town.

Legend:
- Highway commercial
- Regional commercial
- Industrial
- Low-density residential
- Low-to medium-density residential
- Medium-density residential
- Medium-to high-density residential
- Pre-existing planned residential community
- Thorndale Village

WHAT DO YOU THINK?

Suppose that you live next to a 25-hectare (10-acre) horse pasture. There are only a few horses on it, and you enjoy the privacy and quiet. But then the owner sells the pasture to a housing developer who plans to build 10 houses on it. How would you respond? Explain your response.

Zoning One way that planners put their decisions into practice is through **zoning,** the practice of classifying areas for different types of development and land use. For example, zoning may exclude industrial plants from residential neighborhoods in order to keep those neighborhoods cleaner and quieter. Specifying zones for different types of development gives planners a powerful tool for controlling what can be built where. Zoning can restrict areas to a single use, such as "single-family residential only," as is often done with suburban residential neighborhoods. Or, zoning can allow the type of mixed use—residential and commercial, for example—that some planners say can vitalize urban neighborhoods. This is the kind of zoning you often see in cities, in which there are apartments on the same block as stores and restaurants. Zoning can also give homebuyers and business owners security; they know in advance what types of development can and cannot be located nearby. You can see a typical zoning map in **Figure 14.**

Zoning involves a government restriction on the use of private land and limits personal property rights. For this reason, some people feel that zoning violates individual freedoms. In the Central Case, the supporters of Oregon's Measure 37 who wanted compensation for their land felt their property rights had been violated. Other people defend zoning, saying that government has the right to set limitations on property rights for the good of the community. Similar debates arise with endangered species management and other environmental issues. In general, most people support zoning because they feel that the good it yields for communities outweighs the limits it puts on individual property rights.

 Reading Checkpoint *Summarize two arguments in favor of zoning.*

Urban Growth Boundaries An **urban growth boundary (UGB)** is a line that city planners draw on a map to separate urban areas from areas the city would prefer remain rural. As you recall from the Central Case, planners intended Oregon's urban growth boundaries to limit sprawl by containing future growth within existing urban areas, such as Portland. Since Oregon began its experiment, a number of other areas have adopted UGBs, including Boulder, Colorado; Lancaster, Pennsylvania; and many California communities. Though they differ in some ways, all UGBs have similar goals—concentrating development; preventing sprawl; and preserving orchards, ranches, forests, and working farms.

Urban growth boundaries have many advantages. They seem to require less investment in infrastructure than sprawl does. The best estimate nationally is that UGBs save taxpayers about 20 percent on infrastructure costs. In this and other ways, Portland's UGB (**Figure 15**) is working. It has increased the density of new housing inside the UGB by more than 50 percent as residences are built on smaller lots and as apartment buildings are built taller. Such efforts fulfill a vision of "building *up*, not *out*"—promoting development and economic investment in existing urban centers rather than building outward and creating suburbs. Employment in downtown Portland rose by 73 percent between 1970 and 1995 as businesses invested in the central city. And Portland has been able to absorb considerable immigration while avoiding *uncontrolled* sprawl.

But Portland's UGB has not prevented sprawl altogether. The Portland urban area still grew by 101 square kilometers (39 square miles) in the decade after its UGB was established, likely because 146,000 people moved there. Rapid population growth may thwart even the best efforts to prevent sprawl, as you may recall from our earlier discussion of the growth of Los Angeles. The Portland UGB has been expanded 36 times, and continued population growth may lead to more expansion. Many other locations that have UGBs have also expanded them. Given that UGBs are so often expanded, it seems that they are not the complete solution to sprawl.

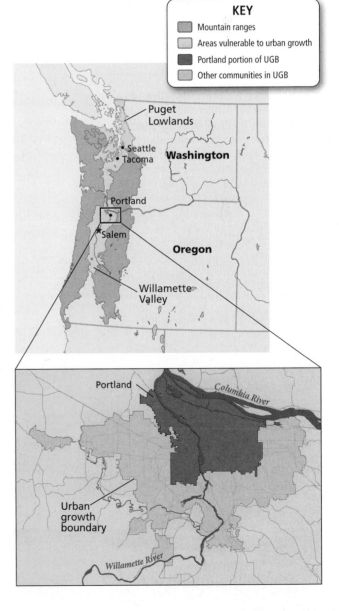

◆▶ **Connect to the Central Case**

FIGURE 15 Urban Growth Boundaries Oregon's urban growth boundaries (UGBs) were a response to fears that sprawl might one day create a megalopolis from Salem, Oregon, up the Willamette Valley and Puget Lowlands to Seattle, Washington (upper map). The Portland area's UGB (lower map) encompasses Portland (dark gray) and portions of 24 other communities and 3 counties (light gray).
Apply Concepts How can a UGB prevent the formation of a megalopolis?

Smart Growth As people have begun to feel the negative effects of sprawl, efforts to control growth have emerged. In 1973, Oregon became one of the first states to pass a law that established statewide land use planning. Dozens of states, regions, and cities have since adopted similar land use policies. Many of the goals of these policies, combined with urban growth boundaries, make up smart growth. **Smart growth** is a philosophy of urban growth that focuses on economic and environmental approaches that lead to sustainable growth and the avoidance of sprawl. Smart growth aims to maintain open spaces by developing and revitalizing existing urban areas, waterfronts, and former industrial sites—a practice called *redevelopment*. Smart growth requires building up, not out. You can see some specific goals of smart growth in **Figure 16**.

"New Urbanism" Related to smart growth is a movement often called "new urbanism." This approach seeks to design neighborhoods with homes, businesses, and schools close together, so that most of a person's needs can be met without driving. Because of this goal, neighborhoods in the new urbanism style are usually near public transit systems. Green spaces, trees, a mix of architectural styles, and creative street layouts add to the visual appeal of new urbanism developments. Ironically, these developments mimic the urban neighborhoods that existed before suburbs became popular. But for urban centers to develop this way, zoning must allow it. Typically, zoning rules limit the density of development, and many exclude retail and commercial business from residential areas. Although well-intentioned, such rules encourage sprawl.

More than 600 new urbanism communities are planned or under construction across North America, and many are now complete. Examples of those that are complete are Seaside, Florida; Addison Circle in Addison, Texas; Mashpee Commons in Mashpee, Massachusetts; Celebration in Orlando, Florida; Orenco Station, Oregon; and Atlantic Station, Georgia.

✓ **Reading Checkpoint** *Give two ways that zoning rules can encourage sprawl.*

Smart Growth...

- … is based on development decisions that are predictable, fair, and cost-effective for the city.

- … mixes land uses to make a more interesting, attractive, and healthy place to live.

- … means building *up,* not *out.*

- … preserves open space.

- … creates walkable neighborhoods.

- … provides a variety of transportation options.

- … creates housing for people of all income levels.

- … encourages cooperation between citizens and businesses to promote a sense of community.

- … strengthens existing communities by promoting redevelopment.

FIGURE 16 Smart Growth and the New Urbanism Smart growth has many goals, all of which promote development and economic investment in existing cities (listed above). The attractive village of Atlantic Station, Georgia (photo below), is a perfect example of redevelopment, because it was built on land once occupied by a steel mill.

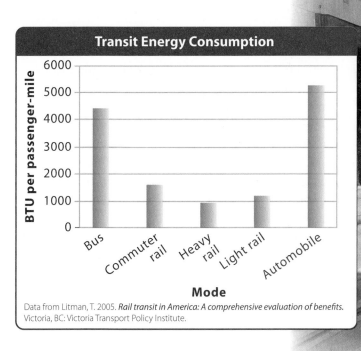

Transit Energy Consumption

y-axis: BTU per passenger-mile (0, 1000, 2000, 3000, 4000, 5000, 6000)

x-axis (Mode): Bus, Commuter rail, Heavy rail, Light rail, Automobile

Data from Litman, T. 2005. *Rail transit in America: A comprehensive evaluation of benefits.* Victoria, BC: Victoria Transport Policy Institute.

FIGURE 17 Energy Consumption of Transit Options As you can see from the graph, rail transit uses much less energy per passenger-mile than bus or automobile transit. This train in Houston, Texas (above), is part of a large passenger rail system in the city.

Transportation Options

Public transportation is a key factor in the quality of urban life. People in cities want public transportation options such as the electric train in **Figure 17** because most city streets were not built to carry the volume of car traffic they now carry. As long as an urban area has been planned in a way that can support mass transit and is large enough to support the infrastructure, mass transit is cheaper, more energy-efficient, and cleaner than roadways filled with cars.

Establishing Mass Transit Establishing mass transit is not always easy, however. Once a road system has been developed and businesses and homes are built alongside those roads, it can be difficult and expensive—or even impossible—to build a mass transit system. And in an existing community, people may resist the change from the car-centered lifestyle they have always known.

To encourage mass transit and discourage urban car use, city governments can raise fuel taxes, tax fuel-inefficient modes of transportation, reward carpoolers with carpool lanes, and encourage bicycle use and bus riding. For example, Geneva, Switzerland, prohibits parking at the workplace; Copenhagen, Denmark, bans all on-street parking; and Paris, France, removed 200,000 parking spaces—all to encourage use of public transportation. Governments can also do their part by reducing their investment in transportation infrastructure that encourages sprawl (such as wider highways). They can also stimulate investment in the renewal of urban centers.

Reading Checkpoint *Describe four ways that city governments can discourage the use of cars in cities.*

Mass Transit Successes This nation's most-used train systems are the extensive heavy rail systems in America's largest cities, such as New York's subways; Washington, D.C.'s Metro; the T in Boston; and the San Francisco area's BART, each of which carries more than one fourth of each city's daily commuters. Portland, Oregon's well-organized bus system carries 66 million riders per year. A single Portland bus is estimated to keep about 250 cars off the road each day. In 1986, Portland introduced a light rail system called MAX, and the city encouraged the development of self-sufficient new urbanism neighborhoods along the rail lines. Light rail ridership has steadily increased as the system has expanded.

There have been many successes outside the United States as well. In Canada, rail systems in Montreal and Toronto are used heavily. Major cities such as Moscow, Beijing, Paris, and Tokyo also have large and well-utilized subway systems. And some cities that formerly had severe traffic problems, such as Bangkok, Thailand, have recently opened new rail systems that carry hundreds of thousands of commuters a day.

Open Space

City dwellers sometimes want to escape from the noise and commotion of urban life. Natural lands, public parks, and open space provide greenery, scenic beauty, freedom of movement, and places for recreation. These lands also keep ecological processes functioning by regulating climate, producing oxygen, filtering air and water pollutants, and providing habitat for wildlife.

Protecting natural lands and establishing public parks become more important as societies become more urbanized. Many urban dwellers feel increasingly isolated and disconnected from nature. In the wake of urbanization and sprawl, people of every industrialized society in the world today have, to some degree, chosen to set aside land for public parks and other open spaces.

(a) Community Garden

FIGURE 18 Open Space Both **(a)** community gardens and **(b)** public rail-trails (next page) help city dwellers feel closer to the environment.

Urban Parks and Forests In urban America around the late 1800s, politicians and citizens alike began to desire ways to make their crowded and dirty cities more livable. U.S. cities began to establish public parks. Many cities are now working to enhance the sustainability of their parks through **ecological restoration,** the practice of restoring native communities. In Portland parks, volunteer teams remove English ivy, an invasive plant that covers trees and smothers native plants on the forest floor. At some Chicago-area forest preserves, scientists and volunteers burn areas of forest under carefully controlled conditions to kill trees so that native prairie grasses can grow again. In the Presidio of San Francisco national park, areas are being restored to the native dune communities that were displaced by urban development.

Other Public Spaces Large city parks and forests are a key component of a healthy urban environment, but even small spaces can make a big difference. Playgrounds provide places where children can be active outdoors and interact with other children. Community gardens, such as the one in **Figure 18a** (on the previous page), are small plots of land where people can grow their own vegetables and flowers in an urban setting. Portland, Seattle, Baltimore, Boston, New York City, and many other cities feature thriving community gardens.

Greenways, strips of vegetated open space that connect parks or neighborhoods, are often located along rivers, streams, or canals. Greenways are extremely valuable both to humans and wildlife. They help protect water quality by providing a buffer between pollution, such as fertilizer runoff, and bodies of water; their attractiveness increases property values; and they serve as corridors between habitats for birds and other wildlife, decreasing habitat fragmentation. One type of greenway is the rail-trail—a former railroad right-of-way that has been converted into a public trail, such as the one in **Figure 18b.** More than 39,000 kilometers (24,223 miles) of 2176 rail lines have been converted to trails for activities such as walking, jogging, and biking.

 What are three benefits of greenways?

(b) Public Rail-Trail

FIGURE 19 Green Buildings Ashland High School in Massachusetts was built to conserve resources in as many ways as possible. Compost bins **(a)** turn plant and food scraps into fertilizer for landscape plants and the student greenhouse. A computer control room **(b)** evaluates data from **(c)** climate stations inside and outside the school and **(d)** solar panels outside the school, and coordinates the school's complex climate control system. Skylights in a central corridor **(e)** provide sunlight to both the first and second floors, since both floors have windows that open onto the corridor. The sunlight provides both light and heat, saving electricity and fuel. In the gymnasium, kitchen, and elsewhere, excess room heat is collected and added to heat from the boiler to help heat the rest of the school, conserving fuel.

Green Building Design

Sustainable architecture, or "green building design," has been successful in residences, and commercial and industrial buildings all over the world. It has also been a major success on high school and college campuses. There is probably a "green" high school or college near you.

One highly efficient green high school is in Ashland, Massachusetts, about 40 kilometers (25 miles) west of Boston. Ashland High School was built in 2005 with the help of a grant from the Massachusetts Technology Collaborative, a state renewable energy and innovation agency. Energy bills at Ashland High are about 20 percent lower than in a similar-sized conventionally built school, saving the school system more than $75,000 a year. Energy-saving features include motion- and light-sensitive lighting and heating systems, rooftop solar panels that generate electricity, a sophisticated climate-control system, and the recycling of excess hot air from rooms into the heating system. The school was also arranged on its lot and built in ways that take advantage of natural light to reduce the use of electric lights and heating. For example, dozens of insulated skylights run above the lobbies, library, and cafeteria, letting in natural light and allowing the sun to warm the interior of the school during the long, cold winters. You can see some of the green features of Ashland High School in **Figure 19.**

Urban Sustainability Successes

Despite the challenges you have been reading about, there has been great success in creating sustainable cities. Many cities have managed to improve both their environmental sustainability and the standard of living of their residents. Curitiba, in Brazil, and New York City show how sustainability can succeed both in the developing world and in the developed world.

Curitiba, Brazil Curitiba, Brazil, shows the kind of success that can result when a city invests in well-planned infrastructure. Besides a highly efficient and well-used bus transit network, the city provides recycling, environmental education, job training for the poor, and free health care. Surveys show that its citizens are unusually happy and better off economically than people living in other Brazilian cities.

New York City Closer to home, on Earth Day 2007, Mayor Michael Bloomberg of New York City unveiled an extensive new plan to make New York "the first environmentally sustainable 21st-century city." OneNYC 2030 is a program that aims to reduce energy use and greenhouse gas emissions, improve mass transit, plant trees, clean up polluted land and rivers, and improve access to parks and greenways. The hope is that New York City will become a better place to live even as it gains 650,000 more people by 2030. In its first couple of years, OneNYC made significant progress, especially in encouraging alternatives to car transportation and in planting trees, as you can see in **Figure 20.**

Progress toward sustainability in places as different as Curitiba and New York City suggests that cities everywhere can be sustainable. Indeed, because they affect the environment in some positive ways and can use resources efficiently, cities can and should be a key element in the progress toward global sustainability.

FIGURE 20 Sustainable Cities Part of OneNYC 2030 is an effort to plant 1,000,000 new trees in New York City by 2030. By 2018, 620,000 had already been planted.

③ Assessment

1. **Describe** Briefly describe how city planners use zoning, UGBs, smart growth, and new urbanism.

2. **Explain** How is a successful mass transit system important to improving the quality of life in a city?

3. **Infer** Give two reasons why open space is important to people who live in cities.

4. **Review** What are four possible features of a green building?

5. **Infer** Give two reasons why the progress toward sustainability in New York City and Curitiba is important to the rest of the world.

REVISIT

6. **INVESTIGATIVE** PHENOMENON Explain how sprawl can contribute to the economic decline of a city.

Geographic Information Systems

A geographic information system, or GIS, is a computer system capable of storing data linked to a specific location and displaying them on a map. GIS maps can visually reveal relationships between data that are not obvious just from looking at the numbers. This makes the maps useful in everything from urban planning to environmental policy.

Data

The first step in creating a GIS map is to gather data. Data can come from a number of sources. In urban areas, data might be gathered by government offices, censuses, or surveys. Data about the environment, such as the amount of pollution in a stream or the population of a species, might be collected by researchers working in the field. Once it has been gathered, the data are entered into a digital mapping program so they can be displayed visually.

Below are three layers of a GIS map of Austin Lake along the Colorado River in Texas. Each layer displays different information about the same place. The geologic layer shows major geologic formations. The satellite layer shows land cover and human development: dark green indicates forests, while the thin white lines represent roads. A digital elevation layer shows the region's topography in three dimensions. Layers such as these can be combined to create a single map, as shown in the illustration on the next page.

Geologic layer

Satellite layer

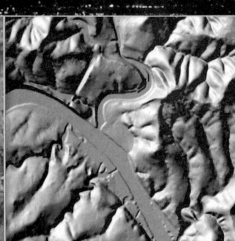

Digital elevation layer

Using GIS Maps

GIS maps are used in a wide range of applications, including research, planning city services, and environmental management. Here's one example of a map used to analyze emergency response times in Salt Lake City, Utah. The map at the top shows where the ground beneath the city is most likely to collapse after an earthquake. These data were combined with a road map (at the bottom) to determine how emergency response times from fire stations (marked *F*) would be affected by an earthquake. This information helped city officials improve the emergency response plans for the city.

Each type of GIS data is called a "layer." Layers can be stacked and combined to create a map containing lots of information.

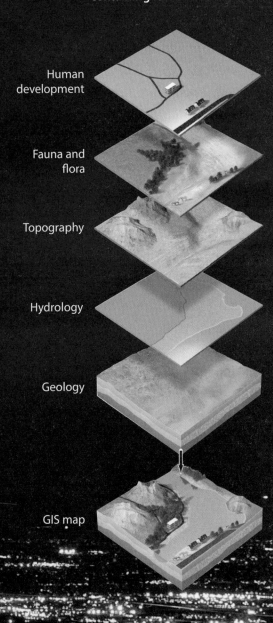

Human development

Fauna and flora

Topography

Hydrology

Geology

GIS map

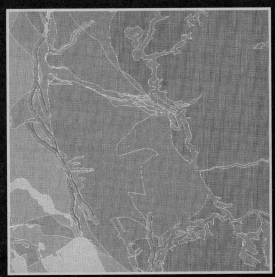

Likelihood of ground collapse—the brighter the red, the more likely a collapse

Road map showing location of fire stations (*F*) and areas most likely to collapse (red).

CAREER **GIS Specialist** A GIS specialist takes geographic data displayed on a map to analyze and automate the information. There are many different career options that are available to someone who specializes in GIS. Go Online and research possible careers that relate to GIS. Write a brief summary of your findings.

INVESTIGATIVE PHENOMENON
How can we balance the ways we use land with the needs of the environment?

Lesson 1
How do we use the land we live on?

Lesson 2
How can the effects of urbanization lead to sprawl?

Lesson 3
What are the characteristics of a sustainable city?

LESSON 1 Land Use and Urbanization

- Land cover refers to the vegetation and manufactured structures that cover land. Land use refers to the human activities that occur on land that are directly related to the land. Land cover influences land use, and humans change both when they build urban areas.
- The shift of population from the countryside to an urban area is called urbanization. Urbanization occurs when people move out of rural areas to an urban area that has more or better jobs.
- Cities have both negative environmental impacts, such as pollution, and positive environmental impacts, such as land preservation.

land cover (292)
land use (292)
urban area (293)
rural area (293)
urbanization (294)
infrastructure (296)
heat island (296)

LESSON 2 Sprawl

- Sprawl is the spread of low-density urban or suburban development outward from a city center. As people move out of cities, population growth and increased per capita land consumption contribute to sprawl. The degree of sprawl can be calculated as the increase in the number of people in an area multiplied by the amount of land the average person lives on.
- Sprawl affects the transportation, pollution, public health, land use, and economics of an area.

sprawl (299)

LESSON 3 Sustainable Cities

- City planners use tools such as zoning, urban growth boundaries, and principles of smart growth and the "new urbanism" to make cities more livable.
- Transportation options are vital to livable cities.
- Parks and open space are key elements of livable cities.
- The goal of a green building is to save energy and other resources without sacrificing people's comfort.
- Cities as different as Curitiba, Brazil, and New York City have made progress toward sustainability, showing that cities can be a key element in progress toward global sustainability.

city planning (305)
geographic information system (GIS) (305)
zoning (306)
urban growth boundary (UGB) (307)
smart growth (308)
ecological restoration (311)
greenway (311)

 GO ONLINE

INQUIRY LABS AND ACTIVITIES

- **Local Land Cover**
  Use maps with satellite imagery on the USGS Web site to find the types of land cover in your area.
- **Patterns of Sprawl**
  Compare maps of the Atlanta area from different years to analyze density and development.
- **Green Building Design**
  Which green building features will you recommend for use in a local school building? Learn their costs and savings.

Chapter Assessment

Defend Your Case

The Central Case in this chapter explored the challenges of maintaining a livable city while respecting the property rights of the people who live in it. Based on what you have learned, what is the next step Portland should take? Use evidence from the Central Case and the lessons to support your ideas.

Review Concepts and Terms

1. Land cover and land use are related, and humans can change
   - **a.** neither.
   - **b.** both.
   - **c.** land cover only.
   - **d.** land use only.

2. The shift of population from the countryside to a city is called
   - **a.** land use.
   - **b.** land cover.
   - **c.** urbanization.
   - **d.** infrastructure.

3. The facilities, services, and installations needed for the functioning of a community make up its
   - **a.** heat island.
   - **b.** infrastructure.
   - **c.** suburbs.
   - **d.** ecosystem services.

4. Which of the following is shown in the photo below?
   - **a.** rural area
   - **b.** city
   - **c.** suburban area
   - **d.** heat island

5. The effects of urban areas on the environment are
   - **a.** negative only.
   - **b.** positive only.
   - **c.** both positive and negative.
   - **d.** nonexistent.

6. The approach to development LEAST likely to result in sprawl is
   - **a.** leapfrog development.
   - **b.** commercial (strip) development.
   - **c.** high-density multi-use development.
   - **d.** low-density single-use development.

7. Sprawl affects which of the following?
   - **a.** pollution
   - **b.** public health
   - **c.** economics
   - **d.** all of the above

8. An attempt to design cities so as to maximize their functionality and beauty is
   - **a.** city planning.
   - **b.** sprawl.
   - **c.** urbanization.
   - **d.** ecological restoration.

9. One way that city planners put their decisions into practice is
   - **a.** zoning.
   - **b.** urbanization.
   - **c.** ecological restoration.
   - **d.** sprawl.

10. A strip of vegetated open space that connects parks or neighborhoods is called a(n)
    - **a.** urban area.
    - **b.** greenway.
    - **c.** heat island.
    - **d.** suburb.

Modified True/False

Write true if the statement is true. If it is false, change the underlined word or words to make the statement true.

11. Developed land covered mostly with buildings and roads is a(n) <u>urban area</u>.

12. The spread of low-density development outward from an urban area is called <u>infrastructure</u>.

13. Two primary causes of sprawl are population growth and <u>ecological restoration</u>.

14. <u>Zoning</u> is a computerized system for storing, manipulating, and viewing geographic data.

15. <u>Greenways</u> are strips of open space that provide pollution buffers, increase property values, and serve as wildlife corridors.

Reading Comprehension

Read the following selection, and answer the questions that follow.

A military base three miles from a medium-sized city is being closed down. The base is large, on the coast, and has small hills, woodlands, wetlands, and a small lake. A railroad and a four-lane highway connect the base with the city. The base has housing, schools, a hospital, shops, and recreational areas for a population of 10,000.

16. A development group wants to turn the whole base area into a recreational resort. Facilities would include an RV campsite, a sports arena, a small harbor for water sports, and a hunting lodge. An important *ecological* concern about this proposal would be

  a. that there would not be enough parking.

  b. that the city might not make enough money from the resort.

  c. that there might be negative effects on the woodlands, wetlands, and wildlife.

  d. whether the development group can attract sports teams to the new arena.

17. Some groups want to restore the buildings and infrastructure on the base and turn the area into a new town. Which of the following would best describe that effort?

  a. smart growth

  b. megalopolis

  c. sprawl

  d. urbanization

18. Which of the following ways might the railroad land be used?

  a. continuing to run the railroad between the city and the base area

  b. removing the tracks and converting it to a cycling and hiking trail

  c. removing the tracks and allowing it to function as a greenway to reduce habitat fragmentation

  d. all of the above

19. City planners could make a decision that *best* balances environmental and economic concerns

  a. by having an advertising campaign funded by the developers and then having citizens vote on the decision.

  b. after holding open town meetings that involved all interested citizens, businesses, and developers.

  c. after city planners have a private meeting with environmental activist groups.

  d. on the basis of the projected tax revenue from the different choices.

Short Answer

20. List six environmental impacts of urbanization.

21. Explain how a heat island occurs.

22. How do city planners use a geographic information system?

23. What is meant by "building up, not out"?

24. List four characteristics of smart growth.

25. What is ecological restoration?

26. Give four reasons why open space is a key element of a livable city.

Critical Thinking

27. Apply Concepts What is one way that densely populated cities can help conserve wildlife habitat?

28. Infer Why do environmental scientists study land cover?

29. Explain What is implied by the term "green building design"?

30. Classify Suppose you were bicycling through a neighborhood made up only of single-family houses set far apart with trees and shrubs separating them. Would you describe this as a rural area, a suburban area, or a city? Explain your answer.

31. Apply Concepts In what ways has infrastructure been important to the progress toward sustainability of Curitiba and New York City?

Analyze Data

The table below shows populations of the world's five most populous cities in 2007 and as projected for 2025. Use the data in the table to answer the questions that follow.

Most Populous Urban Areas	
Urban Area	**2007 Population (millions)**
Tokyo, Japan	35.68
New York, United States	19.04
Mexico City, Mexico	19.03
Mumbai, India	18.98
São Paulo, Brazil	18.85
Urban Area	**2025 Projection (millions)**
Tokyo, Japan	36.40
Mumbai, India	26.39
Delhi, India	22.50
São Paulo, Brazil	21.43
Mexico City, Mexico	21.01

Source: Population Division of the Department of Economic and Social Affairs of the United Nations Secretariat, *World Population Prospects: The 2006 Revision and World Urbanization Prospects: the 2007 Revision.*

32. Calculate Which city's population is expected to grow the most between 2007 and 2025? By how much is it expected to grow?

33. Interpret Tables What population trend are Tokyo, Mexico City, São Paulo, and Mumbai expected to follow?

34. Form a Hypothesis New York City is not projected to be in the top five in 2025, and Tokyo is expected to grow by a smaller percentage than the other cities on the list. Form a hypothesis that might explain these differences.

Write About It

35. Form an Opinion Would you like to live in a city with an urban growth boundary? Explain.

36. REVISIT INVESTIGATIVE PHENOMENON Design an urban area that, in your opinion, balances people's needs with the needs of the environment. You may either write two paragraphs describing how its characteristics work both for people and the environment, or you may sketch the urban area and include the information in labels.

Ecological Footprints

Read the information below. Then copy the data table into your notebook and answer the questions.

One way of reducing your ecological footprint is to change the way you travel. The table shows typical amounts of CO_2 released per person per mile when traveling various ways for a typical distance of 12,000 miles per year.

1. Which of the transportation options shown permits the most miles of travel per pound of CO_2 emissions?

2. Estimate how many of your 12,000 annual miles you think you travel by each method. Enter your estimates in the third column.

3. Based on your estimates, calculate your annual CO_2 emissions for each method. Enter your results in the fourth column.

	Pounds of CO_2 Per Person Per Mile	Estimated Mileage Per Year	CO_2 Emissions Per Year
Automobile (2 persons)	0.413		
Automobile (4 persons)	0.206		
Vanpool (8 persons)	0.103		
Bus	0.261		
Walking	0.082		
Bicycle	0.049		
		Total = 12,000	

4. How could you reduce your ecological footprint? By how many pounds of CO_2 do you think you could reduce it in the next year?

ANCHORING PHENOMENON

These questions will help you apply what you have learned in this Unit to the Anchoring Phenomenon.

1. **Develop and Use Models** Choose a natural disaster and model the impact of the disaster in a densely populated area and a sparsely populated area. Your model should include advantages and disadvantages of being in each area during and after the event. How could you use the advantages to reduce the impacts?

2. **Plan and Carry Out Investigations** Design an investigation to determine how the variable of population size could impact the risk assessment of a chemical hazard. Develop a hypothesis, identify the independent and dependent variables, and write a procedure.

GO ONLINE

For activities that will give you an opportunity to demonstrate what you have learned.

CLAIM-EVIDENCE-REASONING Revisit your Anchoring Phenomenon CER with the information you have learned in this unit.

ANCHORING PHENOMENON PROJECT Design a solution to reduce the impact of population size when an environmental hazard occurs.

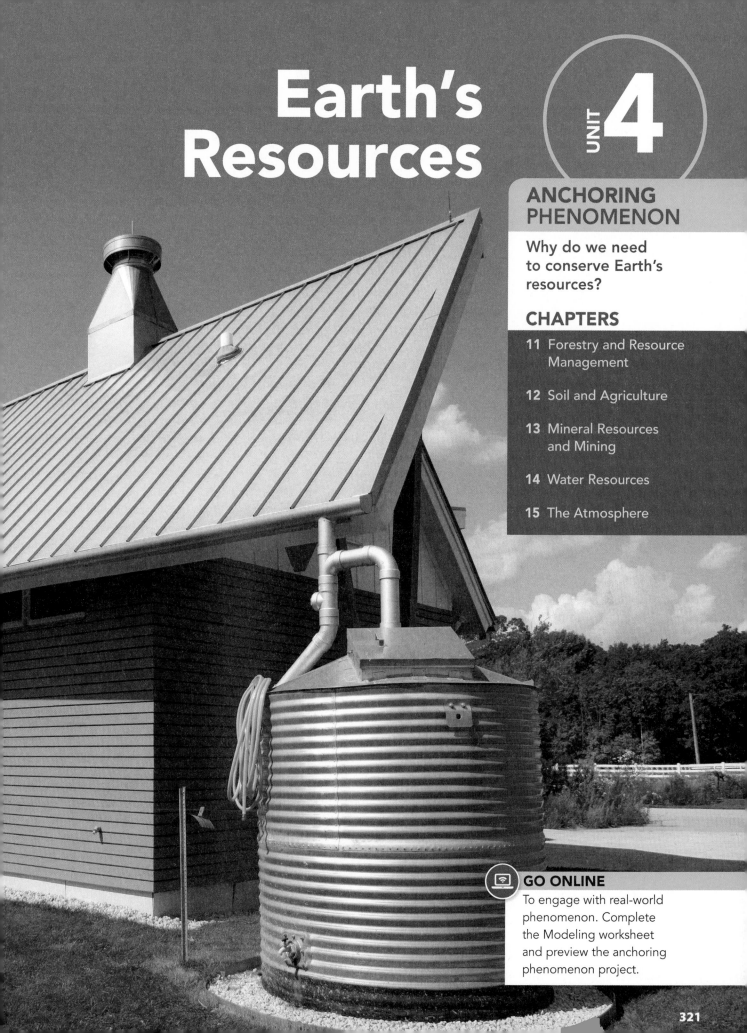

Earth's Resources

ANCHORING PHENOMENON

Why do we need to conserve Earth's resources?

CHAPTERS

GO ONLINE

To engage with real-world phenomenon. Complete the Modeling worksheet and preview the anchoring phenomenon project.

CHAPTER 11

Forestry and Resource Management

INVESTIGATIVE PHENOMENON   Why is it important to manage Earth's resources sustainably?

The old-growth forests of Clayoquot Sound, British Columbia have been designated as an international biosphere reserve.

Lesson 1
Resource Management

Lesson 2
Forests and Their Resources

Lesson 3
Forest Management

Battling Over Clayoquot's Big Trees

IN 1993, the largest act of civil disobedience in Canadian history played out along a beautiful seacoast, at the foot of some of the world's largest trees. At Clayoquot Sound on Vancouver Island, British Columbia, environmentalists blocked logging trucks, chanted slogans, sang songs, and even chained themselves to trees. Loggers complained that the protesters were keeping them from making a living, and, eventually, 850 of the 12,000 protesters were arrested. But this misty, seaside forest had become ground zero in the debate over how we manage forested lands.

Timber had always fueled British Columbia's economy. By 1993, however, the timber industry was eliminating thousands of jobs each year because so much work was being done by machinery. Depletion of the forests threatened to further slow the industry. And as you read above, activists were opposing the logging of some of Canada's oldests forests—those on Clayoquot Sound. An environmental group was even persuading overseas customers to boycott British Columbia forest products. Desperate to save his province's economy, British Columbia's premier tried to persuade European nations not to boycott its timber.

In 1995, it seemed that the conflict had been resolved. British Columbia's government had a plan. It recommended reducing harvests, retaining 15–70 percent of old-growth trees in each stand, decreasing logging roads, designating forest reserves, and managing riverside areas. But in 1997, a new provincial government reversed many of these regulations, denouncing forest activists as "enemies of British Columbia."

Then, in yet another surprising turn of events, environmental advocates and MacMillan Bloedel, a timber company, agreed to limited logging of old-growth forests at Clayoquot Sound using environmentally friendly practices. In 1998, local Native Canadians formed a timber company, Iisaak, in agreement with MacMillan Bloedel's

GO ONLINE
• Take It Local   • 3-D Geo Tour

successor, Weyerhaeuser, and began logging in an even more environmentally sensitive manner. Limiting logging in the Clayoquot Sound forests accomplished just what advocates had predicted.

A million people every year were visiting Clayoquot Sound to watch whales, kayak, and otherwise enjoy the wilderness. Ecotourism, fishing, and aquaculture replaced logging in the local economy. The United Nations designated the site an international biosphere reserve, encouraging land protection and sustainable development. The trees appeared to be worth more left standing than cut down.

The story continues, however. Local forest advocates worry that British Columbia's 2004 Working Forest Policy has increased logging in the region. On the other hand, Iisaak entered into an agreement with the conservation group Ecotrust Canada in 2006, and logging at Clayoquot is now more sustainable. Although the old-growth forest in Clayoquot Sound remains intact, continued demand for lumber, paper, and other forest products has resulted in continued logging in unprotected forested areas of Vancouver Island, the rest of British Columbia, and around the world.

Resource Management

EVERYDAY PHENOMENON How can we manage renewable resources for sustainable use?

Knowledge and Skills

- Explain the importance of managing specific renewable resources.
- Describe three resource management approaches.

Reading Strategy and Vocabulary

✓ **Reading Strategy** Before you read, create an outline using the blue and green headings in this lesson. As you read, fill in key phrases or sentences about each heading.

Vocabulary resource management, maximum sustainable yield (MSY), ecosystem-based management, adaptive management

MOST OF THE RESOURCES we take from the natural world are limited. Recall that resources such as minerals and fossil fuels are nonrenewable on human time scales. Other resources, such as soil, fresh water, wild animals, and timber, are considered renewable. But even renewable resources can run out if they are not harvested *sustainably*—that is, only as rapidly as they can be replaced. In addition, if resources are not harvested sustainably, their entire ecosystem can change. And if the ecosystem changes, some resources may run out. For example, suppose that people in a coastal town relied on a species of fish that only lived in a nearby estuary. But a large fishing company came in and harvested most of those fish. Even if the company were to pay the community, the community would still have lost its most important resource.

Resource managers must balance people's needs for a resource and an ecosystem's need for that resource. This is the importance—and the challenge—of resource management.

Renewable Resource Management

Several types of renewable resources are vital to our civilization. These include soil, fresh water, wild animals, and timber, as shown in **Figure 1.** In addition to fulfilling important human needs, all natural resources, both renewable and nonrenewable, also serve functions in their ecosystems. So to preserve the health of those ecosystems, renewable resources need to be harvested sustainably. When industries that harvest renewable resourcess do so sustainably, they help preserve both the resources and their businesses.

Resource management is the managing of resource harvesting so that resources are not depleted. Resource managers are guided in their decision making by scientific research, but their decisions are also influenced by politics, economics, and social issues.

A key question in managing resources is whether to focus on a specific resource or to consider the entire ecosystem of which the resource is a part. Considering the entire ecosystem makes resource management more complicated, but many scientists say that it is the best way to protect a resource in the long term.

Soil Soil is always being made by natural processes such as the weathering and erosion of rocks and the decomposition of organisms. However, the fertile top layer of soil that plants grow in, called topsoil, is made very slowly—one inch can take hundreds of years to form. Topsoil nourishes the plants we grow for food and fiber, so its quality is essential to our health. Forests and other plant communities also rely on healthy topsoil. So people need to maintain the quantity and quality of existing topsoil. Safeguards against land pollution help protect the fertility of topsoil, and some farming practices can conserve topsoil. You will learn more about soil in the next chapter.

Fresh Water Like soil, fresh water is continually supplied by natural processes. And, as with soil, people need to maintain the quality of water. Because people cannot live without drinking water, ensuring a dependable supply of fresh water is, literally, a matter of life or death. Fresh water is also necessary for agriculture. In fact, we use most of Earth's fresh water not for drinking but for watering crops. Clean waterways and wetlands are also crucial for wildlife and properly functioning ecosystems. People who manage water resources try to maintain clean, adequate supplies for all of these (sometimes conflicting) reasons.

Reading Checkpoint *What are two ways that soil and water are similar as renewable resources?*

FIGURE 1 Renewable Resources
Our civilization depends on many renewable resources, including soil, fresh water, wild animals, and timber.

Fresh Water

Timber

Soil

Wild Animals

Wild Animals People have always hunted animals for food. (Animals that can be hunted legally are called game.) In the United States, state and federal wildlife managers regulate the hunting of game, such as deer and quail, to maintain populations of these animals at desired levels. But, as populations of many animals fall because of habitat loss and other reasons, management of nongame species is becoming increasingly important. Nongame animals provide people with many benefits—wildlife watching, scientific research, and ecosystem services, to name just a few.

▶ *Fishing* People also harvest aquatic animals, including fishes and shellfish. Unfortunately, despite management of fisheries, populations of many aquatic animals have dropped drastically. Fleets of enormous, technologically advanced fishing boats, or trawlers, swarm the oceans. Most use sonar, mechanized nets, and satellite images to find fish. In some ways, the fishing industry has become a victim of its own success, along with the ecosystems in which it operates. For example, in the 1990s, cod populations in some areas dropped to less than 5 percent of their highest levels. Cod fishing is now outlawed in many areas, such as parts of Georges Bank off the New England coast. Unfortunately, even though cod fishing has slowed, North Atlantic cod populations are only at 40 percent of their level of 40 years ago. Because the cod is the top predator in its ecosystem, scientists fear a permanent change to this ecosystem. And in fact, in many areas, fishes that were formerly prey of cod have now become top predators.

▶ *Poaching* Laws are only as effective as their enforcement. Poaching of wild animals, such as the macaws in **Figure 2,** continues. In both developing and developed nations, people kill animals for food and sport in illegal and unsustainable ways. Laws such as the Convention on International Trade in Endangered Species (CITES) have reduced the poaching of endangered animals. Monitoring of trade is difficult in remote areas and some developing nations, however, and CITES is hard to enforce in those places. Poaching of non-endangered animals also continues, affecting their populations and ecosystems.

FIGURE 2 Poaching This zoo employee is holding scarlet macaws that were rescued from poachers. The poachers had intended to sell the macaws as pets.

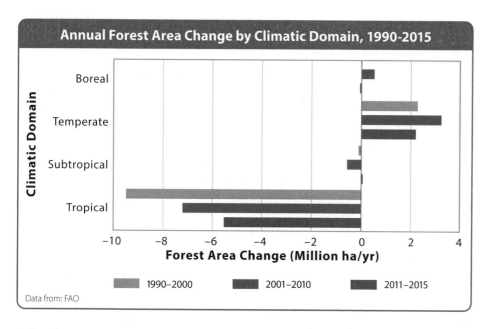

Annual Forest Area Change by Climatic Domain, 1990-2015

Forest Area Change (Million ha/yr)

Climatic Domain

1990–2000   2001–2010   2011–2015

Data from: FAO

FIGURE 3 Deforestation To varying degrees, temperate forests have experienced positive growth between 1990 and 2015. Subtropical forests experienced a small amount of positive growth between 2011 and 2015. **Interpret Graphs** How has the forest area changed for tropical forests between 1990 and 2015?

Timber Wood from trees, or timber, is the raw material for an amazing variety of products you need every day. These products include the wood used to support your house, school, and other buildings; the furniture in those buildings; the paper and cardboard that make up your books and magazines; packaging materials such as boxes, bags, wrappers, and cellophane; rayon fabric; pencils; hamster chew toys; signposts; sponges; doghouses; picture frames; and thousands of others.

The harvesting of timber is essential to our standard of living. In fact, our reliance on products like those above is exactly why we need to carefully manage our forests. Some forest management has been a success. **Figure 3** shows that temperate forests have experienced positive growth from 1990 to 2015. However, tropical forests are still experiencing losses. You will read more about forest resources and efforts to manage them sustainably in the next two lessons.

 Reading Checkpoint *Make a concept map relating some common objects around you to the type of wood product from which they are made.*

Management Approaches

The management of different areas at different times under different political leadership puts different sorts of pressure on resource managers. To try to satisfy these often-conflicting influences and still protect the ecosystem, resource managers use a variety of management approaches. Three of the most common resource management approaches are maximum sustainable yield, ecosystem-based management, and adaptive management.

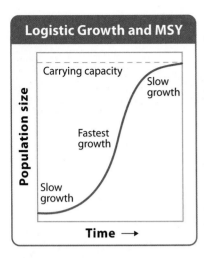

FIGURE 4 Logistic Growth and Maximum Sustainable Yield
The goal of managing for MSY is to maximize harvests without reducing future harvests. With a population that grows according to a logistic growth curve (above), resource managers aim to keep the population well below the carrying capacity, at the point at which the population grows fastest (the steep part of the curve).

WHAT DO YOU THINK?

You have just become the supervisor of a national forest. Ten percent of it is old-growth forest. Your managers are split among preferring maximum sustainable yield, ecosystem-based management, and adaptive management. What questions would you have for scientists? What management approach(es) will you follow?

Maximum Sustainable Yield A common approach to resource management is management for **maximum sustainable yield (MSY).** The aim of MSY is to harvest the maximum amount of a resource without reducing the amount of future harvests. See the logistic growth curve in **Figure 4.** It shows that a population of a resource, such as trees, grows most quickly when it is at an intermediate size (the steep part of the curve). A large population, on the other hand, grows slowly. Once a population reaches the carrying capacity of its environment (the dotted line) growth stops. The goal of harvesting for MSY is to keep a population at an intermediate size, where it will grow fastest.

The maximum sustainable yield approach may at first sound ideal, but in practice it can change the ecosystem that provides the resource. Left alone, a population will stay around the carrying capacity of its environment. But a population managed for MSY is kept far below its carrying capacity. A population that stays below its carrying capacity is not consuming, being consumed by, or competing with other organisms as much as it would if it were not being harvested. So the management of one population for MSY could result in changes for other populations.

In addition, finding the maximum sustainable yield of a population is a matter of trial and error. Some of the errors may result in overharvesting, which can have both economic and ecological effects.

Ecosystem-Based Management Because of the drawbacks of the maximum sustainable yield approach, increasing numbers of managers today have adopted ecosystem-based management. The goal of **ecosystem-based management** is to harvest resources in ways that minimize impact on the ecosystems and ecological processes that provide the resources. The plan approved in 1995 by British Columbia's government for Clayoquot Sound's forests was basically a plan for ecosystem-based management. The plan aimed to allow some timber harvesting while preserving the functioning of the ecosystem. Steps in the plan included carefully managing ecologically important areas such as river valleys, considering patterns in plant cover, and protecting some forested areas. Although ecosystem-based management has gained a great deal of support in recent years, it is challenging for managers to determine how best to put it into action. Ecosystems are complex, and our understanding of how they work is incomplete. As a result, ecosystem-based management can mean different things to different people, and that can result in inconsistent management.

Adaptive Management Any given management approach will succeed in some places and fail in others. **Adaptive management** involves scientifically testing different management approaches in an area, one after the other, and then customizing an approach based on the results. Adaptive management is intended as a true union of science and management because hypotheses about how best to manage resources are tested under controlled conditions.

FIGURE 5 Adaptive Management Adaptive management requires constant monitoring of a resource and adjustments to its management, as the cycle diagram shows. The time and effort can be richly rewarded, however, as in the case of the successful ecological restoration projects at Siuslaw National Forest in Oregon (photo).

ASSESS PROBLEM

Adjust

Design

Evaluate

Implement

Monitor

Source: U.S. Department of the Interior

Adaptive management requires managers and scientists to closely monitor current practices and to continually adjust them. You can see a cycle diagram showing how adaptive management works in **Figure 5.** Because of the large quantity of data that must be processed and the need for adjustments, adaptive management can be time-consuming and complicated. It also poses a challenge for many managers, who, before they can change an approach, must overcome resistance from supporters of existing, failed approaches.

LESSON ① Assessment

1. **Review** Define *resource management*. Why is it important?

2. **Compare and Contrast** Describe the goals of maximum sustainable yield management, ecosystem-based management, and adaptive management. List a drawback of each.

REVISIT

3. **INVESTIGATIVE** PHENOMENON
How may managing a resource for maximum sustainable yield sometimes conflict with what is best for its ecosystem?

Forests and Their Resources

EVERYDAY PHENOMENON Is there a balance between the ecological and economic value of forest resources?

Knowledge and Skills

- List some of the ecological and economical values of forest resources.
- Describe the costs and benefits of the different methods of timber harvesting.
- Discuss the current levels of deforestation in the United States and in developing nations.

Reading Strategy and Vocabulary

✅ **Reading Strategy** Before you read, preview **Figure 8.** Note any questions you have about it, and try to answer them as you read.

Vocabulary even-aged, uneven-aged, clear-cutting, seed-tree approach, shelterwood approach, selection system, deforestation, old-growth forest

FORESTS COVER ABOUT 31 PERCENT of Earth's land surface, as you can see in **Figure 6.** Most of the world's remaining forests are either boreal forest or tropical rain forest. Temperate forests cover a much smaller area, in part because people have already cleared so many of them.

Forests provide habitat for countless organisms; help maintain soil, air, and water quality; and play key roles in our planet's biogeochemical cycles. Forests also have long provided people with wood for fuel, construction, paper production, and other uses.

Resource managers who manage public or private forests are called foresters. Forest management is called *forestry*. Foresters aim to balance the ecological importance of forests with the economic importance of forests as resources for wood products.

FIGURE 6 Earth's Forests About 31 percent of Earth's land area is covered with forests (as indicated by the green areas). Most of Earth's forests are boreal forests in the north and tropical rain forests in the south.

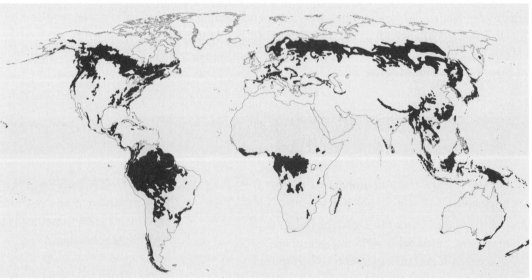

Source: U.S. Geological Survey

Forest Resources

The complexity of forests makes their resources enormously important, both within their ecosystems and in the world economy. A 2005 survey by the United Nations showed that more than one third of the world's forests were used mostly for timber production. But forests provide a wide variety of other services and products, including conservation of biodiversity; protection of soil and water quality; maintenance of biogeochemical cycles; food; medicine; and "social services" such as recreation, tourism, education, and conservation of culturally important sites. In addition, some people live in forests and depend on forests for all their needs.

Ecological Value Because forests are structurally complex, they provide many different habitats for plants and animals. As a result, forest ecosystems have great biodiversity. You can see the complexity of a mature forest's structure and the diverse habitats within it in **Figure 7.** In general, forests with a greater diversity of plants have a greater diversity of other organisms as well. And in general, mature forests, such as the old-growth forests remaining at Clayoquot Sound, have more biodiversity than younger forests.

Forests also provide many vital ecosystem services. Forest plants help prevent soil erosion. They also help regulate the water cycle by slowing runoff, reducing flooding, and purifying water as they take it from the soil and release it to the atmosphere. Forest plants also store carbon and release oxygen, thereby helping to moderate climate. Because they fulfill so many ecological functions, forests are necessary for our survival.

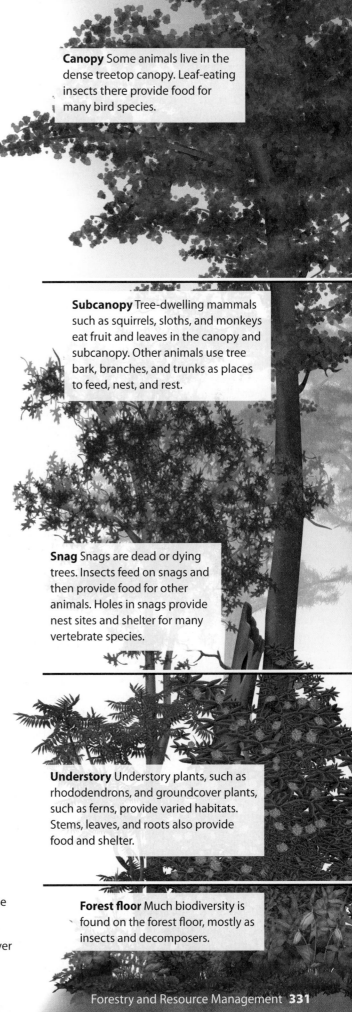

Canopy Some animals live in the dense treetop canopy. Leaf-eating insects there provide food for many bird species.

Subcanopy Tree-dwelling mammals such as squirrels, sloths, and monkeys eat fruit and leaves in the canopy and subcanopy. Other animals use tree bark, branches, and trunks as places to feed, nest, and rest.

Snag Snags are dead or dying trees. Insects feed on snags and then provide food for other animals. Holes in snags provide nest sites and shelter for many vertebrate species.

Understory Understory plants, such as rhododendrons, and groundcover plants, such as ferns, provide varied habitats. Stems, leaves, and roots also provide food and shelter.

Forest floor Much biodiversity is found on the forest floor, mostly as insects and decomposers.

FIGURE 7 Mature Forest Structure Mature forests have complex structures. The crowns of the largest trees form the canopy, and smaller trees beneath them form the shaded subcanopy and understory. Dead or dying trees, or snags, are valuable for nesting and shelter. Shrubs and groundcover grow just above the forest floor.

Economic and Medicinal Value The use of forest resources is essential to our lifestyle. Forests provide timber, which can be made into thousands of economically valuable products. And for thousands of years, wood from forests has fueled the fires that have kept people warm and well fed. Wood has also built the houses that have kept people sheltered. It has built the ships that have carried people and their cultures from one region to another. And wood has enabled us to make paper, which has helped people to share knowledge.

Forest plants also provide food and medicine. Many fruits, nuts, spices, and herbs come from forest plants. Forest plants have also yielded many modern medicines. The drug paclitaxel, which treats several kinds of cancer, was discovered in the Pacific yew tree. Madagascar rosy periwinkle, a flowering forest plant that is endangered in much of its range, is the source of treatments for leukemia and Hodgkin's lymphoma. Other cancer treatments and treatments for other illnesses have also been derived from plants.

Timber Harvesting

Today, most commercial timber harvesting, or logging, takes place in Canada, Russia, and other nations with large boreal forests, and in nations with large tropical rain forests, such as Brazil. In the United States, most logging takes place in the conifer forests of the West and on the pine plantations of the South, on both private and public lands.

Real Data

From Trees to Paper

The invention of the movable-type printing press by Johannes Gutenberg in 1450 created a demand for paper that continues to increase even today. Because most fiber for paper production comes from wood, a high demand for paper results in a high demand for timber. Examine the graph and answer the questions.

1. **Interpret Graphs** About how many millions of tons of paper and paperboard were consumed worldwide in 2016?

2. **Interpret Graphs** Which region(s) of the world showed an increase in paper and paperboard production from 2012 to 2016?

3. **Interpret Graphs** Which region(s) showed a decrease in paper and paperboard production from 2012 to 2016? Provide a possible explanation for the decease in production.

4. **Propose a Solution** List three steps that your school could take to reduce its paper consumption.

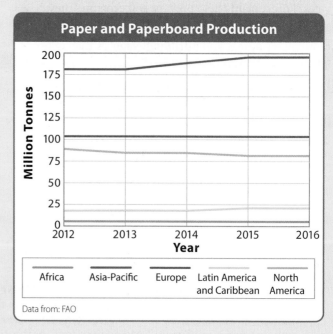

Paper and Paperboard Production

Million Tonnes vs. Year

Africa · Asia-Pacific · Europe · Latin America and Caribbean · North America

Data from: FAO

When timber companies harvest trees, they use one or more of the methods shown in **Figure 8**—clear-cutting, the seed-tree approach, the shelterwood approach, or a selection system. These methods fall into two categories: those that result in even-aged stands of trees and those that result in uneven-aged stands of trees. Even-aged stands result from the regrowth of trees that were mostly all cut at the same time, as with clear-cutting **(Figure 9)**. Uneven-aged stands result from the regrowth of trees that were cut at different times, as with selection systems.

Uneven-aged stands typically have more biodiversity, because the regrown trees of different ages offer a greater variety of habitats. But all methods of logging disturb forest communities. Logging changes forest structure and composition, as the larger trees forming the canopy and subcanopy are often removed. Most logging methods also increase soil erosion, which can lead to muddy waterways that degrade animal habitats and lower drinking-water quality. And most methods also increase runoff, sometimes causing flooding, or even landslides.

FIGURE 9 Clear-Cutting During clear-cutting all the mature trees in an area are cut at once. The result is regrowth that is even-aged, like the short trees in the foreground.

FIGURE 8 Timber Harvesting Methods Different methods of timber harvesting lead to different patterns of regrowth.

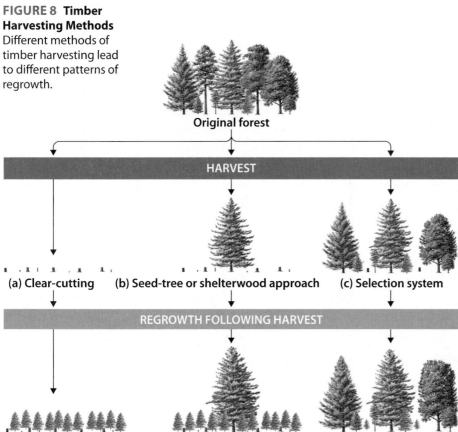

Original forest

HARVEST

(a) Clear-cutting (b) Seed-tree or shelterwood approach (c) Selection system

REGROWTH FOLLOWING HARVEST

Quick Lab

A Tree's History

1. Examine the photo of the tree-trunk slice, or tree cookie, below. Observe the light-colored and dark-colored rings. Each pair of rings represents a year of the tree's growth.
2. Observe areas *A* and *B*. Note any differences.
3. Observe Area *C*, which was blackened by a fire.

Analyze and Conclude

1. **Calculate** Approximately how old was this tree when it was cut down?
2. **Infer** Areas *A* and *B* were both produced by four years of growth. What conditions might account for their difference?
3. **Interpret Visuals** How are the ring widths in Area *C* different from the widths elsewhere? Given these differences, explain how the tree grew after the fire.
4. **Communicate** Using evidence from this tree cookie, write a paragraph that summarizes the history of the tree. Include as many details as possible in your paragraph.

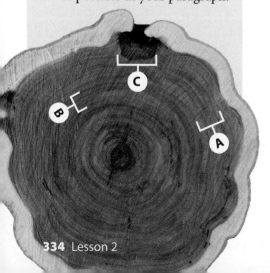

Clear-Cutting From the 1950s through the 1970s, timber was largely harvested by **clear-cutting,** a method in which all of the trees in an area are cut at once. Clear-cutting is generally the most cost-efficient method for timber companies, but it also has the greatest impact on forest ecosystems.

Clear-cutting results in even-aged stands of regrowth. Sometimes clear-cutting can mimic the effects of natural disasters such as fires, tornadoes, or windstorms that knock down large areas of trees. Usually, however, clear-cutting destroys or displaces entire communities of organisms, causes soil erosion, and increases the penetration of sunlight to ground level. Because it changes light, precipitation, wind, and temperature conditions, clear-cutting can lead to a new microclimate. The new microclimate allows different types of plants to replace those of the original forest. Essentially, clear-cutting sets in motion secondary succession in which the resulting climax community may turn out to be different from the original climax community.

Seed-Tree and Shelterwood Approaches When timber is harvested with the **seed-tree approach,** small numbers of mature and healthy seed-producing trees are left standing so that they can reseed the logged area. In the **shelterwood approach,** small numbers of mature trees are left in place to provide shelter for seedlings as they grow. Although both methods are less harmful to forest communities than clear-cutting, both lead to regrowth that is mostly even-aged.

Selection Systems Selection systems, in contrast, result in uneven-aged stands of regrown trees. In a **selection system,** only some of the trees in a forest are cut at once. Selection systems include single-tree selection, in which trees spaced widely apart are cut one at a time, and group selection, in which small patches of trees are cut.

Timber companies pursued a form of selection harvesting at Clayoquot Sound after old-growth advocates applied pressure and the government researched the issue. Not wanting to bring a complete end to logging when so many local people depended on the industry for work, the activists promoted a method they considered more environmentally friendly. After some research, the government agreed.

However, selection systems are by no means ecologically harmless. Moving trucks and machinery over roads and trails to get to individual trees compacts the soil and disturbs the forest floor. In addition, selection methods are unpopular with timber companies because they are more expensive than clear-cutting. For example, cut trees must sometimes be removed by helicopters. Loggers dislike selection systems because they are more dangerous than clear-cutting. In clear-cutting, loggers are largely protected from falling trees by the heavy machinery they operate; when cutting selectively, loggers must spend more time on the ground, in danger both from equipment and from falling trees.

 Reading Checkpoint *What are two different selection systems?*

Deforestation

We all depend on wood, from the herder in Nepal cutting trees for firewood to the American high school student using tons of paper while earning a diploma. For such reasons, people have cut forests for timber for thousands of years. Forests are also cleared to make way for farming. **Deforestation** is the clearing of a forest and the replacement of it by another land use. It has altered the landscapes and ecosystems of much of our planet. Deforestation has provided warmth, shelter, and trade for many human communitites, even as it has caused soil degradation and species population declines for other communities.

The negative effects of deforestation are greatest in tropical regions because of the potential massive loss of biodiversity, and in arid regions because of loss of soil productivity. In addition, deforestation has a global impact. It adds carbon dioxide (CO_2) to the atmosphere in two ways. CO_2 is released when plant matter is burned or decomposed, and after burning, less vegetation remains to use CO_2. Because CO_2 in the atmosphere contributes to the greenhouse effect that can cause global warming, widespread deforestation can contribute to global warming.

United States Deforestation for timber and farmland enabled the United States to expand across the continent. The vast deciduous forests of the East were virtually stripped of their trees by 1850, making way for countless small farms. Timber from eastern forests built the cities of America's East Coast. Later, midwestern cities such as Chicago were constructed with timber cut in the forests of Wisconsin and Michigan.

▶ *The Industrial Revolution* As the U.S. farming economy shifted to an industrial one, wood was used to fuel the Industrial Revolution. Logging operations moved south to Texas, Florida, and the Carolinas. Once most mature trees there were cut, timber companies moved west, cutting the continent's biggest trees in the Rocky Mountains, the Sierra Nevada, the Cascade Mountains, and the Pacific Coast ranges. By the early 1900s, very little **old-growth forest**—forest that has never been logged—remained in the United States, as you can see in **Figure 10.**

FIGURE 10 Deforestation in the United States When Europeans began colonizing the area that would become the United States (left map), the entire eastern half and large parts of the western half were forested (green). By 1920, the vast majority of these forests had been cut (right map).

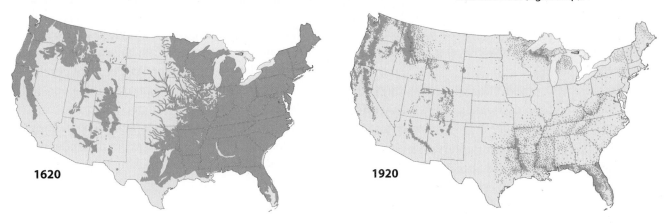

1620

1920

Source: Williams, M. 1989. *Americans and their forests.* Cambridge: Cambridge University Press. As adapted by Goudie, A., 2000. *The human impact.* Cambridge, MA: MIT Press.

▶ *Today* Today, not even the largest oaks and maples in eastern North America, or even most redwoods of the California coast, are old-growth trees. The scarcity of old-growth trees in North America today explains the concern that scientists have for old-growth ecosystems and the passion with which environmental advocates have fought to preserve them in areas such as Clayoquot Sound. While some former farms and pastures of eastern North America are slowly regaining forest cover, this process is basically secondary succession. Once old-growth forest is cut, it may need hundreds of years of undisturbed growth in order to recover.

Developing Nations Old-growth tropical rain forests still remain in many developing nations, and these nations are in the position the United States once was: They have a vast frontier that they can develop and use for income. Today's advanced technology, however, has allowed these nations to exploit their resources much faster than the United States did. As a result, deforestation has been rapid in the tropical rain forests of developing nations, such as Brazil and Indonesia (**Figure 11**). Because rain forests are the most diverse biomes, a great diversity of species—some perhaps still undiscovered—are being affected by, or even lost to, deforestation. And recall that large-scale forest loss has global consequences. It can worsen global warming by increasing carbon dioxide in the atmosphere, especially if trees are cleared by burning, as they often are in tropical rain forests.

FIGURE 11 Rainforest Deforestation
Brazil produces more charcoal than any other nation. Both farmed trees and rainforest trees are cut and burned to make charcoal. About 350,000 Brazilians work in unhealthy, often exploitative conditions in the charcoal industry.

② Assessment

1. **Review** What is one way a forest is ecologically valuable? What is one way a forest is economically valuable?

2. **Compare and Contrast** How are clear-cutting and the shelterwood approach similar? How are they different? How do both differ from selection systems?

3. **Predict** What, generally, is the current level of deforestation in the United States? In developing nations? How would you expect the deforestation in developing nations to change in the next 100 years? Explain.

4. **THINK IT** *THROUGH* People in developed nations often warn people in developing nations to stop destroying rain forests. People of developing nations often respond that this is hypocritical, because many of the developed nations became wealthy by deforesting their land and exploiting its resources. What would you say to the leader of a developing nation that is seeking to clear much of its forest?

Forest Management

EVERYDAY PHENOMENON What challenges does sustainable forestry face?

Knowledge and Skills

- Explain how logging is managed in U.S. national forests.
- Describe where most logging in the United States takes place.
- Discuss the potential effects of fire suppression on an ecosystem and on future fires.
- Explain how consumer demand is important to sustainable forestry.
- Explain how logging is managed in U.S. national parks.

Reading Strategy and Vocabulary

✔ Reading Strategy Before reading the lesson, create a three-column KWL chart. In the first column, write what you know about forest management. In the second column, write what you want to know. After reading the lesson, write what you learned in the third column.

Vocabulary multiple use, monoculture, prescribed burn, salvage logging, sustainable forestry certification

ON AVERAGE, each person in the United States uses about 6200 cubic centimeters of wood each day. It's as if each of us cuts down a tree 15 meters (50 feet) tall every year! Where does all that wood come from? Most of it comes from land owned by logging companies, but some comes from our national forests.

U.S. National Forests

By the early 1900s, the eastern deciduous forests that fueled our nation's growth had all but disappeared. The deforestation caused fear of a "timber famine." This fear led to the formation of our national forest system, which is made up of public lands set aside to grow trees for timber and to protect watersheds. Today, the U.S. national forest system consists of 77.4 million hectares (191 million acres). The national forests in the continental 48 states are shown in **Figure 12.** U.S. national forests are managed by the Forest Service.

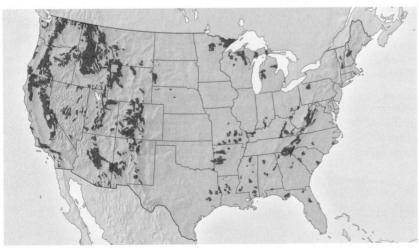

Source: Courtesy of the U.S. Forest Service

FIGURE 12 U.S. National Forests
The national forest system (green areas) was established in 1905.

National Forest Logging You may be surprised to learn that, in the United States, timber is harvested not by the government, but by private timber companies. Forest Service employees plan and manage timber sales and build roads to provide access for logging companies. But the logging companies receive the profits from the sale of the timber. Critics of the Forest Service have protested the fact that taxpayers' money is being used to help private corporations harvest publicly held resources for profit.

In recent decades, increased awareness of this issue has prompted many U.S. citizens to protest the way their public forests are managed. These citizens have urged that national and state forests be managed for recreation, wildlife, and ecosystem health, rather than mostly for timber. They are afraid that public forests have essentially become cropland for timber companies.

National Forest Management Act In theory, the Forest Service has long recognized interests other than timber production. For the past 50 years or so, national forest management has been guided by the policy of multiple use, meaning that the forests were to be managed for recreation, wildlife habitat, mining, and other uses, in addition to timber. In practice, however, timber production has often been the primary use.

In 1976, the U.S. Congress passed the National Forest Management Act (NFMA), which required that plans for renewable resource management be drawn up for every national forest. The plans were required to be consistent with the concepts of multiple use and maximum sustainable yield. You can see some of the law's specific guidelines in **Figure 13.**

FIGURE 13 National Forest Management Act There are many specific guidelines for the plans required by the 1976 National Forest Management Act (NFMA).

Under the NFMA, resource management plans have to:

- consider both economic and environmental factors

- provide for diversity of plant and animal communities and preserve the diversity of tree species

- ensure research and monitoring of management approaches

- allow increases in harvest levels only if sustainable

- ensure that timber will be harvested only where soils and wetlands will not be irreversibly damaged, land will be replanted quickly, and harvest methods will not be determined solely on the basis of financial return

- ensure that logging will occur only where possible impacts have been assessed; cuts will depend on the shape of the land; maximum size limits of cut trees will be established; and cuts will be carried out in a manner consistent with the protection of soil, watershed, fish, wildlife, recreation, and aesthetic resources.

Success Stories In the years following passage of the National Forest Management Act, the Forest Service developed new programs to manage wildlife, nongame animals, and endangered species. It pushed for ecosystem-based management and ran programs for ecological restoration, helping plant and animal communities to recover. Logging methods were brought more in line with the Forest Service's ecosystem-based management goals. In 2006, timber companies harvested 10.7 million cubic meters (378 million cubic feet) of live timber from national forests. Although this is a large amount, it is considerably less than the amount cut from other public forests or private lands. Logging has declined in national forests since the 1980s. In 2006, tree regrowth outpaced tree removal on these lands by more than 11 to 1.

Challenges In the early 2000s, the trend shifted. In 2004, the Bush administration passed regulations that weakened the requirements of the National Forest Management Act. In 2005, the administration also repealed a rule—the so-called "roadless rule"—that limited the building of new roads in national forests. The overall effect of these changes was an increase in logging in national forests. The trend may be shifting back, however. In 2009, the Obama administration reinstated the roadless rule. As of 2010, however, many conflicting court cases pertaining to changes in the NFMA were still being sorted out. Those court decisions will clarify the powers of the NFMA.

✓ Reading Checkpoint *What is the effect of the roadless rule?*

FIGURE 14 U.S. National Forests
National forests benefit directly from the NFMA.

Private Land

Most logging in the United States today takes place on private land, often on land owned by timber companies. Most of this harvesting is from plantations of fast-growing tree species in the Northwest and South. These plantations are typically **monocultures,** or large-scale plantings of a single crop. Also, all the trees in a given stand are planted at the same time, so the stands are even-aged. Stands are cut after a certain number of years, called the *rotation time*, and then the land is replanted with seedlings.

Because there is little variation in tree species or tree age, plantations do not offer as much habitat variety as most forests. As a result, their biodiversity is lower. Most ecologists and foresters view tree plantations as croplands rather than as functioning forestland. However, some plantations are harvested in ways that maintain uneven-aged stands, which are more similar to a natural forest. And the use of tree plantations for timber protects additional natural forests from being cut.

✓ **Reading Checkpoint** *Why is there less biodiversity in a tree plantation than in a similar-sized forest?*

Fire Policies

Ironically, some recent ecosystem management efforts contradict the advice of the Forest Service's lovable spokesbear, Smokey. Smokey's reminder that "only you can prevent forest fires" has done some good; it has probably reduced the number of forest fires caused by people. Unfortunately, the Forest Service also took Smokey's message to heart. For more than a hundred years, it suppressed all fires, both natural and human-caused. Such suppression may have harmed some forests.

Ecosystem Effects Current scientific research shows that many ecosystems depend on fire and that diversity and abundance of species decline without it. For example, certain plants have seeds that germinate only after a fire. The jack pine is one of those plants. The Kirtland's warbler, shown in **Figure 15,** is a songbird that nests only in large stands of young jack pines. When there are fewer fires, there are fewer young jack pines. Currently there are adequate numbers of young jack pines only in small parts of the warbler's former breeding range of Michigan, Wisconsin, and Ontario. The warbler nests primarily in one tiny area in Michigan. Thanks to an intensive recovery plan, Kirtland's warbler populations are now recovering. In 2019, Kirtland's warbler was removed from the Federal List of Endangered and Threatened Wildlife. As you can see, fires can benefit some organisms.

FIGURE 15 Kirtland's Warbler
Kirtland's warbler was North America's most critically endangered songbird. It only nests in young jack pines, and strict control of natural forest fires greatly reduced its habitat, pushing it toward extinction in the 1980s. Only 167 singing males were found in the United States in 1987.

Future Fire Potential In the long term, suppression of small, natural fires can lead to larger, more dangerous fires—ones that permanently damage forests, destroy human property, and threaten human lives. Suppression of small fires allows limbs, sticks, and leaf litter to build up on the forest floor, basically providing kindling for a catastrophic fire. Such fuel buildup helped cause the 1988 fires in Yellowstone National Park, the 2009 fires in southern California, and thousands of other wildfires. Fire suppression and fuel buildup have made catastrophic fires significantly greater problems than they were in the past.

To reduce fuel buildup and improve forest health, the Forest Service and other land management agencies have recently been burning areas of forest under carefully controlled conditions. These **prescribed burns,** or *controlled burns,* have helped restore ecosystems that depend on fire. Prescribed burns also have helped Kirtland's warbler (**Figure 16**) and other fire-dependent species of plants and animals recover from near-extinction. Rarely, a prescribed burn gets out of control, as happened in 2000 when homes and government labs were destroyed at Los Alamos, New Mexico. Such rare accidents have led to public misunderstanding and interference from uninformed politicians, which have limited the use of prescribed burns. This actually increases the risk of injury, property damage, and ecosystem loss from wildfires.

WHAT DO YOU THINK?

Wildfire suppression has left some large forests in danger of catastrophic wildfires. Government agencies will probably never be able to carry out prescribed burns on all this land. Suggest some ways to help protect people's homes near these forests and to decrease the likelihood of major fires.

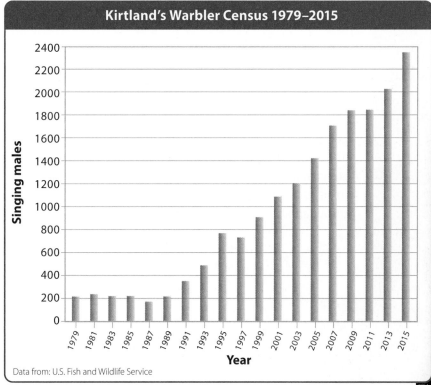

Kirtland's Warbler Census 1979–2015

y-axis: Singing males (0 to 2400)
x-axis: Year (1979 to 2015)

Data from: U.S. Fish and Wildlife Service

FIGURE 16 Kirtland's Warbler and Prescribed Burns Once researchers discovered that Kirtland's warblers only nested in 5–7-year-old jack pines (seedling, right), they came up with a plan. The Kirtland's Warbler Recovery Plan, instituted in 1976 and updated in 1985, includes management of the bird's breeding area, including regularly scheduled prescribed burns. The warbler's population is now more than 10 times its 1987 level (graph above).

Healthy Forests Restoration Act Shortly after the devastating 2003 California fires, Congress passed the Healthy Forests Restoration Act. The goal of the act is to make forests less fire-prone. Although this law encourages some prescribed burning, it primarily promotes the removal of small trees, underbrush, and snags by timber companies. The removal of snags following a natural disturbance is called **salvage logging**.

Economically, salvage logging seems to make good sense. Ecologically, however, snags have immense value; the insects that feed on them provide food for wildlife, and many animals depend on holes in snags for nesting and roosting. Removing timber from recently burned land can also cause severe erosion and soil damage. Salvage logging can also slow forest regrowth and promote more wildfires. And major wildfires can damage both the economic and ecological value of a forest.

Many scientists and most environmental advocates have criticized the Healthy Forests Restoration Act, saying it increases commercial logging in national forests while doing little to reduce catastrophic fires near populated areas. Critics also fear that it makes it easier to log in national forests, decreasing the ability of the government to enforce environmental regulations. In some cases, at least, those fears are well founded. The Forest Service had interpreted the law in such a way that it believed it could stop preparing environmental impact statements before allowing logging in some plots in national forests. In 2007, some environmental groups challenged this assumption in court and won. The environmental groups feared that large timber companies could use the streamlined process as a way to get approval for projects that would not be approved through the usual processes.

✓ **Reading Checkpoint** *What is salvage logging?*

FIGURE 17 Healthy Forests Restoration Act The Healthy Forests Restoration Act encouraged more salvage logging. In this area, which had been burned in a forest fire, salvage logging would remove all the snags and other dying trees.

Sustainable Forestry Products

Any company can claim that its timber harvesting practices are sustainable, but can a consumer know whether they really are? The answer is yes. Several organizations in the United States and elsewhere, such as the Forest Stewardship Council (FSC), now examine the practices of timber companies. These organizations offer **sustainable forestry certification** to products produced using methods they consider sustainable. The FSC has the strictest standards and the most widely accepted certification process of any organization that certifies forest products. Certified wood products carry logos of the certifying organization, as you can see in **Figure 18.** You can look for these logos on wood products and paper products that you purchase.

Some national home-improvement stores and smaller retail stores now carry certified wood because consumers have demanded it. And the decision of these retailers to supply certified wood to consumers requires that timber companies supply it. In British Columbia, Canada, for example, 70 percent of the annual timber harvest now is certified. Although it is more costly for the timber industry to produce certified wood, it seems that they will do so if consumers demand it. So you can protect the environment with your wallet, using the basic economic concept of supply and demand.

FIGURE 18 Certified Forest Products The Forest Stewardship Council has the strictest certification process of any organization that certifies forest products. You can see the FSC certification logo on a box of tissues (above left) and lumber (above right).

LESSON 3 Assessment

1. **Explain** What are the roles of the Forest Service and timber companies in logging U.S. national forests? What are the requirements of the National Forest Management Act?

2. **Infer** Generally, how does a tree plantation's biodiversity differ from that of a natural forest? Give two reasons for your answer.

3. **Pose Questions** Suppose you lived very close to a fire-prone forest where there had been no fire for many years, and the Forest Service wanted to have a prescribed burn there. What are two questions you would ask the Forest Service?

4. **Infer** How do organizations such as the FSC decide whether to certify a product?

5. **THINK IT** *THROUGH* Suppose you were an environmental activist protesting a logging operation that is cutting old-growth trees near your town. Then you find out that if the protest is successful, the company will move to a developing nation and cut its old-growth forest instead. Would you still protest the logging in your town? Would you try any other approaches?

REFORESTING AFRICA

Wangari Muta Maathai was born in the small village of Nyeri, Kenya, in 1940. She became the first woman from East Africa to earn a Ph.D. when she was granted a doctorate of anatomy from the University of Nairobi. In 1977, she became a professor of veterinary anatomy at the University of Nairobi. Throughout Dr. Maathai's life, the environment of Kenya had been in decline. Deforestation was widespread, causing severe soil erosion and biodiversity loss. With the help of the National Council of Women of Kenya, Dr. Maathai launched the Green Belt Movement in 1977 to combat deforestation.

Members of the Green Belt Movement

PLANTING TREES

The Green Belt Movement encourages communities of Kenyan women to plant trees on their land and in their communities. Dr. Maathai and the movement encourages women to start tree nurseries and plant the seedlings. The trees help protect crops, prevent soil erosion, and provide vital fuel for cooking. The Green Belt Movement also trains women in forestry, beekeeping, and other trades that help them earn extra money while protecting the environment.

INTERNATIONAL MOVEMENT

Since the Green Belt Movement began, more than 45 million trees have been planted in Kenya, helping to restore degraded forests, increase water supplies, and provide income for thousands of families. In 1986, the Green Belt Movement began introducing people from other African nations to its approach. There are now more than 4000 communities committed to planting trees across central and eastern Africa.

NOBEL PRIZE

From 2003 to 2007, Dr. Maathai served as the assistant minister for environment and natural resources to the Kenyan president. In 2004, she was awarded the Nobel Peace Prize for promoting democracy and environmental stability across Africa. Dr. Maathai died in 2011.

CAREER **Forester** Foresters manage the overall land quality of forests, parks, and other natural resources. In addition, they monitor forests for insects and disease, and make sure forest activities are complying with government regulations. Go Online and research some of the varied careers that relate to forestry. Write a brief summary of your findings.

INVESTIGATIVE PHENOMENON

Why is it important to manage Earth's resources sustainably?

Lesson 1
How can we manage renewable resources for sustainable use?

Lesson 3
What challenges does sustainable forestry face?

Lesson 2
Is there a balance between the ecological and economic values of forest resources?

LESSON 1 Resource Management

- People need to manage the harvesting of renewable resources in order to ensure their availability.
- Resource management approaches include maximum sustainable yield (MSY), ecosystem-based management, and adaptive management. The aim of MSY is to harvest the maximum amount of a resource without reducing the amount of future harvests. The goal of ecosystem-based management is to harvest resources in ways that minimize impact on the ecosystems and ecological processes that provide the resource. Adaptive management involves scientifically testing different management approaches in an area and then customizing an approach based on the results.

resource management (325)
maximum sustainable yield (MSY) (328)
ecosystem-based management (328)
adaptive management (328)

LESSON 2 Forests and Their Resources

- Forest resources have great ecological and economic value. More than one third of forests are used mostly for timber production. But forests also help conserve biodiversity; protect soil and water quality; maintain biogeochemical cycles; and provide food, medicine, and social services.
- Timber harvesting methods include clear-cutting, seed-tree and shelterwood approaches, and selection systems. Clear-cutting is cheapest and safest, but it reduces biodiversity. Selection systems best conserve biodiversity but are more expensive and more dangerous than clear-cutting.
- Deforestation may help nations develop, but it can be ecologically destructive in the long run.

even-aged (333)
uneven-aged (333)
clear-cutting (334)
seed-tree approach (334)
shelterwood approach (334)
selection system (334)
deforestation (335)
old-growth forest (335)

LESSON 3 Forest Management

- Logging in national forests is managed by the Forest Service, but profits go to the timber companies.
- Most logging in the United States today takes place on tree plantations owned by timber companies. These plantations are usually monocultures, or large-scale plantings of a single variety, which host little biodiversity.
- Suppression of all wildfires can endanger ecosystems, property, and people. Some plants, such as the jack pine, depend on fire to begin their growth cycle. Prescribed burns can help the populations of plants and animals, such as Kirtland's warbler, that depend upon fire.
- The response of timber companies to consumer demand is helping to promote sustainable forestry. The Forest Stewardship Council and other organizations certify wood and wood products from sustainably harvested forests.

multiple use (338)
monoculture (340)
prescribed burn (341)
salvage logging (342)
sustainable forestry certification (343)

 GO ONLINE

INQUIRY LABS AND ACTIVITIES

- **Making Recycled Paper**
  Make new paper from old and compare the fibers under a microscope.

- **How Much Lumber?**
  Measure a tree's diameter. Then use geometric formulas to estimate the volume of its lumber.

- **Your National Forests**
  Find out which national forests are near you. Investigate how they are managed.

Chapter Assessment

Defend Your Case

The Central Case in this chapter has explored the challenges of harvesting the timber we need while preserving irreplaceable forests. Based on what you have learned, how would you recommend that residents of areas with such forests respond to timber harvesting proposals? Use evidence from the Central Case and the lessons to support your ideas.

Review Concepts and Terms

1. Soil, fresh water, wild animals, and timber are examples of
   a. renewable resources.
   b. inexhaustible resources.
   c. nonrenewable resources.
   d. forest resources.

2. Maximum sustainable yield, ecosystem-based management, and adaptive management are three approaches to
   a. poaching.
   b. overharvesting.
   c. resource management.
   d. none of the above.

3. Most of the world's remaining forests are either boreal forest or
   a. tropical rain forest.
   b. temperate forest.
   c. tree plantations.
   d. chaparral.

4. Which of the following logging methods would most likely result in regrowth such as that shown below?
   a. clear-cutting
   b. a selection system
   c. the seed-tree approach
   d. the shelterwood approach

5. Clear-cutting is a timber harvesting method in which
   a. trees that provide shelter to seedlings are left uncut.
   b. only some mature trees in an area are cut.
   c. only immature trees in an area are cut.
   d. all of the trees in an area are cut.

6. Deforestation has the greatest impact on biodiversity
   a. on private lands.
   b. in tropical areas and arid regions.
   c. in densely populated urban areas.
   d. on public lands.

7. The Healthy Forests Restoration Act
   a. encourages salvage logging and prescribed burning on national forest land.
   b. requires that timber companies produce certified wood from national forest land.
   c. does not require environmental impact statements for logging on national forest land.
   d. requires adaptive management on national forest land.

8. Salvage logging can
   a. decrease soil erosion.
   b. decrease commercial logging.
   c. promote wildfires.
   d. speed up forest regrowth.

9. The policy of multiple use requires that national forests be managed for
   a. timber.
   b. wildlife habitat.
   c. recreation.
   d. all of the above.

10. When paper has a Forest Stewardship Council logo on it, the paper is
    a. made from rainforest wood.
    b. not made from wood.
    c. made from sustainably harvested wood.
    d. recycled.

Modified True/False

Write true if the statement is true. If the statement is false, change the underlined word or words to make the statement true.

11. The aim of <u>adaptive management</u> is to harvest the maximum amount of a resource without reducing future harvests.

12. Forests cover about <u>15 percent</u> of Earth's land surface.

13. Clear-cutting results in mostly <u>even-aged</u> stands of trees.

14. Deforestation is still occurring rapidly in some <u>developing</u> nations.

15. Most logging in the United States today takes place on <u>public</u> lands.

Reading Comprehension

Read the following selection and answer the questions that follow.

Natural disasters are unavoidable. People in various regions of the United States must worry about mudslides, fires, hurricanes, tornadoes, and floods. Disasters such as these can directly kill thousands of organisms, including people. Natural disasters also drastically alter habitats of many organisms because the soil, air, and water are all affected.

Unfortunately, people's environmental decisions can worsen the damage done by natural disasters. For example, suppressing all wildfires can lead to larger, more destructive fires because these fires can use fuel that has built up for many years. Another example is deforestation, which makes forest soil more susceptible to erosion. With heavy rain, deforested hillsides can result in mudslides or can increase the risk of floods.

16. Which of the following factors would most likely contribute to an increase in large, destructive forest fires?
   a. an increase in prescribed burns
   b. a decrease in federal funding to fight forest fires in national parks
   c. a decrease in campgrounds
   d. long-term suppression of all fires

17. People's environmental decisions
   a. cause all natural disasters.
   b. could prevent all natural disasters.
   c. can worsen damage from natural disasters.
   d. have no effect on damage from natural disasters.

18. Which of the following human activities most directly contributes to an increased incidence of mudslides?
   a. aquifer depletion
   b. application of nitrogen-containing fertilizers
   c. hunting
   d. deforestation

Short Answer

19. What is the challenge of resource management?

20. Describe the goal of maximum sustainable yield in terms of the logistic growth curve.

21. What is the goal of ecosystem-based management?

22. List six steps in the cycle of adaptive management.

23. Why do uneven-aged stands of trees offer more biodiversity?

24. What was the primary requirement of the National Forest Management Act in 1976?

25. What is a monoculture?

Critical Thinking

26. **Apply Concepts** When managing resources, do you think it is more important to focus on a specific resource or to consider the entire ecosystem of which the resource is one part? Explain.

27. **Form an Opinion** Would you support legislation that banned timber companies from logging in national forests? Explain.

28. **Explain** Why do most ecologists and foresters view tree plantations as croplands?

29. **Compare and Contrast** Explain how wildfires and prescribed burns differ.

30. **Synthesize** How does consumption relate to resource management?

Analyze Data

The graph below compares tree growth and tree removal in the United States in 2006. Private land includes that owned by timber companies, other organizations, and individuals. Use the data to answer the questions.

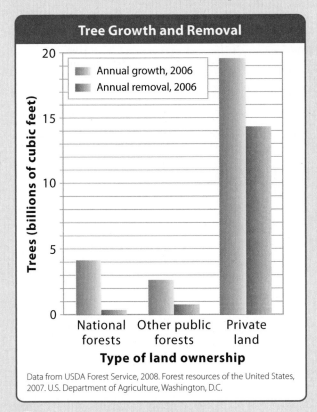

Tree Growth and Removal

Legend:
- Annual growth, 2006
- Annual removal, 2006

y-axis: Trees (billions of cubic feet)

x-axis: Type of land ownership
- National forests
- Other public forests
- Private land

Data from USDA Forest Service, 2008. Forest resources of the United States, 2007. U.S. Department of Agriculture, Washington, D.C.

GO ONLINE
- **Graph It** Forestation Change

31. Interpret Graphs From which type of land was the most timber harvested?

32. Interpret Graphs On which type of land were trees growing the fastest? (*Hint:* Find the lowest ratio of removed trees to new growth.) What was the approximate ratio of removed trees to tree growth on that type of land?

33. Draw Conclusions "Private land" includes both land owned by individuals and land owned by timber companies and other organizations. On land owned by individuals, removal greatly exceeds growth. Of the three resource management approaches, which approach would you expect is most often used on timber company land? Explain your reasoning.

Write About It

34. Persuasion Suppose that you were building a new house, and you wanted to use certified wood. A friend tries to discourage you, saying that you never know if it's really sustainably produced, and it's not worth the extra cost. How would you respond to your friend?

35. REVISIT INVESTIGATIVE PHENOMENON Sketch a new social network Web page for the Forest Service that promotes sustainable use of forest resources. Select one graph and two photographs that support your message. List at least three facts about timber. Also provide a link to Web sites with more information.

Ecological Footprints

Read the information below. Copy the table into your notebook, and record your calculations in it. Then, answer the questions that follow.

Use the data in the table along with the following data to complete the table. Total paper consumed in 2000 (millions of tons) in Asia, Europe, and Latin America was 117, 98, and 20 respectively. Recall that 1 ton is equal to 2000 pounds.

	Population in 2000 (millions)	Total paper consumed in 2000 (millions of tons)	Paper consumed per person in 2000 (pounds)
Africa	840	6	14
Asia	3766		
Europe	728		
Latin America	531		
North America	319	105	
Oceania	32	5	
World	6216	351	113

Source: Population Reference Bureau

1. How many more pounds of paper does a North American use each year compared to an African?

2. About how many tons of paper would North Americans save each year if they consumed paper at the rate of Europeans?

3. About how much paper would be consumed if everyone in the world used as much paper as the average European? As the average North American?

4. Why do you think people in other regions consume less paper, per person, than North Americans?

CHAPTER 12

Soil and Agriculture

How can we balance our growing demand for food with our need to protect the environment?

Harvesting corn
in Mexico

Lesson 1
Soil

Lesson 2
Soil Degradation
and Conservation

Lesson 3
Agriculture

Lesson 4
Food Production

Possible Transgenic Maize in Oaxaca, Mexico

CORN IS A STAPLE of the world's food supply. We can trace it back about 9000 years, when people in the present-day state of Oaxaca, Mexico, first bred wild maize plants for desirable traits. The corn we eat today resulted from their efforts. Oaxaca still grows many native varieties of maize. Preserving native varieties of crops is important for securing the future of our food supply, scientists say, because native varieties serve as sources of genetic diversity—sources we may need to sustain or advance our agriculture.

So when Mexican government scientists conducting routine tests of Oaxacan farmers' maize announced in 2001 that they had found DNA that matched genes from genetically modified (GM) corn, it caused global anxiety. How could GM corn have ended up in Mexico, where it was banned at the time? Corn is one of many crops that scientists have genetically engineered to express desirable traits, such as insect resistance or large size. To genetically engineer crops, scientists extract genes from the DNA of one organism and transfer them into the DNA of another. The transferred genes are called transgenes.

Many people are concerned that crops with transgenes might crossbreed with native crops and "contaminate" their genetic makeup. Two researchers, Ignacio Chapela and David Quist, shared these concerns, and they traveled to Oaxaca to test the native maize. Their analyses seemed to confirm the government scientists' findings, revealing what they argued were traces of DNA from GM corn in native maize plants. Quist and Chapela published their findings in November 2001.

Activists opposed to GM food immediately urged a ban on imports of transgenic crops into developing nations. The GM crop industry defended the safety of GM crops and questioned the validity of the research—as did many scientists. Further research by Mexican government scientists

GO ONLINE

• Take It Local • 3-D Geo Tour

reported that in 15 areas, 3–6 percent of maize contained transgenes, and 37 percent of maize grains distributed by the government to farmers had transgenes, but this research was never published.

In 2003 and 2004, a team of Mexican and American scientists conducted an extensive study. In 154,000 maize seeds, they had found no transgenes at all. However, studies in 2007 and 2009 found transgenes scattered throughout the area. In 2013 transgenic corn was banned from Mexico to protect the native Mexican maize varieties, although it is still imported for livestock feed and found in most human corn-based food products.

Larger, more challenging debates about the genetic modification of crops also continue. How will GM crops affect the environment? How will they affect the future of the world's food supply? Only time will tell.

Soil

EVERYDAY PHENOMENON Why does it take so long for topsoil to form?

Knowledge and Skills

- Explain three processes by which soil forms.
- Describe the horizons that make up a soil profile.
- List the four characteristics used to classify soil.

Reading Strategy and Vocabulary

✔ **Reading Strategy** Before you read, create an outline using the dark blue, green, and light blue headings in this lesson. As you read, fill in key phrases about each heading.

Vocabulary soil, parent material, bedrock, weathering, soil horizon, soil profile, clay, silt, sand, loam

WE USE ABOUT 38 percent of Earth's land surface for agriculture. Our lives depend on agriculture—we must grow most of our food and fiber. And agriculture depends on fertile soil. But what, exactly, is soil?

You might think of soil as an inconvenience—as dirt that you wash off your body and clothes. But soil is much more than dirt. It is a complex, life-filled, life-giving substance. Healthy soil is essential for agriculture, forestry, the cycles of matter, and the flow of energy that keep Earth's ecosystems running. Some soil microorganisms even provide us with medicines, such as antibiotics. **Soil** is a complex plant-supporting system made up of disintegrated rock, remains and wastes of organisms, water, gases, nutrients, and microorganisms. **Figure 1** describes several factors involved in soil formation. Soil is a renewable resource; once its nutrients are used up, it can renew itself over time. But it may take a very long time—hundreds or thousands of years for just one inch of topsoil to form. So if we deplete soil by using up all its nutrients, we ruin it not just for ourselves but for generations to come.

FIGURE 1 **Influences on Soil Formation** Soil formation processes are influenced by outside factors such as climate, organisms, landforms, parent material, and time.

\multicolumn{2}{c}{**Factors That Influence Soil Formation**}	
Factor	**Effects**
Climate	Soil forms faster in warm, wet climates. Heat speeds chemical reactions, weathering, decomposition, and growth of organisms. Moisture is required for many biological processes so it speeds weathering.
Organisms	Earthworms and other burrowing animals mix and aerate soil, add organic matter, and speed decomposition. Plants add organic matter and affect a soil's composition and structure.
Landforms	Hills and valleys affect exposure to sun, wind, and water. Steeper slopes promote runoff and erosion; they also slow leaching, accumulation of organic matter, and formation of soil layers.
Parent material	Chemical and physical attributes of parent material influence properties of the soil formed from it.
Time	Soil formation takes decades, centuries, or millennia.

Adapted from Jenny, H. 1941. *Factors of soil formation: A system of quantitative pedology.* New York: McGraw-Hill, Inc. Reprinted 1994 by Dover Publications, Mineola, New York.

Soil Formation

We often overlook the complexity of soil. Though soil is mostly broken rocks, water, and air, soil also contains a great deal of life (**Figure 2**). Soil consists of roughly 45 percent mineral matter and 5 percent organic (living or once-living) matter. Water and air in the spaces, or pores, between soil particles make up the other 50 percent. The mineral matter in soil is made up of tiny particles of rock. The organic matter includes decomposing organisms as well as living microorganisms. You might be surprised to find that one teaspoon of soil can contain millions of bacteria and thousands of fungi, algae, and protists! Soil also provides a habitat for larger animals, including hundreds of thousands of invertebrate species, amphibians, reptiles, and burrowing mammals.

As you recall, the formation of soil plays a key role in primary succession, which begins when the parent material in an area is exposed. **Parent material** is the base geological material in a particular location. It can be lava or volcanic ash; rock or sediment deposited by glaciers; sand dunes; sediments deposited by rivers, in lakes, or in the ocean; or bedrock. **Bedrock** is the continuous mass of solid rock that makes up Earth's crust. After parent material is exposed to the air, the processes that form most soils are weathering, deposition, and the decomposition of organic matter.

 Reading Checkpoint *List five different types of parent material.*

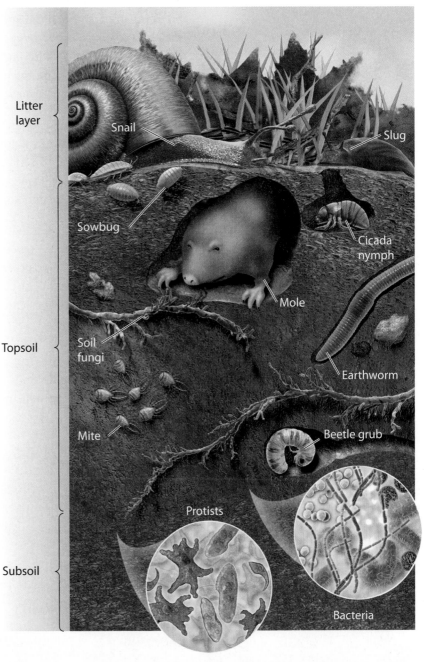

FIGURE 2 Soil Complexity Soil is a complex mixture of abiotic and biotic components, including many organisms whose actions help keep it fertile. Most soil organisms, from bacteria to fungi to insects to earthworms, decompose organic matter. Many, such as moles and earthworms, help to aerate the soil. Entire ecosystems exist in soil.

Weathering The first process in soil formation is often weathering. Weathering describes the physical and chemical processes that break down rocks and minerals into smaller particles.

▶ *Physical Weathering* Anything that touches a rock can cause *physical weathering,* which is the natural breakup of rock without a chemical change. Wind and rain are two main causes of physical weathering. Daily and seasonal temperatures also contribute to physical weathering, since parent material and rocks weaken as they repeatedly expand with heat and contract with cold. For this reason, areas with extreme temperature fluctuations undergo rapid physical weathering. Water that freezes and expands in cracks in rocks also causes physical weathering. Living things, such as a tree whose roots break up rocks as they grow, also add to physical weathering.

▶ *Chemical Weathering* When water and other substances chemically break down parent material and rocks, transforming them into different materials, *chemical weathering* is occurring. Living and once-living things also cause chemical weathering with chemical products of their life processes and decomposition, such as water and carbon dioxide. Warm, wet conditions increase chemical weathering.

Deposition Erosion is often viewed as a destructive process. But it frequently plays a part in soil formation. Erosion may help form soil in one area by depositing material eroded from another. Deposition, as you recall, is the drop-off of eroded material at a new location. You will read more about soil erosion and deposition later in this chapter.

Decomposition The activities of living things—and the decomposition of formerly living things—also help form soil. As plants, animals, and microorganisms deposit waste or die and decompose, nutrients are incorporated into the soil. Deciduous trees, for example, drop their leaves each fall. These dead leaves and other vegetation make up *leaf litter.* Leaf litter is broken down by decomposers and detritivores, and its nutrients become part of the soil. Partially decomposed organic matter is known as *humus,* a dark, spongy, crumbly mass of material made up of complex organic compounds. Soils with high humus content, such as that in **Figure 3,** hold moisture well and contain many plant nutrients.

FIGURE 3 Humus You can tell a lot about a soil's fertility just by looking at it. Very dark soil has a high proportion of humus, so it is very fertile.

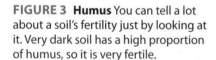

Soil Horizons

As soon as soil begins to form, wind, water, and organisms move the particles. Eventually, the soil is sorted into distinct layers, or **soil horizons.** A cross-section of all the soil horizons in a specific soil, from surface to bedrock, is known as a **soil profile.**

The simplest way to categorize soil horizons is by the A, B, and C horizons, which correspond to topsoil, subsoil, and weathered parent material, respectively. However, soil scientists often subdivide those layers. The six major soil horizons are the O, A, E, B, C, and R horizons (**Figure 4**). Soils from different locations vary, and few soil profiles contain all six of these horizons, but every soil contains at least some of them.

Topsoil A crucial horizon for agriculture and ecosystems is the A horizon, or topsoil. Topsoil consists mostly of mineral particles such as weathered parent material mixed with organic matter and humus from the O horizon. Topsoil is the horizon that has the most plant nutrients available. Its loose texture, dark color, and ability to hold water come from its humus content. The O horizon, or litter layer, and the A horizon are home to most of the countless organisms that give life to soil. For all its vitality, topsoil is fragile. Agriculture practiced carelessly can deplete the nutrients in topsoil or erode it, as you will read in the next lesson.

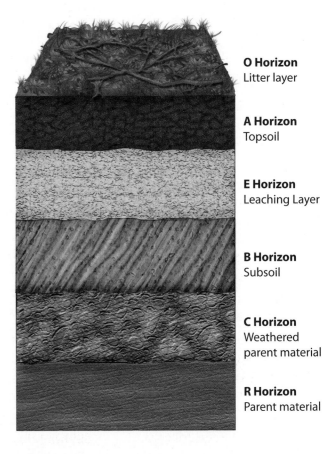

FIGURE 4 Soil Horizons Mature soil consists of horizons that have different compositions and characteristics. The surface layer is the **O horizon,** or litter layer, which consists mostly of organic matter, such as dead leaves. Below it lies the **A horizon,** or topsoil, which consists of organic matter mixed with minerals. Minerals and organic matter tend to leach out of the **E horizon** down into the **B horizon,** or subsoil, where they accumulate. The **C horizon** consists largely of weathered parent material unaltered or only slightly altered by the processes of soil formation. The C horizon may overlie an **R horizon** of parent material.

Lower Horizons Generally, as one moves downward through a soil profile, the particle size increases and the concentration of organic matter decreases. Minerals are generally transported downward as a result of *leaching,* the process whereby solid particles suspended or dissolved in liquid are transported to another location. Soil that undergoes leaching is a bit like the coffee grounds in a filter. When it rains, water filters through the soil, dissolves some soil components, and carries them downward into the lower horizons. Minerals commonly leached from the E horizon include iron, aluminum, and silicate clay. In some soils, minerals may be leached so rapidly that plants are deprived of nutrients. Substances that leach from soils may be carried into groundwater, and some can pose threats to human health.

In which horizon would you expect to find soil like that in ***Figure 3?***

Classifying Soil

1. While wearing safety gloves, collect a small handful of soil from an area chosen by your teacher.

2. Close your fist around the soil as tightly as you can. Put the clump on a sheet of white paper. Observe the speed at which the clump falls apart.

3. Using the tips of two pencils, separate some of the soil into groups of similar-sized particles.

Analyze and Conclude

1. **Observe** Describe the color of the soil.

2. **Classify** Based on particle sizes in your sample, describe the relative amounts of clay, silt, and sand. Which is most common? Would you describe your sample as loam?

3. **Classify** Given the behavior of the soil after you released it, describe its structure. (*Hint:* How clumpy was it?)

4. **Predict** How do you think a farmer would describe the soil's workability? Support your answer with your observations.

Soil Characteristics

The six horizons presented on the previous page make up a common soil profile, but soils display great variety. The characteristics of a region's soil can have as much influence on the region's ecosystems as do the climate, latitude, and elevation. U.S. soil scientists classify soils into 12 major groups, based largely on the processes that form the soils. Scientists further classify soils using properties such as color, texture, structure, and pH.

Color The color of a soil reveals details about its composition and fertility. Dark soils are usually rich in humus and therefore nutrients, whereas pale soils often have less humus and nutrients. Long before scientific tests of soil content were developed, farmers and ranchers often used the color of topsoil as an indicator of a soil's fertility.

Texture Soil texture is based on particle size (**Figure 5**). **Clay** consists of particles less than 0.002 millimeter in diameter, **silt** consists of particles 0.002 to 0.05 millimeter in diameter, and **sand** consists mostly of particles 0.05 to 2 millimeters in diameter. Sand particles are large enough to see individually and do not adhere to one another. Clay particles, in contrast, adhere easily to one another. Most soils are a combination of clay, silt, and sand. Soil with a relatively even mixture of the three particle sizes is known as **loam**.

FIGURE 5 Classifying Soil Texture Scientists use this triangular diagram to classify soil texture. After determining the percentages of sand, silt, and clay particles in a soil sample, you can trace a line inward from each side of the triangle: horizontal for clay, diagonally downward for silt, and diagonally upward to the left for sand. The intersection of the lines reveals the soil texture.

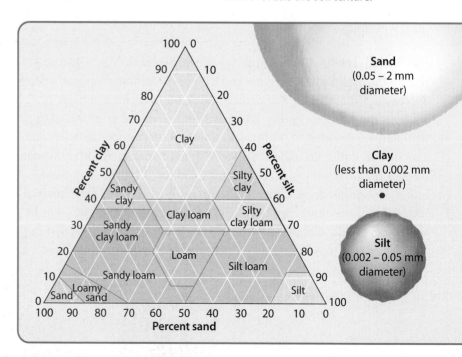

Soil texture influences a soil's *workability*—essentially, how easy it is to plant in and harvest from. Soil texture also indicates how porous a soil is, or the size of the spaces between its particles. In general, the finer the particles, the smaller the spaces and the harder it is for water and air to travel through the soil to roots and soil-nourishing microorganisms. Clay has the finest particles, so it is the least porous soil. Sandy soils are the most porous. Silty soils with medium-sized pores, or loamy soils with a mixture of pore sizes, are generally best for plant growth.

Reading Checkpoint *Using **Figure 5**, classify the texture of a soil that is 40 percent sand, 40 percent silt, and 20 percent clay.*

Structure Soil structure describes the arrangement of soil particles. You can see it in the "clumpiness" of soil. Clumpy soil may have a great deal of humus, indicating that the soil is rich in nutrients and able to hold water. However, soil clumps that become too large or densely compacted, from heavy equipment (**Figure 6**) or grazing cattle, for example, can prevent plant roots from growing.

pH A soil's acidity or alkalinity affects its ability to support plant growth. Different plants require different pH levels, and plants die in soils that are too acidic or alkaline for them. Soil pH varies naturally, but acid precipitation and the subsequent leaching of minerals from the soil can also affect the pH of soil. Few plants can grow in extremely acidic or alkaline soil.

FIGURE 6 Compacted Soil Clumpy soil with a great deal of humus is good for most plants. However, clumpy soil can easily become compacted—by heavy machinery, as in this photo, or by animals. Compacted soil may be too dense for plants to grow in.

LESSON 1 Assessment

1. **Explain** Describe three major processes that contribute to the formation of most soils.
2. **Review** What is a soil profile? Describe the A, B, and C horizons.
3. **Classify** What do each of the four characteristics of soil indicate about its ability to support plant life?
4. **THINK IT** *THROUGH* Recall the analogy between soil and coffee grounds in the section called "Lower Horizons." In this analogy, what do you think the "soil coffee" consists of?

Soil Degradation and Conservation

EVERYDAY PHENOMENON How can erosion be both helpful and harmful to soil formation?

Knowledge and Skills

- Describe some practices that can lead to soil erosion and some that can prevent it.
- Identify the causes and effects of desertification.
- Discuss the activities of U.S. and international agricultural organizations.
- Explain how irrigation and pesticide use can cause soil pollution.

Reading Strategy and Vocabulary

✔ **Reading Strategy** Before you read, preview **Figure 7.** As you read the photo captions, take notes on how each method helps to conserve soil.

Vocabulary soil degradation, intercropping, crop rotation, cover crop, shelterbelt, tilling, terracing, contour farming, overgrazing, desertification, irrigation, salinization, pesticide.

SCIENTISTS' STUDIES and the experiences of farmers have shown that the most *productive* soil, or the type of soil most plants grow best in, is loam with a neutral pH that is workable, contains nutrients, and holds water. Human activities can cause erosion, desertification, and pollution and make soil less productive. The deterioration of the soil characteristics needed for plant growth or other ecosystem services is called **soil degradation.** Soil degradation results in major ecosystem changes. It also makes farming more challenging, so it could make it more difficult to feed Earth's growing human population in the future.

Erosion

Erosion and deposition are natural processes that, in the long run, can help create soil. Flowing water can deposit sediment eroded from other areas into river valleys and deltas, producing rich and productive soils. This is why floodplains are excellent for farming and why preventing floods can decrease long-term farming productivity. But erosion can be a problem because it usually occurs much more quickly than soil is formed. Furthermore, erosion tends to remove topsoil, the most fertile soil layer. And erosion can be gradual and hard to detect. In many parts of the world now, scientists and farmers are carefully measuring soil depth in hopes of identifying areas in danger of serious erosion before they become too badly damaged.

Today, human activities cause more erosion than natural events. More than 19 billion hectares (47 billion acres) of the world's croplands now suffer from erosion and other forms of soil degradation resulting from human activities. People make fertile soils vulnerable to erosion in several ways, including leaving soil bare after harvests, overgrazing rangelands, and clearing forests on steep slopes or with large clear-cuts.

Farming Practices Plant communities, including crops, protect soil from erosion. Plants slow wind and water, and their roots hold soil in place and absorb water. After fields are harvested, and there is no plant cover protecting the soil, wind and water can erode soil, especially if the land is sloped. Erosion rates in the United States are now declining, thanks to soil conservation measures such as those in **Figure 7.**

FIGURE 7 Soil Conservation Techniques

Intercropping

Intercropping is the planting of different crops in mixed arrangements. Intercropping helps slow erosion by providing more plant cover than a single crop does. Intercropping also reduces a field's vulnerability to insects and disease that specialize in certain crops because different crops are planted in the same field. When a nitrogen-fixing crop is planted, intercropping can also replenish the soil's fertility.

Crop Rotation

In **crop rotation,** farmers alternate crops grown in a field. Crop rotation can return nutrients to the soil, break disease and pest cycles, and prevent the erosion that can come from letting fields lie fallow, or unplanted. In a practice similar to crop rotation, farmers plant crops to reduce erosion after a field has been harvested and before the next season's planting. These **cover crops** help prevent erosion and often limit nitrogen loss, because they are often nitrogen-fixing crops such as alfalfa.

Shelterbelts

A widespread technique for reducing wind erosion is to establish **shelterbelts,** or *windbreaks*. These are rows of trees or other tall, perennial plants that are planted along the edges of fields to slow the wind. Fast-growing trees such as poplars are often used in shelterbelts.

Conservation Tillage

Tilling is the turning-over of soil before planting. It creates more pores for air and water but makes soil more susceptible to erosion. To help conserve soil, farmers use no-till or reduced tillage methods. To plant using the *no-till method*, a tractor pulls a drill that cuts furrows through weeds and crop remains and into the topsoil. Seeds and fertilizer are dropped into the furrows, and they are closed. *Reduced-tillage* agriculture disturbs the soil surface slightly more than no-till does. By maintaining organic matter in soil, these techniques can improve soil quality and reduce erosion. They, however, often require substantial use of weed-killers (because weeds remain in fields) and fertilizers (because weeds use soil nutrients).

Terracing

Terracing minimizes erosion on steep hillsides. **Terracing** transforms steep slopes into a series of steps like a staircase, enabling farmers to cultivate slopes without losing huge amounts of soil to water erosion. Terracing is labor-intensive but is probably the only sustainable way to farm mountains.

Contour Farming

Water running down a hillside erodes soil. Contour farming reduces erosion on gently sloping hillsides. **Contour farming** consists of plowing sideways across a hillside, perpendicular to the hill's slope. The plowed furrows follow the contours of the land, and the downhill side of each furrow acts as a dam that catches soil before it is carried away.

Ranching Practices The raising and grazing of *livestock,* animals raised to be used on a farm or sold at a profit, also affects soils and ecosystems. When sheep, goats, cattle, or other livestock graze on open rangelands, they feed primarily on grasses. As long as livestock populations stay within a range's carrying capacity and do not eat grasses faster than the grasses can grow back, grazing may be sustainable. However, when too many animals eat too much of the plant cover, impeding regrowth, the result is **overgrazing**.

▶ *Effects of Overgrazing* Rangeland scientists have shown that overgrazing causes or aggravates several soil problems. Some of these problems give rise to positive feedback cycles that increase damage to soils, natural communities, and the land's productivity (**Figure 8**). When livestock remove too much plant cover, more soil is exposed and made vulnerable to erosion. Soil erosion makes it difficult for vegetation to regrow, allowing yet more erosion. Moreover, non-native weedy plants may invade exposed soils. Livestock often avoid tough non-native plants, leaving the plants to reproduce and outcompete the native plants the livestock eat, further decreasing useful grazing land.

Reading Checkpoint *According to the flowchart in **Figure 8,** which problems does overgrazing directly cause?*

FIGURE 8 Overgrazing In the flowchart below, you can see how overgrazing can set in motion a positive feedback cycle that degrades soils and ecosystems. The effects of overgrazing can be dramatic, as shown in this photo along a fence line separating a grassy, ungrazed plot (left) from a shrubby, overgrazed plot (right).

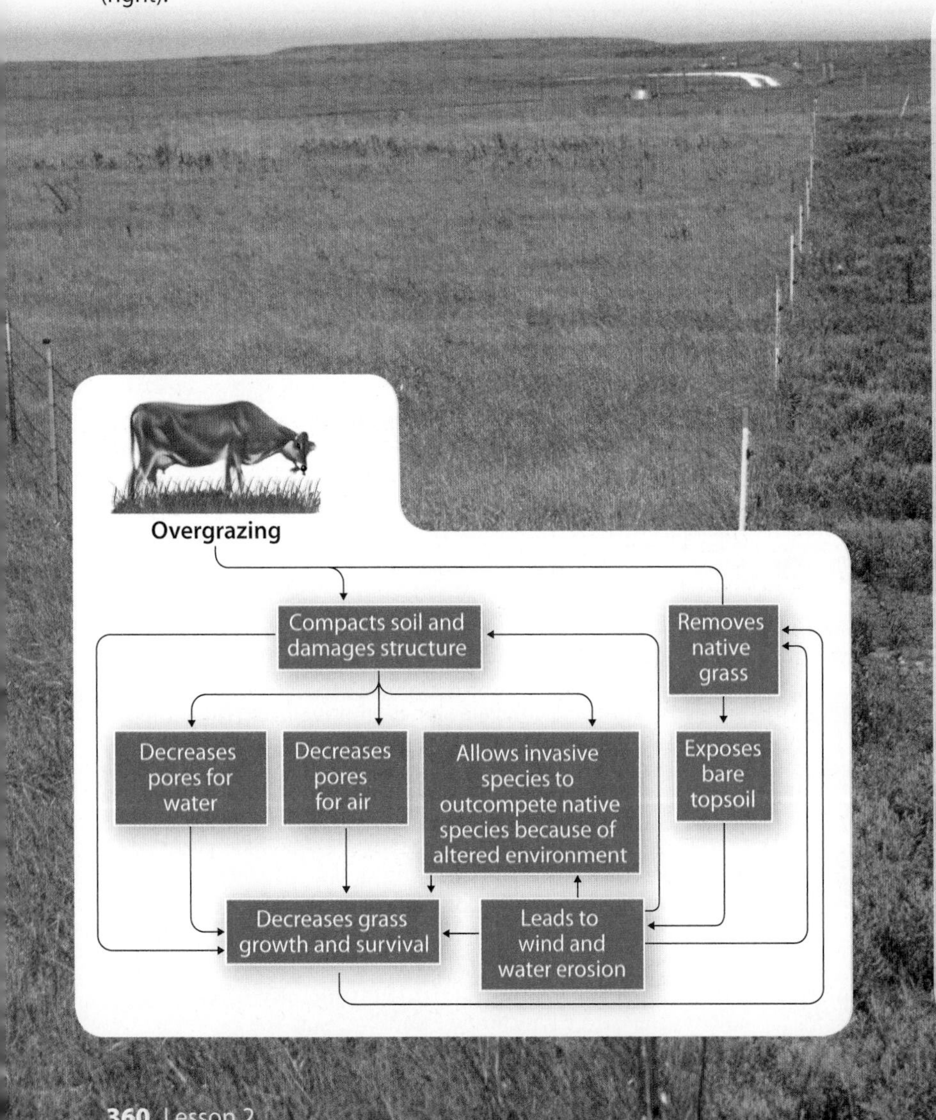

Overgrazing

Compacts soil and damages structure

Decreases pores for water

Decreases pores for air

Allows invasive species to outcompete native species because of altered environment

Removes native grass

Exposes bare topsoil

Decreases grass growth and survival

Leads to wind and water erosion

▶ *Prevention of Overgrazing* Range managers in the United States do their best to assess the carrying capacity of rangelands. They inform ranchers, or livestock owners, of the limits so that they rotate their herds from site to site.

Range managers also can establish and enforce grazing limits on publicly owned land. U.S. ranchers have traditionally had little incentive to limit grazing, since most of their grazing has taken place on public lands leased from the government, not on their own lands. The U.S. government has also heavily subsidized grazing. These two situations have led to extensive overgrazing and resulting environmental problems on many public lands in the American West. Today, however, increasing numbers of ranchers are working cooperatively with government agencies, environmental scientists, and even environmental advocates to find ways to graze their animals more sustainably and safeguard the health of grasslands.

Forestry Practices Forestry can also have substantial impacts on soils. Forestry practices have been altered over the years to try to minimize damage to soils, as you may recall. Nevertheless, some current methods, such as clear-cutting, can lead to severe erosion, particularly on steep slopes. Other logging methods, such as selective systems, tend to lead to less erosion.

Desertification

Soil degradation is especially severe in arid environments, where desertification is a concern. **Desertification** is a loss of more than 10 percent of productivity due to erosion, soil compaction, forest removal, overgrazing, drought, salt buildup, climate change, depletion of water sources, and other factors. Severe desertification can enlarge existing deserts and create new ones in once-fertile regions. This process has occurred in areas of the Middle East that have been inhabited, farmed, and grazed for thousands of years—including the Fertile Crescent region, where agriculture began more than 10,000 years ago. The Fertile Crescent is not so fertile anymore.

Arid and semiarid lands are prone to desertification because they get too little precipitation to meet growing human demands for water. Declines in soil quality in these areas have endangered the food supply and the well-being of more than 1 billion people. In the affected lands, most degradation has been caused by wind and water erosion, as you can see in **Figure 9**.

Global Desertification By some estimates, desertification affects one third of Earth's land area, costing people tens of billions of dollars in crop income each year. China alone loses $6.5 billion annually from desertification. In the western parts of China, desert areas are expanding and combining because of overgrazing from more than 400 million goats, sheep, and cattle. In Kenya, overgrazing and deforestation fueled by rapid population growth has left 80 percent of the land vulnerable to desertification. In an ever-intensifying cycle, soil degradation forces ranchers to crowd their animals onto less-productive land and farmers to keep planting in poor soils, both of which worsen desertification.

A United Nations report estimated that desertification, worsened by climate change, could displace 135 million people by 2045. The report suggested that industrialized nations fund reforestation projects in dryland areas of the developing world. This would slow desertification while gaining these nations carbon credits in emissions trading programs. It would be worth their cost and effort: Desertification knows no national boundaries. In recent years, gigantic dust storms from desertified land in China have blown across the Pacific Ocean to North America, and dust storms from Africa's Sahara have blown across the Atlantic Ocean to the Caribbean Sea.

✔ Reading Checkpoint *List five possible causes of desertification.*

FIGURE 9 Soil Degradation Soil degradation on drylands is due primarily to erosion by wind and water. (Percentages add up to more than 100 percent because of rounding.)

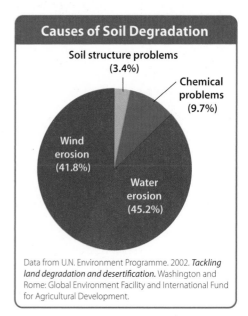

Causes of Soil Degradation

Soil structure problems (3.4%)

Chemical problems (9.7%)

Wind erosion (41.8%)

Water erosion (45.2%)

Data from U.N. Environment Programme. 2002. *Tackling land degradation and desertification.* Washington and Rome: Global Environment Facility and International Fund for Agricultural Development.

FIGURE 10 Dust Bowl In the 1930s, drought combined with poor agricultural practices brought devastation to millions of U.S. farmers in the southern Great Plains. The photo shows towering clouds of dust approaching houses near Stratford, Texas, in a 1935 dust storm. The map shows the Dust Bowl region, with darker colors indicating the areas most affected.

The Dust Bowl Massive dust storms have also occurred in the United States. During the Dust Bowl of the 1930s, desertification shook American agriculture and society as a whole to their very roots.

Prior to large-scale farming on North America's Great Plains, the native prairie grasses there held the soil in place. In the late 1800s and early 1900s, many settlers arrived in Oklahoma, Texas, Kansas, New Mexico, and Colorado hoping to make a living as farmers. Fertile soil formed over many years led the migration. Between 1879 and 1929, the farmed area of the Great Plains increased by 700 percent. Farmers grew abundant wheat, and ranchers grazed thousands of cattle, sometimes on unsuitable land where rainfall was less plentiful. Both types of agriculture contributed to erosion by removing the grasses that had conserved the soil and by breaking down the soil structure.

Then in the early 1930s, a drought occurred, aggravating that erosion. The region's strong winds began to erode millions of tons of topsoil, which would blow around in huge dust clouds **(Figure 10).** Dust storms traveled up to 2000 kilometers (1200 miles) across the continent, blackening rain and snow as far away as New York. Some areas lost as much as 10 centimeters (4 inches) of topsoil in a few years. The most-affected region, the southern Great Plains, became known as the Dust Bowl, a term now also used for the event itself. The Dust Bowl forced thousands of farmers off their land. The land that once had brought an influx of settlers now became a hazard that drove a mass emigration.

Soil Conservation Policies

In response to the devastation of the Dust Bowl, the U.S. government, along with state and local governments, increased support for soil conservation research. In the United States, the Natural Resources Conservation Service works through county conservation districts to promote soil conservation and conservation of other natural resources. Various United Nations programs have similar responsibilities elsewhere.

U.S. Policies In 1935, the U.S. Congress passed the Soil Conservation Act, establishing the Soil Conservation Service (SCS). The SCS began to work with farmers to develop conservation plans for their farms.

In 1994, the SCS was renamed the Natural Resources Conservation Service, and its responsibilities were expanded to include water quality protection and pollution control. The U.S. Congress has also enacted provisions promoting soil conservation through the farm bills it passes every 5 to 6 years. Many of these provisions require farmers to adopt soil conservation plans before they can receive government subsidies. The Conservation Reserve Program (CRP), established in the 1985 farm bill, pays farmers to stop cultivating cropland that erodes easily and to instead place it in conservation reserves planted with grasses and trees. Land under the CRP now covers over 22 million acres, and the U.S. Department of Agriculture (USDA) estimates that each dollar invested in this program saves nearly 1 ton of topsoil. Besides reducing erosion, the CRP generates income for farmers, improves water quality, and provides habitat for wildlife. The CRP marked 35 years of successes, including erosion protection and wetland restoration, in 2020.

International Programs Internationally, the United Nations promotes soil conservation and sustainable agriculture through its Food and Agriculture Organization (FAO). The FAO's Farmer-Centered Agricultural Resource Management Program (FARM) supports creative approaches to resource management challenges in many developing nations. Rather than relying on government control of farming practices, FARM calls upon local leaders to educate and encourage local farmers.

Soil Pollution

Erosion is not the only threat to the health of soils. You might think that watering crops and protecting them from pests would improve soil health, but that is not always the case.

Irrigation The providing of water other than precipitation to crops is known as **irrigation.** Some crops, such as rice and cotton, require large amounts of water, whereas others, such as beans and wheat, require relatively little. By irrigating crops, people have managed to turn previously dry and unproductive regions into fertile farmland.

▶ *Salinization Causes* Irrigation is not without consequences. Too much, or carelessly timed, irrigation can result in waterlogged crops. A more frequent problem is **salinization,** the buildup of salts in upper soil horizons. In dry areas where precipitation is minimal and evaporation rates are high, water evaporating from the soil's A horizon may pull water up from lower horizons by capillary action. As this water rises through the soil, it carries dissolved salts. When the water evaporates at the surface, those salts remain, as you can see in **Figure 11.** Irrigation water also usually contains some dissolved salts, so it adds salt to the soil, increasing the salinization.

FIGURE 11 Salinization In this cross-section of salinized soil, the white crust is salt.

▶ **Salinization Solutions** Salinization currently decreases harvests on 20 percent of all irrigated cropland worldwide, costing farmers $11 billion in crop income each year, so it is a very expensive problem. And it is easier to prevent than to correct. The best way to prevent salinization is to avoid planting crops that require a great deal of water in dry areas. A second way is to irrigate with water that is low in salt content. A third way is to irrigate efficiently, supplying no more water than the crop requires and supplying it as close to the roots as possible. Drip irrigation systems that target water directly at plant roots are one option. Less water evaporates, which means less salt accumulates in the topsoil. Drip irrigation also conserves water and dramatically decreases erosion.

It might seem that the remedy is to stop irrigating and wait for rain to flush salts from the soil. But remember where irrigation is needed. Salinization generally becomes a problem only in dry areas where precipitation is too little to even water crops, never mind to flush salt from the soil. A better option is to plant salt-tolerant plants, such as barley, that can be used as food or pasture. Another option is to bring in large quantities of less-salty water with which to flush the soil. However, too much water can waterlog crops and wash out soil nutrients.

Pesticides Chemicals that kill organisms that attack or compete with plants we value are called **pesticides.** Pesticides may kill plant, animal, fungal, bacterial, or viral pests. (Chemicals that kill other plants are sometimes called *herbicides*.) Some pesticides are toxic to humans. Toxic pesticides and the chemicals they break down into may remain in soil for long periods of time, basically poisoning it. And they can filter through the soil into the groundwater and evaporate into the air. Although pesticides may increase the amount of a crop produced in a given area in the short term, they can be hazardous to humans and other animals in the long term. And broad-spectrum pesticides kill a wide variety of insects, some of which may be helpful to soil. So pesticides can be hazardous to soil health as well. You will read more about pesticides in the next lesson.

LESSON 2 Assessment

1. **Review** Describe one farming practice that can erode soil and one farming practice that can conserve soil.

2. **Relate Cause and Effect** Explain how overgrazing and planting in poor soil can cause a cycle of desertification.

3. **Communicate** In your own words, write one paragraph about the effects of the Conservation Reserve Program.

4. **Explain** How can irrigation and pesticides cause soil pollution?

5. **THINK IT** *THROUGH* You are a land manager with the U.S. Bureau of Land Management and have just been put in charge of 200,000 hectares (500,000 acres) of public lands that have been degraded by decades of overgrazing and poor management. Soil is eroding. Invasive weeds are replacing native grasses. Environmentalists want to end grazing on the land. Ranchers want grazing to continue, but they are concerned about the land's condition. How would you assess the land's condition and begin restoring its soil and vegetation? Would you allow grazing, and if so, would you set limits on it?

Agriculture

EVERYDAY PHENOMENON What are the benefits and environmental consequences of industrial farming?

Knowledge and Skills

- Discuss the beginnings of agriculture.
- Explain the importance of industrial agriculture and the green revolution.
- Identify different types of pest control.
- Explain the importance of pollinators to agriculture.

Reading Strategy and Vocabulary

✓ **Reading Strategy** As you read, fill in a main idea and details chart. List the main ideas of the lesson in the left column. In the right column, note important details about each main idea.

Vocabulary traditional agriculture, yield, industrial agriculture, green revolution, biological pest control, integrated pest management (IPM), pollinator

CAN YOU IMAGINE having to hunt and gather your own food every day? Can you imagine life without cotton? That was life 15,000 years ago. Agriculture arose only about 10,000 years ago. Many aspects of human civilization began about the same time. That is probably not a coincidence. Walking around all day hunting and gathering didn't leave much time for creating art or new technology!

Development of Agriculture

Everything you eat and all the natural fabrics you wear are products of agriculture. If you don't run a farm, you rely on people who do. But agriculture is a relatively new development in human history.

During most of the human species' 200,000-year existence, we have been hunter-gatherers, depending on wild plants and animals for our food and fiber. Then about 10,000 years ago, the climate warmed following an ice age. In the warmer climate, plants grew better. People in the Middle East, China, and other areas began to grow plants from seed and to raise animals.

Agriculture probably began when hunter-gatherers brought wild fruits, grains, and nuts back to their camps. Some of these foods fell to the ground, were thrown away, or were eaten but had seeds that passed through someone's digestive system. The plants that grew from these seeds likely produced fruits larger and tastier than most, because they came from seeds of fruits that people had selected. As these plants bred with others nearby that shared those characteristics, they produced new generations of plants with large and tasty fruits. You can see more details of the evolution of agriculture in **Figure 13** on the next page.

FIGURE 12 Early Farming Tools
The blades in this photo were used to harvest crops about 5000 years ago.

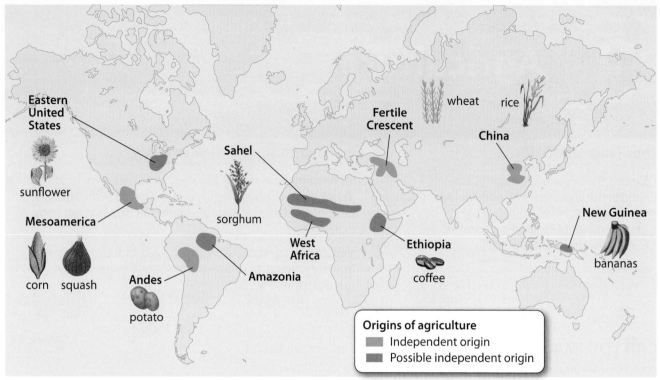

Data from syntheses in Diamond, J. 1997. *Guns, germs, and steel.* New York: W.W. Norton; and Goudie, A. 2000. *The human impact,* 5th ed. Cambridge, MA: MIT Press.

FIGURE 13 **Beginnings of Agriculture** Agriculture originated independently in multiple locations as different cultures selectively bred plants and animals from wild species. Areas where people are thought to have invented agriculture independently are colored green. In areas colored blue, it is not known whether people invented agriculture independently or adopted it from other cultures. The map also shows a few of the crops farmed in each region.

Map it

Origins of Agriculture

The earliest widely accepted evidence of agriculture is from the Fertile Crescent region of the Middle East. Refer to **Figure 13** as you answer the questions that follow.

1. **Interpret Maps** According to the map, in what four areas did agriculture most likely arise independently?

2. **Interpret Maps** In which part of the world were coffee crops first planted?

3. **Infer** Two large rivers, the Tigris and Euphrates, run through the Fertile Crescent. How did those rivers help make it a good place for agriculture?

Selective Breeding and Settlement Eventually, people realized they could control what they grew. Our ancestors then began planting seeds only from those plants whose fruit they liked the most. These were the beginnings of artificial selection, or *selective breeding.* Selective breeding has resulted in all the food crops and livestock that feed you every day.

Once our ancestors learned to cultivate crops, they began to build more permanent settlements, often near water sources. The need to harvest their crops kept them settled, and once they were settled, it made sense to plant more crops. They also began to raise animals as livestock. Increased populations resulted from settlement and more-reliable food supply and reinforced the need for both. Eventually, the ability to grow excess food enabled some people to live away from the farm, leading to the development of professional specialties, commerce, technology, cities, social classes, and political organization. Agriculture ultimately brought us the civilization we know today.

Traditional Agriculture Until the Industrial Revolution of the 1800s, the work of cultivating, harvesting, storing, and distributing crops everywhere was performed by human and animal muscle power, along with hand tools and non-motorized machines such as plows. This biologically powered agriculture is known as **traditional agriculture.** Traditional agriculture may use teams of worker animals and use irrigation and organic fertilizer, but it does not require fossil fuels.

Industrial Agriculture

The Industrial Revolution introduced large-scale mechanization and fossil-fuel engines to agriculture just as it did to industry. Farmers could replace their horses and oxen with faster, more powerful, and more efficient means of harvesting, processing, and transporting crops.

In addition to the efficient farm machinery that resulted from the Industrial Revolution, other changes to agriculture came in the mid-1900s. Many of these were reactions to the Dust Bowl of the 1930s and/or based on wartime technology. There were irrigation improvements and the introduction of synthetic fertilizers. There was also the introduction of chemical pesticides, which reduced competition from weeds and the loss of crops to pests. Because the soil was more productive, and fewer crops were lost to pests, yield increased. **Yield** is the amount of a crop produced in a given area.

The Rise of Industrial Agriculture Mechanized farming technology, the fossil fuels it runs on, manufactured chemicals, and irrigation all allow for **industrial agriculture.** Industrial agriculture produces huge amounts of crops and livestock. It is also known as *high-input agriculture* because it relies on people to "put in" enormous quantities of energy, water, and chemicals. Today, industrial agriculture is practiced on more than 25 percent of the world's croplands and on most of the croplands in the United States.

Because it uses large machinery and chemicals that are customized for a specific crop, to be most efficient, industrial agriculture requires that large areas be planted with a single crop, in a *monoculture*. You can see a monoculture in **Figure 14.** The planting of crops in monocultures makes planting and harvesting more efficient and can thereby increase harvests. However, monocultures have drawbacks as well. Large monocultures reduce biodiversity over large areas, because far fewer wild organisms are able to live in monocultures than in their native habitats or in more-diverse plantings. Moreover, because all the plants in a monoculture are genetically similar, they are vulnerable to the same diseases and pests. For this reason, monocultures carry the risk of catastrophic crop failure.

 Reading Checkpoint *Describe one advantage and one disadvantage of a monoculture.*

FIGURE 14 Monoculture Most crop production in developed nations comes from monocultures such as this cornfield in Texas. Planting crops in large, uniform fields greatly improves the efficiency of planting and harvesting. Unfortunately, it also decreases biodiversity and makes crops susceptible to pests that have adapted to feed on that crop.

FIGURE 15 The Green Revolution
Norman Borlaug, the "Father of the Green Revolution," holds the wheat variety he bred that launched the green revolution. The high-yielding, disease-resistant wheat saved many people in developing nations from starvation.

The Green Revolution In the mid- to late 1900s, the desire for more and better food for the world's growing population led to the **green revolution,** in which agricultural scientists from developed nations introduced new technology, crop varieties, and farming practices to the developing world. (*Green* in this context implies "covered with plants" rather than "environmentally friendly.")

▶ *Technology* The technology sharing began in the 1940s, when U.S. scientist Norman Borlaug introduced Mexico's farmers to a specially bred strain of wheat **(Figure 15).** It produced large seed heads, was short enough to avoid wind damage, resisted diseases, and produced high yields. Within two decades Mexico had tripled its wheat production—in fact, it had surplus wheat it could export. Soon many developing nations were increasing their crop yields using selectively bred strains of wheat, rice, corn, and other crops from developed nations.

Along with new strains of crops, developing nations also imported new methods of industrial agriculture from developed nations. Developing nations began applying large amounts of synthetic fertilizers and chemical pesticides on their fields, liberally irrigating crops, and using heavy equipment powered by fossil fuels. Intensive agriculture of this sort saved millions in India and Pakistan from starvation in the 1970s and eventually turned these nations into net exporters of grain.

▶ *Environmental Effects* The green revolution has saved millions of lives. Its technology comes at a high energy cost, however. Between 1900 and 2008, the energy used by agriculture increased by 7000 percent! On the positive side, the higher productivity of already-cultivated land preserved some ecosystems, because less additional land needed to be cleared for crops. Global cereal grain yields have grown 280 percent from 1961 values; much faster than global population increase of 136 percent. Also, in 2014, only 30% of the land area was needed to grow the same amount of crops that were grown in 1961. So the green revolution has prevented some deforestation and habitat loss and preserved the biodiversity of some ecosystems.

On the negative side, the intensive application of water, inorganic fertilizers, and pesticides has worsened erosion, salinization, desertification, eutrophication, and pollution. In addition, the use of fossil fuels to produce fertilizer and pesticides and to run farm equipment has increased air pollution and contributed to global warming. So the green revolution has saved human lives, but there have been environmental costs. The need to maintain this life-saving productivity while limiting environmental damage has led to attempts at more-sustainable agriculture. You will read more about these in the next lesson.

 Reading Checkpoint   *Describe the green revolution in your own words.*

Pests

What are pests? What are weeds? We call an organism a *pest* when it damages plants that are valuable to us, such as crops. We call a plant a *weed* when it competes with our plants. As you see, these are subjective terms based on our economic interests. Since the beginnings of agriculture, the pests that eat our crops and the weeds that compete with them have taken advantage of the ways we cluster plants in agricultural fields. In a monoculture, a population of a pest adapted to that plant can chew through entire fields. From the viewpoint of a pest adapted to feed on corn, for example, a cornfield is an all-you-can-eat buffet.

Chemical Pesticides To prevent crop losses from pests and weeds, people have developed thousands of chemical pesticides. Roughly 400 million kilograms (900 million pounds) of active ingredients from conventional pesticides are applied in the United States each year. Three quarters of this amount is applied on agricultural land. Since 1960, pesticide use has risen fourfold worldwide. Usage in developed nations has leveled off in the past two decades, but it continues to rise in the developing world.

The ability of a pesticide to reduce a pest population often declines over time as the population evolves resistance to it. Recall that natural selection occurs within populations when individuals vary in their traits. Because the populations of insects and microorganisms in farm fields are huge, it is likely that some individuals have genes that give them immunity to a given pesticide. So even if a pesticide application kills 99.99 percent of the insects in a field, 1 in 10,000 survives. If an insect survives because it is genetically resistant to a pesticide and it passes the resistance trait to its offspring, the trait will become more common in the population. As a larger and larger proportion of the insects in the population become resistant to the pesticide, the chemical becomes less and less effective on that population. As a result, industrial chemists are caught up in an "evolutionary arms race" with the pests they battle, racing to increase the toxicity of pesticides while the pests continue to develop resistance.

Biological Pest Control Because of pesticide resistance and health risks from some pesticides, agricultural scientists increasingly battle pests and weeds with organisms that eat or infect them. This strategy is called biological pest control. For example, parasitoid wasps are natural enemies of many caterpillars. These wasps lay eggs on a caterpillar. The larvae that hatch from the eggs feed on the caterpillar, eventually killing it (**Figure 16**). Some successful biological pest control efforts have led to steep reductions in pesticide use.

FIGURE 16 Biological Pest Control Tomato hornworms are large caterpillars that can destroy a tomato crop very quickly. Here you can see the small white eggs of a parasitoid wasp on a hornworm. When the eggs hatch, the larvae will feed on the caterpillar until it dies—possibly saving a tomato plant!

▶ **Bt** A widespread modern biological pest control effort is the use of *Bacillus thuringiensis (Bt)*. *Bt* is a naturally occurring soil bacterium that produces a protein that kills many caterpillars and the larvae of some flies and beetles. Farmers have used the natural pesticidal activity of this bacterium to their advantage by spraying spores of it on their crops. When used correctly, *Bt* can protect crops from pest-related losses.

▶ *Introduced Predators and Parasites* In some cases, biological pest control requires the introduction of an organism from a different ecosystem. Unfortunately, this means that no one can know for certain in advance what effects the biological pest control organism might have. In some cases, biological pest control organisms have become invasive and harmed nontarget organisms—organisms other than the pests.

▶ *Benefits and Costs* If biological pest control works as planned, it can be a permanent solution that requires no maintenance and is environmentally harmless. However, like all invasive species, invasive biological pest control organisms can have wide-ranging ecological and economic impacts, as did the cactus moth in **Figure 17.** And if nontarget organisms are harmed, the damage may be permanent because halting biological pest control is far more difficult than stopping the application of a pesticide. Because of such concerns, researchers study biological pest control proposals carefully before putting them into action, and government regulators must approve those proposals. But there is never a surefire way of knowing in advance whether a biological pest control program will work as planned.

✔ **Reading Checkpoint** *What is one risk of introducing a predator or parasite from a different ecosystem?*

FIGURE 17 Risks of Biological Pest Control Cactus moth larvae eat the pads of prickly pear cactus. The story of the cactus moth is one of both great success and environmental destruction. The cactus moth was imported from Argentina to Australia in the 1920s to control prickly pear cactus that was invading rangeland. Within just a few years, millions of hectares of rangeland were free of the cactus. Following the cactus moth's success in Australia, it was introduced in other nations. Unfortunately, cactus moths introduced to Caribbean islands spread to Florida and ate many rare native cacti there. If these moths spread to Mexico and the southwestern United States, they could destroy the many native and economically important species of prickly pear there. Biologist Colothdian Tate (inset) has worked to prevent this ecological disaster.

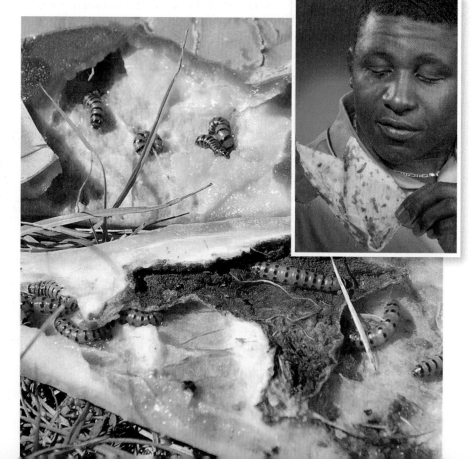

Integrated Pest Management Because both chemical and biological pest control approaches have their drawbacks, agricultural scientists and farmers have developed more-complex strategies that combine the most-useful aspects of each. In **integrated pest management (IPM),** different techniques are combined to achieve the most effective long-term pest reduction. IPM may include biological pest control, close monitoring of populations, habitat alteration, crop rotation, reduced soil tillage, mechanical pest removal, and chemical pesticides.

In recent decades, IPM has become popular in many parts of the world. Indonesia is an important example. Indonesia's government had financially supported chemical pesticide use for years, but its scientists came to understand that the pesticides were actually making the pest problems worse. Pesticides were killing the natural predators of the brown plant-hopper, an insect that devastated rice fields as its population exploded. Concluding that supporting pesticide use was costing money, causing pollution, and decreasing yields, in 1986, the Indonesian government acted. It banned imports of 57 pesticides, slashed financial support for pesticide use, and encouraged IPM. Within four years, Indonesia's pesticide production fell to less than half its 1986 level, pesticide imports fell to one third, and financial support for them was phased out, saving $179 million annually. After these actions, rice yields rose 13 percent.

Pollinators

Pests are such a major problem in agriculture that it is easy to fall into a habit of thinking of all insects as destructive. But in fact, most insects are harmless to agriculture, and some are essential.

Pollination *Pollination* is the process by which male sex cells of a plant (pollen) fertilize female sex cells of a plant. Without pollination, plants cannot reproduce sexually. Plants such as conifer trees and grasses are pollinated by pollen grains carried on the wind. These plants are fertilized when, by chance, pollen grains land on the female parts of other plants of their species. Plants with showy flowers, however, are typically pollinated by animals, such as insects, hummingbirds, and bats. These animals are called **pollinators.** Pollinators are among the most vital, yet least appreciated, factors in agriculture. When pollinators feed on flower nectar, they collect pollen on their bodies and take it to the next flower, which might then be fertilized.

Our important grain crops, such as corn and wheat, are wind-pollinated, but many other crops, such as fruits, depend on insects for pollination (**Figure 18**). The most complete survey to date lists 800 species of cultivated plants that rely on bees and other insects for pollination.

FIGURE 18 Pollinators Many agricultural crops depend on insects to pollinate them. Our food supply, therefore, depends partly on conservation of these vital animals. Flowers such as these apple blossoms have shapes and sweet scents that advertise nectar to pollinators such as honeybees.

FIGURE 19 Pollinator-Safe Gardening
Japanese beetles can destroy rosebushes very quickly. The canister (inset) contains a pheromone (chemical signal) that attracts *only* Japanese beetles, destroying them and conserving pollinators while protecting rosebushes.

Declining Pollinators Unfortunately, pollinator populations have declined. One example is the alkali bee, a native pollinator of Utah, Nevada, and other dry areas of western North America. Alkali bees are a major pollinator of alfalfa, which is a very important livestock feed and cover crop. When pesticide use rose in the mid-1900s, alkali bee populations plummeted, and alfalfa yields fell, threatening both crop and livestock agriculture. Farmers have changed the way they use pesticides in alkali bee habitat, but alkali bees are now extinct in many of their former breeding areas.

Preserving the biodiversity of native pollinators is especially important because our most common domesticated pollinator, the honeybee, is declining sharply. North American farmers regularly hire beekeepers to bring colonies of this introduced bee to their fields when it is time to pollinate crops. Honeybees pollinate more than 130 crops, which together make up one third of the U.S. diet. In recent years, two accidentally introduced parasites have swept through honeybee populations, destroying hives. In addition, starting in 2006, entire hives began dying off for an unknown reason. Scientists are racing to discover the reasons for this mysterious syndrome, which is called *colony collapse disorder*, before it threatens our food supply.

Pollinator Conservation Farmers and homeowners can help maintain populations of insect pollinators, such as bees, by reducing or eliminating pesticide use. Otherwise, they risk killing the "good" bugs along with the "bad" bugs. Pest control measures that target specific pests, such as the pheromone trap in **Figure 19,** are pollinator-safe alternatives to pesticides.

LESSON 3 Assessment

1. **Communicate** Write a paragraph describing when and how agriculture likely began. End with a description of the beginnings of selective breeding.

2. **Infer** How have industrial agriculture and the green revolution affected the world's population?

3. **Compare and Contrast** How do (a) chemical pesticides, (b) biological control, and (c) integrated pest management protect crops from pests?

4. **Review** How are pollinators important to crop agriculture?

5. **THINK IT *THROUGH*** Suppose that you were the resource manager for a national wildlife refuge with a pest problem. You have been told that you can import predators of the pest from Asia to begin a biological pest control program. What three questions would you ask before you began that program?

Food Production

EVERYDAY PHENOMENON How can we increase food
production sustainably?

Knowledge and Skills

- Explain why the world needs to grow more food
  and to grow it sustainably.
- Discuss genetically modified food.
- Describe the advantages and disadvantages of
  industrial food production.
- Discuss sustainable agriculture.

Reading Strategy and Vocabulary

✔ **Reading Strategy** Before reading, create a three-column
KWL chart. In the first column, write what you know about
global food production. In the second column, write what
you want to know. After you read the lesson, write what you
learned in the third column.

Vocabulary arable land, food security, malnutrition,
genetic engineering, genetically modified (GM) organism,
biotechnology, feedlot, aquaculture, seed bank,
sustainable agriculture, organic agriculture

EACH YEAR, EARTH gains about 83 million people and *loses* 5 million
to 7 million hectares (12 million to 17 million acres) of productive cropland. We can expect a world population of 9.8 billion by 2050. In order to
feed the growing human population, we will likely need to increase agricultural production. We cannot keep expanding agriculture into new areas,
because **arable land,** or land suitable for farming, is running out. Especially
in drier regions, degraded soil has made raising crops and livestock more
difficult. We must find ways to increase food production in areas that are
already being used for agriculture and to do so in ways that maintain the
health of our soils and ecosystems. This could involve approaches as diverse
as the use of genetically modified crops and organic farming.

Food Security

Despite increases in global food production, there are still hundreds of
millions of hungry people. Feeding them will require that we continue
improvements in food production and distribution while protecting our
soil and ecosystems.

Food Production Since 1961, despite the loss of arable land, our
ability to produce food has grown faster than the human population. We
have increased food production by devoting more fossil fuel energy to
agriculture; by planting and harvesting more frequently; by increasing
the use of irrigation, fertilizers, and pesticides; by increasing the amount
of cultivated land; and by developing more productive crop and livestock
varieties. But the world's soils are in decline, and nearly all the planet's
arable land is already being farmed. Just because agricultural production
has outpaced population growth so far, there is no guarantee that it will
continue to do so.

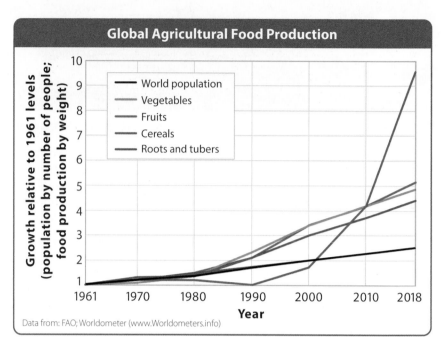

Global Agricultural Food Production

Legend:
- World population
- Vegetables
- Fruits
- Cereals
- Roots and tubers

Y-axis: Growth relative to 1961 levels (population by number of people; food production by weight)

X-axis: Year — 1961, 1970, 1980, 1990, 2000, 2010, 2018

Data from: FAO; Worldometer (www.Worldometers.info)

FIGURE 20 Rising Food Production Global food production rose by more than two and a half times in the last 50 years, even faster than the world population. Production of all types of foods, particularly vegetables, has increased since 1961.

And despite the rise in food production (**Figure 20**), 1 billion people are still hungry. So agricultural scientists and policymakers are aggressively pursuing the goal of **food security,** the guarantee of an adequate and reliable food supply for all people at all times. Making the food supply secure depends on maintaining healthy soil and water, protecting the biodiversity of food sources, and ensuring the safe distribution of food.

Undernourishment and Malnutrition Most people who are undernourished, receiving less than 90 percent of their daily caloric needs, live in the developing world. For most people who are undernourished, the reasons are economic. Hunger is a problem even in the United States. In 2018, the Department of Agriculture classified 37.2 million American households as "food insecure," or lacking the income required to obtain sufficient food at all times.

Just as the *quantity* of food a person eats is important for health, so is the *quality* of food. **Malnutrition,** a shortage of nutrients the body needs, occurs when a person fails to obtain a healthy variety or quantity of nutrients. Malnutrition can lead to disease. When people eat too little protein, a disease called *kwashiorkor* results. Kwashiorkor causes bloating of the abdomen, poor hair quality, skin problems, mental disability, lowered immunity, developmental delays in children, and anemia (**Figure 21**). Protein deficiency and a lack of calories can lead to *marasmus*, which causes wasting of the muscles and many other physical and mental problems. It is most prevalent among children in developing nations.

 Reading Checkpoint *What are three essential steps to global food security?*

FIGURE 21 Malnutrition
Millions of people suffer from hunger and the diseases it can lead to. This woman has kwashiorkor.

Genetically Modified Organisms

Industrial agriculture has enabled us to feed more people, but our continuing population growth demands still more innovation. Some potential solutions arose in the 1980s. For the first time, advances in genetics enabled scientists to directly alter the genes of organisms, including crop plants and livestock. This "gene revolution" could improve world nutrition and the efficiency of agriculture while lessening impacts on ecosystems. But because it is new, it may also pose unexpected risks.

Genetic Modification Any process in which scientists directly manipulate an organism's DNA is called **genetic engineering.** Organisms that have undergone genetic engineering are often called **genetically modified (GM) organisms.** GM organisms are engineered using a technique called *recombinant DNA technology*. Recombinant DNA is DNA taken from multiple organisms and pieced together, or *recombined*. In this process, scientists place genes that code for desired traits into the genomes of organisms lacking those traits. Rapid growth, pest resistance, and frost tolerance are commonly engineered traits in crop plants. Animals can also be genetically modified. For example, the goats in **Figure 22** have been engineered to give milk that can be processed into a drug that treats people whose blood clots abnormally.

The creation of genetically modified organisms is one aspect of **biotechnology,** the use of genetic engineering to introduce new genes into organisms to produce more valuable products. Biotechnology has helped us develop medicines, clean up pollution, understand the causes of diseases, dissolve life-threatening blood clots, and improve crops and livestock.

 Reading Checkpoint *In your own words, define* genetically modified organism.

FIGURE 22 Genetically Modified Organisms These goats look perfectly normal. But their milk can produce a drug that treats people with abnormal blood clotting. (Because the substances are produced only in the goats' mammary glands, the goats are not harmed.)

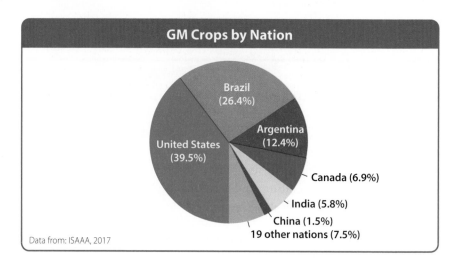

FIGURE 23 GM Crops Are Everywhere The United States devotes the most land area to GM crops.

GM Crops by Nation

Brazil (26.4%)

Argentina (12.4%)

United States (39.5%)

Canada (6.9%)

India (5.8%)

China (1.5%)

19 other nations (7.5%)

Data from: ISAAA, 2017

GM Crops Are Everywhere Many GM crops today are engineered to resist herbicides, so that farmers can kill weeds without worrying about killing their crops. Other crops are engineered to resist insect attack (often with the bacterium *Bt*, which you learned about in Lesson 3). Some are modified to resist both. Plants that are resistant to both herbicides and pests make it more efficient, and in some cases more economical, for large-scale commercial farmers to do their jobs. As a result, sales of GM seeds to these farmers in the United States and other developed nations have risen quickly.

The United States alone grows about 40 percent of the global total of GM crops, as **Figure 23** shows. Today 92 percent of the U.S. corn harvest and more than 90 percent of U.S. soybeans, cotton, and canola crops are genetically modified strains. In the United States, 41 percent of corn and cotton crops are engineered for more than one trait. Worldwide, 70 percent of soybean crops are genetically modified, as are 25 percent of corn crops, 20 percent of canola crops, and nearly 50 percent of cotton crops.

Potential Risks As GM crops were adopted, as research proceeded, and as biotechnology expanded, many citizens, scientists, and policy-makers became concerned. Some feared the new foods might be dangerous for people to eat. Others worried that pests would evolve resistance to the pest-resistant crops and become "superpests." Still others were concerned that GM genes might "escape," pollinating non-GM plants and harming those organisms or others.

That last concern is supported by evidence. A GM grass plant not yet approved by the USDA pollinated wild grass 21 kilometers (13 miles) away from its test growing site in Oregon. Because of this and similar events, such as the discovery of transgenes in Oaxaca, most scientists think GM genes will inevitably make their way from GM crops into wild plants. The consequences (or lack thereof) of this potential event are still being hotly debated, however. Because GM technology is new and changing, scientists are still learning about it. Millions of people eat GM foods every day without obvious signs of harm, and evidence for negative environmental effects is limited so far. Nevertheless, more research is needed before we can dismiss all concerns about GM foods.

Potential Benefits Supporters of GM crops maintain that no ill health effects on people have been demonstrated and that GM crops are, in fact, beneficial for people and the environment. For example, growing insect-resistant *Bt* crops reduces the use of chemical insecticides, because farmers use fewer chemicals if their crops do not need them.

Researchers and biotechnology industry supporters also claim other environmental benefits from GM crops. They say these crops reduce carbon emissions for two reasons: (1) if crops need fewer pesticide applications, then the equipment used to apply pesticides uses less fuel; and (2) if herbicide-resistant crops encourage the adoption of no-till farming, then more carbon (in remnants of plants) remains in the soil and is not released to the atmosphere. One GM crop research agency estimated that in 2018, GM crops prevented carbon emissions equivalent to those of 16.7 million cars.

The Promise of GM Foods But so far, GM crops have not lived up to their promise of feeding the world's hungry. Nearly all commercially available GM crops have either pesticidal properties (for example, *Bt*) or herbicide tolerance (**Figure 24**). These traits help primarily large-scale, commercial farmers in developed nations. Crops with GM traits that might benefit poor small-scale farmers in developing nations—increased nutrients, drought tolerance, and salinity tolerance—have not been widely developed. This may be because corporations have little economic incentive to develop such crops—farmers in developing nations cannot afford to buy expensive GM seed every year. Whereas the green revolution was a largely public venture, the "gene revolution" seems to be largely driven by financial concerns of private corporations.

But environmental activists, policymakers, scientists, and big corporations all agree that lack of food security is a problem and that agriculture should be made more environmentally friendly. They only disagree on appropriate responses to those challenges and the risks that each response would present. Clearly, the future of GM foods will depend on trade-offs and compromises among many people with a wide range of concerns.

✔ **Reading Checkpoint** *Why are today's GM crops unlikely to help feed poor people in developing nations?*

WHAT DO YOU THINK?

Some people think GM products in the United States should be labeled. Given that about 75 percent of processed food now contains GM ingredients, labeling would be more expensive for the food companies, a cost that might be passed on to the consumer. Do you want GM food to be labeled in the United States? Explain your answer.

FIGURE 24 Herbicide-Resistant Crops This field of herbicide-resistant soybeans is being sprayed with an herbicide to kill weeds.

Industrial Food Production

Plant foods make up a large portion of the human diet, but most of us also eat animal products such as meat, fish, milk, and eggs. Raising plants and animals for food affects the environment no matter how it is done. And the larger the scale of the food production, the larger the impact. Feedlots, aquaculture, and crop monocultures are typical methods of industrial food production—the large-scale food production by large corporations. All of these methods have positive and negative environmental impacts.

FIGURE 25 Global Meat and Seafood Consumption Per capita consumption of meat has risen steadily worldwide. Feedlots (background), which are very efficient, and aquaculture may be required in order to meet the demand.

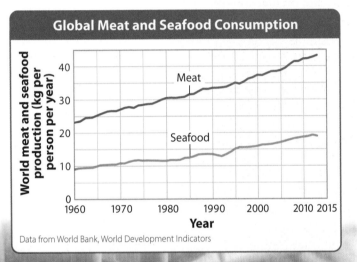

Global Meat and Seafood Consumption

Data from World Bank, World Development Indicators

Feedlots Worldwide, the number of animals raised for food rose from 7.2 billion to 24.3 billion between 1961 and 2007. Since 1950, global meat production has increased by a factor of five, and global meat and seafood consumption per person has nearly doubled since 1960, as you can see in the graph in **Figure 25.**

This growth is both a cause and an effect of industrial agriculture. In traditional agriculture, livestock were kept by farming families near their homes or were grazed on open grasslands by ranchers or herders. These traditions have survived, but industrial agriculture offers a new method. **Feedlots,** also known as *concentrated animal feeding operations* or *factory farms,* are basically huge warehouses or pens designed to deliver energy-rich food to livestock or poultry. Today, more than half of the world's pork and poultry comes from feedlots, as does much of its beef, including most U.S. beef.

▶ *Advantages* Feedlot operations allow for a greater, more efficient production of food and are necessary for a nation with a high level of meat consumption like the United States. Feedlots also have a clear benefit for the environment—cattle and other grazers in feedlots do not degrade soil through overgrazing. Imagine the environmental effects of grazing 10 million cattle across the United States!

Feedlots also reduce the need for chemical fertilizers. One dairy cow can produce 20,400 kilograms (9250 pounds) of waste in a year. Some feedlots hold 100,000 cattle. Where does all that manure go? Feedlot manure is often applied to farm fields as fertilizer.

▶ **Disadvantages** Improper management of feedlot manure, however, can lead to illnesses in feedlot animals and in humans and other animals, often through contamination of bodies of water. Also, because feedlot animals often live in crowded, dirty conditions, the animals need to be given heavy doses of antibiotics to control disease. These antibiotics may make their way into the people who eat animal products. The antibiotics may also leach into groundwater or run off into surface water, affecting ecosystems. In addition, heavy use of antibiotics makes it more likely that bacteria will evolve resistance to them, making the antibiotics less effective. Cattle are also often given steroids to promote growth, and these can also pass into surface water or groundwater through manure.

Some people also question the treatment of animals in feedlots, where they are often packed so densely that they cannot move around or interact normally with other animals. Some animals show signs of stress, such as chickens that peck themselves or others and pigs that chew their neighbors' tails.

Although feedlots have many disadvantages, they are probably a necessary evil. And negative impacts can be lessened if a feedlot is properly managed. To help ensure proper management, the Environmental Protection Agency and state agencies regulate U.S. feedlots.

Aquaculture Not all of our food is grown or raised on land, of course. People also eat aquatic organisms. Fish populations are decreasing throughout the world's oceans as increased demand and new technologies have allowed us to overharvest many species. **Aquaculture,** or fish farming, is the breeding, raising, or harvesting of aquatic plants or animals for food. It may be the only way to meet the increasing demand. Aquaculture is a resource-wise way to provide protein to a growing world. Aquaculture provides 47% of the fish that are eaten by humans, and more than 598 species are farmed. Aquaculture has great benefits, and it can be practiced sustainably, but it also has risks (**Figure 26**).

Global Aquaculture Products, 2014

Aquaculture Products	Million Tonnes
Finfish	49.8
Shellfish	16.1
Frogs and other aquatic animals	7.3
Crustaceans	6.9

Data from: NOAA

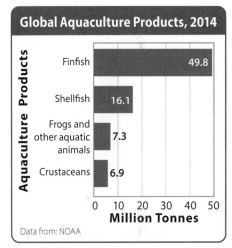

Aquaculture	
Costs	**Benefits**
✘ Diseases spread easily through dense populations, reducing production and profit	✔ On small scale, ensures local people a reliable protein source
✘ Produces enormous amounts of waste that may pollute water outside of farm	✔ Can be sustainable— for example, fish scraps make excellent fertilizer
✘ Escaped organisms may spread disease to wild animals	✔ Reduces harvesting of declining wild aquatic animals
✘ Escaped organisms (such as large GM salmon) may outcompete wild animals and threaten wild populations	✔ Reduces by-catch, the unintended death of nontarget animals
	✔ Uses less fossil fuel than fishing vessels do
	✔ Provides a safer work environment than commercial fishing does

FIGURE 26 Aquaculture Costs and Benefits Many different species of aquatic animals are raised for food (graph above). Like all methods of raising food, aquaculture has costs and benefits (left). For example, GM salmon can be 5 to 50 times larger than wild salmon of the same species (above) and may outcompete them if they were to meet in the wild.

Effects on Plant Diversity As you recall, the efficiency of industrial agriculture relies on monocultures. That means that a disease or pest that specializes in a specific plant could wipe out an entire crop. One concern many people have about GM crops is that GM genes might move by pollination into wild relatives of crop plants, outcompete them, and force them into extinction. If that were to happen, we could eventually be left with a monoculture in the wild as well as on the farms. Then an especially dangerous pest could destroy *all* our corn—GM, conventional, and wild. This would be devastating to the global food supply. But if we still had wild varieties that the pest had not evolved with, those varieties might be less susceptible to the pest. We could save our corn—and many lives.

▶ *Losses* We have already lost a great deal of genetic diversity in our crop plants. Since 1930, the number of Mexico's native maize varieties, from which all of today's corn varieties descend, has decreased by 70 percent. In the United States, we have lost most of our fruit and vegetable varieties—90 percent in less than a century.

A major cause of this loss of diversity is that market forces have discouraged diversity. For example, large food processing and distributing companies prefer items that are of similar size and shape and that are less likely to be damaged during long-distance shipping. For example, many large farms grow the same tomato varieties, often smaller ones with thicker skins, because it is easier to ship them. So next time you are disappointed in the taste of a tomato, check where it was grown. If it was grown more than a couple hundred kilometers away, it might have been grown for thick skin—not flavor!

▶ *Preservation* Protecting areas with high plant diversity is one way to preserve the genetic diversity of our crops. Another is to collect and store seeds from diverse crop varieties. This is what seed banks do. **Seed banks** are organizations that preserve seeds of diverse plants as a kind of insurance policy against a global crop collapse. Seed banks periodically grow plants from their seeds to harvest fresh seeds. The Royal Botanic Garden's Millennium Seed Bank in England holds more than 92,000 seed collections from more than 40,000 species.

Energy Efficiency Our food choices are also energy choices. We have discussed the use of fossil fuels in industrial agriculture. But what we choose to eat also affects how efficiently we use the sun's energy. Recall that every time energy moves from one trophic level to the next, as much as 90 percent of the energy is lost, mainly as heat.

FIGURE 27 Animal Food Products and Resource Use When we choose what to eat, we are also choosing how to use resources. The illustrations in this figure are sized according to the amount of land or water required to produce protein from the given animal source. Beef requires by far the most land and water.

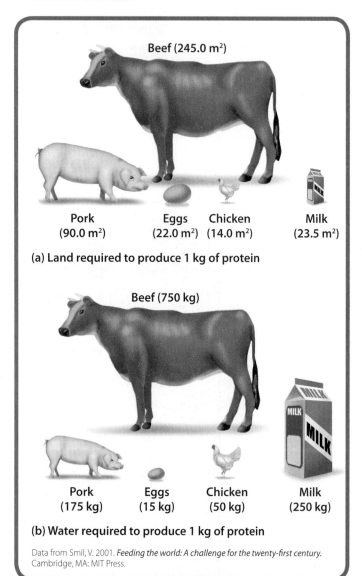

Beef (245.0 m²)

Pork (90.0 m²) Eggs (22.0 m²) Chicken (14.0 m²) Milk (23.5 m²)

(a) Land required to produce 1 kg of protein

Beef (750 kg)

Pork (175 kg) Eggs (15 kg) Chicken (50 kg) Milk (250 kg)

(b) Water required to produce 1 kg of protein

Data from Smil, V. 2001. *Feeding the world: A challenge for the twenty-first century.* Cambridge, MA: MIT Press.

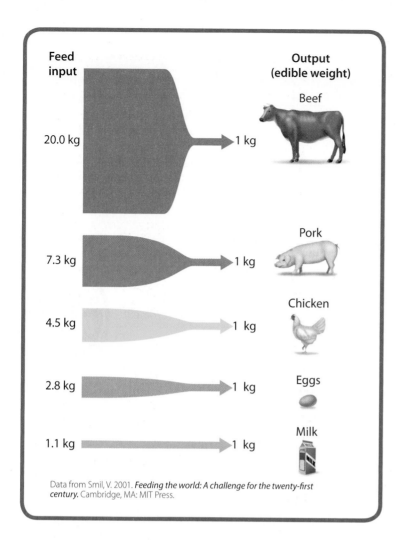

Feed input		Output (edible weight)
20.0 kg		Beef — 1 kg
7.3 kg		Pork — 1 kg
4.5 kg		Chicken — 1 kg
2.8 kg		Eggs — 1 kg
1.1 kg		Milk — 1 kg

Data from Smil, V. 2001. *Feeding the world: A challenge for the twenty-first century.* Cambridge, MA: MIT Press.

FIGURE 28 Animal Food Products and Feed Input It requires much more feed to produce a kilogram of meat than it does to produce a kilogram of eggs or milk.

 GO ONLINE

- **Graph It** Animal Food Production and Food Policy

For example, if we feed grain to a cow and then eat beef from the cow, we have lost 90 percent of the energy in the grain to the cow's metabolism. For this reason, the production of meat for food is extremely inefficient, as you can see in **Figures 27** and **28.**

Sustainable Agriculture

Industrial agriculture can have many adverse environmental impacts, from the degradation of soils to reliance on fossil fuels to problems arising from pesticide use, genetic modification, and feedlot and aquaculture operations. Although industrial agriculture helps relieve certain environmental pressures, it aggravates others. Industrial agriculture seems necessary to feed our planet's almost 7.8 billion people, but we may be better off in the long run by practicing other methods as well.

Farmers and researchers have made great advances toward sustainable agriculture in recent years. **Sustainable agriculture** is agriculture that does not deplete soil faster than it forms. It also does not reduce the amount or quality of soil, water, and genetic diversity essential to long-term crop and livestock production. Simply put, it is agriculture that can be practiced in the same way far into the future.

USDA Organic Criteria	
For crops to be considered organic...	**For livestock to be considered organic...**
• The land where they are grown must be free of prohibited substances for at least 3 years. • They must not be genetically engineered. • They must not be treated with radiation (to kill bacteria). • The use of sewage sludge is prohibited. • They must be produced without fertilizer containing synthetic ingredients, except those approved by the National Organic Standards Board. • Use of most conventional pesticides is prohibited. • Use of organic seeds and other planting stock is preferred. • Pests, weeds, and diseases should be controlled without synthetic substances except those approved by the National Organic Standards Board.	• Mammals must be raised organically from the last third of gestation; poultry, from the second day of life. • Livestock must be fed 100% organic feed; vitamin and mineral supplements are allowed. • Dairy animals must be managed organically for at least 12 months for their products to be sold or labeled as organic. • Cows must be out on pasture for the entire grazing season and must receive at least 30 percent of their feed from pasture. • Animals must have access to the outdoors year-round. They can only temporarily be confined.
Data from: USDA	

FIGURE 29 **USDA Organic Certification** In 2000, the USDA compiled a list of criteria food must meet to be certified organic. The list is updated periodically, and the "USDA Organic" seal indicates the department's certification.

Organic Agriculture Sustainable agriculture that uses smaller amounts of pesticides, fertilizers, growth hormones, water, and fossil fuel energy than are currently used in industrial, high-input agriculture is often called *low-input agriculture*. Food-growing practices that use no synthetic fertilizers, insecticides, fungicides, or herbicides—but instead rely on biological approaches such as composting and biological pest control—are called **organic agriculture.**

Citizens, government officials, farmers, and the agricultural industry debated the meaning of the word *organic* in this context for many years. In 1990, Congress passed the Organic Food Production Act, establishing standards for organic products and facilitating the sale of organic food. As required by that law, the USDA in 2000 issued criteria by which it would certify crops and livestock as organic **(Figure 29)**. These standards went into effect in 2001.

▶ *Growth* Organic foods once made up just a tiny proportion of food sales, but the market is increasing sharply. Although organic foods accounted for only about 4 percent of food purchases in the United States in 2019, that represents an increase of over 200 percent since 1999. Many consumers favor organic products because they are concerned that consuming produce grown with pesticides may pose health risks. Consumers also buy organic produce out of a desire to protect air, water, and land, and to protect nontarget organisms from pesticides and herbicides. And consumers likely have increased confidence that they are buying a truly organic product since the use of the "USDA Organic" seal began in 2001 **(Figure 29)**.

Production is increasing along with demand. Although organic agriculture is practiced on less than 2 percent of farmed land worldwide, that area is increasing. In the United States and Canada, the land used for organic agriculture has been increasing 10–35 percent each year. Farmers in all 50 U.S. states and more than 180 nations now practice organic farming commercially.

▶ *Financial Considerations* Financial obstacles unique to organic farming include the start-up costs of shifting to organic methods. But once it is established, organic farming can yield just as much income as conventional farming. Organic farmers avoid the expense of buying chemical pesticides and herbicides, though some of their costs are higher than those of conventional farmers. And organic foods can sell for higher prices because of a smaller supply than demand.

While many shoppers will not buy organic produce if it is more expensive than conventional produce, many will. Because of the demand, most supermarket chains carry some organic products. In some supermarket chains, organic foods are the norm.

Locally Supported Agriculture In developed nations, increasing numbers of consumers are supporting local, small-scale agriculture. Farmers' markets are multiplying as consumers rediscover the pleasures of fresh, locally grown produce (**Figure 30**). The average food product sold in a U.S. supermarket travels at least 2400 kilometers (1500 miles) between the farm and the shelf, and it is often chemically treated to preserve it during the long trip. In addition, there are few produce varieties in most supermarkets, and as you recall, those varieties are not necessarily grown for their flavor. In contrast, at farmers' markets, consumers can buy a wide variety of local produce grown for taste, texture, and color rather than for durability. And buyers can boost their local economy by supporting local businesses.

Some consumers are also partnering with local farms in an arrangement called *community-supported agriculture (CSA)*. In CSA, consumers pay farmers in advance for a weekly share of their produce yield during the growing season. Consumers get local, fresh, in-season produce, while local farmers get a guaranteed income to invest in their crops—an alternative to taking out loans and being at the mercy of the weather. As of 2012, hundreds of thousands of consumers and over 12,500 farms were involved in CSA programs.

FIGURE 30 Locally Grown Food Farmers' markets, such as this one in Homestead, Florida, have become more widespread as consumers have rediscovered the benefits of buying fresh, locally grown produce.

④ Assessment
LESSON

1. **Explain** Why does the world need to grow more food? Why do the methods need to be sustainable?

2. **Pose Questions** What is a genetically modified organism? What questions would you ask about a food made from genetically modified corn before eating it?

3. **Review** What are two advantages and two disadvantages of industrial food production?

4. **Form an Opinion** Do you think organic foods are worth the extra cost? Explain.

REVISIT

5. **INVESTIGATIVE** PHENOMENON
A *locavore* is a person who eats mostly locally grown or raised food. Give three reasons why a person might become a locavore.

DARK EARTH IN THE
THE AMAZON

SCIENCE BEHIND THE STORIES

As in many tropical regions, farming in the Amazon is difficult—heavy rains tend to wash nutrients out of the exposed soil in just two to three years. Because of its infertile soils, archaeologists once thought that past agriculture in the Amazon could only have supported small villages. But scientists have recently discovered that before South America was colonized in the 1500s, Amazonian Indians created their own super-fertile soil, which grew enough food to support large cities. This soil has lasted for 1000 years, and is still farmed today by locals who call it *terra preta*, or "dark earth" in Portuguese.

Workers till a field fertilized with bio-char. Bio-char can increase the yield of tropical farms.

SUPER SOIL

European archaeologists had known about terra preta since the 1870s. However, almost nothing was known about its chemical properties until 1979, when soil scientist Wolfgang Zech started studying it. The work of archaeologists and soil scientists revealed that the Amazonian people had burned the forest to clear land, and then added their discarded food and wastes to the soil over time, filling it with nutrients. The resulting terra preta was extremely fertile. In fact, crops grown on terra preta can yield as much as eight times more food than crops grown on typical Amazonian soil.

NUTRIENT SPONGE

In the last decade, scientists began using what they've learned from ancient terra preta to improve agricultural soils in South America and Africa. One such scientist is Bruno Glaser, from Bayreuth University in Germany. Dr. Glaser found that charcoal is the key to terra preta's long-lasting fertility. The charcoal acts like a sponge, sucking up nutrients that would otherwise be washed out by rain and keeping them in the soil for hundreds of years.

BIO-CHAR

Dr. Glaser and other researchers think charcoal is the key to improving tropical agriculture. Crop waste can be turned into charcoal, or "bio-char," in special covered ovens, and then mixed into soil with fertilizer. This can help depleted soils retain nutrients and prevent erosion. It can also trap carbon in the soil, helping to slow the release of carbon dioxide, which contributes to climate change. But Dr. Glaser and other researchers caution that bio-char shouldn't be created by cutting down large areas of forest. Rather, the goal of bio-char is to improve the soils of the fields that are already in use, making them as fertile as the terra preta that supported Amazonian cities 1000 years ago.

A dark, fertile layer of terra preta sits atop typical reddish, nutrient-poor Amazonian soil.

Bio-char is a charcoal-rich soil created to imitate the properties of terra preta.

CAREER **Soil Scientist** Soil scientists study the physical and chemical properties of soil, including the distribution, as well as the biological components of the soil. There are many different career options that are available to someone who specializes in Soil Science. Go Online and research possible careers that relate to soil science. Write a brief summary of your findings.

INVESTIGATIVE PHENOMENON

How can we balance our growing demand for food with our need to protect the environment?

Lesson 1
Why does it take so long for soil to form?

Lesson 2
How can erosion be both helpful and harmful to soil formation?

Lesson 3
What are the benefits and environmental consequences of industrial farming?

Lesson 4
How can we increase food production sustainably?

LESSON 1 Soil

- Soil is a complex substance that forms through weathering, deposition, and decomposition.
- A soil profile consists of layers known as horizons.
- Soils can be classified by color, texture, structure, and pH.

soil (352)	soil profile (355)
parent material (353)	clay (356)
bedrock (353)	silt (356)
weathering (354)	sand (356)
soil horizon (355)	loam (356)

LESSON 2 Soil Degradation and Conservation

- Certain farming, ranching, and forestry practices can erode soil, but other practices can protect it.
- Desertification reduces productivity of arid lands.
- U.S. and international agricultural organizations promote soil conservation.
- Irrigation and pesticides can improve soil productivity in the short term but can pollute soil in the long term.

soil degradation (358)	contour farming (359)
intercropping (359)	overgrazing (360)
crop rotation (359)	desertification (361)
cover crop (359)	irrigation (363)
shelterbelt (359)	salinization (363)
tilling (359)	pesticide (364)
terracing (359)	

LESSON 3 Agriculture

- Agriculture began about 10,000 years ago, when humans began to plant seeds and raise livestock.
- Industrial agriculture and the green revolution have saved millions of people from starvation.
- Chemical pesticides, biological pest control, and integrated pest management can all effectively protect crops from pests.
- Many insects and other animals are essential to the reproduction of crop plants.

traditional agriculture (366)
yield (367)
industrial agriculture (367)
green revolution (368)
biological pest control (369)
integrated pest management (IPM) (371)
pollinator (371)

LESSON 4 Food Production

- We need to find a way to increase food production sustainably.
- GM food could be promising, but there are risks.
- Industrial food production is efficient, but it has disadvantages.
- There are sustainable alternatives to industrial agriculture.

arable land (373)	seed bank (380)
food security (374)	sustainable agriculture (381)
malnutrition (374)	organic agriculture (382)
genetic engineering (375)	
genetically modified (GM) organism (375)	
biotechnology (375)	
feedlot (378)	
aquaculture (379)	

 GO ONLINE

INQUIRY LABS AND ACTIVITIES

- **Testing Soil Properties**
  Observe the textures of different types of soil and make a prediction about their permeability. Then test your prediction.
- **Combating Erosion**
  See if you can control soil runoff and erosion with an erosion barrier or with plowing methods.
- **Local Planting Conditions**
  Use hardiness information and growing seasons to design a vegetable garden.

Chapter Assessment

Defend Your Case

The Central Case in this chapter explored issues surrounding the appearance of corn transgenes in Mexico. People are concerned that crops with transgenes could crossbreed with native varieties and contaminate their genetic material. Based on what you have learned, are such concerns valid? Use evidence from the Central Case and the lessons to support your opinion.

Review Concepts and Terms

1. About how much of Earth's land surface is used for agriculture?
   a. 8 percent
   b. 18 percent
   c. 28 percent
   d. 38 percent

2. The organic matter in soil includes
   a. minerals.
   b. living and decomposing organisms.
   c. living organisms only.
   d. bedrock.

3. Crop rotation does all of the following EXCEPT
   a. minimize erosion.
   b. let fields lie fallow.
   c. return nutrients to the soil.
   d. break cycles of disease.

4. Which soil conservation technique is shown in the photo below?
   a. reduced tillage
   b. shelterbelts
   c. contour farming
   d. terracing

5. Arid and semiarid lands are prone to desertification because
   a. the Sahara is expanding.
   b. gigantic dust storms blow sand from China into North America.
   c. the precipitation cannot meet the growing human demand for water.
   d. 10 percent of productivity is lost to erosion.

6. Traditional agriculture may use all of the following EXCEPT
   a. teams of work animals.
   b. irrigation.
   c. fossil fuels.
   d. organic fertilizer.

7. Efficient industrial agriculture requires that large areas be planted with
   a. contoured and well-plowed fields.
   b. a single crop.
   c. native organisms.
   d. cover crops.

8. Because of the green revolution, between 1961 and 2008, food production
   a. increased 150 percent while the population doubled.
   b. kept pace with population growth.
   c. did not increase.
   d. was mostly organic.

9. A secure food supply depends on all of the following EXCEPT
   a. maintaining healthy soil and water.
   b. increased use of fertilizer.
   c. safe distribution of the food.
   d. biodiversity.

10. Industrial food production includes
   a. aquaculture.
   b. monocultures.
   c. feedlots.
   d. all of the above.

Modified True/False

Write true if the statement is true. If it is false, change the underlined word or words to make the statement true.

11. It takes <u>one year</u> to produce one inch of topsoil.

12. Acid precipitation and the leaching of minerals and metals affect the <u>pH</u> of soil and the types of plants that can grow in it.

13. Today, human activities cause <u>less</u> erosion than natural events.

14. Although labor-intensive, <u>intercropping</u> is probably the only sustainable way to farm mountains.

15. Desertification is the loss of more than <u>50</u> percent of soil productivity.

Reading Comprehension

Read the following selection, and answer the questions that follow.

Most GM crops are insect- and/or herbicide-resistant. Farmers are willing to pay higher prices for such GM seeds because they expect to spend less money on pesticides and herbicides. Corn, soybeans, cotton, and canola dominate the GM market. These GM crops are used mostly in animal feed, fabric or yarn, or processed food. For these uses, most people are willing to accept GM crops.

Although GM produce such as strawberries and potatoes has been marketed in the U.S., GM research involving fruits and vegetables has dropped significantly over the past several years. Companies are introducing fewer new GM products. Lack of consumer support means that only a narrow range of GM crops will be produced. If the trend continues, biotechnology may not realize its full potential.

16. Why do soybeans, corn, cotton, and canola dominate the GM crop market?

a. They are mostly inexpensive to produce.

b. Such crops prevent malnutrition and clothe the poor.

c. They are mostly used for animal feed, fabric or yarn, and processed food, so most people accept them.

d. They are the only GM crops exempt from U.S. regulations.

17. Why have most GM crops been modified for resistance to herbicides and insects?

a. Such crops are safer for the environment.

b. Such crops are safer for human health.

c. Farmers expect to save money by planting them.

d. The resistance makes fruits and vegetables taste better.

Short Answer

18. Do you think it is necessary to safeguard native crop varieties? Explain.

19. When it comes to weathering and decomposition, how do the activities of organisms help form soil? Give two examples of how organisms produce the mineral and organic matter in soil.

20. What is intercropping? List three benefits of intercropping.

21. How did growing wheat and grazing cattle contribute to the Dust Bowl?

22. Is it true that monocultures risk catastrophic crop failure? Explain.

23. The green revolution required a large energy investment. In 2008, agriculture used 70 times more energy than it did in 1900. What were two consequences of such an increase in fossil fuel use?

Critical Thinking

24. **Infer** How did agriculture allow for the development of civilization?

25. **Form an Opinion** Would you support legislation that banned GM food crops? Explain.

26. **Explain** How do market forces contribute to the loss of genetic diversity in our crop plants?

27. **Infer** Per kilogram of meat produced, would you expect it to be more expensive to raise pigs for pork or cattle for beef?

28. **Apply Concepts** How would it increase global food security if more crops were engineered to be drought-resistant?

29. **Apply Concepts** Why is it important to support small farms and urban community gardens?

Analyze Data

The graph below shows agricultural land, world population, global food production, and nitrogen fertilizer use from 1965 to 2015. Values in the graph were calculated using the data from the year 2000 as 100%. Use the data to answer the questions.

World Population, Food Production, Fertilizer Use, and Farmland

Data from: FAO World Statistics

30. **Interpret Graphs** Describe the growth rate in world population from 1965 to 2015.

31. **Interpret Graphs** From 1965 to 2015, which variable grew the most and which grew the least? How do you know?

32. **Analyze Data** Write a ratio to compare nitrogen fertilizer use in 1970 and 1990. Write another ratio to compare global food production in 1970 and 1990. How would you compare the trends in these two data sets?

33. **Draw Conclusions** Describe the trends in agricultural land use and food production. Do they seem to be related?

Write About It

34. **Persuasion** Write a video script that argues for engineering GM crops with traits that help small-scale farmers in developing nations. Keep your message brief and compelling.

35. **Summary** In your own words, write a paragraph summarizing the characteristics of livestock raised with organic methods.

36. **REVISIT INVESTIGATIVE PHENOMENON** Do you believe that feedlots are a "necessary evil"? Explain.

Ecological Footprints

Read the information below. Copy the table into your notebook, and record your calculations. Then, answer the questions that follow.

In the 1900s, humans industrialized food production. As a result, we increased the amount of energy used to store food and get it to market. In the United States today, food travels an average of 1500 miles from the field to your table. The price you pay for food covers the long-distance hauling cost. On average, it costs about one dollar per ton per mile. If the average person eats 2 pounds of food per day, calculate the food transportation costs for each category in the table.

1. One recent study found that locally produced food traveled about 50 miles to market and cost 96 percent less to transport than industrial food. Locally grown food is fresher and has less environmental impact. As a consumer, what might be some disadvantages of relying on local food production?

2. Both gasoline and diesel prices can rise suddenly. How might future increases in fuel prices affect food prices in your area?

3. Our current system of food production relies on long-distance transportation. What are some ways that you can support a more sustainable system?

	Population	Daily Cost	Annual Cost
You	1	$1.50	$547.50
Your class			
Your town			
Your state			
United States			

Pirog, R., and A. Benjamin. 2003. *Checking the food odometer: Comparing food miles for local versus conventional produce sales to Iowa institutions.* Ames, IA: Leopold Center for Sustainable Agriculture, Iowa State University.

CHAPTER 13

Mineral Resources and Mining

Can we make the benefits of mining outweigh the costs?

An open pit gold mine in Australia

Lesson 1
Minerals and Rocks

Lesson 2
Mining

Lesson 3
Mining Impacts and Regulation

Mining for ... Cell Phones?

PULLING A CELL PHONE from her pocket, a teenager in the United States calls a friend. Inside her phone is a metal called tantalum—a tiny amount, but no cell phone could operate without it.

Half a world away, a young miner lives in poverty in the heart of Africa. He works all day in a jungle streambed, sifting sediment for particular nuggets called *coltan,* which contain tantalite, a mineral containing the element tantalum. At nightfall, soldiers who are fighting for control of the Congo forcefully take most of the coltan he gathered that day. He's left with little to sell to buy food for his family.

As the teenager chats with her friend, she probably doesn't realize how the high-tech devices she uses are linked to a very battered region of the world. The Democratic Republic of the Congo has been involved in a sprawling conflict that included six other nations and various rebel militias. Beginning in 1998, millions of people died during the war, most from disease and starvation, and millions more fled their homes. It was the latest chapter in the sad history of a nation that is rich in natural resources such as copper, gold, diamonds, uranium, and wood, but whose impoverished people often lose these resources to others.

Global demand for tantalum rose drastically in the 1990s as high-tech industry boomed. Market prices for the metal shot up to $500 per kilogram (about $230 per pound) in 2001. These high prices led some Congolese men to mine coltan by choice, but many more were forced to do it. As the war began in 1998, farmers were chased off their land, villages were burned, and civilians were killed. Soldiers seized control of mines and forced civilians to work in them and live in mining camps with poor conditions. Miners and soldiers streamed into national parks, clearing rain forests and killing already endangered wildlife.

Soldiers and bandits sold coltan to traders who then sold it to companies in Europe and the United States. The companies refined and sold the

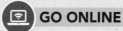

GO ONLINE
• Take It Local   • 3-D Geo Tour

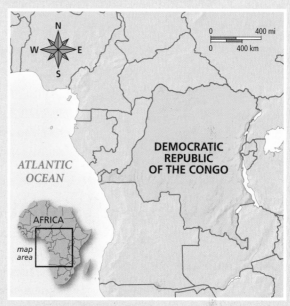

processed tantalum to manufacturers of cell phone parts and computer parts.

In 2001, a United Nations panel concluded that the coltan trade was financing and prolonging the war and urged an U.N. embargo on minerals smuggled from the Congo. Critics complained that an embargo would only hurt the people who had no other way to make money.

Soon, Australia and other nations ramped up industrial-scale tantalum processing. With so much processed tantalum, the price of tantalum dropped considerably to $60 per kilogram ($27 per pound), and stayed low for several years.

In 2003, the war in the Congo was officially declared over, but some fighting continues. Legislation in favor of conflict-free minerals has been passed by several nations, including the United States, the European Union, and China. Tech companies are also working to use conflict-free minerals in their devices. Despite these efforts, many people mining minerals in the Congo are still exploited.

Minerals and Rocks

EVERYDAY PHENOMENON Where do minerals come from?

Knowledge and Skills

- Explain what a mineral is.
- Describe how minerals form.
- Identify types of rocks and the stages of the rock cycle.

Reading Strategy and Vocabulary

✓ **Reading Strategy** As you read, make a two-column table. In the left column, label the properties that all minerals share. In the right column, describe each property.

Vocabulary mineral, precipitation, polymorph, rock, rock cycle

TAKE A QUICK LOOK AROUND. Wherever you are, you are likely surrounded by dozens of manufactured products that contain minerals. A long list of minerals is used in the structure of a laptop, and the intricate pieces that make it work. The glass or bottle you are drinking from, the chair you are sitting in, and the artificial light you are reading by all contain mineral components. Where do all of these minerals come from?

What Are Minerals?

Minerals are used to make products as simple as the graphite in a pencil or as complex as a computer chip. More than 4000 minerals have been identified, and many new ones are identified each year, but only about 1 percent are common in Earth's crust. So, how do geologists—scientists who study the history and structure of Earth—decide whether a newly found substance is a mineral or a different type of naturally occurring substance? For something to be a mineral, it must meet five specific criteria. A **mineral** is naturally occurring, inorganic, and a solid. Each type of mineral has an orderly crystalline structure and a definite chemical composition.

Occur in Nature To be a mineral, a substance must be formed by processes within Earth, on the surface of Earth, or within organisms. Manufactured materials such as synthetic gems aren't minerals.

Be Chemically Inorganic A mineral is formed from inorganic materials which do not contain carbon-carbon and carbon-hydrogen bonds. For example, sugar meets many of the criteria to be a mineral, yet it is not because it contains both of these types of bonds. Coal is not a mineral, because it formed from the remains of ancient plants that contained many carbon-carbon and carbon-hydrogen bonds.

Solids With Orderly Crystalline Structures Minerals are solids within the temperature ranges normally found on Earth's surface. They also have a crystalline structure, which means that their atoms or ions are arranged in an orderly and repetitive manner. Each type of mineral has a unique crystal structure.

Properties of Minerals	
Property	**Description**
Color	A few minerals can be identified by their specific color. But the color of many minerals can vary based on the conditions under which they form.
Streak	The streak of a mineral is the color of its powder. Although the color of a mineral can vary, its streak does not.
Luster	How light is reflected from a mineral's surface is called luster. Terms used to describe luster are metallic, glassy, earthy, silky, waxy, and pearly.
Crystal form	A mineral can be identified by the particular arrangement of its atoms.
Hardness	Hardness is measured using the Mohs hardness scale, a scratch test that ranks the hardness of a mineral on a scale of 1 to 10. Talc, which can be scratched with a fingernail, is rated 1; diamond, which can scratch all known common minerals, is rated 10.
Cleavage	A mineral that splits easily along a flat surface and forms a new "face" is said to have cleavage.
Fracture	Minerals that break apart irregularly, rather than leaving a flat surface, have fracture.
Density	Each mineral has a characteristic density—mass per unit volume.

FIGURE 1 Properties of Minerals The properties in this table can be used to identify particular minerals. For example, one clue that the mineral shown below is mica is that it is has cleavage. In addition to this list, some minerals have special properties such as magnetism, the ability to conduct electricity, or the ability to glow in ultraviolet light.

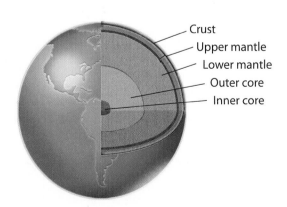

Definite Chemical Composition Most minerals are compounds made of two or more elements. Recall that an element is a substance composed of only one type of atom. Some minerals, such as copper and gold, are made of only one element. Minerals that are made of more than one element always contain the same proportion of these elements. For example, quartz (SiO_2) is made of one atom of silicon for every two atoms of oxygen.

Beyond this common set of criteria, the properties of minerals vary greatly. **Figure 1** describes several of the properties that geologists use to identify specific minerals. Many of these properties are due to how the mineral formed.

Mineral Formation

Minerals can form nearly everywhere on Earth, from deep in the crust or mantle, where temperatures and pressures are high, to warm and shallow ocean waters. **Figure 2** reviews the layers of Earth. In general, minerals can form in four ways.

Crystallization From Magma or Lava Magma is a molten mixture of substances that forms deep within Earth. When magma emerges at Earth's surface, it is called lava. As magma cools inside the crust or lava hardens on the surface, crystallization occurs and minerals can form. The size of the crystals depends on several factors. Magma that remains deep below the surface cools slowly, which leads to the formation of large crystals. Because lava cools more quickly than magma cools, minerals that form from lava typically consist of small crystals.

Crust
Upper mantle
Lower mantle
Outer core
Inner core

FIGURE 2 Earth's Layers Earth consists of three primary layers—the crust, mantle, and core.

Precipitation Elements and compounds that form minerals can be found in solutions—a mixture of substances that are not chemically bonded. Minerals form by **precipitation** when the liquid in a solution evaporates and the remaining solids crystallize. For example, when water evaporates from shallow ocean water, salt crystals can form.

Below Earth's surface, magma can heat water and dissolved substances to high temperatures. The high temperatures can lead to chemical reactions that cause one type of mineral to change into another. Also, dissolved elements and compounds may crystallize as the hot water cools. Metals that crystallize and precipitate from hydrothermal solutions underground often form narrow channels or slabs called *veins* in rock.

Pressure and Temperature When a mineral is subjected to great changes in temperature or pressure, its atoms may rearrange, causing it to become a different type of mineral. Some minerals, called **polymorphs,** consist of the same elements or compounds, but have different crystal structures due to the conditions under which they formed. For example, both graphite and diamond consist of crystallized carbon. When carbon crystallizes in Earth's crust, it forms graphite. When it crystallizes in the mantle at high temperature and under high pressure, it forms diamond.

Produced by Organisms Some organisms form inorganic minerals to produce hard structures that provide protection or support. Examples are calcium carbonate in mollusk shells and coral, and calcium phosphate in the bones of fish and other vertebrates. When they die, the remains of these organisms become sediments.

Minerals are categorized into groups based on the elements or compounds they contain. **Figure 3** includes these groups along with examples of minerals in the groups. Some mineral groups may contain rock-forming minerals that join together with other minerals or other naturally occurring substances and form rocks.

Graphite

Diamond

 Connect to the Central Case

FIGURE 3 Mineral Classes Eight elements—oxygen, silicon, aluminum, iron, calcium, sodium, potassium, and magnesium—make up 99 percent of Earth's crust. These elements form minerals as they combine in different ways. Because the polymorphs diamond and graphite contain only carbon they are native elements. **Interpret Tables** What is one element that must be found in tantalite?

Mineral Groups		
Group	**Chemical Makeup**	**Examples**
Rock Forming		
Silicates	Silicon, oxygen, and one or more other elements (except quartz, which contains only silicon and oxygen)	Quartz, feldspar, mica
Carbonates	Carbon, oxygen, and one or more other elements	Calcite, dolomite
Oxides	Oxygen and one or more other elements	Rutile, hematite, magnetite, bauxite (aluminum oxide), tantalite
Sulfides and sulfates	Sulfur and one or more other elements	Gypsum, anhydrite, pyrite, galena
Non-Rock Forming		
Halides	Halogen ion and one or more other elements	Halite (rock salt), fluorite
Native elements	Contain one nonionized element	Silver, gold, copper, diamond

Rocks

A **rock** is a solid mass of minerals and mineral-like material that occurs naturally. Rocks can be made of one type of mineral or of many different types of minerals and other materials. At first glance, rock appears to be pretty tough stuff that is unlikely to change much. Although people do not live long enough to witness most of these changes, rocks do undergo dramatic transformations.

Earth may feel still under your feet, but this is far from the case. Convection currents in Earth's outer core and the movement of tectonic plates cause rocks to sink deep below Earth's surface and rise again. During a very slow process called the **rock cycle,** rocks are heated, melted, cooled, weathered, and eroded as they slowly change between the three different types of rock—igneous, sedimentary, and metamorphic.

Igneous Rock At very high temperatures within the mantle, rock enters a molten, liquid state called magma. Rock that forms as magma cools and solidifies is called igneous rock. When magma cools slowly well below Earth's surface it forms *intrusive* igneous rock. Granite, shown in **Figure 4,** is a well-known type of intrusive igneous rock. Slow cooling allows minerals of the same type to cluster together. When lava erupts onto Earth's surface, it cools quickly and minerals have little time to cluster together. This kind of igneous rock is called *extrusive* igneous rock. The most common form of this rock is basalt.

(a)

Reading Checkpoint *Did the rock of Torres del Paine form within Earth or on Earth's surface? Explain.*

FIGURE 4 Igneous Rock (a) a chunk of granite. **(b)** Torres del Paine (Towers of Paine) in southern Chile is a granite rock formation.

(b)

Sedimentary Rock Any rock that is exposed on Earth's surface is subjected to factors such as wind, rain, ice, and activities of living things that strip away grains or even chunks of rock. Particles of rock blown by wind or washed away by water finally settle downhill, downstream, or downwind from their sources, forming piles of sediments that can be classified as gravel, sand, or mud depending on the size of the most common particles.

As layers of sediment build up over time, the weight on the earliest layers increases and compacts them. Dissolved minerals seep through sediment layers. Over time, the minerals crystallize and, like glue, bind sediment particles together. This process forms a type of sedimentary rock known as *clastic* sedimentary rock. Similar processes form fossils and fossil fuels, such as coal.

Sedimentary rock can also form when water evaporates and leaves behind minerals and other materials. These components crystallize and form rock known as *chemical* sedimentary rock. Some types of limestone, gypsum, and rock salt form this way.

Remains of marine organisms, such as chunks of dead coral at the base of a reef or shells that blanket regions of ocean floor, may accumulate in an area. These deposits may eventually bond together and form *biochemical* sedimentary rock. Some limestone, such as the white chalk cliffs along the English Channel, formed this way **(Figure 5)**.

Metamorphic Rock When rock is exposed to great heat or pressure, or both, a few kilometers beneath Earth's surface, the rock may become metamorphic rock. The changes occur at temperatures lower than the rock's melting point, but high enough to reshape crystals within the rock and alter its appearance and physical properties. Pressure can change the characteristics of rock by decreasing the space between minerals in the rock or causing the minerals to recrystallize. Common types of metamorphic rock include marble, which was once the sedimentary rock limestone, and soapstone, which was once the igneous rock peridotite.

FIGURE 5 Sedimentary Rock
This white chalk cliff, located near Dover, England, is an example of limestone that is biochemical sedimentary rock.

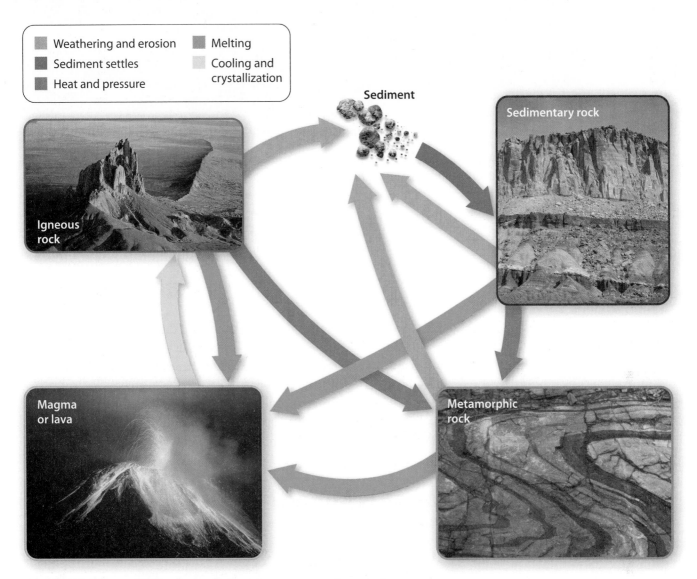

Weathering and erosion
Sediment settles
Heat and pressure
Melting
Cooling and crystallization

Sediment

Sedimentary rock

Igneous rock

Magma or lava

Metamorphic rock

FIGURE 6 The Rock Cycle In the rock cycle, igneous rock is formed when magma or lava cools. Sedimentary rock is formed as sediments from any type of rock are compressed and form new rock. Metamorphic rock is formed when rock is subjected to intense heat and pressure deep underground. Note that there are many pathways by which rocks move through the rock cycle.

LESSON ① Assessment

1. **Infer** Which of the five criteria that define minerals explains why polymorphs are actually different minerals?

2. **Relate Cause and Effect** How is the rate at which magma cools related to the size of the crystals in a mineral?

3. **Sequence** Explain the processes that would cause the material in an igneous rock to become sedimentary rock and then metamorphic rock.

4. **THINK IT** *THROUGH* You may recall that soil is classified by several properties such as color, texture, structure, and pH. Many of the processes that produce soil are related to the activities of living things. Do you think that the types of rocks and minerals found in a particular area could also influence the characteristics of the soil? Explain.

Knowledge and Skills

- Identify the types of resources that are mined.
- Describe different methods used for mining.
- Explain how metals are processed.

Reading Strategy and Vocabulary

✔ **Reading Strategy** Before you read, make an outline using the blue and green headings in this lesson. As you read, fill in information under each heading. Record questions and thoughts in your outline.

Vocabulary ore, strip mining, subsurface mining, open pit mining, mountaintop removal, placer mining, tailings, smelting

BELIEVE IT OR NOT rocks, minerals, and the materials that can be removed from them are valuable resources. But they can be tricky to find because most of these resources are hidden beneath the surface of the ground. Locating mineral resources and fossil fuels can be a scavenger hunt. Mining companies hire geologists who know the clues that may lead to a particular resource. But until the excavation begins, no one knows for sure exactly what and how much of it will be found.

What Is Mined?

Mining involves breaking into the ground to gain access to minerals, fossil fuels, or water, and extracting them. These resources are used in building materials, wiring, appliances, clothing, fertilizers, and an endless list of other goods. Without these resources civilization as we know it would not exist. Although Earth has an immense supply of resources, they are not all accessible. Some minerals, such as silver, are widespread throughout the crust, but in such low concentrations in many places that mining it is not economically practical. One of the goals of mining is to locate areas of concentrated resources. **Figure 7** shows the process by which minerals are mined and used.

Metallic Minerals Most mined metals are a part of minerals or groups of minerals. A mineral or group of minerals that is mined so that a metal or metals can be removed from it is called ore. Most ores are a mixture of desired materials and rocky materials that have no value, which is discarded. For material to be considered ore, the concentration of a mineral must be of a certain level, or mining it would not be economically feasible. Copper, iron, lead, gold, silver, and aluminum are among the valuable metals removed from ores. The tantalum used in high-tech devices is a metal that comes from the mineral tantalite. In nature, tantalite is often found with the mineral columbite. The ore that contains these two minerals is called *coltan.*

Nonmetallic Minerals Many types of minerals are mined because the mineral as a whole has valuable properties. Nonmetallic minerals may actually contain metal as a chemical component, but they are not mined for the metal. For example, sand and gravel may contain aluminum and iron, but these minerals are mined because they are valuable construction materials, not for aluminum or iron. In 2008, $7.6 billion of sand and gravel were mined in the United States alone. About 44 percent of the sand and gravel was used to make concrete. Other valuable nonmetallic minerals include limestone, salt, and gemstones. About 100 minerals are considered gemstones, including garnet, topaz, turquoise, and jade.

Fuel and Water Substances used for fuel sources are also mined. The metal uranium, which can be used to generate nuclear power, is extracted from uranium ore. One of the most commonly mined fuels is coal. Coal is mined in ways similar to minerals. Other fuels, such as petroleum, natural gas, oil sands, and methane hydrates, as well as groundwater, are also extracted from Earth. The methods for mining these substances will be discussed in other chapters.

Mining Methods

Once a good source of a mineral is found, mining companies use a variety of techniques to extract the resource from Earth. Each technique has costs and benefits for the mining industry, the environment, and people living in surrounding communities. The environmental and social impacts of mining will be discussed in the next lesson.

FIGURE 7 Mining and Mineral Use Process The first step in mining is identifying an area that is likely a good source of ore. Once the ore is extracted from the ground, it goes through refinement and processing to free the desired minerals. Minerals are further processed so that they can be used to make products.

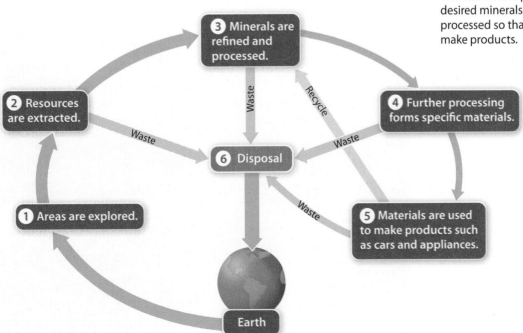

Strip Mining When a resource occurs in shallow horizontal deposits near the surface, the most effective mining method may be strip mining. During **strip mining,** layers of surface soil and rock are removed from large areas to expose the resource. After heavy machinery removes the soil and rock, the resource is extracted. Then, the soil and rock are replaced. Strip mining is commonly used to mine coal, sand, and gravel.

Subsurface Mining When a resource occurs in concentrated pockets or seams deep underground, and the ground allows for safe tunneling, mining companies pursue subsurface mining. In **subsurface mining,** vertical shafts are dug deep into the ground, and networks of horizontal tunnels are dug or blasted out to follow deposits of the resource. Miners remove the resource and transport it out of the mine.

Subsurface mining is used for metals such as zinc, lead, nickel, tin, gold, copper, and uranium, and for nonmetallic minerals such as diamonds, phosphate, and salt. A great deal of coal is also mined using this technique. The size of some subsurface mines can be mind-boggling. Certain gold mines in South Africa extend nearly 4 kilometers into the ground.

Open Pit Mining When a mineral is distributed widely and evenly throughout a rock formation, or when the ground is unsuitable for tunneling, the method of choice is open pit mining. **Open pit mining** involves digging a large hole and removing the ore and the unwanted rock that surrounds the ore. **Figure 8** shows one of the biggest, if not the biggest, open pit mines in the world—Bingham Canyon Mine near Salt Lake City, Utah. This mine is about 4 kilometers wide, 1.2 kilometers deep, and has been seen from space by astronauts. Conveyor systems and immense trucks with tires taller than an average person remove nearly half a million tons of copper ore and waste rock each day.

FIGURE 8 Open Pit Mining
Bingham Canyon Mine, a copper mine in Utah, is an example of a large open pit mine.

FIGURE 9 **Mountaintop Removal** This crater was left behind after a mountaintop was removed at the Samples Mine in West Virginia. This mine closed in the fall of 2009 because of a reduced demand for coal.

Open pit mines are usually expanded until the resource runs out or becomes so difficult to mine that it is unprofitable to continue. This method is used for copper, iron, gold, diamonds, and coal among other resources. Similar methods are used to extract clay, gravel, sand, limestone, granite, marble, and slate, but in these cases the pits are known as quarries.

Mountaintop Removal The method of mountaintop removal is used primarily for coal mining in the Appalachian Mountains (**Figure 9**). In the process of **mountaintop removal,** first, the forests are clear-cut and the timber is sold or burned. Then, the topsoil is removed and rock is blasted away to expose the resource. Repeated cycles of blasting and extraction can eventually remove hundreds of vertical feet of mountaintop. The waste rock is transported to areas that were mined previously or to nearby valleys.

Solution Mining Rather than removing ore from the ground, miners sometimes pump a chemical solution into a mine to leach the desired resource from the ore. Once the solution has reacted with the ore, the liquid is removed from the mine, taking the resource with it. As shown in **Figure 10,** salt miners may use a similar method in which water is pumped into the mine, causing the salt to dissolve into the water. Then the dissolved salt and water mixture, called brine, is pumped out of the mine.

Reading Checkpoint *What are mining sites for marble and slate known as?*

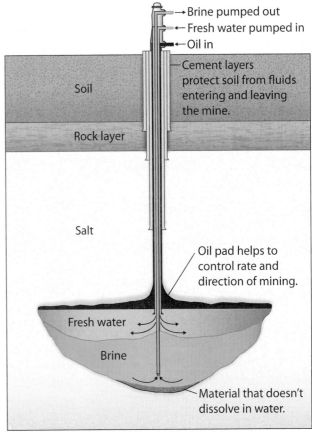

FIGURE 10 **Solution Mining for Salt** In this type of mining, water is used to dissolve salt, and the mixture is extracted from the mine. After mining is complete, these underground caverns are sometimes used to store fuels such as natural gas.

Mineral Resources and Mining **401**

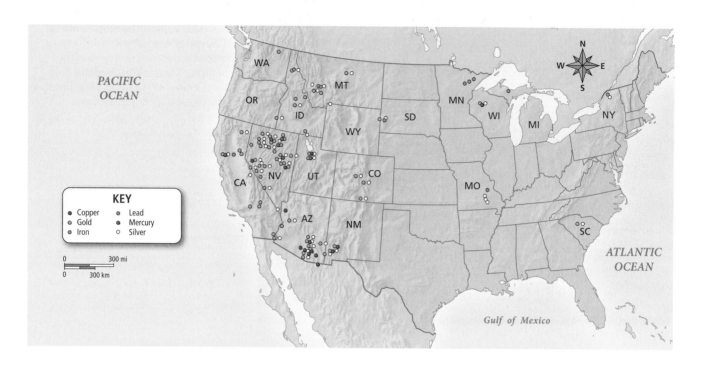

FIGURE 11 **U.S. Metallic Mineral Mining Sites** The map shows some major mining sites of metallic minerals in the continental United States.

Distribution of Minerals

Concentrated sources of valuable minerals are not spread evenly throughout Earth's crust. **Figure 11** shows major mining areas for several important metals in the continental United States.

1. **Observe** In what state is the greatest concentration of copper mines found?

2. **Interpret Maps** What two types of metallic mineral mines are the most common in the western United States?

3. **Develop a Hypothesis** Why do you think that most of the metallic mineral mines in the United States are found in the western part of the nation?

Placer Mining Weathering and other geologic processes can cause metals and gems to break free from their rocky origins. The loose pieces may be carried along by river currents and deposited in riverbeds. Placer mining involves sifting through material in modern or ancient riverbed deposits. The miners usually use running water to separate light-weight mud and gravel from heavier valuable minerals. Placer mining is used in the Congo to collect coltan. It was also used in California during the Gold Rush of 1849 and in Alaska during the Klondike Gold Rush of 1897. In fact, placer mining for gold still takes place in areas of California and Alaska.

Undersea Mining In a process called *dredging,* miners use large machines similar to vacuum cleaners to collect sand and gravel from the sea floor. Miners use other processes to extract sulfur from salt deposits in the Gulf of Mexico and phosphorite from areas near the California coast. Other valuable minerals found on or beneath the sea floor include diamonds, calcium carbonate (used in making cement) and silica (used as fire-resistant insulation and in making glass), as well as copper, zinc, silver, and gold ore. Although the amount of undersea metals is vast, undersea mining is quite limited because it is so expensive to access resources and extract them.

Some companies are exploring hydrothermal vents as a possible concentrated, rich source of metals. Underground volcanic activity causes dissolved metals, such as gold, zinc, and copper to be released through the vents. When the dissolved metals come in contact with the cold water, they crystallize and form chimneys (**Figure 12**).

Processing Minerals and Metals

Removing ores from the ground is just the first step in gaining access to the metals they contain. Mineral processing usually begins at the mining site. Transporting the tons of ore that are removed from the ground would be expensive and wasteful because much of the material in ore will be discarded as waste.

Breakdown of Ore Minerals need to be separated from the ore to gain access to the desired metals. First, ore is crushed and ground into particles. At this point an understanding of the compounds that make up the ore is important to make sure the correct particle size is obtained. If the ore is not ground enough, then it will be difficult to separate the metals.

Separation From Ore Next, processors apply their knowledge of the specific properties of minerals, including density, cleavage, magnetism, and conductivity, to separate minerals from ore. For example, because they know the densities of gold and the other materials usually found in gold ore, they can determine which particles are gold by suspending the ground ore in solution.

A common separation method, called *froth flotation,* involves mixing the finely ground ore with water to form *slurry.* Chemicals and air bubbles are then introduced into the slurry. The chemicals make the desired minerals hydrophobic, so that they do not react with water. Instead, they are attracted to the air bubbles, and float to the surface of the slurry where they can be collected. A froth flotation tank is shown in **Figure 13.**

Once separation is complete, two products remain—the concentrated mineral and a waste product called **tailings.** The amount of tailings left behind can be staggering. The extraction of just a few hundredths of an ounce of gold can produce one ton of tailings. Tailings, which will be discussed more in the next lesson, are controversial because they lead to much of the pollution associated with mining.

 Reading Checkpoint   *What is slurry?*

FIGURE 12 Exploring Hydrothermal Vents The intensely hot solution that emerges from hydrothermal vents solidifies once it comes in contact with cold sea water. Over time, the solid masses containing valuable metals collect in chimney-like structures and on the sea floor. **(a)** A robotic arm grasps part of a chimney so that it can be examined by people at the surface **(b).**

FIGURE 13 Froth Flotation This froth flotation tank is located in a zinc and lead mine in Ireland.

Metal Production Concentrated minerals are shipped from processing sites to metal production plants. Metals such as iron, aluminum, and zinc need to be further separated from the minerals that contain them. Most metal production techniques include smelting—heating ore beyond its melting point and combining it with other metals or chemicals.

For example, to make steel, steelmakers smelt iron ore to extract iron. They then melt and reprocess the mixture, removing precise amounts of carbon and shaping the product into rods, sheets, or wires. During this melting process, other metals may be added to modify the strength, malleability, and other characteristics of the steel. Steel is an *alloy*. Alloys consist of metals that have been melted and fused with other metals or nonmetal substances.

The ability to access minerals, extract metals from them, and process the metals allows us to make products that contribute greatly to modern life. But the toll that mining takes on ecosystems and the pollutants produced from processing metals have also contributed to many of the environmental problems we face today. The next lesson discusses these environmental effects and how mineral resources can be managed to decrease those effects.

LESSON ② Assessment

1. **Explain** In your own words, explain why all sources of valuable metals are not considered to be ore.

2. **Apply Concepts** A mining geologist locates a horizontal seam of coal close to the surface. What type of method will the mining company most likely use to extract it? Explain your answer.

3. **Explain** What are tailings?

4. **THINK IT *THROUGH*** Two terms used to describe the amounts of a mineral are *resources* and *reserves*. Resources are the estimated amount of a mineral on Earth. Reserves are the amount of the mineral that currently can be mined. Which of these estimates would change if a new technology were developed that gave miners new access to a mineral source? Explain.

Mining Impacts and Regulation

EVERYDAY PHENOMENON How can regulations and responsible mineral use reduce the negative impacts of mining?

Knowledge and Skills

- Describe the negative impacts of mining on the environment and society.
- Explain how mining is regulated.
- Describe ways that mineral use can become more responsible.

Reading Strategy and Vocabulary

✔ **Reading Strategy** As you read, make a cause and effect diagram that summarizes the impacts of mining on the environment.

Vocabulary acid drainage

THE PRICE WE PAY from an environmental perspective for the modern-day technologies and goods produced from mined resources is high. Destroyed habitats, air and water pollution, human health problems, and conflicts over limited resources are just a few examples of a long list of negative impacts mining has had on the environment and on the lives of many people.

Negative Impacts of Mining

In many regions of the United States and the world, mining is an important industry that provides the areas with an enormous amount of revenue and jobs for many people. But activities associated with mining, such as destroying forests, disrupting soil, and using chemicals to strip materials from rocks, have environmental effects that have not been well managed historically. Even when regulations have been introduced to prevent further damage from mining, some problems from old mining sites can persist for generations. When new mining methods are implemented, regulations to prevent environmental damage may not be in place right away. Also, not every nation regulates mining in the same way.

Increased Erosion Erosion is a natural process that occurs continuously on Earth's surface. Wind, precipitation, and flowing water move loose soil particles from one area to another. Plants help to keep erosion in check because their roots hold soil together. Over time, other natural processes typically replace the soil that has been lost in an area.

But when people disturb a large area of land, erosion occurs faster than the soil can be replaced. Clearing land and removing soil and rock during strip mining can lead to excessive erosion. Placer mining also causes erosion because it disturbs stream banks. Mountaintop removal leaves areas vulnerable to flashfloods and mudslides. Trees and other plant life may take a long time to reestablish because the soil left behind will have lost a lot of nutrients.

Sediment and Debris Excessive erosion and disturbance of waterways leads to problems for both ecosystems and nearby communities. Placer mining, strip mining, and mountaintop removal can all lead to clogged waterways from excessive sediment and debris. During mountaintop removal large amounts of displaced rocks are placed in surrounding valleys and streams.

The habitats of fish and other wildlife may be damaged as some areas become flooded and other areas experience low water levels. In addition, excess sediment can block sunlight from reaching aquatic plants that need it for photosynthesis.

Water Pollution Strip, subsurface, and open pit mining expose a large amount of rock to air. If iron sulfide is present in the rocks, it reacts with oxygen and water, and a sequence of chemical reactions forms sulfuric acid. The presence of certain bacteria can increase the rate of acid production. **Acid drainage** occurs as the acid and the metals it leaches from rock seep into groundwater or enter streams and lakes as runoff. **Figure 15** shows a waterway that is polluted from acid drainage.

Like erosion, acid drainage is a natural process, but mining greatly accelerates it by exposing a great quantity of rock to air at once. The metals associated with acid drainage can be toxic to wildlife even at low concentrations. They can also make bodies of water unsuitable for drinking water or recreational use.

Tailings contribute significantly to the water pollution caused by mining. At modern processing sites, tailings are stored in impoundments, or dams. Impoundments are designed to keep pollutants from leaching out of the tailings and entering soil and groundwater. But this system isn't perfect, and impoundments sometimes fail.

 Reading Checkpoint *How does mining increase the rate of acid drainage?*

FIGURE 15 Acid Drainage This photograph of acid drainage pollution was taken in 2009 in Colline Metallifere, a region of Italy. The name translates to "hills that produce metals."

FIGURE 16 Infrastructure Damage Residents and geologists discuss the damage caused by the Retsof Salt Mine collapse. The west side of the collapse was centered beneath a highway bridge.

Air Pollution Open pit mining and mountaintop removal can cause air pollution as metal particles are released into the atmosphere. In dry regions of the country, tailings can also cause air pollution as wind disperses these tiny particles. Many processes used for extracting metals from ore also emit air pollution. Of course, miners are the people who receive the most exposure to this air pollution. In subsurface mines, miners inhale toxic fumes and coal dust, which can lead to pneumoconiosis (black lung disease). Deaths from black lung disease have dropped significantly since the mid-twentieth century. But it is estimated that 76,000 miners have died from complications related to black lung disease since 1968.

Possible Impacts of Undersea Mining As land resources become more scarce and undersea mining technology develops, more mining companies will turn to the seas, especially to areas surrounding hydrothermal vents. Some environmental scientists fear that excessive disruption of the sea floor will destroy habitats and organisms that have not been studied yet. Disruption of the sea floor may also cause metals to diffuse into the water and enter the food chain at toxic levels.

Social Impacts Many areas in the United States and around the world rely on the mining industry for jobs and revenue. But mining can have many negative effects on people living in surrounding communities.

▶ *Property Damage* In Appalachia, especially West Virginia, Kentucky, Virginia, and Tennessee, blasts from mountaintop removal crack house foundations and wells, floods damage properties, and loose rock tumbles into yards and homes. Familiar forests and landscapes are lost. Some landowners are pressured to sell their land to mining companies.

In 1994, part of the Retsof Salt Mine in Genesee Valley, New York, collapsed. Groundwater flooded the mine, reducing available water in neighborhood wells. **Figure 16** shows a road damaged from the collapse. The collapse also affected bridges, homes, barns, and farmland. This is not an isolated incident. In many areas of the United States, communities are built on top of old subsurface mines. Over time, the tunnels and shafts collapse. The collapses can occur suddenly and produce sinkholes that can cause property damage and personal injury.

FIGURE 17 Coltan Miners Placer miners in eastern Congo are sifting a creek bed for coltan.
Apply Concepts How could excessive placer mining lead to environmental damage in the Congo?

▶ *Environmental Damage and Conflicts* Internationally, the social impacts of mining can be beneficial to societies. Mining can bring job opportunities and a lot of money into poor areas of the world. But, mining can also be very destructive to the land and water resources that agricultural communities rely on. In nations with weak or corrupt governments, violent conflicts may arise over rights to lands that hold valuable minerals and how the wealth they generate should be shared. In addition to the trade of coltan in the Congo, the trade of gold in Indonesia and diamonds in West Africa has led to violent conflicts.

Mining Regulation

Many people became rich almost overnight when large deposits of valuable metals were discovered throughout the United States in the mid-nineteenth century. Prospectors moved from area to area looking for the next big deposit of minerals, such as silver and gold. Laws governing mining were limited in scope at this time. As the mining industry continued to grow, the technology became more powerful and destructive to the environment. Eventually, laws became necessary to control who had access to mineral resources, the effects of mining on the environment, and the safety of miners. Most federal laws governing mining are set up as guidelines for states to follow as they enact their own laws.

General Mining Law of 1872 This law was enacted partly in response to the chaos of the California Gold Rush of 1849 **(Figure 18).** It created some rules to manage mining activities, but it was also designed to promote mining. At this time, the West was largely unsettled and the government wanted people to have a reason to settle it. The act governs the mining of metallic minerals such as gold, silver, and copper as well as uranium, minerals used for building materials, and diamonds on public lands. Public lands are federally owned lands. Although the United States has changed greatly since 1872, this law has not changed much. Changes that have been made include the prohibition of mining on certain types of public land such as national parks.

FIGURE 18 California Gold Rush
After James Marshall discovered gold in California in 1848, about a half million people from around the world, such as the man shown here, went to California with the hope of striking it rich.

Any United States citizen of legal age, a person who has declared an intent to become a citizen, or a company with permission to do business in the United States can stake a claim on public land that is not exempt from mining. The person or company who owns the claim leases the land from the government and has the sole right to take minerals from the claimed area. Claim owners do not have to pay the government any part of the profits they make on resources taken from the land, and until recently they have not been held accountable for restoring land after mining is complete.

Under the law, claim owners can also file to patent their claim. If a claim is patented, the land becomes privately owned by the patent holder rather than leased from the government. The miner can still purchase the land for the 1872 price of about $5 per acre. However, the government has not accepted applications for new patents since 1994 because of budget constraints.

FIGURE 19 Abandoned Mine
Thousands of abandoned mines dot the landscape of the United States, especially in the West where so many people came down with gold fever.

Mineral Leasing Act of 1920 Because of the high value of fossil fuels, the government realized they should not be managed under the General Mining Law. The Mineral Leasing Act of 1920 governs the leasing of public lands for mining of fossil fuels, phosphates, sodium, and sulfur. The terms of leases differ depending on the substance being mined, but all of those who lease land must pay annual rental fees and royalties on the products they extract.

Amending the General Mining Law Efforts have been under way to significantly amend the General Mining Law for some time. Critics say that the current policy gives away valuable public resources nearly for free. Those who defend the 1872 law argue that mining companies need to be supported because they take on substantial financial risks to locate resources that are important to the U.S. economy.

In 2019, the Hardrock Leasing and Reclamation Act of 2019 was introduced to the House of Representatives. If enacted, the bill would end the patenting process and require miners to pay the government 8 percent of their profits for existing mines and 12.5 percent for new mines. The money would go toward environmental cleanup of mining operations and reimbursement to communities affected by mining. The law would put aside more public land that would be unavailable for mining operations. It also would dictate how mining companies should fix land after mining was complete and would set standards to reduce water pollution.

 Reading Checkpoint *Is coal mining regulated under the General Mining Law of 1872 or the Mineral Leasing Act of 1920? Explain.*

WHAT DO YOU THINK?

Suppose you are a legislator in the U.S. Congress. Would you join an effort to amend the General Mining Law of 1872? Why or why not? If you would join, what would you want to include in the bill?

FIGURE 20 Reclamation More mining sites are being restored today than in the past, but restoration rarely is able to recreate the natural community present before mining. Here, reclamation workers in Ghana, West Africa, plant trees in an abandoned gold mining pit.

Surface Mining Control and Reclamation Act (1977) Because of the negative environmental effects of strip mining, the U.S. government requires that coal mining companies reclaim (restore) the land after mining is complete in an area. The Surface Mining Control and Reclamation Act requires mining companies to post bonds to cover reclamation costs before their mining plans can be approved. This ensures that if a company fails to restore the land for any reason, the government will have the money to do so.

To reclaim a site, companies are required to remove structures built to support the mining operation, replace the soil and rocks that were removed, fill in shafts, and plant vegetation. However, even on sites that are reclaimed, negative effects from mining such as acid drainage can be severe and persist for a long time. Also, restored sites do not generally replace the natural biotic communities that were present before mining. One reason is that fast-growing grasses are typically used to anchor restoration sites. This helps control erosion, but these grasses tend to outcompete slower growing, native plants in the acidic and nutrient-poor soils that remain after mining. Specialized relationships between plants and fungi and between plants and insects are also difficult to restore.

Mining Safety Protecting miners from the hazards of their job has been an ever-expanding role of the federal government. The first law, passed in 1891, established ventilation requirements for coal mines and prohibited hiring children under the age of twelve. Modern day mining safety is regulated under the Federal Mine Safety and Health Act of 1977. In 1977, 273 miners died from accidents at mining sites in the United States. Due to improvements initiated by this act, the number of deaths dropped to 53 in 2008. But the deaths of 29 miners in West Virginia in 2010, following an underground explosion, show that more should be done to protect miners.

Responsible Mineral Use

Minerals are nonrenewable resources because they form over periods that are much longer than human life spans. Like fossil fuels, at some point, there will be no more mineral deposits left to mine. However, there are steps that can be taken for more responsible mineral use.

Many factors influence how long the reserves of a particular mineral will last. New technologies may make some minerals more in demand and others less in demand. For example, increasing popularity of cell phones rapidly boosted the demand for tantalum. But, fiber optics reduced the demand for copper used in wiring. Advances in recycling also help extend the lifetimes of some mineral resources.

Reducing use, reusing, and recycling minerals address both the environmental impacts of mining and the limited supply of minerals. In many cases, reusing and recycling decrease energy use and save consumers and businesses money. For instance, programs for recycling car batteries have recovered so much lead that more than 70 percent of the lead used today comes from recycled materials. Extracting aluminum from ore takes 20 times more energy than obtaining it from recycled sources. Roughly half of the aluminum in use today is also recycled, which saves energy. Also, recycling some metals, such as mercury, means fewer of these toxic metals will end up in landfills and other places where they would pollute the environment.

But more can be done. It is estimated that in the United States there are about 600 million unused cell phones stored in homes and offices. **Figure 21** provides estimates of how many kilograms of minerals can be recycled per one million smart phones. The amount of valuable metals contained in each cell phone is small, but considering that Americans alone stop using about 150 million phones each year, that is a considerable source of minerals that can be recovered and reused.

FIGURE 21 Unused Cell Phones The table shows an estimate of how many kilograms of minerals can be recycled for every one million smart phones.

Minerals Recovered from Recycled Smart Phones

Mineral	Kg/1 million phones recycled
Copper	16,000
Gold	34
Palladium	15
Silver	350

Data from: EPA

LESSON ③ Assessment

1. **Explain** Describe two ways that mines can continue to cause damage to communities even after mining is complete.

2. **Compare and Contrast** Compare and contrast the goals of the General Mining Law of 1872 and the proposed Hardrock Mining and Reclamation Act of 2019.

3. **Apply Concepts** Although both minerals and fossil fuels are nonrenewable resources, how is mineral use more sustainable than fossil fuel use?

REVISIT

4. **INVESTIGATIVE** PHENOMENON
Mining has severe environmental effects. But mining reclamation is costly and difficult. How much reclamation do you think mining companies should be required to do? In your response, consider that mining is a business that operates on profits.

IS IT **SAFE TO MINE** IN **RETSOF, NEW YORK?**

On March 12, 1994, at 5:34 A.M., residents of Cuyler-ville, NY, in the Genesee Valley were woken up by what felt like a 3.6 magnitude earthquake. After being alerted by the local sheriff's office, mine officials discovered that the Retsof Salt Mine, the largest salt mine in North America, had collapsed. The ceiling in one part of the mine caved in, destabilizing the ground above it and releasing a flood of water from the aquifer that sat over the mine. No one was hurt, but the effects of the collapse would be felt across the Genesee Valley for more than 15 years.

Over the next year, the underground aquifer that supplied the region with water drained into the 25-square-kilometer (10-square-mile) mine.

The region's water table dropped as the mine filled with water, and some local wells, which residents relied on for drinking, washing, and watering crops, went dry. Many of the wells that didn't go dry were contaminated with salt and natural gas that seeped out of the flooded mine cavities. The mine collapse also created two sinkholes over 150 meters (500 feet) in diameter and 6 meters (20 feet) deep, and damaged roads, homes, and businesses.

In 1998, a new salt mine was opened 6 miles to the north of Retsof Mine. Some townspeople strongly support the mine, while others are concerned about the threat of another collapse, and want the mine to be closed.

THE OPINIONS

VIEWPOINT 1
The new mine might cause another collapse.

Scientists and some farmers whose land was damaged by the first collapse warn that the new mine is too risky. After all, the area around the first mine hasn't fully returned to normal yet. The U.S. Geological Survey (USGS) estimates that the land will continue to sink over the next century, and it will take at least a decade for groundwater levels to recover. If it has taken this long to recover from the first collapse, people wonder what would happen if there was another one?

And there is reason to worry about another collapse. USGS studies have shown that mines in the Genesee Valley are prone to collapse because they are located directly underneath a permeable groundwater aquifer. That means water can leak out of the aquifer into the surrounding stone, weakening the rock layer above the mine and potentially causing the ceiling to buckle and break.

VIEWPOINT 2
The new mine is profitable and safe.

Town politicians and many of the miners who lost their jobs when the Retsof mine collapsed think that the new mine is good for the region's economy. Before it closed, the Retsof mine employed 300 local miners. Moreover, mining provides some of the highest-paying jobs in the region.

Contrary to USGS reports, supporters of the new mine also argue that the threat of collapse is overblown. The new company claims that the Retsof mine collapsed because the mine operators had switched to a new type of support system. To save money, they had started using supports on the side of the mine shaft instead of large, central pillars, which are stronger. The new mine, however, is built with central supports. It is safe, provides hundreds of jobs, and bolsters the local economy.

In some places, the land sunk into the emptying aquifer, causing roads to crack.

Two workers leave through the new salt mine's shaft.

21st Century Skills

Communication Skills Pick one of the viewpoints relating to the opening of the new mine. Write a short editorial piece from either the perspective of a USGS scientist or as a miner employed by the new mine. In your essay, tell which side you are on and why.

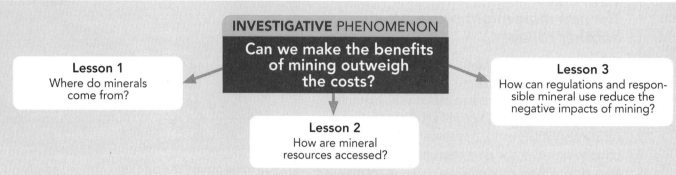

INVESTIGATIVE PHENOMENON

Can we make the benefits of mining outweigh the costs?

Lesson 1
Where do minerals come from?

Lesson 2
How are mineral resources accessed?

Lesson 3
How can regulations and responsible mineral use reduce the negative impacts of mining?

LESSON 1 Minerals and Rocks

- A mineral is a naturally occurring, inorganic solid that has an orderly crystalline structure and a definite chemical composition.
- Minerals can form by crystallization from magma or lava, from precipitation related to evaporation or hydrothermal solutions, or from exposure to high pressure and temperature. They also can be produced by organisms.
- A rock is a solid mass of minerals and mineral-like material that occurs naturally.
- Forces deep inside and at the surface of Earth produce changes in rock that cause the same material to cycle between igneous rock, sedimentary rock, and metamorphic rock stages.

mineral (392)
precipitation (394)
polymorph (394)
rock (395)
rock cycle (395)

LESSON 2 Mining

- Mining companies seek and gather valuable resources such as metals, nonmetallic minerals, and fuel sources.
- Mining companies have developed many techniques to access resources close to the surface of Earth, deep underground, and even underwater.
- After mining, ores and other extracted materials are processed to separate the desired materials, combine them with other materials, or alter their properties.

ore (398)
strip mining (400)
subsurface mining (400)
open pit mining (400)
mountaintop removal (401)
placer mining (402)
tailings (403)
smelting (404)

LESSON 3 Mining Impacts and Regulations

- Environmental impacts of mining include increased erosion, increased sediment and debris, and pollution of water, land, and air. Other negative impacts may arise as undersea mining becomes more prevalent. Mining can also have negative impacts on society, such as property damage and violent conflicts.
- Regulations that govern mining have changed over time. At first, regulations were focused on promoting settlement of the West by making mining an attractive way for settlers to make money. Many modern-day regulations focus on mining safety and reducing the negative environmental effects of mining.
- Because minerals are a nonrenewable resource, we need to be concerned about finite supplies and ways to use them more responsibly, such as reusing and recycling.

acid drainage (406)

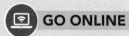 **GO ONLINE**

INQUIRY LABS AND ACTIVITIES

- **Mineral Identification**

  Describe the hardness, color, and streak of several mineral samples. Then design a procedure to classify the samples.

- **Local Geology**

  What sort of rocks and minerals are found in your local area? Research local geology, and then identify samples outdoors.

Chapter Assessment

Central CASE Defend Your Case

Suppose, in the midst of the resource war in the Congo, you were the head of an international aid agency. Explain how you would work with the government of the Congo, the rebel leaders, the United Nations, and mining corporations to help improve the situation in the Congo.

Review Concepts and Terms

1. Which type of rock forms when layers of weathered materials are pressed together over time?
   a. igneous
   c. metamorphic
   b. sedimentary
   d. granite

2. All minerals
   a. have a hardness level of 10.
   b. have cleavage.
   c. have the same crystal form.
   d. are inorganic solids.

3. Compared to minerals that form on the surface of Earth, minerals that form within Earth's crust
   a. have small crystals.
   c. do not have crystals.
   b. have large crystals.
   d. form from lava.

4. Which of the following statements is TRUE of nonmetallic minerals?
   a. They are not mined for their metal content.
   b. They do not contain metals.
   c. They have no value.
   d. They are used as energy sources.

5. Which type of mining would NOT be used to mine coal?
   a. strip mining
   c. solution mining
   b. moutaintop removal
   d. subsurface mining

6. What type of mining would most likely be used when a mineral resource is spread evenly and deeply throughout a rock formation, but the ground is not safe for tunneling?
   a. placer mining
   b. solution mining
   c. subsurface mining
   d. open pit mining

7. Smelting is a process used during
   a. ore extraction.
   c. froth flotation.
   b. metal processing.
   d. grinding ore.

8. Which mining method contributes to excessive erosion, increased sediment, water pollution, and air pollution?
   a. undersea mining
   c. solution mining
   b. placer mining
   d. mountaintop removal

9. A main goal of the General Mining Law of 1872 was to
   a. ensure that limited mining occurred on public land.
   b. ensure the safety of miners.
   c. set up royalty rates for miners to pay on their profits.
   d. outline the rules for mining on public land.

10. Which is NOT a benefit of recycling minerals?
    a. Fewer dangerous metals will get into landfills.
    b. Often recycling costs less than mining.
    c. Recycling fossil fuels increases how long they will be available.
    d. Recycling may have less of an environmental effect than mining.

Modified True/False

Write true if the statement is true. If it is false, change the underlined word or words to make the statement true.

11. Mineral samples of the same type can have different <u>colors</u>, depending on the conditions under which they formed.

12. Granite is an example of <u>extrusive</u> igneous rock because it cooled within Earth's crust.

13. <u>Open pit mining</u> has not become widespread because the costs associated with it are so high.

14. The mining method in which material in riverbeds and streambeds is sifted for deposited resources is called <u>placer mining</u>.

15. A common type of water pollution caused by acidic water leaching metals from strip mining waste is called <u>tailings</u>.

Reading Comprehension

Read the following selection and answer the questions that follow.

In just the two or three centuries since the beginning of the Industrial Revolution, human activity has had major effects on Earth's basic processes. Some geologists have posed the question: "Have these effects been strong enough to justify naming a new geologic epoch after ourselves?" Some have suggested calling the new geologic era the Anthropocene. Through activities such as agriculture, mining, and deforestation, immense amounts of sediment have flowed downstream to oceans. In addition, humans have altered the composition of gases in the atmosphere, which affects Earth's temperature and the acidity of ocean water. Habitat disturbance, pollution, and hunting have also lead to mass extinctions. These changes would appear sudden to a geologist of the future.

16. Which of the following human activities has had the greatest impact to date on the environment?

  a. mining   **c.** burning of fossil fuels

  b. agriculture   **d.** Industrial Revolution

17. How would increased amounts of sediment in the ocean appear to geologists of the future studying the geologic record?

  a. as a sedimentary rock layer

  b. as an igneous rock layer

  c. as a metamorphic rock layer

  d. as granite

Short Answer

18. Describe how metamorphic rocks are formed.

19. What is the difference between magma and lava?

20. Why isn't coal considered to be a mineral?

21. How does increased sediment harm the environment?

22. Describe what a mining company must do to reclaim land after mining is complete.

23. Explain the process of froth flotation.

24. What is an alloy?

25. What are two ways to increase how long the reserves of a particular mineral will last?

Analyze Data

In 2005, U.S. Geological Survey scientists completed a study of tributaries that flow into the Boulder River in Montana. From 1880 to 1907, the area was heavily mined for copper, lead, zinc, silver, and gold. Mining ended in the 1970s, but pollution levels are still high. The map indicates the concentration of zinc in streambed sediments. Use the map to answer Questions 26 and 27.

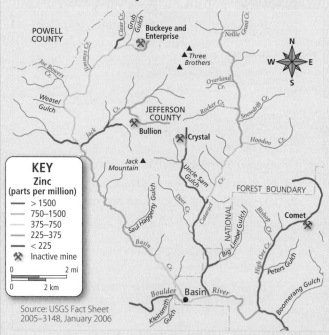

Source: USGS Fact Sheet 2005–3148, January 2006

26. Apply Concepts Pollution in this area is associated with entrances to underground mines and dump sites containing mine waste. What are two possible causes of water pollution in this area?

27. Interpret Data Do the data in this map support the hypothesis that the inactive mines are the source of water pollution in this area? Explain.

Critical Thinking

28. Compare and Contrast Describe how diamond and graphite are alike and different.

29. Form An Opinion Can land that has undergone mountaintop removal truly be reclaimed? Explain your answer.

30. Interpret Diagrams Use the diagram to describe two ways that the particles in a particular sedimentary rock could eventually become metamorphic rock.

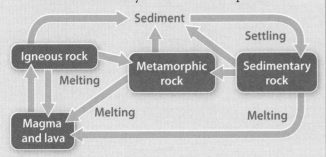

31. Apply Concepts Why is it important that people who process minerals understand the characteristics of the minerals they are processing?

32. Evaluate One of the attractions of space exploration is the possibility of mining minerals from places other than Earth, such as the moon or Mars. Discuss the challenges and benefits.

Write About It

33. Persuasion Some experts think that the reason so few cell phones are recycled is that many people either do not know that cell phones can be recycled or they do not know about available programs. Write to a local environmental agency persuading them to start a cell phone recycling campaign.

34. Opinion Throughout the United States there are many inactive mining areas like the one near the Boulder River in Montana. Some of the worst sites are being cleaned up by the EPA. But such cleanups take a long time and are expensive. Should the government, whose efforts are funded by taxes, be responsible for the cleanup of these areas? Explain.

35. REVISIT INVESTIGATIVE PHENOMENON Describe some ways that you think the environmental costs of mining can be offset.

Ecological Footprints

Read the information below. Copy the table into your notebook and record your calculations. Then answer the questions that follow.

Currently, the average person in the United States consumes metals at a much higher rate than the world average. What would happen to the availability of metals if every individual worldwide started consuming at the rate of an average person in the United States?

1. For each metal, calculate and enter in the fourth column the years of supply left. Then, calculate the years of supply left if the world consumed each metal at the U.S. rate. Enter those values in the sixth column.

2. Which of these seven metals will last the longest at present rates of global consumption? Which will deplete the fastest?

3. The data provided in this table are for 2007. For some metals, availability fluctuates considerably from year to year. What are some factors that would affect the known world reserves and the amount used per year?

Metal	Known World Reserves (thousand metric tons)	Amount Used Per Year (thousand metric tons)	Years of Supply Left	Amount Used Per Year If All Consumed at U.S. Rate (thousand metric tons)	Years of Supply Left
Manganese	5,200,000	11,600.0		20,020.0	
Titanium	1,500,000	6100.0		31,900.0	
Nickel	150,000	1660.0		5082.0	
Tin	11,000	300.0		1290.0	
Tungsten	6300	89.6		316.8	
Antimony	4300	135.0		503.8	
Indium	16	0.5		2.1	

Data are for 2007, from 2008 U.S. Geological Survey Mineral Commodity Summaries. World consumption data are assumed to be equal to world production data. World reserves include amounts known to exist, whether or not they are presently economically extractable.

The low water level of Lake Mead near the Hoover Dam is apparent by the change in rock color along Black Canyon.

Lesson 1
Earth: The Water Planet

Lesson 2
Uses of Fresh Water

Lesson 3
Water Pollution

Looking for Water... in the Desert

THE DESERT is about the last place you would think to mine for water. Yet, the city of Las Vegas is proposing to do just that. The controversial proposal to start mining the Great Basin Desert for water is just one solution Las Vegas is entertaining to try and quench its increasing thirst for water.

Las Vegas is looking to the desert because its main water supply, the Colorado River, is drying up. Drought, dams, and diversion have caused this once raging river to end up a mere dribble. And while Las Vegas's immediate need is to find new water sources, there is a larger, looming question— what can be done to make sure that what was once the West's wildest river doesn't run dry?

Beginning in the high peaks of the Rocky Mountains, the 2300-kilometer (1450-mile) long Colorado River once charged through the Southwest, crossed into Mexico, and rushed into the Gulf of California. Today, however, massive dams regulate its flow. Water is diverted along its length, not only to drink, but also to water crops and lawns, fill backyard swimming pools, and gush through fountains in Las Vegas casinos. What little water is left empties into the Gulf of California. Often, what's left is just a trickle.

But the river didn't dry up overnight. Since 1922, and the signing of the Colorado River Compact, seven western states—Arizona, California, Colorado, Nevada, New Mexico, Utah, and Wyoming—have divided the river's water among themselves. Shares of water were based on the needs and negotiating power each state had at the time. As years passed, California was allowed to take more than its designated amount because the other states didn't need it.

Things have changed. The population of all seven states currently tops 62 million. It is becoming clear that the states depending on the river for water must renegotiate how to divide its dwindling resources. Due to prolonged drought, the Colorado River's flow has been mostly lower

GO ONLINE
• Take It Local   • 3-D Geo Tour

than average since 2000. Reservoirs are at half capacity, and experts predict that climate change will bring still more drought.

Since Nevada was barely populated in the 1920s, it had rights to only 4 percent of the river's water. But with tens of thousands of people coming to the state every year, Nevada needs more water—and fast. The Colorado River, however, is a finite source of fresh water. It simply cannot be stretched to meet the needs of the growing population that depends on it.

Forced to look beyond the Colorado River, Nevada turned to the unlikeliest of places for water—the desert. Officials proposed tapping groundwater sources underneath a scenic area of the Great Basin Desert. The project also required a 300 mile pipeline to pump the water from rural Nevada to Las Vegas. It's a controversial project that may threaten the area's ecology, and after more than 30 years in the courts it appears unlikely to happen. Will the residents of Nevada be able to tap a new well of ideas before the water runs dry?

Earth: The Water Planet

EVERYDAY PHENOMENON How can water be both a renewable resource and be scarce in some regions?

Knowledge and Skills

- Discuss how fresh water can be both renewable and limited.
- Explain the significance of a watershed.
- Explain how most groundwater is accessed.

Reading Strategy and Vocabulary

✓ **Reading Strategy** Before you read, create a main idea and details chart using the sentences under blue headings in this lesson as your main ideas. As you read, fill in the chart with details from the text.

Vocabulary fresh water, surface water, runoff, river system, watershed, groundwater, permeable, impermeable, aquifer, water table, recharge zone, well

"WATER, WATER, EVERYWHERE, nor any drop to drink." The well-known line from the poem *The Rime of the Ancient Mariner* describes the situation on our planet quite well. Water *is* everywhere—it falls from the sky as rain and snow, it covers our poles as ice, and, of course, it fills our oceans. Water even makes up about two thirds of our bodies! However, in many places on Earth, there is not nearly enough of it to meet human needs. One in eight people lack access to clean fresh water. How can there be so little of something so abundant?

Where Is Our Water?

Water may seem abundant to us, but globally, water that we can actually use is quite rare. However, because fresh water is a renewable resource, its supplies can be maintained—as long as we learn to use them sustainably.

A Renewable Resource Water is considered a renewable resource because the water cycle, or hydrologic cycle, constantly recycles it. Cycling water redistributes heat, erodes mountain ranges, builds river deltas, maintains organisms and ecosystems, and shapes civilizations. As water moves, it may change state: from solid ice, to liquid water, to gaseous water vapor, but overall, very little water is ever gained or lost. Water, however, is not always useful or where we want it.

A Limited Resource You can't drink salt water or effectively water crops with ice. Most of people's day-to-day activities rely on fresh, liquid water. However, only a very small portion of Earth's water—about one half of one percent—is both fresh and liquid (**Figure 1**). If a full 2-liter bottle represented all the water on Earth, only about two capfuls would be fresh, liquid water.

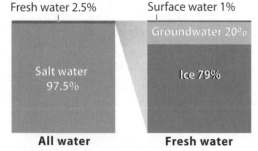

Fresh water 2.5%   Surface water 1%

Groundwater 20%

Salt water 97.5%   Ice 79%

All water   **Fresh water**

Data from the United Nations Environment Programme (UNEP) and World Resources Institute.

FIGURE 1 Water on Earth Only 2.5% of Earth's water is fresh water. Of that 2.5%, most is frozen—tied up in glaciers and ice caps.

FIGURE 2 Water Availability
Developments built near or in deserts often cause a strain on local water sources. In some cases water must be piped in over long distances.

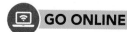

GO ONLINE

- **Graph It** Global Freshwater Resources

About 97.5% of Earth's water is salt water. Most salt water is found in the oceans and is too salty for drinking or watering crops. Only 2.5% of Earth's water is considered **fresh water**, water that is relatively pure with few dissolved salts. Of that tiny proportion of water, more than three quarters is frozen in the form of glaciers and ice caps. The remaining 21%, found in lakes, rivers, the atmosphere, organisms, and soil, is liquid. Only some of this 21% is drinkable or usable for crops. Clearly, useful fresh water is a very limited resource.

People and Water Because water is so critical to our daily lives, you might expect that people would choose to live only in places with ample access to it. Unfortunately, this is not the case. Many areas with high population density, such as Las Vegas and its suburbs, do not have a lot of water. Other areas have plenty of water, but few people. These situations cause inequalities in per capita water resources. For example, India has almost four times as much water as Australia. However, India has almost 55 times the population. So, per capita, Australia has far more water available to its residents than India does.

Seasonal Availability Fresh water is distributed unevenly in time as well as space. Although some areas have access to fresh water, it might not always be there when it is needed. Many parts of the world experience distinct rainy and dry seasons. Portions of western and central India, for example, get around 90 percent of their annual rainfall during the three-month monsoon season. Because fresh water is distributed unevenly in space and time people are often challenged with moving fresh water from its source to where it's needed when it's needed.

FIND OUT MORE

Use the Internet or other resources to find out the following facts about your local water:

1. What major watershed is your hometown part of?
2. Does your area experience any seasonal changes in water availability?
3. Has your hometown experienced any water shortages in the last 10 years?

Surface Water

Water is categorized as either surface water or groundwater depending on where it is located. Just one percent of easily accessible fresh water is surface water, water found on Earth's surface. Sources of surface water include rainfall and melting snow, glaciers, and ice caps. Water travels from these sources to bodies of surface water as runoff. **Runoff** is water that flows over land and has not been absorbed into the ground. Runoff can flow into standing, or still, bodies of surface water such as lakes and ponds, or it can join up with a river system.

River Systems Water moves downhill according to gravity, forming a network of connected streams and rivers called a **river system.** As runoff flows downhill, it can form shallow grooves in the earth. These grooves can deepen and flow together forming streams. Streams can in turn merge into rivers. Smaller rivers, called tributaries, flow into larger rivers. Eventually, running water from a river system empties into a body of water such as a lake or the ocean.

Watersheds Pretend you are standing at a river's mouth, where its waters meet the ocean. Now, picture tracing a drop of water back up the river, through smaller and smaller branches of the river system, right back to the original spot where it fell as precipitation. If you could do that for every drop of water that flows out of a river, you will have defined its watershed. A **watershed** includes all of the land area that supplies water to a particular river system. Watersheds are sometimes called drainage basins because they drain into a river system the same way that rainwater drains into street or house gutters. **Figure 3** shows the major watershed regions in the United States.

 What is a river system?

The Mississippi River Watershed

The Mississippi River Basin is the third largest watershed in the world, covering over 3 million square kilometers (1.2 million square miles). In fact, it drains 41% of the land area of the contiguous United States. Use the map in **Figure 3** to answer the following questions.

1. **Interpret Maps** Trace the path of a raindrop that falls in Billings, Montana, as it makes its way to the Gulf of Mexico. List the rivers it flows through.

2. **Explain** Why does the map of the Mississippi River watershed contain both the river system and the land that surrounds it?

3. **Infer** The Mississippi River watershed is bordered by the Appalachian Mountains to the east and the Rocky Mountains to the west. Why does it make sense that mountain ranges form natural watershed boundaries?

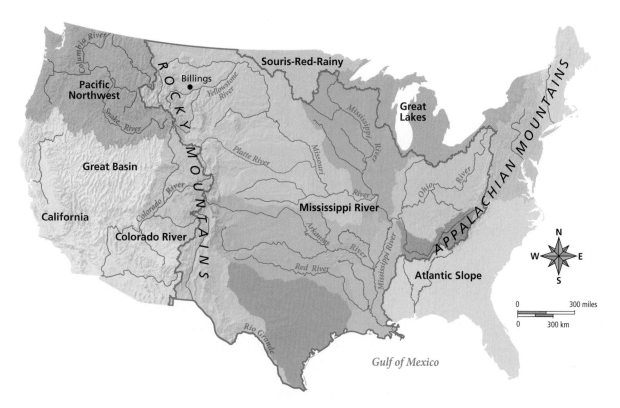

▶ **Watershed Structure** Every waterway, whether a large river or a tiny creek, and the land area that drains into it define a watershed. Notice that the Mississippi River watershed is shown in many shades of green on the map. Inside the enormous Mississippi River watershed are several large watersheds of the river's major tributaries, such as the Ohio River and Missouri River. The Ohio River watershed, shown in lightest green on the map, covers 528,000 square kilometers (204,000 square miles) and parts of 14 states. When the Ohio River drains into the Mississippi River, this large area becomes part of the overall Mississippi River watershed. In fact, each of the watersheds in **Figure 3** is made up of many smaller watersheds. Any river's watershed can, therefore, be thought of as the region drained by it and all of its tributaries. Not shown on the map are the more than 50 smaller watersheds that make up the Ohio River watershed. The Colorado River watershed has two major parts, an upper basin and a lower basin, shown in shades of orange on the map.

▶ **Managing Watersheds** The interconnected nature of watersheds greatly influences how they are managed. Look again at the Mississippi River watershed shown in **Figure 3.** Consider the effect pollution along the Platte River in Nebraska could have on rivers downstream. Once washed into the river, the pollution would flow southeast into the Missouri River. Eventually, it would empty into the Gulf of Mexico. Similarly, the amount of water taken from the Red River in Texas could affect how much is available to people in Louisiana. Clearly, managing water sustainably requires the cooperation of everyone living within the watershed.

◆ **Connect to the Central Case**

FIGURE 3 United States Watersheds This map shows the major watersheds in the continental United States. A watershed consists of all the land that supplies water to a river system. **Interpret Maps** What forms the eastern boundary of the Colorado River watershed?

FIGURE 4 Protect Your Watershed Signs like this one in Canada help raise awareness about watersheds.

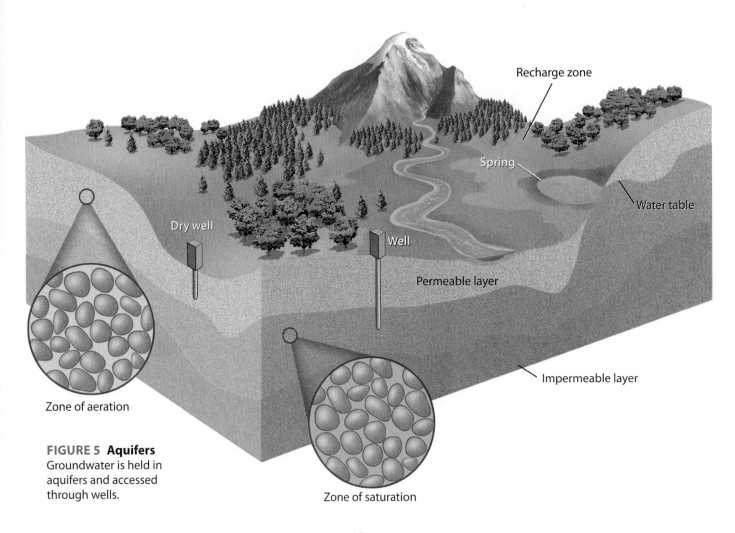

FIGURE 5 Aquifers Groundwater is held in aquifers and accessed through wells.

Groundwater

Any precipitation reaching Earth's land surface that does not evaporate, flow into rivers, or get taken up by organisms soaks into the surface. Some of this water trickles downward through the soil to become **groundwater,** water found below Earth's surface. Groundwater makes up about one fifth of Earth's freshwater supply and plays a key role in meeting human water needs.

Aquifers As water is pulled down into the ground by gravity, it encounters different layers of soil and rock. Layers containing spaces, or pores, through which water can pass are called **permeable.** Layers with few or no pores are called **impermeable.** Water soaks through permeable layers until it reaches an impermeable layer. Once water reaches an impermeable layer, it is trapped and can't move any deeper.

The water then begins to fill up the spaces available in the permeable layers. In this way, groundwater gets contained within **aquifers,** sponge-like formations of rock, sand, or gravel that hold water. Shown in **Figure 5,** an aquifer's upper layer, or *zone of aeration*, contains pores through which water can flow. In the lower layer, or *zone of saturation*, these spaces are completely filled with water. The boundary between the two zones is the **water table.**

A water table's depth is affected by the shape of the land and by the amount of water available. As rock layers rise and dip, so does the water table. The water table rises during times of heavy precipitation or snowmelt and falls with drier weather. Any area where surface water soaks into the ground and reaches an aquifer below is called the **recharge zone.** Once within the aquifer, the typical rate of horizontal groundwater flow might be only about 1 meter (3.2 feet) per day. The rate varies widely with the permeability of the rock and the slope of the aquifer.

Within an aquifer, groundwater may travel horizontally for hundreds of kilometers, remaining underground for a very long time. In fact, the average age of groundwater has been estimated at 1400 years, and some is tens of thousands of years old. This means not only that groundwater is old, but that it can take a long time to recharge once it is depleted.

 Why might a water table drop?

Getting Groundwater to the Surface How do people access groundwater? Sometimes, the water table naturally rises to the surface creating springs. Other times, groundwater bursts to the surface as a geyser, like Old Faithful in Yellowstone Park. Most of the time, however, we have to dig to gain access to groundwater. A hole dug into an aquifer to reach groundwater is called a **well.** Wells are dug deep into the zone of saturation so that they won't dry up during seasonal droughts. But if the water table does drop below the depth of the well, the well will run dry. Dry wells must be dug deeper to keep supplying water to the surface.

Each day in the United States alone, aquifers release 1.9 trillion liters (492 billion gallons) of groundwater through wells, springs, and geysers, into bodies of surface water—nearly as much as the daily flow of the Mississippi River. The world's largest known aquifer is the Ogallala aquifer, which underlies the Great Plains of the United States **(Figure 6).** Water from this massive aquifer has enabled American farmers to create the most bountiful grain-producing region in the world.

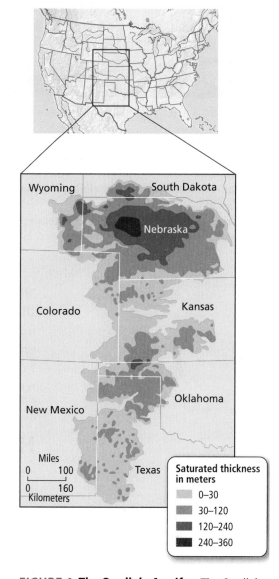

FIGURE 6 The Ogallala Aquifer The Ogallala aquifer is one of the world's largest aquifers. It underlies parts of eight U.S. states from South Dakota to Texas.

---

① Assessment

1. **Explain** Provide details from the text that support the conclusion that liquid fresh water on Earth is a limited resource.

2. **Describe** What is a watershed? Why is it more effective to manage an entire watershed as compared to a single water source?

3. **Relate Cause and Effect** Why might you have to dig a well deeper if it is overused?

REVISIT

4. **INVESTIGATIVE** PHENOMENON
Most civilizations began near a source of fresh water. Over time, however, technology has enabled us to move fresh water great distances. In what ways do you think this kind of technology has contributed to the water shortages many people face today?

2 Uses of Fresh Water

LESSON

EVERYDAY PHENOMENON How can we reduce our own daily water use?

Knowledge and Skills

- List the three primary categories of freshwater use.
- Relate the causes of surface water depletion to their effects.
- Explain the major causes and effects of groundwater depletion.
- Describe strategies for addressing water depletion.

Reading Strategy and Vocabulary

✔ **Reading Strategy** As you read, make a two-column table. In the left column, make notes about how fresh water is being depleted. In the right column, describe possible solutions to water depletion.

Vocabulary water diversion, dam, reservoir, salinization, desalination, xeriscaping

More than half of the world's population will live with water stress by 2050, according to researchers. Data indicate that our current rate of freshwater use is unsustainable in much of the world. Many sources of surface water and groundwater are literally drying up. Where is all of our fresh water going, and what can be done to slow down and eventually reverse water loss?

How We Use Water

Think about what you did today. How much water did you use? You might not think it is a lot—perhaps just some water for a shower, to brush your teeth, to wash your breakfast dishes, and to drink. But in reality, almost everything we use and consume during the day requires water. Globally, about 69% of our fresh water is used on agriculture. Industry accounts for roughly 19%. Personal uses account for 12%. These statistics, however, vary with a region's income and stage of industrial development, as seen in **Figure 7**.

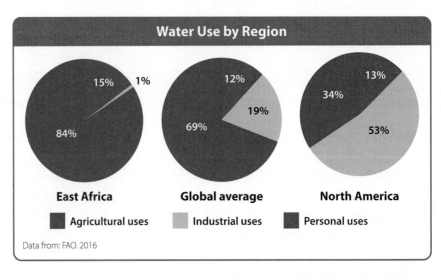

Water Use by Region

East Africa: 84%, 15%, 1%

Global average: 69%, 19%, 12%

North America: 34%, 13%, 53%

■ Agricultural uses   ■ Industrial uses   ■ Personal uses

Data from: FAO. 2016

FIGURE 7 Water Use and Region
The proportion of water consumed in agricultural, industrial, and personal uses varies with a region's economy.

Agricultural Uses No matter a region's income, a lot of fresh water is used for agriculture. Farmers and ranchers who produce the food you eat must use water for their crops and livestock. About 1500 liters (400 gallons) of water are needed to produce just one kilogram (2.2 pounds) of wheat. That's more water than an average person drinks in a year! And ten times as much—about 15,000 liters of water—is needed to produce just one kilogram of grain-fed beef!

Industrial Uses Most manufacturing and industrial processes that create everything from the bed you sleep on to the gasoline that powers the bus you ride to school require water. A standard bottle of water, for example, requires about twice as much water to produce than it holds. Every day, American factories use about 68 billion liters (18 billion gallons) of water to make and transport their products.

The world's energy industries use a lot of water, too. As power plants generate electricity (using coal, oil, natural gas, or nuclear material), the machinery gets very hot. Engineers use water, piped through power plants, to cool off the machinery. Water is also used in the refining processes that generate gasoline and oil. It takes between 1 and 2.5 gallons of water to refine a single gallon of gasoline. Multiply that by the millions of gallons of gasoline used in the United States each day, and you get billions of gallons of water used every day just to keep our motors running.

Personal Uses Every day, an average person in the United States drinks between 2 and 5 liters of water, but we also use water for bathing, cooking, doing laundry, and flushing the toilet. Water keeps lawns green and swimming pools full. Each of these activities is a personal water use because an individual uses the water directly. Many personal uses occur inside the home, so they are sometimes called *residential uses*. **Figure 8** shows how much water is used for some of these activities.

Unless you live in a place with a personal-use well, most of this water comes into your house through pipes after it has been cleaned and treated. For that reason, leaky pipes are also considered a personal use of water. Do you know how much water is used per household just by letting it leak out of our pipes? About 36 liters (9.5 gallons) a day!

✓ **Reading Checkpoint** *What are the three major categories of water use?*

MAKE A DIFFERENCE
your world · your turn ·

One standard 60-watt bulb burning for 12 hours a day every day for a year about 11,000–23,000 liters (3000–6000 gallons) of water. Used in the same way, a compact fluorescent bulb requires only about 4000–8000 liters (1000–2000 gallons) of water and LED lightbulbs will use even less. So, if you want to help conserve water, change your light bulbs!

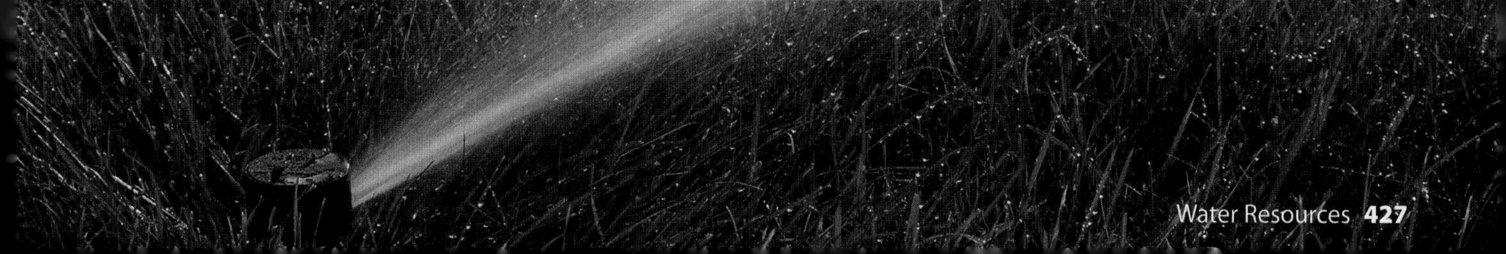

FIGURE 8 Personal Water Uses
A typical American uses more than 250 liters of water a day in various indoor activities such as cleaning and bathing. Outdoor activities such as watering a lawn use even more water. The table lists some personal water uses and the amount of water they require.

How much water does it take to...	
Fill the average swimming pool	72,000 liters (19,000 gallons)
Water the average suburban lawn	2800 liters (750 gallons)
Take a 10-minute shower	150 liters (40 gallons)
Flush the toilet	25 liters (6 gallons)
Run a load of dishes in the dishwasher	25 liters (6 gallons)
Data from H2O Conserve.	

Using Surface Water

In the United States, about 77 percent of the fresh water used—for agricultural, industrial, and personal reasons—comes from surface water sources such as lakes, ponds, rivers, and streams. All of this water has to be pulled from its source and then moved to where it is used. How does that happen?

Diverting Water If you live near a lake or river, it may seem like an easy task to get the water from its source to your house. But if you live in a desert, water has to be transported from much farther away. The process of moving water from its source to places where humans use it, such as homes and farm fields, is called **water diversion.**

Water from the Colorado River is diverted for both agricultural and personal uses. The All-American Canal, shown in **Figure 9**, is the world's largest irrigation canal. It provides water that irrigates over 2000 square kilometers (500,000 acres) of cropland that brings in about $1 billion to the economy. Other canals carry water from the Colorado River to several major cities including Los Angeles, California; Las Vegas, Nevada; and Phoenix, Arizona. People would not be able to live and work in these cities without water diversions. However, water diversions can come at a high cost. For instance, Los Angeles grew by using water diverted from the Owens Valley, Mono Lake, and other rural regions of California. Due to the diversion, these areas have been turned to desert and the local economies have been harmed.

Dams Sometimes it is not possible to rely on a naturally flowing river or stream for water. The flow may be too fast or too slow. Or, the amount of water available may vary too much in different seasons. To help regulate river flow and to build a stable supply of water, a dam may be built. A **dam** is any obstruction placed in a river or stream to block its flow. Dams create artificial **reservoirs,** large lakes that store water for human use. According to the U.S. Army Corps of Engineers, there are currently about 90,000 dams in the United States.

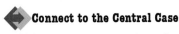

◆ **Connect to the Central Case**

FIGURE 9 Water Diversion There are several major diversions along the Colorado River, including the All-American Canal, shown here in Arizona. Most of the water is used to irrigate farmland in desert regions. **Apply Concepts** How might the All-American Canal affect the flow of water at the mouth of the Colorado River?

Major Costs and Benefits of Dams

Costs	Benefits
✘ **Habitat alteration** Reservoirs flood habitats and displace or kill river species upstream. Shallow warm water downstream from a dam gets flushed with cold reservoir water, stressing or killing many fish.	✔ **Clean power generation** Hydroelectric dams provide inexpensive electricity without greenhouse gas emissions.
✘ **Fisheries decline** Salmon and other fish that migrate up rivers to spawn cannot always get past dams.	✔ **Crop irrigation** Reservoirs can release water for irrigation when farmers need it most.
✘ **Population displacement** Reservoirs have caused approximately 40–80 million people to relocate over the past half-century alone.	✔ **Flood control** Dams can prevent floods by storing seasonal surges.
✘ **Sediment capture** When sediment settles behind dams, downstream flood plains are no longer nourished, and reservoirs fill with silt.	✔ **Shipping** By replacing rocky riverbeds with deep calm pools, dams enable ships to transport goods over longer distances.
✘ **Loss of fertile farmland** Floods create productive farmland by depositing rich sediment. Without flooding, topsoil is lost, and farmland deteriorates.	✔ **New recreational opportunities** People can fish and boat on reservoirs in regions where these activities were not possible before.
✘ **Risk of failure** There is always risk that a dam could fail, causing massive damage and loss of life.	
✘ **Lost recreational opportunities** Tubing, whitewater rafting, fly-fishing, and kayaking opportunities are lost.	

As shown in **Figure 10**, dams involve a complex mix of costs and benefits. Dams can damage river ecosystems, force people from their homes, and fail with devastating results. However, dams can also prevent floods, provide drinking water, facilitate irrigation, and generate electricity. Increasingly, private dam owners and the U.S. government have begun to dismantle dams whose costs seem to outweigh their benefits. More than 750 U.S. dams have been removed in recent years.

There are hundreds of thousands of dams worldwide. The largest is the Three Gorges Dam in China. Only a few major rivers in the world remain undammed, and those run through sparsely populated areas. The Glen Canyon Dam and Hoover Dam created the two great reservoirs along the Colorado River: Lake Powell on the Utah-Arizona border and Lake Mead on the Nevada-Arizona border. The water levels in these reservoirs, however, have been dropping in recent years. This is a sign of surface water depletion and a cause of great concern for cities such as Las Vegas that depend on these reservoirs for water.

 Connect to the Central Case

FIGURE 10 Costs and Benefits of Dams Damming rivers has diverse consequences for people and the environment. The Glen Canyon Dam on the Colorado River is no exception. **Infer** How do you know that the river is flowing from left to right in this photo?

 Using the table above, explain how a dam can have both positive and negative effects on agriculture.

FIGURE 11 A Disappearing Sea Once the world's fourth-largest freshwater body, the Aral Sea in Central Asia is shown in satellite images from **(a)** 1987 and **(b)** 2014. The sea has been shrinking due to over-withdrawal of water to irrigate cotton crops.

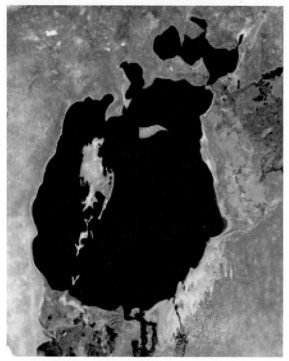

(a) 1987

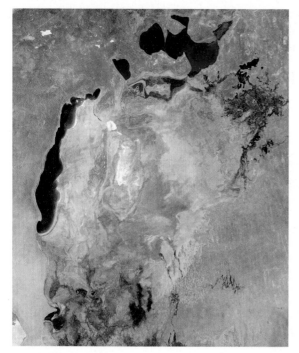

(b) 2014

Surface Water Depletion Drought and overuse have significantly reduced surface water resources. The Colorado River's water is so heavily diverted that it sometimes runs completely dry before reaching the Gulf of California. Reduced water flow has drastically altered the ecology of the lower river and the once-rich delta. Populations of many plants and animals have declined significantly, including those of several fish species endemic to the Colorado River, such as the pikeminnow, humpback chub, and razorback sucker.

▶ *Dried Up Rivers* Sadly, the situation on the Colorado River is not unique. Several hundred miles to the east, the Rio Grande also frequently runs dry, the victim of over-use by Mexican and U.S. farmers coupled with drought. The situation is even worse for China's Yellow River. The Chinese government wants to divert water from the Yangtze River to keep the Yellow River flowing and to supply water to northern China. Even the mighty Nile River in Egypt often dries up before reaching its mouth.

▶ *The Aral Sea* Nowhere are the effects of surface water depletion so evident as in the Aral Sea in Asia, shown in **Figure 11.** Once the fourth-largest freshwater body on Earth, over 90 percent of its volume has been lost since 1960. Cotton is a very "thirsty" crop, requiring a lot of water to grow. To make the land suitable for cotton, it was flooded with water diverted from the two rivers leading into the Aral Sea. For a few decades, this practice boosted Soviet cotton production. Today, however, the Aral Sea lakebed is dry in many places. More than 60,000 fishing jobs are gone, and there is not enough water left to sustain farming.

Using Groundwater

Generally, groundwater recharges so slowly that it takes much longer to replace a given amount of water taken from an aquifer as compared to a lake or pond. Unfortunately, that means that most groundwater use is unsustainable.

Agricultural Uses About 26% of the fresh water used in the United States comes from groundwater. Of that, 40% is used for irrigation. Due to population growth, irrigated land has increased dramatically and contributed to groundwater depletion. In 1950 about 34 billion gallons per day of groundwater were withdrawn. By 2015, more than 82 billion gallons were used. Groundwater is also more likely than surface water to be used for livestock.

Most irrigation is very inefficient. A lot of water is lost to runoff and evaporation. Too much water can also be a bad thing because over-irrigation leads to waterlogging and salinization. Waterlogging occurs when soil becomes saturated with water to the point that oxygen no longer gets in. **Salinization** is the buildup of salts in the surface layers of soil. Too much salinization can make the soil unusable.

Groundwater Mining About 18 percent of groundwater goes to public uses such as drinking water. Las Vegas is trying to win approval to use groundwater from beneath the Great Basin Desert in Nevada to increase its public water supply. Withdrawing groundwater faster than it can be replaced is called *groundwater mining*. Groundwater mining turns groundwater into a nonrenewable resource. However, Las Vegas is running out of water and there isn't enough available in the lower Colorado River to support another surface water diversion. Most residents of the Great Basin region and wildlife advocates oppose the groundwater-mining plan. They are concerned that the project could negatively affect the Great Basin ecosystem. However, life in Las Vegas may not be sustainable for long unless the city can find more water somewhere and institute conservation practices for the water it has.

WHAT DO YOU THINK?

In your opinion, is groundwater mining a sensible solution? How else could Las Vegas meet its future water needs?

✓ **Reading Checkpoint** *What is groundwater mining?*

Real Data

Lake Powell

Lake Powell is a major storage reservoir along the Lower Colorado River. Along with Lake Mead, Lake Powell provides drinking water, power generation, and recreation opportunities. The Colorado River Compact specifies how much water must be released (outflow) from Lake Powell each year.

The normal annual inflow from the Colorado River to Lake Powell from 2010–2018 was 11 million acre-feet (maf). The graph uses this figure as 100% of annual inflow. An acre-foot is the volume required to cover an acre of land in one foot of water.

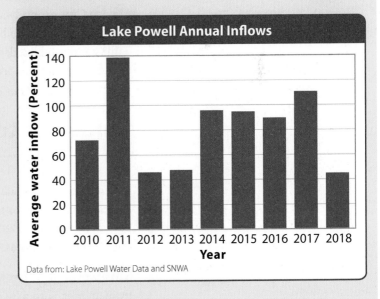

Lake Powell Annual Inflows

Data from: Lake Powell Water Data and SNWA

1. **Calculate** Using 11 maf as 100% of inflow, calculate the inflows for each of the years in the graph.

2. **Infer** What may have accounted for the increase in inflow in 2011?

3. **Analyze the Data** The annual minimum outflow to meet the conditions of the Colorado River Compact is 8.23 maf. For each of the years graphed, determine if Lake Powell had a net gain or loss of water.

4. **Draw Conclusions** Based on your answer to Question 3, how has the Colorado River Compact affected the volume of water stored in Lake Powell?

 MATH SUPPORT For help calculating with percentages, see the Math Handbook.

Groundwater Depletion Many aquifers are being drained as groundwater is mined. As aquifers are depleted, water tables drop and groundwater becomes more difficult and expensive to use. In parts of Mexico, and throughout Asia and the Middle East, water tables are falling 1–3 meters (3–10 feet) per year. When groundwater is over-pumped in coastal areas, salt water can move into aquifers, making water undrinkable. Moreover, as aquifers lose water, the land surface above may subside, causing sections of cities from Venice to Bangkok to actually sink. In Mexico City, groundwater withdrawal is causing streets to buckle, buildings to flood, pipes to break, and buildings to lean, as shown in **Figure 12**. Falling water tables also do vast ecological harm by drying up wetlands vital for wildlife and ecosystem services.

Solutions to Freshwater Depletion

When an area runs out of fresh water, we can do one of two things: increase our supply or decrease our demand. Solutions that increase supply can have immediate effects. Lowering demand is more difficult to do, but will likely be necessary in the long term.

Solutions That Increase Supply As we've seen, diverting water from an area with a lot of it to an area without enough is one way to increase local water supply. Another strategy is to "make" more fresh water by removing salt from seawater. This approach is called **desalination,** or desalinization. One method of desalination uses machines to heat seawater until the water evaporates, leaving the salt behind. The water vapor can then be condensed into liquid fresh water, as shown in **Figure 13**. Another method forces water through artificial membranes to filter out salts. The most common filtering process is called reverse osmosis.

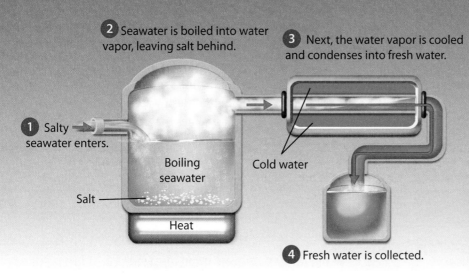

2 Seawater is boiled into water vapor, leaving salt behind.

3 Next, the water vapor is cooled and condenses into fresh water.

1 Salty seawater enters.

Boiling seawater

Cold water

Salt

Heat

4 Fresh water is collected.

FIGURE 13 Desalination One way to "make" fresh water is by heating salty seawater. Fresh water evaporates, leaving the salt behind. The vapor is then condensed into fresh water and collected.

There are more than 20,000 desalination plants worldwide. The process, however, is expensive, requires a lot of energy, and produces a concentrated, salty waste. Because of this, most desalination plants are found in wealthy, energy-rich nations, such as those in the Middle East, that don't have a lot of water. However, the cost of desalination is dropping, and there are now desalination plants in the United States, including 11 in California, as well as a large one in Tampa, Florida.

Solutions That Reduce Demand To reduce the demand for fresh water, agriculture, industry, and individuals need to implement water conservation practices. As water shortages increasingly cause widespread problems, water conservation practices will benefit both the environment and the economy.

FIGURE 14 Saving Water, Drop-by-Drop Drip irrigation systems are one way to reduce water demand in agriculture.

▶ *Agricultural Solutions* Farmers can conserve water by adopting efficient irrigation methods and selecting climate-appropriate crops. Drip irrigation systems (**Figure 14**) target individual plants and introduce water directly into the soil. Drip irrigation reduces water lost to evaporation and runoff. Experts estimate that using drip irrigation instead of traditional methods can cut agricultural water use in half.

Choosing crops that are suitable for the land and climate can also save huge amounts of water. Currently, crops that require a great deal of water, such as cotton, rice, and alfalfa, are often planted in dry areas. Growing these crops mainly in areas with adequate rainfall could greatly reduce the amount of water needed for irrigation.

 Reading Checkpoint *How does drip irrigation save water?*

Connect to the Central Case

FIGURE 15 Xeriscaping Homeowners and businesses can reduce water consumption by xeriscaping their grounds—landscaping them with drought-tolerant plants. To encourage xeriscaping, Las Vegas pays residents $2 per square foot to rip up their lawns. This xeriscaped yard is in Boulder City, Nevada, near Lake Mead.

▶ *Industrial Solutions* Many industries can take water-saving steps that also reduce their costs. Industries are looking at new processes that require less water. Major food and drink manufacturers in the United Kingdom have voluntarily agreed to slash water consumption 20 percent by 2020. This equates to water savings of about 140 million liters (37 million gallons) per day. Some manufacturing plants have made agreements with cities to recycle their wastewater. Finally, recycling water within plant processes can be effective. For example, there are ways in which one supply of water can be used to cool several steps in a manufacturing process.

▶ *Personal Solutions* Individuals can each do a lot to conserve water. Watering at night, for example, prevents a lot of water loss by evaporation. In the American Southwest, home and business owners reduce their outdoor water consumption by choosing outdoor plants adapted for arid conditions, as shown in **Figure 15.** This practice, called **xeriscaping,** requires much less water to maintain landscaping. Inside, low-flow toilets, appliances, and faucets can help reduce water use. Low-flow shower heads, for example, cut the amount of water used for showers in half. Fixing leaky pipes and turning off the tap when brushing your teeth will also save water. These simple steps will go a long way to reducing personal water footprints.

Regardless of how we address the problem, water conservation is starting to pay off. In 2015 water withdrawals in the United States were at the lowest since before 1970, and were 9% lower than 2010 levels. Clearly, conserving water is possible if each person contributes to the solution.

LESSON ② Assessment

1. **Review** What are the three main categories of water use? Give an example of each.

2. **Relate Cause and Effect** Explain how water diversions and dams affect surface water depletion.

3. **Explain** How does agriculture contribute to groundwater depletion?

4. **Classify** For each of the following actions, indicate if the approach increases the supply of water or decreases the demand for water: (a) xeriscaping, (b) desalination, (c) fixing leaky pipes, (d) using drip irrigation.

5. **REVISIT**
   INVESTIGATIVE PHENOMENON
   In this lesson, you've learned many ways we can change how we use water. Which solution mentioned in the lesson do you think would be the most helpful in moving toward global sustainable water use? Explain your answer.

Water Pollution

EVERYDAY PHENOMENON Why do excess nutrients have a negative effect on water health?

Knowledge and Skills

- Discuss the main categories of water pollution.
- Explain why groundwater pollution is difficult to clean up.
- Discuss the sources and effects of major pollutants found in the ocean.
- Describe how water is regulated and treated.

Reading Strategy and Vocabulary

✓ **Reading Strategy** As you read, make a cluster diagram for each category of water pollution.

Vocabulary point-source pollution, nonpoint-source pollution, cultural eutrophication, wastewater, algal bloom, pathogen, red tide, septic system

IT'S A BIG CHALLENGE making sure everyone has the fresh water he or she needs. Ensuring that the quality of that water is good enough for human use makes the challenge even greater. To be safe for humans and other organisms, water must be relatively free of disease-causing organisms and toxic substances. All too often, this is not the case. The United Nations estimates that, around the world, 3800 children (mostly under the age of 5) die every day from diseases associated with unsafe drinking water. What is making these children so sick, and what can be done about it?

Types of Water Pollution

Every type of water pollution comes from either a point or a nonpoint source, as shown in **Figure 16. Point-source pollution** comes from distinct locations, such as a factory or sewer pipe. In contrast, **nonpoint-source pollution** comes from many places spread over a large area. As runoff produced by rain and snowmelt makes its way across farms, lawns, and streets, it picks up accumulated fertilizers, pesticides, salt, oil, and other pollutants. The runoff eventually carries all of this nonpoint-source pollution to bodies of water such as streams, lakes, or the ocean.

(a)

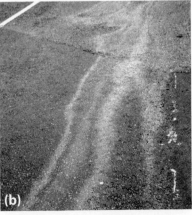
(b)

FIGURE 16 Point and Nonpoint Sources (a) Point-source pollution comes from distinct facilities or locations, usually from single outflow pipes. **(b)** Nonpoint-source pollution originates from numerous sources, such as oil-covered city streets, spread over large areas.

Point and nonpoint water pollution comes in many forms and can have diverse effects. Major categories of pollution include nutrient pollution, toxic chemical pollution, sediment pollution, thermal pollution, and biological pollution.

Nutrient Pollution Bodies of water that have a high nutrient content and low oxygen content are called eutrophic. The word *eutrophic* comes from the Greek for "good food." Indeed, many healthy aquatic ecosystems are eutrophic. However, nutrient pollution by humans can speed up the eutrophication process with negative effects.

▶ *The Process of Eutrophication* Eutrophication occurs naturally when nutrients build up in a body of water. In fresh water, eutrophication usually involves a buildup of sediments and nutrients. This can happen for a number of reasons, and is often part of the normal aging process of a lake or pond. When nutrients build up, the growth rate of algae and aquatic plants increases. More growth means more decomposition as the algae and plants die. Decomposition requires oxygen, so the levels of dissolved oxygen in the water decrease. The result is a body of water that is high in nutrients and low in oxygen. When it occurs naturally, eutrophication takes a long time, sometimes centuries.

▶ *Cultural Eutrophication* Nutrient pollution by humans can dramatically increase the rate at which eutrophication occurs, a situation called cultural eutrophication, or artificial eutrophication. **Figure 17** shows a lake in Ontario, Canada, that suffers from cultural eutrophication. Excess nitrogen and phosphorus is the most common cause of cultural eutrophication in fresh water. Nutrient pollution mostly comes from nonpoint sources such as fertilizers and detergents carried in runoff or wastewater. Wastewater is water that has been used by people in some way. Individuals can help reduce nutrient pollution by using less fertilizer and purchasing phosphate-free detergents.

Cultural eutrophication can severely harm aquatic ecosystems. Excess nutrients cause sudden explosions of algal growth called algal blooms. Although algae are a source of food and oxygen for other organisms, algal blooms can be so thick that they cover the water's surface. When this happens, sunlight can't reach the plants below and they die off. Further, as nutrient levels climb, decomposition increases and overall oxygen levels in the water drop. Eventually, there may not be enough oxygen to support aquatic organisms such as fish and shellfish.

FIGURE 17 Nutrient Pollution Algal blooms, like this one in Lake Simon in Ontario, Canada, are caused by nutrient pollution. Nutrient-rich runoff and wastewater result in foul-smelling blooms in Lake Simon every summer.

Quick Lab

Cultural Eutrophication

1. Label one jar *A* and a second jar *B*. Pour tap water into each jar until it is half full.
2. Add water from a pond or freshwater aquarium to each jar until it is three-quarters full.
3. Add 5 mL of liquid fertilizer to jar *A* only.
4. Cover both jars tightly and place them on a windowsill in the sunlight. Wash your hands with soap and warm water.
5. Observe the two jars every day for a week.

Analyze and Conclude

1. **Observe** Describe the changes you observed in both jars over the week.
2. **Relate Cause and Effect** How did the fertilizer affect the growth of algae in jar *A*?
3. **Control Variables** What was the purpose of jar *B* in this experiment?
4. **Use Models** What is cultural eutrophication? How did this experiment model the process?
5. **Predict** Describe the result you would expect if you were comparing the effects of a high-phosphorus fertilizer to a low-phosphorus fertilizer. Explain your answer.

Toxic-Chemical Pollution Many freshwater supplies have become polluted with toxic chemicals. Toxic chemicals can be organic or inorganic. Petroleum and petroleum products, such as plastics, contain organic chemicals such as Bisphenol-A. Organic chemicals are also found in many pesticides and detergents. Inorganic chemicals include heavy metals such as mercury, arsenic, and lead. Toxic chemicals are released during many industrial and manufacturing processes.

All of these substances can make their way into fresh water through point or nonpoint sources. Toxic chemicals can poison aquatic animals and plants as well as cause a wide array of human health problems, including cancer. Regulating industrial, manufacturing, and agricultural processes to control the amount of toxic chemicals they use and release into the environment will help decrease toxic chemical pollution.

Sediment Pollution Sediment transported by rivers and runoff can harm aquatic ecosystems. Some rivers, like the Colorado River and China's Yellow River, are naturally sediment rich, but many others are not. When a large amount of sediment enters a river, it can cause the aquatic environment to change. Rates of photosynthesis may decline as the water clouds up, causing food webs to collapse. Sediment also degrades water quality, making it less suitable to humans and other organisms.

Sediment pollution is the result of erosion. So, steps taken to decrease erosion, such as avoiding large-scale land clearing, also help decrease sediment pollution. Mining, clear-cutting, clearing land to build houses, and careless farming practices all expose soil to wind and water erosion. **Figure 18** shows a river polluted with sediment runoff from a heavy metal mine in Papua New Guinea. Mine operators have been heavily criticized by international organizations and have been sued for environmental damage by downstream residents.

FIGURE 18 Sediment Pollution
Millions of tons of sediment from the Ok Tedi Mine in Papua New Guinea is deposited into the Ok Tedi River each year. The pollution affects about 50,000 people downstream who rely on the river's water.

Thermal Pollution The warmer water is, the less oxygen it can hold. So, some aquatic organisms may not survive when human activities raise water temperatures. Recall that one of the most common uses of water is for cooling industrial processes and power plants. Water used in this way absorbs a lot of heat. When the water is returned to its source, the temperature of the water will be higher than when it was withdrawn, resulting in thermal pollution. Thermal pollution can also occur when trees and plants that shade bodies of water are removed. Thermal pollution harms fish and other aquatic organisms that cannot tolerate increased water temperatures or decreased oxygen.

Biological Pollution When disease-causing organisms and viruses, called **pathogens,** make their way into our air, soil, and water, it is called *biological pollution*. Drinking water supplies can become contaminated with biological pollution when they are exposed to human or animal waste. Biological pollution causes more human health problems than any other type of water pollution. **Figure 19** lists some of the most common diseases that result from freshwater biological pollution.

The best way of decreasing biological water pollution is to treat water and waste with chemicals or other substances that kill the disease-causing organisms. This already happens in many parts of the world. However, more than 3.4 million people die worldwide each year because of diseases carried in water. Most of these deaths occur in young children living in South Asia and sub-Saharan Africa. Two thirds of people living in these areas do not have access to clean water and waste treatment.

✔ Reading Checkpoint *How many of the diseases listed in* **Figure 19** *are caused by bacteria?*

Illustration of *Giardia lamblia* protozoan

Major Pathogens Found in Water and Their Effects

Pollutant	Disease	Symptoms	Important Facts
Vibrio cholerae (bacteria)	Cholera	Diarrhea, nausea, and vomiting	87% of cholera cases reported to the World Health Organization in 2000 were in African nations.
Shigella dysenteriae (bacteria) or *Entamoeba histolytica* (amoeba)	Dysentery	Diarrhea (sometimes bloody), fever, and nausea	*Shigella* bacteria infections can be treated with antibiotics. *Entamoeba* infections tend to occur in tropical areas and are more difficult to treat.
Escherichia coli (bacteria)	E. coli infection	Severe, often bloody diarrhea	E. coli is more often food borne than waterborne. However, epidemics from contaminated water have occurred.
Giardia lamblia (protozoa)	Giardiasis	Diarrhea, gas, cramping, and nausea	Giardiasis is the most common form of waterborne disease in the United States.
Schistosoma haematobium, S. japonicum, and *S. mansoni* (flatworms)	Schistosomiasis	Rash and itchy skin followed by fever, chills, muscle aches, and cough	According to the World Health Organization, 200 million people are infected worldwide, 80% in sub-Saharan Africa. Reservoirs made by dams provide breeding grounds for the parasites.
Salmonella typhi (bacteria)	Typhoid fever	Fever, headache, and rose-colored spots on the chest	About 17 million people are infected every year. The disease is treatable with antibiotics.

Data from World Health Organization and Centers for Disease Control and Prevention.

FIGURE 19 Biological Pollution More people are affected by biological pollution than any other kind of water pollution. This table lists some common pathogens spread through contaminated water.

Groundwater Pollution

Groundwater sources have become contaminated by pollution from industrial and agricultural practices. Groundwater pollution is largely hidden from view and is extremely difficult to monitor. Often, groundwater contamination is not discovered until drinking water is affected.

Sources of Groundwater Pollution Some chemicals that are toxic at high concentrations, such as aluminum, fluoride, nitrates, and sulfates, occur naturally in groundwater. However, groundwater pollution from human activity is widespread. Because many pollutants enter groundwater from the surface, any of the pollutants already discussed can become groundwater pollutants. Chemicals in fertilizers and pesticides leach through soil and seep into aquifers. Improperly designed wells and leaky storage tanks provide entry for industrial chemicals, raw sewage, gasoline, and other dangerous pollutants.

Cleaning Up Groundwater In general, rivers can flush away pollutants quickly. However, it can take years or even decades for groundwater to get rid of contaminants. The long-lived pesticide DDT, for instance, is still found widely in aquifers in the United States, even though it was banned by the government in 1972. Chemicals break down much more slowly in aquifers than they do in surface water. Groundwater generally contains less dissolved oxygen, microbes, minerals, and organic matter, so decomposition is slower than it is in surface water or soils. For example, concentrations of a certain herbicide called alachlor decline by 50% after 20 days in soil, but in groundwater, a 50% reduction takes four years. Making matters even worse, groundwater moves slowly and takes a long time to recharge.

Most efforts to reduce groundwater pollution focus on preventing it from happening. For example, the U.S. Environmental Protection Agency (EPA) has been working on a nationwide cleanup program to locate and repair leaky gasoline tanks, as shown in **Figure 20.** Over the past 25 years, the agency has closed more than 1.7 million tanks, and has cleaned up more than 380,000 other sites that were exposed to tank leaks. To help prevent future leaks, new sewage and gas tanks are built with strong materials such as fiberglass that don't break down as easily as the plain steel used in older tanks.

✓ **Reading Checkpoint** *Where do groundwater pollutants come from?*

FIGURE 20 Groundwater Pollution
Leaky underground storage tanks are a major source of groundwater pollution. Under an EPA program, hundreds of thousands of tanks are being unearthed and repaired or replaced.

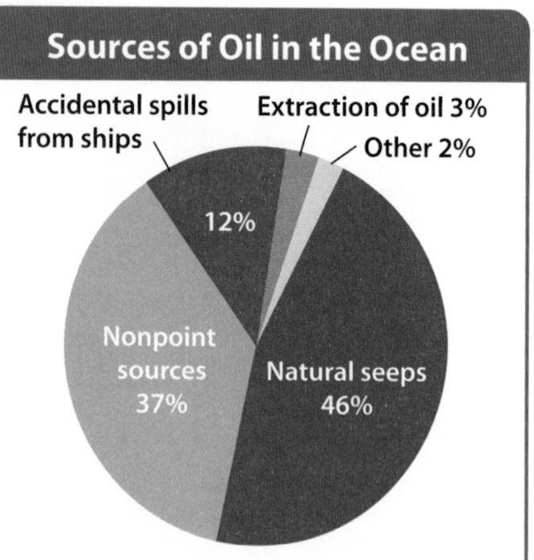

Sources of Oil in the Ocean

Accidental spills from ships

Extraction of oil 3%

Other 2%

12%

Nonpoint sources 37%

Natural seeps 46%

Data from National Research Council. 2003. *Oil in the sea III. Inputs, fates, and effects.* Washington, DC: National Academics Press.

FIGURE 21 Sources of Oil Pollution The National Research Council estimates that on average, 1.3 million tons of oil are released into the oceans every year. Of that, nearly half comes from natural oil seepage. Nonpoint sources, including runoff from land, account for more than three times as much oil as tanker spills.

FIGURE 22 Nutrient Pollution in the Ocean A harmful red tide, like this one along a beach in the Gulf of Mexico, takes a commonly brown or reddish appearance.

Ocean Water Pollution

People have been dumping wastes and pollution into the ocean for centuries. Even into the mid-twentieth century, it was common for coastal U.S. cities to dump trash and untreated sewage into the ocean. Oil, mercury, and excess nutrients can all eventually make their way from land into the oceans through runoff.

Oil Pollution Major oil spills, such as the 2010 *Deepwater Horizon* spill in the Gulf of Mexico about 44 miles off the coast of Louisiana, make headlines and cause serious environmental problems. Yet it is important to put such accidents into perspective. A lot of oil pollution in the oceans comes from many widely spread small sources, not large tanker spills. Small, nonpoint sources include leakage from small boats and runoff from human activities on land. Surprisingly, the largest single source of oil in the oceans may be naturally occurring deposits on the sea floor. This "natural pollution" is called *oil seepage* and, according to one study published in 2003, it accounts for 46 percent of all oil in the ocean, as shown in **Figure 21.**

Minimizing the amount of oil released into coastal waters is important because petroleum pollution harms marine life. Oil can physically coat and kill marine organisms and can poison them when ingested. In 1990, the Oil Pollution Act created a $1 billion prevention and cleanup fund. It also required that by 2015, all oil tankers in U.S. waters have double hulls to help prevent oil leaks.

Mercury Pollution in the Ocean Marine pollution can make some fish and shellfish unsafe for people to eat. A primary concern today is mercury contamination. Mercury is a toxic heavy metal that collects in the tissues of animals. Mercury makes its way up the food chain by biomagnification. As a result, some organisms at high trophic levels, such as swordfish, shark, and albacore tuna, can contain high levels of mercury. Eating a lot of seafood with high levels of mercury can affect humans. Mercury can cause neurological damage, especially in fetuses, babies, and children.

Nutrient Pollution in the Ocean Recall that phosphorus-rich nutrient pollution can cause harmful algal blooms in fresh water. Nutrient pollution is also a problem in the ocean, though it is nitrogen, not phosphorus, that does the most damage. One type of algal bloom is nicknamed red tide because the algae produce reddish pigments. Some red tides and other harmful algal blooms, like the one shown in **Figure 22**, release powerful toxins that make their way through the food chain, causing illness and death among zooplankton, fish, marine mammals, birds, and humans. Harmful algal blooms also hurt the economy. When one occurs, beaches are closed and fishing must stop. Reducing nutrient runoff into coastal waters can lessen the frequency of algal blooms.

(a)

(b)

Controlling Water Pollution

FIGURE 23 Successful Cleanup
Great strides have been made in reducing the pollution in Lake Erie over the last 30 years. **(a)** A sign warns against swimming in August 1973. **(b)** Today, thousands enjoy swimming in Lake Erie. Regulations set by the governments of the United States and Canada have helped to reduce pollution in all the Great Lakes.

As numerous as our water pollution problems may seem, it is important to remember that many of them were worse a few decades ago. Today, legislation, technology, and citizen action are helping to control the harm done by water pollution.

The Clean Water Act The Federal Water Pollution Control Act, which was later amended and renamed the Clean Water Act in 1977, remains the single most important law to prevent water pollution in the United States. The Clean Water Act made it illegal to release pollution from a point source without a permit. It also set standards for pollution levels in surface waters and industrial wastewater, and funded construction of sewage treatment plants. Thanks to this law and others, point-source pollution in the United States has been reduced, and rivers and lakes are cleaner than they have been in decades.

The Great Lakes of Canada and the United States represent a success story in fighting water pollution. In the 1970s these lakes, which hold 18 percent of the world's surface fresh water, were badly polluted. Nutrient and chemical pollution were such a huge problem that Lake Erie was pronounced "dead." Today, efforts by the Canadian and U.S. governments to reduce pollution and increase water treatment have paid off. Nutrient and toxic-chemical pollution have dropped significantly. Bird populations are rebounding, and Lake Erie is now home to the world's largest walleye fishery. **Figure 23** shows just how far Lake Erie has come. The Great Lakes' troubles are by no means over, but the progress shows how conditions can improve when citizens and their governments take action.

 Reading Checkpoint   *What did the Clean Water Act do?*

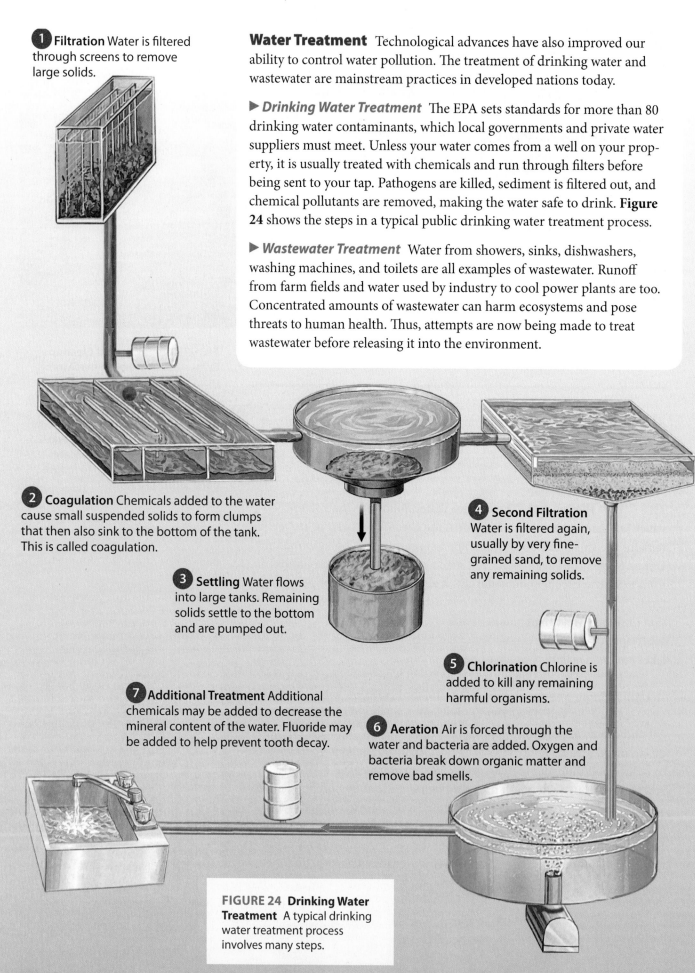

1 Filtration Water is filtered through screens to remove large solids.

Water Treatment Technological advances have also improved our ability to control water pollution. The treatment of drinking water and wastewater are mainstream practices in developed nations today.

▶ *Drinking Water Treatment* The EPA sets standards for more than 80 drinking water contaminants, which local governments and private water suppliers must meet. Unless your water comes from a well on your property, it is usually treated with chemicals and run through filters before being sent to your tap. Pathogens are killed, sediment is filtered out, and chemical pollutants are removed, making the water safe to drink. **Figure 24** shows the steps in a typical public drinking water treatment process.

▶ *Wastewater Treatment* Water from showers, sinks, dishwashers, washing machines, and toilets are all examples of wastewater. Runoff from farm fields and water used by industry to cool power plants are too. Concentrated amounts of wastewater can harm ecosystems and pose threats to human health. Thus, attempts are now being made to treat wastewater before releasing it into the environment.

2 Coagulation Chemicals added to the water cause small suspended solids to form clumps that then also sink to the bottom of the tank. This is called coagulation.

3 Settling Water flows into large tanks. Remaining solids settle to the bottom and are pumped out.

4 Second Filtration Water is filtered again, usually by very fine-grained sand, to remove any remaining solids.

5 Chlorination Chlorine is added to kill any remaining harmful organisms.

7 Additional Treatment Additional chemicals may be added to decrease the mineral content of the water. Fluoride may be added to help prevent tooth decay.

6 Aeration Air is forced through the water and bacteria are added. Oxygen and bacteria break down organic matter and remove bad smells.

FIGURE 24 Drinking Water Treatment A typical drinking water treatment process involves many steps.

In more densely populated areas, sewer systems carry wastewater from homes and businesses to centralized treatment locations. There, pollutants in wastewater are removed by physical, chemical, and biological means (see **A Closer Look**, on the next page). Most often the treated water, called *effluent*, is piped into rivers, reservoirs, or the ocean following primary, secondary, and tertiary treatment. Water that is not released to a body of surface water is called *reclaimed water*. This water might not be treated to drinking water standards, but instead used for irrigation or to cool power plants.

In rural areas, septic systems are the most popular method of wastewater disposal. In a septic system, shown in **Figure 25,** wastewater runs through a pipe from the house to an underground septic tank. Inside the tank, solids and oils separate from water. The water moves downhill to an underground field of gravel where microbes decompose the remaining organic material in the wastewater. The cleansed water eventually makes its way into aquifers. Periodically, solid waste, called *sludge*, is pumped from the septic tank and taken to a landfill or dried and sold as fertilizer.

FIGURE 25 Septic Systems In many rural areas, wastewater flows into a septic tank. In the tank, wastes separate out and bacteria break down organic material.

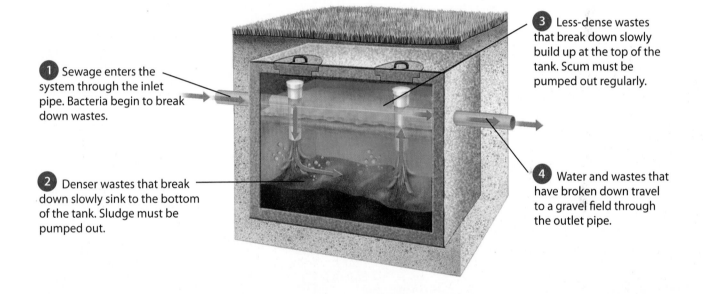

1 Sewage enters the system through the inlet pipe. Bacteria begin to break down wastes.

2 Denser wastes that break down slowly sink to the bottom of the tank. Sludge must be pumped out.

3 Less-dense wastes that break down slowly build up at the top of the tank. Scum must be pumped out regularly.

4 Water and wastes that have broken down travel to a gravel field through the outlet pipe.

LESSON 3 Assessment

1. **Compare and Contrast** What is the difference between point and nonpoint sources of water pollution? Give an example of each.

2. **Explain** Why is groundwater pollution so hard to clean up?

3. **Relate Cause and Effect** Explain how using nitrogen-rich fertilizers can affect algal blooms in the oceans.

4. **Sequence** Describe the steps involved in a typical public drinking water treatment process.

5. **THINK IT** *THROUGH* You run a large farm that is considering using sludge from wastewater treatment plants as fertilizer. You have been told that the sludge can increase the growth rate of your crops, and you know that using the sludge will prevent it from making its way into landfills. However, you have also heard that sludge can contain pollutants such as heavy metals and pathogens. What questions would you want to ask before deciding to use the sludge? Do you feel that the benefits outweigh the costs?

WASTEWATER Treatment

Every day, Americans use more than 13 billion liters (3.5 billion gallons) of water to cook, clean, flush toilets, and bathe. Most of this water isn't consumed—it comes out of the tap and immediately goes down a drain or is flushed down the toilet. In most areas, the water that flows out of our taps has been pulled from a public water supply, such as a reservoir or aquifer, and purified by a multistep water treatment process. But what happens after the water has been used? How does it get back into our waterways and reservoirs? In many communities, it is collected in a sewer system and shuttled to a centralized wastewater treatment plant. Here, water full of soaps, detergents, solids, and many other pollutants is cleaned up and made safe for re-release into aquifers and waterways.

1 Raw sewage enters treatment facility.

2 Screens and grit tank
Solid objects and grit removed

3 Primary clarifier
Oils, greases, and solids removed

Solids sink to the bottom

Liquids float to the top

Solids disposed at landfill

Gases chemically treated to reduce odor

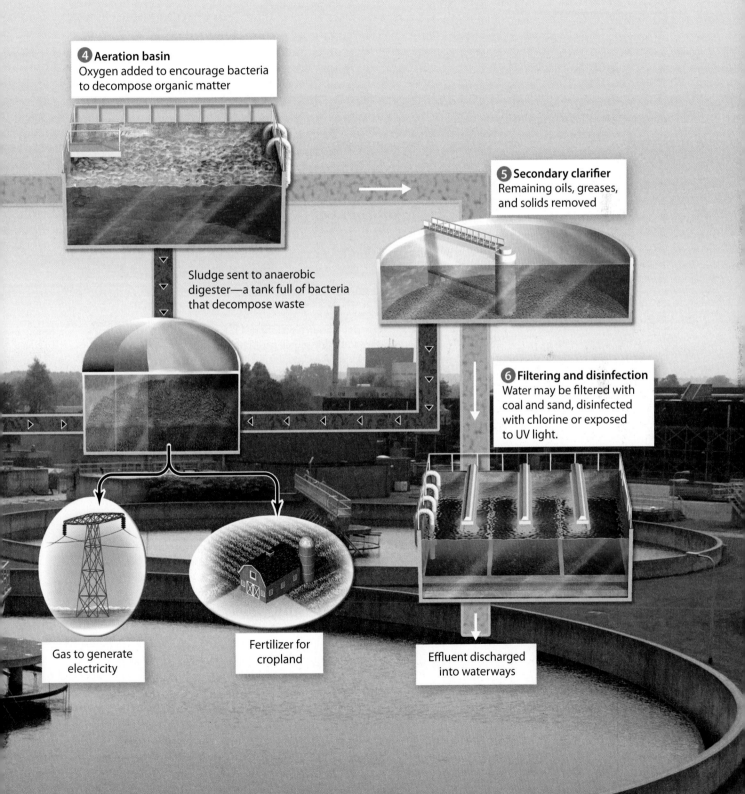

CAREER **Hydrologist** A hydrologist studies how water moves across and through the Earth's crust. Go Online and research careers in hydrology. What do people who work in hydrology do? How does one become a hydrologist? What are some specializations within the field of hydrology? Write a brief report on your findings.

4 Aeration basin
Oxygen added to encourage bacteria to decompose organic matter

5 Secondary clarifier
Remaining oils, greases, and solids removed

Sludge sent to anaerobic digester—a tank full of bacteria that decompose waste

6 Filtering and disinfection
Water may be filtered with coal and sand, disinfected with chlorine or exposed to UV light.

Gas to generate electricity

Fertilizer for cropland

Effluent discharged into waterways

INVESTIGATIVE PHENOMENON

Why is the level of water in the Colorado River so low?

Lesson 1
How can water be both a renewable resource and be scarce in some regions?

Lesson 2
How can we reduce our own daily water use?

Lesson 3
Why do excess nutrients have a negative effect on water health?

LESSON 1 Earth: The Water Planet

- As a natural resource, fresh water is renewable. However, quantities of fresh water on Earth are limited.
- Surface water travels across Earth's surface as runoff and collects in a river system. All of the land that drains water into a river system is called a watershed.
- Water that soaks through permeable layers of soil and rock from the surface is called groundwater. Groundwater is contained within aquifers that can be accessed by wells.

fresh water (421)	permeable (424)
surface water (422)	impermeable (424)
runoff (422)	aquifer (424)
river system (422)	water table (424)
watershed (422)	recharge zone (425)
groundwater (424)	well (425)

LESSON 2 Uses of Fresh Water

- Fresh water is used for agricultural, industrial, and personal activities. Globally, most fresh water is used for agriculture.
- Because of overuse, surface water resources are being depleted. Water diversions and dams move and collect water for human purposes.
- Groundwater is being used, primarily for irrigation, faster than it can be replenished.
- There are many ways to decrease demand for water in agriculture, industry, and at home. Conserving water in each of these areas is necessary to address freshwater depletion.

water diversion (428)
dam (428)
reservoir (428)
salinization (431)
desalination (432)
xeriscaping (434)

LESSON 3 Water Pollution

- Water pollution can come from point or nonpoint sources. Major types of water pollution are nutrient pollution, toxic-chemical pollution, sediment pollution, biological pollution, and thermal pollution.
- Any form of water pollution can affect groundwater. It can take decades to clean up groundwater pollution, so every effort should be made to prevent it from occurring.
- Oceans are polluted with oil, toxic chemicals, and nutrients that run off from land.
- Government regulation and water treatment are two ways of decreasing the effects of water pollution.

point-source pollution (435)
nonpoint-source pollution (435)
cultural eutrophication (436)
wastewater (436)
algal bloom (436)
pathogen (438)
red tide (440)
septic system (443)

🖥 GO ONLINE

INQUIRY LABS AND ACTIVITIES

- **Watershed Boundaries**
  Water always runs downhill. Use this fact and a topographical map to delineate watershed boundaries.
- **The Water You Drink**
  How does your drinking water measure up? Analyze your local EPA-required drinking water quality report.
- **Testing Water Quality**
  Test the waters—literally. Follow these procedures to investigate the water quality of a local water sample.

Chapter Assessment

Defend Your Case

The Central Case in this chapter explored the complex and urgent situation regarding water shortages in Nevada. Based on what you have learned, what do you think Nevada should do? Provide evidence from the Central Case and the lesson to support your ideas.

Review Concepts and Terms

1. More than 97 percent of Earth's total water supply is found in
   a. ice sheets.
   b. the oceans.
   c. the atmosphere.
   d. groundwater.

2. The land area that supplies water to a river system is called a
   a. divide.   c. watershed.
   b. wetland.   d. tributary.

3. The water table is the upper limit of the
   a. zone of saturation.   c. aquifer zone.
   b. zone of aeration.   d. well zone.

4. You must build a model of an aquifer for a science project. What material would be the best to use for the layer that will hold water?
   a. an impermeable material, such as clay
   b. a liquid, such as oil
   c. a permeable material, such as gravel
   d. a material that does not have pores

5. One process used to obtain fresh water from salt water is called
   a. coagulation.   c. recharge.
   b. filtration.   d. desalination.

6. Globally, MOST fresh water used by humans is for
   a. drinking and cooking.
   b. washing and home use.
   c. agricultural irrigation.
   d. electrical production.

7. The All-American Canal, which brings water from the Colorado River to farm fields in California, is an example of a
   a. dam.   c. reservoir.
   b. water diversion. d. well.

8. Which of the following does NOT contribute to water conservation?
   a. drip irrigation
   b. xeriscaping
   c. using low-flow faucets and shower heads
   d. watering lawns during peak sunlight hours, when plants need water most

9. An oil spill is an example of
   a. point-source pollution.
   b. nonpoint-source pollution.
   c. reversible pollution.
   d. natural pollution.

10. Chlorine is often added during water treatment to
    a. make particles form clumps.
    b. kill disease-causing organisms.
    c. improve the taste of water.
    d. remove objects such as fish and trash.

Modified True/False

Write true if the statement is true. If it is false, change the underlined word or words to make the statement true.

11. Most fresh water on Earth is <u>liquid</u>.

12. Water moves through <u>permeable</u> materials.

13. The photo below shows a <u>nonpoint source</u> of pollution.

14. Cultural eutrophication can result from <u>toxic-chemical</u> pollution.

15. Dams create <u>aquifers</u>, artificial lakes that humans use for water storage.

Reading Comprehension

Read the following selection and answer the questions that follow.

On a September day in 1999, people began to notice that Lake Jackson in the Panhandle region of northern Florida was shrinking. Within a few days, it was almost gone. A sinkhole had opened beneath the lake and drained it, along with all of its inhabitants including fish and alligators.

As aquifers lose water, rock and soil layers can become weaker and less capable of supporting overlying layers of earth and any human structures built on them. In such cases, the land surface above may subside, or sink. Sometimes subsidence can occur locally and suddenly in the form of sinkholes, which are areas where the ground gives way with little warning. Once the ground subsides, soil becomes compacted, losing the porosity that enabled it to hold water. Recharging a depleted aquifer may therefore become more difficult.

16. Sinkholes occur when
  a. too much weight above an aquifer causes it to cave in.
  b. the water level in an aquifer rises, pushing through to the surface.
  c. excessive water use lowers a water table and causes subsidence.
  d. new aquifers form.

17. A serious problem that results from the depletion of aquifers is
  a. the water tends to overflow and flood the entire area.
  b. the surrounding soil is compacted and loses its porosity.
  c. the aquifer increases in size, draining a larger surface area and leaving less water in rivers, streams, and lakes.
  d. the aquifer decreases in size and new aquifers form.

Short Answer

18. Why is so little of Earth's water available for human use?

19. Describe three benefits and three costs of damming rivers.

20. Why do many scientists consider groundwater pollution a greater problem than surface water pollution?

21. A substance added to gasoline is found in local wells. Suggest a possible point source and nonpoint source of this pollution.

22. Describe one way farmers can reduce the amount of water lost during irrigation.

23. Explain how desalination "makes" fresh water. Where is the technology primarily being used?

Critical Thinking

24. Apply Concepts Your friend says that we can reduce how much water we use by eating less meat. Is she right? Explain your answer.

25. Form an Opinion To conserve water, should communities limit how often people can do things such as water their lawns or wash their cars? Why or why not?

26. Calculate Growing wheat for one loaf of bread requires about 550 liters of water. If a family eats three loaves a week, how much water would be used to produce the family's bread supply each year?

27. Apply Concepts Define point-source pollution and nonpoint-source pollution. Which of the two is easier to identify? Which is easier to control? In your opinion, which poses the greatest threat to fresh water?

28. Apply Concepts Describe three ways in which your own actions contribute to water pollution. Then, describe three ways in which you could reduce the effects of these actions.

29. Form an Opinion To prevent water pollution, a factory proposes pumping its wastes into the ground instead of into a river. Would you support this proposal? Why or why not?

Analyze Data

The graph below shows how much water per Calorie is needed to produce plant-based food (fruits, vegetables, and grains) and animal-based food (meat and dairy). Use the data to answer the questions.

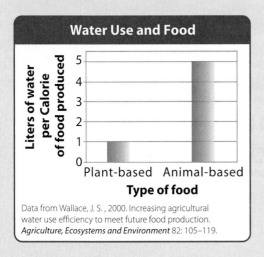

Water Use and Food

Data from Wallace, J. S., 2000. Increasing agricultural water use efficiency to meet future food production. *Agriculture, Ecosystems and Environment* 82: 105–119.

30. Interpret Graphs How many liters of water per Calorie are needed to produce plant-based food?

31. Interpret Graphs How many liters of water per Calorie are needed to produce animal-based food?

32. Calculate Most men require 2700 Calories a day to maintain their weight. How many liters of water are needed to produce one day's worth of food if 2300 of those Calories come from vegetables, and 400 Calories come from meat?

33. Calculate How many liters of water would be saved daily if all 2700 Calories of a man's daily diet came from plant-based foods rather than 2300 from vegetables and 400 from meat?

Write About It

34. Opinion Which is easier, preventing pollution or cleaning up pollution? Give an example to support your answer.

35. Explanation Your community is considering building a dam on a nearby river to reduce flooding. Would you support this proposal? Explain your reasoning.

36. REVISIT INVESTIGATIVE PHENOMENON
Write a public service announcement that teaches people about the effects human activities have on fresh water. The goal of the announcement is to explain the importance of sustainable water practices. Your intended audience is the general public, so you may need to provide background on why fresh water is a renewable, but limited resource. Present your announcement to the class. You may use visuals to support your ideas.

Ecological Footprints

Read the information below. Copy the table into your notebook, record your calculations, and answer the questions.

One of the single greatest personal uses of water is for showering. Older standard shower heads release 17 liters of water per minute, but low-flow shower heads release only 9 liters per minute. Given an average daily shower time of 10 minutes, fill in the footprint table.

1. For the table, you calculated how much water can be saved per person per year by using low-flow shower heads. Use that calculation to determine how much water could be saved per person per day.

2. How much water would you be able to save per day by shortening your average shower time from 10 minutes to 8 minutes? Assume you are using an older standard shower head.

	With Standard Shower Heads (liters per year)	With Low-flow Shower Heads (liters per year)	Savings With Low-flow Shower Heads (liters per year)
You			
Your class			
Your state			
United States			

Data from U.S. EPA, 1995. *Chapter 3—How to conserve water and use it effectively.* EPA 841-B-95-002.

3. Compare your answers to Questions 1 and 2. Is more water saved by showering the full 10 minutes using a low-flow shower head, or by showering for 8 minutes using a standard shower head?

CHAPTER **15** **The Atmosphere**

INVESTIGATIVE PHENOMENON   Does congestion charging work to reduce air pollution?

Transport
for London

Congestion
charging

C

Central
ZONE

Mon - Fri
7 am - 6.30 pm

The congestion charge in London is meant to help reduce air pollution.

Lesson 1
Earth's Atmosphere

Lesson 2
Pollution of the Atmosphere

Lesson 3
Controlling Air Pollution

Charging Toward Cleaner Air in London

AIR POLLUTION is not a new problem in the city of London, England. Even during the Middle Ages, pollution from coal burning was widespread. During the Industrial Revolution in the eighteenth and nineteenth centuries, the use of coal grew. Coal fired the nation's industries, heated people's homes—and polluted the city's air.

In December 1952, weather conditions trapped pollutants over the city for days, creating a thick "killer smog." Londoners breathed the heavily polluted air. Many people became sick. The smog was especially dangerous for people with respiratory or heart problems. The "killer smog" killed at least 4000 people—and by some estimates as many as 12,000 people.

This disaster spurred Great Britain and other developed nations to take steps to control air pollution. Today, Londoners breathe much cleaner air than they did in 1952. Burning coal is no longer a major source of pollution in the city. However, Londoners still battle the pollution released by motor vehicles. About 250,000 vehicles commute into London's downtown every workday, and these cars and trucks spew out air pollutants.

Ken Livingstone, a mayor of London, developed a plan to charge drivers a fee for entering the city. He thought that this measure could reduce traffic congestion and might also reduce air pollution. In February 2003, London's "congestion-charging" program began. People driving into central London on weekdays began to pay a fee every day. The money has gone to improve bus service and encourage people to travel by rail, bicycle, and foot.

Many Londoners were outraged by the program. Some daily commuters complained that the fee was too high. People also argued that the system discriminated against poorer people who cannot afford the fees. Many other Londoners, however, supported the program. Since the program began, traffic congestion has decreased by 25 percent. Fewer private cars are entering the congestion-charging zone in central London.

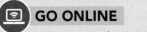

GO ONLINE
- Take It Local
- 3-D Geo Tour

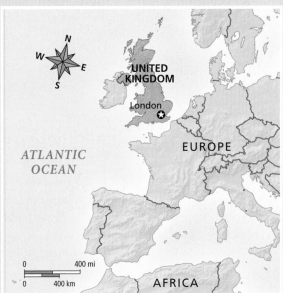

Initially, private hire vehicles, taxis, and zero-emission vehicles were exempt from the congestion charge. However, the number of private hire vehicles and taxis has increased over the years. In 2019, the congestion charge was applied to these vehicles as well. Zero-emission vehicles are still exempt from the congestion charge.

It has been difficult to assess the effect of London's congestion-charging program on air pollution, because it is hard to determine the cause of any change in air quality. A reduction in pollution could be the result of the program. But it could also be caused by some other factor, such as improved vehicle technology. Measurements after one year showed a decrease in some pollutants in London's air. But a study in 2009 indicated little overall change in air quality. Several other cities, including Singapore and Toronto, have adopted a congestion-charging program similar to London's. More cities are considering such a program, hoping to reduce both traffic and pollution.

Earth's Atmosphere

EVERYDAY PHENOMENON How can we describe Earth's atmosphere?

Knowledge and Skills

- Describe the properties of the atmosphere.
- Identify the four main layers of the atmosphere.
- Explain heat transfer and the interaction of air masses in the troposphere.

Reading Strategy and Vocabulary

✅ **Reading Strategy** When you read about the layers of the atmosphere, make a compare/contrast table that compares the four layers. Construct the table with one row for each layer. Include columns for height, temperature characteristics, and other characteristics.

Vocabulary atmosphere, relative humidity, air pressure, troposphere, stratosphere, ozone layer, mesosphere, thermosphere, radiation, conduction, convection, convection current, air mass, front

WHEN PEOPLE WATCH the weather report on TV, what information are they most interested in? Chances are they want to know whether the weather is cloudy or sunny, whether it is likely to rain, and what the air temperature is. Most people also probably pay close attention to the forecast for the weather tomorrow and the next few days. Any weather report, whether you watch it on TV, hear it on the radio, read it in a newspaper, or check it on the Internet, has the same function. A weather report describes the condition of Earth's atmosphere.

Properties of the Atmosphere

The **atmosphere** is the thin layer of gases that surrounds Earth. To get an idea of the size of the atmosphere, imagine that Earth was the size of an apple. You breathe on the apple, and a film of water forms on its surface. Compared to the apple, the film of water is very thin. The atmosphere is about that thin compared to the size of Earth.

We live at the bottom of the atmosphere, which provides us with oxygen, protects us from the most harmful rays in sunlight, and transports and recycles water. It also burns up incoming meteors and helps control climate. To understand the atmosphere, you need to know its composition. Humidity, temperature, and air pressure are also important properties of the atmosphere.

Composition of the Atmosphere You may be surprised to learn that the air you breathe is made up mostly of nitrogen, not oxygen. The atmosphere consists of roughly 78 percent nitrogen gas and 21 percent oxygen gas. The remaining 1 percent is composed of several other gases, as shown in **Figure 1.** Air also contains water vapor, which is water in the form of a gas.

▶ **Nitrogen** In the atmosphere, nitrogen gas occurs as a molecule with the chemical formula N_2. This chemical formula indicates that a molecule of nitrogen gas consists of two nitrogen atoms. All organisms, or living things, contain nitrogen. However, only certain kinds of bacteria can use nitrogen in the form in which it occurs in the atmosphere. These bacteria take nitrogen in and convert it to chemical compounds in a process called nitrogen fixation. These chemicals then become available for other organisms to use.

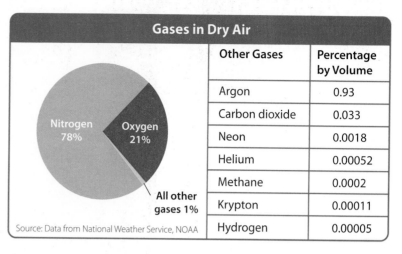

Gases in Dry Air		
Other Gases	Percentage by Volume
Argon	0.93
Carbon dioxide	0.033
Neon	0.0018
Helium	0.00052
Methane	0.0002
Krypton	0.00011
Hydrogen	0.00005

Nitrogen 78%
Oxygen 21%
All other gases 1%

Source: Data from National Weather Service, NOAA

FIGURE 1 Composition of Dry Air Dry air is composed of many gases, as shown in the graph and table.

▶ **Oxygen** Oxygen makes up only about one fifth of the atmosphere. The most common form of oxygen in the atmosphere occurs as a molecule having the chemical formula O_2. Therefore, most molecules of oxygen are made up of two atoms of oxygen. Most living things cannot survive without oxygen. In addition, oxygen is necessary for combustion, or burning. During combustion, oxygen combines chemically with a fuel, such as gasoline, wood, or paper **(Figure 2).** The products of combustion are carbon dioxide and water.

Over Earth's long history, the amount of oxygen in the atmosphere has changed. The atmosphere of early Earth contained almost no oxygen. The early atmosphere was mostly made up of carbon dioxide, nitrogen, carbon monoxide, and water vapor. Oxygen gas began to build up when tiny photosynthetic microorganisms first appeared. These microorganisms produced oxygen during photosynthesis and released it into the atmosphere.

▶ **Water Vapor** Air contains water vapor. The chemical formula for water—whether it is solid, liquid, or gas—is H_2O, indicating that a water molecule consists of two hydrogen atoms and one oxygen atom.

FIGURE 2 Combustion Without oxygen, wood could not burn and there would be no bright, crackling campfire.

FIGURE 3 Condensation After the air becomes cooler, beads of dew form on the flower petals. The process of dew formation, which is also called condensation, occurs when cooled air contains more water vapor than it can hold at that temperature.

Relative Humidity Air does not always hold the same amount of water. **Relative humidity** is the ratio of water vapor the air contains to the maximum amount it could have at that temperature. Average daytime relative humidity in Phoenix, Arizona, is only 31 percent. This means that, in general, the air in Phoenix contains less than a third of the water vapor that it could contain. In contrast, on the tropical island of Guam, the relative humidity rarely drops below 88 percent.

On some hot days, you may have heard people complaining about the humidity. People are sensitive to changes in relative humidity because perspiration cools our bodies. When humidity is high, sweat does not readily evaporate, and the body cannot cool itself efficiently.

▶ *Condensation* In general, warm air can hold more water vapor than cooler air. Suppose warm air contains all the water vapor it can hold, and then the air cools down. When this happens, the water vapor becomes liquid water or ice in a process called *condensation*. If the temperature is above freezing, water droplets form. Ice crystals form when the temperature is below freezing. Dew and frost are both examples of condensation.

▶ *Cloud Formation* In order for condensation to occur, there must be a surface on which water vapor can condense. Dew and frost, for example, form on surfaces such as blades of grass or flower petals, as shown in **Figure 3.** Like dew and frost, clouds are the result of condensation. During the formation of clouds, water vapor condenses on tiny particles in the air. These particles include salt crystals, smoke, and dust.

Air Temperature Like the air's water content, the temperature of the air also varies from place to place, and from time to time. Temperature varies over Earth's surface because the sun's rays strike some areas more directly than others. In the next chapter, you will learn more about factors that affect air temperature.

 Why can't clouds form unless there are tiny particles in the air?

Air Pressure Air is made up of individual molecules of nitrogen and other gases. Each molecule, tiny as it is, weighs something. The weight of a column of air pushes down on the area beneath it, the way the weight of your body pushes down on the ground that you stand on. The force with which something pushes on an area is called pressure. **Air pressure,** or atmospheric pressure, is the force exerted by air on the area below it.

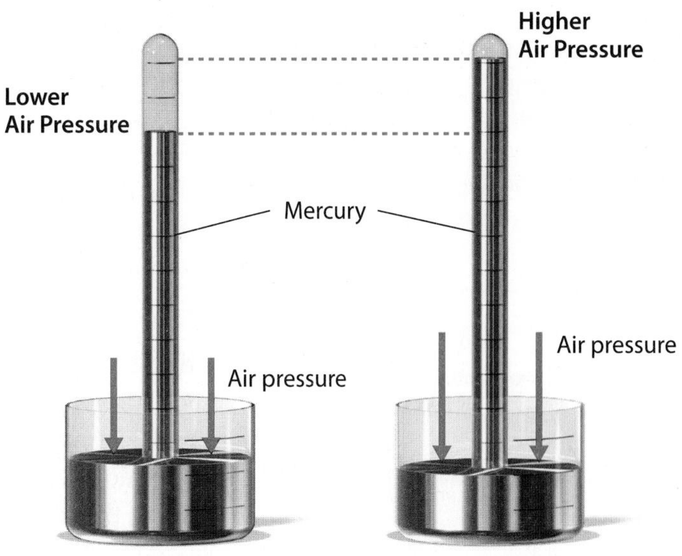

▶ *Measuring Air Pressure* A barometer is an instrument that measures air pressure. There are two common types of barometers: mercury and aneroid. In a *mercury barometer,* which is shown in **Figure 4,** air pressure pushes a column of mercury upward in a tube. The greater the air pressure, the higher the mercury rises. When a mercury barometer is used, air pressure is usually expressed in inches because the height of the mercury column in the barometer is measured in inches. An *aneroid barometer* has a metal chamber whose walls bend inward when air pressure is high. The walls bulge out when air pressure is low. The bending of the chamber walls moves a dial, and the dial indicates the changing air pressure. In an aneroid barometer, air pressure is expressed in units called millibars.

▶ *Altitude and Air Pressure* In general, the lower the altitude, or height above sea level, the higher the air pressure. To understand why this is true, think of a stack of books. The one at the bottom of the pile is under the most pressure because it is bearing the weight of all the books above it. Similarly, the air at the bottom of a column of air is under greater pressure than the air higher up. Air pressure at sea level is about 1000 millibars. In contrast, at the top of Mount Everest, air pressure is just over 300 millibars.

FIGURE 4 Barometers Barometers are instruments that measure atmospheric pressure. The illustration shows how a mercury barometer works. Air pushes down on mercury, as shown by the red arrows. The greater the air pressure, the higher the mercury rises in the tube.

Layers of the Atmosphere

Earth's atmosphere is divided into four main layers, primarily on the basis of changes in temperature. The layers of the atmosphere are the troposphere, stratosphere, mesosphere, and thermosphere.

The Troposphere The lowest layer of the atmosphere, the one directly above the ground, is called the **troposphere.** The troposphere blankets Earth's surface and contains the oxygen we need to live. The movement of air within the troposphere is also largely responsible for Earth's weather. Almost all clouds are found in the troposphere. The troposphere contains three quarters of the atmosphere's mass, even though it is thin compared to the atmosphere's other layers. The troposphere averages about 11 kilometers (7 miles) in height. At the poles, it is about 7 kilometers (4 miles) high, and at the equator, it is about 18 kilometers (10 miles) high.

FIND OUT MORE

What is the weather today in your area? Observe whether it is clear or cloudy, and whether or not precipitation is falling. Then find out the temperature, relative humidity, and air pressure. Use your local newspaper, listen to a TV weather report, or go online to the Web site of the National Oceanic and Atmospheric Administration.

FIGURE 5 Earth's Atmosphere From Space If you view Earth from space, you can see the clouds in the atmosphere.

▶ *Temperature in the Troposphere* Within the troposphere, the higher the air is above Earth, the cooler it becomes. On average, tropospheric air temperature goes down by about 6.5°C for each kilometer in altitude (or 3.6°F per 1000 feet).

▶ *The Top of the Troposphere* At the top boundary of the troposphere, the temperature stops going down. A layer at the top of the troposphere acts like a cap, limiting mixing between the troposphere and the atmospheric layer above it.

The Stratosphere The **stratosphere** is the layer of the atmosphere above the troposphere, as shown in **Figure 6.** The stratosphere extends 11–50 kilometers (7–31 miles) above sea level. The gases in the stratosphere do not mix much. Therefore, once substances including pollutants enter it, they usually stay there for a long time.

▶ *Temperature in the Stratosphere* Unlike the troposphere, the highest part of the stratosphere is warmer than lower levels. However, the stratosphere is definitely not warm. It reaches a maximum temperature of –3°C (27°F) at its highest altitude.

▶ *The Ozone Layer* The most common form of oxygen is O_2, but oxygen also occurs as O_3, which is a gas called ozone. Ozone is concentrated in a portion of the stratosphere called the **ozone layer.** The upper stratosphere is warmer than the lower stratosphere because ozone gas absorbs and scatters the sun's ultraviolet (UV) rays. UV light penetrates the upper stratosphere, but most of it fails to reach the lower stratosphere. The ozone layer greatly reduces the amount of UV light that reaches Earth's surface. UV light can damage an organism's living tissue and cause harmful changes in its DNA. Therefore, the ozone layer's protective effects are vital for life on Earth.

In the stratosphere, ozone occurs naturally and is beneficial to humans, because it filters out UV light. However, in the lower level of the troposphere, ozone does not occur naturally; in the troposphere, ozone is a pollutant. It harms living tissue, including lung tissue, and can interfere with plant growth.

The Mesosphere and Thermosphere Above the stratosphere lies the **mesosphere,** the layer that extends 50–80 kilometers (31–50 miles) above sea level. In this layer, temperatures decrease with altitude, reaching their lowest point at the top of the mesosphere. Air pressure is extremely low.

The **thermosphere** is the top layer, which begins about 80 kilometers (50 miles) above Earth's surface and extends upward into space. Air is very thin, and the thermosphere has only a tiny fraction of the atmosphere's mass. The temperature is very high.

 Reading Checkpoint *Which layer of the atmosphere is located directly above the stratosphere?*

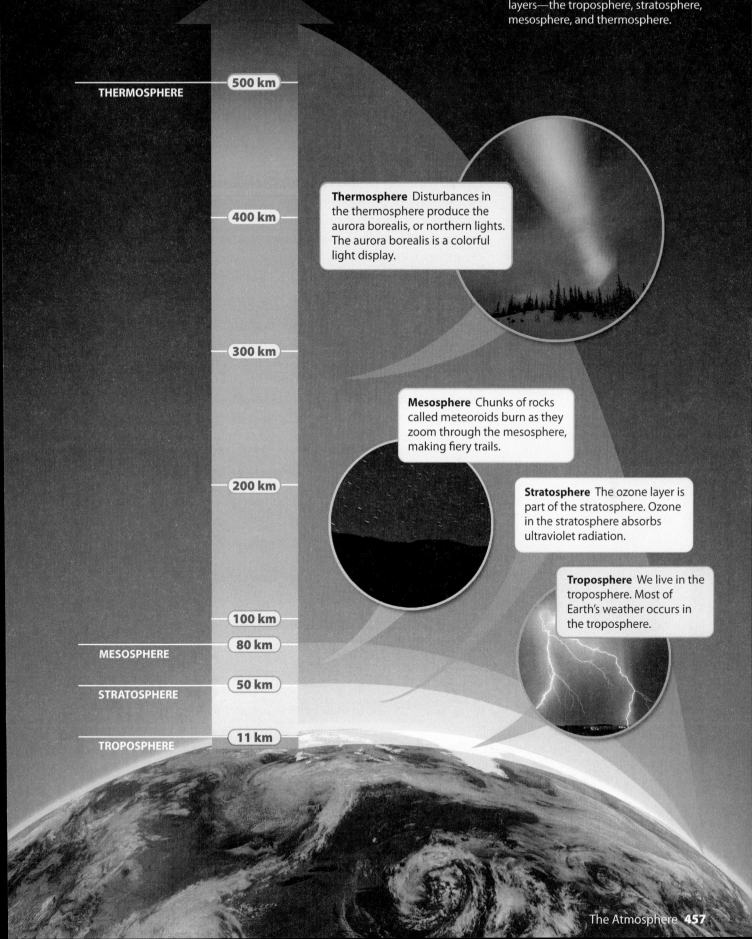

layers—the troposphere, stratosphere, mesosphere, and thermosphere.

500 km

THERMOSPHERE

400 km

Thermosphere Disturbances in the thermosphere produce the aurora borealis, or northern lights. The aurora borealis is a colorful light display.

300 km

Mesosphere Chunks of rocks called meteoroids burn as they zoom through the mesosphere, making fiery trails.

200 km

Stratosphere The ozone layer is part of the stratosphere. Ozone in the stratosphere absorbs ultraviolet radiation.

Troposphere We live in the troposphere. Most of Earth's weather occurs in the troposphere.

100 km

80 km

MESOSPHERE

50 km

STRATOSPHERE

11 km

TROPOSPHERE

The Troposphere and Weather

Weather and climate each involve properties of the troposphere, such as temperature and humidity. *Weather* refers to atmospheric conditions over short time periods, typically hours or days, and within relatively small areas. *Climate,* in contrast, describes the pattern of atmospheric conditions in large geographic regions over long periods. For example, London has a moist, temperate climate. But the weather on summer days in London can sometimes be hot, dry, and sunny.

Heat Transfer in the Troposphere Energy from the sun heats the atmosphere. This energy drives air movement in the troposphere and influences weather and climate. Heat always moves from a warmer substance to something that is cooler. Heat is transferred in three ways— radiation, conduction, and convection. **Figure 7** shows how these processes work in the troposphere.

▶ *Radiation* On a sunny summer day, the handle of a car door becomes hot because of energy from the sun in the form of sunlight. The car door has been heated by **radiation,** which is the transfer of energy through space. Heat travels from the sun to Earth's atmosphere by radiation. When objects are heated by radiation, there is no direct contact between the heat source and the object being heated. Dark objects absorb more radiation than objects that are light in color. Light objects reflect much of the radiation away.

FIGURE 7 Methods of Heat Transfer
Radiation, conduction, and convection all help to transfer heat in the troposphere. Heat from the sun and the heat that moves from an electric burner to the air are both transferred by radiation. Heat moves from a burner to water in a pan by conduction. Within the water in the pan, heat is transferred by convection currents.

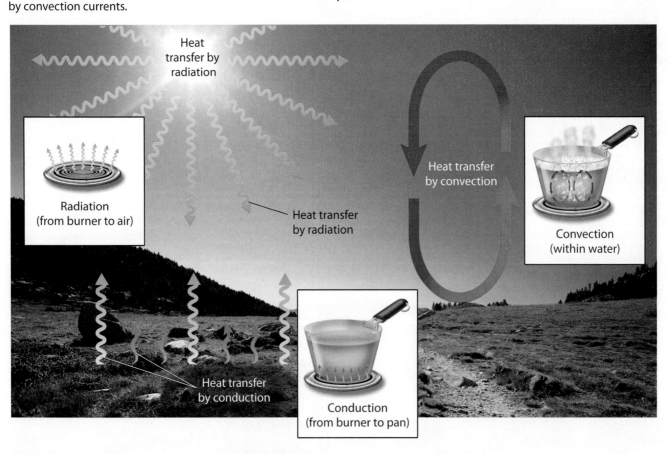

Heat transfer by radiation

Radiation (from burner to air)

Heat transfer by radiation

Heat transfer by convection

Convection (within water)

Heat transfer by conduction

Conduction (from burner to pan)

▶ **Conduction** If you touch the heated handle of the car door, you will feel that it is hot. Heat passes from the handle to your hand through conduction. **Conduction** is the transfer of heat directly between two objects that are in contact with one another. Conduction occurs when molecules collide, and energy is transferred from one molecule to another. In the troposphere, conduction only occurs between Earth's surface and the molecules in the air directly in contact with it.

▶ **Convection** Fluids include liquids and gases, such as the gases in the atmosphere. In fluids, molecules are free to move around. **Convection** is the transfer of heat by the movement of currents within a fluid. Convection is an important method of heat transfer in the troposphere.

▶ **Convection Currents and the Movement of Heat** The process of convection is related to density. Density is the amount of mass of a substance in a given volume. For example, a brick has a greater density than a block of wood that has the same volume, because there is a greater amount of mass in the brick.

When air near the surface of Earth is heated, it becomes less dense than it was before. The cooler air above it is denser than the warmer air at the surface. Because of this difference in density, the cool air sinks and the warm air rises above it. When the cooler air sinks to ground level, it then picks up heat and begins to rise. Sinking cool air and rising warm air form **convection currents.** Convection currents cause winds and move heat through the troposphere.

FIGURE 8 **Conduction** When you touch a hot surface, heat is transferred from the surface to your hand.

Reading Checkpoint   *What is convection?*

 # Quick Lab

How Does the Hot Water Move?

1. Obtain two 100-mL beakers. Fill one of them halfway with cold water.
2. Fill the other beaker halfway with hot water. Squirt a few drops of food coloring into the hot water, until the water is a dark color.
3. Use a dropper to remove some of the hot water that has been colored. Fill the dropper, then wipe it off with a paper towel.
4. Insert the dropper into the cold water so that the dropper's opening is halfway between the surface of the water and the bottom of the beaker.
5. Slowly squeeze the dropper bulb so that you release the colored water into the cold water.
6. Observe the beaker from the side to see what happens to the colored water.

Analyze and Conclude

1. **Observe** How did the hot water move in the beaker?
2. **Relate Cause and Effect** Why did the hot water move the way it did?
3. **Apply Concepts** How is the movement of the hot water similar to the movement of air in the troposphere?

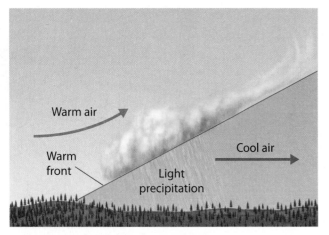

(a) Warm Front

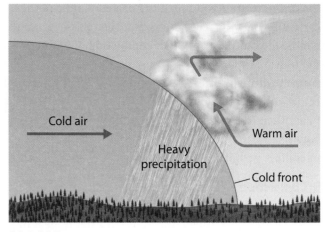

(b) Cold Front

FIGURE 9 Warm and Cold Fronts
When a warm front approaches **(a)**, warmer air rises over cooler air, and light or moderate precipitation may fall. In a cold front **(b)**, colder air pushes beneath warmer air, resulting in heavy precipitation.

Air Masses and Fronts Throughout a large body of air called an **air mass,** properties such as temperature, pressure, and humidity are similar. Weather can change when air masses with different properties come together. The boundary between air masses that differ in temperature and moisture is called a **front.**

▶ *Warm Front* A warm front is a boundary along which a mass of warmer, moister air pushes against a mass of colder, drier air. Because warm air is less dense than cool air, some of the warm, moist air rises over the cold air mass, as shown in **Figure 9a.** The warm air then cools. Because cool air can hold less moisture than warm air can, the water vapor in the cooler air condenses and forms clouds. Light rain may fall.

▶ *Cold Front* A cold front is the boundary along which a colder, drier air mass pushes against a warmer, moister air mass. Because colder air is denser than warmer air, the cold air tends to wedge beneath the warmer air. The warmer air rises. As the air rises, it cools to form clouds. If the rising air contains a lot of water vapor, heavy precipitation—snow or rain—may fall. If there is little water vapor in the air, the cold front may result in clouds only. Cold fronts can produce sudden weather changes, including thunderstorms. Once a cold front passes through an area, the sky usually clears, and the temperature and humidity drop.

 ① Assessment

1. **Use Analogies** Think of a swimming pool with a shallow end and a deep end. The pressure of water on the floor at the shallow end is less than the pressure of water on the floor at the deep end. How is this similar to the way air pressure differs at different altitudes?

2. **Relate Cause and Effect** Why is the temperature in the upper stratosphere higher than the temperature in the lower stratosphere?

3. **Compare and Contrast** How is a warm front different from a cold front?

   REVISIT

4. **INVESTIGATIVE** PHENOMENON
   Winds occur because of convection currents in the troposphere. How do you think winds affect air pollution?

Pollution of the Atmosphere

EVERYDAY PHENOMENON What are the sources of air pollution?

Knowledge and Skills

- Explain how both natural processes and human activities can cause air pollution.
- Describe how air pollutants affect human health.
- Explain what causes smog and how temperature inversions affect it and other forms of air pollution.
- Explain how acid deposition occurs and describe its effects.

Reading Strategy and Vocabulary

✓ **Reading Strategy** Before you read, make a three-column KWL chart. In the first column, write what you already know about air pollution. In the second column, write what you want to learn. After reading, complete the chart by filling in what you have learned in the third column.

Vocabulary air pollution, emission, fossil fuel, primary air pollutant, secondary air pollutant, smog, temperature inversion, acid deposition

CROWDED TOGETHER, the horses in the parade seem to be fighting for space. The horse in the forefront is rearing, possibly frightened by the other horses and riders nearby. The rider, in contrast, appears calm as he looks off into the distance. Thousands of years ago, in ancient Athens, Greek sculptors created this parade in marble to go at the top of the Parthenon, a temple that honored the goddess Athena.

Today the parade of warriors no longer graces the Parthenon. Instead, the sculptures are inside a museum in Athens. The sculptures were moved to protect them from more damage. One cause of damage was pollutants in the air. If you look carefully at **Figure 10,** you can see that some of the stone has been worn away.

FIGURE 10 Damage From Air Pollution Notice that the warriors' faces have been worn away. The damage was caused partly by air pollution.

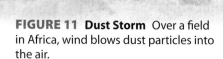

FIGURE 11 **Dust Storm** Over a field in Africa, wind blows dust particles into the air.

Sources of Air Pollution

The cars, trucks, and industries of modern Athens have released pollutants that have contributed to the damage to the Parthenon. Both human activities and natural processes cause outdoor **air pollution,** which is the release of damaging materials into the atmosphere. The substances released are called **emissions.** Some emissions, such as smoke and soot, consist of tiny particles, or particulate matter. Others are gases such as sulfur dioxide and carbon monoxide.

Natural Processes Natural processes produce a great deal of the world's air pollution. Winds sweeping over dry land can create huge dust storms, as seen in **Figure 11.** Winds sometimes blow dust across oceans from one continent to another. Volcanic eruptions release tiny solid particles and gases into the atmosphere. Fires in forests and grasslands also produce smoke, soot, and gases.

Human activities can make some natural pollution worse. For example, some farming and grazing practices strip most plants from the soil. When there are few plant roots to hold soil in place, wind erosion may occur. Wind erosion can lead to dust storms.

Human Sources People's activities have influenced air quality. The way we live—for example, our industries, the cars we drive, and the way we produce electricity—has introduced many sources of air pollution. Air pollution can come from point sources or nonpoint sources. In London, power plants and factories act as point sources of emissions. Millions of cars and trucks together make up a moving nonpoint source.

Most air pollution comes, directly or indirectly, from the combustion of fossil fuels. Fossil fuels are carbon-containing fuels that formed millions of years ago from the remains of living things. Motor vehicles, such as cars and trucks, run by burning fossil fuels. Motor vehicles release an enormous amount of pollutants into the air.

Primary and Secondary Air Pollutants Pollutants may do harm directly, or they may cause chemical reactions that produce harmful compounds. **Primary air pollutants,** such as soot and carbon monoxide, are pollutants released directly into the troposphere. Primary air pollutants may cause damage themselves, or they may react with other products to cause damage. Harmful products produced when primary air pollutants react chemically with other substances are called **secondary air pollutants.** Secondary air pollutants include tropospheric ozone and sulfuric acid. The table in **Figure 12** describes some primary and secondary air pollutants.

FIGURE 12 Air Pollutants Primary air pollutants are released directly into the troposphere. Secondary air pollutants, in contrast, are the products of chemical reactions between primary air pollutants and other substances.

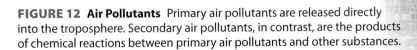

Primary Air Pollutants		
Pollutant	**Source**	**Effect**
Carbon monoxide (CO) A colorless, odorless gas	The incomplete combustion (burning) of fossil fuels by motor vehicles, industries, and other sources	Binds to hemoglobin, the oxygen-carrying chemical in blood; deprives cells of oxygen
Sulfur dioxide (SO_2) A colorless gas with a strong, unpleasant odor	Burning of fossil fuels, especially coal, for electricity generation and industry	Produces secondary pollutants that are part of acid precipitation; causes lung irritation
Nitrogen dioxide (NO_2) A foul-smelling, reddish-brown gas that belongs to a family of compounds called nitrogen oxides	A reaction between atmospheric nitrogen and oxygen in combustion engines and during the production of electricity	Can cause serious lung irritation; contributes to smog and acid precipitation
Volatile organic compounds (VOCs) Carbon-containing chemicals that evaporate easily, producing fumes. Examples include methane, propane, butane, and benzene.	Many sources, including vehicle engines, household cleaning products, some industrial processes, and natural processes	Some can cause cancer; some interact with other chemicals to produce ozone in the troposphere.
Particulate matter Solid or liquid particles that are small enough to float in the atmosphere—soot, dust, tiny bits of metals	Dust blown by wind; soot and chemicals produced by fires and combustion within engines; particles produced during construction and farming	Can affect breathing and damage lungs
Lead A heavy metal that is one type of particulate matter	Industrial refinement of metals; in developing nations, gasoline contains lead	Can damage body tissues, including those in the nervous system

Secondary Air Pollutants		
Pollutant	**Source**	**Effect**
Tropospheric ozone (O_3) A colorless gas with an unpleasant odor	Results from the interaction of sunlight, heat, nitrogen oxides, and volatile organic compounds	Ozone in the stratosphere protects humans from radiation, but ozone in the troposphere can injure living tissues and cause respiratory problems.
Sulfuric acid (H_2SO_4) and nitric acid (HNO_3)	Produced when sulfur dioxide and nitrogen oxides combine with water in the atmosphere	Components of acid precipitation

FIGURE 13 Effects of Air Pollution A runner in the Beijing Olympic Games wears a mask to protect his respiratory system from air pollution. Beijing has severe air pollution. Before the 2008 Olympic Games, the city made a major effort to clean its air.

How Air Pollutants Affect Your Health

Outdoor air pollution is a big health problem. Air pollutants can do serious harm to the respiratory system, which transports oxygen into your body and removes carbon dioxide. Some air pollutants can cause cancer.

Respiratory System Problems Have you ever inhaled dust and then started coughing? Particles in the dust irritated your respiratory system, making you cough. Similarly, air pollutants irritate people's air passages and lungs. If people are exposed over and over to air pollution, they may develop harmful respiratory conditions. Asthma, bronchitis, and emphysema have all been linked to air pollutants.

The Effect of Carbon Monoxide How do the cells of your body obtain the oxygen they need? The air that you inhale contains oxygen. This oxygen passes from the lungs into the bloodstream. There, oxygen binds to hemoglobin. Hemoglobin is a molecule in red blood cells that combines chemically with oxygen. The red blood cells then carry the oxygen to the cells of the body.

However, if there is carbon monoxide in the air, the carbon monoxide will bind to hemoglobin, replacing some of the oxygen that the blood would normally carry. Therefore, carbon monoxide interferes with your body's ability to deliver oxygen to cells. This can cause headaches, tiredness, and nausea. Over time, carbon monoxide can damage the heart because the heart muscle has to work harder than normal to deliver oxygen to cells. In high concentrations, carbon monoxide can be fatal.

Cancer Trace amounts of some air pollutants may contribute to cancer. Soot, for example, can cause cancer if it is inhaled frequently. Benzene, which is a volatile organic compound in gasoline, has also been linked to cancer. Exhaust from cars and trucks contains benzene.

Smog and Temperature Inversions

If you combine the words *smoke* and *fog,* you get the word *smog.* **Smog** is an unhealthy mixture of air pollutants that may form over cities and nearby areas.

Industrial Smog The smog that covered London in 1952 was industrial smog. Industrial smog is produced when soot combines with sulfur compounds and water droplets in air. Because of government regulation, this type of smog is far less common in developed nations than it was 50–100 years ago. However, the situation is different in developing nations, such as China and the nations of Eastern Europe. Industrial technologies in these nations are often older than those in developed nations, and have less ability to control pollution than do newer technologies. Also, there is less government regulation of air quality in these nations. Therefore, industrial smog continues to create health problems in many areas.

Photochemical Smog A photochemical process is one that needs light. Photochemical smog is a thick, brownish haze that forms when sunlight acts on certain air pollutants, such as nitrogen oxides and chemicals called hydrocarbons. Tropospheric ozone is often the most abundant pollutant in photochemical smog. Ozone in the troposphere is chemically identical to ozone in the stratosphere. However, unlike ozone in the stratosphere, which protects living things by filtering ultraviolet light, tropospheric ozone can damage living tissue—especially eye and lung tissues and plant leaves—as well as other materials.

The main source of the pollutants in photochemical smog is the exhaust released by cars and trucks. Governments are acting to reduce motor-vehicle emissions, which will reduce photochemical smog. For example, vehicle inspection programs make drivers fix cars and trucks that release high levels of pollutants.

 Reading Checkpoint *What is the difference between industrial smog and photochemical smog?*

your world • your turn •

WHAT DO YOU THINK?

Should your city, or a city near you, start a congestion-charging program like London's? What are some of the pros and cons of such a program?

 Connect to the Central Case

FIGURE 14 Photochemical Smog Smog shrouds the city of Shanghai in China. **Relate Cause and Effect** What was the main source of the pollutants that caused London's "killer smog" in 1952?

Temperature Inversions Recall that in the troposphere, air temperature usually decreases as altitude increases. Earth's surface warms the air at low altitudes. Since warm air rises, any pollutants in the air are carried away from the surface and higher into the troposphere. This process removes pollutants from low altitudes and helps them disperse.

The situation is different, however, when a temperature inversion occurs. A **temperature inversion,** or thermal inversion, is the condition in the troposphere in which a layer of cooler air is located beneath a layer of warmer air. Since cold air has a greater density than warm air, the air at Earth's surface does not rise and mix with the air higher up. Therefore, temperature inversions can keep air pollutants, including those found in smog, from going away. **Figure 15** shows how a temperature inversion can worsen air pollution. It was a thermal inversion that caused London's "killer smog" of 1952. Inversions regularly cause smog buildup in some cities, such as Los Angeles and Mexico City.

 Reading Checkpoint *During a temperature inversion, why doesn't air at Earth's surface rise?*

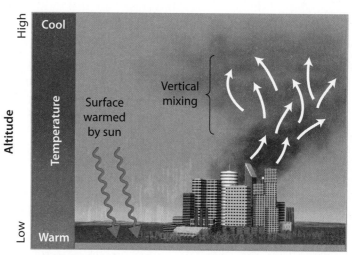

(a) Normal Conditions

 Connect to the Central Case
FIGURE 15 Temperature Inversion
Normally, tropospheric temperature decreases with height above the ground **(a),** and air at the surface mixes with air above it. In a temperature inversion **(b),** cool air stays near the ground, under a layer of warmer air, and little mixing occurs. **Relate Cause and Effect** Why can a temperature inversion, such as the one that occurred in London in 1952, make air pollution worse?

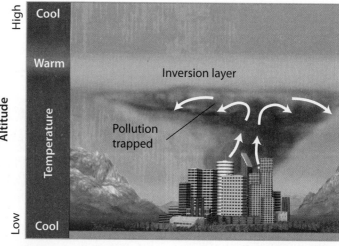

(b) Thermal Inversion

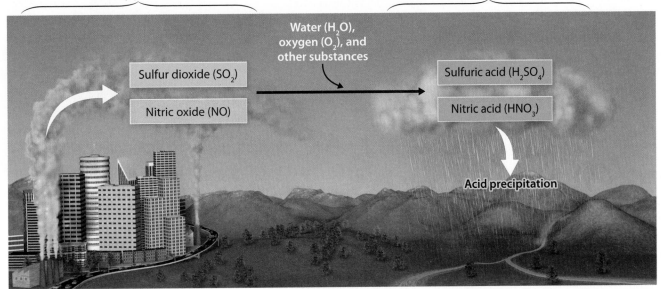

Water (H₂O), oxygen (O₂), and other substances

Sulfur dioxide (SO₂)

Nitric oxide (NO)

Sulfuric acid (H₂SO₄)

Nitric acid (HNO₃)

Acid precipitation

Acid Deposition

FIGURE 16 Formation of Acid Precipitation Acid precipitation starts when sulfur dioxide and nitrogen oxides such as nitric oxide combine with water, oxygen, and other substances. Acid precipitation can affect areas a long way from the original source.

When some pollutants combine with water, oxygen, and other chemicals in the atmosphere, they form compounds called acids. These acids may settle to the surface of Earth as **acid deposition.** Acid deposition may consist of solid or gaseous particles, or the acids may dissolve in fog or precipitation. Acid precipitation is sometimes called acid rain, but any kind of precipitation, such as snow or sleet, can contain acidic pollutants.

The pH Scale and Precipitation The pH scale is used to measure whether solutions are acidic or alkaline. The values on the scale range from 0 to 14. A pH of 7 is neutral, that is, it is neither acidic nor alkaline. If a solution has a pH that is higher than 7, it is alkaline, or basic. An acid is a solution whose pH is lower than 7. The lower the pH number, the higher the acidity.

The pH of precipitation varies. Normal precipitation is slightly acidic, with a pH of about 5.6. Acid precipitation has a lower pH. Some areas in the United States have precipitation with a pH as low as 4.3.

Go Outside

Is the Rainwater Acidic? ⚠

1. On a rainy day, put a clean plastic cup outside where it will collect rainwater.

2. Bring the collected rainwater indoors. Then use pH paper to measure the pH of the water.

3. Compare your results to those of other students.

Analyze and Conclude

1. **Analyze Data** Is rainwater in your area more acidic than normal rainwater? Explain your answer.

2. **Perform Error Analysis** If other students obtained different results from yours, try to figure out why.

FIGURE 17 Effects of Acid Deposition Notice that many trees no longer have any needles—a result of acid deposition.

Sources of Acid Deposition Acid deposition starts mainly with sulfur dioxide and nitrogen oxides. These pollutants are produced largely through the burning of fossil fuels by automobiles, electric power plants, and industries. In the troposphere, these compounds can react with water, oxygen, and other substances to produce acids such as sulfuric acid and nitric acid.

Wind can carry pollutants over long distances. Therefore, acid deposition may fall on areas that are far from where the pollutants were produced. For example, much of the pollution that is produced in Pennsylvania, Ohio, and Illinois falls out in states to the east, including New York, Vermont, and New Hampshire.

Effects of Acid Deposition Acid deposition can harm ecosystems and structures that humans have built. For example, if the pH in lakes becomes too low, neither plants nor fishes can survive. Acid deposition can kill trees and destroy whole forests **(Figure 17).** When acid gets into the soil, harmful chemicals can be released. These chemicals can poison plants growing in the soil. Acid deposition can erode the surfaces of stone buildings and statues, such as the Parthenon sculptures. In addition, acid deposition can increase the acidity of the water that comes into your home. Water with increased acidity can pick up harmful chemicals from metal pipes and contaminate drinking water.

Acid deposition is a problem, but it can be solved. People and governments have taken steps to eliminate or reduce air pollutants that cause acid deposition. The next lesson describes some of those steps.

LESSON

② Assessment

1. **Interpret Tables** Sulfuric acid and sulfur dioxide are both air pollutants. Use **Figure 12** to determine which is a primary pollutant and which is a secondary pollutant. What is the relationship between these two types of pollutants?

2. **Infer** When people work with volatile organic compounds, why should they wear special masks that cover their noses and mouths?

3. **Relate Cause and Effect** Why does a temperature inversion trap smog and prevent it from dispersing?

4. **Apply Concepts** The rain that falls in an area has a pH of 5.8. Is this acid precipitation? Explain your answer.

   REVISIT

5. **INVESTIGATIVE** PHENOMENON
   Why might developing nations be more reluctant than developed nations to take measures to control industrial smog?

Controlling Air Pollution

EVERYDAY PHENOMENON What measures can limit and prevent pollution of the atmosphere?

Knowledge and Skills

- Explain how the provisions of the Clean Air Act have reduced air pollution in the United States.
- Describe international efforts to reduce the ozone hole.

Reading Strategy and Vocabulary

✔ **Reading Strategy** After you read this lesson, write a summary of the goals, provisions, and effects of the Clean Air Act.

Vocabulary Clean Air Act, catalytic converter, scrubber, ozone hole, chlorofluorocarbon (CFC), Montreal Protocol

THE SOUTHERN UTES, a Native American Indian tribe, live in southwestern Colorado, within sight of the La Plata Mountains. Besides being beautiful, this area is rich in natural gas. The removal and processing of this fuel provide income and work for people in the tribe and surrounding communities. However, faulty processing of natural gas can pollute the air.

The Southern Utes want to keep the air clean and safe to breathe. To do that, leaders of the tribe have worked with the state and federal governments to develop an air quality program. The program currently involves monitoring the air for pollutants and identifying point and nonpoint sources of air pollutants on the Southern Ute reservation. In addition, the program conducts inspections of industries and sees to it that industries fix any problems that arise. The Southern Ute Air Quality Program also includes many other activities, such as research into methods of eliminating air pollution.

The Southern Utes are using technology, cooperation, creativity, and determination to preserve air quality. The Southern Ute Air Quality Program focuses on a relatively small area of land. At the national and global level, the United States and other nations are taking steps to deal with air pollution. We have a long way to go, but many of our efforts have been successful. You will read about some of those successes in this lesson.

FIGURE 18 Monitoring Air Quality A scientist with the Southern Ute Air Quality Program examines a device that monitors air quality.

The Atmosphere **469**

The Clean Air Act

To address air pollution in the United States, Congress has passed a series of laws, including the Clean Air Act. The Clean Air Act was first passed in 1963 and has been revised several times since. Revisions in 1970 and 1990 were especially important. Those revisions set stricter standards for air quality and strengthened the government's ability to enforce regulations.

Goal of the Clean Air Act The Clean Air Act protects and improves the quality of air in order to safeguard human health and the environment. The law takes measures to reduce the emission of pollutants that cause health problems such as asthma and cancer. It also limits the release of pollutants responsible for environmental problems such as smog and acid deposition.

Provisions of the Clean Air Act Here are some of the measures taken by the Clean Air Act:

- The Act limits emissions of pollutants by motor vehicles and industries.
- It sets standards for air quality. The law limits the concentration of some specific air pollutants, such as carbon monoxide and particulate matter. The upper limit of each pollutant is based on the maximum amount that humans can tolerate without harm.
- It lets people sue industries that break the rules.
- It sets aside funds for research into pollution control.

Under the Clean Air Act, the U.S. Environmental Protection Agency (EPA) sets nationwide standards governing air pollutants and air quality. However, the states and Native American tribes have the option of developing and enforcing specific regulations that are equivalent to—or exceed—those found in the Clean Air Act.

 Reading Checkpoint *What is the Clean Air Act?*

FIGURE 19 Clean Air in the National Parks Air pollution is partly responsible for the haze over the Blue Ridge Mountains in Shenandoah National Park. The Clean Air Act has provisions that try to reduce haze in national parks.

Real Data

Effects of the Clean Air Act

The Clean Air Act has had major effects on the quality of the air we breathe. To monitor air quality, the EPA tracks emissions of several major air pollutants. The graph shows data for some air pollutants: carbon monoxide, nitrogen oxides, volatile organic compounds, sulfur dioxide, and lead. Look at the graph and then answer the following questions.

1. **Interpret Graphs** What do the green bars represent?

2. **Interpret Graphs** What do the purple bars represent?

3. **Analyze Data** What trend does the graph show?

4. **Analyze Data** Of the pollutants shown on the graph, which has changed by the greatest percentage?

5. **Interpret Graphs** Why is the bar for lead shown separately from the bars for the other pollutants? (*Hint:* Look at the axis labels.)

6. **Infer** Do you think that the general trend shown in this graph is also true for the air in London between 1952 and now? Explain your answer.

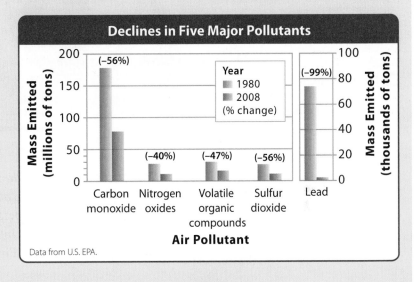

Data from U.S. EPA.

Reduction in Air Pollutants Since the Clean Air Act, the release of the worst air pollutants has gone down by 57 percent. This decrease in pollution has happened even though there are now many more people in the United States, and we use much more energy. The reduction of outdoor air pollution is one of the nation's greatest accomplishments in protecting the environment.

▶ *Motor Vehicles* Cars and trucks now cause less pollution. Catalytic converters have helped bring this about. A **catalytic converter** is a device in a motor vehicle that reduces the amount of air pollutants in emissions. It changes harmful emissions, such as carbon monoxide, into substances that are less harmful, such as carbon dioxide and water. Catalytic converters are usually located between the engine and the muffler of a car. Since 1975, all new cars in the United States have had catalytic converters.

▶ *Cleaner Gasoline* Gasoline once contained lead, and lead was part of the emissions from the exhaust systems of motor vehicles. Lead from vehicle emissions can settle to the ground and contaminate it. If lead gets into the bloodstream of a person—especially a young child—it can cause problems ranging from behavioral disorders to mental retardation. The EPA has been working to phase out lead in gasoline since 1973. Today gasoline used by cars and trucks contains almost no lead.

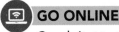 **GO ONLINE**

- **Graph It** Monitoring Major Air Pollutants

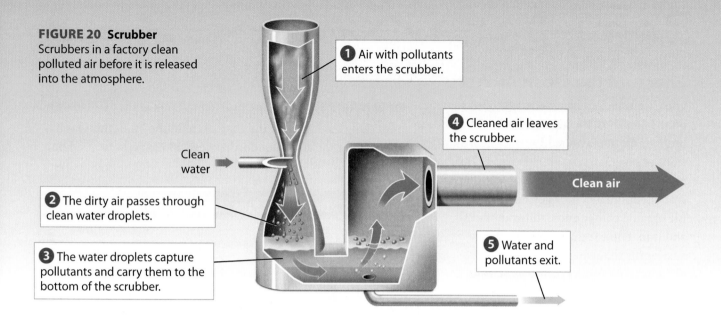

FIGURE 20 Scrubber
Scrubbers in a factory clean polluted air before it is released into the atmosphere.

1 Air with pollutants enters the scrubber.

4 Cleaned air leaves the scrubber.

Clean water

2 The dirty air passes through clean water droplets.

3 The water droplets capture pollutants and carry them to the bottom of the scrubber.

Clean air

5 Water and pollutants exit.

▶ *Industries and Power Plants* As a result of the Clean Air Act, industries and power plants have been required to reduce the amount of pollutants they release. Scrubbers are responsible for much of this reduction. A scrubber removes pollutants or changes them chemically before they leave factory smokestacks. **Figure 20** shows one type of scrubber.

Ozone: A Success Story

Ozone is a pollutant in smog in the troposphere. However, recall that ozone is highly beneficial in the ozone layer of the lower stratosphere. Here, ozone absorbs ultraviolet radiation from the sun. UV radiation can harm living things. For example, it can cause skin cancer in humans by chemically changing the genetic material in skin cells.

The Ozone Hole Late in the twentieth century, scientists noticed that measurements of ozone in the stratosphere were lower than they should have been. By 1985, the level of ozone over Antarctica was 40 to 60 percent lower than it had been 10 years before. People began to use the term ozone hole for the area of lowered ozone concentration over Antarctica that occurs every year from August until October (**Figure 21**).

Chlorofluorocarbons Earlier, in 1974, two scientists, Sherwood Rowland and Mario Molina, had predicted ozone depletion, or loss, and had identified the probable cause. Rowland and Molina suggested that chemicals called chlorofluorocarbons could cause ozone depletion. Chlorofluorocarbons (CFCs) are a family of chemical compounds containing chlorine, fluorine, and carbon. In the 1970s and 1980s, CFCs were manufactured in large amounts. They were used in many ways—for example, in refrigerators and aerosol spray cans.

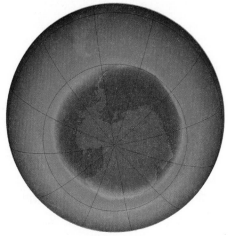
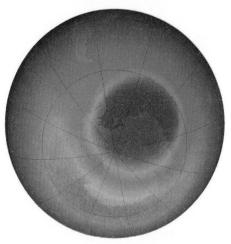

The ozone hole October, 1987

The ozone hole October, 2019

FIGURE 21 The Ozone Hole
The dark blue areas in the photographs show the ozone hole over Antarctica. Notice how the size of the ozone hole decreased between 1987 and 2019.

Molina and Rowland were correct in their prediction. CFCs were rising into the stratosphere and then releasing chlorine atoms that react with ozone. The chemical reactions destroy ozone molecules in the stratosphere. This destruction accounts for the ozone hole over Antarctica.

The Montreal Protocol Scientists and other people became concerned about the possible effects of ozone depletion. They were afraid, for example, that cases of skin cancer would increase. As a result of this concern, many nations, including the United States, began to work together to restrict production of CFCs and other ozone-depleting substances. In 1987, many nations signed the Montreal Protocol. The treaty, strengthened by later amendments, called for major cuts in CFC manufacture. Today the production and use of ozone-depleting compounds has fallen by 95 percent since the late 1980s. Industry was able to shift to different chemicals to perform the functions that CFCs used to perform. The new chemicals have largely turned out to be cheaper and more efficient.

Evidence indicates that the ozone layer is beginning to recover. In the last few years, concentrations of stratospheric ozone have stabilized, and scientists expect that they will soon begin to increase to their former levels. The Montreal Protocol is widely considered the biggest success story in addressing a global environmental problem. The Montreal Protocol is a model for international cooperation in dealing with other worldwide environmental problems, such as climate change.

LESSON ③ Assessment

1. **Relate Cause and Effect** Overall, what has been the effect of the Clean Air Act? Give one reason why this has happened.

2. **Predict** As time passes, what will happen to the amount of ozone in the ozone layer in the stratosphere? Give a reason for your prediction.

3. **THINK IT** *THROUGH* You have just become mayor of your community, and the EPA has informed you that your county has failed to meet the air quality standards for sulfur dioxide and nitrogen oxides. Your community includes an old coal-fired power plant that causes pollution but also provides employment for many people. What measures would you suggest that might deal with the pollution problem but still keep people employed?

THE CLEAN AIR ACT
AND ACID RAIN

SUCCESS STORIES

In 1990, Congress revised the Clean Air Act and gave the EPA authority to control industrial emissions of pollutants that create acid precipitation, particularly sulfur dioxide and nitrogen oxides. These pollutants react with other chemicals in the air to form the acid that falls in precipitation, damaging forests and aquatic ecosystems. In 1995, the EPA began its Acid Rain Program, which put a limit on how much sulfur dioxide and nitrogen oxides could be emitted from power plants nationwide. Coal-burning power plants are the biggest emitters of sulfur dioxide, while vehicles are the biggest emitters of nitrogen oxides.

SULFUR DIOXIDE CAP-AND-TRADE

In addition to placing limits on sulfur dioxide and nitrogen oxide emissions, the Acid Rain Program outlined a system of emissions cap-and-trade for sulfur dioxide. Under the program, power plants were issued a certain number of allowances, each worth one ton of sulfur dioxide emissions. Power plants that emit a lot of sulfur dioxide have to buy more allowances, whereas power plants with fewer emissions can sell their leftover allowances and make a profit. As a result of the program, power plants began to explore new technologies, such as scrubbers, that could help them reduce their sulfur dioxide output.

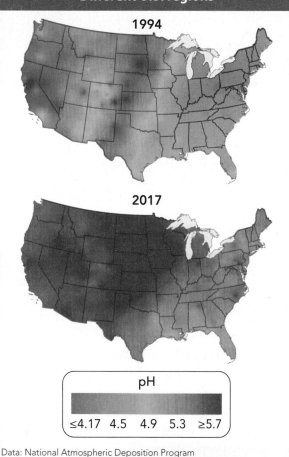

Comparing the pH of Rain in Different U.S. regions

1994

2017

pH

≤4.17 4.5 4.9 5.3 ≥5.7

Data: National Atmospheric Deposition Program

Maps showing the acidity of precipitation in the U.S. in 1994 and 2017. Limits on emissions have reduced acid precipitation across the country.

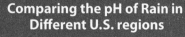

REDUCTIONS

Government regulations currently limit sulfur dioxide emissions from power plants to 50 percent below 1980 levels—a reduction of more than 7 million tons of sulfur dioxide per year. As of early 2010, sulfur dioxide emissions from power plants have decreased to 40 percent below 1980 levels. The Clean Air Act also put a cap on power plant emissions of nitrogen oxides, the other major source of acid pollution.

RECOVERY

The National Atmospheric Deposition Program collects rainwater from around the country and analyzes its pH and chemical content. The program found that acid precipitation has gone down throughout the country, including the heavily damaged Northeast, where the acidity of precipitation has gone down from an average pH of 4.15 to around 4.5. More work is needed to return precipitation across the country to a natural pH of 5.6, but some forests and lakes have started to recover, and water quality has improved. The gains for human health have been even more substantial. The reduction in illnesses caused by sulfur dioxide and nitrogen oxides in the air, such as asthma and bronchitis, save the U.S. billions of dollars annually.

21st Century Skills **Media Literacy** The Clean Air Act requires factories and plants in each state to report their emissions to the EPA, where they become part of the public record. Use the Internet to find out how much sulfur dioxide was emitted in your state last year. Compare this result with that of three other states in different regions of the United States.

Study Guide

Does congestion charging work to reduce air pollution?

Lesson 1
How can we describe Earth's atmosphere?

Lesson 2
What are the sources of air pollution?

Lesson 3
What measures can limit and prevent pollution of the atmosphere?

LESSON 1 Earth's Atmosphere

- Properties of the atmosphere include its composition, relative humidity, temperature, and air pressure.
- Relative humidity is the ratio of water vapor the air contains to the maximum amount it could have at that temperature. Air pressure is the force exerted by air on the area below it.
- The main layers of the atmosphere include the troposphere, stratosphere, mesosphere, and thermosphere. Movement of air within the troposphere is largely responsible for weather.
- The stratosphere, the layer above the troposphere, contains the ozone layer.
- Processes that affect weather in the troposphere include heat transfer and the interaction of air masses.

atmosphere (452)	thermosphere (456)
relative humidity (454)	radiation (458)
air pressure (455)	conduction (459)
troposphere (455)	convection (459)
stratosphere (456)	convection current (459)
ozone layer (456)	air mass (460)
mesosphere (456)	front (460)

LESSON 2 Pollution of the Atmosphere

- Air pollution can be caused by natural processes such as dust storms and human activities such as the combustion of fossil fuels.
- Air pollutants can damage the respiratory system, interfere with the body's uptake of oxygen, and cause cancer.
- Temperature inversions may trap smog and prevent the pollutants from dispersing.
- Acid deposition results when products of combustion combine with water and other substances in the atmosphere.

air pollution (462)	secondary air pollutant (463)
emission (462)	smog (465)
fossil fuel (462)	temperature inversion (466)
primary air pollutant (463)	acid deposition (467)

LESSON 3 Controlling Air Pollution

- The Clean Air Act has provisions that have reduced air pollution in the United States. For example, the Act limits the emissions of pollutants and sets standards for air quality.
- The ozone hole is the area of lowered ozone concentration over Antarctica that occurs every year from August to October. Nations have taken steps to deal with the problem of ozone loss in the stratosphere.
- The Montreal Protocol is an international treaty that has dramatically reduced production of CFCs, the chemicals linked to the development of the ozone hole. Evidence indicates that the ozone layer is beginning to recover.

Clean Air Act (470)
catalytic converter (471)
scrubber (472)
ozone hole (472)
chlorofluorocarbon (CFC) (472)
Montreal Protocol (473)

 GO ONLINE

INQUIRY LABS AND ACTIVITIES

- **Acid Rain and Seeds**

  At what point does acidity in precipitation cause problems? Test vinegar-water dilutions to see how acidity affects seed growth.

- **What's in the Air?**

  Build an air trap and take it outside to capture particles in the air. Observe the particles under magnification to infer their source.

- **Using Your UV Index**

  Checking your forecast involves more than just rain or shine. Monitor the UV index and see what protections the EPA recommends.

Chapter Assessment

Central CASE Defend Your Case

Suppose you live in a city that is going to enact a congestion-charging plan similar to London's. You are on a committee to convince commuters that they and other citizens will benefit from the plan. Use data from the chapter to design a poster or a blog to convey this information.

Review Concepts and Terms

1. Which of the following identifies the layers of the atmosphere in correct order, beginning with the lowest layer?
   a. mesosphere, thermosphere, stratosphere, troposphere
   b. thermosphere, stratosphere, troposphere, mesosphere
   c. troposphere, stratosphere, mesosphere, thermosphere
   d. troposphere, mesosphere, thermosphere, stratosphere

2. A boundary along which a mass of warm, moist air replaces a mass of cool, dry air is called a(n)
   a. air front.   c. cold front.
   b. warm front.   d. convection front.

3. Carbon-containing fuels that formed from the remains of living things are called
   a. fossil fuels.   c. soot.
   b. emissions.   d. smog.

4. Which of the following is the method of heat transfer shown by the arrows in the diagram below?

   a. radiation   c. conduction
   b. convection   d. inversion

5. Which of the following is NOT a primary air pollutant?
   a. particulate matter
   b. lead
   c. carbon monoxide
   d. sulfuric acid

6. Acid deposition is caused mainly by
   a. dust storms.
   b. volcanoes.
   c. burning fossil fuels.
   d. ozone.

7. A scrubber is a device that
   a. prevents temperature inversions.
   b. removes pollutants or changes them chemically before they are released by factories.
   c. reduces the amount of pollutants released by motor vehicles.
   d. removes lead from gasoline.

8. The main chemicals responsible for the ozone hole are
   a. sulfuric acid and nitric acid.
   b. volatile organic compounds.
   c. carbon monoxide and carbon dioxide.
   d. chlorofluorocarbons.

Modified True/False

Write true if the statement is true. If it is false, change the underlined word or words to make the statement true.

9. The force exerted by air on the area below it is called <u>air pressure</u>.

10. The <u>troposphere</u> provides living things with oxygen.

11. <u>Industrial smog</u> is a haze formed when sunlight acts on air pollutants.

12. <u>Lead</u> can bond to hemoglobin and therefore deprive the body of oxygen.

13. As a result of the <u>Montreal Protocol</u>, manufacture of CFCs has fallen dramatically.

Reading Comprehension

Read the following selection and answer the questions that follow.

After World War II, thousands of families moved into Los Angeles and its suburbs. New neighborhoods were springing up, replacing orange groves and open space. Roads and schools were quickly built to keep pace with the rapid population growth. Surrounded by beautiful mountains, the entire Los Angeles basin looked like a new, green, sun-filled paradise to the families moving there.

In the early 1950s, one of the common family chores in Los Angeles was to carry the trash out to the stone incinerator behind the garage, where each family burned its dry trash. "Wet" garbage was collected and taken to the city dump, where it was burned by the city. Everyone throughout the city either used an incinerator or burned things in an open trash pile. There were more than 400,000 back-yard trash incinerators. On warm afternoons, people's eyes would sometimes sting and burn. People would stop, close their eyes, and let the cleansing tears refresh irritated eyes. They accepted this as a normal part of life in suburban Los Angeles.

14. Which of the following would be the BEST title for the selection above?
   a. "The Mountains of Los Angeles"
   b. "Traffic Problems in Los Angeles"
   c. "Burning Trash, Burning Eyes"
   d. "The Lost Orange Groves"

15. Which of the following statements is true about trash in Los Angeles in the early 1950s?
   a. All trash, both wet and dry, was burned.
   b. Only dry trash was burned.
   c. All trash was burned in incinerators.
   d. No trash was burned at the city dump.

16. According to this selection, what made people's eyes burn?
   a. dust storms caused by erosion
   b. pollutants released by burning trash
   c. pollutants released by cars and trucks
   d. warm weather

Short Answer

17. How has the amount of oxygen in Earth's atmosphere changed over time? What has caused this change?

18. In the troposphere, what is the relationship between air temperature and the height above Earth?

19. What is relative humidity?

20. Describe one natural process that causes air pollution.

21. What is the difference between primary air pollutants and secondary air pollutants?

22. How do air pollutants contribute to emphysema, asthma, and other respiratory conditions?

23. Identify two ways in which acid deposition can harm ecosystems.

24. List three provisions of the Clean Air Act.

Critical Thinking

25. **Compare and Contrast** Contrast the effects of stratospheric ozone and tropospheric ozone on people's health.

26. **Relate Cause and Effect** Pollutants generally stay in the stratosphere for a long time. What effect might this characteristic have on the ozone layer?

27. **Infer** Why does it often take a long time for a temperature inversion to end?

28. **Compare and Contrast** Compare industrial smog and photochemical smog. How are these two types of smog similar? How are they different?

29. **Sequence** Describe the sequence of events that led to the Montreal Protocol.

30. **Draw Conclusions** Why is it often difficult for individual states to prevent acid deposition from falling within their boundaries?

31. **Propose a Solution** Suppose a city government wants to start a congestion-charging program similar to London's. However, businesses are fearful of losing money if shoppers are discouraged from going downtown because of the charge. Think of a solution that would keep the congestion-charging program and still encourage shoppers to visit downtown stores.

Analyze Data

The graph shows how several factors related to emission of pollutants changed between 1980 and 2018. Use the data plotted on the graph to answer the questions.

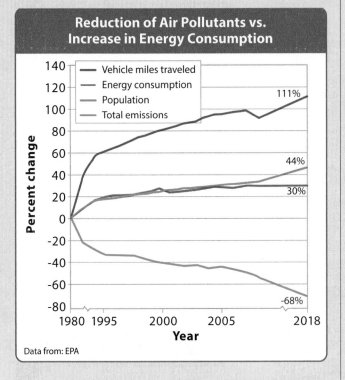

Reduction of Air Pollutants vs. Increase in Energy Consumption

Legend:
- Vehicle miles traveled
- Energy consumption
- Population
- Total emissions

Y-axis: Percent change (−80 to 140)
X-axis: Year (1980, 1995, 2000, 2005, 2018)

Labels: 111%, 44%, 30%, −68%

Data from: EPA

32. Interpret Graphs Between 1980 and 2018, which of the factors plotted on the graph increased?

33. Interpret Graphs During the same period, how did emissions change?

34. Interpret Graphs Which changed more, vehicle miles traveled or energy consumption?

35. Analyze Data On the basis of change in vehicle miles traveled, population, and energy consumption, how would you expect emissions to change during that period? Explain your answer.

36. Draw Conclusions What do you think accounts for the way that the amount of emissions changed?

Write About It

37. Form an Opinion In the area in which you live, is using public transportation a good way to reduce air pollution? Support your answer with information about your area.

38. Creative Writing Sherwood Rowland and Mario Molina won the Nobel Prize for their work in identifying CFCs as the cause of ozone depletion. Suppose you are on the committee overseeing the awards ceremony. Write a speech that you might give explaining why Rowland and Molina are receiving the award.

39. REVISIT INVESTIGATIVE PHENOMENON Draw and label a diagram showing how your school or community might take steps to reduce emissions of pollutants.

Ecological Footprints

According to EPA data, emissions of nitrogen oxides in the United States in 2008 totaled 16.3 million tons. Nitrogen oxides come from many sources, but 9.5 million tons come from motor vehicles. In 2008, the population of the United States was about 304.1 million people. Use this information to calculate the missing values in the table for the year 2008. (*Hint:* 1 ton = 2000 pounds)

1. On the basis of the 2008 data, how many pounds of emissions would be saved per person if driving were reduced by one half?

2. What percentage of the total emissions per person would that be?

3. How might a driver reduce his or her driving by one half?

Source	Population	Total Emissions of Nitrogen Oxides (pounds)	Nitrogen Oxide Emissions From Vehicles (pounds)
You	1		
Your class			
Your state			
United States			

ANCHORING PHENOMENON

These questions will help you apply what you have learned in this Unit to the Anchoring Phenomenon.

1. **Obtain, Evaluate, and Communicate Information**
   According to the International Institute for Sustainable Development, there are 23 key minerals that are needed for the production of sustainable energy technologies such as solar panels, wind turbines, and electric vehicles. Explain why it will be important to manage the extraction of these minerals responsibly. Research information about sustainable mining practices. Write a summary about how these practices depend on the very minerals being mined.

2. **Develop and Use Models** Use examples to explain how air pollution can be a local, national, and international issue. Choose one example, identify solutions enacted to solve the issue, and make a model to show what you would do to improve one of the solutions.

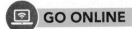

GO ONLINE

For activities that will give you an opportunity to demonstrate what you have learned.

MODELING Revisit your Anchoring Phenomenon Modeling worksheet with the information you have learned in this unit.

ANCHORING PHENOMENON PROJECT Design a solution to improve how a resource is being managed.

Toward a Sustainable Future

GO ONLINE

To engage with real-world phenomenon. Complete the Modeling worksheet and preview the anchoring phenomenon project.

Global Climate Change

Rising sea levels may put homes and lives at risk in the Maldives, an island nation in South Asia.

Lesson 1
Our Dynamic Climate

Lesson 2
Climate Change

Lesson 3
Effects of
Climate Change

Lesson 4
Responding to
Climate Change

Rising Seas May Flood the Maldive Islands

WHEN THE WATER RISES, where will people go? Picture yourself on an island where your family has lived for many generations earning a living by fishing in the surrounding seas. One summer, you notice that the tides are surging higher onto the beach than ever before. At first you think, "No big deal." But as the years pass, the ocean water rises higher and higher. During storms, seawater floods some neighborhoods. Eventually, your whole way of life is threatened. You, your family, and your friends may need to move off the island.

Worldwide the oceans are rising, and one effect of this could be flooding of coastal areas and low-lying islands. Scientists have linked rising sea levels to global warming, which is the increase of the average temperature on Earth's surface. Two factors can account for the rise in sea level. First, warming temperatures make ocean waters expand. In addition, the melting of polar ice and mountain glaciers releases water into the ocean. Both heat expansion and water from melting ice increase the total volume of ocean water. This increase in volume makes sea levels rise.

Higher seas may cause flooding in the Maldives, which are a group of islands in the Indian Ocean. The Maldives are known for their beautiful tropical settings, colorful coral reefs, and sun-drenched beaches. For visiting tourists, the islands seem to be paradise. For the 540,500 people who live there, the islands are home. But residents and tourists alike now fear flooding.

Flooding in the Maldives may cause salt water to contaminate drinking water. But rising sea levels are not the only threat. Warmer water temperatures may make storms worse. If this happens, the storms will erode beaches and cause additional flooding. The storms may also damage the coral reefs that are so vital to the tourism and fishing industries.

Because of possible flooding, the Maldives government has already taken action. Residents have been evacuated from several islands. In 2008, the

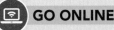

GO ONLINE
• Take It Local • 3-D Geo Tour

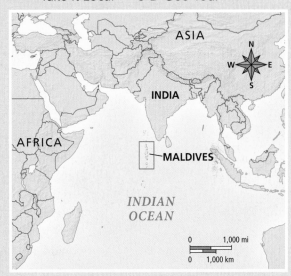

president of the Maldives announced a plan to look for another place for all the people in the Maldives to live in case the islands become uninhabitable. More recently, officials have ramped up tourism and development to raise funds for sea walls, warning systems and other climate change protections.

No one can be certain of what will happen in the future. It is hard to predict the amount of sea-level rise and what the impact will be. Most climate scientists, however, predict that the Maldives will eventually become uninhabitable because of flooding.

Maldives islanders are not the only people who are concerned about rising sea levels. Other island nations, such as the Seychelles, which are off the east coast of Africa, also fear that some day they may need to protect themselves from high waters. Mainland coastal areas of the United States, such as the hurricane-battered coasts of Florida, Louisiana, Texas, and the Carolinas, will face similar challenges.

Islanders and people who live in coastal areas are not the only ones who will be affected by climate change. In one way or another, global climate change will affect all of us for the rest of our lives.

LESSON

1

Our Dynamic Climate

EVERYDAY PHENOMENON Why is the greenhouse effect important for Earth's climate?

Knowledge and Skills

* Describe factors that affect how the sun warms Earth.
* Discuss the role of wind patterns in determining climate.
* Explain how the oceans affect climate.
* Describe how climate is affected by topography, volcanoes, regional vegetation, and periodic changes in Earth's orbit.

Reading Strategy and Vocabulary

✔ **Reading Strategy** Before you read, preview **Figure 1.** Write two questions about the process shown in the illustration. As you read, write answers to the questions.

Vocabulary greenhouse effect, greenhouse gas, thermohaline circulation, El Niño, topography

OF ALL THE ENVIRONMENTAL issues, global climate change may be the one that will have the greatest impact on your future. Recall that while weather refers to the daily changes in temperature, precipitation, air pressure, and so forth, climate is an area's average weather conditions over a long period. To understand why Earth's climate is changing, you first need to know what determines climate. Three factors have more influence on Earth's climate than all others combined—the sun, global wind patterns, and the oceans.

Energy From the Sun

The sun is the source of the energy that determines weather and climate on Earth. Energy from the sun is transferred to Earth by means of radiation. About 30 percent of this incoming radiation is reflected back into space when it strikes land, water, or clouds. This reflected radiation is lost to space and does not contribute to the heating of Earth. The rest of the incoming solar radiation is not reflected. This radiation may be absorbed by Earth and the atmosphere and converted to heat.

The Greenhouse Effect in the Atmosphere If Earth did not have an atmosphere, most of the energy from the sun would be reflected back into space. The **greenhouse effect** is a natural process in which certain gases in the atmosphere keep heat near Earth and prevent it from radiating into space. The gases that do this are called **greenhouse gases.** The major greenhouse gases are water vapor (H_2O) and carbon dioxide (CO_2). Other greenhouse gases include tropospheric ozone (O_3), nitrous oxide (N_2O), and methane (CH_4).

The term *greenhouse effect* is a bit misleading. Greenhouses used for plants hold heat in place by preventing warm air from escaping. In contrast, greenhouse gas molecules in the atmosphere do not trap air or anything else. Instead, they absorb heat and release it slowly.

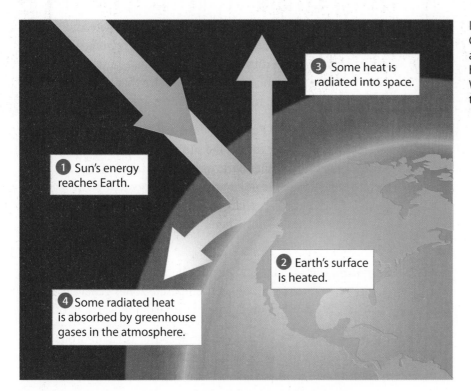

FIGURE 1 Greenhouse Effect
Greenhouse gases, such as water vapor and carbon dioxide, trap some of the heat that radiates from Earth's surface. Without the greenhouse effect, living things could not survive.

1 Sun's energy reaches Earth.

2 Earth's surface is heated.

3 Some heat is radiated into space.

4 Some radiated heat is absorbed by greenhouse gases in the atmosphere.

▶ *Sunlight and Heat* If greenhouse gases keep heat in the atmosphere, why don't they also block solar energy from getting to Earth? The answer lies in what happens to solar energy when it reaches Earth. Greenhouse gases do not stop sunlight from getting through. However, after sunlight hits the surface of Earth, much of its energy is converted to heat. Much of this heat radiates back into the atmosphere. Greenhouse gases absorb some of the heat radiated from Earth's surface. **Figure 1** shows how the greenhouse effect works.

Greenhouse gases prevent some heat from radiating into space as rapidly as it otherwise would. They release the heat slowly, and this slow release of heat warms the troposphere.

▶ *No Life Without Greenhouse Gases* The greenhouse effect is a natural process that is generally beneficial to living things. Greenhouse gases have been present in our atmosphere for billions of years. Without them, life on Earth would be impossible because the surface would be too cold. However, as you will learn, human activities are adding greenhouse gases to the atmosphere and increasing the greenhouse effect.

The Effect of Latitude Latitude has a significant effect on climate. *Latitude* is a measurement of a place's distance from the equator. The equator is located at 0° latitude. The farther you move from the equator, the greater the number of a place's latitude. For example, the latitude of Charlotte, North Carolina, is 35° N. In contrast, Anchorage, Alaska, is located at 61° N latitude, indicating that Anchorage is farther from the equator than Charlotte is. The *N* in the latitude numbers indicates that both Charlotte and Alaska are north of the equator. An *S* would indicate that a place is south of the equator. In general, the farther a place is from the equator, the cooler its climate. Areas close to the equator are generally warm.

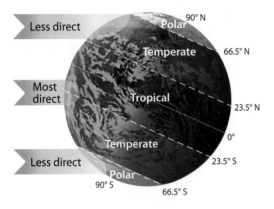

Less direct — Polar — 90° N
— Temperate — 66.5° N
Most direct — Tropical — 23.5° N
— — 0°
Less direct — Temperate — 23.5° S
— Polar — 66.5° S
— 90° S

FIGURE 2 Climate Zones The sun's rays hit different locations on Earth at different angles. As a result, different parts of Earth have different climates.

▶ *Unequal Heating* The relationship between climate and latitude happens because the sun's radiation strikes regions of Earth at different angles. The difference in angles causes unequal heating on Earth. You can see this in **Figure 2.** Notice that there are three general climate regions: tropical, temperate, and polar.

▶ *The Tropics and the Poles* Tropical areas are generally hot. That is because, all year round, the sun's rays hit the equator most directly compared to other parts of Earth. Because of the angle at which the rays strike the polar areas, the energy that polar regions receive is spread out over a larger area than the energy received by regions near the equator. Therefore, polar regions are generally colder than other areas.

▶ *The Temperate Climate Zones* Regions between the poles and the equator are in temperate climate zones. Temperate zones generally have climates that are cool during some parts of the year and warm in others.

▶ *Changing Seasons* The seasons change because, as Earth orbits the sun, the angle at which the sun's rays strike parts of Earth changes. In the Northern Hemisphere in June, the northern end of Earth's axis is tilted toward the sun, and the Northern Hemisphere experiences summer. In December, the northern end of Earth's axis is tilted away from the sun. It is then winter in the Northern Hemisphere.

Quick Lab

Does Latitude Affect the Sun's Rays?

1. Work with a partner. Begin by taping a strip of paper to a globe from the North Pole to slightly below the equator.

2. Divide the paper into three parts. Label the top part *North Pole,* the middle part *mid-latitudes,* and the bottom part *equator.*

3. Tape the end of a toilet-paper roll to the light end of a flashlight and turn the flashlight on. The flashlight represents the sun. Hold the flashlight about 30 cm (12 in.) from the equator. On the paper strip, your partner should draw lines indicating the area the light shines on.

4. Move the flashlight up and aim the beam at the mid-latitudes. Keep the flashlight horizontal. Have your partner mark the lighted area.

5. Repeat Step 4, but shine the light on the North Pole area of the strip.

Analyze and Conclude

1. **Observe** What shape was the lighted area when you pointed the flashlight at the equator?

2. **Compare and Contrast** How did the size and shape of the lighted area change when you moved the flashlight beam to the mid-latitudes and the North Pole?

3. **Relate Cause and Effect** Why did the shape of the lighted area change as you moved the flashlight?

4. **Use Models** How does this activity show why areas near the equator are warmer than areas at the poles?

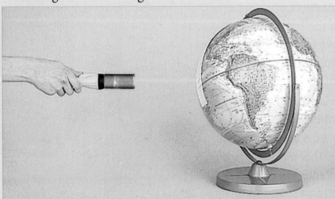

Sunspot Cycles The sun varies slightly in the amount of radiation it emits, over both short and long periods. There is, for example, a relationship between sunspots and radiation emitted. A sunspot is a dark spot on the surface of the sun. The more sunspots present on the surface of the sun, the more energy the sun gives off. The number of sunspots rises and falls in cycles that last about 11 years. Although sunspot cycles have some effect on global climate, scientists think that they do not have a major, long-term effect.

 What accounts for the change in seasons in temperate zones?

Wind Patterns in the Atmosphere

Recall that if air becomes warm, it usually rises. In contrast, if air becomes cool, it sinks. Rising warm air and sinking cool air form convection currents. Convection currents that result from unequal heating produce air currents, or winds. Winds transport both heat and moisture, affecting both temperature and precipitation in the regions they pass over.

Winds and Heat Because the regions near the equator are warm, air rises above them. In contrast, the North and South poles are cold, and air moves downward, toward Earth's surface. The rising of air in equatorial regions and the sinking of air in polar regions help create global wind patterns, called prevailing winds, shown in **Figure 3.** The prevailing winds move huge air masses around the surface of Earth. Warm air moves away from the equator and toward the poles, and cold air moves in the opposite direction.

Winds and Moisture Moisture in the atmosphere occurs in the form of water vapor, which is water in the form of a gas. In the water cycle, water vapor enters the atmosphere through evaporation from Earth's surface from lakes, oceans, and soil. Plants also release water vapor into the atmosphere. In general, warm air can carry more water vapor than cooler air can. When warm, moist air is cooled, the water vapor condenses to form clouds. Rain, snow, or other forms of precipitation may then fall from the clouds.

Winds move moisture from one location to another. For example, when winds move over a large body of water, such as a lake or ocean, they pick up water vapor. The winds may then carry the water vapor a long distance over land, where it falls as precipitation.

FIGURE 3 Prevailing Winds Global wind currents show patterns related to latitude. Trade winds between the equator and 30° latitude blow westward, whereas westerlies between 30° and 60° latitude blow eastward. Because of Earth's rotation, in general winds blow from east to west near the equator and from west to east over temperate zones.

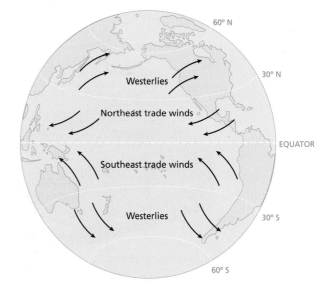

The Oceans and Climate

Like winds, ocean currents transport heat over long distances. In addition, ocean water absorbs carbon dioxide, and this has a cooling effect.

Ocean Circulation   Ocean water exchanges huge amounts of heat with the atmosphere, and ocean currents move heat energy from place to place. A worldwide system of ocean currents is caused by a combination of unequal heating of water and unequal salinity (salt concentration).

▶ *Thermohaline Circulation*   Cool water generally has a greater density than warm water. Saltier water is denser than water with a lower salinity. Therefore, warmer, less salty water moves along the surface of the ocean, and colder, saltier water moves deep beneath the ocean's surface. This pattern is called the **thermohaline circulation.** As part of this pattern, cooler, saltier water at the poles sinks, and warmer, less salty water from the equator moves to take the place of the cooler water. In the Gulf Stream in the Atlantic Ocean, warm surface water flows northward from the equator. The warm water keeps Europe warmer than it would otherwise be.

▶ *El Niño and La Niña*   The interactions between ocean and atmosphere called El Niño and La Niña affect climate. **El Niño** is a change in air pressure, wind patterns, ocean temperature, and ocean circulation in the Pacific Ocean. Normally, prevailing winds blow from east to west along the equator. The winds help move warm surface waters westward. During El Niño, however, equatorial winds weaken, and the surface water in the eastern Pacific Ocean becomes warmer than usual. **Figure 4** diagrams this pattern. El Niño has a major effect on weather worldwide. For example, it causes rainstorms and floods in areas that are usually dry, such as southern California. The pattern known as La Niña is the opposite of El Niño. During La Niña, temperatures in the eastern Pacific Ocean are colder than average. Like El Niño, La Niña disrupts weather worldwide.

FIGURE 4 El Niño (a) Normally, winds push warm waters toward the western Pacific. **(b)** In contrast, under El Niño conditions, the winds weaken and the warm water flows back across the Pacific toward South America. El Niño changes precipitation patterns all over the world.

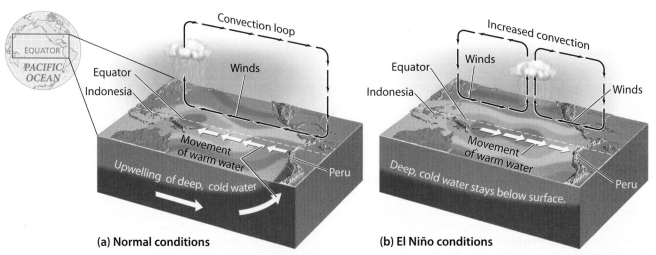

(a) Normal conditions (b) El Niño conditions

Adapted from National Oceanic and Atmospheric Administration, Tropical Atmospheric Ocean Project.

Ocean Absorption of Carbon Dioxide Carbon dioxide moves back and forth between the atmosphere and ocean water. Oceans can hold 50 times more carbon dioxide than is found in the atmosphere. Since carbon dioxide is a greenhouse gas, the absorption of carbon dioxide by the ocean has a cooling effect on the atmosphere. However, the oceans absorb carbon dioxide more slowly than it is being added to the atmosphere. Therefore, carbon absorption by the oceans is slowing global warming but not preventing it.

Other Factors That Affect Climate

Other factors besides the sun, the atmosphere, and the oceans affect climate. Four of these factors are topography, volcanoes, regional distribution of vegetation, and changes in Earth's path around the sun.

Topography A region's topography describes the surface characteristics of the area, including its elevation and features such as mountains, rivers, and lakes. The characteristics of a region's topography affect its climate. Two of these are altitude and the presence of mountain ranges.

▶ *Altitude* Mount Cayambe in South America is located right on the equator. However, its peak is always covered with snow, as are the tops of many high mountains near the equator. In general, the greater the altitude, or elevation, the cooler the air temperature will be. That is why the kinds of plants at the bottom of mountains are usually not the same varieties as those found higher up.

▶ *Mountain Ranges* As winds pass over mountains, the rising air cools and clouds often form. Then, precipitation may fall from those clouds. By the time the air has moved to the other side of the mountains, however, it has usually lost much of its moisture. In general, precipitation falls on the *windward* side of mountain ranges, which is the side that wind first passes over. The *leeward* side of a mountain range, or the downwind side, gets relatively little precipitation.

✓ **Reading Checkpoint** *What is topography?*

FIGURE 5 Snow-Covered Mountain
Even though Mount Cayambe is on the equator, its peak is always covered with snow.

FIGURE 6 Volcanoes and Climate
A volcano erupts in New Guinea. Volcanoes spew out materials that may prevent some sunlight from entering Earth's atmosphere.

Volcanoes An erupting volcano may expel huge amounts of gases and particles, as **Figure 6** shows. Winds can carry these materials to areas that are a long way from the volcano. If the eruption is large enough, the gases and particles may block some sunlight from entering Earth's atmosphere. This blocking of sunlight may, in turn, cool the atmosphere. The cooling is temporary, however, because the volcanic materials remain in the atmosphere for a limited time.

Regional Vegetation Plant life, or vegetation, can influence climate when it covers a large area. For example, the abundant vegetation of the Amazon rain forest promotes cloud formation and rainfall. In addition, plants affect the amount of carbon dioxide in the atmosphere because they use carbon dioxide in the process of photosynthesis. Huge forests take in an especially large amount of carbon dioxide. This intake decreases the amount of carbon dioxide in the atmosphere. However, when large sections of forests are cut down, the loss of trees means that the carbon dioxide they would have used remains in the atmosphere. Therefore, the destruction of forests in one area can increase the temperature of the atmosphere worldwide.

Changes in Earth's Orbit Evidence indicates that during Earth's history climate has changed many times. For example, in the last three million years, Earth has gone through a series of ice ages. During these ice ages, huge glaciers covered large parts of the Northern Hemisphere. Many large mammals that are now extinct, such as woolly mammoths, survived in the frigid climate.

One cause of these climate changes is the periodic variation in Earth's movement and position in space in relation to the sun. Minor changes in Earth's orbit, and in the tilt of Earth's axis, occur in regular cycles. These cyclic changes affect the distribution of solar radiation over Earth's surface. This change in the distribution of sunlight can affect climate. Climate changes caused by these variations may last for thousands of years.

LESSON ① Assessment

1. **Relate Cause and Effect** Why does a region's latitude affect its climate? In your answer, mention the equator, the poles, and the regions in between the equator and the poles.

2. **Compare and Contrast** How is the behavior of warm air different from that of cold air? Relate this difference to global wind patterns.

3. **Explain** What happens during El Niño?

4. **Apply Concepts** What is the relationship between altitude and climate? How does this account for the differences in ecosystems at the base of a mountain and at its peak?

   REVISIT
5. **INVESTIGATIVE** PHENOMENON
   Imagine that you have taken a trip, via spaceship, to a planet that has very little atmosphere, and therefore very little greenhouse effect. Describe what the planet's climate might be like, and how it would probably be different from Earth's climate.

Climate Change

EVERYDAY PHENOMENON How can we determine what the atmospheric greenhouse gas levels were in the distant past?

Knowledge and Skills

- Identify evidence of global warming.
- Explain three methods used to study climate change.
- State the probable cause of global climate change.

Reading Strategy and Vocabulary

✓ **Reading Strategy** Construct a concept map that summarizes the evidence that Earth is becoming warmer. Use the green headings in the lesson as the main subtopics in your map.

Vocabulary global climate change, global warming, proxy indicator, climate model, fossil fuel

IN RECENT YEARS, it seems that almost everybody is noticing evidence of climate change. A person who fishes in the Maldives observes the seas rising higher on the islands' beaches. A rancher in west Texas suffers a dry spell that lasts many years. A homeowner in Florida cannot obtain insurance against the hurricanes that are becoming more frequent. And, in addition to stories such as these, solid scientific evidence confirms that Earth's climate is changing.

Evidence of a Warming Earth

When scientists talk about **global climate change,** they are referring to many climate characteristics, such as temperature, rainfall, wind patterns, and storm frequency. The term **global warming** refers specifically to an increase in Earth's average surface temperature. Global warming is only one aspect of climate change.

In 1988, the United Nations and the World Meteorological Association established the Intergovernmental Panel on Climate Change (IPCC). The IPCC is made up of scientists and government officials from around the world. The group has published several reports, the most recent update in 2019. Hundreds of scientists contributed to the report, and the report was reviewed by 2000 experts. The IPCC has concluded that global warming is indeed occurring, and that human activities have contributed. These conclusions are now widely accepted. Evidence of climate change includes Earth's surface temperatures, precipitation patterns, melting ice, and rising sea levels.

Rising Temperatures The IPCC notes that human activities have caused global temperatures to increase about 1°C (1.8°F) and could be 1.5°C (2.7°F) by 2030 if warming continues at its current rate.

(a)

(b)

FIGURE 7 **A Disappearing Glacier** Both photos show Sperry Glacier in Montana's Glacier National Park. Contrast the sizes of the glacier **(a)** in 1913 and **(b)** in 2008.

Changes in Precipitation Changes in precipitation over the past 100 years have been complex. Some regions of the world, such as the eastern parts of North and South America, are receiving more precipitation than ever before. Other areas, such as the southwestern United States and parts of Africa, are receiving less precipitation than in the past. Meanwhile, heavy rainstorms have increased in both dry and moist regions. These severe storms have caused flooding.

Melting Ice Glaciers are large, slowly moving sheets of ice, and many have taken thousands of years to form. If you go to Glacier National Park in Montana, you can find 26 glaciers. In 1850, there were 150 glaciers in the same area. What happened between 1850 and the present? Much of the glaciers' ice has melted away **(Figure 7).** Throughout the world, most glaciers are shrinking or even disappearing.

Warming temperatures are also reducing the snow and ice that cover the North and South poles. For example, along the coast of Antarctica, edges of glaciers called ice shelves extend into the ocean, where they float. One of these is the Larsen Ice Shelf. Since 1986, this ice shelf has lost an area more than three times the size of Rhode Island. Portions of the ice shelf have broken away and melted.

Rising Sea Levels Sea levels are rising in many parts of the world. Residents of the Maldives and other low-lying areas are anxiously watching this trend. The reasons for the rising seas are complex, but the primary cause according to the IPCC is global warming. When seawater becomes warmer, its volume increases, making sea levels rise. To understand this process, think of the liquid in a thermometer. As temperature increases, the liquid expands and its level goes up. Water from melting ice also contributes to rising sea levels. If ice sheets in the Antarctic and Greenland continue to melt, the liquid water released will soon become the most important part of global sea-level rise.

Studying Climate Change

To understand something that is changing, we need to consider its past and present. Then we can use this information to predict what may happen in the future. Scientists who study climate change can check present-day climate directly. But they have also developed clever ways to infer past climates and to predict future change.

Direct Measurement of Present Conditions To study Earth's climate today, scientists measure conditions directly. You know this if you've ever watched a TV weather report. Every day, weather reports give data about temperature, precipitation, wind patterns, and so forth. Over time, records of data such as air temperature and ocean temperature show that modern climate is changing.

Proxy Indicators: Clues About Past Climates To understand how climate is changing today, scientists must learn what climates were like thousands or millions of years ago. Environmental scientists use clues from the past to do this. **Proxy indicators** are types of indirect evidence that serve as proxies, or substitutes, for direct measurement. Proxy indicators shed light on past climate.

 Reading Checkpoint *What are three kinds of climate data that scientists can measure directly?*

 **GO ONLINE**
- **Graph It** Atmospheric CO_2 and Temperature Change

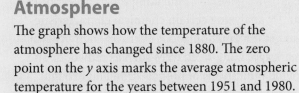

Changing Temperature of the Atmosphere

The graph shows how the temperature of the atmosphere has changed since 1880. The zero point on the *y* axis marks the average atmospheric temperature for the years between 1951 and 1980.

1. **Interpret Graphs** What is the overall trend shown on this graph?

2. **Calculate** Approximately how much has the average air temperature changed since 1880?

3. **Interpret Graphs** Describe the temperature pattern between 1880 and 1930.

4. **Compare and Contrast** Contrast the temperature pattern after 1930 to the pattern before that year.

5. **Predict** How would the trend shown on the graph affect the Maldives?

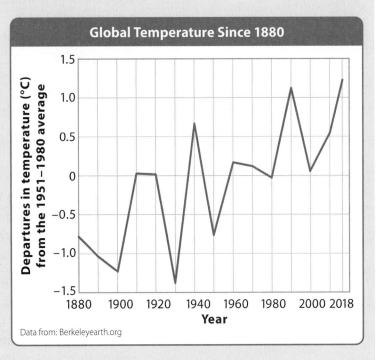

Global Temperature Since 1880

Data from: Berkeleyearth.org

FIGURE 8 Tree Rings as Proxy Indicators Scientists can infer some characteristics of past climates by examining tree rings.

▶ *Clues in Ice* Earth's ice sheets and glaciers hold clues to climate history. As glaciers and ice sheets form, tiny bubbles of air become trapped inside. Scientists use special tools to remove long columns, or cores, of ice. From these ice cores, scientists can determine such things as greenhouse gas concentrations in the ancient atmosphere and temperature trends. Even trapped soot particles have a tale to tell. The soot indicates how often forest fires happened. Frequent forest fires can indicate a time of drought.

▶ *Clues in Sediments* Sediment consists of particles of rock and soil that have been deposited by wind, water, or ice. Researchers take samples from beds of sediment beneath bodies of water. Ancient sediments often preserve pollen grains and other parts of plants that grew in the past. Climate influences the types of plants that grow in an area. Therefore, if scientists know what plants grew in a location at a given time, they can often infer much about the climate at that place and time.

 Reading Checkpoint *How can sediments give information about past climates?*

▶ *Clues in Tree Rings* The scientist in **Figure 8** is examining rings in an old tree. Tree rings in old trees can be a proxy indicator. A pair of light and dark rings represents one year's growth. The width of each ring of a tree trunk reveals how much the tree grew in a particular growing season. A wide ring means more growth, generally indicating a wetter year or in some areas a warmer year. By analyzing certain chemical characteristics of tree rings, scientists can get information about hurricane activity that happened hundreds of years ago. Long-lived trees such as redwoods and bristlecone pines can provide indications of precipitation and drought going back hundreds or thousands of years. And like ice cores, tree rings can show past forest fires. A charred tree ring indicates that a fire took place during that year.

Models: Predicting the Future
Environmental scientists try to understand how climate functions. They then use this understanding to predict future climate change. To do both these tasks, scientists represent climate processes with computer programs known as climate models.

▶ *Climate Models* Programs that combine what is known about the atmosphere and oceans to simulate, or imitate, climate processes are called **climate models.** Climate models use enormous amounts of data and complex mathematical equations. **Figure 9** shows the kinds of information that go into climate models.

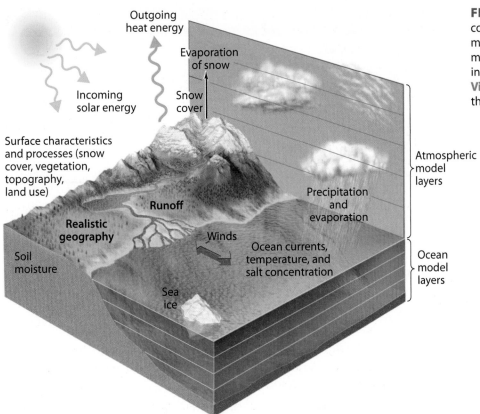

FIGURE 9 Climate Model The computer programs for climate models include information about many factors, such as those shown in the illustration. **Interpret Visuals** In the diagram, where is the runoff coming from?

Labels in the figure: Outgoing heat energy · Incoming solar energy · Evaporation of snow · Snow cover · Surface characteristics and processes (snow cover, vegetation, topography, land use) · Runoff · Precipitation and evaporation · Realistic geography · Winds · Atmospheric model layers · Soil moisture · Ocean currents, temperature, and salt concentration · Sea ice · Ocean model layers

▶ *Testing Models' Accuracy* Researchers use past climate data to test climate models. They compare the results of the climate model with what actually happened in the past. If a model accurately represents past climate, then it may accurately predict future climate. These comparisons show that global climate models can usually produce reliable predictions.

Finding the Cause of Climate Change

In 1958, a scientist named Charles Keeling started to measure carbon dioxide in the atmosphere. Keeling collected air samples every hour at the Mauna Loa Observatory in Hawaii and measured the carbon dioxide in the samples. Since then, scientists have continued to measure levels of carbon dioxide every day at Mauna Loa, around the clock.

The data collected at Mauna Loa show that in 1958, the concentration of carbon dioxide was 315 parts per million (ppm). In contrast, the monthly average concentration was 414 ppm in May 2019. The carefully recorded data of Keeling and his associates show that carbon dioxide concentration in the atmosphere is increasing. According to the IPCC, the rising levels of carbon dioxide and other greenhouse gases are reponsible for most of the increase in atmospheric temperature. The high levels of greenhouse gases are increasing the greenhouse effect.

FIGURE 10 Greenhouse Gases The graph shows how the concentration of different greenhouse gases has changed over time.

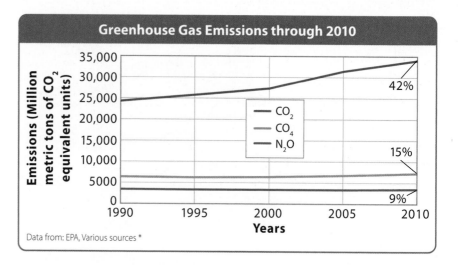

Greenhouse Gas Emissions through 2010

Data from: EPA, Various sources *

Increase in Greenhouse Gases **Figure 10** shows the trends of three different greenhouse gases. Most other greenhouse gases cause more warming than carbon dioxide, molecule for molecule. However, because carbon dioxide is so abundant, it is the greenhouse gas that is most responsible for global warming. Most scientists agree that the extra carbon dioxide in the atmosphere has come from human activities, such as the use of motor vehicles.

Burning Fossil Fuels The main source of extra carbon dioxide in the atmosphere is the burning of carbon-containing fuels, such as oil, natural gas, and coal, for energy. These fuels are called **fossil fuels** because they formed millions of years ago, from the remains of living things.

Use of fossil fuels has been increasing ever since the beginning of the Industrial Revolution about 200 years ago. The Industrial Revolution started a shift from farming to industry as a way of producing the goods that people use. Industry uses machinery, and machinery runs on fossil fuels. During the last two hundred years, people have used an increasing amount of fossil fuels in homes, cars, and industries. As the fossil fuels release carbon dioxide, the greenhouse effect increases and the temperature of the atmosphere continues to rise.

Changes in Use of Land Land-use changes, such as the cutting of forests, have also caused an increase in greenhouse gases. Remember that plants, including trees, take in carbon dioxide. Therefore, the loss of forests contributes to an increase of carbon dioxide in the atmosphere.

LESSON ② Assessment

1. **Use Analogies** What is the main cause of the rise in sea level? How is this similar to the behavior of the liquid in a thermometer?

2. **Apply Concepts** What are climate models? What information do they use to predict what might happen to climate in the future?

3. **Relate Cause and Effect** How has deforestation contributed to climate change?

4. **THINK IT** *THROUGH* Industrialization is the process in which a society develops industry and uses machinery on a large scale. Why has industrialization been a cause of global climate change?

Effects of Climate Change

EVERYDAY PHENOMENON How is climate change affecting food availability for both marine and terrestrial organisms?

Knowledge and Skills

- State ways in which the warming atmosphere affects ecosystems and organisms.
- Explain how climate change is affecting people now.
- Predict future effects of climate change on people.

Reading Strategy and Vocabulary

✓ **Reading Strategy** Make a two-column table. In the left column, write the blue and green lesson headings. In the right column, make notes that summarize the information under those headings.

Vocabulary coral bleaching

DO YOU THINK that global warming is something that may happen in the future? Climate change is affecting the world right now. Ecosystems are changing, and individual organisms are experiencing the effect of those changes. Climate change has also affected people, including how people make their living and even some people's health.

Effects on Ecosystems and Organisms

Think of the ways in which temperature and climate are important to ecosystems and individual organisms. For example, temperature and rainfall both affect animals' food supplies. When the climate changes, the lives of organisms usually change too. The following examples demonstrate this.

Shifting Habitats As ecosystems on land become warmer, the locations in which some organisms live are changing. The habitats of some plants and animals have shifted to places where the climate is cooler—toward the North and South poles or higher up on mountains. For example, in the Santa Rosa Mountains in California, the location of some plant species, such as the Jeffrey pine tree and California lilac, has shifted upward an average of about 65 meters (215 feet) **(Figure 11)**.

FIGURE 11 Changing Range In some places, California lilacs *(Ceanothus)* are growing higher on mountainsides than they once did.

FIND OUT MORE

Are migrating birds in your area arriving earlier in the spring than they did formerly? Contact a state or local chapter of the National Audubon Society or other wildlife organization to find out. Ask for information on how to observe and identify birds.

Changing Migration Times Many species of birds migrate every year in the fall and spring. In the fall, they travel to places where the weather will be warmer and food will be more plentiful. Then in the spring, they fly back to their summer habitat. Some birds are now starting their spring migration earlier than before. Scientists infer that this change in migration is happening because the birds' winter habitat becomes warmer earlier than before. This change in temperature probably sends a signal to the birds to start their migration earlier.

A change in migration time can cause problems for some birds. For example, in the spring, robins arrive on a mountaintop in Colorado about two weeks earlier than they did in the 1970s. However, climate change has caused increased snowfall on the mountain. So when the robins get there, snow still covers the ground. The robins cannot feed until the snow melts.

Problems Obtaining Food Migrating birds are not the only animals whose food supply is threatened by global warming. During the last few decades, temperature changes have been greatest in the Arctic. Ice sheets are melting and sea ice is thinning. Ice-free areas are increasing in the Arctic seas. As sea ice melts earlier and freezes later, it has become more difficult for polar bears to hunt the seals they feed on. Some polar bears have been dying of exhaustion and starvation as they try to swim long distances between ice sheets. Because the number of polar bears is declining, in 2008 the polar bear was listed as a threatened species under the Endangered Species Act. As of April 2020, their status has not changed.

Effects of a Changing Ocean The ocean is becoming warmer. In addition, its chemistry is changing because it is absorbing more and more carbon dioxide. Both these processes have begun to affect organisms in the sea, such as corals. Corals are tiny animals that use chemicals dissolved in water to build hard, stony coverings around themselves. When the animals die, the hard coverings remain. Over time, the stony coverings of millions of corals form the massive ocean structures called coral reefs.

 How is the increase in atmospheric temperature affecting the migration of some bird species?

FIGURE 12 Trouble Finding Food
As polar bears hunt, they swim from one ice sheet to another. The space between ice sheets is increasing, and the polar bears must swim longer distances than before.

Coral reefs provide rich and varied habitats for many marine animals, such as sponges, worms, crabs, and fishes. Many fishes eaten by people, such as flounder, are part of coral-reef food chains. Coral reefs protect beaches against waves and support the tourist industry. Today, coral reefs are dying worldwide, and this loss will affect both ocean biodiversity and the lives of people. There are many causes of coral-reef destruction. Global climate change is one probable cause.

▶ *Warmer Water Temperature* Reef-building corals contain microorganisms called algae within their tissues. During photosynthesis, the algae produce nutrients that supply energy, and the corals use some of the nutrients. Without these algae, corals cannot survive. However, in many places, the algae in corals are dying—a process called **coral bleaching,** because without the algae, the corals lose their bright colors. Scientists do not fully understand why coral bleaching is happening, but evidence indicates that the problem is often related to unusually warm water temperatures.

▶ *Ocean Acidity* Seawater absorbs much carbon dioxide from the atmosphere. As atmospheric carbon dioxide has increased, the amount of carbon dioxide dissolved in the ocean has increased, too. When carbon dioxide dissolves in water, it forms carbonic acid, whose formula is H_2CO_3. The equation for this reaction is shown below.

$$H_2O + CO_2 \rightarrow H_2CO_3$$

Over time, the addition of carbonic acid to ocean water has made the water slightly more acidic. Recall that the acidity of a solution is expressed as its pH. The higher the acidity, the lower the pH. The pH of ocean water is slowly going down, and it will probably continue to do so as long as the ocean keeps absorbing more carbon dioxide. The increased acidity of ocean water may already be harming organisms that live in the ocean, including corals. Ocean acidity limits the ability of corals and other shell-building organisms to build their hard, protective coverings.

The Future of Ecosystems The future effects of climate change on ecosystems will be complex and are hard to predict. For example, an increase in atmospheric carbon dioxide may increase vegetation, since plants use carbon dioxide in photosynthesis. However, if drought and forest fires increase, plant life will be harmed and plants may decrease in number.

Changes will probably continue in the migration patterns of some animals and in the ranges in which specific species can survive. Because they cannot survive in the changed environment, some species may become extinct. Extinction of species will decrease biodiversity.

(a)

(b)

FIGURE 13 Coral Bleaching (a) The color of healthy brain coral comes from algae. **(b)** When the algae die, coral bleaching occurs.

Impact on People Right Now

Extreme weather events, such as severe droughts and heat waves, are becoming more severe in some areas, and this increase may be linked to climate change. People are feeling the impact of bad weather and other problems associated with climate change. These effects will continue into the future.

Agriculture and Forestry The effects of climate change on agriculture have been complex. Some crops, such as melons and sweet potatoes, do well in heat and have probably benefited from longer growing seasons. Other crops, such as spinach and broccoli, are more suited to cooler conditions. In many areas, droughts have reduced crop yields. The forestry industry has also been damaged by extensive forest fires that result in part from longer, warmer, drier fire seasons. Also, forest managers are increasingly battling insect and disease outbreaks.

Economic Effects When yields from agriculture and forestry decrease, people who work in those industries have a hard time earning a living. Huge storms, such as Hurricane Dorian in 2019, cause enormous damage, and this damage has economic consequences, too. Businesses that cater to tourists, such as shops and restaurants, had to shut down because of Dorian and therefore lost money they might have earned. Homeowners, taxpayers, and utility customers had to pay to have damaged homes, highways, and power lines repaired.

The financial consequence of storms is indicated by the amount of money that insurance companies pay to people and companies that have insured their property against weather-related damage. The map in **Figure 14** shows that weather-related events costs billions of dollars across the U.S every year. Between 2015 and 2019 there was an average of 13.8 natural disaster events per year that cost more than a billion dollars in damages.

FIGURE 14 Weather-Related Costs In the map below, the numbers on each state represent the number of weather disasters the state experienced in 2019 that each cost over a billion dollars in relief. Some states, such as Texas, experienced multiple disasters (8). Others, such as California, shown in orange, experienced only one. States like Washington and Oregon, shown in light green, experienced no billion-dollar disasters. The types of weather disasters included wildfires, hurricanes, tropical storms, tornadoes, and floods.

Health Effects As atmospheric temperatures have risen, the probability of severe heat waves has increased. Extreme heat can cause illnesses such as heat exhaustion and heat stroke. Heat stroke is a condition in which the body cannot control its temperature, and body temperature rapidly rises. Heat stroke can cause death if it is not treated quickly. The heat wave season in the U.S. has grown by nearly 50 days since the 1960s, and more than 9000 Americans have died due to heat related causes in that time. Almost 1500 people died in France during a heat wave in 2019 alone.

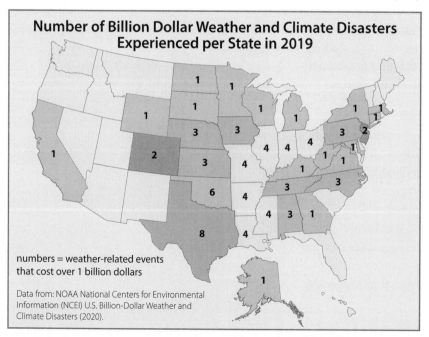

Number of Billion Dollar Weather and Climate Disasters Experienced per State in 2019

numbers = weather-related events that cost over 1 billion dollars

Data from: NOAA National Centers for Environmental Information (NCEI) U.S. Billion-Dollar Weather and Climate Disasters (2020).

Future Impact on People

Computer modeling has enabled scientists to make predictions about climate change. The IPCC report indicates that carbon dioxide in the atmosphere will continue to rise, and so will the temperatures of the atmosphere and ocean. These trends will affect the way people live.

Diseases The ranges of animals that transmit diseases may expand as parts of the world become warmer. Lyme disease, for example, is transmitted to humans by tick bites. In Canada, Lyme disease was once confined to the southern part of the country. The ticks that carry Lyme disease are now able to survive in more northern parts of Canada as milder winters have become more common.

Sea Level As the oceans become warmer and polar ice keeps melting, sea level will continue to rise. People in the Maldives and other coastal areas worldwide are concerned about what will happen eventually. In the United States, 40 percent of the population lives in coastal areas. Many people may need to find new places to live.

Water Supply Rising sea levels increase the possibility that salt water from the ocean will intrude into freshwater aquifers and contaminate people's freshwater supplies. The disappearance of glaciers also threatens water supplies. When glaciers release meltwater slowly, year after year, the meltwater feeds rivers and reservoirs. Therefore, glaciers now indirectly supply many people with water. If glaciers melt too quickly and eventually disappear, this water supply will no longer exist. In addition, dams on many rivers and reservoirs generate electricity. If the amount of water in those rivers and reservoirs decreases significantly, people would need to obtain electricity some other way.

FIGURE 15 Effect on a Lake A dam on Diablo Lake generates electricity for Seattle, Washington. The lake is fed by many glaciers. If the glaciers melt entirely, the lake may disappear, threatening Seattle's supply of electricity.

LESSON 3 Assessment

1. **Relate Cause and Effect** Explain two ways in which global climate change is threatening corals.
2. **Apply Concepts** What are two ways in which climate change is affecting the way in which people earn their living?
3. **Predict** What might happen to coastal tourist industries if sea levels continue to rise?

REVISIT

4. **INVESTIGATIVE** PHENOMENON
Every year, melting water from glaciers helps fill some reservoirs that people use for water. If melting water is the source of the reservoirs' water, why is the glacial melting caused by climate change a threat to water supplies?

Responding to Climate Change

EVERYDAY PHENOMENON What can we personally do to respond to climate change?

Knowledge and Skills

- List ways to reduce greenhouse gases related to the use and generation of electricity.
- Describe some of the ways of reducing greenhouse gases related to transportation.
- Describe other strategies for reducing greenhouse gases.
- Explain how nations are working together to try to address climate change.

Reading Strategy and Vocabulary

✔ **Reading Strategy** How can you save electricity in your home? Write down what you know. Then, as you read the lesson, write additional ways that you and your family can conserve electricity.

Vocabulary carbon footprint, carbon tax, carbon offset, carbon sequestration, Kyoto Protocol

TODAY MOST PEOPLE AGREE that climate change is occurring, and that we need to do something about it. How do we meet this challenge? There are specific things that people and nations can do to address global warming.

Use and Production of Electricity

We can respond to climate change in two basic ways—adaptation and mitigation. One approach, adaptation, involves protecting people from the effects of global warming. For example, residents of the Maldives have built a sea wall around the nation's capital to protect roads and buildings from storms.

FIGURE 16 An Adaptation Strategy
A sea wall is being constructed to protect seaside property from rising sea levels in Sydney, Australia.

Mitigation consists of reducing greenhouse gas emissions. By doing this, we will lessen the severity of future climate change. Mitigation includes strategies such as improving energy efficiency and preventing deforestation. We need to pursue both adaptation and mitigation. However, in the long term, mitigation is more important because it addresses the causes of global warming. Each of us should be trying to reduce our carbon footprints. A **carbon footprint** is the amount of carbon dioxide emissions for which an individual or group is responsible.

A major mitigation strategy addresses how we use and produce electricity. Electricity generation is the largest source of U.S. greenhouse gases. Fossil fuel combustion generates about 70 percent of the electricity in the United States. There are ways to reduce the amount of greenhouse gases released during the generation of electricity. First, we need to encourage energy efficiency and conservation. In addition, we need to switch to energy sources that are cleaner and renewable.

Efficiency and Conservation Efficiency consists of using energy effectively—that is, accomplishing a job using as little energy as possible. Conservation consists of reducing energy use.

▶ *Efficiency* New technologies, such as high-efficiency light bulbs and appliances, provide more effective ways to use electricity. The U.S. Environmental Protection Agency (EPA) offers technological solutions through its Energy Star Program. This program rates household appliances, lights, windows, fans, office equipment, and heating and cooling systems by their energy efficiency. For instance, ratings indicate that by replacing standard light bulbs with light emitting diodes (LEDs), you can reduce energy use for lighting by up to 80%. In addition, certain kinds of appliances, such as air conditioners and refrigerators, must have an EnergyGuide label similar to the one shown in **Figure 17.** EnergyGuide labels give consumers information about the energy efficiency of these appliances.

▶ *Conservation* In addition, individual people can make lifestyle choices that reduce the use of electrical appliances and other devices. Here are just a few things that you and other people can do:
- Turn off lights, computers, and televisions when not in use.
- Wash only full loads in dishwashers and clothes washers.
- Unplug appliances that you seldom use, such as food processors.
- Unplug cell-phone chargers once the phone is charged.
- Don't keep the refrigerator door open. Remove food quickly.
- Use a microwave oven, rather than a conventional oven, to heat food.

✓ **Reading Checkpoint** *What is the largest source of U.S. greenhouse gases?*

Alternate Sources of Electricity Energy sources that produce electricity without using fossil fuels are another way to reduce greenhouse gases. For example, nuclear power comes from reactions that take place within atoms. Solar power uses energy from the sun. Wind power depends on wind to make electricity, and hydroelectric power uses the movement of water. Geothermal power makes use of heat trapped underground. These energy sources do not give off greenhouse gases.

FIGURE 17 EnergyGuide An EnergyGuide label gives consumers an estimate of how much it costs to run an appliance for a year. If the label has the Energy Star logo, the appliance uses less energy than typical models of the appliance.

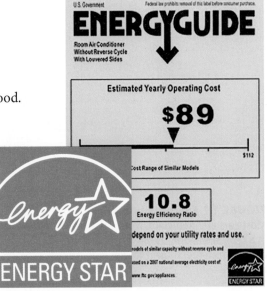

Transportation

Between 1990 and 2017, transportation was the biggest source of greenhouse gas emissions in the U.S. Unfortunately, the typical automobile is not very efficient. More than 70 percent of the fuel does something other than move the car down the road, as shown in **Figure 18.** Automobiles powered by gasoline may always remain somewhat inefficient. However, there are steps we can take to reduce the release of greenhouse gases produced by transportation.

Vehicle Technology The technology exists to make cars and trucks more fuel-efficient than they are now. Vehicles in the United States are generally not as fuel-efficient as they are in many other nations. It will probably take both government regulation and consumer demand to improve fuel efficiency in the United States. As gasoline prices rise, people will demand more fuel-efficient cars.

There are now alternatives to cars that burn only gasoline. For example, hybrid vehicles combine electric motors and gasoline-powered engines. Researchers are investigating alternative fuels such as compressed natural gas. In addition, scientists are working on developing motor vehicles with hydrogen fuel cells that use oxygen and hydrogen. These fuel cells produce only water as a waste product.

Driving Less and Using Public Transportation People can reduce their dependence on cars. For example, some people are choosing to live closer to their workplaces or to work from home. In addition, students can bike or walk to school or to complete their everyday activities.

Still other people use mass transportation, such as buses and subways. According to one study, increasing our use of public transportation may be the most effective strategy for saving energy and reducing pollution. Public transportation in the United States already reduces gasoline use. If people use public transportation more, the United States could significantly reduce its contribution to climate change. Unfortunately, many communities lack good public transportation.

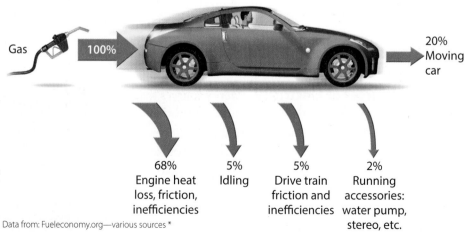

FIGURE 18 Energy Loss in a Car
Most cars are inefficient. Notice that, in a typical car, only 12-30% of the energy from fuel is used to move the car.

Data from: Fueleconomy.org—various sources *

Other Approaches to Reducing Greenhouse Gases

In addressing global climate change, it is important to improve efficiency and conservation in generating electricity and using motor vehicles. But governments, industries, scientists, and individual citizens are also exploring other strategies to reduce greenhouse gas emissions.

Agriculture and Forestry Soil and forests absorb carbon dioxide. Careful farming practices, such as the prevention of erosion, help preserve soil's ability to hold carbon. In addition, agricultural scientists have developed techniques to reduce the greenhouse gases that come from sources such as rice cultivation, livestock, and manure. In forestry, new trees planted to replace those that have been cut down (**Figure 19**) take in carbon dioxide and help prevent soil erosion.

Cap-and-Trade Some industries are better than others in reducing greenhouse gas emissions. In a *cap-and-trade* program, a government puts a limit (cap) on the amount of greenhouse gases that can be released by specific industries and power plants. Industries that release less greenhouse gas than they are allowed can sell their leftover allowances to industries that are less efficient. Suppose, for example, a factory is allowed to release 100 units of carbon dioxide. However, it only releases 75 units. The factory can sell the leftover 25 units to a factory that is having difficulty reducing its emissions as much as is required. Cap-and-trade programs work well only if the caps are progressively lowered.

Carbon Tax Many scientists and policymakers think that cap-and-trade programs are ineffective. A carbon tax is an alternative. A **carbon tax** is a fee that a government charges polluters for each unit of greenhouse gases they emit. This gives polluters a financial incentive to reduce their emissions. Several European nations have established carbon taxes. However, the downside of a carbon tax is that most polluters simply pass the cost along to consumers by charging higher prices for the goods and services they sell.

FIGURE 19 Replacing Lost Trees
Trees take in carbon dioxide, so replacing lost trees prevents some carbon dioxide from entering the atmosphere.

 Reading Checkpoint *How does preventing erosion help limit greenhouse gas emissions?*

FIGURE 20 **Carbon Offsets** Airplane passengers can sometimes buy carbon offsets to compensate for their share of the greenhouse gases released by the airplane.

Carbon Offsets A **carbon offset** is a voluntary payment made when one industry or person, instead of reducing its own greenhouse gas emissions, pays another group or person to do so. Suppose, for example, a person is taking an airplane trip. The airplane passenger finds out how much greenhouse gas the plane will release during the trip and determines one passenger's share of the total emissions. The passenger might pay a carbon-offset organization to plant trees that will take in enough carbon dioxide to compensate for those emissions.

Carbon offsets may seem like a great idea, but in practice it is often difficult to establish effective systems of exchange. At present, there are more potential buyers of carbon offsets than there are sellers. In addition, the offset may not accomplish what it is intended to do. Efforts are being made to create a reliable offset process. If these efforts succeed, then carbon offsets could become an important way to deal with climate change.

Carbon Sequestration Scientists are investigating ways to remove carbon dioxide from power plant emissions. **Carbon sequestration,** or storage, consists of ways of storing this captured carbon. For example, the carbon might be stored underground. However, there is no guarantee that the carbon will not leak out. And some experts doubt that we will ever be able to capture and store enough carbon to make much difference in overall release of carbon dioxide.

Cooperation Among Nations

In 1992, many nations signed the United Nations Framework Convention on Climate Change (UNFCCC). This framework was a voluntary plan for reducing greenhouse gas emissions. By the late 1990s, however, it was clear that a voluntary approach was not likely to succeed. After watching the seas rise, developing nations, including the Maldives, helped begin an effort to create an international treaty to address the problem. This effort led to the Kyoto Protocol.

The Kyoto Protocol The Kyoto Protocol was an international agreement that sought to limit greenhouse gas emissions. Unlike the UNFCCC, the Kyoto Protocol was binding, not voluntary. Nations that signed the treaty committed to reducing emissions of greenhouse gases to levels below those of 1990. The treaty took effect in 2005. Currently, there are 192 nations that have signed the Kyoto Protocol.

The United States did not sign the Kyoto Protocol. Some U.S. leaders called the treaty unfair because the Kyoto Protocol required developed nations to reduce emissions but did not require the same of developing nations, such as China and India. Supporters of the Kyoto Protocol said the different requirements were justified because industrialized nations created the current greenhouse gas problem. Therefore, developed nations, including the United States, should take the lead in solving it.

Paris Agreement On December 12th, 2015 nations gathered in Paris, France for the 21st United Nations climate change conference, also known as the Conference of the Parties (COP-21). In the historic meeting, nations submitted their plans for reducing greenhouse gas emissions. The overarching goal of the Paris Agreement is to prevent global temperatures from increasing more than 2°C (3.8°F) over baseline temperatures recorded before the Industrial Revolution began. By 2017, only Nicaragua and Syria had not signed the agreement. The U.S. initially submitted plans to limit power plant emissions by more than 25%. However, in 2017, President Trump announced that the U.S. would not participate in the Paris Agreement. Currently, 186 of 197 countries have ratified the agreement. More and more scientists and policymakers are saying that immediate action on climate change is necessary. Reducing greenhouse gases is one of the foremost challenges for the world.

◆ **Connect to the Central Case**

FIGURE 21 Underwater Meeting On October 17, 2009, government officials in the Maldives held an underwater meeting. **Infer** The meeting took place shortly before the Copenhagen conference began. What message were the Maldives officials sending to the conference delegates?

---

④ Assessment

1. **Form an Opinion** Which is more important in addressing global climate change: conserving electricity or finding new ways of producing it? Explain your answer.

2. **Infer** What factors are likely to make consumers in the United States prefer small, fuel-efficient cars to large vehicles?

3. **Explain** Describe an example of how you or your family might use a carbon offset.

4. **Form an Opinion** What is a major limitation of the Kyoto Protocol?

5. **REVISIT**
   INVESTIGATIVE PHENOMENON
   You have been appointed as the United States representative to an international conference that will replace the Kyoto Protocol. All nations recognize that the Kyoto Protocol was not fully effective, and most are committed to creating a stronger agreement. What type of agreement will you try to shape? Describe at least three components you would support and at least one you would oppose.

SCIENCE BEHIND THE STORIES

CLIMATE CLUES IN ICE

Ice cores are one of the few ways scientists can study how and why Earth's climate has changed over time. When water turns to ice, it can trap air bubbles, dust, pollen, and other bits of the environment. As ice layers accumulate over thousands of years, these clues of past climates build up, forming a kind of historical record of environmental change.

LONGEST ICE CORE

The longest ice core ever drilled was taken from a site called Dome C in Antarctica by the European Project for Ice Coring in Antarctica (EPICA). The core was more than 3 kilometers (2 miles) long and contained 740,000 years worth of ice! It took EPICA 10 years to retrieve the entire core. To remove the core, the group used a long, hollow drill. Every 6 meters (20 feet), the drill had to be pulled back to the surface so researchers could remove a section of the ice core from inside the drill and place it in storage. There were more than 500 ice core sections in all, with the oldest pieces coming from the bottom of the ice sheet.

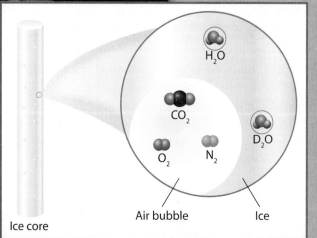

An EPICA researcher examines a section of ice core.

INTERPRETING THE ICE

Researchers used data on Dome C snow accumulation and ice movement to assign approximate dates to the ice core sections based on their depth. Each section contained many materials that could be used as proxy indicators of what the Antarctic climate was like at that time.

The two most important indicators for studying global climate change are carbon dioxide and deuterium. Deuterium is an isotope of hydrogen with an extra neutron. When temperatures are warmer, snow contains more water molecules made with deuterium than when temperatures are cool. (The chemical formula for water containing deuterium is written D_2O instead of H_2O.) EPICA researchers melted sections of the ice cores and analyzed the meltwater for deuterium. The amount of deuterium in the ice helped scientists determine temperature trends in Antarctica for the last 740,000 years.

To see how carbon dioxide and temperature were related in the past, researchers also measured carbon dioxide stuck in the ice. As snow fell and was compacted into ice, tiny bubbles of air became trapped. The EPICA researchers analyzed the air in the bubbles to find the concentration of carbon dioxide in the atmosphere during that time period.

H_2O CO_2 O_2 N_2 D_2O

Ice core Air bubble Ice

PAST CLIMATES

EPICA found that levels of carbon dioxide closely correlated with temperature levels determined from deuterium analysis. The warmer the atmospheric temperature, the more carbon dioxide there was in the air bubbles of the same period. This strengthened the evidence for a link between carbon dioxide and atmospheric temperature. Because it was the longest ice core ever taken, the EPICA core also confirmed that the link between temperature and carbon dioxide found in other ice cores extended for 740,000 years of the atmosphere's history.

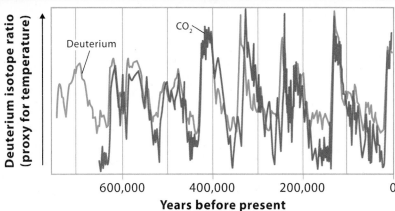

EPICA Ice Core Deuterium and CO_2 Concentrations

Adapted from EPICA community members. 2004. Eight glacial cycles from an Antarctic ice core. *Nature* 429: 623–628; and Siegenthaler, U. 2005. Stable carbon cycle-climate relationship during the late Pleistocene. *Science* 310: 1313–1317.

EPICA used the amount of CO_2 and deuterium in each section of the ice core to plot how CO_2 and temperature in Antarctica changed over time.

CAREER **Climatologist** Climatologists study the Earth's climate. What do people who work in climatology do? How does one become a climatologist? Go online and research careers in climatology. Write a brief report on your findings.

INVESTIGATIVE PHENOMENON

How does climate change impact low-lying areas?

Lesson 1
Why is the greenhouse effect important for Earth's climate?

Lesson 4
What can we personally do to respond to climate change?

Lesson 2
How can we determine what the atmospheric greenhouse gas levels were in the distant past?

Lesson 3
How is climate change affecting food availability for both marine and terrestrial organisms?

LESSON 1 Our Dynamic Climate

- The heating of Earth's atmosphere by the sun is influenced by the greenhouse effect, latitude, and sunspot cycles.
- The greenhouse effect is a natural process in which certain gases in the atmosphere trap heat near Earth.
- In general, the farther a place is from the equator, the cooler its climate.
- Winds distribute heat and moisture globally. Global wind patterns are caused in part by air rising above the equator and air sinking at the poles. Winds move moisture from one location to another.
- Oceans affect climate by transporting heat and absorbing carbon dioxide.
- Global climate may be affected by factors such as topography, volcanic eruptions, regional vegetation, and changes in Earth's orbit.

greenhouse effect (484)
greenhouse gas (484)
thermohaline circulation (488)
El Niño (488)
topography (489)

LESSON 2 Climate Change

- Evidence of global climate change includes rising atmospheric temperature, precipitation trends, melting of glaciers and polar ice, and rising sea levels.
- Scientists study climate change by taking direct measurements, inferring past climate characteristics, and using models to predict future trends.
- Evidence indicates that global warming has been caused largely by the increase in greenhouse gases in the atmosphere.

global climate change (491)
global warming (491)
proxy indicator (493)
climate model (494)
fossil fuel (496)

LESSON 3 Effects of Climate Change

- As the atmosphere warms, ecosystems on land and in the ocean are changing, affecting organisms in various ways.
- Global climate change is affecting aspects of human life such as farming, forestry, the economy, and health.
- Computer modeling predicts that global climate change will continue to affect people.

coral bleaching (499)

LESSON 4 Responding to Climate Change

- Ways of reducing the production of greenhouse gases include conserving electricity and finding new ways to produce electricity.
- By choosing more efficient cars, driving less, and using public transportation, people can reduce greenhouse gas emissions.
- Greenhouse gas emissions can also be reduced through improved agriculture and forestry, cap-and-trade policies, carbon taxes, carbon offsets, and carbon sequestration.
- The Paris Agreement is an agreement among many nations to reduce greenhouse gas emissions.

carbon footprint (503)
carbon tax (505)
carbon offset (506)

carbon sequestration (506)
Kyoto Protocol (507)

 GO ONLINE

INQUIRY LABS AND ACTIVITIES

- **Effects of Greenhouse Gases**

  Use a lamp and plastic soda bottles to simulate the effect on Earth's atmosphere of increased CO_2.

- **Tracking CO_2 and Temperature**

  Do changes in the atmosphere's CO_2 levels correlate to temperature changes? Analyze the data and graph the changes.

Chapter Assessment

Defend Your Case

In the Central Case in this chapter, you learned about the possible crisis facing the Maldives if sea levels continue to rise. What do you think the people of the Maldives should do? Provide evidence from the Central Case and the lessons to support your ideas.

Review Concepts and Terms

1. Which of the following are considered the major greenhouse gases?
   a. water vapor and ozone
   b. water vapor and carbon dioxide
   c. ozone and carbon dioxide
   d. ozone and methane

2. The sun's rays strike Earth most directly at the
   a. poles.
   b. equator.
   c. temperate zones.
   d. Gulf stream.

3. Rising sea levels are a result of
   a. increased amounts of precipitation.
   b. melting ice only.
   c. increased carbon dioxide levels in the water.
   d. melting ice and expansion of heated water.

4. Which of the following does NOT provide clues about Earth's climate in the distant past?
   a. volcanoes
   b. sediments
   c. ice cores
   d. tree rings

5. When large amounts of carbon dioxide dissolve in the oceans, what is the result?
   a. seawater with a higher pH
   b. seawater with a lower pH
   c. rising sea levels
   d. increased coral growth

6. Which activity is the largest source of U.S. greenhouse gases?
   a. vehicle emissions
   b. electricity generation
   c. factory emissions
   d. geothermal power

7. Which of the following is NOT an example of a mitigation strategy?
   a. improving energy efficiency
   b. protecting forests from deforestation
   c. pumping water out of low-lying coastal areas
   d. conserving energy

Modified True/False

Write true if the statement is true. If it is false, change the underlined word or words to make the statement true.

8. In the global wind patterns shown below, warm air rises at the <u>poles</u>.

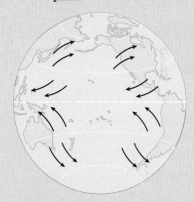

9. <u>Topography</u> refers to surface characteristics of an area, such as the presence of a mountain.

10. When seawater becomes warmer, its volume <u>decreases</u>.

11. <u>Warmer ocean temperatures</u> may lead to the death of algae and coral bleaching.

12. Loss of forests contributes to an increase of <u>oxygen</u> in the atmosphere.

13. The United States <u>did not</u> sign the Kyoto Protocol.

Chapter Assessment

Reading Comprehension

Read the following passage and answer the questions that follow.

Analysts disagree about whether the shift in agricultural locations due to global climate change will raise or lower global agricultural output. Because many nations in higher latitudes are more developed and are more equipped to have higher rates of productivity, more food ought to be produced. On the other hand, much of the arable land in these wealthier nations may have already been developed as urban areas, so some food-production potential may not be realized.

If crops shift locations, poorer nations may become even weaker economically. The gap between rich and poor nations may grow even wider as developing nations become subject to even harsher environmental conditions for growing crops. However, these nations could make positive adaptations, such as increasing use of water-conserving irrigation techniques and cultivating crops that need less water.

14. Based on the way it is used in this passage, what do you think is the closest synonym for *arable*?
    a. free
    c. infertile
    b. dry
    d. fertile

15. Which effect of climate change is most likely to make farmers need to conserve water?
    a. rising sea levels
    b. precipitation pattern changes
    c. changes in migration times
    d. decreased biodiversity

16. Which of the following is an inference that can be made from the information in the passage?
    a. Global climate change is not likely to affect worldwide agriculture.
    b. Poorer nations will benefit from the shift in agricultural locations.
    c. Wealthier nations will suffer from the shift in agricultural locations.
    d. The overall effect of global climate change on agriculture cannot be predicted accurately.

Short Answer

17. What are sunspots? What is the relationship between sunspots and the energy released by the sun?

18. List four examples of evidence that Earth is warming.

19. What is one example of how scientists study the ancient atmosphere?

20. How has the burning of fossil fuels intensified the greenhouse effect?

21. Describe how increased levels of carbon dioxide in the atmosphere can lead to more acidic seawater.

22. What are four ways that you can help to conserve electricity in your home?

23. What is a major limitation of carbon offsets?

24. What is carbon sequestration?

Critical Thinking

25. **Relate Cause and Effect** What is the relationship between latitude, the sun, and climate?

26. **Relate Cause and Effect** Warmer temperatures lead to more evaporation, which leads to more water vapor in the atmosphere. What impact could this have on the greenhouse effect? Explain your answer.

27. **Use Models** What are climate models? What is an advantage of using a climate model? What is a disadvantage?

28. **Infer** Which is a better long-term solution for handling global climate change—adaptation or mitigation? Explain your answer.

29. **Sequence** Describe what happens to the energy from the sun that reaches Earth's atmosphere.

30. **Predict** What is coral bleaching? Do you think coral bleaching will continue to occur? Explain your prediction.

31. **Infer** Why has it been easier to address the problem of ozone depletion than to address global climate change?

32. **Form an Opinion** Did the conference in Paris in 2015 make any progress in addressing climate change? Explain your answer.

Analyze Data

Look carefully at the EnergyGuide label below, and then answer the questions.

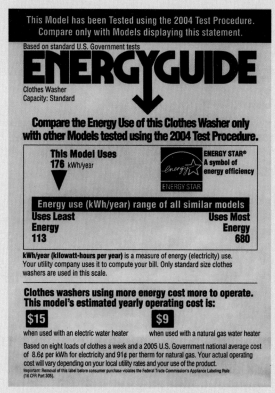

This Model has been Tested using the 2004 Test Procedure.
Compare only with Models displaying this statement.

Based on standard U.S. Government tests

ENERGYGUIDE

Clothes Washer
Capacity: Standard

Compare the Energy Use of this Clothes Washer only with other Models tested using the 2004 Test Procedure.

This Model Uses
176 kWh/year

ENERGY STAR®
A symbol of
energy efficiency

Energy use (kWh/year) range of all similar models

Uses Least Energy	Uses Most Energy
113	680

kWh/year (kilowatt-hours per year) is a measure of energy (electricity) use. Your utility company uses it to compute your bill. Only standard size clothes washers are used in this scale.

Clothes washers using more energy cost more to operate. This model's estimated yearly operating cost is:

$15	$9
when used with an electric water heater	when used with a natural gas water heater

Based on eight loads of clothes a week and a 2005 U.S. Government national average cost of 8.6¢ per kWh for electricity and 91¢ per therm for natural gas. Your actual operating cost will vary depending on your local utility rates and your use of the product.
Important: Removal of this label before consumer purchase violates the Federal Trade Commission's Appliance Labeling Rule (16 CFR Part 305).

33. Interpret Visuals What type of appliance does this label rate?

34. Calculate About how much would it cost to run this appliance for six months?

35. Interpret Visuals Can an EnergyGuide label list the exact cost of running an appliance? Explain your answer.

36. Compare and Contrast How does this model compare to other models in terms of energy efficiency?

37. Pose Questions Besides energy efficiency, what other things might consumers consider when buying this kind of appliance? Write a list of questions that a consumer might ask about the appliance.

Write About It

38. Persuasion Write a letter to your school's principal recommending three ways that your school could use less electricity.

39. Opinion Both supporters and critics of the Kyoto Protocol recognize that it has its limitations. As nations continue to work on the next international agreement that will replace the Kyoto Protocol, what are some factors they should consider?

40. REVISIT INVESTIGATIVE PHENOMENON Make a flowchart that represents the causes and predicted consequences of a warming Earth. (*Hint:* Start your flowchart with the phrase "fossil fuel combustion.")

Ecological Footprints

Read the information below. Copy the table into your notebook and record your calculations. Then, answer the questions that follow.

Everyone can contribute to mitigating global climate change by considering actions they take every day. Find a simple online carbon footprint calculator. Calculate all or part of the annual carbon footprint for yourself and your household. Then, identify one change your household can make to reduce its carbon footprint.

1. Discuss the change you identified that could be made in your household. What are the potential drawbacks of making this change?

2. How would you convince other members of your household to consider making the change?

	Population	Carbon Footprint (kg per person per year)
You	1	
Your household		
Your class's households		
Your state's households		
United States		

3. Do you think it is a change that other households can make? Explain.

MATH SUPPORT For help with calculations, see the Math Handbook.

INVESTIGATIVE PHENOMENON What effect does the use of nonrenewable energy resources have on the environment?

Arctic National
Wildlife Refuge

Lesson 1
Energy: An Overview

Lesson 2
Fossil Fuels

Lesson 3
Consequences of
Fossil Fuel Use

Lesson 4
Nuclear Power

Oil or Wilderness on Alaska's North Slope?

ABOVE THE ARCTIC CIRCLE in Alaska, the land drops steeply down from the mountains of the Brooks Range. From there, a huge area of tundra stretches north until it meets the icy Arctic Ocean. Most of this area, called the North Slope, is wild and undeveloped. But deep under the surface, the North Slope contains petroleum deposits. These deposits have led to controversy. People are struggling to determine whether they can obtain oil and at the same time preserve a wilderness area.

Oil has been extracted from the Prudhoe Bay area since 1977. The drilling and processing of this resource have provided needed fuel for the United States. In addition, the oil industry has created jobs for many Alaskans. However, the oil industry has affected a large area of land in Alaska. There are more than 20 oil fields spread over 160,000 hectares (395,000 acres). The oil is transported across Alaska by a 1300-kilometer (800-mile) pipeline. The pipeline carries the oil south to the port of Valdez, where it is loaded onto tankers.

The Arctic National Wildlife Refuge is another part of the North Slope that contains oil deposits. Years ago, the United States government set aside this part of the North Slope, about the size of South Carolina, as a wilderness area. The Arctic Refuge protects wildlife and preserves ecosystems of tundra, mountains, and seacoast. There are grizzly bears, polar bears, Arctic foxes, timber wolves, and other animals. Many birds nest in this area. In summer, thousands of caribou arrive from the south. Here, the female caribou give birth to their calves.

Millions of U.S. citizens think the Arctic Refuge is priceless because it is the last great wilderness in their industrialized nation. However, for millions of others, this land represents something else—a source of petroleum, the natural resource that fuels our way of life. To these people, it seems wrong to leave such an important resource sitting unused in the ground.

Those who want to drill for oil here accuse wilderness preservationists of neglecting the

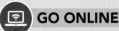

GO ONLINE
- Take It Local   • 3-D Geo Tour

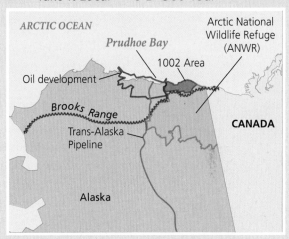

nation's economic interests. Advocates for wilderness do not agree with this point of view. They think that drilling will sacrifice a beautiful, wild area for little gain.

Scientists, oil industry experts, politicians, environmental groups, citizens, and Alaska residents have all been part of the debate. So have the two Native groups in the area, the Gwich'in and the Inupiat. These two groups disagree over whether the Arctic Refuge should be opened to oil development. The Gwich'in depend on hunting caribou. They fear that oil industry activity will reduce caribou herds. In contrast, the Inupiat see oil extraction as one of the few opportunities for economic development in the area.

In 1980, the U.S. Congress tried to compromise. Congress put most of the refuge off limits to development. However, it reserved a 600,000-hectare (1.5-million-acre) area of coastal plain for future decision making. This region, called the 1002 Area, can be opened for oil development by a vote of both houses of Congress. The 1002 Area has been the center of the oil-versus-wilderness debate. In 2017, a tax bill mandated the sale of at least two oil and gas leases on 1002 Area land in next 10 years.

Energy: An Overview

EVERYDAY PHENOMENON What is energy and how is it used?

Knowledge and Skills

- Define *energy* and differentiate between kinetic and potential energy.
- Identify different forms of energy.
- Describe how human society uses energy resources.

Reading Strategy and Vocabulary

✔ **Reading Strategy** As you read about forms of energy, make a two-column table. List the forms of energy in the left column. In the right column, take notes about each form of energy.

Vocabulary energy, kinetic energy, potential energy, combustion, energy efficiency, renewable energy, nonrenewable energy, electricity

KITTY HAWK, December 17, 1903. On a windswept beach in North Carolina, a small, fragile airplane, piloted by Orville Wright, rose into the air. As his brother Wilbur held his breath, Orville managed to keep the tiny airplane aloft for 12 seconds, flying 36 meters (40 yards) across the sand. With that short flight, the Wright brothers forever changed the way people travel and transport materials. Today huge jets carry passengers and cargoes across continents and oceans.

The Wright brothers' tiny plane and modern jets are different in many ways, but they share some characteristics. For one thing, both need fuel to fly, and the fuel they use comes from petroleum. Today's jet is much bigger, and travels much faster and farther, than the first airplane. Therefore, a jet uses a lot more fuel than the plane that took to the air at Kitty Hawk.

FIGURE 1 First Flight Powered by gasoline, the Wright brothers' plane rises above the beach at Kitty Hawk.

(a)

(b)

What Is Energy?

Fuel supplies airplanes, big and small, with energy. Energy is the ability to do work or cause a change. Airplanes do work when they move from one place to another. Energy from the sun changes Earth by warming the atmosphere. The sun's energy also causes a change when, in photosynthesis, it powers chemical reactions in which carbon dioxide and water combine to form food molecules. Energy ran the printing presses that printed this book, and energy enables you to turn these pages. And without energy, you couldn't read the words in this paragraph.

Energy is necessary to change the position, composition, or temperature of something. Most forms of energy fall into one of two categories—kinetic energy or potential energy.

Kinetic Energy On a bright winter day, a skier zooms down a hill. The fast-moving skier has kinetic energy. Kinetic energy is the energy that an object has due to its motion. A whizzing baseball, a train speeding down a track, a jumping frog, and a wave crashing on a beach all have kinetic energy. You can think of kinetic energy as energy in action.

Potential Energy Before the skier took off, she stood at the top of the hill. At that time, before she started moving, she had potential energy, because objects that are high up tend to go downward. Potential energy is energy that an object has because of its position or shape. In contrast to kinetic energy, potential energy is energy that is stored. A stretched rubber band has potential energy. When you release the rubber band, it jumps away from your hand. The rubber band now has kinetic energy because it is moving.

 What is energy?

FIGURE 2 Potential and Kinetic Energy (a) At the top of the hill, the skier has potential energy. **(b)** As she zooms downward, she has kinetic energy.

FIGURE 3 **Different Forms of Energy**
As the hikers move, they use mechanical energy. Chemical energy from food powers their muscles.

Forms of Energy

It's a warm, sunny Saturday, so you and a few friends decide to hike to the top of a hill. You call your parents on your cell phone to let them know what your plans are. Then you pick up your backpack and start climbing. When you get to the hilltop, you and your friends break for lunch, and you eat the sandwich that you packed. On your hike and the lunch break that followed, you used several kinds of energy. Energy comes in many forms, and each of these forms can be converted into other forms.

Mechanical Energy The motions involved in picking up your backpack and hiking involve mechanical energy. *Mechanical energy* is associated with the motion and position of an object. A moving baseball has mechanical energy that is kinetic. So do a speeding bike and a car moving down a street. A compressed spring has mechanical energy that is potential. When you release the spring, the stored energy becomes kinetic, and the spring moves.

Electrical Energy A cell phone uses electrical energy to send messages. *Electrical energy* is energy associated with electric charges. Electrical energy stored in a cell phone's battery is potential energy. When you use the phone to make a call, the energy is kinetic. Electrical energy powers many things you use, such as light bulbs, refrigerators, computers, and hair dryers.

Thermal Energy All materials are composed of tiny particles called atoms and molecules. These particles are moving all the time. *Thermal energy* is the kinetic energy of all the atoms and molecules in an object. The more energy the atoms and molecules have, the faster they move. If the particles in an object start to move faster, the object will become warmer. The particles in hot volcanic lava move very fast.

 Reading Checkpoint *What kind of energy does a compressed spring have?*

Electromagnetic Energy When the sun warms you or you cook food in a microwave oven, you are experiencing or using electromagnetic energy. *Electromagnetic energy* travels through space in the form of waves. Visible light is a type of electromagnetic energy, as are radio waves and ultraviolet radiation.

Chemical Energy The food you and your friends eat while hiking provides your bodies with chemical energy. Food, such as corn, is made of molecules, and *chemical energy* is stored in the bonds that hold the atoms together in molecules. When bonds in molecules break, energy may be released. Chemical energy is potential energy, because it is stored in chemical bonds. When you move your legs and arms during hiking, your body converts chemical energy stored in food into mechanical energy. Like food, fossil fuels contain energy stored in the molecules of chemical compounds.

Nuclear Energy Chemical energy involves bonds between atoms. *Nuclear energy,* in contrast, involves forces within atoms. The nucleus is the central part of an atom. The forces that hold nuclear particles together in the nucleus can store a huge amount of potential energy. You will learn more about nuclear energy later in this chapter.

Energy Conversion Energy can be converted, or changed, from one form to another. For example, when you turn on an electric fan, the blades of the fan turn around. In the fan's motor, electrical energy has been converted to mechanical energy. The mechanical energy of the moving blades produces cooling breezes. When fireworks explode in the night sky, chemical energy has been converted to thermal energy and electromagnetic energy. The electromagnetic energy takes the form of the brightly colored light displays and patterns we associate with fireworks.

▶ *Combustion* Combustion is another example of energy conversion. Combustion is the process in which a fuel burns because it combines rapidly with oxygen. Chemical energy stored in the fuel is converted to thermal and electromagnetic energy. You feel the thermal energy as heat and see the electromagnetic energy as light.

▶ *A Combustion Equation* Many substances can serve as fuels. The fuels you are most familiar with are wood and fossil fuels such as coal and oil. The chemical equation for the combustion of natural gas, a fossil fuel composed mostly of methane (CH_4), is shown below.

$$CH_4 + 2O_2 \rightarrow CO_2 + 2H_2O$$

The principal products of the combustion of methane—and of other fossil fuels—are carbon dioxide and water. Both carbon dioxide and water vapor are greenhouse gases.

FIGURE 4 Renewable Energy
Wind holds the kite aloft. Wind is a renewable energy resource.

Energy Efficiency Airplanes, cars, and fans all require energy to do the jobs they are designed to perform. However, not all the energy supplied is used to do the work for which it is intended. In a car, for example, some of the energy supplied by the fuel is converted to heat rather than motion. **Energy efficiency** is an expression of how much of the energy put into a system actually does useful work. Energy efficiency is usually expressed as a percentage. For example, if an automobile has an energy efficiency of 15 percent, only 15 percent of the energy provided by the fuel actually moves the car forward.

Sources and Uses of Energy

Highly industrialized nations such as the United States use an enormous amount of energy. Where does that energy come from, and how is the energy used?

Renewable and Nonrenewable Energy Energy resources can be divided into two broad categories: renewable energy and nonrenewable energy. Sources of **renewable energy** are nearly always available somewhere on Earth's surface, or they are replaced in a relatively short time. Renewable energy resources include the sun, wind, moving water, wood, and heat that comes from deep within Earth. Sources of **nonrenewable energy**, in contrast, cannot be replaced. Nonrenewable energy resources include fossil fuels, such as coal, oil, and natural gas, and nuclear energy. Once these resources are used up, they are gone forever.

All the renewable and nonrenewable energy resources identified above are primary energy resources. Primary energy resources are found in nature. **Electricity**, which is energy made available by the flow of an electric charge, is considered a secondary source of energy, because it must be produced using a primary energy resource. For example, electricity can be produced by burning coal. Electricity is useful because it can be transferred over long distances and used in many ways.

Quick Lab

Where's the Energy?

1. Obtain a flashlight and remove the batteries.
2. Turn the flashlight's switch on. Observe what happens.
3. Now put the batteries back in the flashlight, and turn the flashlight on. Observe what happens now.
4. Leave the flashlight turned on. After a few minutes, put your hand close to the bulb of the flashlight. What do you feel?

Analyze and Conclude

1. **Infer** When the flashlight did not have batteries, what happened when you switched it on? Why did this happen?

2. **Relate Cause and Effect** After you inserted the batteries into the flashlight, what happened when you turned the switch on? Why?

3. **Apply Concepts** What form of energy lights a flashlight bulb?

4. **Use Analogies** How is a flashlight battery like a box in which you put baseball bats when they are not being used?

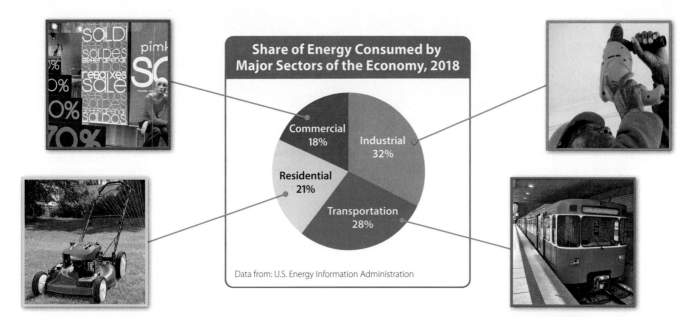

Share of Energy Consumed by Major Sectors of the Economy, 2018

Commercial 18%
Industrial 32%
Residential 21%
Transportation 28%

Data from: U.S. Energy Information Administration

How Energy Is Used The U.S. Department of Energy (DOE) identifies four general ways that energy is used in the United States. As the graph in **Figure 5** shows, energy is used in industry, transportation, residences, and commerce. In industry, energy is used to accomplish jobs such as constructing buildings and making products. Transportation vehicles that use energy include cars and trucks, of course, and also boats, airplanes, trains, and even motorcycles. Residences—including your apartment or house—use electricity to run appliances, light bulbs, and electronic devices. Commercial uses occur in places where business is conducted, such as offices, supermarkets, and shopping malls.

Worldwide Patterns of Energy Use Developed nations generally use far more energy than do developing nations. Per person, nations with the most industry use up to 100 times more energy than do nations with little industry. The United States has about 4.5 percent of the world's population; however, it consumes 17 percent of the world's energy.

Developed and developing nations also tend to use energy differently. Developed nations use about two thirds of their energy on transportation and industry. In contrast, developing nations use most of their energy to provide the basic necessities of life. Such activities include farming, preparing food, and heating homes.

FIGURE 5 How We Use Energy The graph shows the different ways that energy is used in the United States. Notice that industry uses the highest percentage of energy. (Note: The percentages do not add up to 100 due to rounding.)

LESSON

① Assessment

1. **Compare and Contrast** Contrast kinetic energy and potential energy. Give an example of each.

2. **Relate Cause and Effect** Carbohydrate molecules are found in foods. These carbohydrate molecules provide your body with energy. How does this happen?

3. **Explain** Why is electricity considered a secondary source of energy?

   REVISIT

4. **INVESTIGATIVE** PHENOMENON   Is the energy contained in fossil fuels potential energy or kinetic energy? Explain your answer.

Fossil Fuels

EVERYDAY PHENOMENON How did fossil fuels form, and
how are they obtained and used?

Knowledge and Skills

- Explain how fossil fuels formed.
- Describe the uses of coal and how it is removed from the ground.
- Describe the uses of oil and how it is extracted.
- Explain the characteristics and uses of natural gas.
- Predict the future of fossil fuels.

Reading Strategy and Vocabulary

✔ **Reading Strategy** Before you read, preview **Figure 6,** which shows how coal formed. Write any questions you have about the illustration. Answer these questions when you read the lesson.

Vocabulary strip mining, subsurface mining, petroleum, petrochemical, oil sands, oil shale, methane hydrate

"DOWN BY THE STATION, early in the morning, see the little pufferbellies all in a row." When you hear that old children's song, do you ever wonder what a pufferbelly is? *Pufferbelly* is a slang term for a steam locomotive. Many years ago, railroad trains were powered by steam, and that steam usually came from water heated by burning coal.

Today most trains run on diesel fuel or electricity, not steam produced by coal fires. Both diesel fuel and the coal that powered the old steam locomotives are fossil fuels. All fossil fuels are nonrenewable energy resources. These nonrenewable fuels were produced by processes that are still happening today. However, these processes do not create fossil fuels nearly fast enough to replace the ones we are using up. To replenish all the fossil fuels we have used so far would take many millions of years.

How Fossil Fuels Form

Fossil fuels, including coal, oil, and natural gas, are formed from the remains of once-living organisms. The energy in these fuels comes originally from the sun. During photosynthesis, electromagnetic energy from the sun is converted to chemical energy stored in complex molecules. Over millions of years, some of these molecules undergo a series of changes that eventually result in fossil fuels. Fossil fuels are composed mostly of hydrocarbons. Hydrocarbons are chemical compounds made mainly of hydrogen and carbon atoms.

Breakdown Without Oxygen After they die, most organisms do not end up as part of a coal, gas, or oil deposit. Fossil fuels are produced only when the remains of living things are broken down in an environment that has little or no oxygen, such as the bottoms of deep lakes, swamps, and shallow seas. As dead organisms gradually accumulate at the bottoms of these bodies of water, sediments may accumulate on top of the the remains and exert pressure on them.

Different Conditions, Different Fuels The remains of organisms may be converted into crude oil, natural gas, or coal. Various factors, such as temperature, amount of pressure, and the chemical composition of the starting material, determine which fossil fuels are produced. Oil, for example, comes from the remains of organisms such as microscopic animals and algae. These organisms live in oceans and inland seas. Coal forms from plant remains that are compressed under very high pressure. **Figure 6** shows how coal forms. First, peat forms as plants die and fall into a lake, bog, or swamp. Then, coal forms over millions of years, under increasing heat and pressure. Notice that there are different types of coal. Lignite has the lowest energy value, and anthracite typically has the highest.

Coal

Coal is the world's most abundant fossil fuel, and its use goes back to ancient times. People in parts of China have heated with coal for at least 2000 years. In Britain, during the second and third centuries of the modern era, the ancient Roman invading armies used coal for heating. Beginning in the 1300s, in what is now the southwestern part of the United States, Native Americans of the Hopi Nation used coal to heat their homes, cook food, and fire pottery.

North America has abundant coal reserves. One quarter of the world's coal is located in the United States. Asia, too, is rich in coal. Today, China and the United States are the main producers and users of coal.

 Reading Checkpoint *What nations are the main producers of coal today?*

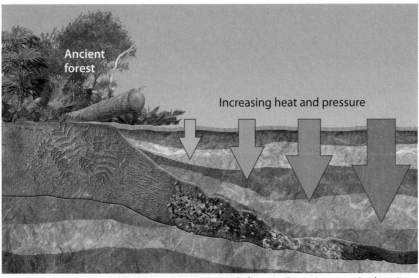

Peat   Lignite   Sub-bituminous   Bituminous   Anthracite

Time →

FIGURE 6 How Coal Forms Coal forms as ancient plant matter is compacted underground. Notice that peat forms before coal, and that there are four types of coal. The type of coal that forms depends on conditions such as heat and pressure.

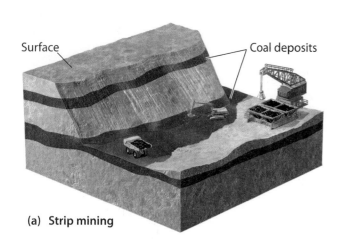

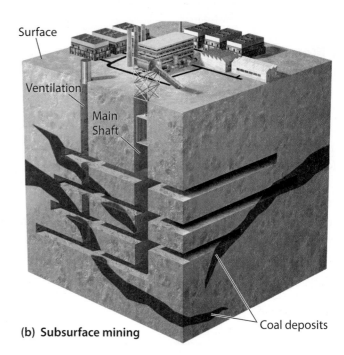

(a) Strip mining

(b) Subsurface mining

FIGURE 7 **Mining for Coal** Coal is mined in two ways. **(a)** Strip mining is used when the coal is near the surface of the ground. **(b)** If the coal is deep underground, it is removed by subsurface mining.

How Coal Is Used Coal provides one fourth of the world's energy. Coal-fired steam engines helped drive the Industrial Revolution, powering factories, trains, and ships. In the 1880s, people began to use coal to generate electricity. Today, coal generates about half the electricity used by Americans. In addition, coal powers many industries. Some of these industries are chemical manufacturing, iron and steel manufacturing, and paper mills.

Mining for Coal We use two major methods to remove coal from the ground. Look at **Figure 7** as you read about these methods.

▶ *Strip Mining* When coal deposits are at or near the surface, strip mining is used. **Strip mining** is the extraction of a mineral by removing a strip of the layers of soil and rock on top of the mineral deposit. Strip mining may remove huge amounts of soil and rock. Once the coal is exposed, it can be extracted. After the coal has been removed, the soil may be put back to fill the holes. Strip mining operations can extend over a large area. In some cases, entire mountaintops are blasted away.

▶ *Subsurface Mining* We reach underground deposits with subsurface mining. **Subsurface mining** is typically the practice of digging shafts deep into the ground to find and remove a mineral. Networks of tunnels are usually blasted with explosives and then dug out so that miners can reach the coal. After miners dig the coal out, it is brought to the surface.

Advantages of Coal There are several reasons why coal is used commonly as an energy source. Compared to other fossil fuels, coal is more abundant and less expensive. It does not need much processing after it has been removed from the ground. Coal can be transported relatively easily in trucks and trains. Unlike the oil taken from Prudhoe Bay in Alaska, coal does not require a pipeline.

FIND OUT MORE

How is your apartment or house heated? Does this method depend on fossil fuels? Ask your parents or the building superintendent for this information. Use a library or Internet resources to find out the advantages and disadvantages of this type of heating.

Oil

Oil, or **petroleum,** is a dark, liquid fossil fuel made up mostly of hydrocarbons. Petroleum is found in underground deposits. The Middle East is especially rich in these deposits. Petroleum is also found in other parts of the world, such as Russia, and North and South America.

How Petroleum Is Used Petroleum is the source of the fuels used for most forms of transportation, such as cars, trucks, airplanes, and ships. Many people heat their homes with fuel oil. Because oil is a complex mix of hydrocarbons, it can be used to make many types of products. **Petrochemicals** are chemical compounds that are derived from oil and used to make products. **Figure 8** shows some petroleum products that are used in and around a home.

Finding Petroleum Deposits Most oil deposits are deep underground. There, the oil is usually found within tiny pores, or holes, in rocks such as sandstone and limestone. Rocks containing oil are a little bit like a sponge that has soaked up water. Scientists look for oil by performing various tests. For example, they send sound waves deep underground and determine how long it takes the waves to be reflected and to reach different surface locations. The length of time can indicate the characteristics of the rocks the waves pass through. Once scientists find a likely location, oil companies drill deep holes and remove rock cores to see whether the rocks contain oil.

 What is petroleum composed of?

FIGURE 8 Petroleum Products
Many products, such as those shown here, are derived from petroleum.

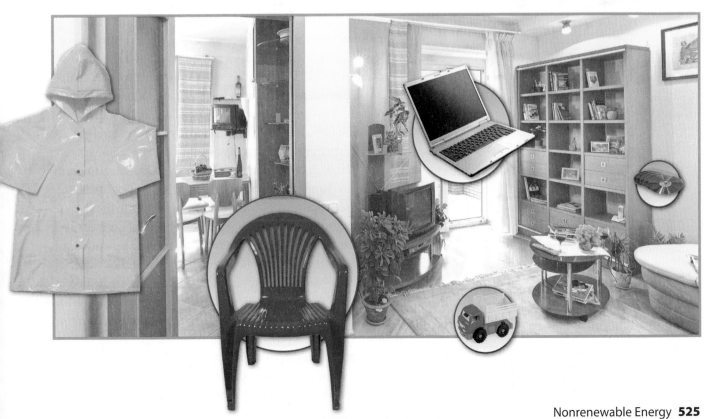

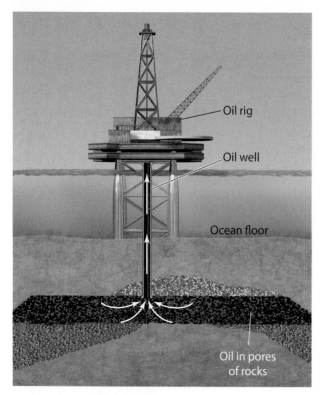

(a) Primary extraction of oil

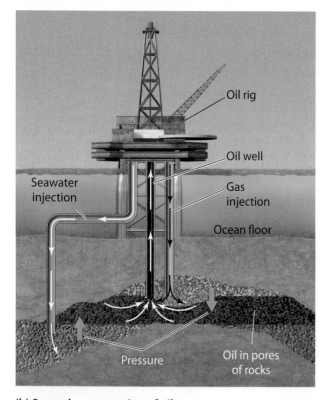

(b) Secondary extraction of oil

 Connect to the Central Case

FIGURE 9 Extracting Oil (a) Primary extraction is used when the oil deposit is already under pressure. **(b)** Once the pressure decreases, secondary extraction is used, which involves injecting water or gas to force the oil upward. **Apply Concepts** Which technique is now used for removing oil from the Prudhoe Bay area?

Drilling for Oil You squeeze a sponge to remove the water. Similarly, pressure is needed to get oil from porous rock. Usually, oil trapped in rocks is already under pressure. So at first, oil will rise in the well, often all the way to the surface, without needing to be pumped out. During that period, a process called *primary extraction* can be used to remove the oil, as shown in **Figure 9.**

Later, once the pressure decreases, oil companies use a process called secondary extraction to get the oil to the surface. In *secondary extraction,* chemicals may be used to dissolve oil. Secondary extraction may also involve pumping water, steam, or gases such as carbon dioxide beneath oil deposits to force the oil to the surface. At Prudhoe Bay in Alaska, seawater is piped into wells to flush out oil. Oil drilling takes place not just on land but on the seafloor in relatively shallow water.

Refining Oil Oil taken out of the ground is called crude oil. Crude oil cannot be used the way it is. It must be refined in order to be usable. Refining involves separating crude oil into different fuels and other substances. This process takes place in a refinery.

✓ Reading Checkpoint   *Describe primary extraction.*

Natural Gas

Natural gas consists of the gas methane mixed in with small amounts of other gases. Its use is growing faster than that of most other fossil fuels today. Natural gas is colorless and odorless. It is much less polluting than coal or oil, and it emits less carbon dioxide per unit of energy produced than either coal or oil. Natural gas produces a large amount of energy. Pockets of natural gas are often located above oil deposits, both on land and offshore. Coal deposits, too, may have natural gas above them. Hydraulic fracturing, or fracking, is another way that natural gas and oil is extracted from rocks. Large amounts of water, chemicals, and sand are forced in the rocks under pressure. The rocks crack and the gas or oil rises to the surface. Within the United States, pipelines carry natural gas from its source to where it is used. If laid end to end, our network of natural gas pipelines would go to the moon and back twice.

About half the homes in the United States are heated by natural gas, as are many businesses. Appliances such as water heaters, stoves, and clothes dryers may use natural gas to produce heat. Increasingly, natural gas is used to generate electricity, because it does not pollute the atmosphere to the extent that coal does. Natural gas goes into products such as paints, plastics, dyes, and fertilizers.

The Supply of Fossil Fuels

Global consumption of coal, oil, and natural gas has risen steadily for years, and it continues to rise. **Figure 10** shows this trend. Right now, all the coal, oil, and natural gas that will be available to human society have already formed. What will happen when easily obtainable supplies of fossil fuels begin to run out?

Dwindling Deposits No one knows the exact amount of fossil fuels that are left or how long they will last. The most accessible reserves of natural gas, oil, and coal have already been used up. Remaining deposits of fossil fuels are often difficult and expensive to extract. The technology for extracting and producing fossil fuels will probably continue to improve. However, as people continue to remove fossil fuels, it is becoming harder and harder to find new sources.

Some scientists and oil-industry experts calculate that we have already extracted nearly half of the world's oil reserves. Many scientists predict that the worldwide production of oil will decrease over the next few decades. **Figure 11** shows a graph of one prediction for what will happen to oil production. And many scientists and experts think that we will face a crisis long before the last drop of oil is pumped from a well. If the demand for oil continues to increase, there will be a shortage when the rate of oil production first starts going down. Reserves of coal are expected to last significantly longer than oil. In fact, one projection indicates that coal supplies will last 130 years in the United States. But even supplies of coal, the most abundant fossil fuel, will not last forever.

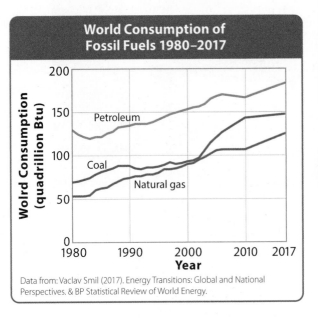

World Consumption of Fossil Fuels 1980–2017

Data from: Vaclav Smil (2017). Energy Transitions: Global and National Perspectives. & BP Statistical Review of World Energy.

FIGURE 10 Consumption of Fossil Fuels The graph shows how the use of petroleum, coal, and natural gas increased between 1980 and 2017.

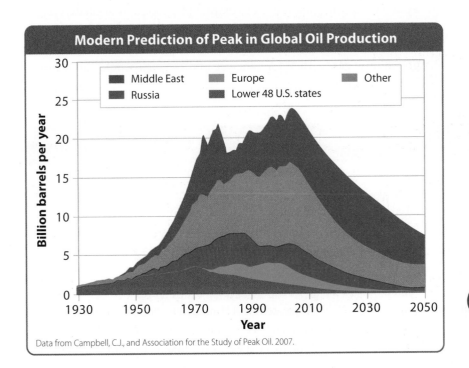

Modern Prediction of Peak in Global Oil Production

Data from Campbell, C.J., and Association for the Study of Peak Oil. 2007.

◆➤ **Connect to the Central Case**

FIGURE 11 Oil Production The graph shows how much oil has been produced worldwide since 1930 and one prediction for the amount of oil to be produced in the future. **Interpret Graphs** Does this graph affect your opinion about drilling in the Arctic Refuge? Explain your answer.

🔲 **GO ONLINE**

• **Graph It** Global Oil Production and the Hubbert Curve

Nonrenewable Energy **527**

FIGURE 12 Oil Shale If it is lighted, oil shale will continue to burn on its own. Oil shale may be a future source of oil.

New Sources of Fossil Fuels Are there other fossil fuels that can replace or supplement oil, natural gas, and coal? Oil sands, oil shale, and methane hydrate may be alternative sources of fossil fuels.

▶ *Oil Sands* Oil sands are deposits of moist sand and clay containing bitumen. Bitumen is a thick, heavy form of petroleum that is rich in carbon. Oil sands are generally removed by strip mining. After extraction, bitumen is refined into a more valuable synthetic crude oil. Petroleum prices are rising, and this fact makes oil sands more profitable than they once were.

▶ *Oil Shale* Oil shale is rock filled with a mixture of hydrocarbons. Once mined, oil shale can be burned directly, like coal. Alternatively, it can be processed to extract liquid petroleum. The world's known deposits of oil shale may be able to produce a large amount of oil. As crude oil prices rise, oil shale is attracting a large amount of attention.

▶ *Methane Hydrate* The deep ocean floor contains a possible source of energy, methane hydrate. Methane hydrate is an icelike solid that consists of molecules of methane within a crystal network of water molecules. Methane hydrate can be burned to release energy. Scientists think there is a huge amount of methane hydrate on Earth. However, they still need to find a way to extract methane hydrate safely, without causing underwater landslides.

▶ *Drawbacks* Alternative fossil fuels are abundant, but they will not solve our energy challenges. They are expensive to extract and process. Because it takes a lot of energy to extract alternative fossil fuels, they provide much less net energy than conventional fossil fuels do. (*Net energy* is the energy provided by a source after the energy used to obtain the source has been subtracted.) In addition, the extraction of alternative fossil fuels can cause environmental damage. For example, strip mining is used to extract oil sands and oil shale, and strip mining removes topsoil and vegetation. The most serious environmental effect of these fuels is that their combustion releases greenhouse gases. Therefore, the use of these fuels would speed up climate change.

LESSON ② Assessment

1. **Review** Where did the energy in fossil fuels originally come from? What type of energy is stored in fossil fuels?

2. **Compare and Contrast** What are two major methods of obtaining coal from the ground? Compare these two methods.

3. **Use Analogies** How are rocks that contain oil similar to a sponge?

4. **Apply Concepts** What is one advantage that natural gas has over coal and oil?

5. **Relate Cause and Effect** Why is the supply of fossil fuels dwindling?

   REVISIT

6. **INVESTIGATIVE** PHENOMENON The cost of researching technology to extract alternative fossil fuels, such as oil sands and oil shale, is high. Do you think this is a wise investment? Explain your answer.

Consequences of Fossil Fuel Use

EVERYDAY PHENOMENON What problems are associated with fossil fuel use?

Knowledge and Skills

- Explain how pollutants released by fossil fuels damage health and the environment.
- Describe the environmental and health effects of mining and drilling.
- Explain the implications of dependence on foreign nations for fossil fuels.
- Explain why energy conservation is important.

Reading Strategy and Vocabulary

✔ **Reading Strategy** As you read, draw a concept map about the harmful effects of fossil fuels. Be sure to include all the blue and green headings in your map.

Vocabulary acid drainage, energy conservation

ON AUGUST 5, 2010, a chunk of stone broke off the side of a mountain in the Chilean Atacama Desert. The chunk of stone, weighing almost 800,000 tons, landed on a mine, trapping thirty-three miners 700 meters (2300 feet) underground. For seventeen days, no one knew if the miners were alive or not. Then, a drill reached the shelter area in the mine. The miners tied a note to the drill letting people know they were safe in the shelter, sharing small amounts of food and water.

The next day, a second drill reached the shelter. Miners were supplied with food and water, and could now communicate with people at the surface. Rescue plans were enacted, including drilling a channel large enough to lift the miners out of the mine. Throughout September, various drills were used to carve a hole in the rock to reach the miners. On October 13, 2010, the first miner was brought to the surface in a capsule after a 15 minute journey. The remaining 32 miners were also successfully rescued after spending 69 days underground.

The Chilean mine accident is a reminder that fossil fuels come with costs as well as benefits. Workers risk their lives to obtain the fuels we need. And use of the fuels can cause damage.

FIGURE 13 Rescue! One of the Chilean miners is carried to safety.

Real Data

Carbon Dioxide From Fossil Fuels

The combustion of fossil fuels releases carbon dioxide into the atmosphere. Carbon dioxide is the major greenhouse gas that is increasing in the atmosphere because of human activities. The graph shows how the release of carbon dioxide by the burning of oil, coal, and natural gas has changed since 1800. Study the graph and then answer the questions.

1. **Interpret Graphs** What does the purple line on the graph represent?

2. **Relate Cause and Effect** Around what year did the total emissions of carbon dioxide from fossil fuels begin to go up dramatically? What do you think accounts for this dramatic change? (*Hint:* Around that time, how did people's lifestyles begin to change?)

3. **Analyze Data** Which two fossil fuels release the most carbon dioxide into the atmosphere?

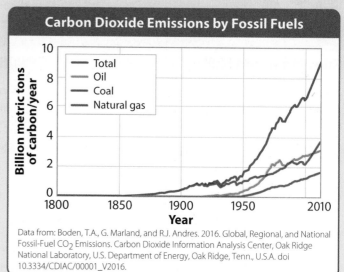

Carbon Dioxide Emissions by Fossil Fuels

Data from: Boden, T.A., G. Marland, and R.J. Andres. 2016. Global, Regional, and National Fossil-Fuel CO_2 Emissions. Carbon Dioxide Information Analysis Center, Oak Ridge National Laboratory, U.S. Department of Energy, Oak Ridge, Tenn., U.S.A. doi 10.3334/CDIAC/00001_V2016.

4. **Predict** Do you think the overall trend shown on the graph will change? Explain your answer.

Pollution From Fossil Fuels

When they are burned, fossil fuels release substances that contribute to climate change and cause pollution. In addition, the processes involved in obtaining and refining fuels can harm human health and the environment. Some of these effects are described below.

Releasing Greenhouse Gases All fossil fuels contain carbon. When fossil fuels burn, they release carbon dioxide into the atmosphere. As you have learned, carbon dioxide is a greenhouse gas. Carbon dioxide produced by the combustion of fossil fuels warms the atmosphere and drives changes in global climate. Because of its role in global climate change, carbon dioxide pollution is becoming recognized as the greatest environmental impact of fossil fuel use.

Air Pollution The burning of coal and oil releases sulfur dioxide and nitrogen oxides, which contribute to industrial and photochemical smog and cause acid deposition. However, catalytic converters have cut down the release of pollutants by motor vehicles. To reduce pollution by power plants, the U.S. government and industries are working to develop a coal-fired power plant that does not release pollutants.

Water Pollution Fossil fuels pollute water as well as air. For example, some oil from nonpoint sources, such as industries, homes, and cars, runs off from its sources. This oil in runoff can contaminate water in or on the ground. Eventually, this runoff oil enters rivers and streams. From there, the oil may be carried to the ocean. Huge oil spills from ships and platforms also can severely damage marine environments. This was the case with the *Exxon Valdez* spill in 1989. Oil from Alaska's North Slope had been piped to the port of Valdez and loaded onto the ship. Leaving the port, the ship grounded, causing a huge oil spill. The spilled oil caused massive long-term environmental damage to Alaska's Prince William Sound. Twenty-one years later, the *Deepwater Horizon*, an offshore drilling rig, exploded in the Gulf of Mexico. The resulting oil spill will likely be more devastating than the *Valdez* spill.

Effects on Health Numerous health risks are associated with fossil fuels. Mercury, for example, which is present in coal in trace amounts, is released from coal-fired power plants. Mercury can damage the central nervous system and the kidneys, and can cause severe nausea. Motor vehicles release pollutants that irritate the nose, throat, and lungs. Gases such as hydrogen sulfide can evaporate from certain kinds of crude oil and irritate the eyes and throat. Crude oil also often contains trace amounts of poisons such as lead and arsenic.

✔ **Reading Checkpoint**

How do fossil fuels affect water?

FIGURE 14 The *Exxon Valdez* and **Deepwater Horizon Oil Spills** **(a)** Two days after the Exxon Valdez spill began, a smaller tanker tries to offload oil from the ship to prevent more oil from spilling into Prince William Sound. **(b)** A man becomes covered with oil while helping to clean a beach in Alaska. **(c)** An explosion destroys the Deepwater Horizon oil rig, killing 11 workers and allowing oil to spurt directly from the sea floor into the Gulf of Mexico. **(d)** Workers clean a brown pelican at the Fort Jackson Wildlife Rehabilitation Center in Louisiana.

(a)

(d)

(c)

Prince William Sound, 1989

(b)

Gulf of Mexico, 2010

Damage Caused by Extracting Fuels

In most cases, it isn't easy to remove fossil fuels from the ground. Tunnels often must be dug, and holes must be drilled. Expensive technology is needed, energy is required, and the process takes a long time. Jobs in mining and oil operations can be dangerous. And damage to the environment can result from the extraction of fossil fuels.

Dangers of Mining Underground coal mining today is one of our society's most dangerous occupations. As the Quecreek accident and other mining accidents show, miners risk injury or death from collapsing shafts and tunnels. In addition, miners risk their health by inhaling coal dust, which can lead to respiratory diseases, including black lung disease.

Strip Mining and the Environment Strip mining can destroy large areas of habitat and cause extensive soil erosion. **Acid drainage** occurs when sulfide minerals in exposed rock surfaces react with oxygen and rainwater to produce sulfuric acid. As the acid runs off, it removes metals from the rocks, and both the acid and metals enter groundwater and water bodies. In high concentrations, many of these metals are toxic to living things. Acid drainage occurs through natural processes as well as mining. However, it speeds up when mining exposes many new rock surfaces at once. Regulations in the United States require mining companies to restore land that has been strip mined. However, the effects are still severe and last a long time.

Mountaintop removal can have an even greater impact than ordinary strip mining. Tons of rock and soil are removed from the top of a mountain. This material may accidentally slide downhill, or it may be deliberately dumped downhill in order to dispose of it. The rock and soil may destroy land habitats and clog waterways.

 Describe the effects of acid drainage.

FIGURE 15 Mountaintop Removal
Part of the summit of this mountain in West Virginia has been blasted away to get to a coal deposit.

FIGURE 16 **Oil Technology in the Tundra** A caribou wanders across a field near buildings used in the oil industry near Prudhoe Bay in Alaska.

Damage From Oil and Gas Extraction Developing an oil or gas field involves much more than drilling. For example, roads must be built, and housing for workers must be constructed. Workers build pipelines to carry the fuel. These activities may harm plants and animals.

▶ *Prudhoe Bay* Tundra vegetation at Prudhoe Bay still has not fully recovered from temporary roads that have not been used in 30 years. Experts do not agree on whether the region's caribou have been harmed. Surveys show that the caribou population has increased since Prudhoe Bay was developed. Other studies, however, show that female caribou and their calves avoid all parts of the Prudhoe Bay oil complex.

▶ *Possible Impact on the Arctic Refuge* To predict the ecological effects of drilling in the Arctic National Wildlife Refuge, scientists have examined the effects in similar environments in Alaska. In addition, they have conducted some experiments to determine what might happen. Based on these studies, many scientists predict that wildlife and plants will be damaged. Oil spills can harm plants, and sometimes plants may be buried under gravel pits or roads. Roads can break up habitats. Other scientists, however, think that drilling in the Arctic Refuge will not affect the environment that much. For example, they point out that most drilling would take place in the winter, when caribou are not in the area. They also note that the technology has improved in the time since the Prudhoe Bay oil fields were developed, and claim that development of the Arctic Refuge would be more sensitive to the environment.

KEY
**Proven reserves
at end of 2008**
(thousand million barrels)

- Asia Pacific 42.0
- North America 70.9
- South America
  and Central America 123.2
- Africa 125.6
- Europe and Eurasia 142.2
- Middle East 754.1
- —— National border

Data from British Petroleum. *Statistical Review of World Energy 2009.*

FIGURE 17 World Oil Distribution
The map shows the approximate oil reserves, in thousand million barrels, in different regions of the world.

Map it

Imports and Exports

Study the map in **Figure 17** and answer the questions.

1. **Interpret Maps** Which region of the world has the least oil? Approximately how much oil can be found in this part of the world?

2. **Interpret Maps** How do the oil reserves in North America compare to those in the rest of the world?

3. **Infer** Which part of the world probably exports the most oil to other areas?

Dependence on Foreign Sources

Fossil fuels are not evenly distributed worldwide, as shown in **Figure 17.** Some nations have more deposits of a fossil fuel than others. The United States, for example, has extensive coal resources. However, Middle Eastern nations such as Saudi Arabia and Iran have far more crude oil reserves than does the United States. Almost all our modern technology and services depend in some way on fossil fuels. This means that a nation can suffer when its supplies become unavailable or very costly.

Disadvantages of Foreign Dependence Nations that lack adequate fossil fuels are especially at risk. For instance, Germany, France, South Korea, and Japan consume far more energy than they produce. Therefore, nations such as these rely almost entirely on fuel imports for their economic well-being. In recent years, the United States has relied more and more on foreign energy. Today the United States imports two thirds of its crude oil. Such reliance means that seller nations can control energy prices. They can force buyer nations to pay more and more as supplies of fossil fuels decrease.

Reducing Dependence on Foreign Oil The United States government has enacted policies to reduce dependence on oil from some foreign nations. One policy calls for developing additional resources within the United States, such as some of those in Alaska.

In addition, the United States has diversified its sources of petroleum. It now receives much of its petroleum from nations other than those in the Middle East. For example, we now import a lot of oil from Canada, Mexico, Venezuela, and Nigeria. Another way to reduce dependence on foreign oil is to develop renewable energy sources, such as solar and wind power. You will learn more about renewable energy in the next chapter.

Energy Conservation

We want supplies of fossil fuels to last as long as possible, and one way to accomplish that is to reduce our use of them. In addition, if we are less dependent on fossil fuels, we can prevent some of the environmental damage they do. Energy conservation is the practice of reducing energy use to meet those goals.

Conservation and Transportation Transportation accounts for two thirds of oil use in the United States. One way to conserve energy is to design and sell motor vehicles that use less gasoline. In addition, if taxes on gasoline were increased, gasoline would become more expensive, and people would then have a powerful reason to conserve gasoline. Drivers in many European nations pay much higher gasoline taxes than do drivers in the United States.

Many critics of oil drilling in the Arctic National Wildlife Refuge point out that our cars and trucks waste huge amounts of oil. They argue that a small amount of conservation would save the nation far more oil than it could obtain from the oil deposits in the Arctic Refuge.

Personal Choices Individual people can make choices that save energy. In addition to driving less, we can take other actions. For example, we can turn lights off in rooms that aren't being used. By turning down thermostats, we can reduce the energy needed to heat homes. We can buy appliances that conserve energy. All these actions save people money and reduce fossil fuel use.

FIGURE 18 Gas Guzzlers Huge recreational vehicles use a lot of gas, increasing our need for oil.

LESSON 3 Assessment

1. **Explain** Describe how oil in runoff from a city street might eventually reach the ocean.

2. **Infer** U.S. government regulations require companies to restore land after strip mining. In spite of these regulations, why does strip mining still have a severe impact on the environment?

3. **Relate Cause and Effect** Why can it be a disadvantage for a nation to depend on foreign oil?

4. **Apply Concepts** What effect might an increase in gasoline taxes have on the way people get to work? Explain your answer.

5. **THINK IT THROUGH** You have been elected United States Senator from Alaska. The other senator from Alaska has just proposed a law that would open the Arctic National Wildlife Refuge to oil drilling. Would you vote in favor of this law? Why or why not?

Nuclear Power

EVERYDAY PHENOMENON What are the advantages and disadvantages of nuclear energy?

Knowledge and Skills

- Relate nuclear fission to the production of energy.
- Describe how a nuclear power plant generates electricity.
- Identify the advantages and disadvantages of nuclear power.
- Contrast nuclear fusion with nuclear fission, and explain the issues related to nuclear fusion.

Reading Strategy and Vocabulary

✔ **Reading Strategy** As you read about the process of generating electricity with nuclear power, construct a flowchart to show what happens in a nuclear power plant. Use the flowchart to help answer **Question 2** at the end of the lesson.

Vocabulary nuclear energy, nuclear fission, nuclear reactor, meltdown, nuclear waste, nuclear fusion

IN THE DEBATE over energy, nuclear power occupies an odd position. It doesn't pollute the air, so some people think it is an environmentally friendly alternative to fossil fuels. Yet nuclear power's great promise has been clouded. People worry about radioactive waste disposal and nuclear power plant accidents. Concerns for public safety have limited the development of this energy source.

Of all nations, the United States generates the most electricity from nuclear power. However, only 20 percent of United States electricity comes from nuclear power. A number of other nations rely more heavily on nuclear power. France leads the list, receiving 78 percent of its energy from nuclear power.

FIGURE 19 Light Up the Night The Eiffel Tower in Paris is illuminated with nuclear power.

Nuclear Energy

Matter is made up of tiny particles called atoms. The center of an atom is called the nucleus. The nucleus is composed of tiny particles called protons and neutrons. **Nuclear energy** is the energy that holds these particles together in the nucleus. We use this energy by converting it to thermal energy, which can then be used to generate electricity.

The reaction that drives the release of nuclear energy in power plants is nuclear fission. **Nuclear fission** is the splitting of an atom's nucleus into two smaller nuclei.

Bombardment by Neutrons To produce nuclear fission, the nuclei of large, unstable atoms, such as uranium or plutonium, are bombarded with neutrons. When a neutron smashes into the large atom's nucleus, the large nucleus breaks apart into smaller nuclei. The breakup of the large nucleus releases energy in the form of heat and radiation. In addition, as it breaks up, the large nucleus emits neutrons. **Figure 20** shows a nuclear fission reaction. An atom of one form of uranium called uranium-235 (U-235) is broken apart. The smaller nuclei produced by this reaction are nuclei of krypton and barium.

Nuclear Chain Reaction The neutrons emitted from the broken-apart nucleus can then go on to split other atomic nuclei. In **Figure 20,** for example, the three neutrons can go on to split other U-235 nuclei that are nearby. Each time a nucleus is split, the process releases more energy and more neutrons. If there are enough uranium atoms nearby, the repeated release of neutrons can cause a chain reaction. With each step in the chain, the amount of energy increases. If a chain reaction is not controlled, a huge explosion happens. The explosion of a nuclear bomb is the result of an uncontrolled fission chain reaction.

FIGURE 20 Nuclear Fission In the process of nuclear fission, the nucleus of a large atom splits into the nuclei of smaller atoms. The reaction releases a great deal of energy.

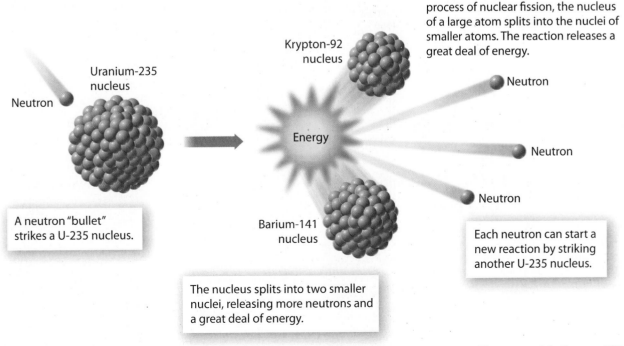

Neutron

Uranium-235 nucleus

Krypton-92 nucleus

Energy

Neutron

Neutron

Neutron

Barium-141 nucleus

A neutron "bullet" strikes a U-235 nucleus.

The nucleus splits into two smaller nuclei, releasing more neutrons and a great deal of energy.

Each neutron can start a new reaction by striking another U-235 nucleus.

Generating Electricity

A nuclear power plant contains a **nuclear reactor,** which generates electricity by controlled fission reactions. Uranium-235 is used as fuel. Because the supply of U-235 is limited, nuclear power is a nonrenewable energy resource. **Figure 21** shows how a nuclear reactor works.

❶ *Nuclear Fission Takes Place* The reactor contains fuel rods, which are made of U-235. Neutrons released by U-235 begin fission reactions. The fission reactions generate heat, which is transferred to the water that surrounds the rods. The water is kept under pressure, so it cannot boil.

If the reactions produce too much heat, control rods are inserted between the fuel rods. The control rods absorb neutrons and therefore slow down the chain reaction.

❷ *Steam Is Produced* The super-heated water passes through a pipe (primary loop) into the steam generator. In the steam generator, heat from the pipe boils the surrounding liquid water, changing it to steam. The steam flows through the secondary-loop pipe to the turbine.

❸ *Electricity Is Generated* The steam makes the turbine rotate. The rotating turbine makes the generator move, producing electricity.

❹ *Water Is Cooled* From the turbine, steam flows into the condenser, where it is cooled by water from the cooling tower. The cooling changes the steam to liquid water. This water is piped back into the reactor.

FIGURE 21 Nuclear Power Plant
A nuclear power plant uses fission reactions to produce the energy necessary for generating electricity.

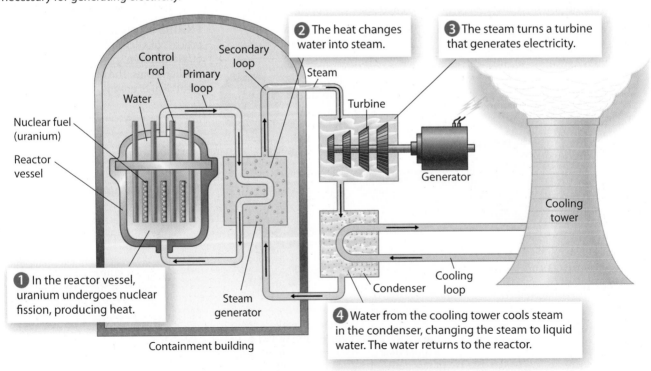

❷ The heat changes water into steam.

❸ The steam turns a turbine that generates electricity.

❶ In the reactor vessel, uranium undergoes nuclear fission, producing heat.

❹ Water from the cooling tower cools steam in the condenser, changing the steam to liquid water. The water returns to the reactor.

Containment building

Benefits and Costs of Nuclear Power

When nuclear power was first developed and used in the 1950s, many people thought it would be a safe, nonpolluting source of energy. But today, people are concerned about the possibility of accidents in nuclear power plants. In addition, there is no really good way of disposing of leftover nuclear material.

Benefits of Nuclear Power Nuclear power plants generate electricity without producing air pollution. In contrast, the combustion of fossil fuels releases pollutants such as carbon dioxide, nitrous oxides, sulfur dioxide, and particulate matter. Scientists from the International Atomic Energy Agency (IAEA) estimate that nuclear power reduces carbon emissions worldwide each year by 600 million metric tons. That amount is equal to 8 percent of worldwide greenhouse gas emissions.

Small amounts of uranium can produce far more energy than the same amount of coal. Therefore, to produce the same amount of energy, less uranium than coal needs to be mined. Under normal conditions, nuclear power plants are safer for workers than coal-fired plants are.

 Reading Checkpoint *Identify three benefits of nuclear power.*

Costs of Nuclear Power Nuclear power also has its costs. For example, nuclear power plants are very expensive to build and maintain. In addition, people fear the possibility of nuclear accidents. Another problem is the disposal of the waste materials left over after nuclear energy has been produced.

▶ *Accidents at Power Plants* On March 11, 2011, a large nuclear accident occurred at the Fukushima Daiichi nuclear power plant in Japan. A powerful earthquake and its resulting tsunami caused the cooling systems at Fukushima to fail. The fuel rods produced so much heat that they melted, a condition known as a **meltdown.** High amounts of radiation were released over the next several days. The Japanese government evacuated more than 100,000 people within 20 km of the plant. Japanese officials and plant employees worked for months to contain the radiation and safely shut down the plant. In December 2011, the plant was shut down and, fortunately, no deaths from radiation exposure have been recorded.

In 1986, there was an accident at the Chernobyl plant in the Ukraine, which was then a part of the Soviet Union. Human mistakes, combined with unsafe reactor design, led to the disaster. Part of the power plant exploded, and clouds of dust rose into the air. The dust included material that was radioactive. The accident killed 31 people directly. Thousands of other people developed cancer and other illnesses caused by radiation.

FIGURE 22 Fukushima The earthquake and tsunami in March 2011 caused damage to both the nuclear power plant and the surrounding buildings as shown in this photograph.

▶ **Temporary Storage of Nuclear Waste** Nuclear power plants produce **nuclear waste,** which is radioactive material left over from the production of energy and other processes. This material will continue to release radiation for thousands of years. Currently, nuclear waste from power generation is being held at nuclear power plants all over the world. Used fuel rods are sunk in deep pools of cooling water to prevent radiation from leaking out. This storage, however, is only a temporary solution.

▶ **Long-Term Disposal** The United States government is trying to solve the problem of nuclear waste. When wastes are stored at many locations throughout the nation, each of those places is a potential nuclear hazard. Therefore, it would be better to keep all the waste in one safe site. After extensive study by scientists and policy makers, in the 1980s Congress chose a possible location for disposing the nuclear waste—Yucca Mountain, a remote place in the Nevada desert. Yucca Mountain was chosen for many reasons—its location is far from where people live, and it can be protected from sabotage. Also, there is little rainfall or risk of earthquakes. Because the water table is very deep, water is unlikely to become contaminated with radioactivity.

However, some scientists and people who live in Nevada have protested that Yucca Mountain isn't a good place to store hazardous waste. They have argued that the site isn't as geologically stable as has been claimed. They are concerned that earthquakes and volcanoes could open underground cracks, and that waste could leak from the cracks. As yet, the United States has no central place for disposing of radioactive waste from nuclear power plants. Therefore, for now, the nuclear waste will remain stored at numerous locations across the nation.

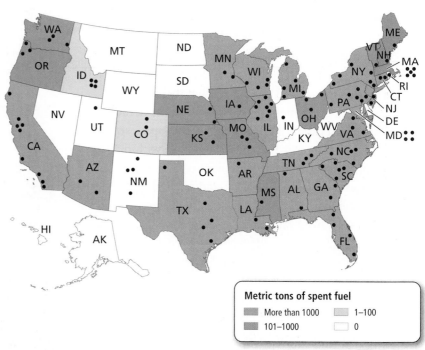

FIGURE 23 Nuclear Waste Sites
The dots on the map show where radioactive wastes are stored in the United States. (Note that some of the sites store radioactive wastes that are not spent nuclear fuel.)

Metric tons of spent fuel

More than 1000	1–100
101–1000	0

Data from Office of Civilian Radioactive Waste Management, U.S. Department of Energy; and Nuclear Energy Institute, Washington, D.C.

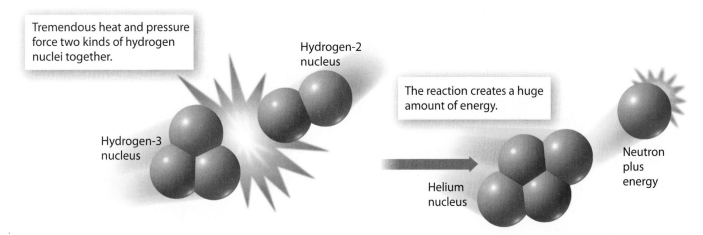

Tremendous heat and pressure force two kinds of hydrogen nuclei together.

Hydrogen-2 nucleus

Hydrogen-3 nucleus

The reaction creates a huge amount of energy.

Helium nucleus

Neutron plus energy

FIGURE 24 **Nuclear Fusion** In nuclear fusion, two hydrogen nuclei are forced together. This reaction, which releases energy and a neutron, forms a nucleus of helium.

Nuclear Fusion: The Future?

Nuclear fusion reactions generate the energy released by the sun. In nuclear fission, an atomic nucleus is split apart. The opposite happens in **nuclear fusion**—small nuclei of lightweight elements are forced together to form a heavier nucleus. **Figure 24** shows a fusion reaction in which two hydrogen atoms with different numbers of neutrons are fused together to form helium. This fusion reaction releases a neutron and huge amounts of energy.

Nuclear fusion could produce much more energy per amount of fuel than nuclear fission can. However, fusion reactions require a temperature of many millions of degrees Celsius. This extremely high temperature and other requirements have made it impossible to use fusion to generate electric power. Despite much research, fusion reactions in the lab still require more energy than they produce.

Fusion's possible payoffs, however, make scientists keep trying. Theoretically, in a controlled fusion reactor, water could serve as a fuel to produce vast amounts of energy. The process would create only small amounts of radioactive waste. It would not pollute the air. However, power from nuclear fusion is probably a long way off.

LESSON ④ Assessment

1. **Apply Concepts** What is a nuclear chain reaction?
2. **Sequence** List the steps involved in using nuclear fission to generate electricity. Begin with the role of the fuel rods.
3. **Infer** Why is the disposal of nuclear waste a greater problem than the disposal of the trash that you and your family need to get rid of?

4. **Compare and Contrast** Compare and contrast nuclear fusion and nuclear fission. How are they similar? How are they different?

   REVISIT
5. **INVESTIGATIVE** PHENOMENON Which do you think has more advantages: electricity generated by nuclear power or electricity generated by coal? Support your opinion with specific details.

Using Coal to Generate ELECTRICITY

Coal generates more than half of the electricity used in the United States. But how is coal converted into electricity? Coal power is cheap and abundant, but it has a big environmental cost. When coal is burned, it creates ash and smoke containing pollution particles and toxic metals. The smoke is released from smokestacks, while the ash is sent to a toxic waste disposal site.

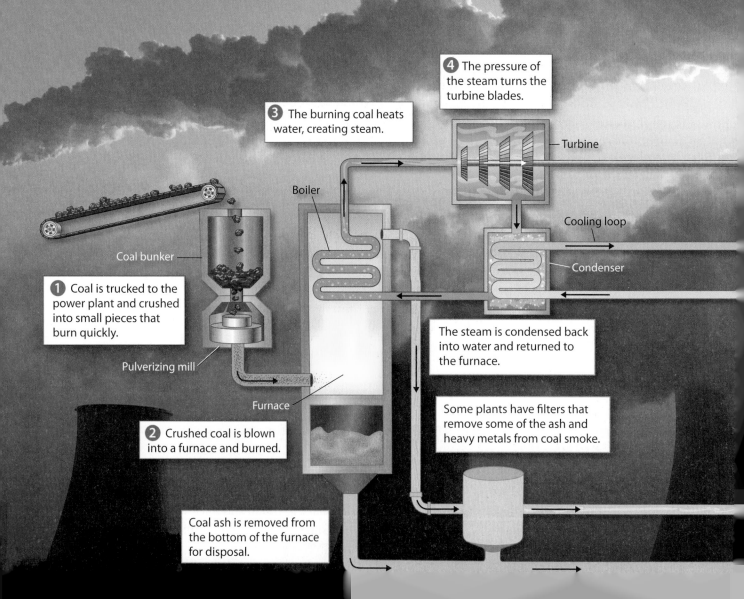

4 The pressure of the steam turns the turbine blades.

3 The burning coal heats water, creating steam.

Turbine

Boiler

Cooling loop

Coal bunker

Condenser

1 Coal is trucked to the power plant and crushed into small pieces that burn quickly.

Pulverizing mill

The steam is condensed back into water and returned to the furnace.

Furnace

Some plants have filters that remove some of the ash and heavy metals from coal smoke.

2 Crushed coal is blown into a furnace and burned.

Coal ash is removed from the bottom of the furnace for disposal.

After coal is mined, it is shipped by train to power plants across the nation.

5 The turbine makes magnets inside a generator spin near stationary copper coils, which generates electricity.

Generator

6 Power lines deliver electricity to homes and businesses.

Cooling tower

Smoke is released from smokestacks.

Stack

Ash disposal

Toxic ash is taken to a hazardous waste disposal site.

21st Century Skills **Media Literacy** A small number of power plants have adopted "clean coal" technology, using scrubbers and chemical reactions to remove more of the toxins from coal smoke. However, some environmental groups say there is no such thing as "clean coal." Use the Internet to find three news articles on clean coal. List both the benefits and costs of the technology. Based on what you read, do you think clean coal is really "clean"? Why or why not?

INVESTIGATIVE PHENOMENON

What effect does the use of nonrenewable energy resources have on the environment?

Lesson 1
What is energy and how is it used?

Lesson 2
How did fossil fuels form, and how are they obtained and used?

Lesson 3
What problems are associated with fossil fuel use?

Lesson 4
What are the advantages and disadvantages of nuclear energy?

LESSON 1 Energy: An Overview

- Energy, which is the ability to do work, can be classified as kinetic or potential.
- Forms of energy include mechanical energy, electrical energy, thermal energy, electromagnetic energy, chemical energy, and nuclear energy.
- Human society uses renewable and nonrenewable energy resources in industry, transportation, commerce, and residences.

energy (517)
kinetic energy (517)
potential energy (517)
combustion (519)
energy efficiency (520)
renewable energy (520)
nonrenewable energy (520)
electricity (520)

LESSON 2 Fossil Fuels

- Fossil fuels form from the remains of organisms that lived millions of years ago.
- Coal, which is used mainly to generate electricity, is obtained by mining.
- Petroleum, which is obtained by drilling, is a major source of energy and is used to make a variety of products.
- Natural gas yields a large amount of energy and is less polluting than other fuels.
- The supply of fossil fuels is limited.

strip mining (524)
subsurface mining (524)
petroleum (525)
petrochemical (525)
oil sands (528)
oil shale (528)
methane hydrate (528)

LESSON 3 Consequences of Fossil Fuel Use

- The burning of fossil fuels causes pollution that affects health and the environment.
- Mining and drilling for fuels can endanger people and change ecosystems in harmful ways.
- Since fossil fuels are unevenly distributed in the world, many nations need to depend on foreign sources.
- To save fossil fuels and limit the damage they cause, we need to conserve energy.

acid drainage (532)   energy conservation (535)

LESSON 4 Nuclear Power

- The process of nuclear fission releases energy.
- In a nuclear power plant, nuclear fission is used to generate electricity.
- Nuclear power does not cause air pollution, but its problems include risk of accidents and disposal of wastes.
- Nuclear fusion has advantages over fission, but the technology does not yet exist to use fusion to generate power.

nuclear energy (537)   meltdown (539)
nuclear fission (537)   nuclear waste (540)
nuclear reactor (538)   nuclear fusion (541)

 GO ONLINE

INQUIRY LABS AND ACTIVITIES

- **Home Energy Use**
  Graph your monthly energy use and follow U.S. Department of Energy recommendations for lowering your household consumption.

- **Fossil Fuel Use**
  Will oil supplies soon peak and then decline? Form your own conclusions from a variety of data.

- **Identifying Insulators**
  Which insulation materials conserve heat? Test a variety—from rubber to steel wool. See how each affects heat loss.

Chapter Assessment

Defend Your Case

The Central Case in this chapter explored the issue of whether or not Alaska's Arctic National Wildlife Refuge should be developed to obtain oil. Based on what you have learned, develop two lists—Benefits and Costs. The Benefits list should identify the advantages of drilling for oil. The Costs list should identify the disadvantages. Be sure to include information you have learned about the benefits and costs of using oil as a fuel. Then, as a class, discuss the benefits and costs of drilling for oil in the Arctic National Wildlife Refuge.

Review Concepts and Terms

1. Energy is defined as the ability to
   a. burn fuel.
   b. lift heavy objects off the floor.
   c. do work or make a change.
   d. cook food over a campfire.

2. Which of the following exhibits kinetic energy?
   a. a ball rolling down a ramp
   b. the bonds that hold food molecules together
   c. a bike rider waiting for a red light to turn green
   d. a compressed spring

3. Chemical energy is stored in a match tip. In the photo, what has this chemical energy been converted into?

   a. electrical and mechanical energy
   b. thermal and electromagnetic energy
   c. electromagnetic and nuclear energy
   d. only electromagnetic energy

4. The world's most abundant fossil fuel is
   a. coal.   c. oil.
   b. natural gas.   d. uranium.

5. The Middle East is especially rich in deposits of
   a. coal.   c. methane hydrate.
   b. oil.   d. uranium-235.

6. Rock filled with a mixture of hydrocarbons is called
   a. methane hydrate.   c. oil sands.
   b. petrochemicals.   d. oil shale.

7. Which of the following is NOT caused by the burning of fossil fuels?
   a. air pollution
   b. water pollution
   c. release of carbon dioxide
   d. a meltdown

8. Chemical compounds derived from oil are called
   a. petrochemicals.
   b. fossil fuels.
   c. renewable energy resources.
   d. secondary energy resources.

9. In a nuclear power plant, which process is used to generate electricity?
   a. the burning of coal
   b. the burning of natural gas
   c. nuclear fission
   d. nuclear fusion

Modified True/False

Write true *if the statement is true. If it is false, change the underlined word or words to make the statement true.*

10. Mechanical energy is associated with the forces that hold particles together in an atom's nucleus.

11. Electricity is a primary source of energy.

12. Fossil fuels form in an environment with little or no oxygen.

13. Coal is used to generate about half the electricity in the United States.

14. In strip mining, miners dig shafts deep underground to reach the fossil fuel deposit.

15. When sulfide in rock surfaces reacts with oxygen and rainwater, acid drainage occurs.

Reading Comprehension

Read the following selection and answer the questions that follow.

In 1979, an accident happened at the Three Mile Island nuclear power plant in Pennsylvania. Through a combination of mechanical failure and human error, cooling water drained from the reactor vessel, temperatures rose inside the reactor core, and metal surrounding the uranium fuel rods began to melt, releasing radiation. This partial meltdown proceeded through half of one reactor core.

Area residents stood ready to be evacuated. Fortunately, however, most radiation remained trapped inside the building that contained the nuclear reactor. The accident was brought under control within days. The damaged reactor was shut down. It took years, and about a billion dollars, to clean up the damage.

16. Which of the following best describes the sequence of events at Three Mile Island?
   a. partial meltdown, followed by loss of cooling water, followed by rising temperatures in the reactor core
   b. partial meltdown, followed by the release of radiation, followed by an explosion
   c. partial meltdown, followed by cleanup, followed by rising temperatures in the reactor core
   d. loss of cooling water, followed by rising temperatures in the reactor core, followed by partial meltdown

17. People were not evacuated because
   a. the cleanup had begun.
   b. most of the radiation did not leak out.
   c. the evacuation would have cost billions of dollars.
   d. only one reactor was affected.

18. Which of the following was NOT involved in the accident at Three Mile Island?
   a. an explosion
   b. reactor damage
   c. nuclear fission
   d. mistakes by people

Short Answer

19. What is thermal energy?

20. What is combustion? What is the equation for the combustion of methane?

21. What are the advantages of coal as a source of energy?

22. Over the next few decades, what is likely to happen to the world's production of oil?

23. Identify at least three ways in which fossil fuels can damage human health.

24. What is mountaintop removal?

25. Identify two reasons why energy conservation is important to practice.

26. Describe what happens during nuclear fission.

Critical Thinking

27. **Apply Concepts** Look at the photo below. When water reaches the top of the waterfall, does it have kinetic energy, potential energy, or both? Explain your answer.

28. **Apply Concepts** When you turn an electric burner on, what happens to the electrical energy?

29. **Compare and Contrast** Compare and contrast the conditions under which coal and oil form. How are they similar? How are they different?

30. **Relate Cause and Effect** Why is the use of natural gas increasing?

31. **Apply Concepts** Under what circumstances must oil drillers switch from primary extraction to secondary extraction?

32. **Pose Questions** An energy expert has come to your house or apartment to evaluate how well your home is constructed to conserve energy. What are two questions you would ask the expert?

Analyze Data

Nuclear fuel rods are usually made of uranium oxide. The United States produces some fuel rods from uranium oxide mined in the United States. It also imports uranium oxide from other nations. Finally, the United States exports some uranium oxide. The graph shows the production and trade of uranium oxide from 1949 to 2010.

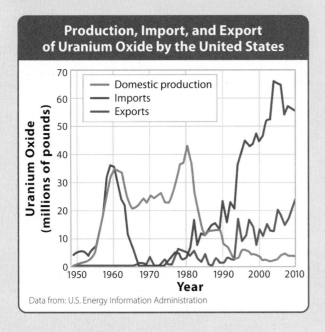

Production, Import, and Export of Uranium Oxide by the United States

— Domestic production
— Imports
— Exports

Data from: U.S. Energy Information Administration

33. **Interpret Graphs** About how much uranium oxide did the United States import in 2000? About how much did it export?

34. **Interpret Data** In 2010, how does the amount of uranium oxide produced in the United States compare to the amount imported?

35. **Interpret Data** Describe the trend in uranium oxide production since 1950.

36. **Infer** How do the amounts of uranium oxide imported in 1950 and 2010 compare? Why do you think this has happened?

Write About It

37. **Explanation** Explain why electricity is considered a secondary source of energy.

38. **Creative Writing** A film company is going to make an animated film showing how coal forms. Your job is to create storyboards and text that can provide information for the animator. Sketch three or four storyboards that show the process of coal formation, and write an explanatory caption for each storyboard.

39. **REVISIT** **INVESTIGATIVE** PHENOMENON Choose one fossil fuel. Draw a concept map showing the costs and benefits of this form of energy.

Ecological Footprints

Read the information below. Copy the table into your notebook and record your calculations. Then answer the questions that follow.

Each person in the United States and Canada uses about 3 gallons of oil every day. Calculate the amount of oil, in gallons, that you probably use during a year. Then calculate the daily and yearly use for your class, your hometown, your state, and the United States.

1. In other developed nations, the average person uses about 1.4 gallons of oil per day. What do you think accounts for the difference between other developed nations and the United States and Canada?

2. The average person in a developing nation uses about 0.2 gallons of oil per day. In a year, about how much more oil do you use than a person in a developing nation?

	Population	Gallons of Oil Per Day	Gallons of Oil Per Year
You (or the average American)	1	3	
Your class			
Your hometown			
Your state			
United States			

Data from Energy Information Administration, Official Energy Statistics from the U.S. Government.

3. In your opinion, who has more responsibility for limiting consumption of fossil fuels—people in developed nations or people in developing nations? Justify your opinion.

Renewable Energy Alternatives

An offshore wind farm in Germany

Lesson 1
Biomass and
Geothermal Energy

Lesson 2
Hydropower and
Ocean Energy

Lesson 3
Solar and Wind
Energy

Lesson 4
Energy From
Hydrogen

Germany's Big Bet on Renewable Energy

GERMANY, a nation of over 83 million people, uses vast amounts of energy. Germans are betting on renewable sources of energy—wind, water, sunlight, and plant material—to supply their energy needs and cut down on greenhouse gas emissions. In 2000, Germany passed the Renewable Energy Law, which specified that the nation must obtain a minimum of 10 percent of its energy from renewable energy sources by 2020.

The law has had a wide impact and has been revised several times in recent years. It has meant that Germany must burn less coal, despite the nation's plentiful coal deposits. In addition, Germany is shutting down its nuclear power plants, even though they emit no greenhouse gases and once produced one quarter of the nation's electricity.

Germany's policy has increased renewable energy and reduced greenhouse gas emissions. In 2018, about 38 percent of Germany's electricity came from renewable sources. That switch to renewable energy reduced emissions of greenhouse gases by 385 million metric tons, about 30.8 percent lower than 1990 levels. And Germany's economy has benefited. Renewable-energy industries have annual sales worth billions of dollars and provide jobs for hundreds of thousands of people.

In spite of its successes, however, Germany's policy has disadvantages. For example, energy prices have increased somewhat. Germans pay among the highest price for power in Europe. And there have been environmental costs. Most of Germany's renewable energy comes from wind turbines. Wind turbines are altering the landscape. They may be harming populations of birds and bats and causing other kinds of ecological damage.

Germany is not the only nation that is trying to reduce their reliance on fossil fuels and diversify their energy sources. The European Union has set a

GO ONLINE
• Take It Local • 3-D Geo Tour

target for all of its countries for at least 32 percent of total energy use to be from renewable sources. The government of Estonia offers generous subsidies to its citizens that use renewable energy. Latvia relies heavily on hydropower for its electricity. Sweden, a front runner in green energy, reached its 2020 goal of using 50 percent renewable energy by 2012. Its new target is 100 percent renewable energy by 2040.

The United States has also been increasing renewable sources of energy. In many areas of the U.S., customers can choose which energy supplier provides their electricity, including renewable options. Federal tax credits offer incentives to homeowners to use renewable energy, and citizens who have installed solar panels can sell surplus energy to the electric companies. Many states now have renewable energy portfolios. Increasing renewable energy options is critical for the environment and can keep an economy strong. Germany is a nation that has led the way for others, into a future in which people can depend on clean, renewable energy sources.

Biomass and Geothermal Energy

EVERYDAY PHENOMENON How can we use the heat from the Earth to both warm and cool our homes?

Knowledge and Skills

- Explain the benefits and current status of renewable energy resources.
- Define biomass energy and explain how it is used.
- Describe how geothermal energy is harnessed and used.

Reading Strategy and Vocabulary

✓ **Reading Strategy** As you read, make a two-column table. In the left column, write the blue and green lesson headings. In the right column, write notes that summarize the information in the text that follows each heading.

Vocabulary biomass energy, biofuel, biopower, geothermal energy, ground source heat pump

RENEWABLE ENERGY RESOURCES are sometimes called *alternative energy resources*, because they are an alternative to fossil fuels and nuclear energy. Why is it important to provide an alternative? Fossil fuels will not last forever. In addition, their use causes pollution, including greenhouse gas emissions. Nuclear power is a relatively pollution-free alternative to fossil fuels, but it has its own problems, including waste disposal and the possibility of accidents.

The Reasons for Alternative Energy

You are familiar with some kinds of renewable energy. When you see a sailboat gliding across a bay, you are observing wind energy in action. Since ancient times, people have harnessed wind and moving water to do work. Hundreds of years ago, in Europe, America, and other parts of the world, windmills and water wheels turned machinery that ground grain into flour. And long before that, people burned wood to cook food and keep warm.

Today wind, water, and wood still provide people with energy. In addition, if you have seen solar panels on roofs, you know that people have found ways to capture energy from the sun. Scientists are looking into new ways of using renewable resources to fill modern energy needs.

Benefits of Renewable Energy Renewable energy resources provide several benefits. For one thing, most of them are unlikely to run out. Also, if renewable energy resources replace fossil fuels, they will help decrease air pollution and greenhouse gas emissions. And if our nation develops renewable energy resources, we will be less dependent on other nations to supply us with fuel. Finally, the development of renewable energy will create jobs for people to design, build, and maintain the needed technology. Maybe you will one day have a career in a renewable-energy industry.

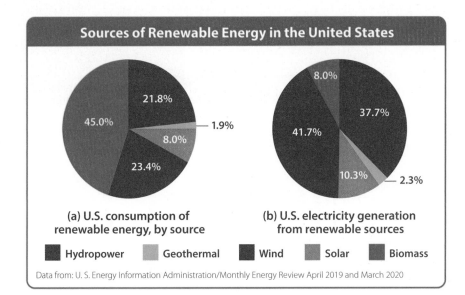

Sources of Renewable Energy in the United States

(a) U.S. consumption of renewable energy, by source

- 21.8%
- 45.0%
- 1.9%
- 8.0%
- 23.4%

(b) U.S. electricity generation from renewable sources

- 8.0%
- 37.7%
- 41.7%
- 10.3%
- 2.3%

■ Hydropower ■ Geothermal ■ Wind ■ Solar ■ Biomass

Data from: U. S. Energy Information Administration/Monthly Energy Review April 2019 and March 2020

◆ **Connect to the Central Case**

FIGURE 1 Renewable Energy in the United States The graphs show **(a)** U.S. consumption of renewable energy and **(b)** U.S. generation of electricity from renewable energy sources. **Compare and Contrast** About 17 percent of the energy in the United States comes from renewable sources. How does this compare with Germany's renewable energy use in 2018?

Renewable Energy Today Today the world is powered mainly by fossil fuels. Oil, coal, and natural gas supply 80 percent of our energy. These three fuels also generate two thirds of the world's electricity. However, use of renewable energy sources is generally growing much faster than use of nonrenewable energy. The leader in growth is solar power, which has averaged 25% growth per year between 2015 and 2020.

Renewable energy will probably keep growing rapidly. That will happen because the world population will keep increasing and—along with it—the need for energy. In addition, reserves of fossil fuels are decreasing. Furthermore, citizens want a cleaner environment. In spite of growth, though, it will take renewable energy sources some time to catch up. At present, even though renewable-energy technology is rapidly improving, renewables cannot yet produce enough power to replace fossil fuels and nuclear energy.

Biomass Energy

Biomass is material that makes up living organisms or comes from organisms. Wood, manure, and grain are all examples of biomass. **Biomass energy** is energy that is produced from this material. Recall that fossil fuels, too, come from living things. However, unlike energy from fossil fuels, biomass energy is renewable.

Using Biomass as an Energy Source There are many ways of using biomass to produce energy. More than 1 billion people still burn wood from trees as their main energy source. In developing nations, families gather wood to burn in their homes for heating, cooking, and lighting. Wood, charcoal, and manure account for 35 percent of energy use in developing nations. In the poorest nations, these forms of biomass supply up to 90 percent of energy. Industrialized nations are developing new ways to use biomass as a source of energy. Biomass energy can now power motor vehicles and generate electricity.

FIGURE 2 Biomass for Fuel Women in Mozambique, Africa, collect wood to use as fuel.

Biodiesel

The graph shows the percentage reductions in several major automotive pollutants when two kinds of diesel fuel are burned. One kind, B20, is a mixture that consists of 20 percent biodiesel and 80 percent conventional, petroleum-based diesel. The other, B100, is 100 percent biodiesel.

1. **Interpret Graphs** In the graph, what do the percentages refer to? (*Hint:* Look at the label for the vertical axis and think about what both fuels are being compared to.)

2. **Interpret Graphs** If B20 is used, by what percentage are carbon monoxide emissions reduced?

3. **Compare and Contrast** Of the two fuels shown on the graph, which reduces pollution most?

4. **Interpret Graphs** Can you use this graph to determine the actual amount of each pollutant released when the fuels are burned? Explain your answer.

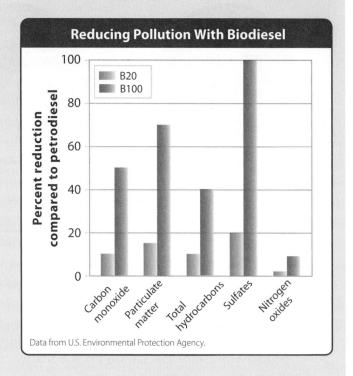

Reducing Pollution With Biodiesel

Data from U.S. Environmental Protection Agency.

FIGURE 3 Electricity From Switchgrass Fast-growing switchgrass, shown here, may one day be a source of biopower.

Biofuels Liquid fuels from biomass sources, known as **biofuels,** are helping to power millions of vehicles on today's roads. The two primary biofuels are *ethanol,* which is used in gasoline engines, and *biodiesel,* which runs diesel engines.

▶ *Ethanol* Ethanol is produced by the fermentation of starches or sugars. The result of this type of fermentation is pure alcohol. Ethanol can be used either by itself or as a supplement to gasoline to power cars. The ethanol that is used as an energy source in the United States is produced mainly from corn. A blend of gasoline and alcohol called *gasohol* is widely used in the United States because it releases smaller amounts of many pollutants, such as carbon monoxide and particulate matter, than does pure gasoline.

▶ *Biodiesel* Biodiesel is produced from vegetable oil, such as soybean oil. Although biodiesel can be used in its pure form, it is usually mixed with conventional petroleum-based diesel fuel. Biodiesel cuts down on emissions compared with conventional diesel fuel.

Biopower Electricity that is generated by the combustion of biomass is called **biopower.** Many of the sources used for biopower are the waste products of existing industries or processes. For instance, the timber industry generates sawdust and other woody debris. Cornstalks, corn husks, and biomass waste from landfills can also be burned to generate electricity. Besides using waste, we also grow crops to produce biopower. These crops include fast-growing trees and grasses, such as the switchgrass in **Figure 3.**

The decomposition of biomass by microorganisms produces gas that can be used to generate electricity. The breakdown of waste in landfills produces methane. This "landfill gas" is being captured at many landfills and sold as fuel. Power plants that burn methane and other kinds of biomass operate similarly to those powered by fossil fuels. The combustion heats water, creating steam to turn turbines that power generators.

Benefits of Biomass Energy Because biomass is a valuable energy resource, the German government has established a research center to explore and promote its use. There are many benefits to biomass energy. For one thing, the carbon produced by the combustion of biomass is the same amount of carbon that was removed from the atmosphere by photosynthesis to make the biomass in the first place. Therefore, the combustion of biomass releases no net carbon into the atmosphere. Biomass energy can also benefit nations economically. Unlike oil and other fossil fuels, biomass is distributed worldwide. Therefore, it should help reduce many nations' dependence on imported fuels.

Costs of Biomass Energy Biomass energy has disadvantages, too. Biofuel crops take up land that might be used for growing food or left in its natural condition. Deforestation, soil erosion, and desertification can result if wood is cut down too rapidly for fuel. In reality, biomass is not renewable if it is used up faster than it is produced. Biomass is not an efficient source of energy, and its use can cause indoor air pollution.

▶ *Inefficiency* Growing corn for ethanol requires a substantial input of energy, partly because farmers use fossil fuels to run farm equipment. Corn ethanol provides only a small amount more energy than the energy needed to produce it. It takes 1 unit of input energy to gain 1.5 units of energy from ethanol.

▶ *Indoor Air Pollution* Indoor air pollution can result if wood and other biomass fuels are burned inside buildings. In developing nations, the burning of biomass indoors is a major threat to health. It increases the risk of respiratory system problems such as lung cancer and infections.

✓ **Reading Checkpoint** *How can biomass energy cause indoor pollution?*

Geothermal Energy

Deep beneath the surface of Earth, high pressure combined with the breakdown of radioactive elements produces heat. This heat is geothermal energy, which heats rocks below Earth's surface, sometimes melting them to form liquid rock called magma. In some places, heated rocks or magma in turn heat underground water. Hot water and steam may spurt from beneath the ground to the surface, as shown in **Figure 4.** Hot springs and geysers are the result of geothermal energy.

your world • your turn •

WHAT DO YOU THINK?

Corn and other crop plants can be used to produce ethanol for fuel. This means that the land on which the crops are grown cannot be used to grow crops that feed people. Do you think that the use of crops and land to produce ethanol is justified? Would you attach any conditions to this use?

FIGURE 4 Geyser Eruptions of geysers such as this one in Yellowstone National Park are the result of geothermal energy.

FIGURE 5 A Geothermal Power Plant In some locations, magma heats groundwater. Steam from that heated groundwater can be used to generate electricity.

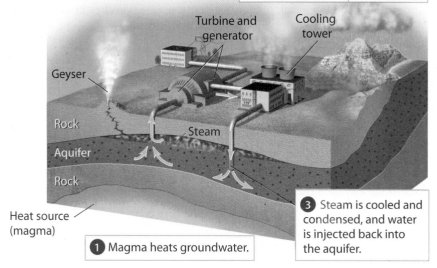

2 Wells tap underground heated water or steam. The water turns turbines and generates power.

Turbine and generator

Cooling tower

Geyser

Rock

Aquifer

Steam

Rock

Heat source (magma)

1 Magma heats groundwater.

3 Steam is cooled and condensed, and water is injected back into the aquifer.

Harnessing Geothermal Energy Geothermal energy can be harnessed to produce electricity in two basic ways. In some cases, steam from geysers at the surface is used to supply energy. Usually, however, wells must be drilled down hundreds or thousands of meters toward heated rocks and water. For example, Germany does not have many locations where magma comes close to the surface. In Germany, therefore, deep drilling is the main method of getting access to geothermal energy.

Generating Electricity Figure 5 shows how geothermal energy can be used to generate electricity. In this illustration, a geothermal power plant taps into steam below ground. The steam turns the blades of a turbine, which makes a generator produce electricity. After being used, the steam is often cooled and condenses into liquid water. The water is then returned to the aquifer from which it came.

Some geothermal power plants actually create the steam that is used to generate electricity. Cold water from the surface is pumped deep underground, where it reaches heated rocks. Heat from the rocks converts the water to steam. The steam then rises to the power plant, where it turns the blades of a turbine.

Using Heat Directly Hot groundwater can be used directly for heating homes, offices, and greenhouses. Hot water is piped from its source into buildings. Therefore, heating with groundwater is practical only where geothermal energy sources are nearby.

Ground Source Heat Pumps Geothermal energy can be used even in areas without heated underground rocks. A **ground source heat pump** takes advantage of the fact that the temperature of soil a few feet underground stays about the same all year, even though the air temperature changes with the seasons. This steady underground temperature is what enables a ground source heat pump to work.

FIGURE 6 Ground Source Heat Pump A ground source heat pump takes advantage of the fact that the temperature of soil far below the ground remains about the same in winter and summer.

Winter
In winter, the soil deep underground is warmer than the air at the surface. Water flowing through the pipe transfers heat from the ground to the house. This warms the house.

Summer
In summer, the soil underground is cooler than the air above the ground. Water in the pipe cools the house by transferring heat from the house to the ground.

In a ground source heat pump, water circulates through underground pipes, as shown in **Figure 6**. In the winter, the water picks up heat from the ground and transfers it to a building. The opposite happens in the summer. Water transfers heat from a building to the ground, cooling the building in the process. More than 600,000 ground source heat pumps are already used to heat homes in the United States.

Benefits and Costs of Geothermal Energy The use of geothermal energy can help replace the use of fossil fuels. Like other renewable sources, geothermal power causes far less air pollution than fossil fuel combustion. And geothermal power releases a much smaller quantity of greenhouse gases than does the burning of fossil fuels.

On the negative side, geothermal sources may not always be truly sustainable. If a geothermal power plant uses heated water more quickly than groundwater is replaced, the plant will eventually run out of water. In addition, the water of many hot springs contains chemicals that damage equipment and add to pollution. Some geothermal energy projects may trigger earthquakes. Moreover, geothermal power plants are generally limited to areas where heated groundwater can be tapped fairly easily. Most of the world's nations, including Germany, have few such areas.

LESSON 1 Assessment

1. **Relate Cause and Effect** Why will the use of renewable energy probably keep increasing?

2. **Explain** What is biomass energy? Give an example.

3. **Sequence** Describe how geothermal energy is used to generate electricity from steam that is produced naturally underground. Include what often happens to steam after it is used to produce electricity.

REVISIT

4. **INVESTIGATIVE** PHENOMENON
Suppose you are a planner who is working for the German government. You and other planners must decide how to use tax money to develop renewable resources. Would you spend tax money on developing sources of geothermal energy? Why or why not?

Hydropower and Ocean Energy

EVERYDAY PHENOMENON How can the movement of water be used to generate electricity?

Knowledge and Skills

- Explain how river water can be used to generate electricity.
- Identify benefits and costs of hydropower.
- Describe how energy from the ocean can generate electricity.

Reading Strategy and Vocabulary

✔️ **Reading Strategy** After you have read the lesson, construct a concept map to show the lesson's ideas and how they are related. Use the blue headings as main topics.

Vocabulary hydropower, tidal energy, ocean thermal energy conversion (OTEC)

IN A SERIES OF RAPIDS upriver from Lowell, Massachusetts, the Merrimack River plunges more than 9 meters (about 30 feet) within about 1.5 kilometers (1 mile). In the 1820s, a few smart manufacturers made use of this drop in water level. They built mills that harnessed the water's energy, using the energy to run looms that wove cotton thread into cloth. Those mills on the Merrimack helped start the Industrial Revolution in the United States.

The manufacturers needed workers to operate the looms. At first, most mill workers were young women from New England villages and farms. Later, immigrants came to Lowell from Europe, lured by the hope of jobs in the mills. All the mill workers, no matter where they came from, were looking for a better way of life. Helped by the power of falling water, many of them would make a new beginning.

Today the water-powered looms are silent. Tourists visit the old mills, which are part of Lowell National Historic Park. But we still use the kinetic energy of moving water as a source of power.

FIGURE 7 Waterfall on the Merrimack Falling water has kinetic energy. During the Industrial Revolution, this energy ran looms that made cloth.

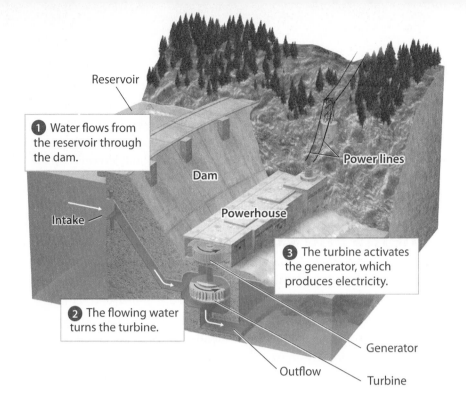

Reservoir

1 Water flows from the reservoir through the dam.

Dam

Intake

Powerhouse

3 The turbine activates the generator, which produces electricity.

2 The flowing water turns the turbine.

Power lines

Generator

Outflow

Turbine

FIGURE 8 Hydropower Dam
In a powerhouse of a hydroelectric dam, the movement of water provides the energy to generate electricity.

Generating Electricity With Hydropower

Next to biomass, we draw more renewable energy from the motion of water than from any other resource. In **hydropower,** or hydroelectric power, we use the kinetic energy of moving water to turn turbines and generate electricity. In the United States, about 6 percent of the electricity we use is generated by hydropower. In Germany, hydropower produces about 3.5 percent of the electricity.

There are two basic approaches to generating electricity from moving water. In the first way a dam blocks a river, and water is stored in a reservoir behind the dam. In the second way, a river is not blocked. Instead, the natural movement of river water is used to produce electricity.

Using Water Stored Behind Dams Figure 8 shows how a hydroelectric dam uses moving water to generate electricity. As the river water passes through the dam, the water turns the blades of turbines. The turbines, in turn, cause generators to produce electricity. After the water has passed through the turbines, it flows back into the river from which it came. Because dams store water in reservoirs, they ensure a steady supply of electricity at all times. Most hydropower is generated by dams.

FIGURE 9 Hydroelectric Dam in Germany
The Jettenbach 2 hydropower station is located on the Inn River.

Using the Natural Flow of a River The second way of producing hydroelectric power also uses flowing water to turn turbines. However, this method, called the run-of-the-river approach, takes advantage of a river's natural flow. Some of the water may be diverted through a pipe, which carries the water to the turbines. This method does not disturb natural habitats as much as the reservoir-storage method. However, in seasons when the river is low, little electricity is generated.

Benefits and Costs of Hydropower

Unlike other renewable energy alternatives, the use of hydropower is unlikely to grow. Most of the rivers that offer the best opportunity for hydropower are already dammed. Like all the ways in which humans produce and use energy, hydropower has both benefits and costs.

Benefits of Hydropower Hydropower is renewable. As long as there are rivers, we can use water to turn turbines. When electricity is generated with hydropower, nothing is burned. Therefore, hydropower is "clean." It does not pollute the atmosphere or release greenhouse gases. Electricity generated by running water is relatively inexpensive. The dams that are built to generate electricity may also control floods. Hydropower is an especially useful source of energy in nations that have a lot of rivers and the money to build dams. Canada, Brazil, Norway, and Venezuela all produce more than half their electricity using hydropower.

Costs of Hydropower Because dams and reservoirs interrupt the natural flow of water, they drastically change ecosystems. For example, the populations of many fishes, such as salmon, have been reduced or eliminated in dammed waterways throughout the world. In addition, the process of dam construction damages the landscape. This damage can cause erosion as well as landslides.

Dams can prevent important sediments and nutrients from getting downstream. Before the Aswan High Dam was constructed in Egypt in the 1960s, the Nile River flooded every year, depositing nutrient-rich mud over a strip of agricultural land. The nutrients in the mud made the soil fertile. Now, the mud is trapped behind the dam, and farmers must use chemical fertilizers to improve the quality of the soil.

FIGURE 10 Monuments Saved From Flooding In the 1960s, the ancient monuments at Abu Simbel were moved to higher ground after the Aswan High Dam was constructed on the Nile River in Egypt. The monuments were threatened by the rising waters of the reservoir behind the dam.

Three Gorges Dam: An Example The Three Gorges Dam on China's Yangtze River, which was completed in 2008, illustrates both the benefits and costs of hydropower. The reservoir is approximately 600 kilometers (370 miles) long—about as long as Lake Superior. This project generates enough hydroelectric power to replace dozens of large coal or nuclear plants. It controls floods and enables boats to travel farther upstream than before.

However, the Three Gorges Dam cost $26 billion to build. The reservoir has flooded many cities and destroyed the homes of 1.3 million people. These people had to move to new homes, often far from the areas where they once lived and worked. In addition, the reservoir has flooded 10,000-year-old archaeological sites. The rising waters have destroyed farmlands and wildlife habitats. Many scientists worry that water pollutants will be trapped in the reservoir, making the water undrinkable.

FIGURE 11 Farmland Under Water • Villagers in China row past a cornfield flooded after the construction of the Three Gorges Dam.

Energy From the Ocean

Twice a day, as ocean tides rise and fall, large amounts of water move upward and then draw back. This daily cycle of tidal motion can be harnessed to generate electricity. And energy that ocean water absorbs from the sun is another potential way to produce electricity.

Tidal Energy The term **tidal energy** refers to using the movement of tidal water to generate electricity. There are different ways to accomplish this. In one method, a dam is built across a bay or tidal river. As the tide rises, water moves through the dam and enters the bay. When the tide falls, water leaves the bay. As the water from the receding tide passes through the dam, it is channeled through a system of turbines. The moving water turns the turbines.

 Reading Checkpoint *Describe how tidal energy can be used to generate electricity.*

 **FIND OUT MORE**

Dams are constructed for many purposes. Find information about dams in your community or state. Learn why the dams were built, how they are maintained, and what, if anything, was done to compensate people whose lives were disrupted by the construction of the dams.

(a) Low tide

(b) High tide

FIGURE 12 Bay of Fundy Because of the large difference between low and high tides, the Bay of Fundy is a good location for harnessing tidal energy.

▶ *Best Locations* Harnessing tidal energy works best in long, narrow bays such as Alaska's Cook Inlet or the Bay of Fundy in Canada. In those places, the differences in height between high and low tides are especially great. Partly because there are few locations with the right characteristics, tidal energy is not yet being used much in the world. Some rivers have tides, and these rivers may be appropriate for generating electricity from tidal energy.

▶ *Costs and Benefits* Tidal electricity stations have the benefit of releasing few or no pollutants. However, the production of tidal energy can harm the ecology of the bay or river. And with the technology we have now, there are few places where tidal energy can be harnessed effectively.

Thermal Energy From the Ocean Each day, ocean water near the equator absorbs radiation from the sun. In fact, the heat content absorbed daily by tropical oceans is equivalent to the heat content of 250 million barrels of oil. If this heat were harnessed to produce electricity, it could, in theory, provide 20,000 times the electricity used in the United States every day.

Ocean thermal energy conversion (OTEC) is a process that converts the thermal energy in ocean water to electrical energy that people can use. The ocean's surface water is warmer than deep water. The temperature decreases gradually with increasing depth. This gradual change in temperature is called a temperature gradient. OTEC methods use this temperature gradient to generate electricity.

In one approach, warm surface water circulates around pipes that contain substances, such as ammonia, that boil at temperatures that are lower than the boiling point of water. The heat from the water makes the substances evaporate. The gases spin turbines to generate electricity, similar to the way steam does. Cold water piped in from the ocean depths then condenses the gases so they can be used again.

Research on OTEC systems has been conducted in Hawaii and other places. However, costs remain high. Therefore, no OTEC facility yet produces electricity to sell to customers.

LESSON ② Assessment

1. **Compare and Contrast** What are the two basic ways of generating electricity with hydropower? How are they similar? How are they different?

2. **Explain** What are the benefits of hydropower?

3. **Infer** Why are there relatively few stations for generating electricity with tidal power?

REVISIT
4. **INVESTIGATIVE** PHENOMENON
How does the Three Gorges Dam demonstrate that renewable energy resources have both benefits and costs?

Solar and Wind Energy

EVERYDAY PHENOMENON How does both solar and wind energy depend upon radiation from the sun?

Knowledge and Skills

- Describe techniques for using solar energy to heat buildings and generate electricity.
- Analyze the benefits and costs of solar energy.
- Explain how wind energy can be used to produce electricity.
- Analyze the benefits and costs of wind energy.

Reading Strategy and Vocabulary

✅ **Reading Strategy** Before you read, skim the lesson headings, illustrations, and vocabulary. Write down what you think this lesson will be about. Then, as you read, write down the things you read that are most surprising to you.

Vocabulary passive solar heating, active solar heating, flat-plate solar collector, photovoltaic (PV) cell, concentrating solar power (CSP), wind turbine, wind farm

WILLIAM KAMKWAMBA loves to read. When he was 14 years old, he needed electricity to power a light bulb so that he could read after sunset. William and his family live in a village in Malawi, a developing nation in Africa. Few people in rural Malawi have electricity.

In a nearby library, William found an old science textbook that described how wind energy could be used to generate electricity. So he decided to build a windmill that would do this. He constructed a slender wooden tower. On top of it he placed a generator he put together using plastic pipe, bicycle parts, and a few other things he found in trash piles.

His mother thought he was crazy, until one day he connected a light bulb to the generator. As the windmill's blades began to spin, light flickered in the bulb. Since that day, William has built other windmills that power light bulbs and radios and charge cell phones. Electricity from the windmills even pumps water for people in his village.

The wind energy that can run an electric generator ultimately comes from the sun, because the sun heats different parts of Earth unequally, and this unequal heating creates air currents. Both the sun and the wind provide energy that can be put to use.

William Kamkwamba and his windmill

Harnessing Solar Energy

The sun provides energy for almost all life processes on Earth, from the reproduction of tiny bacteria to the opening of flower buds. Every day, Earth receives a huge amount of energy from the sun. If we could harness one day's energy, it would power human consumption for 25 years. We may someday be able to use sunlight to meet many of our energy needs. However, we are still developing the technologies to do this.

When we use sunlight directly as a source of energy, without involving mechanical or electrical devices, we are using passive solar energy collection. This is the most common way that we harness solar energy. In contrast, active solar energy collection uses technology to focus, move, or store solar energy. The house in **Figure 13** uses both passive and active solar energy collection.

Passive Solar Heating We use passive solar energy to heat homes and buildings. **Passive solar heating** involves designing a building to collect, store, and distribute the sun's energy naturally. Greenhouses are designed to do this. Houses that are designed to use solar heating often have windows that face south and east to capture sunlight in winter. At night, window shades help keep the heat inside. Features such as these conserve energy and save energy costs.

Active Solar Heating An **active solar heating** system uses technology to collect, move, and store heat derived from the sun. One method of active solar heating uses devices called flat-plate solar collectors, which are sometimes called solar panels. A **flat-plate solar collector** generally consists of a black, heat-absorbing metal plate in a flat box with a glass cover. Sunlight passes through the glass, heating the metal plate. A long tube passes through the collector. Fluid in the tube absorbs heat from the metal plate. A pumping system circulates the fluid, transferring heat throughout the building. Heated water can be pumped to tanks to store the heat for later use. Flat-plate solar collectors are usually installed on rooftops, and they can be used to heat both water and air inside buildings.

 How does a flat-plate solar collector work?

Generating Electricity With Solar Energy Because passive and active solar heating methods supply heat to buildings, they can reduce the need for electricity and other forms of energy. However, neither passive nor active solar heating produces electricity. Two ways of using the sun's energy to generate electricity are photovoltaic cells and concentrating solar power.

▶ *Photovoltaic Cells* In a **photovoltaic (PV) cell,** solar energy is converted directly into electricity. Photovoltaic cells contain two plates. The plates of a typical PV cell are made mainly of silicon. One of the plates is rich in electrons. When sunlight strikes this plate, it knocks some electrons loose. These electrons are attracted to the other plate. The flow of electrons from one plate to another creates an electric current.

FIGURE 13 Going Solar Any house can be adapted to use active and passive solar techniques for heating and for generating electricity. **Apply Concepts** In Germany, how can homeowners profit from extra electricity generated by photovoltaic cells?

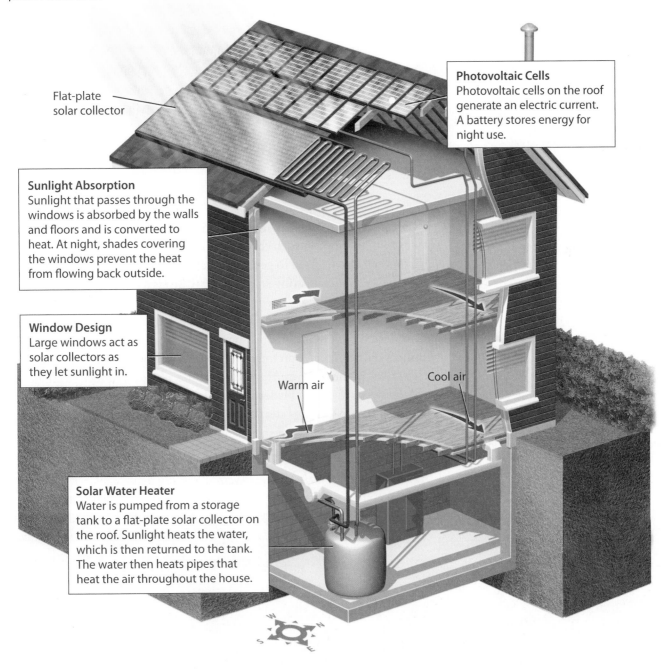

Flat-plate solar collector

Photovoltaic Cells
Photovoltaic cells on the roof generate an electric current. A battery stores energy for night use.

Sunlight Absorption
Sunlight that passes through the windows is absorbed by the walls and floors and is converted to heat. At night, shades covering the windows prevent the heat from flowing back outside.

Window Design
Large windows act as solar collectors as they let sunlight in.

Warm air

Cool air

Solar Water Heater
Water is pumped from a storage tank to a flat-plate solar collector on the roof. Sunlight heats the water, which is then returned to the tank. The water then heats pipes that heat the air throughout the house.

PV cells have many uses. You may be familiar with small PV cells that power your watch or your calculator. Some power plants use PV cells to generate electricity for a wide area. In addition, individual households and businesses can use PV cells to obtain all or part of the electricity they use. On top of the roofs of homes and other buildings, PV cells are arranged in panels or contained in special roofing tiles.

Go Outside

Does the Temperature Change? ⚠️

1. Obtain two clear, resealable plastic bags. Pour 250 mL of water into each bag.

2. Use a thermometer to measure the water temperature in each bag. Record the temperatures.

3. Put one bag in a shady place outdoors. Put the other bag in a sunny place.

4. Form a hypothesis about what will happen to the water temperature in each bag.

5. After 30 minutes, measure and record the water temperature in each bag.

Analyze and Conclude

1. **Observe** How did the water temperature change in each bag?

2. **Form a Hypothesis** How did the results correspond to your hypothesis?

3. **Apply Concepts** What energy conversion did you observe?

4. **Control Variables** Why was it important to measure the water temperature in both bags at the beginning of the experiment as well as the end?

▶ **Concentrating Solar Power (CSP)** You probably think of a mirror as something you use to check your appearance before you go out. Mirrors can also be used to generate electricity through concentrating solar power. **Concentrating solar power (CSP)** is a technology that uses mirrors to focus sunlight in order to generate electricity. In one kind of CSP, hundreds of mirrors are positioned in a large area surrounding a tall tower, called a "power tower," as shown in **Figure 14.** The mirrors focus sunlight onto a receiver on top of the tower. The concentrated sun's rays heat a fluid in the receiver. The heated fluid is used to produce steam, and the steam turns the blades of a turbine, which powers a generator. Because this process uses steam, it is similar to the way a coal power plant produces electricity. However, the sun, not a coal fire, is the source of the heat that produces the steam.

 Reading Checkpoint *What is a power tower?*

FIGURE 14 Concentrating Solar Power In this CSP facility in Spain, hundreds of mirrors focus sunlight toward the power tower to generate electricity.

Benefits and Costs of Solar Power

The sun will continue burning for another 4 to 5 billion years. Therefore, it is an inexhaustible energy source. In spite of this, solar energy contributes only a small part of today's energy production. However, solar energy worldwide has grown by 28 percent every year since 1971, a growth rate second only to that of wind power.

Benefits of Solar Power Solar energy has many benefits besides its endless source. PV cells and other solar technologies use no fuel. They are quiet and safe. Solar technology does not release greenhouse gases, and it does not pollute the air or water. Solar devices require little maintenance. An average unit can produce energy for 20–30 years. Homes, businesses, and isolated communities can use solar power to produce their own electricity. This production reduces dependence on power plants. Solar power is especially attractive in developing nations, because many of these nations have a lot of sun but few power plants.

In the developed world, most PV systems are connected to a regional electric grid. In Germany, owners of houses with PV systems can sell their excess solar electricity to the local power company. And in many states in the United States, consumers can lower their electric bill if they supply some electricity to their local electric company. Finally, the development of solar power is creating many new jobs.

FIGURE 16 Sunlight in the United States Notice that some locations receive more sunlight than others. Therefore, harnessing solar energy is more profitable in some areas than in others.

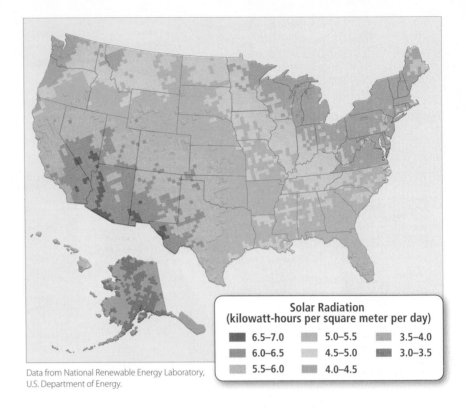

Solar Radiation
(kilowatt-hours per square meter per day)

6.5–7.0	5.0–5.5	3.5–4.0
6.0–6.5	4.5–5.0	3.0–3.5
5.5–6.0	4.0–4.5	

Data from National Renewable Energy Laboratory, U.S. Department of Energy.

Costs of Solar Power The manufacturing of solar-energy devices creates some pollution. In addition, with the technology we now have, some regions are not sunny enough to provide much solar power. Seattle, for example, often has cloudy and rainy weather. Therefore, Seattle might find it difficult to depend on solar power.

Currently, solar equipment is expensive, so the investment cost for solar power is higher than that for fossil fuels. In fact, solar power is the most expensive way to produce electricity today. However, prices for solar equipment are falling fast. In addition, solar technologies are becoming more efficient. This increased efficiency is making it possible to produce energy for less money.

 Reading Checkpoint *Look at **Figure 16**. Which part of the United States is most likely to benefit from solar energy?*

Harnessing Wind Power

Indirectly, wind energy is a form of solar energy. The sun heats the atmosphere, and unequal heating of air masses causes winds to blow. People have used wind power for thousands of years. Windmills have ground grain into flour and pumped water to drain wetlands and irrigate crops. Even today, farms and ranches in parts of the United States use windmills to draw water up for thirsty cattle.

Windmills in the Netherlands

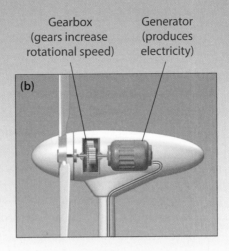

(a)

Blades

Tower

(b)

Gearbox
(gears increase
rotational speed)

Generator
(produces
electricity)

FIGURE 17 How a Wind Turbine Generates Electricity Wind spins the blades of a wind turbine **(a).** The spinning motion is transferred to a gearbox **(b),** which in turn activates a generator.

Modern Wind Turbines Recall that electricity is often generated by using a turbine's rotating motion. A **wind turbine** is a device that converts the wind's kinetic energy, or energy of motion, into electrical energy. Wind blowing into a turbine turns blades that connect to a gearbox, as shown in **Figure 17.** The gearbox connects to a generator that produces electricity. Wind turbines are located on top of towers. Some of these towers are taller than a football field is long. Wind turbines are most often built in groups called **wind farms.** The world's largest wind farms contain hundreds of turbines **(Figure 18).**

Offshore Wind Turbines Average wind speeds are approximately 20 percent greater over water than over land. For this and other reasons, offshore wind turbines are becoming more common. Costs to erect and maintain wind turbines in water are higher than for wind turbines located on land. However, the stronger winds produce more power and may make offshore wind turbines more profitable than wind turbines on land.

FIGURE 18 A Wind Farm This wind farm is located in California.

Percentage of World's Wind Power From Leading Nations

India 5.9%
Spain 4.0%
China 35.5%
Germany 10.0%
U.S. 16.3%
Rest of world 28.2%

Data from: REN21. 2019. Renewables 2019 Global Status Report

Connect to the Central Case

FIGURE 19 Where Wind Energy Is Significant The graph shows the percentage of world wind power supplied by various nations. **Interpret Graphs** What percentage of the world's wind power does Germany supply?

Benefits and Costs of Wind Power

The graph in **Figure 19** shows that five nations account for about three-fourths of the world's wind power output. Like other forms of energy that we use, wind power has both benefits and costs. Some of these advantages and disadvantages are described below.

Benefits of Wind Power Like solar power, wind power does not cause pollution. The U.S. Environmental Protection Agency (EPA) has calculated that during a year, a 1-megawatt wind turbine prevents the release of more than 1500 tons (1361 metric tons) of carbon dioxide, 6.5 tons (5.9 metric tons) of sulfur dioxide, 3.2 tons (2.9 metric tons) of nitrogen oxides, and 60 pounds (27.2 kilograms) of mercury. Under the best conditions, wind power appears to be highly efficient. One study found that wind turbines produce 23 times more energy than they use. Wind-turbine development can range from one or two turbines to huge wind farms. Small-scale development can help make local areas more self-sufficient, just as small-scale solar energy can. Startup costs of wind farms generally are higher than those of plants powered by fossil fuels, but wind farms are less expensive once they are up and running.

Map it

Wind Patterns

The map shows how wind conditions compare in different parts of the United States. Use the map to answer the following questions.

1. **Interpret Maps** In general, which part of the United States—the eastern part or the western part—has winds with the highest density?

2. **Interpret Maps** Find your state on the map. Do you think your state could obtain a lot of its energy from wind? Explain your answer.

3. **Infer** Do you think the southeastern part of the United States has many wind farms? Explain your answer.

4. **Infer** On the basis of the circle graph in **Figure 19,** what can you infer about the state of the wind-energy industry in the United States?

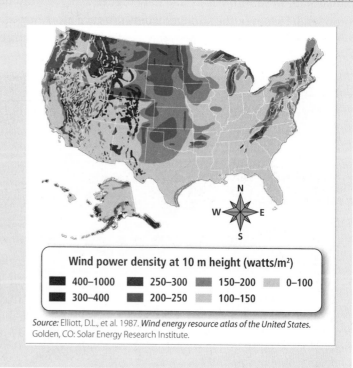

Wind power density at 10 m height (watts/m²)

400–1000	250–300	150–200	0–100
300–400	200–250	100–150	

Source: Elliott, D.L., et al. 1987. *Wind energy resource atlas of the United States.* Golden, CO: Solar Energy Research Institute.

FIGURE 20 Wind Energy Job
Wind power provides work for many people. Here, a technician works atop a wind turbine high above the ground.

Costs of Wind Power We have no control over when wind will occur. This unpredictability is a major limitation of wind as an electricity source. Some areas are windier than others, and wind power is not a good choice in places with little wind. The wind-power industry has located much of its generating capacity in states with high wind speeds, but these areas are often far from the large population centers that need the electricity.

Other factors besides unpredictability can prevent the use of wind power. For example, when wind farms are proposed near communities, the people living in the area often oppose them. Many people think that wind turbines clutter the landscape and are too noisy. In addition, birds and bats can be killed when they fly into the rotating blades on wind towers. This is a negative effect scientists are not certain about how to handle. The best strategy may be to avoid constructing wind farms in certain places, such as along bird and bat migration routes.

LESSON ③ Assessment

1. **Compare and Contrast** What is the main difference between passive solar heating and active solar heating?

2. **Identify** List four benefits of solar power.

3. **Explain** Explain how a wind turbine generates electricity.

4. **Identify** List two benefits and two costs of wind power.

5. **THINK IT *THROUGH*** You work for a company that develops wind farms. Officials in a major city have asked you to evaluate the possibility of constructing a wind farm on a ridge top among the city's suburbs. What questions would you want answered before deciding whether or not to recommend the site?

Energy From Hydrogen

EVERYDAY PHENOMENON How can a reaction that produces water also generate electricity?

Knowledge and Skills

- Describe how hydrogen fuel can be produced.
- Explain the way fuel cells work and how they are used.

Reading Strategy and Vocabulary

✔ **Reading Strategy** Construct a Venn diagram comparing electrolysis and the breakdown of methane as ways to obtain hydrogen.

Vocabulary electrolysis, fuel cell

Hydrogen is the simplest and the most abundant element in the universe. In its elemental form, hydrogen is a gas with the chemical formula H_2. Hydrogen gas can be burned to release energy that, in turn, can generate electricity. When it is burned to produce energy that people can use, hydrogen gas is called hydrogen fuel. Its combustion is clean compared to fossil fuels. The U.S. space flight programs have used hydrogen fuel since the 1960s.

Hydrogen gas is rare on Earth. Hydrogen atoms bind to the atoms of other elements, forming compounds such as water (H_2O) and methane (CH_4). To release hydrogen, the compounds that contain it must be broken down chemically.

Why are environmental scientists interested in hydrogen as a source of energy? One reason is that hydrogen fuel can be stored and transported from one place to another, unlike most other sources of renewable energy. We can't transport the wind from North Dakota to North Carolina, and we can't move the sun from Arizona to the state of Washington. Some day, however, energy from the wind in North Dakota may be used to create hydrogen fuel. The hydrogen fuel can then be transported to places like North Carolina. The portability of hydrogen fuel is the key to its potential usefulness.

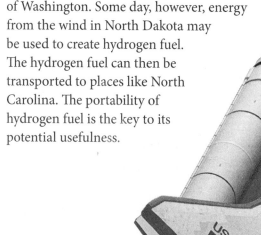

FIGURE 21 Power From Hydrogen Hydrogen fuel powered the rockets that blasted vehicles such as the space shuttle into space.

Producing Hydrogen Fuel

To produce hydrogen fuel, hydrogen-containing compounds must be forced to release their hydrogen atoms. The chemical breakdown of hydrogen-containing compounds requires an input of energy.

Electrolysis One process that releases hydrogen is electrolysis. In electrolysis, water molecules are broken down into oxygen gas (O_2) and hydrogen gas (H_2) by an electric current that runs through the water. This reaction can be expressed by the following chemical equation:

$$2\,H_2O \rightarrow 2\,H_2 + O_2$$

Electrolysis produces pure hydrogen gas. The process does not emit greenhouse gases or pollutants. However, the electrolysis of water is a costly way to obtain hydrogen.

 Reading Checkpoint   *What is electrolysis?*

Breakdown of Methane Hydrogen can also be extracted from the methane in natural gas. This process is less expensive than electrolysis and is now the most common way of obtaining hydrogen. The following equation summarizes the reaction:

$$CH_4 + 2\,H_2O \rightarrow 4\,H_2 + CO_2$$

This reaction produces carbon dioxide, a greenhouse gas. Therefore, energy experts do not see methane as a desirable long-term source of hydrogen.

Other Methods There are disadvantages to both methods described above. Therefore, scientists are investigating other ways to obtain hydrogen. For example, the heat given off by a nuclear reactor may one day be used to split water into hydrogen and oxygen. Researchers are also looking into using algae to produce hydrogen (**Figure 22**).

FIGURE 22 Hydrogen From Algae
Microorganisms called algae give the solutions in the bottles their green color. The algae in the solutions are producing hydrogen from water.

Benefits and Costs of Energy From Hydrogen As a fuel, hydrogen has a number of benefits. Because it is the most abundant element in the universe, it will never run out. Depending on how it is made, it produces few greenhouse gases or pollutants. Water and heat may be the only waste products generated by using hydrogen as fuel. Hydrogen can be stored and transported from one place to another. Hydrogen gas can catch fire, but if it is stored properly, it is probably no more dangerous than gasoline.

However, processes that break compounds down to release hydrogen, such as electrolysis, require energy inputs. With the technology now available, hydrogen fuel is expensive to produce. In addition, to be useful in a motor vehicle, hydrogen needs to be compressed, or squeezed into a smaller volume. Scientists are working on ways to do this safely.

 Reading Checkpoint *Why are hydrogen-powered motor vehicles uncommon?*

Fuel Cells

Hydrogen gas can be used to produce electricity within **fuel cells.** The chemical reaction that takes place in a fuel cell is the reverse of the reaction for electrolysis. Two hydrogen molecules and an oxygen molecule combine to form two water molecules:

$$2\,H_2 + O_2 \rightarrow 2\,H_2O$$

Inside a Fuel Cell A fuel cell has a positive (+) electrode and a negative (−) electrode, as you can see in **Figure 24.** Reactions in a fuel cell result in an electric current flowing through a wire from one terminal to the other.

FIGURE 23 Hydrogen-Powered Scooter This electric scooter runs on a fuel-cell battery.

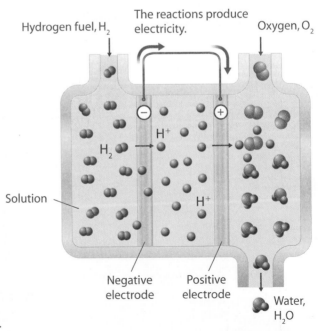

Hydrogen fuel, H_2

The reactions produce electricity.

Oxygen, O_2

− H_2 H^+

+ H^+

Solution

Negative electrode

Positive electrode

Water, H_2O

FIGURE 24 A Fuel Cell A fuel cell uses hydrogen and oxygen to produce electricity. Inside the fuel cell, hydrogen molecules are split into ions, and an electric current flows from one terminal of the cell to the other.

FIGURE 25 Fuel Cell Bus The city of Hamburg in Germany has buses that run on energy obtained from hydrogen.

Hydrogen gas enters the side of the cell with the negative electrode. Each hydrogen molecule then splits into two positively charged hydrogen ions (H^+). Meanwhile, oxygen gas enters the cell on the side with the positive electrode. A series of reactions occurs that makes two things happen. The reactions cause an electric current to flow from the negative terminal to the positive terminal. As this is taking place, the oxygen and hydrogen ions combine to form molecules of water.

How Fuel Cells Are Used Fuel cells can be used in many ways. They provide power for moving vehicles. The city of Hamburg in Germany has buses powered by fuel cells as shown in **Figure 25.** In fact, vehicles ranging from cars to space vehicles use hydrogen fuel cells as an energy source. However, such vehicles are uncommon.

Fuel cells can supply power in places that are far from conventional utility companies that produce electricity. Other technologies can be combined with fuel cells to accomplish this. One example is the system built on Stuart Island in the state of Washington. There, solar power produces hydrogen, which is then used in fuel cells to produce electricity.

LESSON ④ Assessment

1. **Apply Concepts** Write the equation for the reaction in which hydrogen is obtained from methane. Use this equation to explain why this method of obtaining oxygen could contribute to global climate change. (*Hint:* Look at the products of the reaction.)

2. **Explain** Explain how electricity is produced inside a fuel cell.

3. **THINK IT** *THROUGH* When hydrogen fuel is ignited, the result can be a huge explosion that causes enormous damage. Suppose you are on a commission evaluating the safety of hydrogen fuel. Your specific focus is transportation of hydrogen. What safety measures would you recommend? Think about issues such as the design of transportation vehicles, the routes they might take, and the time of day during which the transportation would take place.

ARE BIOFUELS BETTER FOR THE ENVIRONMENT?

In the last decade, reducing carbon dioxide (CO_2) emissions has become a goal of many nations. Around the world, gasoline-powered cars and trucks are among the biggest producers of carbon dioxide. That's why some nations have started considering plant-based biofuels as an alternative to fossil fuels. Because plants absorb carbon dioxide from the air, biofuels are carbon neutral—the amount of carbon dioxide released when they burn is the same as the amount the plant originally took in and used during photosynthesis.

Many businesses and governments worldwide have already invested millions of dollars in biofuel production in an effort to curb climate change. However, some research has shown that biofuels may not be as "green" as initially thought. A fierce debate has sprung up between those who argue biofuels are a useful tool for limiting carbon dioxide emissions, and those who say biofuels ultimately do more harm than good.

Most of the ethanol fuel produced in Brazil comes from sugar cane.

THE OPINIONS

VIEWPOINT 1 *Biofuels are an effective alternative to fossil fuels.*

Many farmers, businesses, and governments have embraced biofuels as the best available alternative to fossil fuels. Also, there is a considerable environmental benefit, because burning biofuels produces fewer pollutants, such as carbon monoxide and particulates, than fossil fuels do. Beyond the environmental benefit, the biofuel industry has created new jobs and businesses. Many farmers in developing nations have successfully increased their income by selling oil palm, corn, and sugar cane to be turned into biofuel.

Brazil has shown that biofuels can be used successfully on a large scale. As of 2015, all cars in the country run on a mixture of 73% gasoline and 27% ethanol made from sugar cane. Brazil has reduced its use of fossil fuels proving that biofuels can be an affordable and effective replacement.

VIEWPOINT 2 *Biofuels won't reduce CO_2 emissions and will waste fertile land.*

Some environmental groups and scientists have argued that the costs of biofuels outweigh the benefits. First, growing crops to make biofuels requires large areas of land. This leads to deforestation as natural areas are cleared to make room for farmland. Besides accelerating loss of habitat and biodiversity, deforestation also releases large amounts of carbon dioxide. Machinery used to harvest crops, particularly corn, also uses fossil fuels, offsetting the benefits gained from turning those crops into biofuels. So, while the biofuel itself may be carbon neutral, the processes involved in producing biofuel are not so eco-friendly.

Biofuels affect people, too, because biofuel crops are often grown on land that used to grow food crops. Some researchers have estimated that growing enough corn to power a car for one year would take about 4.5 hectares (11 acres) of fertile farmland. Over-reliance on biofuels could raise food prices and increase hunger and malnourishment around the world. This has led researchers, environmentalists, and human rights groups to argue that the benefits of biofuels are outweighed by the huge requirements of arable land.

Some gas stations offer E85 fuel, which is 85% ethanol; however, cars need specially designed engines to run on E85.

The need for fertile land to grow biofuels can lead to deforestation.

21st Century Skills

Communication Skills Suppose lawmakers in your state are considering legislation to build new ethanol plants. Write a letter to your representative either in support or opposition to the legislation. Explain your reasoning.

CHAPTER 18 · Study Guide

INVESTIGATIVE PHENOMENON

Do the benefits of renewable energy outweigh the costs?

Lesson 1
How can we use the heat from the Earth to both warm and cool our homes?

Lesson 4
How can a reaction that produces water also generate electricity?

Lesson 2
How can the movement of water be used to generate electricity?

Lesson 3
How does both solar and wind energy depend upon radiation from the sun?

LESSON 1 Biomass and Geothermal Energy

- Alternative energy resources are needed to replace fossil fuels, reduce air pollution, and reduce the emission of greenhouse gases.
- Energy derived from biomass is used for cooking, heating, powering motor vehicles, and generating electricity.
- Liquid fuels made from biomass, known as biofuels, help to power millions of vehicles. Ethanol is used in gasoline engines, and biodiesel is used in diesel engines.
- Biopower is electricity generated from the combustion of biomass.
- Steam and hot water produced by geothermal energy can be used for generating electricity and for heating.
- A ground source heat pump uses underground soil temperature to heat and cool buildings.

biomass energy (551)
biofuel (552)
biopower (552)
geothermal energy (553)
ground source heat pump (554)

LESSON 2 Hydropower and Ocean Energy

- The movement of river water can be used to generate electricity. Electricity can be generated by using water stored behind a dam in a reservoir or by using the natural movement of a river.
- Hydropower is nonpolluting and relatively inexpensive, but dams can alter ecosystems and disrupt people's lives.
- The movement of tides and ocean thermal energy can be used to generate electricity. Harnessing tidal energy works best where there is a large difference between the height of the water at low and high tides.
- Ocean thermal energy conversion (OTEC) is a process that converts thermal energy in ocean water to electrical energy.

hydropower (557)
tidal energy (559)
ocean thermal energy conversion (OTEC) (560)

LESSON 3 Solar and Wind Energy

- The sun's energy can be used to heat buildings and generate electricity.
- Solar power has many benefits, such as its limitless supply, but it depends on weather and is expensive.
- Wind turbines convert wind's kinetic energy to electricity.
- Wind power is nonpolluting and efficient, but its supply is unpredictable, and it may damage landscape and wildlife.

passive solar heating (562)
active solar heating (562)
flat-plate solar collector (562)
photovoltaic (PV) cell (562)
concentrating solar power (CSP) (564)
wind turbine (567)
wind farm (567)

LESSON 4 Energy From Hydrogen

- Hydrogen fuel can be produced from the breakdown of water or methane.
- Fuel cells are used to generate electricity.

electrolysis (571)
fuel cell (572)

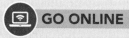 **GO ONLINE**

INQUIRY LABS AND ACTIVITIES

- **Regional Renewable Energy**
  Think of a logical source of renewable energy in your region. Then, research a local provider of this type of energy.
- **Compare Biofuels**
  Research the advantages and disadvantages of various biofuels to replace petroleum-based fuels. Make a recommendation.
- **Energy From Wind**
  Design the rotor and blades for a model wind turbine and test its efficiency at lifting weights.

Chapter Assessment

Defend Your Case

Germany's Renewable Energy Sources Act specifies that Germany has to obtain at least 40–45 percent of its energy from renewable energy resources by 2025. Write a paragraph explaining the benefits and costs of the law.

Review Concepts and Terms

1. Which of the following is NOT a renewable source of energy?

   a. wind   **c.** coal

   b. sunlight   **d.** wood

2. Energy produced from material that comes from living organisms is known as

   a. geothermal energy.   **c.** electrical energy.

   b. biomass energy.   **d.** wood energy.

3. The plant shown below can be a source of

   a. ethanol.   **c.** hydropower.

   b. ground source heat.   **d.** photovoltaic power.

4. Geothermal energy is obtained by harnessing

   a. sunlight.

   b. wind energy.

   c. energy from tides.

   d. hot underground water or steam.

5. The run-of-the-river approach to generating hydroelectric power

   a. requires construction of a dam.

   b. takes advantage of a river's natural flow.

   c. causes more extensive habitat destruction than the reservoir storage method does.

   d. involves burning fossil fuels.

6. Concentrating solar power uses

   a. a building's design to capture solar energy.

   b. a heat-absorbing metal plate to capture solar energy.

   c. passive solar heating techniques to generate electricity.

   d. mirrors that focus sunlight to generate electricity.

7. Offshore wind turbines are useful because

   a. they do not need gearboxes.

   b. they are easier to build than wind turbines on land.

   c. average wind speeds are greater over water than land.

   d. they do not require a generator to produce electricity.

8. Which of the following is NOT an advantage of hydrogen as a source of energy?

   a. It usually produces few pollutants.

   b. Hydrogen is the most abundant element in the universe.

   c. It can be stored and transported.

   d. It is inexpensive to produce.

Modified True/False

Write true if the statement is true. If it is false, change the underlined word or words to make the statement true.

9. Tidal energy works best in places where the differences in height between low and high tides are <u>small</u>.

10. <u>Active</u> solar heating uses devices such as pumps to move heat derived from the sun.

11. <u>PV cells</u> can be incorporated into roof tiles.

12. In a fuel cell, <u>water</u> molecules split to release hydrogen ions.

13. Hydropower uses the <u>potential energy</u> of water to generate electricity.

Reading Comprehension

Read the following selection and answer the questions that follow.

In Idaho, resource planners decided that the state's power future lies in generating electricity from wind. Idaho has turned its citizens into "wind prospectors," asking them to identify potential areas for wind farms. People who join the program collect data on wind speed and direction, and share those data with the state.

To obtain wind data, Idaho lends landowners devices called anemometers. Anemometers measure wind speed and direction. To measure wind speed, anemometers have three or four hollow cups that catch the wind and rotate around a vertical rod. The greater the wind speed, the faster the cups rotate.

14. Which of the following is the BEST title for the selection?

a. "Anemometers and Barometers"

b. "Collecting Wind Data"

c. "Idaho's Weather"

d. "Alternative Energy"

15. Which of the following is the BEST description of what people use an anemometer for?

a. to find a potential location for a wind farm

b. to convert wind energy into electrical energy

c. to measure wind speed and direction

d. to collect information about how frequently the wind blows

16. On one day, the same anemometer was used to measure wind speed in two different locations. In Location *A*, the anemometer's cups rotated faster than they did in Location *B*. How did the wind speeds compare in the two locations?

a. Wind speed was greater in Location *A*.

b. Wind speed was greater in Location *B*.

c. Wind speed was the same in both locations.

d. An anemometer's cups are not used to measure wind speed.

Short Answer

17. List four benefits of renewable energy resources.

18. Explain what biodiesel is and why biodiesel is a form of biomass energy.

19. What is biopower? Give an example of how it can be produced.

20. What are the costs of hydropower?

21. Explain what ocean thermal energy conversion (OTEC) is.

22. Describe the construction of a wind turbine. Alternatively, make a diagram with labels and captions.

23. What is a photovoltaic cell? How does it work?

24. What are two problems associated with solar power?

25. What are the products of the electrolysis of water?

Critical Thinking

26. Predict In ten years, do you think there will be more jobs in renewable energy industries than there are now? Explain your answer.

27. Apply Concepts A greenhouse such as the one below uses glass panes to trap heat inside. Is this an example of passive solar heating or active solar heating? Explain your answer.

28. Relate Cause and Effect Why is the production of electricity from geothermal energy practical only in certain parts of the world?

29. Pose Questions You and your family are thinking of building a home that uses both active and passive solar heating. What questions should you ask the building contractor before you make the decision?

30. Apply Concepts Besides solar energy itself, what forms of alternative energy can trace their origin to energy from the sun? Explain your answer.

Analyze Data

The graph shows how different sources of energy grew annually worldwide from 1971 to 2004. Use the graph to answer the questions.

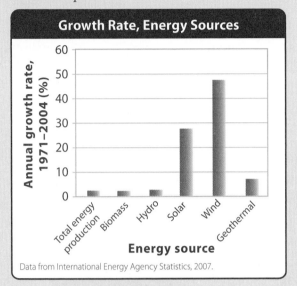

Growth Rate, Energy Sources

Annual growth rate, 1971–2004 (%)

Energy source

Data from International Energy Agency Statistics, 2007.

31. **Interpret Graphs** Which source of energy had the most rapid growth rate for the years shown?

32. **Relate Cause and Effect** Which two forms of renewable energy had the lowest growth rate? What is the probable reason? (*Hint:* Before the period shown on the graph, what renewable energy sources were already widely used?)

33. **Interpret Graphs** Taken as a whole, did renewable energy resources grow slower or faster than nonrenewable energy resources? How does the graph show this?

34. **Infer** Do you think the overall trend shown for the growth of renewable energy sources has continued? Explain your answer.

Write About It

35. **Creative Writing** Suppose you are writing a magazine article about the Three Gorges Dam in China. Your article will focus on the effects the dam has had on people's lives. Plan interviews that you might conduct with two people: one person whose job depends on the dam, and one person who had to move because the dam has flooded his or her town. Write a list of questions you might ask each person.

36. **Explanation** Explain how a ground source heat pump regulates the temperature in a building.

37. **REVISIT** **INVESTIGATIVE** PHENOMENON
A community that borders the ocean is deciding whether to construct an offshore wind farm that can be seen from the community. Write a letter to the editor of the local newspaper. Your letter should either support the development of the wind farm or be against it. Support your opinion with facts and reasons.

Ecological Footprints

Read the information below. Copy the table into your notebook and record your calculations. Then answer the questions that follow.

Assume that in the United States, photovoltaic cells cost $800 per square meter to install. Also assume that the average person needs 25 square meters of photovoltaic cells to supply the electricity that he or she needs. Use this information to fill in the footprint table.

1. The actual number of PV cells needed per person depends on where the person lives. Why is this true?

2. Find the area where you live on the map in **Figure 16**. Do you think that you would need more than the average number of PV cells, an average number, or fewer? Explain.

	Population	Area of Photovoltaic Cells Needed (m²)	Cost of Photovoltaic Cells Needed
You	1		
Your class			
Your state			
United States			

3. The cost of a photovoltaic system is high. Besides cost, what else would you consider when thinking about installing photovoltaic cells for your home?

INVESTIGATIVE PHENOMENON   What can we do with old landfills?

Freshkills Park in Staten Island,
NY used to be a landfill.

Central CASE Transforming New York's Fresh Kills Landfill

THE CLOSURE OF A LANDFILL is not the kind of event that normally draws politicians and the press, but the Fresh Kills Landfill was no ordinary dump. The largest landfill in the world, Fresh Kills was the primary repository of New York City's garbage for half a century. On March 22, 2001, New York City Mayor Rudolph Giuliani and New York Governor George Pataki were on hand to celebrate as a barge arrived on the western shore of New York City's Staten Island and dumped the final load of trash at Fresh Kills.

The landfill's closure was a welcome event for Staten Island's 450,000 residents, who had long viewed the landfill as a bad-smelling eyesore, health threat, and civic blemish. The 890-hectare (2200-acre) landfill featured six gigantic mounds of trash and soil. The highest, a 69-meter (225-foot) mound was taller than the nearby Statue of Liberty.

New York City had big plans for the Fresh Kills site. It planned to transform the old landfill into a world-class public park—a verdant landscape of rolling hills and wetlands teeming with wildlife, and a mecca for recreation for New York's residents.

Meanwhile, with its only landfill closed, New York City had to find another place to send its trash. The city found itself paying contractors exorbitant prices to haul its garbage away to landfills and incinerators in New York, New Jersey, Virginia, Pennsylvania, and Ohio. The city sanitation department's budget nearly doubled and the city raised taxes. Concerned citizens began to resent the increases in taxes and suggested reopening Fresh Kills.

Plans for the park moved ahead. A draft master plan was released in 2006. In 2008, an

GO ONLINE
- Take It Local
- 3-D Geo Tour

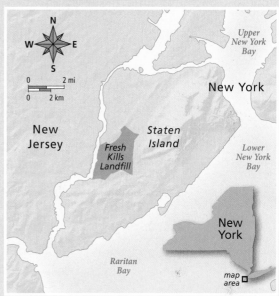

environmental impact statement was released that underwent public comment. The plan involved everything from ecological restoration of the wetlands to the construction of roads, ball fields, sculptures, bicycle trails, and scenic overviews.

In 2012, parts of the park began opening to the public. Native grasses were planted on the capped landfill mounds. These grasses attract grassland birds. Upon completion, the 2200 acre park will be the largest park developed in New York City in over 100 years. It will be three times larger than Central Park and will be a world-class center for recreation and urban ecological restoration.

Municipal and Industrial Waste

EVERYDAY PHENOMENON How does our current waste disposal impact our environment?

Knowledge and Skills

- Identify the three categories of waste.
- Describe conventional waste disposal methods.

Reading Strategy and Vocabulary

✔ **Reading Strategy** Before you read, use the headings in this lesson to make an outline about waste management. As you read, fill in details that provide key information.

Vocabulary waste, municipal solid waste, industrial waste, hazardous waste, sanitary landfill, leachate, incineration

DID YOU EVER THINK about all the items you throw in the trash each day? A paper napkin and empty yogurt container at breakfast; the contents of your lunch tray; the empty water bottle and apple core from an afternoon snack. And those are just items related to your meals! How about the plastic wrap that surrounds your news magazine? Or those dried-up pens and markers you threw in the trash? The list is probably much longer than you ever imagined. Now, think about the other people who live in your house … your city or town. Suddenly, the amount of garbage becomes overwhelming.

What Is Waste?

As the world's human population increases, and as we produce and consume more material goods, we generate more waste. But, what exactly is waste? For the purpose of this chapter, **waste** is any unwanted material or substance that results from a human activity or process. Waste pollutes our water, air, and soil. It's ugly to look at and even worse to smell. In order to safeguard public health and protect the environment, we need safe and effective waste management. In this lesson, you will learn about where our waste comes from and where it ends up.

There are three main categories of waste. **Municipal solid waste** is nonliquid waste that comes from homes, institutions, and small businesses. **Industrial waste** is waste that comes from the production of consumer goods, mining, agriculture, and petroleum extraction and refining. **Hazardous waste** refers to solid or liquid waste that is toxic, chemically reactive, flammable, or corrosive. It includes everything from paint and household cleaners to medical waste to industrial solvents. Another type of waste is wastewater. *Wastewater* includes the water we use in our households, businesses, industries, or public facilities and drain or flush down our pipes, as well as the polluted runoff from our streets and storm drains. In this chapter, we will limit our focus to the three main categories of waste.

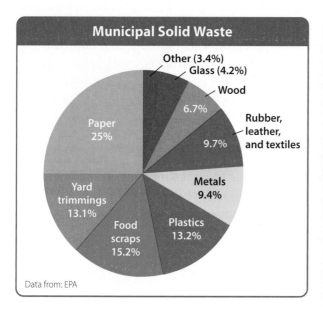

Municipal Solid Waste

Other (3.4%)
Glass (4.2%)
Wood 6.7%
Rubber, leather, and textiles 9.7%
Metals 9.4%
Plastics 13.2%
Food scraps 15.2%
Yard trimmings 13.1%
Paper 25%

Data from: EPA

Municipal Solid Waste Municipal solid waste is waste that is produced by consumers, public facilities, and small businesses. It is what we commonly refer to as "trash" or "garbage." Everything from paper, to tires, to food scraps, to roadside litter, to old appliances and furniture is considered municipal solid waste.

In the United States, paper, yard debris, food scraps, and plastics are the main components of municipal solid waste. Even after recycling, paper is the largest component of U.S. municipal solid waste. The average American generates more than 2.0 kilograms (4.5 pounds) of trash per day, or 745 kilograms (1643 pounds) per year!

▶ *Packaging and Nondurable Goods* A large portion of municipal solid waste comes from packaging and nondurable goods. Packaging includes bubble wrap, blocks of styrofoam, and packing "peanuts." Nondurable goods are products that we discard after a short period of use. Nondurable goods include items such as pens, disposable cameras, clothing, and furniture.

In addition, we throw away old durable goods and outdated equipment as we purchase new products. For example, do you know someone who got a new cell phone just because his or her contract had expired or because a new model became available? The "old" cell phone was probably in good working condition, but the person wanted something new. As we acquire more goods, we generate more waste.

▶ *Plastic Products* During the 1970s, plastic products became widely available to consumers. They were inexpensive, nondurable goods. Most plastic products were made for temporary use. They wore out quickly and soon piled up in dumps. Since the 1970s, plastic products have accounted for a significant increase in solid waste.

 Reading Checkpoint *Which type of material is the largest single contributor to municipal solid waste?*

FIGURE 1 Components of Municipal Waste Paper products make up the largest component of the municipal solid waste stream in the United States. (Note: The percentages in the graph do not add up to 100 due to rounding.) Tires are not accepted with regular garbage collection anymore and they pile up in dumps.

Industrial Waste The U.S. Environmental Protection Agency (EPA) classifies industrial waste as waste that is neither hazardous nor municipal solid waste. Industrial waste includes waste from factories, farms, mines, and refineries, as well as materials from construction sites. Industrial waste can also include medical waste, such as used surgical gloves and needles that have been used for drawing blood or giving injections.

Each year, U.S. industrial facilities generate about 7.6 billion tons of waste. Almost 97 percent of that waste is wastewater. The rest is solid waste—about 228 million tons. This amount almost equals the amount of municipal solid waste we dispose of each year. Most of the time, private companies collect and dispose of industrial waste.

Methods of Solid Waste Disposal

Historically, people dumped their garbage wherever it suited them. As cities and towns became more crowded, the garbage began to pile up. Local authorities took on the task of consolidating trash into open dumps at specified locations to keep other areas clean. To decrease the volume of trash, these dumps would be burned from time to time.

Open dumping and burning still occur throughout much of the world, as shown in **Figure 2.** As populations and consumption rise, waste is increasing and dumps are growing larger. As cities and suburbs expand, more people end up living next to dumps. These residents are repeatedly exposed to the harmful, toxic, and foul-smelling smoke from dump burning. As a result, more people are aware that unregulated dumping and burning damages their health and degrades the environment. In response to these hazards, many nations are improving their methods of waste disposal. Most industrialized nations now bury waste in landfills or use incinerators to burn waste.

FIGURE 2 Burning Garbage In many nations, people still burn their garbage.

Sanitary Landfills In modern sanitary landfills, waste is buried in the ground or piled up in large, carefully engineered mounds. In contrast to open dumps, sanitary landfills are designed to prevent contamination of groundwater and to reduce soil and air pollution. Most municipal landfills in the United States are regulated locally or by the states, but they must meet national standards set by the EPA. Fresh Kills was a sanitary landfill.

You can see the parts of a sanitary landfill in **Figure 3.** In a sanitary landfill, waste is partially decomposed by bacteria and compressed under its own weight to take up less space. Waste is layered along with soil, a method that speeds decomposition, reduces odor, and reduces infestation by pests. Some infiltration of rainwater allows for biodegradation by different types of bacteria. However, if too much water gets in, some contaminants may escape as the excess water flows out.

To protect against environmental contamination, U.S. regulations require that landfills be located away from wetlands and earthquake-prone faults and be at least 6 meters (20 feet) above the water table. The bottom and sides of sanitary landfills must be lined with heavy-duty plastic and 60 to 120 centimeters (2 to 4 feet) of impermeable clay to help prevent contaminants from seeping into aquifers. Sanitary landfills must also have systems of pipes, collection ponds, and treatment facilities to collect and treat leachate. **Leachate** is the liquid that results when substances from the trash dissolve in water as rainwater percolates downward. Landfill managers are required to maintain leachate collection systems for 30 years after a landfill has closed. Regulations also require that area groundwater be monitored regularly for contamination.

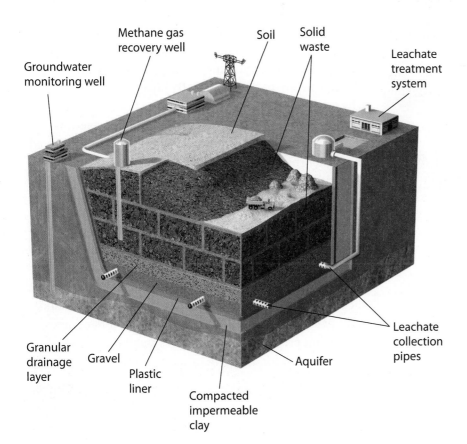

Groundwater monitoring well

Methane gas recovery well

Soil

Solid waste

Leachate treatment system

Granular drainage layer

Gravel

Plastic liner

Compacted impermeable clay

Aquifer

Leachate collection pipes

FIGURE 3 Sanitary Landfills
Sanitary landfills are engineered to prevent waste from contaminating soil and groundwater. Waste is laid in a large depression lined with plastic and impermeable clay to prevent liquids from leaching out. Leachate collection pipes draw out these liquids from the bottom of the landfill. Waste is layered along with soil until the depression is filled, and it continues to be built up until the landfill is capped. Landfill gas produced by bacteria may be recovered, and waste managers monitor groundwater for contamination.

FIGURE 4 Closed Landfills Old landfills, once properly capped, can serve other purposes. A number of them, such as Corona Park in Flushing Meadows (Queens, New York) have been developed into recreation areas.

FIGURE 5 Do They Ever Break Down? Landfills are often kept free of moisture. As a result, items that are buried in landfills take long periods of time to break down. Some, such as this newspaper from 1957, have hardly changed since they were dumped.

▶ *Closing Landfills* After a landfill is closed, it is capped with an engineered cover that must be maintained. This cap consists of a hydraulic barrier of plastic that prevents water from seeping down and gas from seeping up; a gravel layer above the hydraulic barrier that drains water, lessening pressure on the hydraulic barrier; a soil barrier of at least 60 centimeters (24 inches) that stores water and protects the hydraulic layer from weather extremes; and a topsoil layer of at least 15 centimeters (6 inches) that encourages plant growth, helping to prevent erosion.

Today thousands of landfills lie abandoned. One reason is that waste managers have closed many smaller landfills and consolidated the trash into fewer, much larger, landfills. In 1988 the United States had nearly 8000 landfills, but today it has fewer than 1300. Some landfills have been converted to recreational areas **(Figure 4)**.

▶ *Drawbacks of Landfills* Despite improvements in liner technology, many experts believe that leachate will eventually escape even from well-lined landfills. Liners can be punctured, and leachate collection systems eventually cease to be maintained. Moreover, landfills are kept dry to reduce leachate, but the bacteria that break down material thrive in wet conditions. Dryness, therefore, slows waste decomposition. In fact, it is surprising how slowly some materials biodegrade when they are tightly compressed in a landfill. Innovative archaeological research has revealed that landfills often contain food that has not decomposed and old newspapers that are still legible **(Figure 5)**.

Another problem is finding suitable areas to locate landfills, because most communities do not want them nearby. This not-in-my-backyard (NIMBY) reaction is one reason why New York decided to export its waste and why residents of states receiving that waste are increasingly protesting. As a result of the NIMBY syndrome, landfills are rarely located in neighborhoods that are home to wealthy and educated people with the political clout to keep them out.

Capturing Energy From Landfills Deep inside landfills, bacteria decompose waste in an oxygen-deficient (anaerobic) environment. This anaerobic decomposition produces landfill gas, a mix of gases of which almost 50 percent is methane. We can collect, process, and use landfill gas the same way we use natural gas. At Fresh Kills, collection wells pull landfill gas upward through a network of pipes by vacuum pressure. This tapped gas should soon provide enough energy for 25,000 homes.

 Reading Checkpoint *What are two benefits and two costs of landfills?*

Incineration Just as sanitary landfills are an improvement over open dumping, incineration in specially constructed facilities can be an improvement over open-air burning of trash. **Incineration** is a controlled process in which mixed garbage is burned at very high temperatures (see **Figure 6** on next page). Pollution control technology removes most, but not all, of the pollutants from the emissions. At incineration facilities, waste is generally sorted and metals removed. Metal-free waste gets chopped into small pieces so that it burns more easily. Incinerating waste reduces its weight by up to 75% and its volume by up to 90%.

As a result of real and perceived health threats from incinerator emissions—and of community opposition to these plants—engineers have developed several technologies to mitigate emissions. *Scrubbers* chemically treat the gases produced in combustion to remove hazardous components and neutralize acidic gases, such as sulfur dioxide and hydrochloric acid, turning them into water and salt. Scrubbers generally do this either by spraying liquids formulated to neutralize the gases or by passing the gases through dry lime. These scrubbers are similar to the ones used to treat smokestack emissions from coal-fired plants.

Particulate matter is physically removed from incinerator emissions in a system of huge filters known as a *baghouse*. These tiny particles, called fly ash, often contain some of the worst dioxin and heavy metal pollutants. In addition, burning garbage at especially high temperatures can destroy certain pollutants, such as PCBs. Even all these measures, however, do not fully eliminate toxic emissions.

▶ *Drawbacks of Incineration* Simply reducing the volume and weight of trash does not get rid of the toxins. The ash remaining after trash is incinerated therefore must be disposed of in hazardous waste landfills. Moreover, when trash is burned, hazardous chemicals—including dioxins, heavy metals, and PCBs—can be created and released into the atmosphere. Such releases caused a backlash against incineration from citizens concerned about health hazards. Most developed nations now regulate incinerator emissions, and some have banned incineration outright.

▶ *Energy From Incineration* Incineration was initially practiced simply to reduce the volume of waste, but today it serves as a way to generate electricity as well. Most North American incinerators today are waste-to-energy (WTE) facilities. These incinerators use the heat from burning waste to boil water, which creates steam that then drives a generator to make electricity. Steam from incinerators can also fuel heating systems. Burning waste equals almost 35 percent of the energy from burning coal.

Revenues from power generation, however, are usually not enough to offset the financial cost of building and running incinerators. Because it can take many years for a WTE facility to make a profit, many companies that build and operate these facilities require municipalities to guarantee a minimum amount of garbage. On occasion, such long-term commitments can defeat efforts to reduce waste through recycling because towns are required to "guarantee" a certain amount of trash.

FIND OUT MORE

Do you know where your trash goes? Where is your municipality's landfill or incinerator located? Contact your local public works department to find out.

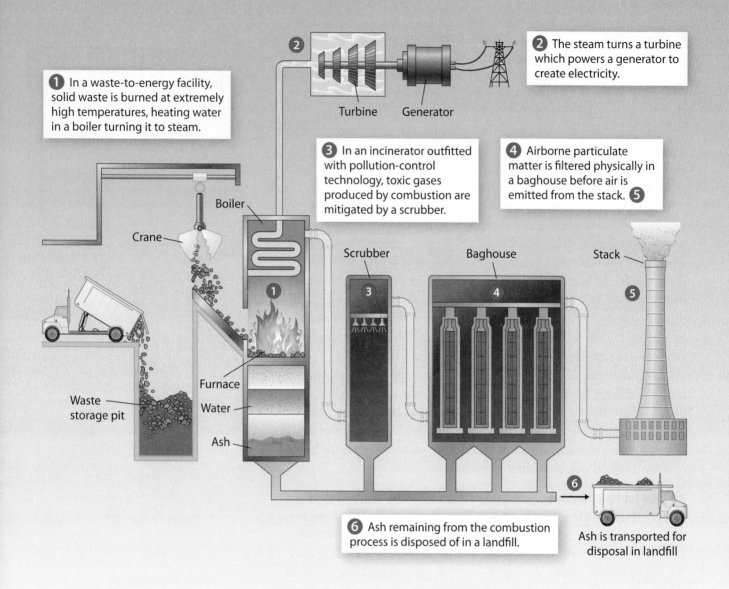

① In a waste-to-energy facility, solid waste is burned at extremely high temperatures, heating water in a boiler turning it to steam.

② The steam turns a turbine which powers a generator to create electricity.

③ In an incinerator outfitted with pollution-control technology, toxic gases produced by combustion are mitigated by a scrubber.

④ Airborne particulate matter is filtered physically in a baghouse before air is emitted from the stack. ⑤

⑥ Ash remaining from the combustion process is disposed of in a landfill.

Ash is transported for disposal in landfill

Turbine   Generator

Boiler

Crane

Scrubber   Baghouse   Stack

Furnace

Waste storage pit

Water

Ash

FIGURE 6 Incineration Incinerators reduce the volume of solid waste by burning it, but as a result may emit toxic compounds into the air. Many incinerators are waste-to-energy (WTE) facilities that use the heat of combustion to generate electricity.

① Assessment

1. **Review** Define waste. What are the three main categories of waste?

2. **Explain** When it comes to solid waste disposal, how does incineration affect landfills?

3. **THINK IT** *THROUGH* Do the costs of incineration outweigh the benefits? (*Hint:* Prepare a cost-benefit analysis to help you answer the question.)

LESSON 2

Minimizing Solid Waste

EVERYDAY PHENOMENON What is the best way to manage our solid waste?

Knowledge and Skills

- Discuss the importance of reducing waste.
- Describe how composting and recycling help reduce the amount of waste.

Reading Strategy and Vocabulary

✓ **Reading Strategy** As you read, draw a concept map showing the big ideas of waste management.

Vocabulary source reduction, biodegradable, composting, recycling, material recovery facility (MRF)

WASTE CAN DEGRADE water quality, soil quality, and air quality, thereby degrading human health and the environment. Waste is also a measure of inefficiency, so reducing waste can potentially save industries, municipalities, and consumers both money and resources. And finally, waste is ugly to look at. For these and other reasons, waste management has become a vital pursuit.

There are two main strategies for managing solid waste—reducing the amount of solid waste, and recovery. Recovery includes both composting and recycling. Recycling is not a concept that humans invented; recall that all materials are recycled in ecosystems. Therefore, recycling is a fundamental characteristic of the way natural systems function.

Waste Reduction

Many industrialized nations must deal with the issue of ever-increasing waste. Waste managers are now relying on reduction, reuse, recycling, and composting to deal with their waste. As a result, they are greatly reducing the amount of solid waste that gets disposed of in sanitary landfills or incinerators.

When we reduce the amount of waste, we lower the costs of disposal and recycling. We also conserve resources and produce less pollution. Preventing waste generation this way is called **source reduction.** One way to achieve source reduction is through less consumption. Other strategies for source reduction include less packaging, banning certain plastics, and designing goods that last longer.

To reduce waste, you can save items to use again or substitute disposable goods with durable ones. Habits as simple as bringing your own coffee cup to coffee shops or bringing sturdy reusable cloth bags to the grocery store can, over time, have substantial effect. You can also donate unwanted items and shop for used items yourself at yard sales and resale centers. Over 6000 reuse centers exist in the United States, including stores run by organizations that resell donated items. Besides being good for the environment, reusing items is often economically advantageous. Used items can be as functional as new ones, and much cheaper.

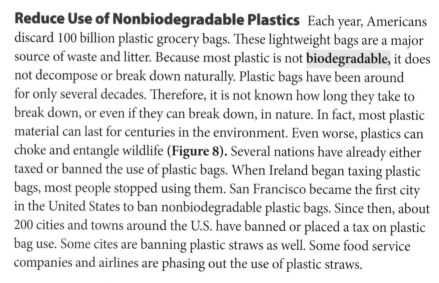

FIGURE 7 Less Packaging By choosing fruits and vegetables with less packaging—like those sold at farmers' markets or farm stands—you can reduce the amount of garbage caused by excess packaging.

Reduce Packaging Reducing packaging cuts down on waste, but how, when, and how much should we reduce? Packaging can serve very worthwhile purposes, such as preserving freshness, preventing breakage and tampering, and providing information. But, too much packaging is extraneous.

Consumers can help reduce packaging waste by choosing goods with minimal packaging. You can also buy foods in bulk, and buy unwrapped fruits and vegetables **(Figure 7)**. Manufacturers can also help by using packaging that is more recyclable. They can also reduce the size or weight of goods and materials. This reduction in size has been successful with aluminum cans, plastic soft drink bottles, and personal computers.

Reduce Use of Nonbiodegradable Plastics Each year, Americans discard 100 billion plastic grocery bags. These lightweight bags are a major source of waste and litter. Because most plastic is not **biodegradable,** it does not decompose or break down naturally. Plastic bags have been around for only several decades. Therefore, it is not known how long they take to break down, or even if they can break down, in nature. In fact, most plastic material can last for centuries in the environment. Even worse, plastics can choke and entangle wildlife **(Figure 8).** Several nations have already either taxed or banned the use of plastic bags. When Ireland began taxing plastic bags, most people stopped using them. San Francisco became the first city in the United States to ban nonbiodegradable plastic bags. Since then, about 200 cities and towns around the U.S. have banned or placed a tax on plastic bag use. Some cites are banning plastic straws as well. Some food service companies and airlines are phasing out the use of plastic straws.

FIGURE 8 Effect of Plastics in the Environment
Plastic grocery bags, as well as other plastics, are found in coastal areas as well as inland. Plastic six-pack rings and plastic bags often entangle wildlife, sometimes with fatal results.

Quick Lab

Reduce, Reuse, Recycle

1. Collect one day's worth of dry trash.
2. Sort the trash into items that can be reused, recycled, or discarded because they can't be reused or recycled.

Analyze and Conclude

1. **Analyze Data** Look at the trash you have sorted. Roughly what percentage of the total does each type represent?

2. **Predict** What do you think happens to the trash you produce? Think of at least three ways trash can affect living things.

3. **Evaluate** List three ways you can reduce the amount of trash you produce.

Design Goods to Last Increasing the lifetime and durability of goods also helps reduce waste. Consumers generally choose goods that will last longer. To maximize sales, however, some companies intentionally design goods that will quickly wear out or become outdated. As a result, we buy new goods to replace them. Examples include computers, technical gadgets, the latest sneaker, the coolest sports gear; and disposable goods such as pens, cameras, and cell phones.

Financial Incentives Some states or municipalities use economic incentives to reduce waste. For example, the "pay-as-you-throw" approach to garbage collection uses a financial incentive to influence consumer behavior. In these programs, municipalities charge residents for home trash pickup according to the amount of trash they put out. The less waste the household generates, the less the resident has to pay. More than 7000 of these programs now exist in the United States.

"Bottle bills" represent another approach that uses financial incentives. Ten U.S. states have these laws, which allow consumers to return empty bottles and cans to stores or collection facilities and receive a refund on the deposit required per bottle—generally 5 cents per bottle or can. The first bottle bills were passed in the 1970s to cut down on litter, but they have also served to decrease waste. Data show that containers with deposits are recycled in greater amounts then containers without deposits **(Figure 9).** In fact, bottle bills are recognized as among the most successful state legislation of recent decades. States with bottle bills have reported that their beverage container litter has decreased by 69–84% and their total litter has decreased by 30–64%.

FIGURE 9 Success of Financial Incentives Data suggest that deposits on containers increase recycling rates. In the case of PET plastic bottles and glass bottles, recycling rates are more than double on bottles with a deposit compared to bottles without a deposit.

Percent of U.S. Recycling Rates by Deposit Status, 2015		
Container Type	Deposit	Non-deposit
Aluminum cans	82.5	46.1
PET plastic bottles	63.4	17.8
HDPE plastic bottles	40.5	34.2
Glass bottles	72.0	11.8

Data from: 2015 Beverage Market Data Analysis. Container Recycling Institute, 2017.

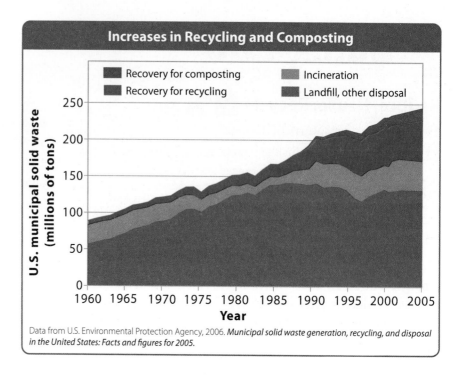

Data from U.S. Environmental Protection Agency, 2006. *Municipal solid waste generation, recycling, and disposal in the United States: Facts and figures for 2005.*

Waste Recovery

Recovering our solid waste is the second strategy for waste reduction. When we recover waste, we take material out of the waste stream so that it does not end up in a landfill or incinerator. Prime examples of recovery include composting and recycling. Industrial waste is not regulated in the same way as municipal solid waste. As a result, materials that could have been recovered end up incinerated or in a landfill.

According to the EPA, in 2007 we recovered almost one third of our municipal solid waste by recycling or composting it. The data for 2005 are shown in **Figure 10.** That amount of recovered waste comes to almost 85 million tons. By recycling and composting this waste, we saved energy equal to more than 10 billion gallons of gas. We also prevented the release of more than 190 million metric tons of carbon dioxide (CO_2). That's about the same amount of CO_2 that 35 million cars release each year.

Composting Composting is the conversion of organic waste into mulch or humus through natural biological processes of decomposition. The compost can then be used to enrich soil. People can place waste in compost piles, underground pits, or specially constructed containers. As wastes are added, heat from microbial action builds up in the interior, and decomposition proceeds. Banana peels, coffee grounds, grass clippings, autumn leaves, and countless other organic items can be converted into rich, high-quality compost through the actions of earthworms, bacteria, soil mites, sow bugs, and other detritivores and decomposers. Home composting is a prime example of how we can live more sustainably by mimicking natural cycles and incorporating them into our daily lives.

FIGURE 11 Composting Straw, grass clippings, leaves, wood chips, and kitchen wastes (eggshells, vegetable and fruit peels, and coffee grinds, for example) are all good things to include in a compost pile.

Municipal composting programs—3800 across the United States as of 2010—divert food and yard waste to central composting facilities, where the wastes decompose into mulch that community residents can use for gardens and landscaping. Nearly half of U.S. states now ban yard waste from the municipal trash collection, helping accelerate the drive toward composting. Approximately one fifth of U.S. waste is made up of materials that can easily be composted. Composting reduces landfill waste, enriches soil and helps it resist erosion, encourages soil biodiversity, makes for healthier plants and more pleasing gardens, and reduces the need for chemical fertilizers.

Recycling Recycling is the collection of materials that can be broken down and reprocessed to make new items. Recycling reduces the amount of waste that ends up in landfills and incinerators. As **Figure 12** shows, the recycling loop contains three basic steps: collection and processing, manufacturing, and purchasing recycled products. All three steps are needed for a successful recycling program.

▶ *Collection and Processing* The first step in a successful recycling program is the collection of recyclable items. Some communities have locations where residents can drop off their recyclables. Other communities have curbside recycling in which trucks pick up recyclables items in front of homes. Curbside recycling is rapidly growing because its convenience increases recycling rates. About 9000 curbside recycling programs across all 50 states now serve nearly half of all American households.

Collection and processing of recyclable materials by municipalities and businesses

Consumer purchase of products made from recycled materials

Use of recyclables by industry to manufacture new products

FIGURE 12 Recycling The familiar recycling symbol represents the three components of a sustainable recycling strategy.

FIGURE 13 Recycled Products To complete the recycling loop, consumers must purchase goods made from recycled materials, such as these bags out of candy wrappers and snack bags, or this fleece made out of recycled water bottles.

your world · your turn

WHAT DO YOU THINK?

Should recycling programs be subsidized by governments even if they are run at an economic loss? What types of external costs—costs not reflected in market prices—do you think would be involved in not recycling, say, aluminum cans? Do you feel these costs justify sponsoring recycling programs even when the programs are not financially self-supporting? Why or why not?

▶ *Manufacturing* The second step of the recycling process begins at a material recovery facility. **Material recovery facilities (MRFs)** are places where collected recyclables are sorted and prepared for reprocessing. Workers and machines sort items using automated processes. Magnetic pulleys, optical sensors, water currents, and air classifiers separate items by weight and size. MRFs clean the materials and shred them so that industries can use the reprocessed materials to manufacture new goods and materials.

▶ *Purchasing Recycled Products* In order for the recycling loop to function, consumers and businesses must complete the third step in the cycle. Recycled material is also called post-consumer waste. In step 3, industry uses post-consumer waste to create new goods for consumers to buy. Many textbooks are made from some post-consumer paper. Many glass and metal containers are now made from recycled materials. In some city parks, there are benches and pedestrian bridges made from recycled plastics. Glass is sometimes mixed with asphalt to create a new material called "glassphalt" for paving roads and making paths. Even clothing can be made from recycled plastic bottles as shown in **Figure 13.**

▶ *Limits of Recycling* Recycling rates vary from one product or material to another. Recycling rates also vary from state to state. Recycling rates among U.S. communities are anywhere from less than 5% to almost 50%. The rapid growth in recycling over the past two decades is due to three factors: economic forces, the need to reduce waste, and the satisfaction of protecting the environment by "doing the right thing."

Recycling's growth has been propelled in part by economic forces as established businesses see opportunities to save money and as entrepreneurs see opportunities to start new businesses. It has also been driven by the desire of municipalities to reduce waste and by the satisfaction people take in recycling.

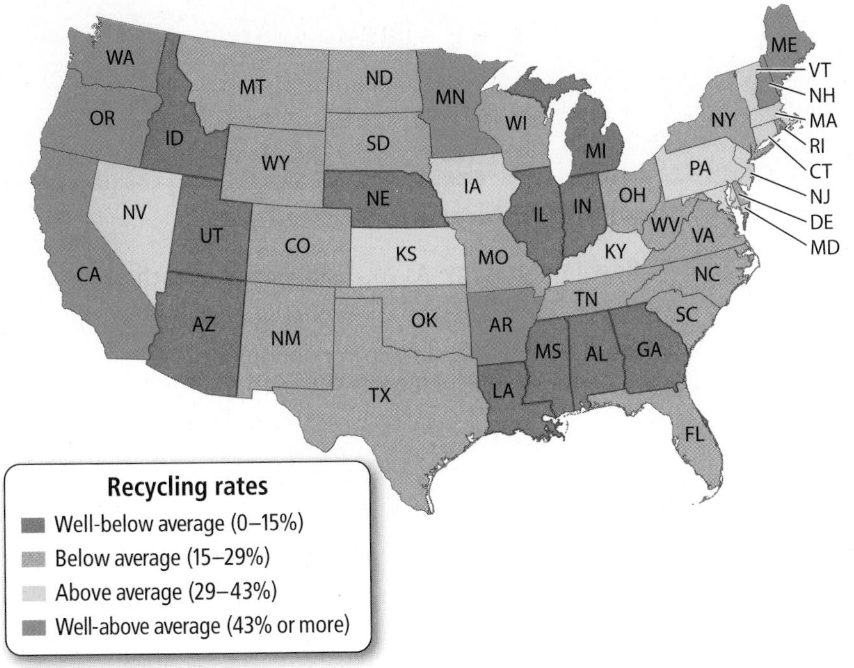

FIGURE 14 Recycling in the United States U.S. states vary greatly in the rates at which their citizens recycle.

Recycling rates
- Well-below average (0–15%)
- Below average (15–29%)
- Above average (29–43%)
- Well-above average (43% or more)

Data from: BioCycle, July 2018

These two forces have driven recycling's rise even though it has often not been financially profitable. In fact, many of the increasingly popular municipal recycling programs are run at an economic loss. The expense required to collect, sort, and process recycled goods is often more than recyclables are worth on the market. Furthermore, the more people recycle, the more glass, paper, and plastic is available to manufacturers for purchase, driving down prices and profits.

Recycling advocates, however, point out that market prices do not take into account external costs—in particular, the effects that *not recycling* has on human health and the environment. For instance, it has been estimated that globally, recycling saves enough energy to power 6 million households per year. And recycling aluminum cans saves 95 percent of the energy required to make the same amount of aluminum from mined virgin bauxite, its source material.

As more manufacturers use recycled products and as more technologies and methods are developed to use recycled materials in new ways, markets should continue to expand, and new business opportunities may arise. The steps we have taken in recycling so far are central to this transition, which many analysts view as key to building a sustainable economy.

LESSON ② Assessment

1. **Explain** Why is it so important to reduce the amount of our waste?

2. **Apply Concepts** How does recycling save energy and money?

3. **THINK IT** *THROUGH* Suppose you are the director of a company that makes boxes that hold soups and juices. These containers are not easy to recycle because they are made up of layers of paper, polyethylene (plastic), and aluminum foil. These are hard to separate in recycling efforts. How can you improve the company's environmental practices while not cutting into profits?

LESSON 3

Hazardous Waste

EVERYDAY PHENOMENON How can we best reduce the impact of hazardous waste?

Knowledge and Skills

- Define hazardous waste.
- Describe some of the sources of hazardous wastes.
- Describe current methods for hazardous waste disposal.
- Describe the danger of radioactive wastes.
- Identify agencies that regulate hazardous waste.

Reading Strategy and Vocabulary

✔ **Reading Strategy** As you read, stop after each paragraph. Write a quick summary of what you have just read.

Vocabulary e-waste, surface impoundment, deep-well injection, radioactive waste, Superfund

HAZARDOUS MATERIALS are found just about everywhere—in your home, in schools and businesses, and in the environment. Hazardous materials can harm human health and environmental quality. They can damage ecosystems and pollute the atmosphere. Toxic wastes in lakes and rivers have caused fish to die off and have closed important domestic fisheries. And the scary part is, people are not always aware of what hazardous materials really are.

What Is Hazardous Waste?

There are many harmful substances and chemicals that qualify as hazardous wastes. These wastes may be liquid, solid, sludge, or gas. By EPA definition, hazardous waste is ignitable, corrosive, reactive, or toxic.

▶ **Ignitable** Ignitable substances are those that can easily catch fire under certain conditions. These substances include natural gas, gasoline, waste oils from automotive shops and restaurants, oil-based paints, solvents (e.g. paint thinners), and alcohol.

▶ **Corrosive** Corrosive substances are those that can eat through or dissolve metal storage tanks and equipment. They are strong acids, such as sulfuric acid and hydrochloric acid. Or, they are strong bases, such as potassium hydroxide and sodium hydroxide. These wastes are particularly difficult and dangerous to dispose of because of their corrosive properties.

▶ **Reactive** Reactive substances are chemically unstable and can easily react with other compounds. When mixed with water, compressed, or heated, these substances can explode or produce toxic fumes. Examples include old ammunition or fireworks, lithium-sulfur batteries, wastes containing cyanides or sulfides, and chlorine bleach and ammonia.

▶ **Toxic** Toxic substances are harmful or fatal when inhaled, ingested, or absorbed through the skin. Toxic wastes can contaminate groundwater. Some toxins can also be highly reactive and corrosive.

Sources of Hazardous Wastes

Industry, mining, households, small businesses, agriculture, utilities, and building demolition all create hazardous waste. Industry produces the largest amounts of hazardous waste, but in most developed nations industrial waste generation and disposal is highly regulated. This regulation has reduced the amount of hazardous waste entering the environment from industrial activities. As a result, households currently are the largest source of unregulated hazardous waste.

Household hazardous waste includes a wide range of items, such as paints, batteries, oils, solvents, cleaning agents, lubricants, and pesticides **(Figure 15).** American citizens generate tons of household hazardous waste annually. The average home contains close to 45 kilograms (100 pounds) of it in sheds, basements, closets, and garages.

Although many hazardous substances become less hazardous as they degrade chemically over time, two classes of chemicals are particularly hazardous because their toxicity persists over time: organic compounds and heavy metals.

Organic Compounds In our day-to-day lives, we rely on synthetic organic compounds and petroleum-derived compounds to resist bacterial, fungal, and insect activity. Items such as plastic containers, rubber tires, pesticides, solvents, and wood preservatives are useful to us precisely because they resist decomposition. We use these substances to protect our buildings from decay, kill pests that attack crops, and keep stored goods intact. However, the resistance of these compounds to decay also makes them persistent pollutants. Many synthetic organic compounds are toxic because they can be readily absorbed through the skin of humans and other animals and can act as mutagens, carcinogens, teratogens, and endocrine disruptors.

FIGURE 15 Hazardous Wastes in the Home Many items are considered hazardous by EPA definition, including paint, cleaning supplies, and even nail polish. These items should not be disposed of with your regular garbage.

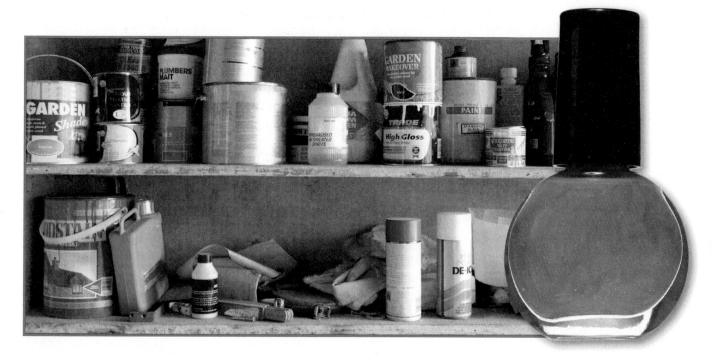

FIGURE 16 E-waste Discarded electronic waste is considered to be hazardous waste. As a result, many stores now offer drop-off locations where you can bring your outdated electronic equipment, including cell phones and computers.

Heavy Metals Heavy metals such as lead, chromium, mercury, arsenic, cadmium, tin, and copper are used widely in industry for wiring, electronics, metal plating, metal fabrication, pigments, and dyes. Heavy metals enter the environment when paints, electronic devices, batteries, and other materials are disposed of improperly. Lead from fishing weights and from hunters' lead shot has accumulated in many rivers, lakes, and forests. In older homes, lead remains a problem—from the pipes that contaminate drinking water to peeling paint. Heavy metals that are fat-soluble break down slowly and are prone to bioaccumulate in human and animal tissues.

E-waste When we first began to conduct much of our business, learning, and communication with computers and other electronic devices, many people predicted that our waste would decrease. But that has not happened. Instead, the proliferation of computers, printers, game systems, cell phones, MP3 players, and other gadgets has created a substantial new source of waste. People quickly judge these devices obsolete, and most are discarded after only a few years.

The amount of this electronic waste—called **e-waste**—is growing rapidly. On average, each household in the United States owns 24 electronic products. Each person in the U.S. generates about 20 kg of e-waste every year. In 2017, over 44 million tonnes of e-waste were produced worldwide. E-waste is estimated to increase by about 5 percent each year, reaching 120 million tonnes by 2050.

Most e-waste is disposed of in landfills as conventional solid waste. However, most electronic products contain heavy metals and toxic flame-retardants. Recent research suggests that e-waste should instead be treated as hazardous waste. The EPA and a number of states are now moving toward keeping e-waste out of conventional sanitary landfills.

In many North American cities, businesses, nonprofit organizations, or municipal services now collect used electronics for reuse or recycling. So next time you upgrade to a new computer, TV, or cell phone, find out what opportunities exist in your area for recycling your old one **(Figure 16).**

Disposal of Hazardous Waste

We have developed three primary means of hazardous waste disposal: landfills, surface impoundments, and injection wells. None of these methods lessen the hazards of the substances, but they do help keep the waste isolated from people, wildlife, and ecosystems.

Hazardous wastes should not be disposed of with your regular trash. Since the 1980s, many communities have designated sites or special collection days to gather household hazardous waste **(Figure 17).** Some areas have special facilities for the exchange and reuse of substances.

Once hazardous waste is gathered, it is transported for treatment and ultimate disposal. Transport, treatment, and disposal costs have encouraged responsible businesses to invest in reducing their hazardous waste.

Landfills The most common method of dealing with hazardous waste is to dump it in a specially designed landfill. Construction standards for hazardous waste landfills are stricter than those for ordinary sanitary landfills. Hazardous waste landfills must have several solid and watertight liners and leachate removal systems. They also must be located far from aquifers.

Dumping of hazardous waste in ordinary landfills has long been a problem. In New York City, Fresh Kills largely managed to keep hazardous waste out. However, after the September 11, 2001, terrorist attacks, Fresh Kills was reopened temporarily. Almost two million tons of rubble from the collapsed World Trade Center towers was taken by barge to Fresh Kills. Part of this rubble was considered hazardous waste. Many older landfills are now considered hazardous waste sites because of past toxic waste dumping.

FIGURE 17 Community Collection of Hazardous Waste Many communities designate collection sites or collection days for household hazardous waste.

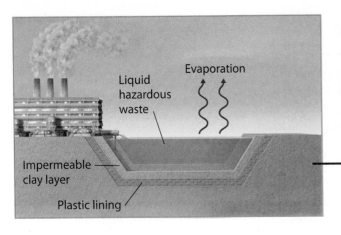

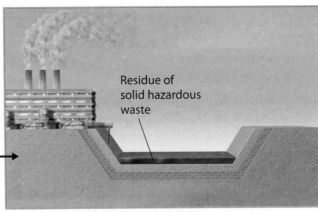

FIGURE 18 Surface Impoundment Surface impoundments are a strategy for temporarily disposing of liquid hazardous waste. The waste, mixed with water, is poured into a shallow depression lined with plastic and clay to prevent leakage. When the water evaporates, leaving a crust of the hazardous substance, new liquid is poured in and the process repeated. This method alone is not satisfactory because waste can potentially leak, overflow, evaporate, or blow away.

Surface Impoundment The second method for managing hazardous waste disposal is surface impoundment. **Surface impoundments** are shallow pits lined with plastic and an impermeable material, such as clay. Water mixed with hazardous waste is placed in the pit. When the water evaporates, it leaves behind a residue of solid hazardous waste on the bottom. This process is repeated over and over. Eventually, the residue is removed and transported elsewhere for permanent disposal. Surface impoundments are not ideal. The underlying layer can crack and leak waste. Some harmful substances may evaporate or get blown into surrounding areas. Rainstorms can cause waste to overflow and contaminate nearby areas. For these reasons, surface impoundments provide only a temporary storage solution. We rely on this strategy to reduce the volume of liquid hazardous waste.

Deep-Well Injection The third method of hazardous waste disposal is intended for long-term disposal. In **deep-well injection,** a well is drilled deep beneath the water table, into porous rock. Wastes are then injected into it. The waste is meant to remain deep underground, isolated from groundwater and human contact. However, wells can corrode and leak wastes into the soil, contaminating aquifers. Roughly 34 billion liters (9 billion gallons) of hazardous waste are pumped into U.S. injection wells each year.

 Reading Checkpoint *What are the three main ways to dispose of hazardous waste?*

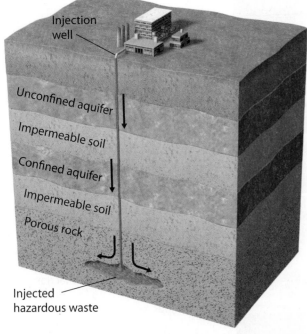

FIGURE 19 Deep-Well Injection Liquid hazardous waste may be pumped deep underground for long-term disposal. The injection well must be drilled below aquifers, into porous rock separated by impermeable soil (usually clay). The technique is expensive and waste may leak from the well shaft into groundwater.

Radiation and Human Health

In 1986, an accident at the Chernobyl nuclear power plant in Ukraine caused the release of radiation into the atmosphere. Since then, scientists have studied how radiation exposure affects human health. The graph shows the rate of thyroid cancer in people who were children at the time of the accident.

1. **Interpret Graphs** In which year did the incidence of thyroid cancer start increasing dramatically in Belarus, a nation that borders Ukraine?

2. **Interpret Graphs** In which year did Belarus show the highest number of cases? In which year did Ukraine show the highest number of cases?

3. **Apply Concepts** Many cancers usually do not appear for at least 10–15 years after radiation exposure. How does that relate to the data in the graph?

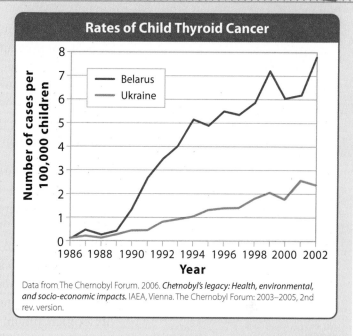

Rates of Child Thyroid Cancer

Data from The Chernobyl Forum. 2006. *Chernobyl's legacy: Health, environmental, and socio-economic impacts.* IAEA, Vienna. The Chernobyl Forum: 2003–2005, 2nd rev. version.

Radioactive Waste

Radioactive waste is waste that gives off radiation and is harmful to humans and the environment. Radioactive waste is often classified into one of two categories: high-level and low-level. Radioactive wastes that emit large amounts of radiation are called high-level wastes. High-level wastes include wastes from nuclear power plants. These wastes are very dangerous to handle and dispose of. Low-level wastes are not as radioactive as high-level wastes. Low-level radioactive wastes are produced by hospitals, laboratories, and uranium mines, as well as contaminated clothing of nuclear power plant workers. Although low-level wastes pose less known danger, they are more common, and therefore may cause more danger than we know.

Because of the long half-life of many elements in radioactive waste, radioactive wastes are difficult to dispose of safely. They must be sealed in containers that will not corrode for thousands of years. They also must be stored deep under ground.

Almost all of the high-level radioactive waste that exists currently is stored in tanks outside nuclear power plants. Yucca Mountain in Nevada has been discussed as a possible single-site repository for all U.S. nuclear waste in the future.

FIGURE 20 Sources of Radiation
Radiation in the environment comes from many sources. The largest source is radon.

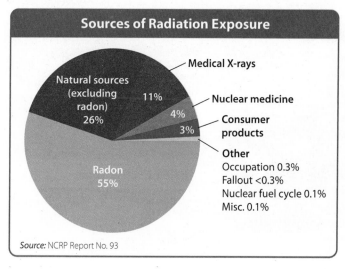

Sources of Radiation Exposure

Source: NCRP Report No. 93

Hazardous Waste Regulation

Current U.S. law makes disposing of hazardous waste quite costly. As a result, some companies illegally dump waste or ship their hazardous waste to developing nations. Either means of disposal endangers us all. Shipping hazardous waste creates health risks for everyone along the way. The costs to local governments forced to deal with illegal dumping are very high. The hazardous waste contaminates groundwater and soil. Residents and farm animals become sick, and crops fail to thrive.

Resource Conservation and Recovery Act (RCRA) The Resource Conservation and Recovery Act (RCRA) became law in 1976. Under the act the EPA sets standards by which states are to manage hazardous waste. The RCRA also requires industries that generate large amounts of hazardous waste to obtain permits and mandates that hazardous materials be tracked "from cradle to grave." As hazardous waste is generated, transported, and disposed of, the producer, carrier, and disposal facility must each report to the EPA the type and amount of material generated; its location, origin, and destination; and the way it is being handled. This process is intended to prevent illegal dumping and to encourage the use of reputable waste carriers and disposal facilities.

Fortunately, the high costs of disposal have encouraged businesses to invest in reducing their hazardous waste. Many biologically hazardous materials can be broken down by incineration. Some hazardous materials can be treated by exposure to bacteria that break down harmful components and synthesize them into new compounds.

Comprehensive Environmental Response Compensation and Liability Act (CERCLA) In 1980, the U.S. Congress passed the Comprehensive Environmental Response Compensation and Liability Act (CERCLA). This legislation established a federal program to clean up U.S. sites polluted with hazardous waste from past activities. The EPA administers this cleanup program, called the **Superfund.** With EPA support, experts identify sites polluted with hazardous chemicals. The EPA then takes action to protect groundwater near these sites, and clean up the pollution. Later laws also charged the EPA with cleaning up *brownfields*, lands whose reuse or development are complicated by the presence of hazardous materials.

FIGURE 21 Love Canal, New York Love Canal was a residential neighborhood in Niagara Falls, New York. Families were forced to evacuate their homes after toxic chemicals buried by a company and the city in past decades rose to the surface, contaminating homes and an elementary school.

Two well-publicized events spurred the creation of the Superfund legislation. In Love Canal, a residential neighborhood in Niagara Falls, New York, families were evacuated after toxic chemicals buried by a company and the city in past decades rose to the surface, contaminating homes and an elementary school. In Missouri, the entire town of Times Beach was evacuated and its buildings demolished after being contaminated by dioxin from waste oil sprayed on its roads.

Once a Superfund site is identified, EPA scientists evaluate how close the site is to human habitation, whether wastes are currently confined or likely to spread, and whether the site threatens drinking water supplies. Sites that appear harmful are placed on the EPA's National Priority List, ranked according to the level of risk to human health that they pose. Cleanup proceeds on a site-by-site basis as funds are available. Throughout the process, the EPA is required to hold public hearings to inform area residents of its findings and to receive feedback.

The objective of CERCLA was to charge the polluting parties for cleanup of their sites. For many sites, however, the responsible parties cannot be found or held liable, and in such cases, Superfund activities have been covered by taxpayers' funds and from a trust fund established by the government. As funding dwindles and the remaining cleanup jobs become more expensive, fewer cleanups are being completed.

As of early 2020, 424 of the 1335 Superfund sites on the National Priority List had been cleaned up. Many sites are contaminated with hazardous chemicals we have no effective way to deal with. In such cases, cleanups simply involve trying to isolate waste from human contact by two ways: (1) by excavating contaminated material or placing it in industrial-strength containers, and (2) shipping it to a hazardous waste disposal facility. For all these reasons, the current emphasis in the United States and elsewhere is on preventing hazardous waste contamination in the first place.

FIGURE 22 Hazardous Waste Disposal Workers need to wear protective clothing when dealing with hazardous wastes.

LESSON ③ Assessment

1. **Review** What is hazardous waste?

2. **Explain** What is the largest source of unregulated hazardous waste in the United States?

3. **Evaluate** Of the three methods of hazardous waste disposal, which one do you believe is the safest? Explain.

4. **Apply Concepts** Why is radioactive waste so dangerous?

5. **Form an Opinion** Who should be responsible for cleaning up brownfields? Explain.

REVISIT

6. **INVESTIGATIVE PHENOMENON** In this lesson, you have learned about the issues of hazardous waste management. Why is it important to have a global approach to deal with hazardous waste?

The Recycling Process

In 2017, Americans generated more than 267 million tons of waste. Of that, 35.2 percent, or 94 million tons, was recycled or composted. This might sound like a lot, but we could be recycling more. Improving our recycling habits can help reduce energy costs, conserve resources, and reduce pollution by using resources we already have to make new products. So how do all the plastic bottles, newspapers, and aluminum cans we recycle become something we can use again?

1 Residential recycling is brought by truck and loaded on a conveyor belt. Workers pull out cardboard and plastic bags. All along the conveyor belt, workers remove stray trash, which is collected and sent to a landfill.

2 The screening machine is made of three levels of spinning rollers. Bottles and cans fall through the rollers onto the lower conveyor belt. Large sheets of newspaper stay on top, while mixed paper falls to the middle level.

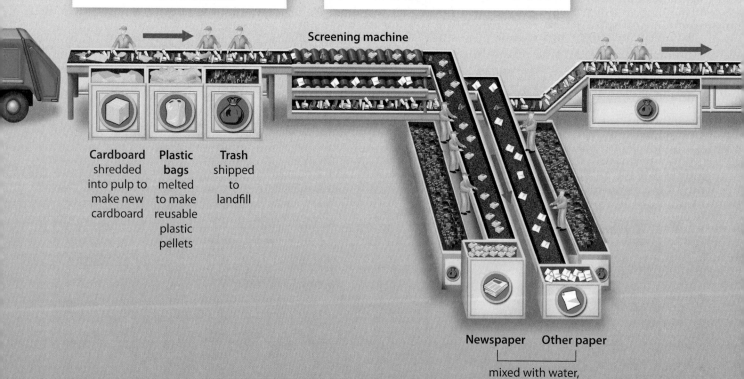

Screening machine

Cardboard shredded into pulp to make new cardboard

Plastic bags melted to make reusable plastic pellets

Trash shipped to landfill

Newspaper **Other paper**

mixed with water, shredded into pulp, and made into new paper

As materials make their way down the conveyor belt, workers check that recyclables have been properly sorted and remove any stray trash. Glass, metals, and plastics need to be as pure as possible before they get reused, so picking out trash is an important part of the sorting process.

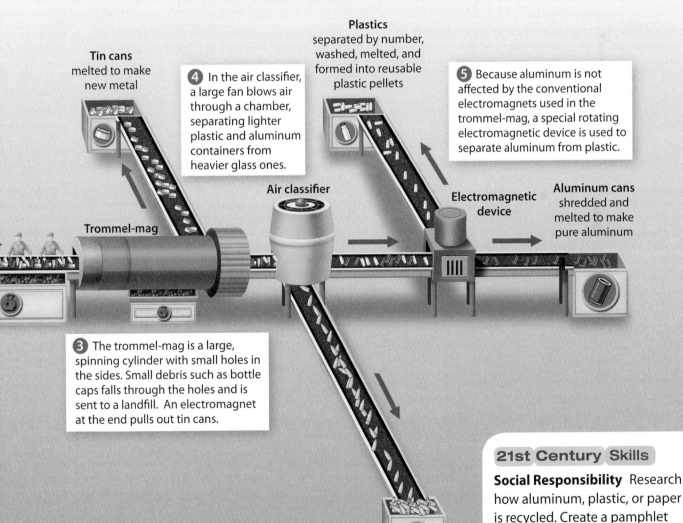

Tin cans
melted to make new metal

Plastics
separated by number, washed, melted, and formed into reusable plastic pellets

4 In the air classifier, a large fan blows air through a chamber, separating lighter plastic and aluminum containers from heavier glass ones.

5 Because aluminum is not affected by the conventional electromagnets used in the trommel-mag, a special rotating electromagnetic device is used to separate aluminum from plastic.

Air classifier

Electromagnetic device

Aluminum cans
shredded and melted to make pure aluminum

Trommel-mag

3 The trommel-mag is a large, spinning cylinder with small holes in the sides. Small debris such as bottle caps falls through the holes and is sent to a landfill. An electromagnet at the end pulls out tin cans.

Glass bottles
melted and reformed

21st Century Skills

Social Responsibility Research how aluminum, plastic, or paper is recycled. Create a pamphlet that explains the recycling process for the item you selected, and why it is important to recycle.

INVESTIGATIVE PHENOMENON

What can we do with old landfills?

Lesson 1
How does our current waste disposal impact our environment?

Lesson 2
What is the best way to manage our solid waste?

Lesson 3
How can we best reduce the impact of hazardous waste?

LESSON 1 Municipal and Industrial Waste

- The three main categories of waste include municipal solid waste, industrial waste, and hazardous waste. Municipal solid waste is nonliquid waste that comes from homes, institutions, and small businesses. Industrial waste is waste that comes from the production of consumer goods, mining, agriculture, and petroleum extraction and refining. Hazardous waste is solid or liquid waste that is toxic, chemically reactive, flammable, or corrosive.
- Current solid waste disposal methods are based on ancient practices of dumping, burying, or burning waste. In sanitary landfills, waste is buried in the ground or piled up in large mounds. Incineration is a controlled process in which mixed garbage is burned at very high temperatures.

waste (582)
municipal solid waste (582)
industrial waste (582)
hazardous waste (582)
sanitary landfill (585)
leachate (585)
incineration (587)

LESSON 2 Minimizing Solid Waste

- One of the best ways to manage solid waste is to reduce the amount we generate. One way to reduce the amount of solid waste we generate is to consume less. Other strategies include using less packaging, banning certain plastics, and designing goods that last longer.
- The amount of waste can also be reduced by composting and recycling. Composting is the conversion of organic waste into mulch or humus through decomposition. Recycling is the collection of materials that can be broken down and reprocessed to make new items.

source reduction (589)
biodegradable (590)
composting (592)
recycling (593)
material recovery facility (MRF) (594)

LESSON 3 Hazardous Waste

- Waste that is ignitable, corrosive, chemically reactive, or toxic is considered to be hazardous waste.
- Both industry and the private sector produce hazardous wastes. Organic compounds and heavy metals are particularly hazardous because they remain toxic for long periods of time. The amount of e-waste is growing rapidly.
- There are three main ways to dispose of hazardous wastes—landfills, surface impoundments, and injection wells.
- Radioactive waste is particularly dangerous to human health and is persistent in the environment.
- Hazardous waste is regulated and monitored, but illegal dumping is a problem. The two main laws that govern hazardous waste are the Resource Conservation and Recovery Act (RCRA) and the Comprehensive Environmental Response Compensation and Liability Act (CERCLA), otherwise known as the Superfund.

e-waste (598)
surface impoundment (600)
deep-well injection (600)
radioactive waste (601)
Superfund (602)

 GO ONLINE

INQUIRY LABS AND ACTIVITIES

- **Where Waste Goes**
  What gets recycled, reused, or removed? Use your town's guidelines for disposal to create your own household recommendations.
- **Overpackaging**
  Single-serving packs may be convenient, but do they make ecological or environmental sense? Use area and volume to find out what they really cost.
- **Observing a Compost**
  Make your own compost container from a 2-liter plastic bottle. Predict what will happen as materials decompose.

Chapter Assessment

Defend Your Case

The Central Case in this chapter looked at what happened to a landfill in one our nation's largest cities. Ultimately, all landfills meet their capacity. Based on what you have learned about reducing the waste stream, would you advocate federal regulations mandating recovery (reuse, recycle, compost)? Use evidence from the Central Case and the lesson to support your stand.

Review Concepts and Terms

1. Which of the following produces the largest amount of hazardous waste?
   a. farms
   c. industries
   b. households
   d. utility companies

2. To safeguard against groundwater contamination, sanitary landfills are
   a. located far from populated areas.
   b. lined with plastic and clay.
   c. covered with cement.
   d. located on slopes so that water runs downhill.

3. Which item should you NOT put in your compost pile?
   a. food scraps
   c. coffee grinds
   b. autumn leaves
   d. plastic

4. U.S. industrial waste
   a. is mostly wastewater.
   b. excludes mining waste.
   c. is shipped overseas.
   d. is regulated the same as municipal waste.

5. Items that are not easily broken down in nature are
   a. biodegradable.
   c. toxic wastes.
   b. nonbiodegradable.
   d. corrosive.

6. Substances that can eat through metals are
   a. ignitable.
   c. corrosive.
   b. toxic.
   d. reactive.

7. Heavy metals
   a. are less hazardous after incineration.
   b. are only harmful when radioactive.
   c. pose no threat after repeated exposure.
   d. bioaccumulate in animal tissues.

8. Which of the following represents the largest source of unregulated hazardous waste?
   a. farms
   c. industries
   b. households
   d. utility companies

9. E-wastes, such as the discarded computer parts below, are a source of

   a. radioactive materials.
   b. heavy metals.
   c. compostable organic compounds.
   d. corrosive acids.

10. All of the following are methods of disposal of solid wastes EXCEPT
    a. landfills.
    c. incineration.
    b. open dumping.
    d. recovery.

Modified True/False

Write true if the statement is true. If it is false, change the underlined word or words to make the statement true.

11. Plant materials can be put into a compost pile instead of municipal garbage.

12. The waste management practice of recycling involves burning garbage at high temperatures.

13. In the United States, a large portion of municipal solid waste comes from packaging and nondurable goods.

14. Currently in the United States <u>plastic</u> products are the largest component of municipal solid waste.

15. The law that helps identify and clean up hazardous waste sites is <u>CERCLA (Superfund)</u>.

Reading Comprehension

Read the following selection and answer the questions that follow.

Our society's "throwaway" mentality has fueled the demand for paper and plastic goods. It has also added to our waste disposal problem. Recycling has value as long as the recycling loop is closed. It works when people purchase the recycled items. From recycled paper, we can make paper towels and paperboard for packaging cereal, shoes, and toys. From recycled plastic, we can make carpets, pillows, and new bottles.

In order for recycling to be profitable, there can be no cross-contamination. For example, adding food, plastic, or paperboard to the paper collection reduces the paper's value. Even glass bottles must be sorted by color.

Plastic grocery bags (recycling symbol #4, LDPE) are the most widely used plastic, but not the most recycled plastic. The most widely recycled plastics are beverage bottles (#1, PET and #2, HDPE). Containers for toxic substances, such as motor oil and pesticides, are not included in recycling due to contamination risks. Styrofoam is not collected with other plastics because it is also a contaminant.

16. LDPE is the
 a. most widely recycled plastic.
 b. toxin found in plastics.
 c. plastic used to make grocery bags.
 d. only plastic that cannot be recycled.

17. Closing the recycling loop means that we must
 a. avoid contaminating collected materials for recycling.
 b. find ways to compost biodegradable plastics.
 c. purchase items made from recycled goods.
 d. stop making disposable goods.

Short Answer

18. What is the best solution for reducing the solid waste problem?

19. Why were the first bottle bills introduced and passed into law?

20. What is a WTE facility? Explain what it does and what WTE means.

21. What is composting and what are its advantages?

22. Describe the growing problem with e-waste.

23. What are the three parts of a successful recycling program?

24. What four criteria are used to define hazardous wastes?

25. Why are heavy metals and synthetic organic compounds particularly dangerous?

Critical Thinking

26. **Explain** How can we reduce the amount of material that ends up in landfills?

27. **Form an Opinion** Some nations make manufacturers responsible for reducing e-waste. Companies must recover used and discarded electronic equipment that they sell to consumers. Do you think this is a good idea? Would you support it? Why or why not? If you do not support it, offer an alternate means of reducing e-waste.

28. **Draw Conclusions** The Resource Conservation and Recovery Act requires large generators of hazardous waste to track hazardous materials "from cradle to grave." Explain what this means.

29. **Apply Concepts** U.S. households generate a great deal of hazardous waste. Most of this waste ends up in ordinary landfills or incinerators. What sort of policies do we need in place to ensure safer waste management?

Analyze Data

The graph below shows trends in managing municipal solid waste from 1960 to 2005. Use the data to answer the questions.

Municipal Solid Waste Trends (in millions of tons)						
Activity	1960	1970	1980	1990	2000	2005
Recycling	5.6	8.0	14.5	29.0	52.8	58.6
Composting	*	*	*	4.2	16.5	20.6
Incineration	0.0	0.4	2.7	29.7	33.7	33.4
Landfill	82.5	112.7	134.4	142.3	135.3	135.6
Total Waste	88.1	121.1	151.6	205.2	238.3	248.2

Source: U.S. Environmental Protection Agency, Facts and Figures for 2006.

*Negligible amount

30. Compare and Contrast Look at trends in municipal solid waste (MSW) from 1960 to 1990. How does landfill use compare to incinerator use? What happened from 1990 to 2005?

31. Interpret Tables What activities show an upward trend after 1990?

32. Draw Conclusions How do you account for the slight decline in incinerated MSW from 2000 to 2005? Was this due to declining MSW overall? Explain.

Write About It

33. Description Speculative fiction is based on projecting from current trends and facts. Describe two possible scenarios for waste management in the year 2040. Base one on the current trend of ever-increasing waste per person. Base the other on the assumption that people will generate less waste in the future.

34. REVISIT **INVESTIGATIVE** PHENOMENON
The choices we make as consumers affect our environment. How we handle the waste we produce also affects our environment. When it comes to managing waste, what do you think are the most important issues? Pick one and develop a Web page that supports that issue.

Ecological Footprints

Read the information below. Copy the table into your notebook, and record your calculations. Then, answer the questions that follow.

The "State of Garbage in America" survey shows how much municipal solid waste (MSW) U.S. residents generate. Results vary from state to state. In 2006, the daily average was 7.56 pounds MSW per person. By comparison, other high-income nations generate 2.64 pounds of waste a day. The world average is 1.47 pounds per day. Calculate the amount of MSW generated in 1 day and in 1 year by each of the groups if they generated waste at the rate of the U.S., other high-income nations, and the world average. For the U.S., convert the pounds of MSW to tons. (*Hint:* Divide pounds by 2000.)

1. Suppose you are a town manager in a town of 50,000 people. The council wants to have a landfill built nearby.

The town's landfill will hold up to 1 million tons of MSW. How many years will it take to fill the landfill? To calculate, use the average amount of MSW generated in the U.S. What other assumptions are you making in your calculations?

2. Suppose your town of 50,000 people generated the same amount of MSW as the world average. How many tons of MSW would the town generate per day? per year? How much longer would a landfill of the same capacity serve the town?

Groups Generating Municipal Solid Waste	Population	Per Person MSW Generation Rates					
		U.S. Average (lb)		Average of High–income Nations (lb)		World Average (lb)	
		Day	Year	Day	Year	Day	Year
You	1	7.56	2760	2.64	963.6	1.47	536.5
Your class							
Your state							
United States							

Data from Simmons, P., et al. 2006. The State of Garbage in America. *BioCycle.* 47:26.

ANCHORING PHENOMENON

These questions will help you apply what you have learned in this Unit to the Anchoring Phenomenon.

1. **Obtain, Evaluate, and Communicate Information** Choose a nonprofit organization that advocates for the environment. Research more about the organization. What is their mission statement? How do they reach people? What actions do they take to protect the environment? How do they raise funds to run the organization? What else interests you about this organization? Write a summary report on your findings.

2. **Develop and Use Models** Suppose your town has a coal-burning power plant. You would like to form a nonprofit organization to raise awareness about the benefits of renewable energy, with the long-term goal of replacing the coal-burning plant with energy from renewable sources. List steps you would take to form your organization. What would you need to make your organization run successfully? How would you obtain what you need? How would you reach people in your town? How would you address concerns about job losses associated with closing the plant? Use a flowchart to model how you would start your organization.

🖥 GO ONLINE

For activities that will give you an opportunity to demonstrate what you have learned.

MODELING Revisit your Anchoring Phenomenon Modeling worksheet and update it with the information you have learned in this unit.

ANCHORING PHENOMENON PROJECT Model a nonprofit organization with a mission to address climate change.

Skills and Reference HANDBOOK

Math Handbook

THROUGHOUT YOUR STUDY OF SCIENCE, you will often need to solve math problems. This handbook is designed to help you quickly review the basic math skills you will use most often.

Fractions

Adding and Subtracting Fractions

To add or subtract fractions that have the same denominator, add or subtract the numerators, and then write the sum or difference over the denominator. Express the answer in lowest terms.

Examples

$$\frac{3}{10} + \frac{1}{10} = \frac{3+1}{10} = \frac{4}{10} = \frac{2}{5}$$

$$\frac{5}{7} - \frac{2}{7} = \frac{5-2}{7} = \frac{3}{7}$$

To add or subtract fractions with different denominators, find the least common denominator. Write an equivalent fraction for each fraction using this least common denominator. Then add or subtract the numerators. Write the sum or difference over the least common denominator and express the answer in lowest terms.

Examples

$$\frac{1}{3} + \frac{3}{5} = \frac{5}{15} + \frac{9}{15} = \frac{5+9}{15} = \frac{14}{15}$$

$$\frac{7}{8} - \frac{1}{4} = \frac{7}{8} - \frac{2}{8} = \frac{7-2}{8} = \frac{5}{8}$$

Multiplying Fractions

When multiplying two fractions, multiply the numerators to find the product's numerator. Then multiply the denominators to find the product's denominator. It helps to divide any numerator or denominator by the greatest common factor before multiplying. Express the answer in lowest terms.

Examples

$$\frac{3}{5} \times \frac{2}{7} = \frac{3 \times 2}{5 \times 7} = \frac{6}{35}$$

$$\frac{4}{14} \times \frac{6}{9} = \frac{2 \times 2}{7 \times 2} \times \frac{2 \times 3}{3 \times 3} = \frac{2 \times 2}{7 \times 3} = \frac{4}{21}$$

Dividing Fractions

To divide one fraction by another, first invert the fraction you are dividing by. Then multiply the two fractions. Express the answer in lowest terms.

Examples

$$\frac{2}{5} \div \frac{3}{4} = \frac{2}{5} \times \frac{4}{3} = \frac{2 \times 4}{5 \times 3} = \frac{8}{15}$$

$$\frac{9}{16} \div \frac{5}{8} = \frac{9}{16} \times \frac{8}{5} = \frac{9 \times 1}{2 \times 5} = \frac{9}{10}$$

Ratios and Proportions

A ratio compares two numbers or quantities. A ratio is often written as a fraction expressed in lowest terms. A ratio also may be written with a colon.

Examples

The ratio of 3 to 4 is written as 3 to 4, $\frac{3}{4}$, or 3 : 4.

The ratio of 10 to 5 is written as $\frac{10}{5} = \frac{2}{1}$, or 2 : 1.

A proportion is a mathematical sentence that states that two ratios are equivalent. To write a proportion, place an equals sign between the two equivalent ratios.

Examples

The ratio of 6 to 9 is the same as the ratio of 8 to 12.

$$\frac{6}{9} = \frac{8}{12}$$

The ratio of 2 to 4 is the same as the ratio of 7 to 14.

$$\frac{2}{4} = \frac{7}{14}$$

You can set up a proportion to determine an unknown quantity. Use *x* to represent the unknown. To find the value of *x*, cross multiply and then divide both sides of the equation by the number that comes before *x*.

Example

Two out of five students have blue notebooks. If this same ratio exists in a class of twenty students how many students in the class have blue notebooks?

$$\frac{2}{5} = \frac{x}{20} \qquad \leftarrow \textbf{Cross multiply.}$$
$$2 \times 20 = 5x \qquad \leftarrow \textbf{Divide.}$$
$$8 = x$$

Percentages and Decimals

Calculating Percents

A percentage is a ratio that compares a number to 100. The word percent (%) means "parts of 100" or "per 100 parts." Another way to think of a percentage is as a part of a whole expressed in hundredths. Thus, the number 0.41 ("41 hundredths") can also be expressed as 41%, or "41 per 100 parts."

$$0.41 = \frac{41}{100} = 41\%$$

You can calculate a percentage by multiplying the ratio of the part to the whole by 100%.

$$Percent = \frac{Part}{Whole} \times 100\%$$

Examples

The fraction $\frac{7}{10}$ is equivalent to 70%.

The fraction $\frac{5}{8}$ is equivalent to 62.5%.

The fraction $\frac{15}{200}$ is equivalent to 7.5%.

You have probably seen data expressed in the form of a percentage. For instance, nutrition labels on packaged foods include a column title "% Daily Value." In this column, the nutrients (such as fat, cholesterol, and fiber) contained in a single serving are compared to the recommended daily intake. You also encounter percentages when you go shopping (items on sale might be labeled "20% off"), or when you receive test scores.

Example

A student answers 34 questions correctly on a 40-question exam. What is the student's score expressed as a percent?

$$Percent = \frac{Part}{Whole} \times 100\%$$

$$= \frac{Number\ of\ correct\ answers}{Number\ of\ questions\ asked} \times 100\%$$

$$= \frac{34}{40} \times 100\%$$

$$= 85\%$$

Calculating Between Percentages and Decimals

To convert a percentage to a decimal value, write the number without the percent sign and move the decimal point two places to the left. Add a zero before the decimal point.

$$38\% = 0.38$$
$$13.92\% = 0.1392$$

You can convert a decimal value to a percentage by moving the decimal point two places to the right and adding the percent sign.

Examples

$$0.46 = 46\%$$
$$0.8215 = 82.15\%$$

Converting between percentages and decimals is often necessary when solving word problems involving composition or concentration.

Example

A nighttime cold medicine is 22% alcohol by volume. How many milliliters of alcohol are in a 250-mL bottle of this medicine?

$$22\% = 0.22 \quad \leftarrow \textbf{Convert percent to a decimal.}$$

$$\frac{Part}{Whole} = \frac{Part}{250\ mL} = 0.22$$

$$Part = 250\ mL \times 0.22$$

$$Part = 55\ mL$$

Example

During a flu epidemic, 28% of the students at a school were absent. If 238 students were absent, what was the school's attendance?

$$28\% = 0.28 \quad \leftarrow \textbf{Convert percent to a decimal.}$$

$$\frac{Part}{Whole} = \frac{238\ students}{Whole} = 0.28$$

$$Whole = \frac{238\ students}{0.28}$$

$$Whole = 850\ students$$

Math Handbook

Exponents

A base is a number that is used as a factor. An exponent is a number that tells how many times the base is to be used as a factor. In the example below, 2 is the base and 5 is the power.

Example

$2^5 = 2 \times 2 \times 2 \times 2 \times 2 = 32$

A power is any number that can be expressed as a product in which all of the factors are the same. Any number raised to the zero power is 1. The only exception is the number 0, which is zero regardless of the power it is raised to. Any number raised to the first power is that number.

Exponents	
Powers of 2	**Powers of 10**
$2^4 = 16$	$10^4 = 10{,}000$
$2^3 = 8$	$10^3 = 1000$
$2^2 = 4$	$10^2 = 100$
$2^1 = 2$	$10^1 = 10$
$2^0 = 1$	$10^0 = 1$
$2^{-1} = \frac{1}{2}$	$10^{-1} = \frac{1}{10}$
$2^{-2} = \frac{1}{4}$	$10^{-2} = \frac{1}{100}$
$2^{-3} = \frac{1}{8}$	$10^{-3} = \frac{1}{1000}$
$2^{-4} = \frac{1}{16}$	$10^{-4} = \frac{1}{10{,}000}$

Multiplying With Exponents

To multiply exponential expressions with the same base, add the exponents. The general expression for exponents with the same base is $x^a \times x^b = x^{a+b}$.

Example

$3^2 \times 3^4 = (3 \times 3) \times (3 \times 3 \times 3 \times 3) = 3^6 = 729$

To raise one power to another power, keep the base and multiply the exponents. The general expression is $(x^a)^b = x^{ab}$.

Example

$(3^2)^3 = (3^2) \times (3^2) \times (3^2) = 3^6 = 729$

To raise a product to a power, raise each factor to the power. The general expression is $(xy)^n = x^n y^n$.

Example

$(3 \times 9)^2 = 3^2 \times 9^2 = 9 \times 81 = 729$

Dividing With Exponents

To divide exponential expressions with the same base, keep the base and subtract the exponents. The general expression is:

$$\frac{x^a}{x^b} = x^{a-b}$$

Example

$$\frac{5^6}{5^4} = 5^{6-4} = 5^2 = 25$$

When the exponent of the denominator is greater than the exponent of the numerator, the exponent of the result is negative. A negative exponent follows the general expression:

$$x^{-n} = \frac{1}{x^n}$$

Example

$$2^3 \div 2^5 = 2^{3-5} = 2^{-2} = \frac{1}{2^2} = \frac{1}{4}$$

Metric conversions often involve multiplication or division of exponential expressions. Make sure to keep track of the sign of the exponent when performing operations with exponential expressions.

Example

Convert 3.49×10^2 μm to meters. ($1 \text{ μm} = 10^{-6}$ m) Based on the equivalence $1 \text{ μm} = 10^{-6}$ m, you can write the ratio $1 \text{ μm}/10^{-6}$ m, which equals one.

$$3.49 \times 10^2 \text{ μm} \times \frac{10^{-6} \text{ m}}{1 \text{ μm}} = 3.49 \times 10^2 \times 10^{-6} \text{ m}$$

$$= 3.49 \times 10^{2-6} \text{ m}$$

$$= 3.49 \times 10^{-4} \text{ m}$$

Scientific Notation

Scientific notation is used to express very large numbers or very small numbers. In scientific notation, a number is written as the product of two numbers: a coefficient that is greater than or equal to one and less than ten, and 10 raised to a power. For example, the number 710,000 written in scientific notation is 7.1×10^5. The coefficient in this number is 7.1. The power of ten, or the exponent, is 5. The exponent indicates how many times the coefficient must be multiplied by 10 to equal the number 710,000.

To convert a large number to scientific notation, move the decimal point to the left until it is located to the right of the first nonzero number. The number of places that you move the decimal point becomes the positive exponent of 10.

Example

$18,930,000 = 1.893 \times 10^7$

To write a number less than 1 in scientific notation, move the decimal point to the right of the first nonzero number. Use the number of places you moved the decimal point as the negative exponent of 10.

Example

$0.0027 = \dfrac{2.7}{10 \times 10 \times 10} = 2.7 \times 10^{-3}$

When you convert a number to scientific notation, remember that you are not changing the value of the number. You are only changing the way that it is written.

Examples

$500,000 = 5 \times 10^5$
$0.000\,000\,042 = 4.2 \times 10^{-8}$
$0.030\,06 = 3.006 \times 10^{-2}$
$285.2 = 2.852 \times 10^2$
$0.0002 = 2 \times 10^{-4}$
$83,700,000 = 8.37 \times 10^7$

Adding and Subtracting

To add or subtract numbers in scientific notation, the exponents must be the same. If they are different, rewrite one of the numbers to make the exponents the same. Then write the answer so that only one number is to the left of the decimal point.

Examples

$$(3.20 \times 10^3) + (5.1 \times 10^2) = (32.0 \times 10^2) + (5.1 \times 10^2)$$
$$= 37.1 \times 10^2$$
$$= 3.71 \times 10^3$$

$$(3.42 \times 10^{-5}) - (2.5 \times 10^{-6})$$
$$= (34.2 \times 10^{-6}) - (2.5 \times 10^{-6})$$
$$= 31.7 \times 10^{-6}$$
$$= 3.17 \times 10^{-5}$$

Multiplying and Dividing

To multiply or divide numbers in scientific notation, the exponents are added or subtracted.

Examples

$$(1.2 \times 10^3) \times (3.4 \times 10^4) = (4.1 \times 10^{3\,+\,4})$$
$$= 4.1 \times 10^7$$

$$(5.0 \times 10^9) \div (2.5 \times 10^6) = (2.0 \times 10^{9\,-\,6})$$
$$= 2.0 \times 10^3$$

$$\dfrac{(1.2 \times 10^{-3})^2}{(10^{-2})^3 \times (2.0 \times 10^{-3})} = \dfrac{1.2^2 \times (10^{-3})^2}{(10^{-6}) \times (2.0 \times 10^{-3})}$$

$$= \dfrac{1.44 \times 10^{-6}}{2.0 \times 10^{-6\,+\,3(-3)}}$$

$$= \dfrac{1.44 \times 10^{-6}}{2.0 \times 10^{-9}}$$

$$= 0.72 \times 10^{-6\,-\,(-9)}$$

$$= 0.72 \times 10^3$$

$$= 7.2 \times 10^2$$

Significant Figures

When measurements are combined in calculations, the uncertainly of each measurement must be correctly reflected in the final result. The digits that are accurate in the answer are called significant figures. When the result of a calculation has more significant figures than needed, the result must be rounded down or up. If the first digit after the last significant digit is less than 5, round down. If the first digit after the last significant digit is 5 or more, round up.

Examples

1577 rounded to three significant figures is 1580.
1574 rounded to three significant figures is 1570.
2.458462 rounded to three significant figures is 2.46.
2.458462 rounded to four significant figures is 2.458.

Examples

Each of the measurements listed below has three significant figures. The significant figures are underlined.

456 mL
0.305 g
70.4 mg
0.000457 g
5.64×10^3 km
444,000 µg
1.30×10^{-2} m
0.00406 dm

Adding and Subtracting

In addition and subtraction, the number of significant figures in the answer depends on the number with the largest uncertainty.

Example

$$
\begin{array}{r}
25.34 \text{ g} \\
152 \text{ g} \\
+ \quad 4.009 \text{ g} \\
\hline
181 \text{ g}
\end{array}
$$

The measurement with the largest uncertainty is 152 g and it is measured to the nearest gram. Therefore, the answer is given to the nearest gram.

Example

189.427 g − 19.00 g = 170.427 g ≈ 170.43 g

The measurement with the larger uncertainty is 19.00 g, which is measured to the nearest hundredth of a gram. Therefore, the answer is given to the nearest hundredth of a gram.

Multiplying and Dividing

In multiplication and division, the measurement with the smallest number of significant figures determines the number of significant figures in the answer.

Example

$(5.3 \text{ m}) \times (1.54 \text{ m}) = 8.162 \text{ m}^2 \approx 8.2 \text{ m}^2$

Because 5.3 m has only two significant figures, the answer must be rounded to two significant figures.

Example

$$
\begin{aligned}
\text{Density} &= \frac{\text{Mass}}{\text{Volume}} \\
&= \frac{20.79 \text{ g}}{5.5 \text{ mL}} \\
&= 3.78 \text{ g/mL} \\
&\approx 3.8 \text{ g/mL}
\end{aligned}
$$

Because 5.5 mL has only two significant figures, the answer must be rounded to two significant figures.

Example

Calculate the perimeter [(2 × length) + (2 × width)] and the area (length × width) of a rectangular garden plot that measures 3.28 m by 16 m. Round each answer to the correct number of significant figures.

$$
\begin{aligned}
\text{Perimeter} &= (2 \times 32.8 \text{ m}) + (2 \times 16 \text{ m}) \\
&= 65.6 \text{ m} + 32 \text{ m} \\
&= 97.6 \text{ m} \\
&\approx 98 \text{ m}
\end{aligned}
$$

Area = 32.8 m × 16 m = 524.8 m² ≈ 5.2×10^2 m²

Formulas and Equations

An equation is a mathematical sentence that contains one or more variables and one or more mathematical operators (such as +, −, ÷, ×, and =). An equation expresses a relationship between two or more quantities.

A formula is a special kind of equation. A formula such as $V = l \times w \times h$ states the relationship between unknown quantities represented by the variables V, l, w, and h. The formula means that volume (of a rectangular solid) equals length times width times height. Some formulas have numbers that do not vary, such as the formula for the perimeter of a square, $P = 4s$. In this formula, the number 4 is constant.

To solve for a quantity in an equation or formula, substitute known values for the variables. Be sure to include units.

Example

$$\text{Speed} = \frac{\text{Distance}}{\text{Time}}$$

$$v = \frac{d}{t}$$

An airplane travels in a straight line at a speed of 600 km/h. How far does it fly in 3.5 hours? Write the formula that relates speed, distance, and time.

To solve for distance, multiply both sides of the equation by t.

$$v = \frac{d}{t}$$

$$v \times t = \frac{d}{t} \times t$$

$$v \times t = d$$

Substitute in the known values.

$$600 \text{ km/h} \times 3.5 \text{ h} = d$$
$$2100 \text{ km} = d$$

Conversion Factors

Many problems involve converting measurements from one unit to another. You can convert units by using an equation that shows how units are related. For example, 1 in. = 2.54 cm relates inches and centimeters.

To write a conversion factor, divide both sides of the equation by 1 in.

$$\frac{1 \text{ in.}}{1 \text{ in.}} = \frac{2.54 \text{ cm}}{1 \text{ in.}}$$

$$1 = 2.54 \text{ cm/in.}$$

Because the conversion factor is equal to 1, you can multiply one side of an equation by it and preserve equality. You can make a second conversion factor by dividing both sides of the equation by 2.54 cm.

$$\frac{1 \text{ in.}}{2.54 \text{ cm}} = \frac{2.54 \text{ cm}}{2.54 \text{ cm}} = 1$$

$$1 = 0.394 \text{ in./cm}$$

One conversion factor converts inches to centimeters and the other converts centimeters to inches. Choose the conversion factor that cancels out the unit that you have a measurement for.

Example

Convert 25 inches to centimeters. Use the conversion factor 2.54 cm/in. so that the inches units cancel.

$$25 \text{ in.} \times \frac{2.54 \text{ cm}}{1 \text{ in.}} \approx 64 \text{ cm}$$

Math Handbook

Some conversions are more complicated and require multiple steps.

Example

Convert 23°F to a Celsius temperature.
The conversion formula is $°F = (\frac{9}{5} \times °C) + 32°F$.

First solve the equation for °C.

$$°F = (\frac{9}{5} \times °C) + 32°F$$

$$°F - 32°F = \frac{9}{5} \times °C$$

$$\frac{5}{9}(°F - 32°F) = °C$$

Now substitute in 23°F:

$$°C = \frac{5}{9}(23°F - 32°F) = \frac{5}{9}(-9) = -5$$

Thus, 23°F is equivalent to -5°C.

Example

A grocer is selling oranges at a price of 3 for $1.00. How much would 10 oranges cost?

Use the equality 3 oranges = $1.00 to write a conversion factor. The desired conversion factor should have dollars in the numerator so that the oranges units cancel.

$$10 \text{ oranges} \times \frac{\$1.00}{3 \text{ oranges}} = \$3.33$$

Example

Water runs through a hose at a rate of 2.5 gallons per minute. What is the rate of water flow in gallons per day?

To convert gal/min to gal/d, you must use conversion factors based on the following equalities.

60 min = 1 h

24 h = 1 d

$$\frac{2.5 \text{ gal}}{\text{min}} \times \frac{60 \text{ min}}{1 \text{ h}} \times \frac{24 \text{ h}}{1 \text{ d}} = 3600 \text{ gal/d}$$

Graph Skills

PRESENTING DATA in ways that reveal trends and patterns is a vital part of science. For scientists—or anyone presenting investigation results—the primary tool for showing data trends and patterns is the graph. Graph interpretation, therefore, is a skill you will want to develop and improve. This section shows you how to read graphs and surveys, the most common types of graphs, and their typical uses.

Navigating a Graph

A graph is a diagram that shows relationships among variables, which are factors of an investigation that can change. The most common types of graphs relate values of a dependent variable to those of an independent variable. When a researcher changes the values of an independent variable, values of the dependent variable may change in response. A dependent variable is so named because its values "depend on" the values of an independent variable. The values of the independent variable are known or specified, and the values of the dependent variable are unknown and are what we are interested in obtaining or measuring. Graphing the data from an investigation helps reveal relationships—or the lack thereof—among variables.

Usually, independent variables are represented on the horizontal axis, or *x*-axis, of a graph, while dependent variables are represented on the vertical axis, or *y*-axis. Numerical values of variables generally become larger as one proceeds rightward on the *x*-axis or upward on the *y*-axis. In many cases, independent variables are not numerical at all, but categorical. For example, in a graph presenting population sizes of several nations, the nations make up different "values," or categories, of the independent variable. Population size, in numerical data, is the dependent variable.

Figure 1 shows a typical graph presenting data from an experiment. In the experiment, a researcher investigated population growth among yeast cells.

The *x*-axis shows values of her independent variable, which in this case was time expressed in units of hours. The researcher was interested in how many bacterial cells would propagate over time, so the dependent variable presented on the *y*-axis, is the number of bacterial cells present. For each hour at which data were measured during the course of the experiment, a data point on the graph is plotted to show the corresponding number of bacterial cells present. In this particular graph, a line (purple curve) was then drawn through the actual data points (orange dots), showing how closely the empirical data matched the logistic growth curve.

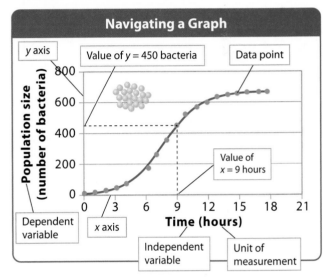

FIGURE 1

Now that you're familiar with the basic building blocks of a graph, let's review a few basic concepts of graphing while surveying the most common types of graphs and their uses.

GO ONLINE

• Graph It

Take advantage of the Graph It tutorials on the Realize course. The Graph It tutorials allow you to plot your own data, and help you further expand your comprehension of graphs.

Graph Skills

Line Graphs

A line graph is often used when a data set involves a sequence of some kind, such as a series of values that occur one by one and change through time or across distance (**Figure 2**). Line graphs are most appropriate when the *y*-axis expresses a continuous numerical variable, and the *x*-axis expresses either continuous numerical data or categories that occur in sequence (such as years).

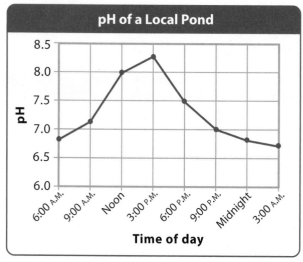

FIGURE 2

One useful technique is to plot two or more data sets together on the same graph (**Figure 3**). This allows us to compare trends in the data sets to see whether and how they may be related.

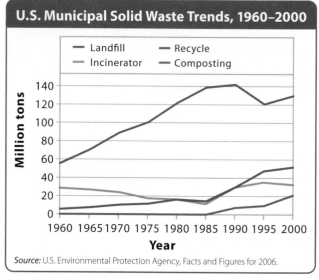

Source: U.S. Environmental Protection Agency, Facts and Figures for 2006.

FIGURE 3

To create a line graph, follow these steps:

1. On graph paper, draw a horizontal, or *x*-axis and a vertical, or *y*-axis.

2. Label the horizontal axis with the name of the independent variable. Label the vertical axis with the name of the dependent variable. Include units of measurement.

3. Create a scale on each axis by marking off equally spaced numbers that cover the range of the data collected.

4. Plot a point on the graph for each piece of data.

5. Connect the plotted points with a solid line. In some cases, it may be more appropriate to draw a line that shows the general trend of the plotted points. In those cases, some of the points may fall above or below the line. Also, not all graphs are linear. It may be more appropriate to draw a curve to connect the points.

6. Add a title that identifies the variables of the relationship in the graph.

Projections

Besides showing observed data, we can use graphs to show predicted, or projected, data that are based on models, simulations, or extrapolations from observed data. Often, projected data on a line graph are shown with dashed lines, as in **Figure 4**, to indicate that they are less certain than observed data.

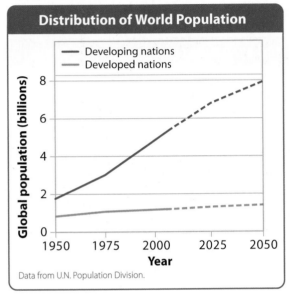

Distribution of World Population

Data from U.N. Population Division.

FIGURE 4

Circle Graphs

A circle graph (sometimes called a pie chart) is a good choice when you need to compare the proportions of a whole that is made up of several categories (**Figure 5**). Each category is graphed as a wedge of a circle (or slice of a pie), the width of which represents the percentage of the whole represented by that category.

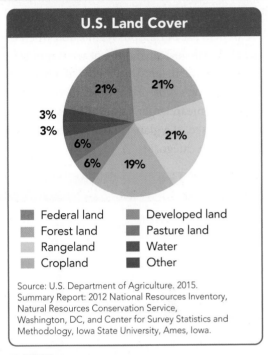

U.S. Land Cover

- Federal land
- Forest land
- Rangeland
- Cropland
- Developed land
- Pasture land
- Water
- Other

Source: U.S. Department of Agriculture. 2015. Summary Report: 2012 National Resources Inventory, Natural Resources Conservation Service, Washington, DC, and Center for Survey Statistics and Methodology, Iowa State University, Ames, Iowa.

FIGURE 5

To create a circle graph, follow these steps.

1. Use a compass to draw a circle. Mark the center with a point. Then, draw a line from the center point to the top of the circle.

2. Determine the size of each slice by setting up a proportion where x equals the number of degrees in a slice. Note: a circle contains 360 degrees.

3. Use a protractor to measure the angle of the first slice, using the line you drew to the top of the circle as the 0 line. Draw a line from the center of the circle to the edge for the angle you measured.

4. Continue around the circle by measuring the size of each slice with the protractor. Start measuring from the edges of the previous slice so the wedges do not overlap. When you are done, the entire circle should be filled in.

5. Determine the percentage of the whole circle that each slice represents. To do this, divide the number of degrees in a slice by the total number of degrees in a circle (360) and multiply by 100%.

6. Use a different color for each slice. Label each slice with the category and with the percentage of the whole it represents.

7. Add a title to the circle graph.

Bar Graphs

Researchers use bar graphs most often when one variable is categorical and the other is numerical. In a bar graph, the height (or length) of a bar represents the value of one category of the categorical variable; longer bars mean larger values (**Figure 6**). Bar graphs allow us to see, at a glance, how values of a variable differ among categories.

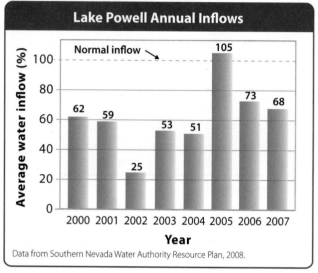

FIGURE 6

Graphing two or more data sets together on a bar graph sometimes helps reveal patterns and relationships. A bar graph such as **Figure 7** allows us to compare two data sets: average number of vultures in early month and average number of vultures in late month. A graph that does double duty in this way allows for higher-level analysis. Many bar graphs in this text illustrate multiple types of information at the same time.

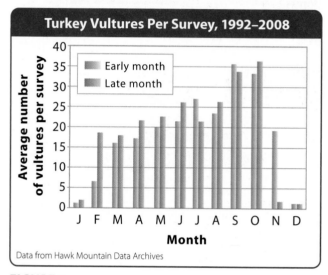

FIGURE 7

Figure 8 illustrates another way in which a bar graph can be modified. First, note that the bars are arranged horizontally instead of vertically. In this arrangement, the independent variable (category) is along the *y*-axis, and the dependent variable (data) is along the *x*-axis. Second, note that the bars extend in both directions from a central *x*-axis value of zero, representing either positive (right) or negative (left) values. Depending on your type of data and the points you want to make, one or both of these modifications can make for a clearer presentation of your data.

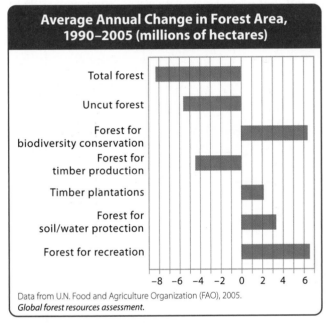

Average Annual Change in Forest Area, 1990–2005 (millions of hectares)

Data from U.N. Food and Agriculture Organization (FAO), 2005.
Global forest resources assessment.

FIGURE 8

One specific type of horizontal bar graph is the age structure pyramid. This specialized bar graph shows the distribution of a nation's population across different age groups and sexes (**Figure 9**). Age categories are displayed on the *y*-axis, while there are bars on the *x*-axis representing the population size by age group and sex.

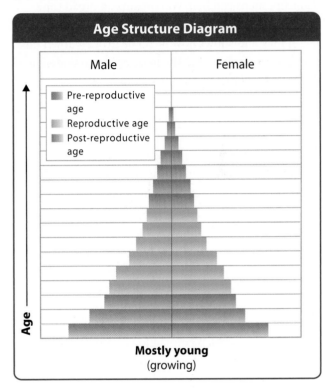

Age Structure Diagram

Mostly young
(growing)

FIGURE 9

To create a bar graph, follow these steps:

1. On graph paper, draw a horizontal, or *x*-axis and a vertical, or *y*-axis.

2. Write the names of the categories to be graphed along the horizontal axis. Include an overall label for the *x*-axis as well.

3. Label the vertical axis with the name of the dependent variable. Include the unit of measurement. Then, create a scale along the axis by marking off equally spaced numbers that cover the range of the data collected.

4. For each category, draw a solid bar using the scale on the vertical axis to determine the height. Make all the bars the same width.

5. Add a title that describes the graph.

AT THE BEGINNING OF EACH LESSON, you will find a reading strategy to help you study. Each strategy uses a graphic organizer to help you stay organized. The following strategies and graphic organizers are used throughout the text.

Concept Maps

Concept maps can help you organize a broad topic having many subtopics. A concept map begins with a main idea and shows how it can be broken down into specific topics. It makes the ideas easier to understand by presenting their relationships visually.

You construct a concept map by placing the concept words (usually nouns) in boxes and connecting the boxes with linking word(s). The most general concept usually is placed at the top of the map or in the center. The content of the other boxes becomes more specific as you move away from the main concept. The linking word(s), which describe the relationship between the linked concepts, are written on a line between two boxes. If you follow any string of concepts and linking words down through a map, they should read approximately like a sentence.

Some concept maps may also include linking words that connect a concept in one branch to another branch. Such connections, sometimes called cross-linkages, show more complex interrelationships.

Flowcharts

A flowchart can help you represent the order in which a set of events has occurred or should occur. Flowcharts are useful for outlining the steps in a procedure or stages in a process with a definite beginning and end.

To make a flowchart, list the steps in the process you want to represent and count the steps. Then, create the appropriate number of boxes, starting at the top of a page or on the left. Write a brief description of the first event in the first box, and then fill in the other steps, box by box. Link each box to the next event in the process with an arrow. Then, add a title to the flowchart.

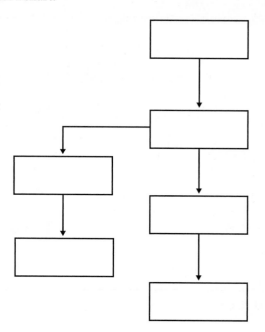

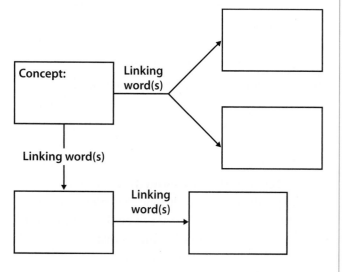

Cause and Effect Diagrams

A cause-and-effect diagram can be used to visually represent cause-and-effect relationships. To create a simple cause-and-effect diagram, write down one cause. Then think of all the effects that could result from that cause. Remember that a single cause can have multiple effects, just as several causes can contribute to a single effect.

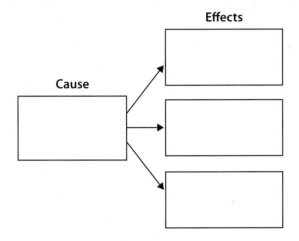

Cluster Diagrams

A cluster diagram shows how concepts are related to one another. To create a cluster diagram, write the main idea or topic in the center of a sheet of paper. Circle it. Next, draw lines branching off the main idea, connected to circles that contain concepts or characteristics related to the main topic. Continue adding facts and details in a branching pattern, connecting related ideas and facts.

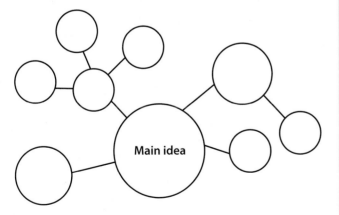

Compare/Contrast Tables

Compare/Contrast tables are useful for showing the similarities and differences between two or more objects or processes. The table provides an organized framework for making comparisons based on specific characteristics.

To create a compare/contrast table, list the items to be compared across the top of the table. List the characteristics that will form the basis of your comparison in the column on the left. Complete the table by filling in information for each item.

	Item:	Item:	Item:
Characteristic:			
Characteristic:			
Characteristic:			
Characteristic:			

Cycle Diagrams

A cycle diagram shows a sequence of events that is continuous, or cyclical. A continuous sequence does not have a beginning or an end; instead, each event in the process leads to another event. The diagram shows the order of the events.

To create a cycle diagram, list the events in the process and count them. Draw one box for each event, placing the boxes around an imaginary circle. Write one of the events in a box, and then draw an arrow to the next box, moving clockwise. Continue to fill in the boxes and link them with arrows until the descriptions form a continuous circle. Then, add a title.

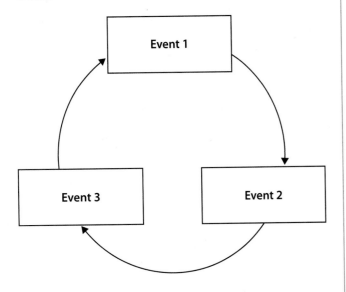

KWL Charts

KWL charts help you activate prior knowledge, gather information and check for understanding. To fill in a *KWL* chart, before the lesson fill in what you know about the topic in the *K* column. Next, fill in what you want to know about the topic in the *W* column. After you have read the lesson, fill in the *L* column with what you learned about the topic.

K	W	L
I Know.	I Want to Know.	I Learned.

Main Ideas and Details Charts

You can use this type of chart to organize lesson concepts by main ideas and supporting details. Use clues from the text such as headings and topic sentences to determine main ideas. First draw a line down the center of a sheet of paper to divide it into two columns. In the left column, write the main ideas of the topic or reading. In the right column, write the supporting details for each main idea.

Main Ideas	Details

T-Charts

A T-chart can be used to organize lesson information including concepts, vocabulary, questions, and facts. To create a T-chart, divide a sheet of paper into two columns. Write a heading for each column based on the information being organized. For example, "Key Term" and "Definition." As you read, fill in the chart.

Venn Diagrams

Another way to show similarities and differences between items is with a Venn diagram. To create a Venn diagram, draw two overlapping circles or ovals. Label them with the names of the objects or the ideas they represent. Write the unique characteristics in the part of each circle or oval that does not overlap. Write the shared characteristics within the area of overlap.

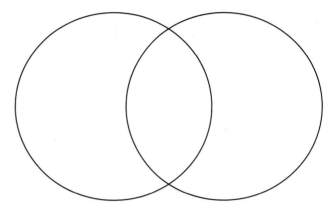

Science Skills

Basic Process Skills

During an environmental science course, you often carry out short lab activities as well as lengthier experiments. Here are some skills that you will use as you work.

Observing

In every science activity, you make a variety of observations. Observation uses one or more of the five senses to gather information. Many observations involve the senses of sight, hearing, touch, and smell.

Sometimes you will use tools that increase the power of your senses or make observations more precise. For example, hand lenses and microscopes enable you to see things in greater detail. Rulers, balances, and thermometers help you measure key variables. Besides expanding the senses or making observations more accurate, tools may help eliminate personal opinions or preferences.

In science, it is customary to record your observations at the time they are made, usually by writing or drawing in a notebook. You may also make records by using computers, cameras, videotapes, and other tools. As a rule, scientists keep complete accounts of their observations, often using tables to organize their observations.

Inferring

In science, as in daily life, observations are usually followed by inferences. Inferring is interpreting an observation or statement based on prior knowledge. For example, suppose you're on a mountain hike and you see footprints like the ones illustrated above right. Based on their size and shape, you might infer that a large mammal had passed by. In making that inference, you would use your knowledge about the shape of animals' feet. Someone who knew much more about mammals might infer that a bear left the footprints. You can compare examples of observations and inferences in the table.

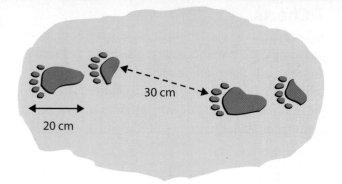

Comparing Observations and Inferences	
Sample Observations	**Sample Inferences**
The footprints in the soil each have five toes.	An animal made the footprints.
The larger footprints are about 20 cm long.	A bear made the footprints.
The space between each pair of footprints is about 30 cm.	The animal was walking, not running.

Notice that an inference is an act of reasoning, not a fact. An inference may be logical but not true. It is often necessary to gather further information before you can be confident that an inference is correct. For scientists, that information may come from further observations or from research done by others.

Predicting

People often make predictions, but their statements about the future could be either guesses or inferences. In science, a prediction is an inference about a future event based on evidence, experience, or knowledge. For example, you can say, *On the first day next month, it will be sunny.* If your statement is based on evidence of weather patterns in the area, then the prediction is scientific. If the statement was made without considering any evidence, it's just a guess.

Predictions play a major role in science because they provide a way to test ideas. If scientists understand an event or the properties of a particular object, they should be able to make accurate predictions about that event or object. Some predictions can be tested simply by making observations. At other times, carefully designed experiments are needed.

Measuring

Measurements are important in science because they provide specific information and help observers avoid bias. Measuring is comparing an object or process to a standard. Scientists use a common set of standards called the International System of Units, abbreviated as SI (for its French name, Système International d'Unités).

Calculating

Once scientists have made measurements, calculations are a very important part of analyzing data. How fast is a ball moving? You could directly measure the speed of a ball by using probeware such as a motion sensor. But you could also calculate the speed using distance and time measurements. Calculating is a process in which a person uses mathematical operations to manipulate numbers and symbols.

Classifying

If you have ever heard people debate whether a tomato is a fruit or a vegetable, you've heard an argument about classification. Classifying is the process of grouping items that are alike according to some organizing idea or system. Classifying occurs in every branch of science, but it is especially important in environmental science because living things are so numerous and diverse.

You may have the chance to practice classifying in different ways. Sometimes you will place objects into groups using an established system. At other times, you may create a system of your own by examining a variety of objects and identifying their properties. For example, you could group household cleaners into those that are toxic and those that are not. Ammonia is toxic, whereas vinegar is not.

Using Models

Some cities refuse to approve any new buildings that could cast shadows on a popular park. As architects plan buildings in such locations, they use models that can show where a proposed building's shadow will fall at any time of day at any season of the year. A model is a mental or physical representation of an object, process, or event. In science, models are usually made to help people understand natural objects and processes.

Models can be varied. Mental models, such as mathematical equations, can represent some kinds of ideas or processes. For example, the equation for the surface area of a sphere can model the surface of Earth, enabling scientists to determine its size. Physical models can be made of a huge variety of materials; they can be two-dimensional (flat) or three-dimensional (having depth).

Physical models can also be made "to scale," which means they are in proportion to the actual object. Something very large, such as an area of land being studied, can be shown at 1/100 of its actual size. A tiny organism can be shown at 100 times its size.

Conducting an Experiment

A science experiment is a procedure designed to test a prediction. Some types of experiments are fairly simple to design. Others may require ingenious problem solving.

Posing Questions

A gardener noticed that her flowers seemed to flourish on one side of the garden, but not the other. The gardener wondered, *Why did more flowers bloom on one side of the garden than the other?*

An experiment may have its beginning when someone asks a specific question or wants to solve a particular problem. Sometimes the original question leads directly to an experiment, but often researchers must restate the problem before they can design an appropriate experiment. The gardener's question about the flowers, for example, is too broad to be tested by an experiment, because there are so many possible answers. To narrow the topic, the gardener might think about several related questions: *Were the seeds the same on both sides of the garden? Was the sunlight the same? Is there something different about the soil?*

Developing a Hypothesis

In science, a question about an object or event is answered by developing a possible explanation called a hypothesis. The hypothesis may be developed after long thought and research, or it may come to a scientist in a flash. How a hypothesis is formed doesn't matter; it can be useful as long as it leads to predictions that can be tested.

In this case, the gardener decided to focus on the quality of the soil on each side of her garden. She did some tests and discovered that the soil had a lower pH on the side where the plants did not produce well. That led her to propose this hypothesis: *If the pH of the soil is too low, fewer flowers will bloom.* The next step is to make a prediction based on the hypothesis, for example, *If the pH of the soil is increased using lime, more flowers will bloom.* Notice that the prediction suggests the basic idea for an experiment.

Designing an Experiment

A carefully designed experiment can test a prediction in a reliable way, ruling out other possible explanations. As scientists plan their experimental procedures, they pay particular attention to the factors that must be controlled and the procedures that must be defined.

The gardener decided to study three groups of plants:

- *Group 1:* 20 plants on the side of the garden with a low pH
- *Group 2:* 20 plants on the side of the garden with a low pH, but with lime added; and
- *Group 3:* 20 plants on the side of the garden with a high pH.

Controlling Variables

As researchers design an experiment, they identify the **variables**, factors that can change. Some common variables include mass, volume, time, temperature, light, and the presence or absence of specific materials. An experiment involves three categories of variables. The factor that scientists purposely change is called the **independent variable**. An independent variable is also known as a manipulated variable.

The factor that may change because of the independent variable and that scientists want to observe is called the **dependent variable**. A dependent variable is also known as a responding variable. Factors that scientists purposely keep the same are called controlled variables. Controlling variables enables researchers to conclude that the changes in the independent variable are due exclusively to changes in the dependent variable.

For the gardener, the independent variable is the pH of the soil. The dependent variable is the number of flowers produced by the plants. Among the variables that must be controlled are the amount of sunlight received each day, the time of year when seeds are planted, and the amount of water the plants receive.

What is a "Control Group"?

When you read about certain experiments, you may come across references to a control group (or a "control") and the experimental group. All of the groups in an experiment are treated exactly the same except for the independent variable. In an experimental group, the independent variable is being changed. The control group is used as a standard of comparison. It may consist of objects that are not changed in any way, or objects that are being treated in the usual way. For example, in the gardener's experiment, Group 1 is the control group because for these plants nothing is done to change the low pH of the soil.

Forming Operational Definitions

In an experiment, it is often necessary to define one or more variables explicitly so that any researcher could measure or control the variable in exactly the same way. An operational definition describes how a particular variable is to be measured or how a term is to be defined. In this context, the term *operational* means, "describing what to do."

The gardener, for example, has to decide exactly how much lime to add to the soil. *Can lime be added after the seeds are planted or only before planted? At what pH should no more lime be added to the soil?* In this case, the gardener decided to add lime only before planting, and to add enough lime to make the pH equal in Groups 2 and 3.

Interpreting Data

The observations and measurements that are made in an experiment are called **data**. Scientists usually record data in an orderly way. When an experiment is finished, the researcher analyzes the data for trends or patterns, often by doing calculations or making graphs, to determine whether the results support the hypothesis.

For example, the gardener regularly measured and recorded data such as the soil moisture, daily sunlight, and pH of the soil. She found that the soil pH in Groups 2 and 3 started the same, but after two months the soil pH for Group 3 was a little higher than the soil pH for Group 2.

The gardener then recorded the numbers of flowers produced by each plant. She totaled the number of flowers for each group. Her results were the following:

- *Group 1:* 67 flowers
- *Group 2:* 102 flowers
- *Group 3:* 126 flowers

The overall trend was clear: The gardener's prediction was correct.

To be sure that the results of an experiment are correct, scientists review their data critically, looking for possible sources of error. Here, *error* refers to differences between the observed results and the true values. Experimental error can result from human mistakes or problems with equipment. It can also occur when the small group of objects studied does not accurately represent the whole group. For example, if some of the gardener's seeds had been exposed to a herbicide, the data might not reflect the true seed germination pattern.

Drawing Conclusions

If researchers are confident that their data are reliable, they make a final statement summarizing their results. That statement—called the *conclusion*—indicates whether the data support or refute the hypothesis. The gardener's conclusion was: *Adding lime to soil with a low pH will improve the production of flowering plants.* A conclusion is considered valid if it is a logical interpretation of reliable data.

Communicating Results

When an experiment has been completed, one or more events often follow. Researchers may repeat the experiment to verify the results. They may publish the experiment so that others can evaluate and replicate their procedures. They may compare their conclusion with the discoveries made by other scientists. And they may raise new questions that lead to new experiments. For example, *Why does the pH level decrease over time when soil is treated with lime?*

Evaluating and Revising

Scientists must be flexible about the conclusions drawn from an experiment. Further research may help confirm the results of the experiment or make it necessary to revise the initial conclusions. For example, a new experiment may show that lime can be effective only when certain microbes are present in the soil. Scientists continuously evaluate and revise experiments based on the findings in new research.

Science Safety

Working in the laboratory can be an exciting experience, but it can also be dangerous if proper safety rules are not followed at all times. To prepare yourself for a safe year in the laboratory, read the following safety rules. Make sure that you understand each rule. Ask your teacher to explain any rules you don't understand.

General Safety Rules and First Aid

1. Read all directions for an experiment several times. Follow the directions exactly as they are written. If you are in doubt about any part of the experiment, ask your teacher for assistance.

2. Never perform unauthorized or unsupervised labs, or handle equipment, unless you have specific permission.

3. When you design an experiment, do not start until your teacher has approved your plan.

4. If a lab includes physical activity, use caution to avoid injuring yourself or others. Tell your teacher if there is a reason that you should not participate.

5. Never eat, drink, or bring food into the laboratory.

6. Immediately report all accidents, no matter how minor, to your teacher.

7. Learn the correct ways to deal with a burn, a cut, or acid splashed in your eyes or on your skin.

8. Be aware of the location of the first-aid kit. Your teacher should administer any required first aid due to injury. Your teacher may send you to the school nurse or call a physician.

9. Report any fire to your teacher at once. Find out the location of the fire extinguisher, fire alarm, and phone where emergency numbers are listed.

Dress Code

10. Always wear safety goggles to protect your eyes when working in the lab. Avoid wearing contact lenses. If you must wear contact lenses, ask your teacher what precautions you should take.

11. Wear a laboratory apron or coat to protect your skin and clothing from harmful chemicals or heated substances.

12. Wear disposable plastic gloves to protect yourself from contact with chemicals that can be harmful. Keep your hands away from your face. Dispose of the gloves according to your teacher's instructions.

13. Tie back long hair and loose clothing. Remove any jewelry that could come in contact with chemicals and flames.

Heating and Fire Safety

14. Hot plates, hot water, and hot glassware can cause burns. Never touch hot objects with your bare hands. Use an oven mitt or other hand protection.

15. Use a clamp or tongs to hold hot objects. Test an object by first holding the back of your hand near it. If you feel heat on the back of your hand, the object may be too hot to handle.

16. Tie back long hair and loose clothing, and put on safety goggles before using a burner. Follow instructions from your teacher for lighting and extinguishing burners. If the flame leaps out of a burner as you are lighting it, turn the gas off. Never leave a flame unattended or reach across a flame. Make sure your work area is not cluttered with materials.

17. If flammable materials are present, make sure there are not flames, sparks, or any exposed sources of heat.

18. Never heat a chemical without your teacher's permission. Chemicals that are harmless when cool can be dangerous when heated. When heating a test tube, point the opening away from you and others in case the contents splash or boil out of the test tube.

19. Never heat a closed container. The expanding hot air, vapors, or other gases inside may blow the container apart, causing it to injure you or others.

Using Chemicals Safely

20. Do not let any corrosive or poisonous chemicals get on your skin or clothing, or in your eyes. When working with poisonous or irritating vapors, work in a well-ventilated area and wash your hands thoroughly after completing the activity.

21. Never test for an odor unless instructed by your teacher. Avoid inhaling a vapor directly. Use a wafting motion to direct vapor toward your nose.

22. Never mix chemicals for "the fun of it." You might produce a dangerous, possibly explosive substance.

23. Never touch, taste, or smell a chemical that you do not know for certain to be harmless.

24. Use only those chemicals needed in the investigation. Keep all container lids closed when a chemical is not being used. To avoid contamination, never return chemicals to their original containers. Notify your teacher if chemicals are spilled.

25. Take extreme care not to spill any chemical. If a spill occurs, immediately ask your teacher about the proper cleanup procedure. Dispose of all chemicals as instructed by your teacher.

26. Be careful when working with acids or bases. Pour such chemicals from one container to another over the sink, not over your work area. Immediately notify your teacher of any acid or base spill. If an acid or base gets on your skin or clothing, rinse it with water.

27. When diluting an acid, pour the acid into water. Never pour water into the acid.

Science Skills

Using Glassware Safely

28. Handle fragile glassware, such as thermometers, test tubes, and beakers, with care. Do not touch broken glass. Notify your teacher if glassware breaks. Never use chipped or broken glassware.

29. Never force glass tubing into a stopper. Your teacher will demonstrate the proper methods.

30. Never heat glassware that is not thoroughly dry. Use a wire screen to protect glassware from any flame.

31. Keep in mind that hot glassware will not appear hot. Never pick up glassware without first checking to see if it is hot.

32. Never eat or drink from laboratory glassware. Thoroughly clean glassware before you put it away.

Using Sharp Instruments

33. Handle scalpels or razor blades with extreme care. Never cut material toward you; cut away from you.

34. Notify your teacher immediately if you cut yourself when in the laboratory.

Working With Live Organisms

35. No experiments that will cause pain, discomfort, or harm to animals should be done in the classroom or at home.

36. Your teacher will instruct you how to handle each species that is brought into the classroom. Animals should be handled only if necessary. Special handling is required if an animal is excited or frightened, pregnant, feeding, or with its young.

37. Clean your hands thoroughly after handling any organisms or materials, including animals or cages containing animals.

End-of-Experiment Rules

38. When an experiment has been completed, clean up your work area and return all equipment to its proper place.

39. Wash your hands before and after every experiment.

40. Turn off all burners before leaving the laboratory. Check that the gas line leading to the burner is off.

Safety Symbols

 Safety Goggles
Always wear safety goggles in the laboratory.

 Lab Apron
Wear a laboratory apron to protect your skin and clothing.

 Plastic Gloves
Wear disposable plastic gloves to protect your hands from harmful chemicals or organisms.

 Breakage
Handle breakable materials such as glassware with care.

 Heat-Resistant Gloves
Never touch hot objects with your bare hands.

 Heating
Be careful using sources of heat.

 Sharp Object
Use caution with sharp or pointed tools.

 Electric Shock
Avoid the possibility of electric shock.

 Corrosive Chemical
Work carefully with acids or other corrosive chemicals.

 Poison
Do not let any poisonous chemical get on your skin, and do not inhale its vapor.

 Flames
Work carefully around open flames.

 No Flames
Flammable materials may be present.

 Fumes
Avoid inhaling dangerous vapors.

 Physical Safety
Use caution in physical activities.

 Animal Safety
Treat live animals with care to avoid injuring the animals or yourself.

 Plant Safety
Handle plants only as your teacher directs.

 Disposal
Follow the instructions from your teacher for disposal.

 Hand Washing
Wash your hands thoroughly with soap and warm water when finished with the activity.

 General Safety
Follow all safety instructions.

SVALBARD
(Norway)

CTIC OCEAN

ARCTIC CIRCLE

RUSSIA

80° N

Moscow

JROPE

Astana

ASIA

KAZAKHSTAN

Ulaanbaatar

MONGOLIA

60° N

UZBEKISTAN
Tashkent · Bishkek
KYRGYZSTAN

Beijing

NORTH
KOREA
P'yongyang
Seoul
SOUTH
KOREA

JAPAN

40° N

TURKEY

TURKMENISTAN

TAJIKISTAN

Tunis
UNISIA

IRAQ
Baghdad

Ashgabat
Dushanbe

CHINA

Tokyo

Tripoli

Cairo

Kuwait
KUWAIT
BAHRAIN
QATAR
Riyadh

Manama
Doha

Tehran

Kabul

IRAN AFGHANISTAN

Islamabad

Kathmandu

BHUTAN

PAKISTAN

New
Delhi

NEPAL

Thimphu

Dhaka

Taipei

PACIFIC

OCEAN

LIBYA

EGYPT

Abu Dhabi
Muscat

TAIWAN

TROPIC OF CANCER

20° N

AFRICA

SAUDI
ARABIA

OMAN

INDIA

MYANMAR

ERITREA

UNITED
ARAB
EMIRATES

BANGLADESH

LAOS

Hanoi

Khartoum

Sanaa

Vientiane

CHAD

SUDAN

YEMEN

Asmara

Yangon

THAILAND VIETNAM

Manila

MARSHALL
ISLANDS

N'Djamena

DJIBOUTI

Bangkok

CAMBODIA

Majuro

CENTRAL
AFRICAN
REPUBLIC

Djibouti

SRI
LANKA

Phnom Penh

PHILIPPINES

Addis Ababa

PALAU

Palikir

Bangui

ETHIOPIA

SOMALIA

Colombo

BRUNEI

Melekeok

FEDERATED STATES
OF MICRONESIA

KIRIBATI

REPUBLIC
OF THE
CONGO

Kampala
UGANDA
Kigali
KENYA

Male
MALDIVES

Kuala Lumpur

Bandar Seri Begawan

MALAYSIA

Tarawa

EQUATOR

0°

ville

RWANDA
Bujumbura
BURUNDI

Nairobi

SEYCHELLES

Singapore SINGAPORE

NAURU

Yaren

DEMOCRATIC
REPUBLIC OF
THE CONGO

Dodoma

Victoria

INDONESIA

SOLOMON
ISLANDS

da

TANZANIA

Jakarta

PAPUA NEW
GUINEA

TUVALU

MALAWI

COMOROS

INDIAN

Dar es Salaam

ANGOLA

ZAMBIA
Lusaka

Lilongwe

Moroni

OCEAN

Dili

EAST TIMOR

Honiara

Funafuti

Harare

Antananarivo

Port
Moresby

ZIMBABWE

MAURITIUS

VANUATU

FIJI

AMIBIA

dhoek

BOTSWANA

MADAGASCAR

Port Louis

Port-Vila

Suva

20° S

Gaborone

Maputo

RÉUNION
(France)

NEW
CALEDONIA
(France)

Bloemfontein

Pretoria
Mbabane

AUSTRALIA

SOUTH
AFRICA

SWAZILAND

LESOTHO

e Town

Maseru

0   2,000 mi

0   2,000 km

Robinson Projection

Canberra

NEW
ZEALAND

40° S

Wellington

20° E   40° E   60° E   80° E   100° E   120° E   140° E   160° E

60° S

SOUTHERN OCEAN

ANTARCTIC CIRCLE

80° S

ANTARCTICA

KEY
- National border
- State border
- ⊗ Capital city
- ★ State capital
- ○ Other city

ARCTIC OCEAN

RUSSIA

CANADA

Alaska

Yukon R.

Bering Sea

○ Anchorage

Juneau ★

Gulf of Alaska

0   300 mi
0   300 km
Lambert Azimuthal
Equal-Area Projection

Kauai

Honolulu ★

Hawaii

Molokai

Maui

Hilo ○

Hawaii

PACIFIC OCEAN

Same scale as main map

PACIFIC OCEAN

Seattle ○
Olympia ★
Spokane ○
Washington

Portland ○
Salem ★
Columbia R.
Eugene ○
Oregon

Helena ★

Mont

Billings

Snake R.

Boise ★
Idaho

Pocatello ○

Wyo

Great Salt Lake

Salt Lake City ★
Provo ○

Carson City ★
Sacramento ★
Nevada
Utah

San Francisco ○
San Jose ○

Fresno ○

California

Colorado River

Col

Las Vegas ○

Los Angeles ○

Arizona

San Diego ○

Phoenix ★

Santa
Albuquerque ○

Tucson ○

MEXI

0   200 mi
0   200 km
Albers Conic Projection

The Metric System

SI (Système International d'Unités) is a revised version of the metric system, which was originally developed in France in 1791. SI units of measurement are used by scientists throughout the world. The system is based on units of 10. Each unit is 10 times larger or 10 times smaller than the next unit. The table lists the prefixes used to name the most common SI units.

Common SI Prefixes

Prefix	Symbol	Meaning
kilo-	k	1000
hecto-	h	100
deka-	da	10
deci-	d	0.1 (one tenth)
centi-	c	0.01 (one hundredth)
milli-	m	0.001 (one thousandth)

Commonly Used Metric Units

Length

To measure length, or distance from one point to another, the unit of measure is a meter (m). A meter is slightly longer than a yard.

Useful equivalents:
1 kilometer (km) = 1000 (10^3) meters (m)
1 meter (m) = 100 (10^2) centimeters (cm)
1 meter (m) = 1000 millimeters (mm)
1 centimeter (cm) = 0.01 (10^{-2}) m
1 millimeter (mm) = 0.001 (10^{-3}) meter

Metric to English conversions:
1 km = 0.62 miles
1 m = 1.09 yards
1 m = 3.28 feet
1 m = 39.37 inches
1 cm = 0.394 inch
1 mm = 0.039 inch

English to metric conversions:
1 mile = 1.61 km
1 yard = 0.914 m
1 foot = 0.305 m
1 foot = 30.5 cm
1 inch = 2.54 cm

Area

The measurement of the perimeter of an object is its area.

Useful equivalents
1 square meter (m^2) = 10,000 square centimeters
1 square centimeter (cm^2) = 100 square millimeters

Metric to English conversions
1 m^2 = 1.1960 square yards
1 m^2 = 10.764 square feet
1 cm^2 = 0.155 square inch

English to metric conversions
1 square yard = 0.8361 m^2
1 square foot = 0.0929 m^2
1 square inch = 6.4516 cm^2

Volume

To measure the volume of a liquid, or the amount of space an object takes up, the unit of measure is a liter (L). A liter is slightly more than a quart.

Useful equivalents:
1 liter = 1000 milliliters (mL)
1 kiloliter (kL) = 1000 liter
1 mL = 0.001 liter
1 mL = 1 cubic centimeter (cm^3)

Metric to English conversions:
1 kL = 264.17 gallons
1 L = 0.264 gallons
1 L = 1.057 quarts

English to metric conversions
1 gallon = 3.785 L
1 quart = 0.946 L
1 quart = 946 mL
1 pint = 473 mL
1 fluid ounce = 29.57 mL

Mass

To measure the mass, or the amount of matter in an object, the unit of measure is the gram (g). A paper clip has a mass equal to about one gram.

Useful equivalents:

1 metric ton (t) = 1000 kilograms
1 kilogram (kg) = 1000 grams (g)
1 gram (g) = 1000 milligrams
1 milligram (mg) = 0.001 gram

Metric to English conversions:

1 t = 1.103 ton
1 kg = 2.205 pounds
1 g = 0.0353 ounce

English to metric conversions

1 ton = 0.907 t
1 pound = 0.4536 kg
1 ounce = 28.35 g

Temperature

To measure of the hotness or coldness of an item, or its temperature, you use the unit degrees. The freezing point of water is 0°C (Celsius). The boiling point of water is 100°C.

Metric to English conversion:

$°C = 5/9 (°F - 32)$

English to metric conversion:

$°F = 9/5°C + 32$

Appendix D: Periodic Table

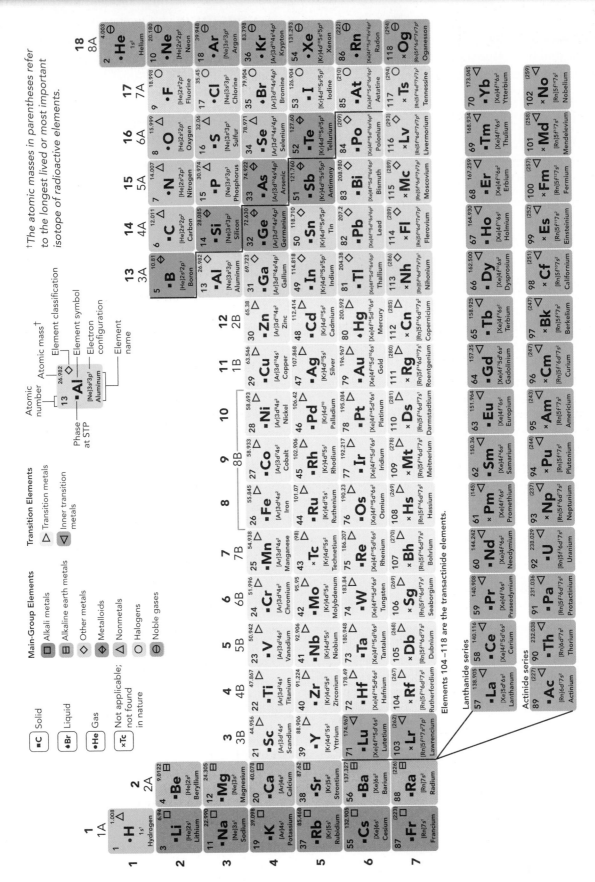

English/Spanish Glossary

A

abiotic factor: any part of an ecosystem that has never been living, 103
factor abiótico: cualquier parte de un ecosistema que no ha tenido nunca vida

acid deposition: water vapor containing acids that falls to the ground as rain, snow, sleet, or hail, 467
deposición ácida: vapor de agua que contiene ácidos y cae al suelo en forma de lluvia, nieve, aguanieve o granizo

acid drainage: a type of mining pollution that occurs when oxygen and rainwater react with newly exposed rock that contains iron sulfide, forming sulfuric acid that removes metals from rocks and leaches into groundwater or enters water bodies as runoff, 406, 532
drenaje ácido: tipo de contaminación que ocurre cuando el oxígeno y el agua de lluvia reaccionan con la nueva roca expuesta que contiene sulfuro de hierro y forman ácido sulfúrico que remueve los metales de la roca y se filtra en aguas subterráneas o ingresa en cuerpos de agua por escurrimiento

active solar heating: the use of technology to collect, store, and distribute the sun's energy, 562
calefacción solar activa: el uso de la tecnología para captar, almacenar y distribuir la energía solar

adaptation: a heritable trait that increases the likelihood of an individual's survival and reproduction, 129
adaptación: rasgo hereditario que aumenta las probabilidades de supervivencia y reproducción de un individuo

adaptive management: a customized approach to managing resources that has been developed through scientific testing, 328
gestión adaptativa: enfoque personalizado para la gestión de recursos desarrollado mediante la experimentación científica

age structure: the relative number of organisms of each age within a population; also called *age distribution*, 108
estructura por edad: el número relativo de organismos de cada grupo etario dentro de una población; también conocida como *distribución por edad*

age structure diagram: a chart that shows the age distribution of a population; also called *age pyramid*, 108
diagrama de estructura por edad: gráfica que muestra la distribución por edad de una población; también conocida como *pirámide de edades*

air mass: a large body of air in which properties such as temperature, pressure, and humidity are similar, 460
masa de aire: gran volumen de aire con propiedades de temperatura, presión y humedad similares

air pollution: the release of damaging materials into the atmosphere, 462
contaminación del aire: liberación de materiales dañinos hacia la atmósfera

air pressure: the force exerted by air on the area below it; also called *atmospheric pressure*, 455
presión de aire: fuerza ejercida por el aire sobre el área que se encuentra debajo; también conocida como *presión atmosférica*

algal bloom: the rapid growth of algae in an area that can cover the surface of the water and block sunlight from reaching plants below, 436
floración de algas: crecimiento rápido de las algas en una zona de modo tal que las algas pueden cubrir la superficie del agua e impedir que la luz del sol llegue a las plantas de abajo

aphotic zone: the layer below the photic zone in an aquatic ecosystem, where no sunlight penetrates so photosynthesis cannot occur, 182
zona afótica: capa que está debajo de la zona fótica en un ecosistema acuático, donde no penetra la luz solar y, por lo tanto, no se puede realizar la fotosíntesis

aquaculture: the raising of aquatic organisms for food in a controlled environment; also called *fish farming*, 379
acuicultura: cultivo de organismos acuáticos para consumo humano en un ambiente controlado; también conocido como *piscicultura*

aquifer: a spongelike formation of rock, sand, or gravel that holds water, 82, 424
acuífero: formación esponjosa de rocas, arena o grava que retiene agua

arable land: land that is suitable for farming, 373
tierra arable: tierra apta para el cultivo

artificial selection: a human-controlled process to produce individuals with certain traits, 130
selección artificial: proceso controlado por los seres humanos para producir individuos con rasgos específicos

asbestos: a mineral that forms long, thin, microscopic fibers; used as an insulator against heat and sound, 271
asbesto: mineral que forma fibras microscópicas largas y delgadas; se usa como aislante térmico y acústico

atmosphere: the thin layer of gases that surrounds Earth, 74, 452
atmósfera: capa delgada de gases que rodea la Tierra

atom: the basic unit of matter; the smallest unit that maintains the chemical properties of an element, 64
átomo: unidad básica de la materia, la unidad más pequeña de un elemento que mantiene sus propiedades químicas

avalanche: the rapid movement of snow sliding down a slope, 282
avalancha: movimiento rápido de nieve que se desliza por una ladera

B

bedrock: the mass of solid rock that makes up Earth's crust, 353
lecho rocoso: masa de roca sólida que compone la corteza terrestre

benthic zone: the bottom layer of an aquatic ecosystem, 182
zona bentónica: capa del fondo de un ecosistema acuático

bioaccumulation: the buildup of large concentrations of poisons in the body, 275
bioacumulación: acumulación de grandes concentraciones de veneno en el cuerpo

biodegradable: able to decompose or break down naturally, 590
biodegradable: que tiene la capacidad de descomponerse o desintegrarse naturalmente

biodiversity: the variety of organisms in an area, by species, genes, populations, and communities; also called *biological diversity,* 200
biodiversidad: la variedad de organismos en un área considerando las especies, la genética, las poblaciones y las comunidades; también conocida como *diversidad biológica*

biodiversity hotspot: an area that supports a large number of native species, 215
punto caliente (*hotspot*) de biodiversidad: área que sostiene una gran cantidad de especies nativas

biofuel: fuel from organic sources, 552
biocombustible: combustible proveniente de fuentes orgánicas

biogeochemical cycle: the circulation of nutrients through the atmosphere; also called *nutrient cycle,* 83
ciclo biogeoquímico: circulación de nutrientes en la atmósfera; también conocido como *ciclo de nutrientes*

biological pest control: the use of organisms to battle pests and weeds, 369
control biológico de plagas: uso de organismos para combatir plagas y malas hierbas

biomagnification: the increased concentration of pollutants at each step up a food chain, 275
biomagnificación: aumento en la concentración de contaminantes en cada eslabón de una cadena alimentaria

biomass: the total amount of living tissue in a trophic level, 145
biomasa: cantidad total de tejido vivo en un nivel trófico

biomass energy: the energy produced from organic materials (e.g., plants and human wastes), 551
energía de biomasa: energía producida a partir de materiales orgánicos (p. ej., desechos de plantas y animales)

biome: a grouping of ecosystems with similar abiotic and biotic conditions, 164
bioma: grupo de ecosistemas con condiciones abióticas y bióticas similares

biopower: electricity generated by the combustion of organic materials, 552
bioenergía: electricidad generada por la combustión de materiales orgánicos

biosphere: the Earth and all of its organisms and environments, 74, 102
biósfera: la Tierra y todos sus organismos y medio ambientes

biotechnology: the use of genetic engineering to increase the value of products, 375
biotecnología: el uso de la ingeniería genética para aumentar el valor de los productos

biotic factor: any part of an ecosystem that is living or used to be living, 102
factor biótico: cualquier parte de un ecosistema que tiene, o alguna vez tuvo, vida

biotic potential: the growth rate of a population under ideal conditions, 117
potencial biótico: la tasa de crecimiento de una población en condiciones ideales

C

canopy: the dense covering of trees, 50 to 80 meters above the ground, in a rain forest, 168
dosel: capa densa de árboles, entre 50 y 80 metros sobre el suelo, en una selva tropical

cap-and-trade: a system the U.S. government uses first to determine an acceptable amount of a specific pollutant and then assigns (via permits) a fraction of that amount to industrial sources of the pollutant, 53
limitación y comercio de emisiones: sistema que el gobierno de los Estados Unidos usa, primero, para determinar la cantidad aceptable de un contaminante específico y, luego, para asignar (por medio de permisos) una fracción de esa cantidad a las fuentes industriales de ese contaminante

captive breeding: the process of breeding and raising organisms under controlled conditions, 214
reproducción en cautiverio: proceso de reproducción y cría de organismos en condiciones controladas

carbohydrate: an organic compound that consists of atoms of carbon, hydrogen, and oxygen, 68
carbohidrato: compuesto orgánico formado por átomos de carbono, hidrógeno y oxígeno

carbon footprint: the total carbon dioxide emissions produced by an individual, group, or location, 503
huella de carbono: el total de emisiones de dióxido de carbono producidas por un individuo, un grupo o un lugar

carbon offset: a voluntary payment made to compensate for greenhouse gas emissions, 506
compensación de emisiones de carbono: pago voluntario que se realiza para compensar las emisiones de gases de efecto invernadero

carbon sequestration: a method of storing carbon emissions to prevent their release into the atmosphere, 506
captura de carbno: método de almacenamiento de las emisiones de carbono para evitar su liberación en la atmósfera

carbon tax: a fee that the government charges polluters for each unit of greenhouse gas they emit, 505
impuesto sobre el carbiono: tributo que el gobierno impone a los contaminadores por cada unidad de gas de efecto invemadero que emiten

carcinogen: a chemical that causes cancer, 268
carcinógeno: producto químico que provoca cáncer

carnivore: an animal that kills and eats other animals, 143
carnívoro: animal que mata y come a otros animales

carrying capacity: the largest population a given environment can support, 115
capacidad de carga: la población más grande que un medio ambiente dado puede sostener

catalytic converter: a device in a motor vehicle that reduces the amount of pollutants in emissions, 471
catalizador: dispositivo de un automóvil que reduce la cantidad de contaminantes en las emisiones

cellular respiration: the process by which organisms use oxygen to release the chemical energy of sugars, producing carbon dioxide and water, 85, 143
respiración celular: proceso mediante el cual los organismos usan el oxígeno para liberar la energía química de los azúcares y producen dióxido de carbono y agua

chemosynthesis: the process by which bacteria use energy stored in bonds of hydrogen sulfide to convert carbon dioxide and water into sugars, 142
quimiosíntesis: proceso mediante el cual las bacterias usan la energía almacenada en los enlaces del ácido sulfhídrico y convierten el dióxido de carbono y el agua en azúcares

chlorofluorocarbon (CFC): a chemical compound containing chlorine, fluorine, and carbon; developed for use in refrigeration and spray-can propellants, 472
clorofluorocarbono (CFC): compuesto químico formado por cloro, flúor y carbono; desarrollado para su uso en refrigeración y propelentes para aerosoles

city planning: the process of designing cities to maximize their functionality and beauty, 305
planificación urbana: proceso de diseño de las ciudades que tiene como objetivo maximizar su funcionalidad y belleza

clay: soil particles that are less than 0.002 mm in diameter, 356
arcilla: partículas de tierra con un diámetro menor a 0.002 mm

Clean Air Act: an act that sets strict standards for air quality and strengthens the government's ability to enforce regulations, 470
Ley del Aire Limpio: ley que fija niveles estrictos para la calidad del aire y refuerza la capacidad del gobierno para hacer cumplir las normas

clear-cutting: a method of harvesting trees in which all trees in an area are cut at once, 334
corta a hecho: método de explotación forestal mediante el cual se cortan de una vez todos los árboles de un área

climate: the average conditions, including temperature and precipitation, over long periods in a given area, 165
clima: condiciones promedio, que incluyen la temperatura y la precipitación, durante períodos largos en un área dada

climate model: a program that combines what is known about the atmosphere and oceans to simulate, or imitate, climate processes, 494
modelo climático: programa que combina el entendimiento que se tiene de la atmósfera y los océanos para simular o imitar procesos climáticos

climatograph: a diagram that shows an area's average temperature and precipitation, 165
climograma: diagrama que muestra la temperatura y la precipitación promedios de un área

coevolution: the process by which two species evolve in response to changes in each other, 137
coevolución: proceso mediante el cual dos especies evolucionan una en respuesta a los cambios de la otra y viceversa

combustion: burning; the chemical reaction when fuel combines rapidly with oxygen, 519
combustión: quema; reacción química que ocurre cuando un combustible se combina rápidamente con oxígeno

command-and-control approach: an approach to environmental policy in which a government body sets rules and threatens punishment for violations, 50
enfoque de comando y control: enfoque de la política ambiental por el cual un órgano de gobierno fija las normas y requiere su cumplimiento bajo sanciones determinadas

commensalism: a relationship between two organisms from different species in which one benefits and the other is unaffected, 140
comensalismo: relación entre dos organismos de especies diferentes en la cual uno se beneficia y el otro no se ve afectado

community: all of the population in a particular area, 101
comunidad: la población total de un área específica

composting: the conversion of organic wastes into mulch or humus through natural biological processes of decomposition, 592
compostaje: transformación de desechos orgánicos en mantillo o humus mediante procesos biológicos naturales de descomposición

compound: a substance combining atoms of two or more different elements, 66
compuesto: sustancia que combina átomos de dos o más elementos diferentes

concentrating solar power (CSP): a technology that uses the heat of the sun to generate electricity; mirrors focus the sun's energy, which is used to heat the water that fuels electric power plants, 564
energía solar concentrada: tecnología que utiliza el calor del sol para generar electricidad; unos espejos concentran la energía solar, que se usa para calentar el agua que alimenta las plantas de energía eléctrica

condensation: a change in state from a vapor to a liquid, 81
condensación: cambio del estado gaseoso al estado líquido

conduction: the transfer of heat directly between two objects that are in contact with each other, 459
conducción: transferencia directa de calor entre dos objetos que están en contacto

coniferous: a tree bearing cones that typically does not lose its leaves, 173
conífera: árbol que porta conos y que generalmente no pierde sus hojas

consumer: an organism that relies on other organisms for energy and nutrients; also called *heterotroph*, 84, 142
consumidor: organismo que depende de otros organismos para obtener energía y nutrientes; también conocido como *heterótrofo*

contour farming: a soil conservation method in which furrows are plowed across a hillside, perpendicular to its slope, 359
cultivo en curvas de nivel: método de conservación del suelo mediante el cual los surcos se aran en una ladera de forma perpendicular a la pendiente

controlled study: a study in which only one factor is manipulated, or changed, 18
estudio controlado: estudio en el cual sólo se manipula o modifica un factor

convection: the transfer of heat in a fluid as warm parts of the fluid rise from the heat source and expand, 76, 459
convección: transferencia de calor en un fluido que ocurre cuando sus partes calientes se elevan de la fuente de calor y se expanden

convection current: the movement in a fluid as warm parts of the fluid rise and cool parts sink, 459
corriente de convección: movimiento que se da en un fluido cuando sus partes calientes se elevan y sus partes frías se hunden

coral bleaching: the death or expulsion of the algae that live in coral reefs and give the coral its bright color; often caused by a change in water temperature or other conditions, 499
blanqueamiento de coral: muerte o expulsión de las algas que viven en los arrecifes de coral y dan al coral su color brillante; a menudo se produce por un cambio en la temperatura del agua u otras condiciones

core: the layer of Earth below the mantle, 76
núcleo: capa de la Tierra que está debajo del manto

cost-benefit analysis: a method in which decision-makers compare what will be sacrificed and gained by taking a specific action, 37
análisis de costo-beneficio: método por el cual quienes toman decisiones comparan qué se sacrificará y qué se ganará al realizar una acción específica

cover crop: a fast-growing crop that is planted in the interval between harvest and the next season's planting to prevent erosion and limit the loss of nitrogen, 359
cultivo de cobertura: cultivo de crecimiento rápido que se siembra en el intervalo entre la cosecha y la siembra de la temporada siguiente para evitar la erosión y limitar la pérdida de nitrógeno

crop rotation: a soil conservation method in which the type of crop grown in a field is alternated from one season or year to the next, 359
rotación de cultivos: método de conservación del suelo por el cual el tipo de cultivo que se siembra en un campo se alterna de un año a otro o de temporada en temporada.

crust: the thin layer of rock that forms Earth's outer surface on land and in the ocean, 76
corteza terrestre: capa delgada de rocas que forma la superficie externa de la Tierra sobre el suelo y en el océano

cultural eutrophication: the pollution of a body of water as a result of human activity; also called *artificial eutrophication,* 436
eutrofización cultural: contaminación de una masa de agua como resultado de la actividad humana; también conocida como *eutrofización artificial*

D

dam: an obstruction placed in a river or stream to block its flow, 428
dique: obstrucción colocada en un río o arroyo para bloquear su flujo

data: information collected using scientific methods, 19
datos: información recopilada mediante métodos científicos

deciduous: a tree that loses its leaves and stops photosynthesis during part of the year, 170
caducifolio: árbol que pierde sus hojas y deja de realizar la fotosíntesis durante una parte del año

decomposer: an organism (e.g., a fungus or bacterium) that breaks down nonliving matter into simple parts that can then be taken up and reused by primary producers, 84, 143
descomponedor: organismo (p. ej., un hongo o una bacteria) que descompone la materia sin vida en partes simples que luego los productores primarios pueden tomar y reutilizar

deep-well injection: a method of hazardous waste disposal in which the waste is pumped into a well that has been drilled deep beneath the water table, into porous rock, 600
inyección en pozo profundo: método de desecho de residuos peligrosos mediante el cual los residuos se bombean dentro de un pozo que se ha perforado en las rocas porosas, debajo del nivel freático

deforestation: clearing a forest for another land use, 335
deforestación: acción de despejar un bosque para darle otro uso al suelo

demand: the amount of a product or service people will buy at a given price if free to do so, 37
demanda: cantidad de un producto o servicio que las personas comprarán a un precio dado si son libres de hacerlo

demographic transition: a theory that links lower birthrates and death rates in a population to improvements in education, economic conditions, and health care, 238
transición demográfica: teoría que relaciona la disminución de las tasas de natalidad y mortalidad de una población con las mejoras en la educación, las condiciones económicas y la atención de salud

demography: the study of human populations, 232
demografía: estudio de las poblaciones humanas

density-dependent factor: a limiting factor whose influence changes with population density; includes competition, predation, and disease, 116
factor dependiente de la densidad: factor limitante cuya influencia varía según la densidad de población; incluye la competencia, la depredación y las enfermedades

density-independent factor: a limiting factor whose influence is not affected by population density; includes catastrophic events, 116
factor independiente de la densidad: factor limitante cuya influencia no se ve afectada por la densidad de población; incluye las catástrofes

dependent variable: the variable that changes in response to the conditions set in an experiment, 17
variable dependiente: variable que cambia en respuesta a las condiciones fijadas en un experimento

deposition: the movement and accumulation of eroded soil, 77
sedimentación: movimiento y acumulación del suelo erosionado

desalination: the process of removing salt from seawater; also called *desalinization,* 432
desalinización: proceso de extraer la sal del agua de mar; también conocido como *desalación*

desertification: a loss of more than 10 percent in the productivity of soil due to erosion, deforestation, overgrazing, drought, or other factors, 361
desertificación: pérdida de más del 10 por ciento de la productividad del suelo a causa de la erosión, la deforestación, el sobrepastoreo, las sequías u otros factores

detritivore: an organism (e.g., a millipede or soil insect) that scavenges the waste products or dead bodies of other community members, 143
detritívoro: organismo (p. ej., un milpiés o un insecto rastrero) que hurga en los desechos o en el cuerpo sin vida de otros miembros de la comunidad

dose: the level of exposure to a pollutant or other hazardous substance, 258
dosis: nivel de exposición a un contaminante u otra sustancia peligrosa

dose-response relationship: the effect on an organism at different levels of exposure to a pollutant or other hazardous substance, 258
relación dosis-efecto: efecto sobre un organismo de los distintos niveles de exposición a un contaminante u otra sustancia peligrosa

E

earthquake: the movement of earth caused by shifting tectonic plates, 277
terremoto: movimiento de la tierra causado por el desplazamiento de las placas tectónicas

ecolabeling: a labeling system that tells consumers which brands are made with processes that do not harm the environment, 41
etiquetado ecológico: sistema de etiquetado que informa a los consumidores qué marcas usan procesos que no causan daño al medio ambiente

ecological economics: the field of economics that recognizes the relationships between ecosystems and economic systems, 39
economía ecológica: campo de la economía que reconoce la relación entre los ecosistemas y los sistemas económicos

ecological footprint: the environmental impact of an individual or population in terms of the total amount of land and water required (1) to provide the raw materials the individual or population consumes and (2) to dispose of or recycle the waste the individual or population produces, 9
huella ecológica: impacto ambiental de un individuo o una población en términos de la cantidad total de tierra y agua que se necesita para (1) proveer las materias primas que consume el individuo o la población y (2) eliminar o reciclar los desechos que produce el individuo o la población

ecological restoration: the practice of rebuilding native communities, 311
restauración ecológica: práctica de restablecer las comunidades nativas

ecology: the study of how organisms interact with one another and with their environments, 100
ecología: estudio de la forma en que los organismos interactúan entre sí y con su medio ambiente

economics: the study of how resources are converted into products and services and of how those products and services are distributed and used, 36
economía: estudio de la forma en que los recursos se convierten en productos y servicios, y de cómo se distribuyen y se usan esos productos y servicios

ecosystem: all living things and their physical environments within a particular area, 101
ecosistema: todos los seres vivos y el medio ambiente físico dentro de un área determinada

ecosystem diversity: the number and variety of ecosystems within a particular area, 202
diversidad de ecosistemas: número y variedad de ecosistemas en un área determinada

ecosystem-based management: harvesting resources in ways that minimize the impact on the ecosystems that provide them, 328
gestión basada en los ecosistemas: explotación de los recursos de forma tal que se minimice el impacto sobre los ecosistemas que los proveen

electricity: the energy produced by the flow and interaction of electrons, 520
electricidad: energía producida por el flujo y la interacción de los electrones

electrolysis: a process that releases hydrogen by using an electric current to break down water molecules, 571
electrólisis: proceso que libera hidrógeno al usar una corriente eléctrica para descomponer las moléculas de agua

element: a chemical substance with a unique set of properties that cannot be broken down into substances with other properties, 64
elemento: sustancia química con un conjunto de propiedades específicas que no se puede descomponer en sustancias con otras propiedades

El Niño: a periodic change in air pressure, wind patterns, ocean temperature, and ocean circulation in the Pacific Ocean, 488
El Niño: cambio periódico en la presión del aire, los patrones de viento, y la temperatura y la circulación del agua en el océano Pacífico

emergent layer: the few tall trees that extend above the canopy in a rain forest, 168
capa emergente: los pocos árboles altos que se elevan sobre el dosel en una selva tropical

emerging disease: a disease that is appearing in the human population for the first time or that has existed for a while, but is spreading rapidly, 263
enfermedad emergente: enfermedad que aparece en la población humana por primera vez o que ha existido durante un tiempo pero se propaga más rápidamente

emigration: the movement of individuals away from a given area, 112
emigración: traslado de individuos desde un área dada

emission: a substance that is released into the atmosphere; the cause of air pollution, 462
emisión: sustancia liberada en la atmósfera; causa de la contaminación del aire

endangered species: a species that is at serious risk of extinction, 208
especie en peligro de extinción: especie que corre un grave riesgo de desaparecer

Endangered Species Act (ESA): the major law in the United States that protects biodiversity, 212
Ley de Especies en Peligro de Extinción: la principal ley de los Estados Unidos que protege la biodiversidad

endemic: found in one area of the world, 215
endémico: propio de determinada parte del mundo

energy: the ability to do work or cause a change, 517
energía: capacidad de realizar un trabajo o producir un cambio

energy conservation: reducing energy use to prolong the supply of fossil fuels, 535
conservación de energía: reducción del consumo de energía para asegurar la disponibilidad de combustibles fósiles

energy efficiency: an expression of how much of the energy put into a system actually does useful work, 520
eficiencia energética: expresión que indica cuánta de la energía que se le proporciona a un sistema genera verdaderamente un trabajo útil

environment: all the living and nonliving things with which an organism interacts, 4
medio ambiente: todos los seres vivos y no vivos con los que interactúa un organismo

environmental economics: the field of economics that links environmental and economic costs, 39
economía ambiental: campo de la economía que relaciona los costos económicos con los costos ambientales

English/Spanish Glossary

environmental ethics: the application of ethical standards to relationships between humans and their environment, 25

ética ambiental: aplicación de las normas éticas a las relaciones entre los seres humanos y su medio ambiente

environmental health: the study of how environmental factors affect human health and quality of life, 256

salud ambiental: estudio de la forma en que los factores ambientales afectan la salud y la calidad de vida de los seres humanos

Environmental Impact Statement (EIS): a description of the effects a proposed project (e.g., a new dam or highway) will have on the environment, 46

Evaluación del Impacto Ambiental (EIA): descripción de los efectos que tendrá un proyecto (p. ej., una nueva represa o carretera) en el medio ambiente

environmental policy: a general plan and principle related to the interactions between humans and the environment, 42

política ambiental: plan y principio generales relacionados con las interacciones entre los seres humanos y el medio ambiente

environmental science: the study of how the natural world works, how the environment affects humans, and how humans affect the environment, 5

ciencias del medio ambiente: estudio de cómo funciona el mundo natural, cómo el medio ambiente afecta a los seres humanos y cómo los seres humanos afectan al medio ambiente

environmentalism: a social movement dedicated to protecting the natural world—and by extension, people—from the harmful changes produced by human activities, 6

ambientalismo: movimiento social dedicado a proteger al mundo natural y, por extensión, a las personas, de los cambios dañinos producidos por la actividad humana

epidemiology: the study of disease in human populations, 258

epidemiología: estudio de las enfermedades en las poblaciones humanas

epiphyte: a plant that grows on other plants instead of in soil, 169

epifita: planta que crece sobre otras plantas y no en el suelo

erosion: the removal of soil by water, wind, ice, or gravity, 74

erosión: desgaste del suelo por acción del agua, el viento, el hielo o la gravedad

estivation: the deep sleeplike state that an animal enters when conditions are dry, 170

estivación: estado profundo de letargo en el que entra un animal cuando las condiciones del clima son secas

estuary: body of water, partly enclosed by land, that occurs where fresh water meets the water of an ocean or inland sea, 186

estuario: cuerpo de agua parcialmente rodeado de tierra, que se forma donde el agua dulce se encuentra con el agua de mar

ethics: the branch of philosophy that involves the study of good and bad, and of right and wrong, 24

ética: rama de la filosofía que trata del estudio del bien y el mal, y de lo correcto y lo incorrecto

eutrophication: the introduction of phosphorus and nitrogen into a body of water that leads to an overgrowth of algae and other producers, 86

eutrofización: introducción de fósforo y nitrógeno en una masa de agua que lleva a la proliferación de algas y otros productores

evaporation: a change in state from a liquid to a gas, 81

evaporación: cambio del estado líquido al gaseoso

even-aged: a condition in timber plantations in which all the trees are the same age, 333

coetánea: condición de una plantación forestal en la que todos los árboles tienen la misma edad

evolution: in general terms, change over time, 126

evolución: en términos generales, el cambio a lo largo del tiempo

e-waste: electronic equipment and appliances that are no longer being used; also called *electronic waste,* 598

e-desechos: equipos y aparatos electrónicos que ya no se utilizan; también conocidos como *desechos electrónicos*

exponential growth: the pattern of population growth in which a population increases by a fixed percentage each year, 114

crecimiento exponencial: patrón de crecimiento de una población por el cual ésta crece a un porcentaje fijo cada año

extinction: the disappearance of a species from Earth, 132

extinción: desaparición de una especie de la Tierra

extirpation: the disappearance of a particular population from a particular area, 207

extirpación: desaparición de una población específica de un área determinada

F

feedback loop: a circular process that describes how an event is both a cause and an effect in the same system; can be a positive feedback loop or a negative feedback loop, 73

retroacción: proceso circular que describe cómo un suceso es tanto una causa como un efecto dentro del mismo sistema; puede haber retroacción positiva o negativa

feedlot: a huge warehouse or pen designed to deliver energy-rich feed to livestock or poultry; also called concentrated animal feeding operations (CAFOs) or factory farms, 378

cebadero: enorme depósito o corral diseñado para proveer de alimentos ricos en energía al ganado o las aves de corral; también conocido como "operaciones de engorde de animales en confinamiento", o granjas industriales

fitness: the degree to which an organism can reproduce successfully in its environment, 129

eficacia biológica: medida en la que un organismo se puede reproducir exitosamente en su medio ambiente

flat-plate solar collector: a metal box that absorbs the sun's energy to heat water or air, 562

colector solar de placa plana: caja de metal que absorbe la energía del sol para calentar agua o aire

flood plain: an area alongside a river that periodically floods, 185

llanura de inundación: área junto a un río que se inunda periódicamente

food chain: a linear series of feeding relationships, 146

cadena alimentaria: serie lineal de relaciones de alimentación

food security: the guarantee of an adequate and reliable food supply for all people at all times, 374

seguridad alimentaria: la garantía de un suministro adecuado y confiable de alimentos para todas las personas en todo momento

food web: a diagram of feeding relationships and energy flow showing the paths by which nutrients and energy pass from organism to organism as one consumes another, 146

red alimentaria: diagrama de las relaciones de alimentación y el flujo de energía que muestra las vías por las cuales los nutrientes y la energía pasan de organismo a organismo a medida que uno consume al otro

fossil fuel: a carbon-containing fuel formed over millions of years from the remains of living things, 8, 462, 496

combustible fósil: combustible que contiene carbono, formado durante millones de años a partir de restos de seres vivos

fresh water: relatively pure water; water with few dissolved salts, 421

agua dulce: agua relativamente pura; agua con pocas sales disueltas

front: the boundary between air masses that differ in temperature and moisture, 460

frente: límite entre masas de aire que difieren en temperatura y humedad

fuel cell: a device that converts hydrogen or another fuel into electricity, 572

célula de combustible: dispositivo que transforma el hidrógeno u otro combustible en electricidad

G

gene: a sequence of DNA that codes for a particular trait, 126

gen: secuencia de ADN que codifica un rasgo determinado

genetic diversity: differences in DNA among individuals within a species or population, 202

diversidad genética: diferencias en el ADN entre los individuos de una especie o población

genetic drift: biological evolution that occurs by chance, 127

deriva genética: evolución biológica que ocurre de manera aleatoria

genetic engineering: a process in which scientists directly manipulate an organism's DNA, 375

ingeniería genética: proceso por el cual los científicos manipulan de forma directa el ADN de un organismo

genetically modified (GM) organism: an organism whose DNA has been manipulated by scientists, 375

organismo modificado genéticamente (MG): organismo cuyo ADN ha sido manipulado por científicos

geographic information system (GIS): a computerized system for storing, manipulating, and viewing geographic data, 305

sistema de información geográfica (SIG): sistema computarizado para el almacenamiento, la manipulación y la observación de datos geográficos

English/Spanish Glossary

geosphere: all of the rock at and below Earth's surface, 74
geósfera: la totalidad de las rocas que se encuentran en la superficie terrestre y debajo de ella

geothermal energy: a type of renewable energy that is generated deep within the earth; produced by the breakdown of radioactive elements and high pressure together, 553
energía geotérmica: tipo de energía renovable que se genera en las profundidades de la Tierra; se produce por la acción conjunta de la desintegración de elementos radiactivos y la alta presión

global climate change: a change in global weather patterns; includes changes in temperatures, wind patterns, rainfall, and the frequency of storms, 491
cambio climático global: cambio en los patrones globales del clima; incluye cambios en la temperatura, los patrones de viento, las lluvias y la frecuencia de las tormentas

global warming: an increase in Earth's average surface temperature, 491
calentamiento global: aumento de la temperatura promedio de la superficie de la Tierra

green revolution: the introduction of new technologies, crop varieties, and farming practices to the developing world in the third quarter of the twentieth century, 368
revolución verde: introducción de prácticas agrícolas, variedades de cultivos y tecnologías nuevas en el mundo en vías de desarrollo durante el último trimestre del siglo XX

green tax: a tax levied on companies that participate in activities or produce products that are harmful to the environment, 52
impuesto verde: impuesto aplicado a las empresas que participan en actividades o fabrican productos que dañan el medio ambiente

greenhouse effect: a natural process in which certain gases in the atmosphere trap heat near Earth, preventing the heat from radiating back into space, 484
efecto invernadero: proceso natural por el cual ciertos gases de la atmósfera atrapan calor cerca de la Tierra y así evitan que se irradie de vuelta al espacio

greenhouse gas: a gas that traps heat near Earth, preventing the heat from radiating back into space; includes carbon dioxide and methane, 484
gas de efecto invernadero: gas que atrapa calor cerca de la Tierra y así evita que se irradie de vuelta al espacio; incluye el dióxido de carbono y el metano

greenway: a strip of vegetation that connects parks or neighborhoods; often located along rivers, streams, or canals, 311
corredor verde: franja de vegetación que conecta parques o vecindarios; a menudo se encuentra cerca de ríos, arroyos o canales

ground-source heat pump: a network of pipes that circulates water from the ground (for heating) and back into the ground (for cooling), 554
bomba de calor geotérmica: red de cañerías que transportan agua desde el suelo (para calefacción) y hacia el suelo (para refrigeración)

groundwater: fresh water found below Earth's surface, 82, 424
agua subterránea: agua dulce que se encuentra debajo de la superficie terrestre

growth rate: the change in size of a population over a specific period, 231
tasa de crecimiento: cambio en el tamaño de una población durante un período específico de tiempo

H

habitat: the specific environment in which an organism lives, 103
hábitat: medio ambiente específico en el que vive un organismo

habitat fragmentation: the division of a habitat into smaller patches, 209
fragmentación del hábitat: división de un hábitat en zonas más pequeñas

hazard: something that threatens or is harmful to human health, 256
peligro: algo que pone en riesgo la salud humana o resulta perjudicial para ella

hazardous waste: solid or liquid waste that is toxic, chemically reactive, flammable, or corrosive, 582
desecho peligroso: desecho sólido o líquido que es tóxico, químicamente reactivo, inflamable o corrosivo

heat island: an area in which the temperature generally is several degrees higher than that of the surrounding area; often found in large cities, where structures and materials (e.g., concrete and asphalt) retain heat, 296
isla de calor: área en la que la temperatura suele ser varios grados mayor que en las áreas circundantes; se halla a menudo en ciudades grandes, donde las estructuras y los materiales (p. ej., concreto y asfalto) retienen el calor

herbivore: an organism that eats plants, 143
herbívoro: organismo que se alimenta de plantas

herbivory: the act of feeding on a plant, 138
herbivoría: acción de consumir plantas

hibernation: the deep sleeplike state that an animal enters for most of the winter, 174
hibernación: estado profundo de letargo en el que entra un animal durante la mayor parte del invierno

hurricane: a powerful storm that forms over the ocean in the tropics, 280
huracán: tormenta fuerte que se forma sobre el océano en los trópicos

hydrocarbon: an organic compound combining hydrogen and carbon, 66
hidrocarburo: compuesto orgánico que combina hidrógeno y carbono

hydropower: electricity generated from the energy of moving water, 557
energía hidroeléctrica: electricidad generada por la energía del agua en movimiento

hydrosphere: all of the water—salt water and fresh water, in the form of liquid, ice, or vapor—above and below Earth's surface and in the atmosphere, 74
hidrósfera: toda el agua — agua salada y dulce, en forma de líquido, hielo o vapor — que se encuentra sobre y bajo la superficie de la Tierra y en la atmósfera

hypothesis: a testable idea that attempts to explain a phenomenon or answer a scientific question, 15
hipótesis: idea verificable que intenta explicar un fenómeno o responder una pregunta científica

I

immigration: the movement of individuals to a given area, 112
inmigración: traslado de individuos hacia un área dada

impermeable: not allowing water or other substances to pass through, 424
impermeable: que no permite el paso del agua u otras sustancias

incineration: a controlled process in which mixed garbage is burned at very high temperatures, 587
incineración: proceso controlado por el cual se quema basura mezclada a temperaturas muy altas

independent variable: the variable that is manipulated, or changed, in an experiment, 17
variable independiente: variable que se manipula o cambia en un experimento

industrial agriculture: a type of farming that relies on technology and chemicals to increase yields and reduce costs; also called *high-input agriculture,* 367
agricultura industrial: tipo de agricultura que se basa en la tecnología y las sustancias químicas para aumentar el rendimiento y reducir los costos; también conocida como *agricultura de altos insumos*

Industrial Revolution: introduction of machinery powered by fossil fuels, marked by the shift from a rural, agriculture-based society to an urban, industry-based society, 229
revolución industrial: introducción de máquinas alimentadas con combustibles fósiles, marcada por la transformación de una sociedad rural basada en la agricultura en una sociedad urbana basada en la industria

industrial waste: waste that comes from the production of consumer goods, mining, agriculture, and petroleum extraction and refining, 582
desechos industriales: desechos provenientes de la producción de bienes de consumo, la minería, la agricultura y la extracción y refinación de petróleo

infant mortality: the number of infants per 1000 live births in a population that do not survive the first year of life, 230
mortalidad infantil: número de niños por cada 1000 nacimientos en una población en la que mueren antes de cumplir su primer año de vida

infectious disease: a disease caused by a pathogen, 261
enfermedad infecciosa: enfermedad causada por un agente patógeno

infrastructure: the facilities, services, and installations needed for a community to function; includes transportation systems, communications systems, water, power, waste removal, and schools, 296
infraestructura: prestaciones, servicios e instalaciones necesarios para que una comunidad funcione; incluye los sistemas de transporte, los sistemas de comunicación, el agua, la energía, el desecho de basura y las escuelas

integrated pest management (IPM): the use of both biological and chemical methods to control pests safely and economically, 371
manejo integrado de plagas (MIP): uso de métodos tanto biológicos como químicos para controlar las plagas de forma segura y económica

intercropping: a soil conservation method in which two or more crops are planted in one field, 359
cultivo intercalado: método de conservación del suelo por el cual se siembran dos o más cultivos en un campo

invasive species: a nonnative species that spreads widely in a community, 153
especie invasora: especie no nativa que se propaga ampliamente en una comunidad

irrigation: using a source other than precipitation to water crops, 363
irrigación: uso de una fuente que no es la precipitación para regar los cultivos

K

keystone species: a species that has a strong or wide-ranging impact on a community, 148
especie clave: especie que tiene un impacto fuerte o de gran alcance en una comunidad

kinetic energy: the energy produced by motion, 517
energía cinética: energía producida por el movimiento

Kyoto Protocol: an international agreement drafted in 1997 to limit greenhouse gas emissions, 507
Protocolo de Kioto: acuerdo internacional redactado en 1997 para limitar las emisiones de gases de efecto invernadero

L

land cover: the vegetation and manufactured structures that cover land, 292
cobertura de la tierra: la vegetación y las estructuras manufacturadas que cubren la tierra

land use: human activity that occurs on and is directly related to the land; includes farming, grazing, logging, recreation, and residential and industrial development, 292
uso del suelo: actividad humana que ocurre en el suelo y está directamente relacionada con éste; incluye la agricultura, el pastoreo, la explotación forestal, la recreación y el desarrollo residencial e industrial

landform: a mountain, island, or continent formed by the collisions and separations of tectonic plates, 77
accidente geográfico: una montaña, una isla o un continente formado por las colisiones y separaciones de las placas tectónicas

landslide: the rapid movement of rock and soil sliding down a slope, 278
desprendimiento de tierras: movimiento rápido de rocas y suelo que se deslizan por una pendiente

law of conservation of matter: the principle that states that matter can change form but cannot be created or destroyed, 83
ley de conservación de la materia: principio que establece que la materia puede cambiar de forma pero no se puede crear ni destruir

leachate: the liquid that forms in a landfill as trash dissolves in rain or snow; a source of groundwater contamination, 585
lixiviado: líquido que se forma en un vertedero a medida que la basura se disuelve con la lluvia o la nieve; fuente de contaminación del agua subterránea

life expectancy: the average number of years an individual can expect to live, 230
esperanza de vida: promedio de la cantidad de años que un individuo puede esperar vivir

limiting factor: a characteristic of the environment that restricts population growth, 115
factor limitante: característica del medio ambiente que restringe el crecimiento de la población

limnetic zone: the portion of the photic zone that is farther from shore than the littoral zone; no rooted plants are found in this zone, 183
zona limnética: parte de la zona fótica que se encuentra más alejada de la costa que la zona litoral; no se encuentran plantas con raíces en esta zona

lipid: chemically diverse compound that does not dissolve in water, 69
lípido: compuesto químicamente diverso que no se disuelve en agua

lithosphere: sphere of Earth made up of the hard rock on and just below Earth's surface; the outermost layer of both Earth and its geosphere, 74
litósfera: esfera de la Tierra compuesta por la roca dura que se encuentra sobre y apenas debajo de la superficie terrestre; la capa más externa de la Tierra y su geósfera

littoral zone: the shallow near-shore portion of the photic zone, 183
zona litoral: parte poco profunda, cercana a la costa, de la zona fótica

loam: soil that is approximately equal parts clay, silt, and sand, 356
marga: suelo que se compone de partes casi iguales de arcilla, limo y arena

lobbying: efforts to influence an elected official into supporting a specific interest, 54
cabildeo: esfuerzos para convencer a un funcionario electo de que apoye un interés específico

logistic growth: the pattern of population growth in which exponential growth is slowed and finally stopped by limiting factors, 115
crecimiento logístico: patrón de crecimiento de la población por el cual el crecimiento exponencial se desacelera y finalmente se frena debido a factores limitantes

M

macromolecule: a large organic molecule; includes proteins, nucleic acids, carbohydrates, and lipids, 67
macromolécula: molécula orgánica grande; incluye las proteínas, los ácidos nucleicos, los carbohidratos y los lípidos

malnutrition: a shortage of essential nutrients, 374
desnutrición: falta de nutrientes esenciales

mantle: the layer of very hot but mostly solid rock beneath Earth's crust, 76
manto: capa de roca muy caliente pero mayormente sólida que se encuentra bajo la corteza terrestre

market failure: a situation in which a free economy, operating on its own, does not distribute resources fairly, 40
falla del mercado: situación en la que una economía libre, operando por sí misma, no distribuye equitativamente los recursos

materials recovery facility (MRF): a plant where collected recyclables are sorted and prepared for reprocessing, 594
centro de recuperación de materiales: planta donde se clasifican y se preparan los materiales reciclables recolectados para su reproceso

matter: any material that has mass and occupies space, 64
materia: cualquier material que tiene masa y ocupa espacio

maximum sustainable yield (MSY): the amount of a resource that can be harvested without reducing the amount of future harvests, 328
rendimiento máximo sostenible (RMS): cantidad de un recurso que se puede explotar sin reducir la explotación futura

meltdown: the accidental melting of the uranium fuel rods inside the core of a nuclear reactor, causing the release of radiation, 539
fusión del núcleo de un reactor: fusión accidental de las barras de combustible de uranio dentro del núcleo de un reactor nuclear, que produce la liberación de materiales radiactivos

mesosphere: the layer of the atmosphere above the stratosphere; extends 50 to 80 km above sea level, 456
mesósfera: capa de la atmósfera que está sobre la estratósfera; se encuentra entre los 50 y los 80 km de altura sobre el nivel del mar

methane hydrate: an icelike solid that consists of molecules of methane within a crystal network of water molecules; can be burned to release energy, 528
hidrato de metano: sólido de aspecto similar al hielo que se compone de moléculas de metano dentro de una red cristalina de moléculas de agua; se lo puede quemar para que libere energía

migration: the seasonal movement of organisms into and out of an area, 112
migración: desplazamiento estacional de organismos desde y hacia un área

mineral: an inorganic solid that has an orderly crystalline structure and a specific chemical composition, 392
mineral: sólido inorgánico con una estructura cristalina ordenada y una composición química específica

molecule: a combination of two or more atoms, 66
molécula: combinación de dos o más átomos

monoculture: the large-scale plantings of a single crop, 340
monocultivo: plantación a gran escala de un único cultivo

Montreal Protocol: a treaty that limits the production of chlorofluorocarbons, 473
Protocolo de Montreal: tratado que limita la producción de clorofluorocarbonos

mountaintop removal: a type of mining in which plants and soil are removed from the top of a mountain and then explosives are used to reach seams of coal, 401
remoción de cimas de montañas: tipo de minería en la que se remueven las plantas y el suelo de la cima de una montaña y luego se utilizan explosivos para llegar a las vetas de carbón

multiple use: a policy that states that the national forests must serve a number of uses (e.g., recreation, wildlife habitat, mining, grazing, and timber), 338
  uso múltiple: política que establece que los bosques nacionales deben servir para una cantidad de usos (p. ej., recreación, hábitat para la vida silvestre, minería, pastoreo y explotación forestal)

municipal solid waste: nonliquid waste that comes from homes, institutions, and small businesses, 582
  desechos sólidos urbanos: desechos no líquidos provenientes de hogares, instituciones y pequeñas empresas

mutation: a change in DNA, 127
  mutación: cambio en el ADN

mutualism: a relationship between two organisms from different species in which both organisms benefit, 139
  mutualismo: relación entre dos organismos de distinta especie en la que ambos organismos se benefician

N

natural resource: any of the natural materials and energy sources provided by nature that humans need to survive, 6
  recurso natural: cualquiera de los materiales naturales y las fuentes de energía provistos por la naturaleza que el ser humano necesita para sobrevivir

natural selection: the process by which traits that improve an organism's chances for survival and reproduction are passed on more frequently to offspring than those that do not, 127
  selección natural: proceso mediante el cual los rasgos que mejoran las probabilidades de supervivencia y reproducción de un organismo se transmiten con más frecuencia a los descendientes que los rasgos que no tienen esta característica

net primary production: the organic matter, or biomass, that remains after cellular respiration, 167
  producción primaria neta: materia orgánica, o biomasa, que queda después de la respiración celular

neurotoxin: a chemical that can damage the nervous system, 268
  neurotoxina: sustancia química que puede dañar el sistema nervioso

niche: an organism's habitat, resource use, and fundamental role in a community, 133
  nicho: el papel fundamental en la comunidad, el uso de los recursos y el hábitat de un organismo

nitrogen fixation: the conversion of nitrogen gas into ammonia, 88
  fijación del nitrógeno: transformación del nitrógeno gaseoso en amoníaco

non-market value: the value that is not included in the price of a product or service, 40
  valor no comercial: valor que no se incluye en el precio de un producto o servicio

nonpoint-source pollution: pollution that comes from many places over a large area, 435
  contaminación no puntual: contaminación proveniente de muchos lugares en un área grande

nonrenewable energy: an energy resource that cannot be replaced in a relatively short time; includes fossil fuels and nuclear energy, 520
  energía no renovable: recurso energético que no se puede reemplazar en un período relativamente corto de tiempo; incluye los combustibles fósiles y la energía nuclear

nonrenewable natural resources: a resource that is formed much more slowly than it is used, 7
  recurso natural no renovable: recurso que se forma mucho más lentamente de lo que se consume

nuclear energy: the energy that holds protons and neutrons together in the nucleus of an atom, 537
  energía nuclear: energía que mantiene unidos los protones y los neutrones en el núcleo de un átomo

nuclear fission: the conversion of the energy within an atom's nucleus to usable thermal energy by splitting apart atomic nuclei, 537
  fisión nuclear: transformación de la energía dentro del núcleo de un átomo en energía térmica utilizable mediante la división de núcleos atómicos

nuclear fusion: the conversion of the energy within an atom's nucleus to usable thermal energy by forcing together the small nuclei of lightweight elements under high temperature and pressure, 541
  fusión nuclear: transformación de la energía dentro del núcleo de un átomo en energía térmica utilizable mediante la unión forzada de pequeños núcleos de elementos livianos a altas temperatura y presión

nuclear reactor: a facility within a nuclear power plant that generates electricity through controlled nuclear fission, 538
reactor nuclear: instalación dentro de una planta nuclear que genera electricidad mediante la fisión nuclear controlada

nuclear waste: the radioactive material left over from the production of energy and other processes in a nuclear power plant, 540
desecho nuclear: material radiactivo que queda como subproducto de la generación de energía y otros procesos en una planta nuclear

nucleic acid: the macromolecule that carries hereditary information; includes DNA and RNA, 68
ácido nucleico: macromolécula que contiene la información hereditaria; incluye el ADN y el ARN

nucleus: the central core of an atom; consists of protons and neutrons, 65
núcleo: parte central de un átomo; formado por los protones y los neutrones

nutrient: matter that organisms need to carry out their life processes, 83
nutriente: materia que necesitan los organismos para llevar a cabo sus procesos vitales

O

ocean thermal energy conversion: the process of changing the solar energy stored in the ocean to electric power, 560
conversión de energía térmica oceánica: proceso de transformación de la energía solar almacenada en el océano en energía eléctrica

oil sand: a deposit of moist sand and clay that can be mined to extract bitumen, an oil-rich hydrocarbon, 528
arenas petrolíferas: depósito de arcilla y arena húmeda que se puede explotar para extraer betún, un hidrocarburo rico en petróleo

oil shale: rock that contains hydrocarbons; can be burned directly or processed to extract liquid petroleum, 528
pizarra bituminosa: roca que contiene hidrocarburos; se puede quemar directamente o procesarse para extraer petróleo líquido

old-growth forest: a forest that has never been logged, 335
bosque primario: bosque que nunca ha sido talado

omnivore: an animal that eats both plants and animals, 143
omnívoro: animal que come plantas y animales

open pit mining: a type of mining in which a large hole (versus a shaft or tunnel) is dug to extract ore and the rock around it, 400
explotación a tajo abierto (metales): tipo de minería en la cual se excava un gran hoyo (en contraste con la minería subterránea o de túneles) para extraer la mena y la roca que la rodea

ore: a mineral or grouping of minerals that is mined to extract one or more valuable metals, 398
mena: mineral o grupo de minerales que se explota para extraer uno o más metales valiosos

organic agriculture: a type of sustainable agriculture in which only biological methods (e.g., biological pest control and composting) are used, 382
agricultura orgánica: tipo de agricultura sostenible en la cual sólo se utilizan métodos biológicos (p. ej., control biológico de plagas y compostaje)

overgrazing: allowing animals to eat so much of the plant cover in a field or pasture that the plants cannot regrow, 360
sobrepastoreo: acción de permitir que los animales coman tanto de la cobertura vegetal de un campo o una pradera que las plantas no puedan volver a crecer

ozone hole: the area of lowered ozone concentration over Antarctica, 472
agujero en la capa de ozono: la zona de concentración reducida de ozono sobre la Antártida

ozone layer: the concentration of ozone in the stratosphere, 456
capa de ozono: concentración de ozono en la estratósfera

English/Spanish Glossary

P

parasitism: a relationship between two organisms from different species in which one organism (the parasite) depends on the other (the host) for nourishment or some other benefit, 138
parasitismo: relación entre dos organismos de distinta especie en la que un organismo (el parásito) depende del otro (el huésped) para obtener alimento o algún otro beneficio

parent material: the base geological material in a particular location, 353
material precursor: material geológico básico de una ubicación determinada

passive solar heating: using the design of a building (versus technology) to collect, store, and distribute the sun's energy, 562
calefacción solar pasiva: uso del diseño de un edificio (en lugar de la tecnología) para captar, almacenar y distribuir la energía solar

pathogen: a disease-causing organism, 256, 438
patógeno: organismo que causa enfermedades

peer review: the formal process of submitting research for examination by the scientific community, 22
revisión por pares: proceso formal de presentar una investigación para que la examine la comunidad científica

permafrost: permanently frozen soil, 178
permafrost: suelo que se encuentra siempre congelado

permeable: having spaces or pores that allow water or other substances to pass through, 424
permeable: que tiene espacios o poros que permiten el paso del agua u otras sustancias

pesticide: a chemical used to kill organisms that attack or compete with plants that humans value, 364
pesticida: sustancia química utilizada para matar a los organismos que atacan a las plantas de valor humano o compiten con ellas

petrochemical: a chemical compound derived from oil that is used to make plastics, detergents, and other products, 525
petroquímico: compuesto químico derivado del petróleo que se usa para fabricar plásticos, detergentes y otros productos

petroleum: a liquid fossil fuel made up mostly of hydrocarbons; the primary source of gasoline, 525
petróleo: combustible fósil líquido compuesto principalmente por hidrocarburos; fuente primaria de la gasolina

pH: a measure of the acidity or alkalinity (basicity) of a solution, 71
pH: medida de la acidez o alcalinidad (basicidad) de una solución

photic zone: the uppermost layer of an aquatic ecosystem, where there is enough sunlight for photosynthesis to occur, 182
zona fótica: capa superior de un ecosistema acuático, donde hay luz solar suficiente para que se pueda realizar la fotosíntesis

photosynthesis: the process by which primary producers use sunlight to convert carbon dioxide and water into sugars, releasing oxygen, 84, 142
fotosíntesis: proceso por el cual los productores primarios usan la luz solar para transformar el dióxido de carbono y el agua en azúcares, liberando así oxígeno

photovoltaic (PV) cell: a device that converts solar energy directly into electricity, 562
célula fotovoltaica: dispositivo que transforma la energía solar en electricidad

pioneer species: one of the first species to colonize newly exposed land, 150
especie pionera: una de las primeras especies que coloniza un nuevo terreno expuesto

placer mining: a type of mining that involves sifting through sand and gravel in a riverbed or streambed to extract metals, minerals, or precious stones, 402
minería aluvial: tipo de minería que implica el filtrado de arena o grava en el lecho de un río o arroyo para extraer metales, minerales o piedras preciosas

poaching: the illegal capture or killing of an organism, 211
caza furtiva: matanza o captura ilegal de un organismo

point-source pollution: pollution that comes from a specific location (e.g., a factory or a sewer pipe), 435
contaminación puntual: contaminación proveniente de una ubicación específica (p. ej., una fábrica o un tubo de desagüe)

policy: a formal set of general plans and principles that guides problem solving and decision making in specific instances, 42
política: un conjunto formal de planes y principios generales que orientan la resolución de problemas y la toma de decisiones en instancias específicas

pollinator: an insect or other animal that transfers pollen from one plant to another, 371
polinizador: insecto u otro animal que transfiere el polen de una planta a otra

pollution: matter or energy that is harmful to the environment, 267
contaminación: materia o energía que daña el medio ambiente

polymorph: a mineral that crystallizes in different forms because of differences in temperature or other conditions, 394
polimorfo: mineral que se cristaliza de distintas maneras debido a las diferencias en la temperatura u otras condiciones

population: the members of a species that live in the same area, 101
población: miembros de una especie que viven en la misma área

population density: the number of individuals in a population per unit of area, 106
densidad de población: número de individuos de una población por unidad de área

population distribution: how organisms are arranged within an area; sometimes called *population dispersion,* 107
distribución de la población: forma en que se distribuyen los organismos dentro de un área; también conocida como *dispersión de la población*

population size: the number of individual organisms present in a population at a given time, 104
tamaño de la población: número de organismos individuales presentes en una población en un momento dado

potential energy: the energy that an object has because of its position or shape, 517
energía potencial: energía que tiene un cuerpo por su posición o su forma

precipitation: the return of water from the atmosphere to Earth's surface in the form of rain, snow, sleet, or hail, 81; the process of separating a solid substance (precipitate) from a solution, 394
precipitación: regreso del agua desde la atmósfera a la superficie de la Tierra en forma de lluvia, nieve, aguanieve o granizo; proceso de separar una sustancia sólida (precipitado) de una solución

predation: the process by which individuals of one species (the predators) hunt, capture, and feed on individuals of another species (the prey), 136
depredación: proceso mediante el cual los individuos de una especie (depredadores) persiguen, capturan y comen a los individuos de otra especie (presa)

prediction: a statement of what a scientist expects to observe if a hypothesis is true, 16
predicción: enunciado que indica lo que un científico espera observar si una hipótesis se confirma

prescribed burn: the process of setting fire to an area of forest under carefully controlled conditions; also called *controlled burn,* 341
quema prescrita: proceso de prender fuego a una zona de bosque en condiciones cuidadosamente controladas; también conocida como *quema controlada*

primary air pollutant: a pollutant released directly into the troposphere; can cause damage itself or react with other substances to cause damage, 463
contaminante primario del aire: contaminante liberado directamente a la tropósfera; puede causar daños por sí mismo o en combinación con otras sustancias con las que reacciona

primary producer: an organism that can capture energy from the sun or from chemicals and store it; also called *autotroph,* 84, 141
productor primario: organismo que puede captar la energía del sol o de las sustancias químicas y almacenarla; también conocido como *autótrofo*

primary succession: the somewhat predictable series of changes in a community that follows a disturbance so severe that no vegetation or soil life remains, 150
sucesión primaria: serie de cambios más o menos predecibles en una comunidad que ocurre después de una alteración tan grave que no queda vida en el suelo ni vegetación

protein: an organic compound made up of carbon, oxygen, hydrogen, nitrogen, and sometimes sulfur, 67
proteína: compuesto orgánico formado por carbono, oxígeno, hidrógeno, nitrógeno y, a veces, azufre

proxy indicator: type of indirect evidence that serves as a substitute for direct measurement, 493
indicador *proxy* o sustituto: tipo de evidencia indirecta que se utiliza en lugar de una medición directa

English/Spanish Glossary

R

radiation: the transfer of energy through space, 458
radiación: transferencia de energía a través del espacio

radioactive waste: waste that gives off radiation that is harmful to humans and the environment, 601
desecho radiactivo: desecho que emite radiaciones dañinas para los seres humanos y el medio ambiente

radon: a colorless, highly toxic radioactive gas, 271
radón: gas radiactivo incoloro, altamente tóxico

recharge zone: an area where surface water soaks into the ground and reaches an aquifer, 425
zona de recarga: área en la que el agua superficial es absorbida por el suelo y llega a un acuífero

recycling: collecting materials that can be broken down and reprocessed to make new items, 593
reciclaje: recolección de materiales que se pueden descomponer y reprocesar para hacer elementos nuevos

red tide: a harmful algal bloom caused by algae that produce reddish pigments, 440
marea roja: floración dañina de algas causada por algas que producen pigmentos rojizos

relative humidity: the ratio of water vapor in the air to the maximum amount of water vapor the air could hold at that temperature; expressed as a percentage, 454
humedad relativa: razón del vapor de agua en el aire a la cantidad máxima de vapor de agua que el aire puede contener a esa temperatura; se expresa como porcentaje

renewable energy: an energy resource that is readily available or that can be replaced in a relatively short time; includes wind, moving water, sunlight, and wood, 520
energía renovable: recurso energético que se encuentra fácilmente o que se puede reemplazar en un período relativamente corto de tiempo; incluye el viento, el agua en movimiento, la luz solar y la madera

renewable natural resource: a resource that is replenished, or renewed over short periods of time, 7
recurso natural renovable: recurso que se repone, o se renueva, en un período corto de tiempo

replacement fertility: the birthrate at which a nation's population size stays the same, 235
fertilidad de reemplazo: tasa de natalidad a la que el tamaño de la población de una nación se mantiene estable

reservoir: an artificial lake where water for human use is stored, 428
embalse: lago artificial donde se almacena agua para consumo humano

resource: anything an organism needs; includes nutrition, shelter, mates, and breeding sites, 103
recurso: todo lo que necesita un organismo; incluye nutrición, refugio, pareja y lugar para la reproducción

resource management: using resources without depleting them, 324
gestión de recursos: uso de los recursos sin agotarlos

resource partitioning: a process that allows different species to share common resources, 135
repartición de recursos: proceso que permite que distintas especies compartan recursos comunes

response: the effect on an organism of exposure to a pollutant or other hazardous substance, 258
respuesta: efecto sobre un organismo de la exposición a un contaminante u otra sustancia peligrosa

risk: the probability that a hazard will cause a harmful response, 260
riesgo: la probabilidad de que un peligro provoque una respuesta dañina

risk assessment: the process of measuring risk, 260
evaluación de riesgos: proceso de medición de los riesgos

river system: a network of connected streams and rivers, 422
sistema fluvial: red de arroyos y ríos interconectados

rock: a solid mass of minerals or mineral-like materials that occurs naturally, 395
roca: masa sólida de minerales o materiales similares a los minerales que existe de forma natural

rock cycle: a very slow process in which rocks are heated, melted, cooled, weathered, and eroded as they change type—igneous, sedimentary, or metamorphic—in response to changes in environmental conditions, 395
ciclo de las rocas: proceso muy lento por el cual las rocas se calientan, derriten, enfrían, desgastan y erosionan al tiempo que cambian de tipo —ígnea, sedimentaria o metamórfica— en respuesta a los cambios en las condiciones ambientales

runoff: water that flows over land and collects in a stream or river, 422
escurrimiento: agua que fluye sobre el suelo y se acumula en un arroyo o un río

rural area: undeveloped land or a settlement of fewer than 2500 people, 293
área rural: tierra no urbanizada o asentamiento de menos de 2500 personas

S

salinity: a measurement of the amount of salts dissolved in water, 181
salinidad: medida de la cantidad de sales disueltas en agua

salinization: the buildup of salts in the surface layers of soil, 363, 431
salinización: acumulación de sales en las capas superficiales del suelo

salvage logging: the removal of dead trees following a natural disturbance, 342
corta de recuperación: extracción de los árboles muertos después de una alteración natural

sand: soil particles that are 0.05 to 2 mm in diameter, 356
arena: partículas del suelo que tienen un diámetro de entre 0.05 y 2 mm

sanitary landfill: a facility in which waste is buried in the ground or piled up in large, carefully engineered mounds, 585
relleno sanitario: instalación en la que se entierran desechos o se los apilan en grandes montículos cuidadosamente diseñados

scrubber: a device that removes pollutants or changes them chemically before they leave factory smokestacks, 472
desulfuradora: dispositivo que remueve los contaminantes o los modifica químicamente antes de que salgan de las chimeneas de las fábricas

secondary air pollutant: a harmful substance produced when a primary pollutant reacts with other substances, 463
contaminante secundario del aire: sustancia nociva que se produce cuando un contaminante primario reacciona con otras sustancias

secondary succession: the somewhat predictable series of changes in a community that follows a disturbance (e.g., a fire, logging, or farming) that dramatically alters the community but does not destroy all vegetation or soil life, 151
sucesión secundaria: serie de cambios más o menos predecibles en una comunidad que ocurre después de una alteración (p. ej., incendio, tala o cultivo) que modifica de forma drástica a la comunidad pero no destruye toda la vegetación o la vida del suelo

seed bank: an organization that preserves the seeds of diverse plants in case of a global crop collapse, 380
banco de semillas: organización que preserva las semillas de plantas diversas por si llegara a ocurrir un colapso global de los cultivos

seed-tree approach: a method of harvesting trees in which a small number of mature and healthy seed-producing trees are left standing so they can reseed an area that has been logged, 334
método de árboles padres: método de explotación forestal por el cual un número pequeño de árboles semilleros maduros y sanos se dejan en pie para que puedan dispersar las semillas y repoblar un área que se ha talado

selection system: a method of harvesting trees in which only some of the trees in a forest are cut at one time, 334
sistema selectivo: método de explotación forestal por el cual sólo algunos de los árboles de un bosque se cortan al mismo tiempo

septic system: a method of wastewater disposal, 443
sistema séptico: método de eliminación de aguas residuales

sex ratio: the proportion of males to females in a population, 109
proporción de sexos: proporción de machos y hembras en una población

shelterbelt: one or more rows of trees or other tall, perennial plants planted along the edge of a field to prevent wind erosion; also called a *windbreak*, 359
cortina forestal: una o más hileras de árboles u otras plantas perennes altas que se plantan a lo largo del borde de un campo para evitar la erosión del viento; también conocida como *cortavientos*

shelterwood approach: a method of harvesting trees in which a small number of mature trees are left in place to provide shelter for seedlings as they grow, 334
corta por aclareo sucesivo: método de explotación forestal por el cual un número pequeño de árboles maduros se dejan en su lugar para que brinden protección a las plántulas mientras crecen

silt: soil particles that are 0.002 to 0.05 mm in diameter, 356
limo: partículas del suelo que tienen un diámetro de entre 0.002 y 0.05 mm

smart growth: a philosophy of urban growth that focuses on sustainable growth and the avoidance of sprawl, 308
crecimiento inteligente: filosofía de crecimiento urbano que se concentra en el crecimiento sostenible y en evitar la expansión descontrolada

smelting: the process of extracting metal from ore by heating the ore beyond its melting point, 404
fundición: proceso de extracción del metal de una mena que consiste en calentar la mena más allá de su punto de fusión

thunderstorm: a localized storm that produces both lightning and thunder, 282

tormenta eléctrica: tormenta localizada que produce tanto rayos como truenos

tidal energy: electricity generated from the movement of the tides, 559

energía mareomotriz: electricidad generada a partir del movimiento de las mareas

tilling: the turning-over of soil before planting, 359

labranza: acción de remover el suelo antes de la siembra

tolerance: the ability to survive and reproduce under changing environmental conditions, 134

tolerancia: capacidad de sobrevivir y reproducirse en condiciones ambientales cambiantes

topography: the surface characteristics of an area, 489

topografía: características superficiales de un área

tornado: a type of windstorm in which a funnel of rotating air drops down from a storm cloud and touches Earth's surface, 280

tornado: tipo de tormenta de viento en la que un embudo de aire en rotación desciende de una nube de tormenta y toca la superficie terrestre

total fertility rate: the average number of children a female member of a population gives birth to during her lifetime, 235

tasa de fertilidad total: número promedio de hijos que da a luz un miembro femenino de una población durante su vida

toxicant: any chemical that harms an individual's health; also called a *chemical hazard*, 267

sustancia tóxica: cualquier sustancia química nociva para la salud de un individuo; también conocida como *peligro químico*

toxicity: the degree to which a substance is harmful to an organism, 258

toxicidad: medida en que una sustancia es perjudicial para un organismo

toxicology: the study of how poisons affect an organism's health, 258

toxicología: estudio de la forma en que los venenos afectan la salud de un organismo

traditional agriculture: a type of farming that relies on human and animal power, along with hand tools and nonmotorized machines (e.g., plows), 366

agricultura tradicional: tipo de agricultura que se basa en la fuerza de los seres humanos y los animales, junto con herramientas manuales y máquinas sin motor (p. ej., arados)

transpiration: the release of water vapor by plants through their leaves, 81

transpiración: liberación de vapor de agua de las plantas a través de las hojas

trophic level: a rank in a feeding hierarchy, 144

nivel trófico: posición en una jerarquía alimentaria

troposphere: the lowest layer of the atmosphere; extends 0 to 11 km above sea level, 455

tropósfera: la capa más baja de la atmósfera; se encuentra a una altura de entre 0 y 11 km sobre el nivel del mar

tsunami: a large ocean wave produced by an earthquake or other disturbance on the ocean floor, 278

tsunami: gran ola oceánica producida por un terremoto o por otra alteración en el fondo del océano

U

urban area: mostly developed land or a settlement with more than 2500 people; a city and the suburbs around it, 293

área urbana: tierra urbanizada en su mayor parte o asentamiento de más de 2500 personas; una ciudad y sus suburbios

urban growth boundary (UGB): a line used by city planners to separate areas that will remain urban from areas that will remain rural, 307

límite de crecimiento urbano: línea utilizada por los urbanistas para separar las áreas que seguirán siendo urbanas de las que seguirán siendo rurales

urbanization: a population shift from living in the country to living in cities, 294

urbanización: cambio que hace que una población pase de vivir en el campo a vivir en las ciudades

understory: the shorter trees and plants found in a tropical rain forest, 168

sotobosque: árboles y plantas más bajos de la selva húmeda tropical

upwelling: the flow of cold, nutrient-rich water toward the surface of the ocean, 188

corriente de ascenso: corriente de agua fría y rica en nutrientes que fluye hacia la superficie del océano

uneven-aged: a condition in timber plantations in which trees are all different ages, 333

no coetánea: condición de una plantación forestal en la que todos los árboles tienen distintas edades

V

volcano: an opening in Earth's crust through which molten lava, ash, and gases are ejected, 279
volcán: abertura de la corteza terrestre por la cual salen expulsados lava líquida, cenizas y gases

W

waste: any unwanted material or substance produced by an organism's activity or process, 582
desecho: material o sustancia no deseada producida por una actividad o un proceso de un organismo

wastewater: water that has been used in households, businesses, industries, or public facilities and drained or flushed down the pipes, as well as the polluted runoff from streets and storm drains, 436
aguas residuales: agua que se ha usado en las viviendas, empresas, industrias o instalaciones públicas y se ha desagotado o eliminado por los tubos de desagüe, así como el escurrimiento contaminado de las calles y los desagües pluviales

water diversion: the process of moving water from its source to places where humans can use it (e.g., homes and farm fields), 428
desviación de las aguas: proceso de mover el agua de su fuente hacia los lugares donde los seres humanos puedan usarla (p. ej., hogares y campos de cultivo)

water table: the boundary between the zone of aeration and the zone of saturation in an aquifer, 424
nivel freático: límite entre la zona de aireación y la zona de saturación en un acuífero

watershed: all of the land area that supplies water to a particular river system, 422
cuenca hidrográfica: toda el área de terreno que suministra agua a un sistema fluvial determinado

wealth gap: the difference in assets and income between individuals in a society or between nations, 244
brecha en la distribución de la riqueza: diferencia en los bienes e ingresos entre los individuos de una sociedad o entre diferentes naciones

weather: the day-to-day conditions in Earth's atmosphere, 165
tiempo meteorológico: condiciones diarias de la atmósfera terrestre

weathering: the physical and chemical processes that break down rocks and minerals into smaller particles, 354
desgaste: los procesos químicos y físicos que erosionan la roca y los minerales y los convierten en partículas más pequeñas

well: a channel dug into an aquifer to reach groundwater, 425
pozo: canal excavado en un acuífero para llegar al agua subterránea

wetland: an area of land that is flooded with water at least sometime during the year, 184
humedal: área de tierra que se inunda al menos una vez en el año

wind farm: a power plant that uses wind turbines to generate electricity, 567
parque eólico: central eléctrica que utiliza aerogeneradores para generar electricidad

wind turbine: a device that converts the wind's kinetic energy into electrical energy, 567
aerogenerador: dispositivo que transforma la energía cinética del viento en energía eléctrica

X

xeriscaping: landscaping using plants adapted to dry conditions, 434
xerojardinería: paisajismo que utiliza plantas adaptadas a condiciones secas

Y

yield: the amount of a crop produced in a given area, 367
rendimiento: cantidad de cultivo producido en un área dada

Z

zoning: the practice of classifying areas for different types of development and land use, 306
zonificación: práctica de clasificar áreas de acuerdo con diferentes tipos de desarrollo y uso del suelo

Index

A

Abiotic factors, **103**

Acid deposition, **467**–468

Acid drainage, **406, 532**

Acid rain, 53, 467, 474–475

Acids, 71, 467, 499

A Closer Look
  coal and electricity, 542–543
  geographic information systems (GIS), 314–315
  nutrients, 90–91
  recycling, 604–605
  U.S. Census, 248–249
  wastewater treatment, 444–445

Active solar heating, **562**

Adaptations, **129**
  benthic ecosystems, 191
  and genetic diversity, **202**
  polar fish, 179
  predators and prey, 137
  rainforest plants, 169
  salinity, 181

Adaptive management, **328**–329

Addo Elephant National Park, 163, 164, 176, 193

Aeration, 442

Affluence, 242, 244–245

Africa, 11, 243, 344–345

African elephants, 163, 171, 176

Age structure, **108**, 111, 235–236

Age structure diagrams, **108**–109, 236–237

Agricultural Revolution, 8

Agriculture, 365–383. *See also* Food production.
  and artificial selection, 130
  and biodiversity, 205
  and climate change, 500
  community-supported, 383
  development of, 228–239, 365–366
  farming practices, 359, 505
  and fresh water, 325
  genetically modified (GM) crops, 351, 375–377, 380
  and grasslands, 175
  green revolution, **368**
  high-input, 367
  industrial, **367**–368, 373, 378–381
  loss of cropland, 373
  low-input, 382
  organic, **382**–383
  pests, 369–371
  pollinators, **371**–372
  and population growth, 228, 373
  reduced-tillage, 359
  sustainable, **381**–383
  traditional, **366**
  and water use, 427, 430–431, 433

AIDS, 261

Air
  composition of, 67, 452–453
  and heat transfer, 458–459
  pressure, **455**
  temperature, 454

Air mass, **460,** 487

Air pollution, 270–273, 461–473
  acid deposition, **467**–468
  acid rain, 467, 474–475
  and biomass fuels, 553
  Clean Air Act, **470**–472, 474
  defined, **462**
  and fossil fuels, 530
  and health, 464
  indoor, 270–271
  and mining, 406
  monitoring, 469
  Montreal Protocol, 25, 49, **473**
  and ozone hole, **472**–473
  primary and secondary, **463**
  reduction in, 471
  smog, 66, 451, **465**, 472
  sources of, 462–463
  temperature inversions, **466**
  and traffic, 451, 462, 465

Air pressure, **455**

Alachor, 439

Alaska, 402, 515

Alfalfa, 372

Algae
  brown, 190
  and corals, 499
  eutrophication, 86
  and fungi, 150
  hydrogen from, 571
  photosynthetic, 205

Algal blooms, **436, 440**

Alkaline solutions, 71

All-American Canal, 428

Allergens, 269

Allopatric speciation, 131

Alloy, 404

Aloe vera, 172

Alternative energy, 503, 550. *See also* Renewable energy.

Altitude, 455, 489

Aluminum, 411, 595

Amazon, 384–385

Ammonia, 88

Anderson, James, 18–19, 21

Aneroid barometer, 455

Ancient sediments, 494

Anglerfish, 191

Animals
  and antibiotics, 379
  boreal forest, 177

desert, 172
  and food production, 378–379
  grassland, 175
  nocturnal, 172
  rainforest, 169
  and resource management, 326
  temperate forest, 174

Antarctica, 3, 20, 205, 472, 492, 508

Antarctic Treaty System of 1959, 49

Anthropocentrism, 26

Antibiotic resistance, 264

Antibiotics, 229, 379

Aphotic zone, **182,** 188, 191

Appalachian Mountains, 401, 407

Aquaculture, **379**

Aquatic ecosystems, 181–191
  aquatic layers, 182
  biomes, **164**–180
  classification of, 181–182
  estuaries, **186**–187
  flowing and standing water, 182
  freshwater, 183–185
  mangrove forests, 186–187
  oceans, 188–191
  salt marshes, 186–187
  and temperature, 182
  wetlands, **184**

Aquatic succession, 152

Aquifers, **82, 424**–425, 432, 439, 600

Arable land, **373**

Aral Sea, 430

Arctic, 211, 498

Arctic National Wildlife Refuge, 515, 533, 535

Arizona, 172

Arms race, evolutionary, 137

Index

C

Cacti, 172, 370

Cactus moths, 370

Calcium, 91

Calcium carbonate, 394

Calcium phosphate, 394

Calculating, SH-19

California, 176, 273, 402, 419, 428, 567

California Academy of Science, 24

California condors, 218

California Floristic Province, 215

Camouflage, 174

Canada, 236, 501

Canals, 428

Cancer, 268, 289, 472

Cane toads, 154

Canola plants, 376

Canopy, **168**, 331

Cap-and-trade programs, **53**, 474, 505

Captive breeding, **214**–215

Carbohydrates, **68**

Carbon, 65–66, 90

Carbonates, 394

Carbon cycle, 83–85

Carbon dioxide, 335, 484

and atmospheric temperature, 495–496, 509

and combustion, 519

and forest loss, 490

and fossil fuels, 530

molecular structure, 66

ocean absorption of, 85, 489, 499

in photosynthesis, 84

Carbon emissions, 302, 377, 574

Carbon footprint, **503**

Carbonic acid, 499

Carbon monoxide, 272, 463, 464

Carbon offsets, **506**

Carbon sequestration, **506**

Carbon sink, 85

Carbon tax, **505**

Carcinogens, **268**

Caribou, 178, 514, 533

Carnivores, **143**

Carrying capacity, **115**, 231, 328

Carson, Rachel, 45, 255

Caspian Sea, 183

Catalytic converters, **471**, 474

Cause-and-effect diagrams, SH-15

Cell phones, 391, 411

Cells, 101

Cellular respiration, **85**, **143**, 167

Cellulose, 68

Census, U.S., 248–249

Centers for Disease Control and Prevention (CDC), 265

Central Case

air pollution in London, 451

China's one-child policy, 227

DDT, 255

elephants in South Africa, 163

flooding in Maldive Islands, 483

forest management in British Columbia, 323

Fresh Kills Landfill, 581

golden toads in Costa Rica, 99

Gulf of Mexico dead zone, 63

land use in Portland, Oregon, 291

oil in Alaska, 515

ozone layer, 3

renewable energy in Germany, 549

Siberian tiger, 199

tantalum mining, 391

Tijuana River pollution, 35

transgenic maize in Oaxaca, Mexico, 351

water in Great Basin Desert, 419

zebra mussels in Great Lakes, 125

Centrally planned economics, 36

Central Valley of California, 273

Certified forest products, 343

Chain reaction, 537

Chaparral, 164, 166, 176

Chapela, Ignacio, 351

Character displacement, 135

Charcoal, 384–385

Chatham Island Black Robins, 218

Chemical energy, 519

Chemical hazards, 257, 260, 267–276. *See also* Hazardous waste.

biomagnification, 275–276, 440

biomediation, 64

incineration, 588

indoor, 270–272

outdoor, 273–274

and pollution, 267, 437, 439–440

types of, 268–269

Chemical mutagens, 268

Chemical pesticides, 369

Chemical pollution, 267, 437, 439–440

Chemical sedimentary rock, 396

Chemical weathering, 354

Chemistry, 64–71

atoms, **64**–65

bonding, 65

compounds, **66**–67

elements, **64**–65

macromolecules, **67**–69

molecules, **66**–69

solutions, **67**

Chemosynthesis, **142**

Chernobyl nuclear plant accident, 607

Chesapeake Bay, 186

Chicago, 294

China, 227, 235, 245, 361, 421

Chitin, 68

Chlorination, 442

Chlorine monoxide, 16, 18–19

Chlorofluorocarbons (CFCs), 3, 14–20, 25, 27, **472**–473

Cholera, 262–263, 438

Chromosomes, 68

Chytrid fungi, 119

Circle graphs, SH-11

Cities, 293, 297–298. *See also* Sustainable cities; Urbanization.

City planning, **305**–308

Class, 201

Classification

biomes, 166, 179

minerals, 394

rocks, 396

soils, 356

species, 101

taxonomic groups, 201

Classifying, SH-19

Clastic sedimentary rock, 396

Clay, **356**

Clayoquot Sound, 322, 323, 328, 334

Index

Index

Index

Index

Index

Index

Pollination, 139, 371

Pollinators, **371**–372

Pollution, **267**. *See also* Air pollution; Chemical hazards; Emissions; Water pollution.
and biodiversity, 210
biological, 438
and biomagnification, 275
gasoline, 66, 439, 451, 462, 465, 471
groundwater, 439
light, 295
mercury, 440
noise, 295
nutrient, 436, 440
oil, 66, 440
ozone, 472–473
persistent organic pollutants (POPs), 276
point-source/nonpoint-source, **435**–436, 441, 462
sediment, 406, 437
soil, 363–364, 468
thermal, 438
urban, 295, 302
and waste management, 587–588

Polycarbonate plastic, 284–285

Polycyclic aromatic hydrocarbons (PAHs), 66

Polymers, 67

Polymorphs, **394**

Ponds, 183

Population, **101**. *See also* Human population; Population growth.
age structure, **108,** 111
and biodiversity, 209
epidemiology, **258**
geographic isolation of, 131
population cycles, 136

population density, **106,** 232, 300, 302
population distribution, **107,** 232, 240
population size, **104**–105, 111, 232
and predation, 73, 136
and resource management, 328
sex ratio, **109,** 237
urban, 293–294

Population Bomb, The, 9

Population ecology, **101**
describing populations, 104–109
levels of ecological organization, 100–102

Population growth, 110–117. *See also* Human population.
and agricultural production, 228, 373
biotic potential, **117**
birth and death rates, 111
calculating, 113
developing nations, 240
exponential, **114**
factors determining, 110–113
global, 8, 229, 231–232, 240
growth rate, 230, **231**
immigration and emigration, **112**
and industry, 229
and infant mortality, **230**
limiting factors, **115**–116
logistic, **115,** 328
and natural selection, 128
in nature, 115
and poverty, 243
and resource use, 9
and urban sprawl, 300

Portland, Oregon, 290, 291, 307, 310

Positive feedback loops, 74

Post-consumer waste, 594

Potassium, 90

Potential energy, **517**–519

Poverty
environmental impact of, 243–244
and global resource distribution, 245
and urban pollution, 295

Power tower, 564

Prairies, 175

Precipitation, **81,** 487
acid, 467–468
and biome classification, 166
changes in, 492
and mountain ranges, 489
savanna, 171
temperate rain forest, 173
tropical dry forest, 170
tropical rain forest, 168–169

Precipitation (of minerals), **394**

Predation, 73, **136**–137

Predator-prey cycles, 136

Predators, 136–137, 204, 370

Predictions, scientific, **16,** SH-18

Prescribed burns, **341**

Pressure, air, **455**

Prevailing winds, 487

Prey, 73, 136–137

Primary air pollutants, **463**

Primary consumers, 143

Primary energy resources, 520

Primary producers, **84, 141**–144, 167

Primary succession, **150,** 353

Prince William Sound, 440, 531

Producers, 84

Projections, SH-11

Property rights, 306

Proportions, SH-2

Protein deficiency, 374

Proteins, **67**

Protons, 65, 537

Proxy indicators, **493**–494

Prudhoe Bay, 533

Public health, 303

Public parks, 310–311

Public transportation, 504

Pyramid of energy, 145

Q

Quagga mussels, 125

Quality of life, 246

Quantitative data, 19

Quarries, 401

Quartenary period, 208

Quartz, 393

Quecreek mining accident, 529

Questions, SH-20

Quetzal, 104

Quick Lab
age structure, 237
cost-benefit analysis, 37
cultural eutrophication, 437
ecological succession, 152
energy sources, 520
heat movement in water, 459
infectious diseases, 263
latitude and sunlight, 486
replication, 22

Index

Index

Index

Credits

Photography

Photo locators denoted as follows: Top (T), Center (C), Bottom (B), Left (L), Right (R), Background (Bkgd)

Covers

Front: Marg Wood/Design Pics/Shutterstock

Front Matter

iii: Courtesy of Jay Withgott; xv: ElementalImaging/iStockphoto; xxii: Courtesy of Jay Withgott; xxiiiBkgrd: Martin Shields/Alamy Inc.; xxiiiT: Bay Ismoyo/AFP/NewsCom; xxiiiC: John Walker/The Fresno Bee/NewsCom; xxiiiB: Greg Vaughn/Perspectives/Getty Images; xxivBkgrd: Rebecca Grella/Brentwood High School; xxivT: Rebecca Grella/Brentwood High School; xxivBL: Rebecca Grella/Brentwood High School; xxivBR: Rebecca Grella/Brentwood High School; xxvT: Rebecca Grella/Brentwood High School; xxvCL: Rebecca Grella/Brentwood High School; xxvCR: Rebecca Grella/Brentwood High School; xxvBL: Rebecca Grella/Brentwood High School; xxvBR: Rebecca Grella/Brentwood High School; xxviBkgrd: Christin Brown/Cape Hatteras Secondary School; xxviT: Amber Bradshaw/Cape Hatteras Secondary School; xxviTC: Olivia Gaskins/Cape Hatteras Secondary School; xxviBC: Olivia Gaskins/Cape Hatteras Secondary School; xxviB: Tracy Shisler/Cape Hatteras Secondary School; xxviiBkgrd: Christin Brown/Cape Hatteras Secondary School; xxviiTL: Olivia Gaskins/Cape Hatteras Secondary School; xxviiTR: Tracy Shisler/Cape Hatteras Secondary School; xxviiC: Tracy Shisler/Cape Hatteras Secondary School; xxviiBL: Tracy Shisler/Cape Hatteras Secondary School; xxviiBR: Amber Bradshaw/Cape Hatteras Secondary School; xxviiiT: Romeo Gacad/AFP/NewsCom; xxviiiTCR: Jeff Greenberg/PhotoEdit, Inc; xxviiiTR: Joel Sartore/National Geographic Stock; xxviiiBCR: Greg Wood/AFP/Getty Images; xxviiiBL: United Nations Environment Programme; xxviiiBR: Jeff Greenberg/PhotoEdit, Inc.;

Units

U1: 001: Steven David Miller/Nature Picture Library/Alamy Stock Photo; **U2:** 096: Steven David Miller/Nature Picture Library/Alamy Stock Photo; 097: Alfie1981/Alamy Stock Photo; **U3:** 224: Alfie1981/Alamy Stock Photo; 225: Tzido Sun/shutterstock; **U4:** 320: Tzido Sun/shutterstock; 321: Thomas Barrat/Shutterstock; **U5:** 480: Thomas Barrat/Shutterstock;

Chapter 1

002: Li Jizhi/Xinhua/Alamy Stock Photo; 004: NASA Goddard Space Flight Center/Reto Stockli (land surface, shallow water, clouds). Enhancements: Robert Simmon (ocean color, compositing, 3D globes, animation); 005C: Tuul and Bruno Morandi/The Image Bank/Getty Images; 005L: Gerald Nowak/Westend61; 005R: Jim Richardson/National Geographic Stock; 006L: Wheatley/WENN Rights Ltd/Alamy Stock Photo; 006R: Brian J. Skerry/National Geographic Stock; 008L: Library of Congress Prints and Photographs Division [LC-USZ62-54516]/Library of Congress; 008R: NanoStock/Shutterstock; 009: Umesh Goswami/The India Today Group/Getty Images; 010: Worldmapper; 011: NewsCom; 012: Carsten Peter/National Geographic Stock; 013: STR New/Reuters America LLC; 017: Roy Toft/National Geographic Stock; 018T: Jim Ross ED06-0117-24/NASA; 018B: Steve Woods Photography/Cultura/Getty Images; 020L: Ozone Watch/NASA; 020R: Ozone Watch/NASA; 021: Axel Schmidt/AFP/Getty Images; 023: Lynn Johnson/National Geographic Stock; 024: David Paul Morris/Getty Images; 025: Axel Schmidt/AFP/Getty Images; 027: Phil Dent/Redferns/Getty Images; 028: Troy Blaisden/GNS Science; 029T: Angelo Cavalli/AGE Fotostock; 029B: Cindy Miller Hopkins/Danita Delimont/Alamy Inc.;

Chapter 2

034: Tijuana River NERR/NOAA; 038B: Trekandshoot/Shutterstock; 038TL: Dean Turner/iStock International, Inc.; 038TR: jacus/iStock International, Inc.; 039: Lenny Ignelzi/AP Images; 040T: Lindsay Snow/Shutterstock; 040C: Gary Whitton/Shutterstock; 040B: Marvin Dembinsky Photo Associates/Alamy Inc.; 041: Simon de Trey-White/eyevine/NewsCom; 043L: The Print Collector/AGE Fotostock; 043R: Keith Srakocic/AP Images; 044T: Bettmann/Getty Images; 044B: Nathan Chor/Shutterstock; 045T: MPI/Stringer/Getty Images; 045C: Alfred Eisenstaedt/The LIFE Picture Collection/Getty Images; 045B: Bettmann/Getty Images; 046: Ryan Hasler/AP Images; 049Bkgrd: NASA; 049BL: Pinchuk Alexey/Shutterstock; 049BR: COP21/Alamy Stock Photo; 049TL: RonaldNaar/AGE Fotostock; 049C: Eric Isselee/Shutterstock; 049TR: Eco Print/Shutterstock; 050: Givaudan; 052: Alden Pellett/AP Images; 053: Oliver Strewe/The Image Bank/Getty Images; 055: Sundry Photography/Shutterstock; 056Bkgrd: Ron Chapple Stock/Photolibrary Royalty Free; 056: Nancee E. Lewis/SDU-T/ZUMA Press/NewsCom; 057: K.C. Alfred/SDU-T/ZUMA Press/NewsCom;

Chapter 3

062: RGB Ventures/SuperStock/Alamy Stock Photo; 066T: Vadim Volodin/Shutterstock; 066B: Imaginechina Limited/Alamy Stock Photo; 067: Niall McDiarmid/Alamy Royalty Free; 068: Kenneth Eward/BioGrafx/Science Source; 069T: David Murray/Dorling Kindersley Ltd; 069B: Lepas/Shutterstock; 070B: Melissa King/Shutterstock; 70T: AlasdairJames/E+/Getty Images; 071T: Mjay/Shutterstock; 071B: OlgaLis/Shutterstock; 073: Michele and Tom Grimm/Alamy Stock Photo; 078: Imageshop/Alamy Royalty Free; 079: NASA; 082: Jim Wark/AGE Fotostock; 085: Mana Photo/Shutterstock; 088: Matthew D White/Photodisc/Getty Images; 090Bkgrd: Guenter Fischer/Photolibrary Royalty Free; 090: John Giustina/The Image Bank/Getty Images; 091T: Aquapix/Shutterstock; 091B: Susumu Nishinaga/Science Source;

Chapter 4

098: Education Images/Universal Images Group/Getty Images; 103: Fred Grover Jr./Alamy Inc.; 104: imagebroker/Alamy Royalty Free; 105T: G. I. Bernard/Science Source; 105B: Wisconsin Historical Society, WHS14277 ; 106: Dr. Paul A. Zahl/Science Source; 107T: SuperStock; 107C: All Canada Photos/Alamy Inc.; 107B: Oxford Scientific/Getty Images; 109: Jeremy Woodhouse/Photolibrary Royalty Free; 110: Photoshot/AGE Fotostock; 110 inset: Fancy/Alamy Royalty Free; 112: Ray Hennessy/Shutterstock; 114: Gary Cook/Alamy Inc.; 116: WILDLIFE GmbH/Alamy Stock Photo; 117T: Aquabluedreams/Shutterstock; 117C: Fotolia, LLC; 117B: moodboard/SuperStock Royalty Free; 118: Jan Csernoch/Alamy Royalty Free; 119: Joel Sartore/National Geographic Stock; 119 Inset: Joel Sartore/National Geographic Stock; 122: dave stamboulis/Alamy Royalty Free; 124: Valley Journal/Shutterstock; 126: Elena Elisseeva/Shutterstock;

Chapter 5

124: Valley Journal/Shutterstock; 133: Paul Prince Photography/Alamy Inc.; 134L: Mauritius images GmbH/Alamy Stock Photo; 134R: Ted Smykal; 137TL: Tobias Bernhard/Oxford Scientific/Getty Images; 137TR: Tobias Bernhard/PhotoLibrary Group Inc.; 137TC: Nathan A Shepard/Shutterstock; 137B: Thomas Kitchin & Victoria Hurst/Glow Images; 138T: Papilio/Alamy Inc.; 138B: Javarman/Shutterstock; 139T: Dr. Jeremy Burgess/Science Source; 139B: Millard H. Sharp/Science Source; 140: Stone Nature Photography/Alamy Inc.; 141: Monika Gniot/Shutterstock; 142: Bill Whelan/Photolibrary Royalty Free; 143T: Thomas Dressler/AGE Fotostock; 143C: Russell Burden/Photolibrary/Getty Images; 143B: David Chapman/Alamy Inc.; 143BR: Vinicius Tupinamba/Shutterstock; 144: Ted Kinsman/Science Source; 149: imagebroker/Alamy Royalty Free; 150: Michael DeYoung/Glow Images; 151: Michael P. Gadomski/Photo Researchers, Inc.; 153: James P Blair/Photolibrary Royalty Free; 154L: Peter Arnold, Inc./Alamy Inc.; 154R: Brian Cassey/AP Images; 155T: Pat Canova/Alamy Stock Photo; 155B: Wallenrock/Shutterstock; 156–157: Fraser Hall/Robert Harding World Imagery/getty Images; 156L: STR New/Reuters America LLC; 156R: Universal Images Group Limited/Alamy Inc.; 157: Tony Gardner;

Chapter 6

162: EcoPrint/Shutterstock; 167: Demetrio Carrasco/Dorling Kindersley Ltd; 168T: Berndt Fischer/AGE Fotostock; 168B: Nigel Hicks/Dorling Kindersley Ltd; 169: adrian davies/Alamy Royalty Free; 170Bkgrd: Milse/AGE Fotostock; 170R: Morley Read/Alamy Stock Photo; 171Bkgrd: Getty Images/Getty Images; 171BL: Gallo Images/Alamy Royalty Free; 171BR: Fabian von Poser/AGE Fotostock; 172Bkgrd: Chris Curtis/Shutterstock; 172BL: Ivan Chantler/Alamy Royalty Free; 172BR: Rusty Dodson/Shutterstock; 173Bkgrd: Steffen Foerster/Shutterstock; 173T: Petar Tasevski/Shutterstock; 173B: FLPA/Bob Gibbons/AGE Fotostock; 174Bkgrd: Enigma/Alamy Royalty Free; 174L: Yvonne Duffe/Alamy Royalty Free; 174R: Nialat/Shutterstock; 175Bkgrd: Clint Farlinger/Alamy Inc.; 175L: Geoffrey Kuchera/Shutterstock; 175R: Derek Croucher/Alamy Inc.; 176Bkgrd: George Ostertag/AGE Fotostock; 176L: Sharon Lumpkin/Shutterstock; 176R: Arto Hakola/Shutterstock; 177Bkgrd: Mike Grandmaison/AGE Fotostock; 177T: Andrew McLachlan/AGE Fotostock; 177B: M Delpho/AGE Fotostock; 178Bkgrd: Timothy Epp/Shutterstock; 178L: Juniors/Superstock; 178R: Joel Sartore/National Geographic Stock; 179: Sue Flood/The Image Bank/Getty Images; 180: Trekandshoot/Shutterstock; 182: Scubadesign/Shutterstock; 184Bkgrd: Deco/Alamy Royalty Free; 184T: Zdorov Kirill Vladimirovich/Shutterstock; 184C: Paul S. Wolf/Shutterstock; 184B: Rod McLean/Alamy Inc.; 186L: Cameron Davidson/The Image Bank/Getty Images; 186R: Kuznetsov Alexey/Shutterstock; 190T: Camille Lusardi/Glow Images; 190B: Wolfgang Amri/Shutterstock; 191: Getty Images; 192: Four Oaks/Shutterstock; 193T: James Pomfret/Reuters America LLC; 193B: AfriPics.com/Alamy Inc.; 195: Pawe Borowka/Shutterstock; 196: You Touch Pix of EuToch/Shutterstock;

Chapter 7

198: Simonlong/Moment/Getty Images; 202T: Cardaf/Shutterstock; 202B: Frank Krahmer/Corbis/Getty Images; 204: Iofoto/Shutterstock; 205T: Sue Cunningham Photographic/Alamy Stock Photo; 205R: Nigel J. Dennis/Science Source; 206: Martin Moxter/AGE Fotostock Royalty Free; 208: Tom Brakefield/Stockbyte/Getty Images; 210: Leon Neal/Stringer/AFP/getty Images; 211: Norbert Rosing/National Geographic Stock; 213L: Pjmorley/Shutterstock; 213R: All Canada Photos/SuperStock, Inc.; 214: Juniors Bildarchiv/AGE Fotostock; 215: Sundry Photography/Shutterstock; 217L: Australian Rainforest Foundation; 217R: Dave Pinson/Alamy Stock Photo; 218T: Philippe Psaila/Science Source; 218Bkgrd: Rigucci/Shutterstock; 218B: Roy Toft/National Geographic Stock; 219: Brent Stephenson/Nature Picture Library/Alamy Stock Photo; 221: AWPhoto/Alamy Inc.;

Chapter 8

226: Didier Marti/Getty Images; 229: Library of Congress Department of Prints and Photographs [LC-DIG-ppmsca-05944]/Library of Congress; 230: imageBROKER/Alamy Stock Photo; 233T: Konstantin Karchevskiy/Shutterstock; 233B: ErickN/Shutterstock; 234T: Guillermo Granja/Reuters America LLC; 234B: Rhoda Sidney/The Image Works; 239T: ULTRA.F/Getty Royalty Free; 239B: Chris Zahniser/Centers for Disease Control and Prevention; 241L: Taylor S. Kennedy/AGE Fotostock Royalty Free; 241R: Robert Harding Picture Library/AGE Fotostock; 243: Mbrand85/Shutterstock; 244L: Walter Bibikow/AGE Fotostock; 244R: Mike Fei/Shutterstock; 245: Natalie Behring-Chisolm/Stringer/Getty Images; 246: Muellek Josef/Shutterstock; 247L: Jeff Gentner/AP Images; 247R: Pixtal Images/Photolibrary Royalty Free; 248–249Bkgrd: Gary718/Shutterstock; 248T: Andrew P. Scott/Sipa USA/Alamy Stock Photo; 249T: Jim West/Alamy Stock Photo; 249B: UPI Photo/Bill Greenblatt/NewsCom;

Chapter 9

254: Cristina Aldehuela/AFP/Getty Images; 257Bkgrd: Sascha Burkard/Shutterstock; 257T: Christian Zachariasen/Getty Royalty Free; 257C: Janice Haney Carr/Centers for Disease Control and Prevention; 257B: Daniel Loiselle/iStock International, Inc.; 259T: Stuart Wong/KRT/Newscom; 260: Evgeny Murtola/Shutterstock; 262Bkgrd: Mujahid Safodien/AP Images; 262T: James Gathany/Centers for Disease Control and Prevention; 262B: Tsvangirayi Mukwazhi/AP Images; 265T: Smith Collection/Gado/Getty Images; 265B: Allison Shelley/For The Washington Post/Getty Images; 266: Karen Sherlock/Milwaukee Journal Sentinel/MCT/NewsCom; 267L: John Kaprielian/Science Source; 267R: Stuart Monk/Shutterstock; 268: Leonard Mccombe/The LIFE Picture Collection/Getty Images; 271T: Lloyd Sutton/Alamy Inc.; 271B: Ted Kinsman/Science Source; 272: Joy Fera/Shutterstock; 273: Ingmarsan/Shutterstock; 274: DedMityay/Shutterstock; 278: Aflo Co., Ltd./Alamy Stock Photo; 279Bkgrd: NASA; 279B: Itsuo Inouye/AP Images; 280: Chris White/Alamy Royalty Free; 281: Scott Olson/Getty Images; 282: Comstock/Jupiter Unlimited; 283: Walter Quirtmair/Alamy Royalty Free; 284L: Sandra van der Steen/Shutterstock; 284C: Ussr79/Shutterstock; 284R: ShutterWorx /iStock International, Inc.; 285T: Dan Lamont/Alamy Inc.; 285B: David McNew/Getty Images; 287: Javier Larrea/AGE Fotostock;

Chapter 10

290: Nick Gammon/Alamy Stock Photo; 294T: Corbis Premium RF/Alamy Royalty Free; 294B: Frank Zullo/Science Source; 295: Harold R. Stinnette Photo Stock/Alamy Inc.; 297L: VStock LLC/

Credits

AGE Fotostock Royalty Free; 297R: Kim Steele/Getty Royalty Free; 298Bkgrd: Dennis W Donohue/Shutterstock; 298L: Ferenc Cegledi/Shutterstock; 298R: David Watkins/Shutterstock; 299: Craig Mayhew (NASA/GSFC) and Robert Simmon (NASA/GSFC); 300: Rodney Grubbs/NASA; 301T: Tim Roberts Photography/Shutterstock; 301BC: David R. Frazier Photolibrary, Inc.; 301TC: Thinkstock Images/Stockbyte/Getty Images; 301TC: Getty Images; 301B: Aldo Torelli/The Image Bank/Getty Images; 303: dbimages/Alamy Inc.; 304B: Olivier Laban-Mattei/AFP/Getty Images/NewsCom; 304T: NewsCom; 308: Atlantic Station/Cohn & Wolfe; 309: Mastering_Microstock/Shutterstock; 310: Gary Crabbe/Alamy Inc.; 311: Dorothy Alexander/Alamy Inc.; 312a: Maxim_Kovalev/Shutterstock; 312b: Russ Lappa/Ashland High School; 312c: Russ Lappa/Ashland High School;312d: Russ Lappa/Ashland High School; 312e: Russ Lappa/Ashland High School; 312f: Russ Lappa/Ashland High School; 312g: Russ Lappa/Ashland High School; 313: A Katz/Shutterstock; 314: Davewright321/Shutterstock; 317: Getty Images;

Chapter 11

322: Francesco Riccardo Iacomino/Moment/Getty Images; 325T: Nikita Rogul/Shutterstock; 325BC: Craig Stocks Arts/Shutterstock; 325BL: Lane V. Erickson/Shutterstock; 325BR: Evok20/Shutterstock; 326: Kent Gilbert/AP Images; 329: Bob Pool/Shutterstock; 333: Theodore Clutter/Science Source; 334: Kenneth M. Highfill/Science Source; 336: Christopher Pillitz/The Image Bank/Getty Images; 338: Malachi Jacobs/Shutterstock; 340: William Leaman/Alamy Inc.; 341: Don Johnston/Alamy Inc.; 342: Cathleen Allison/AP Images; 343L: Steven May/Alamy Inc.; 343R: Betastock/Alamy Stock Photo; 344: William Campbell/Sygma/Getty Images; 345: Gianluigi Guercia/Stringer/AFP/Getty Images;

Chapter 12

350: Ruslan Bustamante/Alamy Stock Photo; 354: Aeolos Image/Shutterstock; 357: Francesco Carucci/Shutterstock; 359T: Jeff Carroll/AGE Fotostock; 359TC: David Wall/Alamy Stock Photo; 359C: Ron Giling/PhotoLibrary Group Inc.; 359BC: Keren Su/The Image Bank/Getty Images; 359B: Kevin Horan/The Image Bank/Getty Images; 360: W. Perry Conway/Corbis/Getty Images; 362: George E. Marsh Album/NOAA; 363: Jim Richardson/National Geographic Stock; 365: The Granger Collection Ltd.; 367: Sherry Moore/Alamy Royalty Free; 368: Micheline Pelletier/Sygma/Getty Images; 369: Stephen Bonk/Shutterstock; 370: Phil Coale/AP Images; 371: Gorillaimages/Shutterstock; 372T: Steven Chadwick/Alamy Inc.; 372B: Chamille White/Shutterstock; 374: Dr. Lyle Conrad/Centers for Disease Control and Prevention; 375: GTC Biotherapeutics, Inc.; 377: Bill Barksdale/Agstockusa/Age fotostock; 378: Design Pics Inc./Alamy Royalty Free; 379: AquaBounty Technologies; 383: Jeff Greenberg/AGE Fotostock; 384Bkgrd: Julie Major/International Biochar Initiative; 384: Travel Pix Collection/AGE Fotostock; 385T: Biqing Liang/Institute of Earth Sciences, Academia Sinica; 385B: Jeff Hutchens/Getty Images; 387: David Wall/Alamy Stock Photo;

Chapter 13

390: Symbiosis Australia/Shutterstock; 393: Chip Clark/Smithsonian National Museum of Natural History; 394T: Colin Keates/Courtesy of the Natural History Museum, London; 394B: Harry Taylor/Dorling Kindersley Ltd; 395T: Michal812/Shutterstock; 395B: Patrick Poendl/Shutterstock; 397TL: Francois Gohier/Science Source; 397TR: Simon Fraser/Science Source; 397BL: Ammit/Alamy Stock Photo; 397BR: Philip Dombrowski; 400: David R. Frazier/The Image Works; 403TL: Nautilus Minerals, Inc.; 403TR: Nautilus Minerals, Inc.; 403B: Dr. Ian Geoffrey Stimpson; 404: M. E. Warren/Science Source; 406: Elbardamu/Alamy Inc.; 407: Rochester Committee for Scientific Information; 408T: Gamma/Eyedea/Zuma Press; 408B: Private Collection/Peter Newark American Pictures/Bridgeman Images; 409: Darren J. Bradley/Shutterstock; 410: Greenshoots Communications/Alamy Inc.; 411: Maxx-Studio/Shutterstock; 412: David Duprey/AP Images; 413T: David Duprey/AP Images; 413B: Rochester Committee for Scientific Information;

Chapter 14

418: Benedek/E+/Getty Images; 421: Jim Parkin/Alamy Stock Photo; 423: Jessie Eldora Robertson/Shutterstock; 427: L Rider/Shutterstock; 429: Vlad Turchenko/Shutterstock; 430T: Jesse Allen/Goddard Level 1 and Atmospheric Archive and Distribution System (LAADS); 430B: World History Archive/Alamy Stock Photo; 432: gianmarco maggiolini/AGE Fotostock; 433: James L. Stanfield/National Geographic Stock; 434: Rich McMahon; 435L: Mark Winfrey/Shutterstock; 435R: Ian Francis/Alamy Royalty Free; 436: Don Johnston/AGE Fotostock; 437: Wayne G. Lawler/Science Source; 438: SciePro/Shutterstock; 439: Greg Pease/The Image Bank/Getty Images; 440: Mark Winfrey/Shutterstock; 441L: James L. Amos/National Geographic Stock; 441R: Jeff Greenberg/Alamy Inc.; 444: Rob Bouwman/Shutterstock; 445: David Hoffman Photo Library/Alamy Inc.;

Chapter 15

450: PjrTravel/Alamy Stock Photo; 453: Zia Soleil/Iconica/Getty Images; 454: EVasilieva/Shutterstock; 456: GOES Project Science Office/NASA; 457Bkgrd: GOES Project Science Office/NASA; 457L: Morten Hilmer/Shutterstock; 457C: Chad Graham/Getty Royalty Free; 457B: Mike Rurak/Shutterstock; 458: Xavi Arnau/iStock International, Inc.; 459: Huntstock, Inc /Alamy Royalty Free; 461: Nimatallah/Art Resource, NY; 462: Jenny Elia Pfeiffer/Corbis Documentary/Getty Images; 463: Don Despain/rekindlephoto/Alamy Inc.; 464: AFP PHOTO/Frederic J. Brown/NewsCom; 465: Michal Staniewski/Shutterstock; 468: DBA Images/Alamy Stock Photo; 469: Jeremy Wade Shockley/Southern Ute Drum; 470: Jim West/Alamy Inc.; 473L: NASA; 473R: NASA; 474: JTB Photo/AGE Fotostock; 475: Goncalo Veloso de Figueiredo/Shutterstock;

Chapter 16

481: Klaus Vedfelt/DigitalVision/Getty Images; 482: Stockphoto-graf/Shutterstock; 486: Savvas Learning Company LLC.; 489: Danita Delimont/Alamy Inc.; 490: redbrickstock.com /Alamy Inc.; 494: Jeff Geissler/AP Images; 497: FlowerPhotos/Universal Images Group/Getty Images; 498: Incredible Arctic/Shutterstock; 499T: imagebroker/Alamy Inc.; 499B: NOAA; 501: Pierdelune/Shutterstock; 502: Daniel Munoz/Reuters America LLC; 503L: Rich McMahon; 503R: Federal Trade Commission; 505: C Borland/PhotoLink; 505inset: Dave McAleavy Images/Alamy Inc.; 506: Justin Sullivan/Getty Images; 507: Mohammed Seeneen/AP Images; 508Bkgrd: The Alfred Wegener Institute for Polar and Marine Research; 508: Karim Agabi/Science Source; 513: Federal Trade Commission;

Chapter 17

514: Cathy Hart/Design Pics/Getty Images; 516: Wright Brothers collection/LC-DIG-ppprs-00626/Library of Congress; 517L: Erik Isakson/Getty Royalty Free; 517R: Erik Isakson/Getty Royalty Free; 518T: Ligia Botero/The Image Bank/Getty Images; 518C: Stephen Mcsweeny/Shutterstock; 518B: Beboy/Shutterstock; 519T: Keren seg/Shutterstock; 519B: Manzrussali/Shutterstock; 520: LightShaper/Shutterstock; 521TL: magicinfoto/Shutterstock; 521TR: Africa Rising/Shutterstock; 521BL: Travis manley/Shutterstock; 521BR: Blaz Kure/Shutterstock; 522: Bram van Broekhoven/Shutterstock; 525a: HamsterMan/Shutterstock; 525b: Steve Shott/Dorling Kindersley Ltd; 525c: Bojan Pavlukovic/Shutterstock; 525d: Ene/Shutterstock; 525e: AXL/Shutterstock; 525f: Beneda Miroslav/Shutterstock; 528: Douglas C. Pizac/AP Images; 529: Hugo Infante/UPI/Alamy Stock Photo; 531TL: USFWS Photo/Alamy Stock Photo; 531TR: Stapleton/AP Images; 531BL: Everett Collection Historical/Alamy Stock Photo; 531BR: John Gaps III/AP Images; 532: 2008 by Toronto Star/NewsCom; 533: Al Grillo/AP Images; 535: NewsCom; 536: Walter Bibikow/AGE Fotostock; 539: GAMMA/Gamma-Rapho/Getty Images; 542: Danicek/Shutterstock; 545: Bernd Juergens/Shutterstock; 546: Rkriminger/Shutterstock;

Chapter 18

548: Rob Arnold/Alamy Stock Photo; 551: Obert/AGE Fotostock; 552: Peggy Greb/USDA Agricultural Research Service; 553: Jim Peaco/Yellowstone National Park; 556: Steve Dunwell/AGE Fotostock; 557: Clynt Garnham Renewable Energy/Alamy Inc.; 558: Takashi Hagihara/amanaimagesRF; 559: Greg Baker/AP Images; 560: Laszlo Podor/Alamy Inc.; 561: Tom Rielly/Moving Windmills Project; 564: FOURMY MARIO/SIPA/NewsCom; 565: Alison Wright/Corbis Documentary/Getty Images; 566: Eric Gevaert/Shutterstock; 567: Greg Randles/Shutterstock; 569: Greg Smith/Corbis/Getty Images; 570: GRIN/NASA; 571: Dr. Michael Seibert/National Renewable Energy Laboratory; 572: Yoshikazu Tsuno/AFP/Getty Images; 573: Sarah Leen/National Geographic Stock; 574: Glowimages RF/AGE Fotostock Royalty Free; 575T: David R. Frazier Photolibrary, Inc./Alamy Inc.; 575B: Martin Harvey/Science Source; 577: Sandra Cunningham/Shutterstock; 578: Jan kranendonk/Shutterstock;

Chapter 19

580: Andrew Lichtenstein/Corbis/Getty Images; 583: Paul Prescott/Shutterstock; 584: Anupam Nath/AP Images; 586T: Tina Fineberg/AP Images; 586B: John Homer Thiel; 590TL: Ange/Alamy Inc.; 590TR: Alex Segre/Alamy Inc.; 590B: John Cancalosi/Photolibrary/Getty Images; 593: Gary K. Smith/AGE Fotostock; 594L: Angela Hampton/AGE Fotostock; 594R: Marco Ugarte/AP Images; 597L: Justin Kase z08z/Alamy Royalty Free; 597R: Kedrov/Shutterstock; 598L: Sergio Azenha/Alamy Stock Photo; 598R: Enrique Marcarian/Reuters America LLC; 599: Hans Gutknecht/NewsCom; 602: Bettmann/Getty Images; 603: Dennis R.J. Geppert/The Holland Sentinel/AP Images; 604: Mike Flippo/Shutterstock; 605: Rolf Adlercreutz/Alamy Inc.; 607: Michael Conroy/AP Images; 610: Klaus Vedfelt/DigitalVision/Getty Images;

End Matter

SH-01: Photoshot Holdings Ltd/Alamy Inc.; SH-19: Savvas Learning Company LLC.; SH-20: Paul Debois/AGE Fotostock; SH-22: F Hecker/AGE Fotostock;

Text Credits

Chapter 1

014, 015, 016, 019, 020, 021, 022: Adapted from the Understanding Science Infographic, ©University of California Museum of Paleontology, Berkeley; 024: Data from CSIRO Atmospheric Research and Cape Grim Baseline Air Pollution Station, Australian Antarctic Division and Australian Bureau of Meteorology as appears in Understanding Science Infographic, ©University of California Museum of Paleontology, Berkeley; 027: Adapted from Understanding Science Infographic, ©University of California Museum of Paleontology, Berkeley;

Chapter 2

041: Fair trade logo. Copyright © Fair Trade USA. Published with permission.

Chapter 4

112: Data from Hawk Mountain Data Archives; 115: Adapted from Scheffer, Victor B. 1951. The Rise and Fall of a Reindeer Herd. THE SCIENTIFIC MONTHLY 73: 6, 356–362, Fig 1. Reprinted with permission from AAAS.;

Chapter 5

132: From Raup, D.M. and J.J. Sepkoski. 1998. Mass extinctions in the marine fossil record. SCIENCE 215: 1501–1503, Fig 2. Reprinted with permission from AAAS and the author.;

Chapter 6

169–173: Adapted from Breckle, S.W. and H. Walter, trans. by G. Lawlor. 2002. *Walter's Vegetation Of The Earth: The Ecological Systems Of The Geo-Biosphere*, 4/e. Originally published by Eugen Ulmer KG, 1999, used by permission.; 174–175: Source: Climatograph adapted from Breckle, S.W. 2002. *Walter's Vegetation Of The Earth: The Ecological Systems Of The Geo-Biosphere*, 4th ed. Berlin: Springer-Verlag.; 176–178: Adapted from Breckle, S.W. and H. Walter, trans. by G. Lawlor. 2002. *Walter's Vegetation Of The Earth: The Ecological Systems Of The Geo-Biosphere*, 4/e. Originally published by Eugen Ulmer KG, 1999, used by permission.;

Chapter 8

232: Source: Center for International Earth Science Information Network (CIESIN), Columbia University, and Centro Internacional de Agricultura Tropical (CIAT), 2005.; 238: Source: Kent, M. M. and K.A. Crews. 1990. World population: Fundamentals of growth. Population Reference Bureau.;

Chapter 10

302: Data from Kenworthy, J., et al. 1999. An international sourcebook of automobile dependence in cities. Boulder, CO: University Press of Colorado, as cited by Sheehan, M.O. 2002. What will it take to halt sprawl? Washington, DC: Worldwatch Institute.;

Chapter 17

527: Source: Campbell, C.J., and Association for the Study of Peak Oil, 2007.;